Amphibious Realities

Amphibious Realities

The Documentary Poetics of Allan Sekula

Gail Day and Steve Edwards

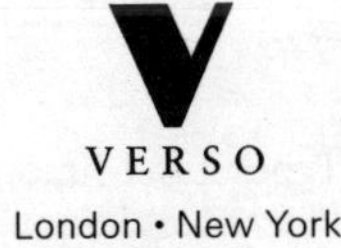

London • New York

First published by Verso 2025

The manufacturer's authorized representative in the EU for product safety (GPSR) is LOGOS EUROPE, 9 rue Nicolas Poussin, 17000, La Rochelle, France Contact@logoseurope.eu

1 3 5 7 9 10 8 6 4 2

Verso
UK: 6 Meard Street, London W1F 0EG
US: 207 East 32nd Street, New York, NY 10016
versobooks.com

Verso is the imprint of New Left Books

ISBN-13: 978-1-80429-504-5
ISBN-13: 978-1-80429-506-9 (US EBK)
ISBN-13: 978-1-80428-505-2 (UK EBK)

British Library Cataloguing in Publication Data
A catalogue record for this book is available from the British Library

Library of Congress Cataloging-in-Publication Data

Names: Day, Gail author | Edwards, Steve, 1959- author
Title: Amphibious realities: the documentary poetics of Allan Sekula / Gail Day and Steve Edwards.
Description: London; New York: Verso, 2025. | Includes bibliographical references and index.
Identifiers: LCCN 2025025169 (print) | LCCN 2025025170 (ebook) | ISBN 9781804295045 paperback | ISBN 9781804295069 ebook
Subjects: LCSH: Sekula, Allan--Criticism and interpretation | Sekula, Allan--Philosophy
Classification: LCC NX512.S45 D39 2025 (print) | LCC NX512.S45 (ebook)
LC record available at https://lccn.loc.gov/2025025169
LC ebook record available at https://lccn.loc.gov/2025025170

Typeset in Minion by Hewer Text UK Ltd, Edinburgh
Printed and bound by CPI Group (UK) Ltd, Croydon CR0 4YY

In memory of Fred Orton,
Jeroen Verbeeck, Marina Vishmidt

Heaven is for thee too high / To know what passes there; / be lowlie wise.

John Milton

Everything comes down to Aesthetics and political economy.

Stéphane Mallarmé

Contents

Acknowledgements xi

List of Illustrations xv

Introduction: 'Against the grip of advanced capitalism' 1

1 'Capitalism's inability to deliver the conditions of a fully human life' 29

2 'A horizontal sort of beast' 103

3 A poetics in realist language 167

4 Amphibious (ir)realities and capitalism's dreamworld 227

Index 285

Acknowledgements

Our first thanks go to the much-missed Allan Sekula, with whom we were fortunate to share time reflecting on photography, art, film, history and politics – and the many other things that attracted his keen intelligence. Sally Stein and Ina Steiner helped hugely with our research, supplying information, pictures and ideas. We are extremely grateful for their incredible sacrifice of time; this book is made possible because of them. And it is made much better for the insightful critical engagement of our readers: Fred Orton, Alex Potts, Ross Truscott and Marina Vishmidt. Unfortunately, neither Fred nor Marina lived to see it in print. We have long discussed Sekula with Alberto Toscano, who remains such an intellectually generous comrade. Jürgen Bock at Maumaus in Lisbon has been hugely supportive (and curated some of the very best Sekula exhibitions). Luiz Renato Martins, Ana Paula Pacheco and Marcos Soares enabled important visits to São Paolo and Santos to debate aesthetics and politics.

Thanks are due to the friends, colleagues and interlocutors with whom we have shared ideas, or who stimulated earlier iterations by inviting us to contribute to their conferences and publications: Larne Abse Gogarty, Shahidul Alam, Fiona Allen, Jamie Allinson, Tilo Amhoff, Elise Archias, Caroline Arscott, Jairus Banaji, Pascal Beausse, Dave Beech, Nick Beech, John X. Berger, Mathilde Bertrand, Guillaume Blanc, Roger M. Buergel, Benjamin H. D. Buchloh, Liam Campling, Richard Checketts, Justin Carville, Paulo Catrica, Amy Charlesworth, Danny Child, James Christie, Alex Colás, Simon Constantine, Luisa Lorenza Corna, Mark Crinson, David Cunningham, Taous Dahmani, the late Neil Davidson, Mary Ann Doane, Manthia Diawara, Angela Dimitrakaki, Nesrin Değirmencioğlu, Patrizia di Bello, Ed Dimendberg, Bart De Baere, Carol Duncan, Kodwo Eshun, Marcos Fabris, Ângela Ferreira, Andy Fisher, Marnie Flemming, Maki Fukuoka, Duncan Forbes, Tamar Garb, the late Martin Gaughan, Hilde Van Gelder, Craig Gilmore, Ruth Wilson Gilmore, Helen Graham, Jorge Grespan, Carmela Gross, Carles Guerra, Adam Hanieh, Harry Harootunian, Dan Hartley, Danny Hayward, Andrew Hemingway, Brenda Hollweg, Sarah James, Laleh Khalili, Nick Lawrence, Patricia Leal, Kirstin Lloyd, Katie Lloyd Thomas, Fred Lonidier, Stewart Martin, David McNally, David Mabb, Michael Mack, Grant Mandarino, the late Margarida Medeiros, Antigoni Memou, Tom Mitchell, Colin Mooers, John Mowitt, Laura Mulvey, Molly Nesbit, Ben Noys, Nizan Shaked, Gill Perry, Clare Pettitt, Charlie Post, Jorge Ribalta, Olivier Richon, Alistair Rider, Adrian Rifkin, Bill Roberts, John Roberts, Justin Rosenberg, Martha Rosler, Kristin Ross, Anja Isabel Schneider, Fred Schwartz, Stephanie Schwartz, Alan Sears, Susan Siegfried, Claudia Sternberg, Blake Stimson, Emilia Tavares, Richard Taws, the late Jeroen Verbeeck, Julia Welbourne, Paul Wood and Benjamin Young. At an earlier stage, we benefitted from significant conversations with Stanley Mitchell and Jo Spence. Our sincerest apologies to anyone we have overlooked.

We wish to thank: Sebastian Budgen at Verso for supporting this book; Karen Francis for excellent work on the manuscript; Melissa Weiss for the careful cover design; Danny Hayward for the index; and Nick Walther for guiding a complex project through to realisation.

Financial support and invaluable time to write was provided by: the University of Leeds's Faculty of Arts, Humanities and Culture and the School of Fine Art, History of Art and Cultural Studies; the Departments of History of Art at the Open University; Birkbeck, University of London; The Courtauld Institute of Art; and República Portuguesa – Cultura/Direção-Geral das Artes and Câmara Municipal de Lisboa. A Getty Library Grant enabled Gail Day to examine Sekula's notebooks in Los Angeles, and thanks are due to the incredible support received there from the librarians.

Although the authors have published independently over the years, their arguments emerged through a sustained and intense intellectual collaboration; one does not prise apart the study into 'personal possessions' without doing considerable violence to the fully dialogic constitution of the research. All earlier texts have been substantially reworked and rewritten for *Amphibious Realities* and most of book is entirely new material. We are indebted to the editors and readers of:

Gail Day and Steve Edwards, 'Global Dissensus: Art and Contemporary Capitalism', *Exploring Art and Visual Culture: From Modernity to Globalisation*, eds Steve Edwards and Paul Wood (London: Tate Publishing, 2012), 285–315.

Gail Day and Steve Edwards, 'Differential time and aesthetic form: uneven and combined capitalism in the work of Allan Sekula', *Cultures of Uneven and Combined Development*, eds James Christie & Nesrin Değirmencioğlu (Leiden: Brill, 2019), 253–88. A different version is published as "'Recoding the Sea": Uneven and Combined Capitalism in the work of Allan Sekula (Telegraph Version)', *Scrambled Images: Coding and Representation from the Nineteenth Century to the Present*, eds Anne Chapman and Natalie Hume (London: Routledge, 2021), 161–88.

Gail Day, 'Realism, Totality, and the Militant *Citoyen*: Or, What Does Lukács Have to do with Contemporary Art?', *The Fundamental Dissonance of Existence: New Essays on the Social, Political and Aesthetic Theory of Georg Lukács*, eds Timothy Bewes and Timothy Hall (New York and London: Continuum, 2011), 203–19. Republished: 'Realism, Totality, and the Militant *Citoyen*: Or, What Does Lukács Have to do with Contemporary Art?', *ReNew Marxist Art History: Essays for Andrew Hemingway*, eds Frederic J. Schwartz, Barnaby Haran, Warren Carter (London: Art/Books, 2013), 478–93.

Gail Day, 'Allan Sekula's Transitive Poetics: Metonymy and Metaphor in *Lottery of the Sea*, *Ship of Fools* and *The Dockers' Museum*', *Allan Sekula: Ship of Fools/Dockers' Museum*, ed. Hilde Van Gelder (Leuven: Leuven University Press, 2015), 57–70; (Rennes: La Criée centre d'art contemporain, 2015), 57–71; (Lisbon: Maumaus, 2015), 57–70. Republished: *Revue Période* (November 2015).

Gail Day, 'Allan Sekula: Industries of Architecture/Architectures of Industry', *Industries of Architecture*, eds Tilo Amhoff, Nick Beech and Katie Lloyd Thomas (London: Routledge, 2015), 13–24.

Steve Edwards, 'Optical Truths and Visual Pleasures: Allan Sekula and a Theory for Photography', *Ten.8* 26 (1987): 37–9.

Steve Edwards, 'Photography out of Conceptual Art', *Themes in Contemporary Art*, eds Gill Perry and Paul Wood (New Haven: Yale University Press, 2004), 136–80.

Steve Edwards, 'Commons and Crowds: Figuring Photography from Above and Below', *Third Text*, 23:4 (2009): 447–64. Republished: *Crítica Marxista* (2017).

Steve Edwards, 'Allan Sekula's Chronotopes: Uneven and Combined Capitalism', *Allan Sekula: Ship of Fools/The Dockers' Museum*, ed. Hilde Van Gelder (Leuven: Leuven University Press, 2015), 31–43; (Rennes: La Criée centre d'art contemporain, 2015), 31–44; (Lisbon: Maumaus, 2015), 31–44. Republished: *Revue Période* (September 2015); *Traduzioni Marxiste* (September 2016).

Steve Edwards, 'Allan Sekula: *Fish Story*', *Kunst und Politik Jahrbuch der Guernica-Gesellschaft, Icons of 20th-Century Political Art/Politische Kunst des 20. Jahrhunderts*, eds Andrew Hemingway & Norbert Schneider (Göttingen: V&R unipress, 2016), 147–57.

Steve Edwards, 'White Collar Blues: Allan Sekula Casts an Eye Over the Professional-Managerial Class', *Nonsite* 8 (2021).

List of Illustrations

All images are generously supplied courtesy of the Allan Sekula Studio, unless otherwise stated.

1–2
***Short Autobiography* (1971)** – selection of two panels.
Complete work: Ten silver-gelatine prints (18.5 x 25 cm); each print pairing two photographs with the addition of autographic text in black ink.

3–4
***Box Car* (1971)**
Single black-and-white photograph and text (62.1 x 52.3 cm framed).

5–6
***Meat Mass* (1972)** – selection of two photographs.
Complete work: Performance documentation. Twelve black-and-white photographs and text panel (83 x 154.3 cm framed).

7–8
***Two, three, many . . . (terrorism)* (1972)** – selection of two photographs. Complete work: Six black-and-white photographs (15.4 x 22.7 cm) in single frame (80.4 x 130.2 cm).

9–20
***Aerospace Folktales* (1973)** – selection of twelve photographs.

Complete work: Fifty-one black-and-white photographs in twenty-three frames (55.9 x 71.5 cm framed). Three red canvas director's chairs, six potted fan palms. Three CD players, three speakers, three simultaneous, unsynchronised CD recordings. CD total playing time seventeen minutes, twenty-one minutes and twenty-three minutes. Edition of two.

21–6
***This Ain't China: A Photonovel* (1974)** – selection of six photographs. Complete work: Twenty-nine black-and-white photographs (20.3 x 25.3 cm card-mounted) and a single colour photograph (79.7 x 70 cm card-mounted), compiled in eight frames (five 58 x 73.5 cm; three 79.7 x 70 cm). Nine colour photographs in single frames (112.5 x 132 cm). Two chairs. Text in two booklets.

27
***California Stories: Attempts to correlate class with the elevation of the main harbor channel (San Pedro, July 1975)* (1975/2011)**
Panel of six archival pigment prints (10.6 x 101.6 x 3.81 cm).

28–34
***Sketch for a Geography Lesson* (1983)** – selection of six photographs and one photocopy.
Complete work: nine colour photographs in one frame (137 x 107 x 5 cm); two individually framed text panels (58 x 114 x 5 cm); two individually framed gelatin silver prints (63 x 52 x 5 cm). Edition of two.

35–47
***Geography Lesson: Canadian Notes* (1987)** – selection of thirteen photographs. The 1997 book contains seventy-five pictures in a distinct edit, the order of which our selection follows. The exhibition adopted and alternative itinerary.
Complete work: Seventy-nine photographs: forty colour (27.94 x 35.56 cm) and thirty-nine black-and-white (20.32 x 25.4 cm). Compiled in eighteen frames (five 81 x 36 cm; two 81 x 50.5 cm; four 81 x 71 cm; three 81 x 102 cm; four 81 x 152 cm).

35
Photographer with two views of Parliament Hill from Hull, Quebec.

36
Fertilizer, Garden Court, Bank of Canada.

37
Bank of Canada, August 1985.

38
Worker's lounge overlooking Parliament Hill, Bank of Canada.

39
Garden Court, Bank of Canada.

40
Inco Smelter.

41
Reception room, Eldorado Resources Limited (uranium mining and processing firm), Ottawa. Landscape paintings by A. Y. Jackson.

42
President's office, Mine, Mill and Smelter Workers Union, Local 598, Sudbury. Landscape painting by A. Y. Jackson.

43
Louis-Phillipe Herbert, *The Last Indian*, 1901. National Gallery of Canada, Ottawa.

44
Current series of Canadian paper money (1985). Currency Museum, Bank of Canada.

45
Service station, Sudbury.

46
Big Nickel Mine, Sudbury.

47
Sudbury.

48–97

***Fish Story* (1995)** – selection of forty-eight photographs from Sekula's published sequence. Numbers in brackets (e.g., #2) indicate the plate numbers used in the publication (to which we refer in our discussion).

Exhibition: One-hundred-and-five colour photographs in ninety-two frames, organised in seven sections. Variable dimensions. Seventeen text panels; seven caption panels; two quotation panels. *Dismal Science* and *Walking on Water*: two slide projections, each a sequence of eighty transparencies, booklet with the captions and an accompanying text. Vitrines with Sekula's publications. Screenprint on wall of a newspaper map of riots in Newcastle.
Book: Richter Verlag: Düsseldorf, 1995. Ninety-six colour photographs, with texts, quotations, and image captions. Includes an illustrated long-form essay, 'Dismal Science', in two parts and an essay by Benjamin H. D. Buchloh. The recent republication (Mack Edition, London, 2018) reproduces the original format, with an additional Foreword by Laleh Khalili.

48
Installation view, Witte de With, Rotterdam, Netherlands, 1995.

49
Installation view, Busan Biennial, Busan, South Korea, 2012.

50–1
(*Fish Story* plate numbers: #1–2)
Boy looking at his mother. Staten Island Ferry. New York harbor. February 1990. (Each 59.2 x 83.2 x 4.5 cm.)

52 (#3)
Welder's booth in bankrupt Todd Shipyard. Two years after closing. Los Angeles harbor. San Pedro, California. July 1991. (59.2 x 83.2 x 4.5 cm.)

53 (#5)
Pipe fitters finishing the engine room of a tuna-fishing boat. Campbell Shipyard. San Diego harbor. August 1991. (59.2 x 83.2 x 4.5 cm.)

54 (#6)
Welder's booth in bankrupt Todd Shipyard. Two years after closing. Los Angeles harbor. San Pedro, California. July 1991. (59.2 x 83.2 x 4.5 cm.)

55 (#7)
Remnants of a movie set. Abandoned shipyard. Los Angeles harbor. Terminal Island, California. January 1993. (59.2 x 83.2 x 4.5 cm.)

56 (#8)
The rechristened *Exxon Valdez* awaiting sea trials after repairs. National Steel and Shipbuilding Company. San Diego harbor. August 1990. (59.2 x 83.2 x 4.5 cm.)

57 (#9)
'Lead Fish'. Variant of a conference room designed for Chiat/Day advertising agency. Architect: Frank Gehry. Installation at the Museum of Contemporary Art, Los Angeles. May 1988. (76.8 x 68 x 4.5 cm.)

58 (#10)
Remnants of a Roman harbor near Minturno, Italy. June 1992. (62.9 x 79.4 x 4.5 cm.)

59 (#11)
Hammerhead crane unloading forty-foot containers from Asian ports. American President Lines terminal. Los Angeles harbor. San Pedro, California. November 1992. (62.9 x 79.4 x 4.5 cm.)

60 (#12)
Shipyard-workers' housing – built during the Second World War – being moved from San Pedro to South-Central Los Angeles. May 1990. (59.2 x 83.2 x 4.5 cm.)

61 (#14)
Koreatown, Los Angeles. April 1992. (59.2 x 83.2 x 4.5 cm.)

62 (#15)
Workers cleaning up chemical spill after refinery explosion. Los Angeles harbor. Wilmington, California. October 1992. (59.2 x 83.2 x 4.5 cm.)

63 (#17)
'Pancake', a former shipyard sandblaster, scavenging copper from a waterfront scrapyard. Los Angeles harbor. Terminal Island, California. November 1992. (62.9 x 79.4 x 4.5 cm.)

Loaves and Fishes

64 (#23)
Palace of Culture and Science. Warsaw, Poland. November 1990. (59.2 x 83.2 x 4.5 cm.)

65 (#24)
Unemployment office. Gdańsk, Poland. November 1990. (59.2 x 83.2 x 4.5 cm.)

Middle Passage – Voyage 167 of the container ship M/V *Sea-Land Quality* from Port Elizabeth, New Jersey, to Rotterdam. November 1993.

66 (#27)
Detail. Inclinometer. Mid-Atlantic. (62.8 x 99.6 x 4.5 cm.)

67 (#28)
Panorama. Mid-Atlantic. (62.8 x 99.6 x 4.5 cm.)

68 (#29)
Chief mate checking temperatures of refrigerated containers. Mid-Atlantic. (59.2 x 83.2 x 4.5 cm.)

69 (#30)
Filling lifeboat with water equivalent to weight of crew to test the movement of the boat falls before departure. Port Elizabeth, New Jersey. (59.2 x 83.2 x 4.5 cm.)

70 (#31)
Third assistant engineer working on the engine while underway. (59.2 x 83.2 x 4.5 cm.)

71 (#37)
Engine-room wiper's ear protection. (76.8 x 68 x 4.5 cm.)

72 (#38)
Figurine based on the television series *Star Trek* mounted on engine-room control console. (76.8 x 68 x 4.5 cm.)

73 (#42)
Ship models in vitrine with linear scale. Maritiem Museum Prins Hendrik, Rotterdam. (76.8 x 68 x 4.5 cm.)

Seventy in Seven – South Korea. September 1993.

74–5 (#54–5)
Doomed fishing village of Ilsan. (Each 62.9 x 145.5 x 4.5 cm.)

76 (#61)
Outer perimeter of monument to Hyundai construction workers killed building the Kyung-bu Highway from Seoul to Pusan. Keum-kang rest stop. (62.9 x 79.4 x 4.5 cm.)

Message in a Bottle – Vigo, Galicia, Spain. May 1992.

77 (#64)
Jewelry store. Rúa Príncipe. (59.2 x 83.2 x 4.5 cm.)

78 (#65)
Shop occupied by women clerks for eighteen months in dispute over pay. Rúa Príncipe. (62.9 x 79.4 x 4.5 cm.)

79 (#68)
Workers gathering on the waterfront at the end of a nationwide general strike opposing the Socialist government's cutbacks in unemployment benefits. (62.9 x 79.4 x 4.5 cm.)

True Cross – Veracruz. March 1994.

80 (#70)
Waterfront vendor and docker in container storage area. (62.9 x 79.4 x 4.5 cm.)

81 (#72)
Monument to the defenders of Veracruz against the US Marines in 1914. Pemex headquarters. Malecón. (62.9 x 145.5 x 4.5 cm.)

82–3 (#73–4)
Surveying new container storage area. (Each 62.9 x 145.5 x 4.5 cm.)

84–5 (#75–6)
Drilling core samples from the coral walls of the fortress. San Juan de Ulúa. (Each 62.9 x 145.5 x 4.5 cm.)

86 (#77)
Truckload of Volkswagens from factory in Puebla awaiting arrival of car-carrier ship for export. (62.9 x 145.5 x 4.5 cm.)

87 (#78)
Containers used to contain shifting sand dunes. (62.9 x 145.5 x 4.5 cm.)

88–9 (#79–80)
Waterfront vendors living in containers. (Each 62.9 x 145.5 x 4.5 cm.)

90 (#82)
Coral sample from the fortress walls. San Juan de Ulúa. (62.9 x 79.4 x 4.5 cm.)

Dictatorship of the Seven Seas

91–2 (#85–6)
Kaiser steel mill being dismantled after sale to Shougang Steel, People's Republic of China. Fontana, California. May and December 1993. (Each 62.9 x 79.4 x 4.5 cm.)

93 (#87)
Chinese dismantling crew being bussed to their motel at the end of the day shift. Kaiser steel mill. Fontana, California. December 1993. (62.9 x 79.4 x 4.5 cm.)

94 (#91)
Man sleeping under a eucalyptus tree. Embarcadero Park. San Diego harbor. July 1994. (62.9 x 79.4 x 4.5 cm.)

95 (#92)
Brazilian steel slab headed inland through South-Central Los Angeles to remaining rolling mill in Fontana. Los Angeles harbor. Wilmington, California. July 1994. (62.9 x 79.4 x 4.5 cm.)

96 (#93)
Mike and Mary, an unemployed couple who survive by scavenging and who, from time to time, seek shelter in empty containers. South-Central Los Angeles. August 1994. (62.9 x 79.4 x 4.5 cm.)

97 (#94)
Chair designed for since-demolished Channel Heights shipyard-workers housing in San Pedro, 1943. Architect: Richard Neutra. Decorative arts collection, Los Angeles County Museum of Art. (62.9 x 79.4 x 4.5 cm.)

98–103
***Dead Letter Office* (1997–98)** – selection of nine photographs from the published sequence.
Complete work: Cibachrome prints presented in twelve diptychs, two triptychs and two single prints. Variable dimensions.

98–9 Hyundai container factory and trucker's graffito, Tijuana. Diptych. (62.9 x 167.6 x 6.3 cm framed.)

100–1 Twentieth Century Fox set for *The Titanic* and mussel gatherers, Popotla. Diptych. (62.9 x 167.3 x 6.3 cm framed.)

102–3 Coffin factory, Tijuana. Diptych. (62.9 x 167.6 x 6.3 cm framed.)

104–15
***Freeway to China (Version 2, for Liverpool)* (1998–99)** – selection of twelve photographs.
Complete work: twenty-three colour photographs in eighteen frames, text. Variable dimensions. Edition of five. (Many images have long captions, here abbreviated with ellipses.)

104
Freeway to China 3. Mason Davis and a co-worker loading welding-gas cannisters aboard the *Teal*. (75 x 102.3 cm framed.)

105
Freeway to China 2 (Portrait 1). Mason Davis . . . (75 x 102.3 cm framed.)

106
Freeway to China 5. Container cranes welded and braced for the difficult ocean-crossing aboard the *Teal* . . . (59 x 102.3 cm framed.)

107

Freeway to China 4. The *Teal* berthed at Pier 300 . . . (49.2 x 102.3 cm framed.)

108

Freeway to China 6. Russian sailor Yuri Smolin (left) and a shipmate loading supplies aboard the *Teal* . . . (75 x 102.3 cm framed.)

109

Portrait 2. Louisa Gratz . . . Matson Terminal, Terminal Island, Port of Los Angeles, May 1998. (75 x 102.3 cm framed.)

110

One Thousand Trucks . . . Fontana, California, May 1996 (75 x 102.3 cm framed.)

111–12

Dockers Looking (Diptych). Mickey Tighe (front) and Marty Size (rear) . . . Liverpool, July 1999. (76.2 x 182.9 cm framed.)

113

Shipspotter . . . New Brighton, July 1999. (75 x 102.3 cm framed.)

114

Portrait 3. John Stanson . . . Albert Dock, Liverpool, July 1999. (42.5 x 52.7 cm framed.)

115

Queen of the Pirates. Albert Dock, July 1999. (112 x 182.3 cm framed.)

116

***Waiting for Tear Gas [white globe to black]* (1999–2000)** – selection of thirty-eight slides.
Complete work: Slide project of eighty-one 35mm transparencies. Fourteen minutes looped. Sequence co-editor Sally Stein. Edition of five.

117–19

***TITANIC's wake* (1998–2000)** – selection of three photographs.
Complete work: thirty-one colour photographs (nine diptychs and fourteen single images). Variable dimensions.

117, 119
Bilbao. Diptych. (74 x 173 cm.)

118
Shipwreck and Worker, Istanbul. (115 x 150 cm.)

120–2
***Black Tide/Marea Negra* (2002–3)** – selection of seven photographs. Complete work: twenty colour photographs in ten frames, plus text. Three single photographs, four diptychs and three triptychs. Cibachrome prints. Variable dimensions. Edition of five.

120–1
Volunteer watching, volunteer smiling (Isla de Ons, 12/19/02). Diptych. (67 x 171.6 x 6.35 cm.)

122
Dripping black trapezoid (Lendo, 12/22/02). (104.3 x 73.1 x 6.35 cm.)

123
***The Lottery of the Sea* (2006)** – selection of twenty-four video stills from *Prologue* and *Athens, December 2003* (00:00:00–00:09:54).
Complete work: One-hundred-and-eighty-minute single-channel video. English, Spanish & Gallego (with English subtitles).

124–8
***Ship of Fools* (2010)** – selection of five photographs. Complete work: thirty-three framed chromogenic prints mounted on alu-dibond and two projections. Variable dimensions.

124–6
Engine Room Eyes 1–3, 1999/2010. Triptych. (Each 101.6 x 127 cm.)

127
Sugar Gang (Santos) 6, 2010. (76.2 x 76.2 cm.)

128
Working (Santos), 2010. (101.6 x 149.9 cm.)

129–34

***The Dockers' Museum* (2010–13)** – selection of five objects (and installation view).
Complete work: Multiple objects purchased through eBay. Variable dimensions. Courtesy Allan Sekula Studio & M HKA, Antwerp. Details based on accession data for M KHA's collection.

129

Exhibition view of Allan Sekula, *The Dockers' Museum*, Lumiar Cité, Lisbon, 2013. Photo: DMF. Courtesy of the Estate of Allan Sekula and Maumaus/Lumiar Cité.

130

Anon., *Loading Coffee, Santos.* Sekula's title. Colour postcard, date unknown (probably circa 1908), 8.8 x 13.8 cm. Purchased by Allan Sekula through eBay on 21 April 2010. (TDM 30.)

131

Anon., *From the Sculpture by Constantin Meunier*, an Antwerp dockhand. Black-and-white print on paper, c. 1906, 25 x 17.5 cm. Purchased by Sekula through eBay on 6 May 2010. (TDM 11.)

132

Anon., *Sea Lion in the Antwerp Zoo.* Sekula's title. Black-and-white postcard, ed. NELS Bromurite (now Thill), c. 1930–50, 9 x 14 cm. Purchased by Sekula through eBay on 6 May 2010. (TDM 13.)

133

Dock-Worker Cup (Portugal), Burlap Bags of Unroasted Coffee (Santos). Sekula's title. Ceramics and burlap bags with coffee beans. Producers and dates unknown (probably c. 2010): cup 11 x 8 x 7 cm; 7 bags: 18 x 10 x 5 cm. Purchased by Sekula through eBay on 29 March (cup) and 30 April (bags). (TDM 38.)

134

(Homer) Van Pelt, *Production Still of the Film-Musical 'The Thrill of Brazil'.* Sekula's title. Black-and-white photograph, 1946. 20.5 x 25.5 cm. Purchased by Sekula through eBay on 6 May 2010. (TDM 10.)

Introduction

'Against the grip of advanced capitalism'

A question for 'cultural studies'.
'Can the battle between materialism and idealism be fought out over the image of a fish?'[1]

Allan Sekula posed this problem in a notebook jotting from 1999. Beneath this note-to-self, he sketches two schemata. The first suggests the Christian 'sign of the fish', although Sekula diverges from its usual form of two intersecting arcs – their ends touching at the nose and crossing at the tail joint – preferring, instead, a single cursive loop. The second depicts a simplified piscine endoskeleton – with a roughly triangular head and ribs hatched across the spine perpendicularly – the type of thing that Top Cat tosses from his garbage-can home. Christ as Saviour, resurrection and immortality, on the idealist side. On the materialist side: brute creaturely death, base materiality, a life curtailed, consumed and consigned to the trash. The element of animated caricature should not be overlooked. While Top Cat, 'TC', is our point of reference for a cartoon consumed fish, not (necessarily) Sekula's, it touches on his thinking about popular comic forms, the film studios and the interconnection of animated with still images. Two words accompany the drawings: 'Icthus/Icthys'. The distinction he attempted here likely drew on memory and is not accurate, but nonetheless carries palaeontological and archival resonances. He

1 Allan Sekula Papers 1960–2013. Getty Research institute Special Collections. Catalogue Reference: 2016. M.22. Notebook Number S.1.05:02. 1999. (Hereafter, abbreviated to Sekula Papers with notebook descriptor.)

clearly had in mind the Latinised Greek word for 'fish' ('Ichthys' or 'Ichthus'), which is commonly used for the 'Jesus fish'. He probably also had in mind the taxonomic term, often classifying primordial fossil fish or extinct fish-lizards.[2] Sekula's 'idealist fish', like an elongated loop of string, is reminiscent of visual instructions for knotting rope – and especially like the one he used for the frontispiece to his epic photographic cycle of 1995, *Fish Story*: a reproduction of a plate from Diderot and d'Alembert's *Encyclopédie ou Dictionnaire raisonnée des sciences, des arts et des métiers*, showing 'Fishing, Fabrication of Nets'. A further clue to the significance of Sekula's note – repeating the same inverted commas around 'cultural studies' – can be found in his withering comment of 1997 concerning 'the ongoing academic institutionalization of "cultural studies" as a field of happily roving "interdisciplinarity" that too often evades the grim and contested and oh-so-boring terrain of the economic'.[3]

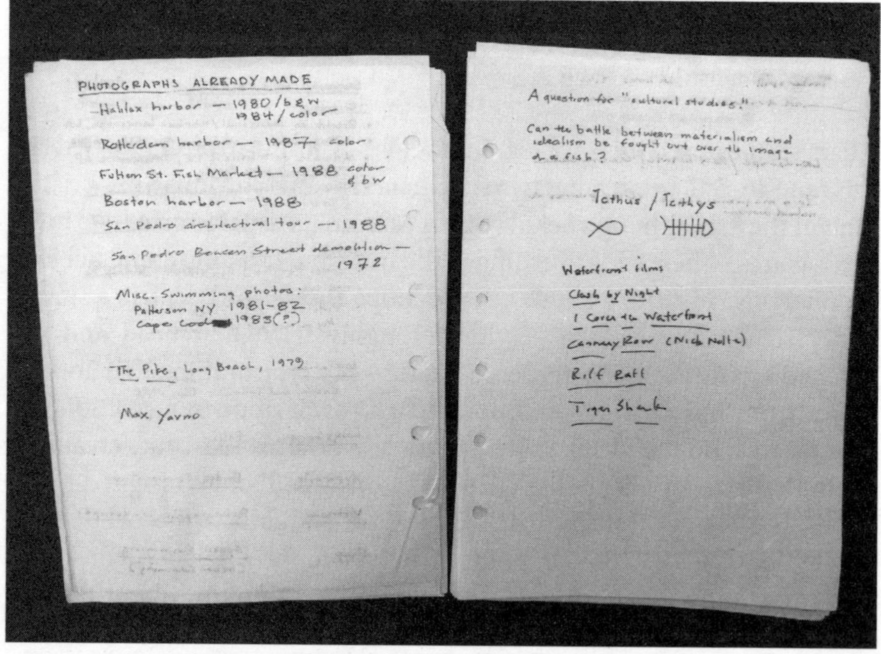

PHOTOGRAPHS ALREADY MADE
Halifax harbor — 1980/b&w
1984/color
Rotterdam harbor — 1987 color
Fulton St. Fish Market — 1988 color & bw
Boston harbor — 1988
San Pedro architectural tour — 1988
San Pedro Beacon Street demolition — 1972
Misc. Swimming photos:
Patterson NY 1981–82
Cape Cod 1985(?)
The Pike, Long Beach, 1979
Max Yavno

A question for "cultural studies!"
Can the battle between materialism and idealism be fought out over the image of a fish?
Icthus / Icthys
Waterfront films
Clash by Night
I Cover the Waterfront
Cannery Row (Nick Nolte)
Riff Raff
Tiger Shark

Figure 1: Page spread from Sekula's notebook, Sekula Papers, S.1.05:02, 1999

2 The suffix ('-ichthys') is used for fish and the prefix ('ichthyo-') for both fish and fish-like creatures, as with the ichthyosaurs ('fish-lizards').

3 Allan Sekula, 'On *Fish Story*: The Coffin Learns to Dance', *Camera Austria* 59/60 (1997): 49–69 (52).

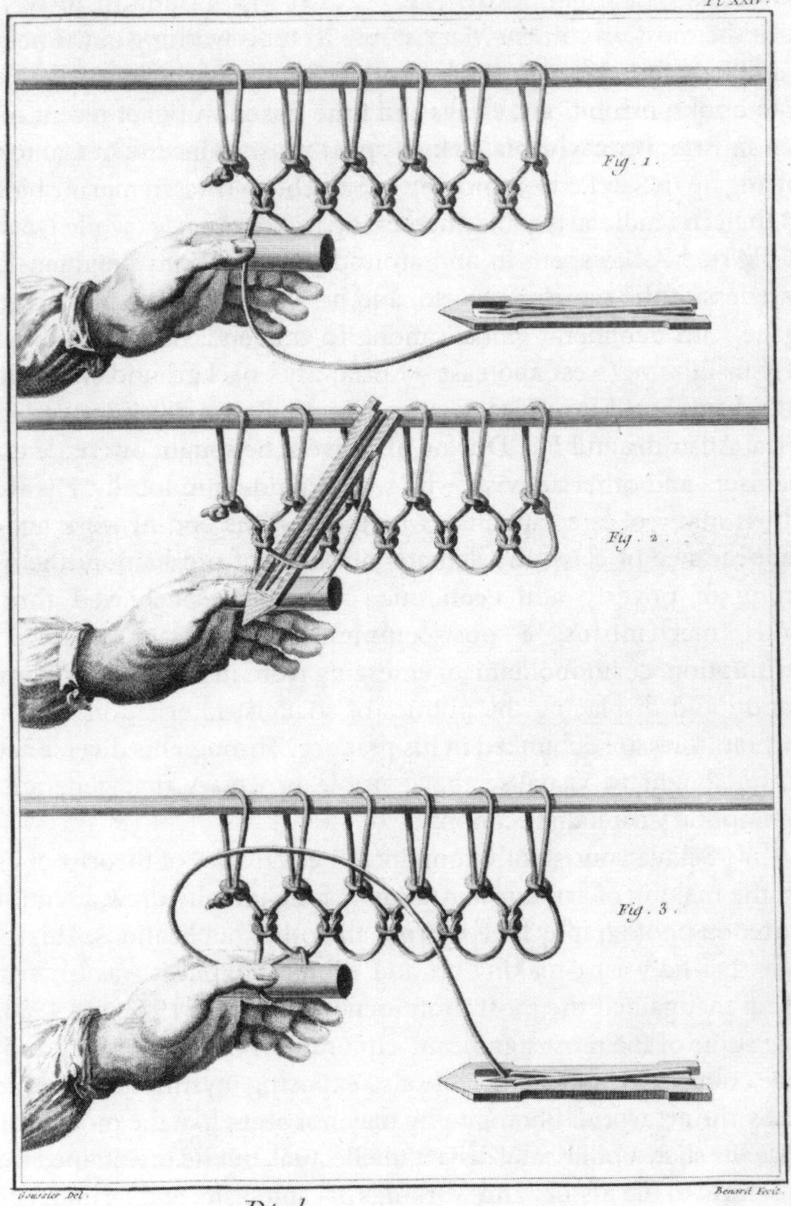

Figure 2: Frontispiece to Fish Story *(1995)*
Diderot and d'Alembert's Encyclopédie ou Dictionnaire raisonnée des sciences, des arts et des métiers, *'Fishing, Fabrication of Nets'*

The North American photographer, cultural theorist, filmmaker and political activist Allan Sekula (1951–2013) was for almost forty years one of the most prominent Marxist intellectuals working in the fields of art and lens-based practices. He produced some of the most significant photo books, exhibitions, essays and time-based works of recent times. Born in Erie, Pennsylvania, Sekula spent most of his life in California: growing up in San Pedro; studying in San Diego (first in marine biology and then in studio arts); and then living in Los Angeles while teaching at CalArts.[4] A life spent in and around port locations heightened his awareness of the maritime world, and he was one of the first artists to engage with neoliberal globalisation. To this end, he travelled extensively in Europe (west and east – his family's background was Polish); Central and South America; East and South-East Asia; as well as South Africa, Australia and Fiji. During his travels, he sought out trade union organisers and other activists who would guide him locally. His works address many of late capitalism's mythemes: the end of work and the disappearance of class; the dematerialisation of production; the overcoming of poverty and economic 'convergence' achieved through market mechanisms; a post-communist democracy attained by consumption; cosmopolitanism emerging from instantaneous communication and displacing the politics of socialist internationalism – so many fantasies are debunked in his practice. Through his diverse activities, he sought to visualise the invisible processes that generate the contemporary capitalist economy.

While Sekula consistently combined the activities of theorist or critic with the making of art, it is fair to say that he initially drew attention as a writer on photography for *Artforum* and other publications. This is not to say that he wasn't making art and exhibiting, but it was his critical writing that gained the most prominence.[5] Between 1973 and 1983, he wrote some of the most significant explorations of photography and the image culture of capitalism, while also exposing mystifications perpetuated by the art world. Photography may not seem like the most obvious choice for such a politically driven intellectual, but he maintained that it was central to the history and workings of capitalism, and he understood his project as brushing photography 'against the grain', to use his

4 For short periods he lived in New York and Ohio, while fellowships took him to Nova Scotia, Saché (France) and Lisbon.

5 One rather foolish reviewer suggested he would be best remembered for his essays: Steve Edwards, 'The Condition of Photographic Culture: The Work of Allan Sekula', *Art History* 9:4 (1986): 545–52.

favourite adage from Walter Benjamin.[6] His essays from this period are collected in *Photography Against the Grain* (1984).[7] From the early 1970s, his critical essays and photo works ran in tandem, but in the mid-1990s, his attention increasingly shifted to the production of exhibitions and photo books, and then to video and film works. The early photo works already engaged text–image relations (scripto-visual work in the post-conceptual or political-conceptual lineage), but, over time, the barriers between these genres became ever more porous. His writing become increasingly associative, looser, absorbing the horizontal-montage form of his artworks. Meanwhile, some of his artworks adopt an essayistic form, such as *The Lottery of the Sea* and *The Forgotten Space*, while *Black Tide/Marea Negra* was imagined through the model of an operetta.

Sekula became antagonistic towards the political quietude and epistemological scepticism associated with dominant versions of 'postmodernism'. As realism and documentary became subject to intense intellectual suspicion and hostility during the 1980s and 1990s, Sekula deepened his engagement with these modes. He began thinking about and working in photography in the 1970s, at a time when critical intellectuals were rediscovering the historical avant-gardes and reworking the legacy of Bertolt Brecht. Sekula notes, in an interview with Benjamin H. D. Buchloh, that his approach – combining Hegelian and structuralist Marxism – 'wouldn't have passed muster in the more strict British

6 Sekula alludes to Thesis VII in Walter Benjamin, 'Theses on the Philosophy of History' (1940), in *Illuminations* (London: Fontana, 1973), 255–66 (259); retranslated as 'On the Concept of History', in *Selected Writings Volume 4, 1938–1940* (Cambridge, MA: The Belknap Press, 2003), 389–400 (392).

7 Allan Sekula, *Photography Against the Grain: Essays and Photo Works 1973–1983* (Halifax, Nova Scotia: The Press of Nova Scotia College of Art and Design, 1984). The volume is republished (London: MACK Books, 2016) with a Preface by Sally Stein. MACK has taken the trouble to replicate the original appearance and the paginations are identical except for Sekula's 'Introduction', where we give page references to both editions. There are two other major essays from the period: 'Photography Between Labour and Capital' (1983) and 'The Body and the Archive' (1986). The second was the last of his more formal academic essays; thereafter, essayistic writing became incorporated into his creative practice. Allan Sekula, 'Photography Between Labour and Capital', *Mining Photographs and Other Pictures, A Selection from the Negative Archives of Shedden Studio, Glace Bay, Cape Breton, 1948–1969*, eds Benjamin H. D. Buchloh and Robert Wilkie (Halifax, Nova Scotia: The Press of Nova Scotia College of Art and Design, 1983); 'The Body and the Archive', *October* 39 (1986): 3–64. Both essays are now available, along with many others, including *Geography Lesson: Canadian Notes*, in Allan Sekula, *Art Isn't Fair: Further Essays on the Traffic in Photographs and Related Media*, eds Sally Stein and Ina Steiner (London: MACK Books, 2020). In *Amphibious Realities*, we have largely referenced earlier publications; most of these now rare essays are readily available in the MACK editions.

context that had developed around *Screen* magazine'.[8] From today's perspective, his lack of orthodoxy and open intellectual constellation looks more productive. Indeed, Sekula's theoretical concerns now appear especially prescient, even if some of the specific political details seem to belong to a previous era. From the early 1970s, his work engaged with precarious labour, biopolitics, social reproduction and anti-imperialism. As his work developed in the 1980s, other issues emerged for him: cognitive mapping, borders and migration, globalisation, critical logistics, abstraction and the value form.

Following the completion, in 1995, of his epic project *Fish Story* – which was, arguably, the centrepiece of the hugely significant *Documenta 11*, curated by Okwui Enwezor in 2002 – he gained international recognition as an artist. Combining essays on the imaginary of the sea with photographic sequences made around the world, *Fish Story* presented a multi-layered reflection on global capitalism. This realist interrogation of the global marketplace or capitalist world system spoke to a new generation of activists and thinkers who were experiencing the devastating impacts of neoliberalism. His consistent engagement with the military-industrial complex – from *Aerospace Folktales* (1973) through *War Without Bodies* (1991/96) to *The Lottery of the Sea* (2006) – engaged with the hot wars of the new imperialism. His strong emphasis on the role of social relations anticipates the rise of relational practices in contemporary art. He stood with the protesters at Seattle in *Waiting for Tear Gas* (1999–2000); he sailed with campaigners for the rights of maritime workers in *Ship of Fools* (1999/2010), and, in *Black Tide/Marea Negra* (2002–3), recorded Galician fishing communities and environmental volunteers attempting to clear an oil spill. He persistently explored the labour–capital relation, from *Aerospace Folktales* through to his final films. He examined the global interconnections of maritime work, and the transformations wrought on it by containerisation and the flag-of-convenience system: *Fish Story*, *TITANIC's wake* (1998–2000), *The Lottery of the Sea*, *The Dockers' Museum*, and, with Noël Burch, *The Forgotten Space* (2010).

In the revivified political climate around art in the first decades of the twenty-first century, the model of Jean-Luc Godard, so prominent

8 Allan Sekula in 'Allan Sekula and Benjamin H. D. Buchloh Conversation', in Allan Sekula, *Performance Under Working Conditions* (Vienna: Generali Foundation, 2003), 20–55 (35).

during the 1970s, was supplemented or displaced by other figures, including: Jo Spence, Black Audio Film Collective, Harun Farocki, Martha Rosler, Mrinal Sen, Jean-Marie Straub and Danièle Huillet, Chris Marker, Med Hondo, Alexander Kluge, and Laura Mulvey. To this list should be added Allan Sekula as a key critical intellectual interrogating capital with and in photography, film and art. His works – including *Fish Story*, *Waiting for Tear Gas*, *The Lottery of the Sea*, and *The Forgotten Space* (the film that he made with Noël Burch won the Orizzonti Jury Prize at the Venice Film Festival) – bear comparison with any works of art or film made within the last twenty years. As a sustained project holding together a radical investigation of capitalist social reality and critical thinking about representation, his work is quite probably unrivalled. It is difficult now to imagine many of the directions taken in recent art and photography without the formative impact of his practice. It is not so much that he has produced a raft of imitators – his has been a singular intervention – but rather that growing numbers have come to understand the importance of the questions he raised concerning aesthetics and politics.

Discussions of Sekula's work typically focus on his militant social critique and his explicit themes: the maritime industries, globalisation, deindustrialisation, containerisation, logistics and class conflict. While commentary of this type is certainly welcome, Sekula's project is not reducible to economics and politics; focusing solely on these topics makes it difficult to see what is actually distinctive about his practice. Our book is centrally conceived as an engagement with a dialectics of form. We consider what is at stake for a thoroughgoing commitment to socio-political art. Asking questions about the sea, painting and socialism as well as representation and historical anachronism, and navigating the risk of 'the additional charge of "naïve realism" or reflectionism', Sekula remarks: 'The economic questions are relatively easy to answer, while the aesthetic questions are more difficult.'[9] And herein – within the 'aesthetic questions' – is to be found all the interesting stuff that gives Sekula's work its granularity, singularity, fascination and

9 Allan Sekula, 'Dismal Science: Part 1', *Fish Story* (Rotterdam: Witte de With, and Düsseldorf: Richter Verlag, 1995), 41–54 (48). A second edition was produced in 2002 by Richter Verlag. MACK Books published the third revised edition *Fish Story* with a new Foreword by Laleh Khalili (London: MACK, 2018). Paginations are consistent across these editions.

importance.[10] In this book, we want to hold fast to and explore some – if not all – of the difficult aesthetic questions that Sekula's work presents.

The problem that confronts us can be posed through the maritime hazard that appears in classical literature: how to navigate the Strait of Messina, between rock shoal and whirlpool, personified by the monsters Scylla and Charybdis. Which is to say, tacking too close to 'art' brings the dangers of small-world elitism, preciousness, internalised reflection or aestheticisation. Steering too closely towards social-political topics risks reducing Sekula's practice to illustration, transparency and instrumentalism. This problem or concern is posed in his notebooks. In 1998, he worried that *Fish Story* was being read solely in terms of its content: 'absence of plans for esthetic commentary on work. Risk of treating FS transparently.'[11] Sekula remained sensitive to the difficulties faced by some of his readers and viewers in grasping not only the socio-political content of his work but also its aesthetic and poetic dimensions. Benjamin H. D. Buchloh wrote of the illegibility of Sekula's work in and for the art world of that time (existing in the non-space 'between discourse and document').[12] That situation was to change – to a degree. At stake, we argue, is not how to steer the 'safe' middle course between reductive notions of the social and narrow understandings of the aesthetic. It is far messier than that; and becoming an expert navigator is no solution. It is not so much (to change the metaphor) 'how to strike a balance?' – a question that invites us to find ways and means of achieving harmony between these two situations or requirements. Sometimes footing is lost, the tightrope walker trips; sometimes cartoons fall flat. On 18 August 1989, he wrote in his notebook: 'My parochialism. My anti-modernism. My recourse to anecdote. My failure to universalize. What can be rescued from the particular and the local? What false refuges, illusory totalities

10 Ariella Aïsha Azoulay has also sought to counter the conventional opposition of 'aesthetics and politics'. See *Civil Imagination: A Political Ontology of Photography* (London: Verso, 2012). In Azoulay's thinking, the potentialities of the 'political imagination' have been circumscribed by the ongoing denigration of the aesthetic (here she includes Walter Benjamin's critique of the 'aestheticisation of politics'); hence, she advocates for '*civil* imagination'. However, her concerns are primarily animated by the Kantian and Habermasian frameworks that shaped the 'modernity-postmodernity' debates of the 1980s. We do not take these as foundational. We refuse the aesthetics–politics dichotomy as a starting point, while still acknowledging its socio-material, historical and discursive functioning, placing emphasis on the tensility of the relationship. Politics is always aesthetic; aesthetics always political.

11 Sekula Papers, S.1.08:01, 1998.

12 Benjamin H. D. Buchloh, 'Allan Sekula: Photography between Discourse and Document', *Fish Story*, 189–200.

are offered by this? Retreat? Advance?'[13] It seems that he was ventriloquising criticisms aimed at his work – whether by unsympathetic foes or, more constructively, by friends. But these might equally be self-criticisms, or ones imagined through inner dialogues with the aesthetic, theoretical and political debates he engaged in.

One motivation for this book has been our frustration with the cursory attention given to Sekula's actual creative output, to his image work, but also to his modes of writing. Commentaries generally 'speak around it'. Admittedly, our frustration has only partially been assuaged – in some senses, further aggravated – by our rationale for and the scale afforded by this project. To provide a full *explication de texte* for Sekula's major works – even just one – would require a book many times the size of this volume. One thinks of the differing models represented by Barthes's *S/Z* or Sartre's study of Flaubert.[14] Indeed, it would be an impossible project, and one probably bordering on insanity (even if productively so). We sometimes focus into detailed work, reading units of meaning that the author of *S/Z* might call *lexia*. And, in places, we entertain crazier temptations. If attention to form risks a kind of 'formalism' (narrowly understood), we hope that our discussions will prove to be a very different kettle of fish. A dialectics of form is not formalism. Even formalism itself comes in several guises. Sergei Eisenstein, for his part, pointed out that the antonym of 'form' is not, as is frequently assumed, 'content', but 'formlessness' – by which he meant badly articulated ideas.[15] The 'formless' – in the aesthetic and psychoanalytic senses – as we will show, has an active place in Sekula's thinking.

We want to get at the cultural logics of these works, to think alongside Sekula and to reconsider the relation of aesthetics and politics. We have used his personal notebooks and library not to supply fixed meaning but as guides in our research. This engagement, in turn, commits us to attempt some detailed descriptions of Sekula's diverse and multilayered works. If philosophy involves the elaboration of concepts, one of the tasks immediately facing art historians is *ekphrasis*: a labour of speech or writing that aims to guide the eye or the senses. That is not all

13 Sekula Papers, S.1.05:04, 1989–90.

14 Roland Barthes provided a paragraph-by-paragraph commentary on Balzac's novella *Sarrasine* in *S/Z: An Essay* (1970; New York: Hill and Wang, 1974).

15 Sergei Eisenstein, 'The Problem of a Materialist Approach to Form' (1925), in *Sergei Eisenstein Selected Works. Vol. 1: Writings, 1922–34*, ed. Richard Taylor (London: I.B. Tauris, 2010), 59–64.

a history of art should be, of course, but the labour of description (or description-meets-analysis-meets-interpretation) is by no means a straightforward undertaking. It entails more than filling a gap or oversight in the Sekula literature. 'Description' is at the heart of the problems presented and explored by Sekula. It is political, not pre-political. The documentary photograph poses that problem in a way that other kinds of image do not. To put it another way, and in the simplest terms, were we to describe a painting, no one would doubt that it was a painting being described – even if we did a poor job of describing it and said nothing about painting *qua* painting. The photograph – above all, the photograph that aspires to document – always risks disappearing. Like a vanishing mediator, viewers seem to slide through the invisible surface or screen. From the perspective of description (as a project) this tends to result in the works appearing as mere illustrations to accounts with other gravitations: economic, social, political, theoretical. We do not look, let alone watch or see; we seem just to acknowledge and check the boxes. 'Maritime industries': tick; got it. Working activities: tick; spot some folks labouring. Protesters: tick; move on to the next. The image tends to be little more than a confirmation of the ideas discussed. So, what if, instead, we slow down?[16] A favourite approach of Sekula's was to retard capitalist momenta, to deliberately refuse or interrupt their temporalities; to find antidotes to the profit-driven hubris, the culture of spectacle or the serialities of assembly-line production, or manipulations of consumerist desire. He practised a militant aesthetic go-slow. He actively values the role of the 'simple descriptive',[17] of 'portrayal' and 'more modest descriptive strategies'.[18] He finds significant, to use Alex Potts's observations on realism, 'the referential, outwardly directed, representational aspects of an artwork'; the 'density and vividness of reference to some larger world or reality'.[19] He aspires, and these are his words, to 'a "poetics" of sequenced descriptive photographs';[20] and, while being no narrow empiricist, seeks 'the radical wisdom that follows from close and sustained attention to observation'.[21]

16 For another argument advocating slow looking, see T. J. Clark, *The Sight of Death: An Experiment in Art Writing* (New Haven, CT: Yale University Press, 2006).

17 *Waiting for Tear Gas [white globe to black]*, in *Art Isn't Fair*, 170 (note to reader: where the author is not identified in these shortened citations, it is Sekula).

18 'On *Fish Story*', 56.

19 Alex Potts, *Experiments in Modern Realism: World Making in Postwar European and American Art* (New Haven, CT: Yale University Press, 2013), 2, 24.

20 'On *Fish Story*', 52.

21 Ibid., 51.

Sekula's project takes us to the heart of the intractable problem facing any artist committed to a critical-realist epistemology: the materiality of capitalism's social relations exceeds empirical detectability. The question of how to represent capitalism, and increasingly its terraqueous form, is at the heart of his practice. His video essay *The Lottery of the Sea* (2006) asks how to reveal the 'hidden hand' of the global market.[22] Rendering visible the abstract processes that shape our world is not an easy task, and it is one that usually eludes even the most committed of image makers. As Fredric Jameson notes – generalising from Marx's comment on value – capitalism can be seen 'only in its symptoms'.[23] How, then, are we to show accumulation, socially necessary labour time, exchange value, fictitious capital, the geopolitical system of states, or even classes? How might we confront a situation or condition not given to immediate understanding? In its classic articulation, this problem has centred on the motif of industrial architecture – more specifically, the *photographing of* manufacturing buildings. Sekula often returned to Brecht's comment:

> A photograph of the Krupp works or the AEG reveals almost nothing about these institutions. Reality as such has slipped into the domain of the functional. The reification of human relations, the factory, for example, no longer discloses those relations. So, there is indeed 'something to construct', something 'artificial', 'invented'. Hence, there is in fact a need for art.[24]

The citation was reiterated by Walter Benjamin and, as Brecht acknowledged, derived from Fritz Sternberg.[25] As many radical documentarians

22 *The Lottery of the Sea* (2006) takes its title from Adam Smith's *The Wealth of Nations* (1776). This interest in the critique of political economy also manifests in his essay and projects called 'Dismal Science' (from Thomas Carlyle): 'Dismal Science', in *Fish Story*, 41–54 and 105–37; *Dismal Science: Photoworks 1972–1996* (Normal, IL: University Galleries, 1999).

23 Fredric Jameson, *Representing Capital: A Reading of Volume One* (London: Verso, 2011), 6.

24 Bertolt Brecht, 'The *Threepenny* Lawsuit' (1932), in *Bertolt Brecht on Film and Radio*, ed. Marc Silberman (London: Methuen, 2000), 147–99 (164–5); cf. ibid., 'No Insight Through Photography' (1930), 144. Sekula opens an essay with an abridged version of this quotation ('On *Fish Story*', 49–69).

25 Walter Benjamin, 'A Short History of Photography' (1931), *Screen* 13:1 (1972): 5–26 (24); retranslated as 'Little History of Photography', in *Selected Writings Volume 2, 1927–1934* (Cambridge, MA: The Belknap Press, 1999), 507–30 (526); Brecht, 'No Insight Through Photography', 144.

have experienced, corporate control increasingly determines how, or whether, workplace environments may appear in photography or film. However, the point is not so much that we do not (or cannot) see the working activities inside these spaces. The question of the seen and the unseen, of what enters or fails to enter photographic representation – be that inside the factory, downstream at the new container terminals or onboard the cruise ship – is not simply a matter of where photographers and filmmakers choose (or are allowed) to point their cameras. Relying on 'empirical' or 'naturalistic' approaches to documentary is insufficient, and – to pierce the occluding masks of capitalist appearance, to scratch at its reifications and to solve its representational 'riddles' – Brecht therefore emphasised the 'something to construct'. The tensions between photography's figured and non-figured aspects animate Sekula's thinking.

Sekula was highly alert to the 'complexity of meaning' occasioned by reading images, image sequences and text–image conjunctions.[26] When he began writing and making photographic sequences, documentary practice was widely viewed as politically dubious. During the core decades of neoliberalism, attachment to the documentary or other realist modes was viewed as an indication of theoretical naivety and an adherence to a sentimental humanism, mired in a nostalgic class politics; it was seen as a masquerade of power-knowledge, in which 'truth claims' provided a pretext for the authority of the individuals and institutions that made them. In addition, representations of violence or atrocity were viewed as akin to pornography; the depiction of suffering was criticised as a passive spectator sport in which victims were presented for the pleasure or sympathy of detached viewers. This prevailing attitude was contradictory, even incoherent, on at least two counts: if the practice in its traditional forms was thought to objectify working people, subjecting them to a condescending gaze or moral authority, the proposed solution was to give up on attempts to depict the working class. Instead of a 'counter-investigation', the result was what, in another context, Siegfried Kracauer called 'the abyss of imageless oblivion'.[27] The abandonment of documentary was the form the 'retreat from class' took in visual culture.[28] The second related point

26 'On *Fish Story*', 57.

27 Siegfried Kracauer, *The Salaried Masses: Duty and Distraction in Weimar Germany* (1929/30; London: Verso, 1998), 94.

28 For 'counter-investigation', see Matthew Fuller and Eyal Weizman, *Investigative Aesthetics: Conflicts and Commons in the Politics of Truth* (London: Verso, 2021). Elsewhere,

entailed a criticism of realist epistemology, as though truth claims can ever be suspended. Documentary is an evidential mode; it points and directs attention to the overlooked, but, like all evidentiary forms, it exists in a dialogical condition of 'word' and 'answering word'.[29] Propositions of this kind, like any other truth claim, do not 'prove' anything; rather, they are conditions for disputation and verification. And if, as the critics of the mode argued, documentary is a practice of representation like any other, there is no reason not to take those representations seriously, to read them. As one sceptical commentator of the prevailing critique put it, documentary was said to be 'a fiction like any other – it's just more ashamed of the company it keeps and tries to hide it'.[30] In many cases during that period, a smug irony replaced moral seriousness. Documentary was thought vulgar: as Sekula later noted, it came to be treated as 'a necessary bad object for contemporary art'.[31] His interventions have long been key to challenging the all too easy 'suspicion' towards documentary, anticipating more recent debates.[32]

In opposition to realist practices, some artists and filmmakers at the time attempted to combine avant-garde techniques with political commitments, believing that radical formalist devices could break the grip of ideology on spectators – the way it interpellates subjects; the

---

Weizman distinguishes *Veritas* from verification: highlighting a difference between reified claims to 'Truth' and a process of critical investigation (Studio B: Unscripted, 'Art, surveillance and investigation: Trevor Paglen and Eyal Weizman', 14 May 2023, aljazeera.com). The latter seems closer to Sekula's project of critical realism. For one influential account of the retreat from class, see Ellen Meiksins Wood, *The Retreat from Class: A New 'True' Socialism* (London: Verso, 1986).

29 V. N. Vološinov, *Marxism and the Philosophy of Language* (1929; Cambridge, MA: Harvard University Press, 1986); M. M. Bakhtin, *The Dialogic Imagination: Four Essays* (Austin, TX: University of Texas Press, 1981).

30 Bill Nichols, *Representing Reality: Issues and Concepts in Documentary* (Bloomington, IN: Indiana University Press, 1991), xi.

31 Allan Sekula in Debra Risberg, 'Imaginary Economies: An Interview with Allan Sekula', in Sekula, *Dismal Science*, 235–51 (237).

32 We have in mind here the understanding of documentary as an enabling condition of democratic politics. Along with John Roberts, we see no reason why this important argument should be limited to 'liberal' claims on democracy. John Roberts, *Photography and Its Violations* (New York: Columbia University Press, 2014). See also Ariella Azoulay, *The Civil Contract of Photography* (New York: Zone Books, 2008) and *Civil Imagination*; Robert Hariman and John Louis Lucaites, *No Caption Needed: Iconic Photographs, Public Culture, and Liberal Democracy* (Chicago, IL: University of Chicago Press, 2007), and *The Public Image: Photography and Civic Spectatorship* (Chicago, IL: University of Chicago Press, 2016). Complementary arguments have been advanced by scholars working across the fields of anthropology, critical Black studies and the history of photography, such as Tina Campt, Elizabeth Edwards, Susie Linfield, Leigh Raiford, Deborah Poole and Blake Stimson.

ways we experience, feel and conceptualise our place in the world – even effect a non-bourgeois subjectivity. Drawing on Althusser and Lacan, theorists of the cinematic apparatus transformed this idea into an account of vision and power, suggesting that the mainstream cinematic *dispositif* sutured a centred, bourgeois subject.[33] This project of 'political modernism', as Sylvia Harvey styled it, called for work on the politics of representation (rather than the representation of politics) that would reveal the hidden articulations, procedures and interests that underpinned conventional media. Some of the techniques employed against realism or mimetic naturalism include: displaying the apparatus and laying bare the device; breaking up diegesis through fragmentation and temporal disordering; dislocated montage of imagetrack and soundtrack; using direct address to the beholder; dispersing points of view; breaking empathy or identification through a *Verfremdungseffekt* (estranging or alienation effect).[34] The aim was the defiguration of the imaginary coherence of text or image.

Sekula wrote in 1984, introducing a collection of writings and photo works for *Photography Against the Grain*:

> I wanted to construct works from *within* concrete life situations, situations within which there was either an overt or active clash of interests and representations. Any interest I had in artifice and constructed dialogue was part of a search for a certain 'realism', a realism not of appearances or social facts but of everyday experience in and against the grip of advanced capitalism.[35]

As this passage indicates, Sekula was one of a handful of radical artists who questioned the political-modernist consensus. For him, the techniques of montage (editing and sequencing) could be allied with a

---

33 Key texts – including those of Christian Metz, Jean-Louis Baudry, Jean-Louis Comolli, Mary Ann Doane, Stephen Heath and Kaja Silverman – are collected in Philip Rosen, ed., *Narrative, Apparatus, Ideology: A Film Theory Reader* (New York: Columbia University Press, 1986). For photography, the debate is articulated in Victor Burgin, 'Photography, Phantasy, Function', *Screen* 21:1 (1980): 43–80.

34 Sylvia Harvey, 'Whose Brecht? Memories for the Eighties', *Screen* 23:1 (1982): 45–59. See also David N. Rodowick, *The Crisis of Political Modernism: Criticism and Ideology in Contemporary Film Theory* (Berkeley, CA: University of California Press, 1994); Steve Edwards, *Martha Rosler, The Bowery in two inadequate descriptive systems* (London: Afterall, 2013).

35 Sekula, 'Introduction', in *Photography Against the Grain*, ix–xv (x). (Page xii in MACK edition.)

critically reflexive conception of documentary and an allegorical awareness.[36] We concur with John Roberts, who suggests that, although Sekula treats photography as 'a figured/nonfigured language', this is understood under the political (and not positivist) imperative of 'the documentation of the world'.[37] That said, it is evident that Sekula's earlier 'performative' or 'staged' work had already grappled with these problems, albeit from the other direction. Here is an extract from *This Ain't China* (1974), his photographic study of a San Diego fast-food outlet:

> everyone was satisfied that the first photograph constituted the truth and that the second was a clever piece of propaganda. and from that point on all the photos had a staged look. not because of a moral or esthetic commitment to fiction but because it was no longer possible to photograph inside the boss's kitchen nor was it possible to work there.[38]

This comment was not an external commentary on the work (an interview, a talk, an introduction and so on) but an element of its scripto-visual composition (hence, in part, the non-standard formatting).

Once more, we find ourselves on the terrain of the modernism–realism debate. Montage has been a privileged cultural mode on the left and, unsurprisingly, it has been subject to extensive debate. Both realism and modernism can be seen as responses to the conditions of capitalist culture: the former as a primarily cognitive approach for de-reification through displaying the occluded connections of the social field ('cognitive mapping'), the latter as critical work on subject and suture. Individual thinkers have adopted distinct approaches towards each torn half. Whereas Walter Benjamin saw montage as a defetishising form, capable of tearing open the capitalist dreamworld, Theodor Adorno and Georg Lukács saw it as a fetishistic parallel for the

36 We are not able to explore the matter here, but thinking about documentary troubles post-Adornian accounts of art's autonomy. For consideration of autonomy–heteronomy: John Roberts, 'Autonomy and the Avant-Garde', *Radical Philosophy* 103 (2000): 25–8; Stewart Martin, 'The Absolute Artwork Meets the Absolute Commodity', *Radical Philosophy* 146 (2007): 15–25; Gail Day, 'The Fear of Heteronomy', *Third Text* 23:4 (2009): 393–406; Peter Osborne, 'The Postconceptual Condition, or, the cultural logic of high capitalism today', *Radical Philosophy* 184 (2014): 19–27; Marina Vishmidt, *Speculation as a Mode of Production: Forms of Value Subjectivity in Art and Capital* (Leiden: Brill, 2019).

37 Roberts, *Photography and Its Violations*, 70.

38 Sekula, '*This Ain't China*', in *Photography Against the Grain*, 188 (formatting original).

fragmented consciousness produced by commodity culture – it was one of the few things they agreed on. In 'Realism in the Balance', Lukács suggested the approach was restricted to the surface of reality.[39] Already in 1977, Jameson was arguing that the opposition between modernism and realism had gone stale. There was something slippery about the whole debate, whether we come at it from the perspective of montage or that of documentary. Documentary is a diverse genre, with variants that are observational, direct, poetic, subjective, reflexive or performative. Compared with the scripted fiction film, documentary 'can sustain far more gaps, fissures, cracks, and jumps in the visual appearance of its world', cutting together distinct times and places.[40] Compiled from distinct materials – talking heads and interviews that can represent differing points of view, observational images, voice-over, archive material, songs and diverse other elements – it is the argument or research method that provides unity by weaving together these different materials and voices. The political modernism of the 1970s, whatever its strengths and fascinations, adhered to a rather myopic view of realist forms.

The strategies of political modernism, as we have seen, were meant to disrupt imaginary coherence; in some accounts, they were intended to produce a critical (even a revolutionary) subject.[41] In late twentieth-century photography, however, these strategies sometimes overlaid the growing prominence of the staged dioptric (lens-based) tableau. Although distinct projects, political modernism and the tableau similarly opposed documentary. (Though they all use the tableau, Victor Burgin and Jeff Wall, for example, have radically different relations to Godardian political modernism.) Theorisation of the tableau dates back to Denis Diderot, for whom it constrains or disciplines vision under a uniting point of view.[42] This spectatorial position might now read as a

39 Georg Lukács, 'Realism in the Balance' (1934), in *Aesthetics and Politics* (1977; London: Verso, 1980), 28–59; and 'The Ideology of Modernism', in *The Meaning of Contemporary Realism* (1957; London: Merlin Press, 1963), 17–46; Walter Benjamin, 'Surrealism' (1931), in *One Way Street and Other Writings* (London: Verso, 1985), 225–39, republished in *Selected Writings Volume 2, 1927–1934* (Cambridge, MA: The Belknap Press, 1999), 207–21; Theodor W. Adorno, 'Looking Back on Surrealism' (1956), in *Notes to Literature Vol.1* (New York: Columbia University Press, 1991), 86–90.

40 Nichols, *Representing Reality*, 19.

41 Rodowick suggests that the argument depends on an unfounded analogy, collapsing text with subject, so that disrupting narrative structure comes to be seen as performing critical reconstruction of the bourgeois self.

42 Denis Diderot, 'The Salons', *Selected Writings on Art and Literature* (London:

rather paranoid effort to exclude heteroglossia.[43] As Hubert Damisch suggests, it may be that all perspective pictures – rather than fixing the knowing (Cartesian) or desiring (Lacanian) subject – allow for a locating and dislocating of the self.[44] Perhaps being in one place enables us to imagine another; in this regard, perspective and the historical imagination may be closely bound together.

If the locating–dislocating process described by Damisch can be found in any perspectival image, it is especially emphasised in diptychs and montage, with their comparisons and alternating points of view. Pairings of photographs can undertake various functions, such as comparing or contrasting, or employing temporal ellipses. Sekula's methods – montaged adjacencies, page spreads, diptychs, triptychs, 'double diptychs' and so forth – actively multiply or disperse points of view.[45] Sekula's photographs are not intended as isolated shots, and his low-plane vision systematically avoids transcendental framing devices. This is why complaints that he is no 'great image maker' – no Sebastião Salgado – entirely miss the point of his enterprise. Sekula said that he did not think of himself as working in a 'signature style'.[46] If, at first glance, his quotation of other photographers seems close to 'postmodern' appropriation, it is important to recognise that these citations are resituated within larger complexes or narrative frames. He explains that his working method involves editing on a light box to assemble sequences that link images through techniques of metonymic relay, transference and transcoding.[47] Another way of putting this is to say that he rejected the modernist idea of expressive originality for a practice that reworked existing genres, modes and styles. Sekula substitutes the sociolect for the modernist idiolect. Even with those images that are visually arresting in the conventional sense – such as the prow of a container ship pushing forward into the ocean expanse – we understand that he is referring to a genre of such

---

Penguin, 1994). Michael Fried, *Absorption and Theatricality: Painting and Beholder in the Age of Diderot* (1761–69; Chicago, IL: University of Chicago Press, 1980).

43 Jeff Wall appeared flummoxed when Tim Clark put this criticism to him: 'Representations, Suspicions and Critical Transparency: Interview with T.J. Clark, Claude Gintz, Serge Guilbaut and Anne Wagner', in *Jeff Wall* (London: Phaidon, 2002), 112–23 (114).

44 Hubert Damisch, *The Origin of Perspective* (Boston, MA: MIT Press, 1994).

45 On double diptychs, see Sekula's lecture 'Globalism's Discontents and the Return of the Sea', AA School of Architecture, 10 November 1999, youtube.com.

46 Sekula, in Katarzyna Ruchel-Stockmans, 'Interview with Allan Sekula', in *Critical Realism in Contemporary Art: Around Allan Sekula's Photography*, eds Jan Baetens and Hilde Van Gelder (Leuven: Leuven University Press, 2006), 138–151 (148).

47 'Working at the Light Table', dir. Guillaume Blanc, 1999, dailymotion.com.

images; and that this picture will find its place alongside other, less eye-catching photographs, sometimes as counterpoint or as elements of a dialectical image.

The photo essay has been widely misunderstood. Like film, photo essays consist of discontinuous elements (shots) that are edited in sequences, establishing chains of association and temporal direction, where the viewer fills in gaps in diegesis. In this sense, the photo sequence is a modernist form. Sekula could be scathing about the journalistic picture essay, which he considered 'cliché-ridden': 'Photo essays are an outcome of a mass-circulation picture-magazine esthetic, the esthetic of the merchandisable column-inch and rapid, excited reading, reading made subservient to visual titillation.'[48] Yet, in an expanded and critical form (slowed down, opened up), the photo sequence is central to his project, and he drew on the precedent of the photobook, photo essay or picture story. Discussing the spreads in picture magazines, Siegfried Kracauer said that photography's reality 'is to be found solely in the mosaic that is assembled from single observations'.[49] The 'photo mosaic' feels far from 'rapid, excited reading'. Perhaps, even more than narrative film – where, however disjunctive the montage, the filmic forward flow asserts some sense of unity – the photo sequence consists of adjacent-but-*separate* shots. Sekula described his approach to the slide reel *Aerospace Folktales* (1973) as making a 'disassembled movie', evading the 'unilinear dictatorship of the projector'.[50] Sekula's work involves a particularly thoughtful exploration of essayistic and open-form approaches.[51] In this mode, he works the seam/seme to develop a version of documentary that is multi-dimensional and multi-vocal. This is montage as concatenation, involving associations, sequential arrangement and image–text relations.

---

48 Sekula, 'Dismantling Modernism, Reinventing Documentary (Notes on the Politics of Representation)', in *Photography Against the Grain*, 53–75 (60). The essay dates from 1976/78. For extended reflection on Sekula and photojournalism, see: Stephanie Schwartz, 'Anti-Photojournalism: Working Against the Grain', *Waiting for Tear Gas 1999–2000 by Allan Sekula*, 2016, tate.org.uk.

49 Kracauer, *The Salaried Masses*, 32. See also Sergei Tret'iakov, 'From the Photo-Series to Extended Photo-Observation' (1931), *October* 118 (2006): 71–7.

50 Sekula, 'Introductory Note to *Aerospace Folktales*', in *Photography Against the Grain*, 106; 'On *Fish Story*', 57. Young observes that Sekula first referred to a 'disassembled movie' in an artist's statement accompanying *Aerospace Folktales* and then incorporated it into the published version: Benjamin J. Young, 'Sympathetic Materialism: Allan Sekula's Photo-Works, 1971–2000' (unpublished PhD, University of California, Berkeley, 2018), 85 n. 61.

51 For an introduction to debates over montage, see: Jacques Aumont, *Montage* (Montreal: Caboose, 2020). See also 'Working at the Light Table'.

The critical issues at stake turn on understanding montage as either essentially 'closed' or 'open', 'smooth' or 'interruptive' – a distinction appearing in film discourse as découpage versus montage. Setting aside single-take novelties, all films involve joining separate shots or shot sequences into a larger continuum. Noël Burch argues that 'shot transition', the passage from frame to frame, is the basic element of cinema.[52] In mainstream narrative cinema, 'match cutting' seeks narrative coherence and self-effacing construction, normalising apparently seamless narrative (découpage or 'transparent montage'). In contrast, montage – especially as practised in different ways by Vertov, Dovzhenko and Eisenstein (sometimes known as 'productive' montage)[53] – prioritised the role of editing in the production of narrative form and meaning. During the 1920s, and arguably until *Bezhin Meadow*, Eisenstein regarded shots and shot clusters as components within an assembly: 'the frame [shot] is a *cell* of montage'.[54] His emphasis was on the interaction of shots: 'The expressive effect of cinema is the result of juxtapositions.'[55] In all forms of montage, the seam/seme is of great importance; the issue is whether stress falls on continuity or ellipse.[56]

Despite his criticisms of political modernism, Sekula's practice owes more to the understanding of montage as contradiction and fragment. Totalising is important (and here he modifies political modernism's overstating of disjuncture), but it is negatively charged and ever motile – repeatedly adjusting to revive representational strategies. Closer to a negative dialectic, the 'whole' never settles; it is understood not as a 'thing' or 'end', but as an animating horizon shaping critical reflection. In this sense, then, the interplay of simultaneity and singularity, the integrative and the disjunctive, the synchronous and non-synchronous,

---

52 Noël Burch, *Theory of Film Practice* (London: Secker & Warburg, 1973), 12; Stephen Heath, 'Notes on Suture', *Screen*, 18:4 (1977): 48–76; 'Narrative Space', in *Questions of Cinema* (London: Macmillan, 1981), 19–75.

53 Timothy Barnard, *Découpage* (Montreal: Caboose, 2009).

54 Pascal Bonitzer cited in Jacques Aumont, *Montage Eisenstein* (Bloomington, IN: Indiana University Press, 1987), 37–8.

55 Sergei Eisenstein, 'Béla Forgets the Scissors' (1926), in *Film Factory: Russian and Soviet Cinema in Documents 1896–1939*, eds Richard Taylor and Ian Christie (London: Routledge and Kegan Paul, 1988), 145–9 (147). Eisenstein's categories – montage of attractions; intellectual montage; tonal and overtonal montage; vertical and horizontal montage; polyphonic or 'contrapuntal' montage; and so forth – are all as essential as they are elusive. Sergei Eisenstein, *Towards a Theory of Montage* (London: I.B. Tauris, 2010).

56 Burch, *Theory of Film Practice*; Roger Leenhardt, 'Cinematic Rhythm', in *French Film Theory: A History/Anthology 1907–1929 Vol. 2*, ed. Richard Abel (Princeton, NJ: Princeton University Press, 1988), 200–5.

might be understood to manifest in aesthetic form. This awareness and sensitivity enables Sekula to develop a vision of an unevenly differentiated and internally contradictory, but nonetheless simultaneously 'totalising' (synchronising), modernity.

Still on the terrain of the (political) modernism–realism debates, while emphasising the descriptive and observational, it is important to register that Sekula's realism is not a practice of mimesis. Nor is it a formal style. It is, rather, a processual and critical orientation towards and against global capitalism; it is a militant research programme of de-reification, relinkage and anti-fetishism. These qualities constitute a 'critical realism' – where Sekula draws not only on Lukács's essay (which tried to advance a mode avoiding both socialist realism and modernism) but also on Brecht's epistemology and on more recent philosophy of science.[57] There are also echoes of the distinction made by Roman Jakobson between realism and verisimilitude, for whom there could be no such thing as 'naive realism'.[58] Instead, Jakobson stressed realism's motility. The 'realistic' gauge must be constantly recalibrated, existent forms de-formed and re-formed.[59]

Sekula's realism involves mediating abstract and concrete; general and particular; the local within the world system, with each term viewed from a partisan and materialist perspective. There are efforts to recognise and describe the totality of global capitalism – attempts to break through its veneers. He gives us details, fragments and singularities, which he builds into chains of contiguity, demolishing and rebuilding to thicken meaning.[60] There are interesting shifts across his practice in photography and film, which we will explore in due course, but, throughout his work, he insisted on the cognitive role of

57 Georg Lukács, 'Critical Realism and Socialist Realism' (1956), in *The Meaning of Contemporary Realism*, 93–135; Roy Bhaskar, *Reclaiming Reality: A Critical Introduction to Contemporary Philosophy* (London: Verso, 1989) and *A Realist Theory of Science* (London: Verso, 1997); *Critical Realism: Essential Readings*, Margaret Archer, Roy Bhaskar, Andrew Collier, Tony Lawson and Allan Norrie, eds (London: Routledge, 1998).

58 Roman Jakobson, 'On Realism in Art' (1921), in *Language in Literature*, eds Krystyna Pomorska and Stephen Rudy (Cambridge, MA: The Belknap Press, 1987), 19–27. For Sekula's understanding of Jakobson's text, see: 'Epilogue: A Debate on Critical Realism Today', in *Critical Realism: Around Allan Sekula's Art*, Hilde Van Gelder and Jan Baetens, eds (Leuven: Leuven University Press, 2006) 121–37 (126–7).

59 Richard Shiff traversed the terrain in 'Phototropism (Figuring the Proper)', *Studies in the History of Art* 20 (1989): 161–79.

60 Fredric Jameson, *Signatures of the Visible* (New York: Routledge, 2007), 200.

documentary realism, while attending to its character as formal construction, emphasising both truth-telling and form-giving. His comparisons through immediate spatial or temporal adjacencies, as well as through intertextual recollections, help summon up the economic and historical integration of diverse locales and histories. The connections might turn on some small anecdote or episode reported by those he had met, or on the artist's own reflections, just as much as on socio-economic logic. To employ Roberto Schwartz's words, the approach involves attending to both 'relations and forms'.[61] Understood like this, Sekula's documentary habitus allows for the production of fluid and multi-accented representations.

Neither reflection nor fabrication, Sekula's works interlace intra- and extra-aesthetic concerns. Part of his brilliance is as a connective thinker. He had real difficulty halting the processual character of this dialectical mode of working. There was always one more link; another possible juxtaposition; a different arrangement. It was almost an affliction that sometimes pushed his work to the edge of intelligibility. His exhibition displays were subject to revisions – not in search of some ideal form, but to respond to a site or the possibilities offered by the shape of a room.[62] Ideas gestated and led down long digressive tracks, sometimes idiosyncratic paths that just held personal weight. As a photographer, Sekula was a compulsive collector of incidents – and, understood like this, the collection of ephemera he assembled as *The Dockers' Museum* (2010–13) is not such an anomaly in his practice.

It comes as no surprise to learn that Sekula was exceptionally well read. 'Bibliophile' is an understatement. His gargantuan library, including 15,000 books, was dispersed around and beyond his modest home. Depending on your perspective, this provokes feelings either of deep comfort or of oppressive anxiety. The collection has been preserved, but it is now turned into a 'visually stunning art installation' (a large decorative wall) at the Clark Art Institute in western Massachusetts.[63] Several critical thinkers are important for him, but his apparent 'eclecticism' – not the best word – was thoughtful and rigorous. Sekula maintained a

61 Roberto Schwarz, *Misplaced Ideas: Essays on Brazilian Culture* (London: Verso, 1992), 101.

62 Evidence of this thinking can be found in his notebooks (for example: Sekula Papers, S.1.05:06, 1991–2, or S.1.05:04, 1989–90) and his discussion of his methods in 'Working at the Light Table'.

63 The Clark, 'Allan Sekula Library', clarkart.edu.

dialectical address, employing seemingly contrary intellectual paradigms or practices (structuralism and dialectics, for example), transcoding distinct bodies of thought within the horizon of Marxism. We suggest that Sekula's thoughtful and rigorous eclecticism is understood not as comprising a diverse range of themes, sources and references, and so on, but as a dialectical 'matrix', which can be diagrammatised by a 'Greimasian square'. Recourse to this semiotic schema helps to capture the distinctively fluid, conceptual and political coordinates of Sekula's work.[64]

The Greimasian square is typically generated from an initial term (for example, 'black'), which is then twice denied: negated first as antonym ('white'), and then as simple difference (anything that is 'non-black'). That process produces three terms. The challenge facing the semiotician turns on identifying the fourth term in the square. We do not need to get lost in the intricacies of Greimasian logic to note an interesting and important consequence: Jameson sees a parallel between this fourth moment and the dialectic's 'negation of the negation'.[65] In the classic threefold movements of the dialectic – thesis-antithesis-synthesis; affirmation-negation-sublation (*Aufhebung*) – the 'negation of the negation' is typically understood as the third moment (that is, as 'synthesis' or 'sublation'). Still, that classic 'third' has increasingly been viewed as entailing both a third and a fourth moment – it is 'supplemented' or 'prised open'.[66] It is worth recalling that Hegel's *Aufhebung* embraces both destruction and preservation, as well as a raising to a new level, making it both a temporary conclusion and a fresh initiation. Jameson's point is that this fourth instance manifests a qualitative shift. It drives a deduction, say, or provokes an intuitive connection; it is a 'semiotic slippage' or 'creative slippage', and a 'great leap' into the unexpected.[67] This fourth is, Jameson suggests, the 'alchemical transmutation' or 'magical term', which transforms, transcodes and resets the entire array of interrelations in the Greimasian matrix.[68] He describes this as an 'amphibious reality'.[69] Jameson surely alludes to the Introduction to Hegel's *Aesthetics*,

64 A. J. Greimas, *On Meaning: Selected Writings in Semiotic Theory* (Minneapolis, MN: University of Minnesota Press, 1987).

65 Jameson, 'Foreword to A. J. Greimas', *On Meaning: Selected Writings in Semiotic Theory*', in *The Ideologies of Theory* (London: Verso, 2008), 524–31.

66 Slavoj Žižek, 'Why Should a Dialectician Learn to Count to Four?', *Radical Philosophy* 58 (1991): 3–9.

67 Jameson, 'Foreword to A. J. Greimas', 527, 528, 531.

68 Ibid., 523, 531. Jameson's example of the fourth term is irony.

69 Ibid., 524.

where Hegel described the modern human as 'an amphibious animal' who must 'live in two worlds which contradict one another'.[70] This familiar discordance is where, on the one hand, life and consciousness are 'imprisoned in the common world of reality and earthly temporality' (in objectivity) and, on the other, modern thought (spirit) subjectively aspires to freedom.[71] Amphibiousness results from consciousness striving to move beyond the rigidity of this and other oppositions (object/subject, matter/freedom, nature/spirit, intellectual/affective, concept/intuition, concrete/abstract, finite/infinite, and so forth). Jameson's characterisation of 'amphibious reality' – and we should note his Marxist- or left-inspired twist on Hegel – speaks to Sekula's creative approach. (On a coincidental biographical note: Sekula was very much at home in water; he was a strong swimmer and body surfer, having grown up as a 'harbour rat' – the term port workers used for children who played around the wharves and breakwaters.)

Sekula often tarries in the interstices of seeming oppositions: documentary/art; montage/record; realism/modernism; Brecht/Lukács; heteronomy/autonomy; everyday/aesthetic; art/politics; theory/practice; objective/subjective; base materialism/imaginative flight; labour/capital; local/global; abstract/concrete. And his discussions often traverse other social topographies in art and culture, which invariably have political implications: low/high; below/above; enslaved/enslaver; production/consumption; occlusion/appearance; agent/spectator; active/passive. If this all looks a bit 'binary' (and this is a mistake made by some readers), that is not because Sekula subscribed to a dualist metaphysic – quite the contrary – but because the dualisms are born of capitalist social relations, not only as ideas but as material forms, which are constantly being resurrected, reshaped, reframed and always accumulated afresh.[72] Sekula's

70 G. W. F. Hegel, *Aesthetics: Lectures on Fine Art*, Vol. 1, translated by T. M. Knox (1835; Oxford: Oxford University Press, 1975), 54.

71 Ibid.

72 Philosophers dispute the reading of Hegel's passage on the 'amphibious animal': whether Hegel proposes that art (or philosophy) can reconcile what cannot be reconciled in actuality; or whether he falls into error and contradicts himself (caught between his argument on irreconcilability and the accepted 'reconciliatory' mores of his day); or whether aesthetic reconciliation should be distinguished from social reconciliation; or what weight Adorno gives in his reading of Hegel. In light of the points made by Jameson, we would err towards left interpretations. Importantly, in the debates over Hegel's passage, 'consciousness' shuttling between the two opposing states is not taken to reinforce dualism (as initially appears to be the case by the array of contrasting terms). On the contrary, the focus is on the very movements to resist dualism. The amphibian, then, opposes ontological dualities produced by modern life. This account accentuates the amphibious condition not as

project entails holding these contrasting registers in tension, suspending their poles, mixing or cross-infecting their terms; he swims betwixt and treads the water in between them, while also being tugged by the internal currents they generate. To be clear: this 'between' is not the same as those recurrent aesthetic fashions where ambiguity and indeterminacy are celebrated as ends in themselves.

The fluidity of Sekula's thought becomes, of course, highly schematised by this 'semiotic square', which – it is important to keep in mind – is simply a device to help visualise a complex field. Nonetheless, delineating coordinates helps to locate the seemingly incongruous elements of Sekula's imagination and to discern some interrelations between them. We also employ Greimas's square with tongues in cheeks. The device privileges, from the outset, one of its own internal vectors; it is essentially a structuralist method. Yet, despite structuralism's synchronic bias, the 'heuristic value' of the approach has been advocated by Jameson – and specifically its value for 'a historicizing and dialectical criticism'.[73] The square, he argues, departs from structuralism's more static approach to binary oppositions: it possesses a 'powerful mediatory capacity' and offers a symptomatic map of 'social contradiction'; it is a way to make visible the antinomies of bourgeois thought, ideology and the 'political unconscious'.[74] These words are Jameson's, but they could also describe some of Sekula's methods.

We are in danger of overplaying the Greimasian square (and that would endow it with more weight than it warrants in this context and more than we intend). We accept that there are problems with the technique itself – and with the version we have drawn: there are gaps, and there could be other coordinates. If there is a single figure who haunts Sekula's imagination, it is probably Walter Benjamin with his injunction

---

metaphysical but as historical. Hegel's amphibious passage can thus be described as characterising the problem of the dialectic and the problem of 'aesthetics and politics'. See: Robert B. Pippin, *After the Beautiful: Hegel and the Philosophy of Pictorial Modernism* (Chicago, IL: University of Chicago Press, 2014); J. M. Bernstein, '"Our Amphibian Problem": Nature in History in Adorno's Hegelian Critique of Hegel', in *Hegel on Philosophy in History*, eds Rachel Zuckert and James Krienes (Cambridge: Cambridge University Press, 2017), 193–212.

73 Fredric Jameson, *Valences of the Dialectic* (London: Verso, 2009), 489; *The Political Unconscious: Narrative as a Socially Symbolic Act* (London: Methuen, 1981), 47. Sekula encountered Jameson at University of California, San Diego (UCSD) while a student. Although Sekula reported not being enamoured with his coterie of postgraduates, he continued to read Jameson's dialectical studies.

74 Jameson, 'Foreword to A.J. Greimas', 527; *Political Unconscious*, 83.

to brush ideology against the grain. We have placed him under the 'History' coordinate, but Benjamin's contributions traverse all poles, highlighting the schema's intrinsic limitations. The square did not 'come first'; it did not 'lead' our thinking but represents a 'later' distillation of our reflections and discussions. It is an effort to make sense of them. One of us would have removed it altogether once it had done its work in the collaborative process, consigning it to a drawer or file along with the working notes; the other is committed to its retention. But, in the spirit of 'baring the device' for the organisation of this book – or, simply because one co-author was the more stubborn (ever a hazard of dialogic collaboration) – here it is:

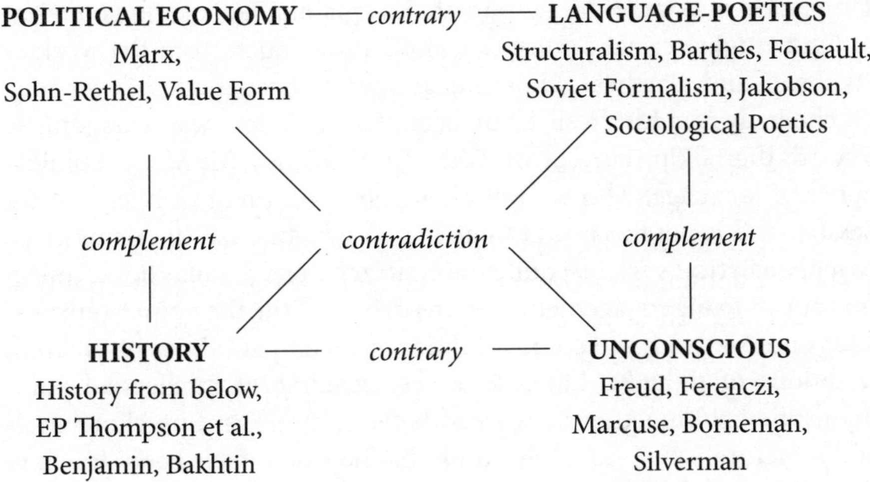

Figure 3: Authors' conceptual matrix for Sekula

In Sekula's historical hermeneutics, the critique of political economy is probably the instance that inflects all the others. That is where we start. As we will see, this is not a crude materialism or an appeal to brute facticity that punches through to some tangible reality independent of signification; rather, in capitalist society economic relations – the accumulation process and the nexus of class – exert a gravitational force on all other relations. Ideologies, political values, social forms and cultural practices are not reducible to these relations, but neither are they independent of them. In this sense, Sekula often referred to 'imaginary economies' or 'imaginary geographies', the layered assumptions and images through which economic processes are understood. This engagement with political economy is consistent across Sekula's work, linking production, social reproduction, circulation and consumption (contrary to those debates – prominent in the late twentieth century – that challenged Marx's supposed 'productivist bias' and turned to focus solely on consumption).

Sekula brings the critique of political economy into dialogue with other, seemingly incompatible, methodologies. Michel Foucault, for example, clearly exists in a strained relation with many of the other thinkers that constitute Sekula's web. The same might be said of the socialist humanism of a Lukács or E. P. Thompson and the anti-humanism of Barthes and Foucault. Sekula's debt to synchronic structuralist thought is unquestionably difficult to square with the processual qualities of the dialectic. As well as engaging the critiques of semiotics by Timpanaro and Jameson, he nonetheless maintained a serious interest in (and taught) visual semiotics. Sekula drew much from the work of Jakobson and Barthes, whose ideas figure throughout his writing. Psychoanalysis adds fresh challenges. Foucault too was antagonistic towards the 'talking cure', as was Valentin Vološinov, the Marxist philosopher of language, who was another important point of reference for Sekula. This is not to say that there are no structuralist Marxisms or no psychoanalytical variants; quite the contrary – and Sekula's book collection attests to his engagement with the debates. Still, the point to emphasise is not so much the compatibilities or incompatibilities of different traditions of thought, but Sekula's *constellating* of intellectual paradigms: he held together or worked between Marxism, psychoanalysis and structuralism. One might think that he would have been drawn to the Althusserian attempt to synthesise Marx with structuralism and psychoanalysis, but Sekula remained closer to the more dialectical variants of Marxism, again underscoring the tensions and contradictions in play across his conceptual grid.

Our book is not a systematic explication of the individual studies and artworks; it does not aim to offer a complete overview of Sekula's career, or a full discussion of his works – and some significant projects barely feature in our discussion. As explained at the outset, that is not our project. Rather, our aim is to bring to the surface the intellectual shaping of Sekula's dynamic exploration of the relation of aesthetics and politics. Each of the four chapters is organised around one coordinate of our square. Those acquainted with Sekula's work will recognise some coordinates, while others may be less familiar with the shaping elements – they may be surprised. Our book moves from the more widely recognised towards the less. The elements need to be thought of together. As

Jameson aptly remarks, 'for good or ill, the dialectic requires you to say everything simultaneously'.[75] Questions of aesthetic figuration grow, although they are inevitably there from the outset. Discussions are rarely discrete; they cross-weave and mutually inflect. In the process, we consider elements of Sekula's practice that have hitherto received little or no attention to his employment of the dialectic; his reading of photography through the value form; his systematic purview 'from below'; the role of psychoanalysis; and, last in this listing but not least, his 'critical *ir*realism'.

75 Fredric Jameson, *The Modernist Papers* (London: Verso, 2007), ix.

1

'Capitalism's inability to deliver the conditions of a fully human life'

SECTION 1: STAGING THE MIDDLE

Performative Documentary

Sekula produced his first significant artworks while he was a student at the University of California, San Diego (UCSD), during the period when conceptual art assumed a new political mood. He took art classes with John Baldessari and philosophy with Herbert Marcuse; he argued with Fredric Jameson's students; and worked closely with a like-minded group of postgraduates including Martha Rosler and young faculty members Fred Lonidier and Phil (later Phel) Steinmetz.[1] The climate at UCSD was framed by anti-war activism and the countervailing surveillance and terror; the pall of violence hangs over his early works.[2] Sekula's practice took shape in this situation alongside a heady mix of avant-garde art, leftist political theory, second-wave feminism and Marcuse's Freudo-Marxism. He cleaved to these commitments throughout his life, even as they were inflected by subsequent intellectual configurations.

---

1 Sekula spent six years at UCSD (1968–74), initially registering for marine biology before majoring in studio arts and eventually undertaking an MFA. Marcuse taught at UCSD from 1965–70; Baldessari, 1968–70.

2 For the intellectual and political context in San Diego, see: Mike Davis, Kelly Mayhew and Jim Miller, *Under the Perfect Sun: The San Diego Tourists Never See* (New York: The New Press, 2003); *The Uses of Photography: Art, Politics and the Reinvention of a Medium*, ed. Jill Dawsey (La Jolia, CA: Museum of Contemporary Art San Diego, 2016); Benjamin J. Young, 'Sympathetic Materialism: Allan Sekula's Photo-Works, 1971–2000' (unpublished PhD, University of California, Berkeley, 2018).

Initially performing art actions like his immediate circle, he was drawn to photography. From the outset, he rejected the photographic ideologies of transparency and objectivity. Sekula began by employing photographs to document sculptures and performances or actions, including the collaborative *Body Bags* (1970, also called *Meat Piece*); *Box Car* (1971 – it is important to note in passing that this is a 'Box Car' not a 'boxcar'); and *Meat Mass* (1972). *Box Car* is a single black-and-white photograph with the caption: 'made from the open door of a rail-freight wagon as it passed a chemical research and development plant where I had worked as a technician more than two years earlier'.[3] Almost certainly, he was riding the freight car illegally, recalling the outlaw mobility of the hobos and Wobbly organisers of an earlier time. This action points forward to the role of the container in his later work. Riding a goods wagon figures the author as a movable commodity and, in passing the factory, labour power momentarily faces off against fixed capital. As another example, *Meat Mass* consists of twelve black-and-white photographs and a typed caption: 'Over a period of several weeks, expensive cuts of meat were stolen from a supermarket and stored in a freezer. The thawed steaks were thrown beneath the wheels of freeway traffic.' The images depict: wrapped meat; Sekula exiting the supermarket; passing traffic, with the artist at the roadside; and splatted meat; finally, we see Sekula exiting the freeway and clambering up the embankment. At the time it was made, the United Farm Workers were conducting a unionising campaign and Safeway was targeted for selling non-union lettuce. Perhaps there is a connection and recoding made with the shift from lettuce to steak, vegetable to flesh. Buchloh calls *Meat Mass* an 'enigmatic performance', which alerts us to 'the deep connection between ecological destruction and socially enforced compulsive consumption'.[4] It is a good point, but the juxtaposition is probably broader, joining machines and flesh in a time of war, paralleling Rosler's montage *Bringing the War Home* (1967–72).

Sekula's works between 1972 and 1975 follow two parallel lines of development: conceptual gestures infused with politics and staged, or performed, micronarratives. Along with other politicised US-based artists, Sekula's photoworks joined a militant ethos to the conceptual

---

3 Sekula in 'Allan Sekula and Benjamin H. D. Buchloh Conversation', in Allan Sekula, *Performance Under Working Conditions* (Vienna: Generali Foundation, 2003), 20–55 (21).

4 Benjamin H. D. Buchloh, 'Passages: Allan Sekula, 1951–2013', *Artforum* 52:5 (2014): 45.

puns and visual conundrums of John Baldessari, Keith Arnatt and Jan Dibbets. In Sekula, consciously de-aestheticised forms are combined with socially charged subjects, straddling or oscillating affect and affectlessness. Take *Attempt to correlate social class with elevation above main harbor channel (San Pedro, July 1975)*, now incorporated into *California Stories*: here the viewpoint or sight line is seemingly matched to social topography, gesturing to the role of real-estate speculation in urban politics.[5] Like Fred Lonidier's *29 Arrests* (1972), this is a work that ridicules the formalist residues in conceptual art, its adherents 'sleep through the deluge that threatens them'.[6]

Commentators often over-emphasise the role of conceptual art in the formation of the San Diego group, with the emphasis placed on the canonical figures of Ed Ruscha, Robert Smithson and Dan Graham. If conceptual art was significant for Sekula, it was in relation to those figures with whom he became close around *The Fox* and the New York branch of Art & Language: Ian Burn, Carole Condé and Karl Beveridge.[7] The art-historical focus on the banal photographs of Ruscha and the others minimises the wider histories of realism in Sekula's work. Long before the 'documentary turn', the San Diego group contributed to the recovery and re-evaluation of the documentary mode, considering Jacob Riis, Lewis Hine, the Farm Security Administration (FSA) and the Photo League, and critically evaluating the mannered and subjectivist orientations of the Museum of Modern Art (MoMA) *New Documents* exhibition of 1967. Over the course of Sekula's career, important for him were: Winslow Homer and Constantin Meunier, Herman Melville's *Moby Dick*, Studs Terkel's aural histories and Peter Weiss's *Aesthetics of Resistance*, Joris Ivens, Jean Vigo and Chris Marker, Hartmut Bitomsky, Billy Woodberry, Harun Farocki, Rithy Panh, Fernando Solanas, Jean Rouch and Jon Jost. As he wrote, 'the most developed critiques of the illusory facticity of photographic media have been cinematic, stemming

---

5 See Mike Davis's excoriating essay: 'The Next Little Dollar: The Private Governments of San Diego', in *Under the Perfect Sun*, 17–144. The book includes the group work *Body Bags* (1970) and *Photo Chronicle: 1970–1997* by Fred Lonidier.

6 Theodor W. Adorno, 'Commitment' (1965), in Bloch et al., *Aesthetics and Politics* (1977; London: Verso, 1980), 177–95 (177).

7 Burn introduced him to Condé and Beveridge in 1976. See '. . . The Red Guards come and go, Talking of Michelangelo, in *Condé and Beveridge: Class Works*' (2008), in Allan Sekula, *Art Isn't Fair: Further Essays on the Traffic in Photographs and Related Media*, eds Sally Stein and Ina Steiner (London: MACK Books, 2020), 283–90. *The Fox* was the journal of the Art & Language group in New York as it increasingly became involved with radical politics.

from outside the tradition of still photography'.[8] In an interview with Benjamin Buchloh, Sekula counters the conceptual art frame, stressing his engagement with other sequential image presentations – Muybridge and the photographic book form, from the FSA to Larry Clark. Sekula, Rosler and the rest of the San Diego group possessed a broad understanding of photography's diverse histories. Sekula said 'Godard's take on the pathetic lumpen-imperialist blandishments of photography' in *Les Carabiniers* 'seemed much more compelling than anything I could find in conceptual art'.[9] This understanding of photography enabled this group to look for their models outside the pages of *Artforum* – the mouthpiece of US avant-garde art in the 1960s (as *Art News* had been in the later 1940s and 1950s).

The presence of Ed Ruscha on the Los Angeles art scene makes his bookworks a regular point of comparison for commentators. Sekula displays an ambivalence towards Smithson, but otherwise conceptual art appears as a negative example in his practice. Benjamin Young perceptively suggests Ruscha's books are a game with late-modernist criticism – flatbed, drip, stain, grid – but this observation must be expanded.[10] John Roberts provides a suggestive reading of the 'eradication of empathy and identification' in Ruscha's bookworks, and, by extension, others working with vernacular photo forms. This 'commodity-vision', he argues, involved 'numbness, inertness, and repetition', where an earlier identification with photographers as witnesses to 'every-day experience and struggle' was replaced by 'empathy and identity with the photographer's *field of vision*'.[11] In a related vein, Sekula notes that he was 'annoyed' by the 'neutron bomb' approach of the New Topographics, which eradicated people while preserving property.[12] The prefabricated tract housing and industrial units in the images had a bureaucratic commodity logic – an idea developed in his later work. This criticism marks a difference from photography's

8 Sekula, 'Dismantling Modernism, Reinventing Documentary (Notes on the Politics of Representation)', in *Photography Against the Grain*, 53–75 (62).

9 Sekula in 'Allan Sekula and Benjamin H. D. Buchloh Conversation', 23.

10 Benjamin J. Young, 'Arresting Figures', *Grey Room* 55 (2014): 78–115 (92).

11 John Roberts, *Photography and Its Violations* (New York: Columbia University Press, 2014), 136–7. It is somewhat unclear whether Roberts sees this as a consciously critical perception by Ruscha or as the echo of the commodity form.

12 The 'neutron bomb' reference comes from Sekula's retrospective note (2011–12) for *California Stories* in *Art Isn't Fair*, 293. Cf. his other comments on the New Topographics: 'Dismantling Modernism, Reinventing Documentary', 63–4, and *School Is a Factory*, 233–4, in *Photography Against the Grain*.

commodity-masochism. To parody and irritate this affectless conceptual aesthetic, Sekula and his co-workers injected realist elements.

Alongside Sekula's conceptual gestures, he developed a narrative presentation, which would become the enduring form for his practice. These micronarratives include *Short Autobiography* (1971); *Two, three, many . . . (terrorism)* (1972); *California Stories* (1973–5, clustering some smaller works); and, perhaps, *Untitled Slide Sequence* (1972). These black-and-white photographs, ordered in a sequence and usually with text, draw on the popular genre of the photo narrative. In the six silver gelatine prints comprising *Two, three, many . . . (terrorism)*, Gregg Arreguin poses in everyday settings holding a toy gun and wearing a Vietnamese *nón lá*. The title evokes Che Guevara's 1967 speech to the Tricontinental in which he predicted 'a bright future should two, three or many Vietnams flourish throughout the world'.[13] The work shows – and shares with others Sekula made at the time – a concern with anti-imperialist struggle, 'Third World' revolution, guerrilla organisation and the 'base' or 'foco'. *A Short Autobiography* notes, 'We're looking at Godard and reading Mao' and presents copies of Lenin's *Imperialism* and Fanon's *Wretched of the Earth*. These works mix forms and media, high and low, politics and everyday life. They stage and perform scenarios, and evidence some of the mores of documentary. In a moment, we will discuss two significant works of this period, *This Ain't China* and *Aerospace Folktales*.

'Dismantling Modernism, Reinventing Documentary (Notes on the Politics of Representation)' articulates claims for politico-performative documentary against the prevailing formalism of the time, associated especially with John Szarkowski's tenure as curator of photography at MoMA. Written in the militant voice of the 1970s, it is a kind of manifesto for the San Diego group; if Sekula authored the text, it seems evident that the essay emerged from collective discussion, perhaps even involving direct input from his collaborators. The essay rejects modernist common sense: 'idealist esthetics', romantic genius, 'the cult of private experience' and 'the transformation of the photographic print into a privileged commodity'.[14] As Sekula noted, 'only formalism can unite all the photographs in the world in one room, mount them behind glass, and *sell* them.'[15] In contrast, he advocated:

13 Che Guevara, 'Message to the Tricontinental', Havana, 16 April 1967, marxists.org.

14 'Dismantling Modernism, Reinventing Documentary', 53–4.

15 Ibid., 59–60.

> an art that documents monopoly capitalism's inability to deliver the conditions of a fully human life, for an art that recalls Benjamin's remark . . . that 'there is no document of civilization that is not at the same time a document of barbarism'. Against violence directed at the human body, at the environment, at working people's ability to control their own lives, we need to counterpose an active resistance, simultaneously political and symbolic, to monopoly capitalism's increasing power and arrogance, a resistance aimed ultimately at socialist transformation.[16]

All photographs are performative, involving the conjuncture of an apparatus and the pro-filmic event to constitute an image. Sekula's works of the 1970s and early 1980s accentuate that condition through explicit theatricalisation, in part taking up the neo-Brechtian or Godardian project articulated by authors associated with *Screen* magazine.[17] Sekula's works in this period combine techniques intended to disrupt imaginary coherence of the work (disjuncture of image and text, humour and clowning, gaps, fragments, splitting, over-writing and performance) with political themes (class, imperialism, family, education, militarism). The lineage of political modernism is now well known, but attention to 'Dismantling Modernism' highlights Sekula's significant difference: he rejected pejorative characterisations of documentary, advocating for realist representations – such as the work of Chauncey Hare and Jon Jost – that were anathema to European political modernists.[18] This new critical orthodoxy took a dim view of 'realism' – characterised, at best, as naïve, and, at worst, as complicit with totalitarian power. This commitment to a reinvented documentary realism would subsequently distinguish Sekula from the emerging critical 'postmodern' consensus. As he described his earlier work retrospectively in 1999:

16 Ibid., 74.

17 We suggest that when authors at *Screen* spoke of Brecht, they translated his practice via Godard, employing a reductive notion of realism; see, for example: Peter Wollen, 'Godard and Counter-Cinema: *Vent d'Est*', *Afterimage* 4 (1972): 6–17; Christine Gledhill, 'Notes for a Summer School: Godard, Criticism and Education', *Screen* 14:3 (1973): 67–74; Colin MacCabe, ed., *Godard: Images, Sounds, Politics* (BFI, 1980); MacCabe, 'Realism and the Cinema: Notes on Some Brechtian Theses', *Screen* 15:2 (1974): 7–27; and in the same issue, Stephen Heath, 'Lessons from Brecht', 103–28.

18 For critiques, see: Rodowick, *The Crisis of Political Modernism*; Edwards, *Martha Rosler, the Bowery in Two Inadequate Descriptive Systems* (London: Afterall, 2013).

> I was drawn to a very mundane idea of documentary: something very direct, uninflected by obvious esthetic treatment. And I began to think that it might be possible to photograph everyday life – leaving a factory, or housework – as if it were performance.[19]

The balancing of these two modes – staged and documentary – shifts in emphasis over time, as we will see, although this is far from a march from theatricalisation to documentary, from ironic humour to seriousness. It is notable how Sekula treated the documentary elements of his practice. Unlike some one-dimensional approaches to 'performative documentary' (if this is even an appropriate term to use), he does not focus on simply ironising documentary rhetoric.[20] The early works parody, at once, the rhetoric of documentary and the performative, while both modes also seem to be tackled with a degree of respect. His interest develops around what he called the 'ambiguity of the documentary function', and how quotidian events already involve fiction or theatre (the 'as if' performance).[21]

This Ain't China: A Photonovel (1974)

This Ain't China: A Photonovel (1974) is Sekula's most evidently Godardian work – Sekula later thought it too much so.[22] Made in a fast-food restaurant where he worked, the narrative sequence depicts a unionisation struggle in a low-paid, casualised sector. Given the predominance of aerospace engineering, electronics industries and steel in the economy of San Diego, this focus on the service sector is noteworthy, pointing to more than student employment. Throughout Sekula's work, labour is invariably precarious. Even secure workers face this risk, their employment always in danger of being withdrawn as

19 Allan Sekula in Debra Risberg, 'Imaginary Economies: An Interview with Allan Sekula', in Allan Sekula, *Dismal Science: Photo Works 1972–1996* (Normal, IL: University Galleries, 1999), 235–51 (240). His point of reference for thinking about performance was both Bertolt Brecht as well as Erving Goffman's *The Presentation of Self in Everyday Life* (New York: Anchor, 1959) rather than J. L. Austin's account of speech acts.

20 For 'performative documentary', see Stella Bruzzi, *New Documentary: A Critical Introduction* (London: Routledge, 2000).

21 Sekula in Risberg, 'Imaginary Economies: An Interview with Allan Sekula', 240. Indeed, Sekula sees not only the ironising of social documentary by neo-Brechtian antinaturalists and would-be postmodern sceptics but also from a very different direction: from Szarkowski.

22 Sekula in 'Allan Sekula and Benjamin H. D. Buchloh Conversation', 24.

capital roves the planet in search of better rates of profit. *This Ain't China* counters the heroic plenitude of the labouring body in realist art.

There is an important political point at stake here. Marxism has often been thought to entail a focus on waged factory work, often emphasising the role of the industrial male 'breadwinner'. This is a peculiar assumption, because, as Marx observed:

> Political economy . . . does not recognize the unoccupied worker, the working man in so far as he is outside this work relationship. The swindler, the cheat, the beggar, the unemployed, the starving, the destitute and the criminal working man are *figures* which exist not *for it*, but only for other eyes – for the eyes of doctors, judges, grave-diggers, beadles, etc. . . . Therefore as far as political economy is concerned, the requirements of the worker can be narrowed down to one: the *need to support him while he is working* and prevent the *race of workers* from dying out.[23]

It is political economy that reduces the proletariat to the wage relation, not Marx. As living labour, the proletarian is an antagonistic element of the commodity labour power (the prime use value for capital).[24] Realist heroicisations of the worker tend to turn work into a *positive* category, underplaying class struggle. 'Labour' is a creation of capitalism and, for Marx, the proletariat is a self-abolishing class. Further, as Michael Denning notes, the problem with the social-democratic normalisation of wage labour was that 'much of capitalism's multitude was unrecognizable to a labour movement that had been reconstituted by state apparatuses into an employment movement'.[25] This attitude has resulted in a lack of attention to women's reproductive work, and the 'surplus population': the unemployed and underemployed, the would-be-employed and what Ambalavaner Sivanandan calls the 'never employed'; informal and precarious labour, migrant wage seekers and the continued existence of other regimes of labour exploitation, such as indenture or enslavement.[26]

---

23 Karl Marx, 'Economic and Philosophical Manuscripts' (1844), in *Early Writings* (London: Penguin, 1975), 279–400 (335); cf. 288.

24 Chris Arthur calls this antagonistic or counterproductive labour: *The New Dialectic and Marx's Capital* (Leiden: Brill, 2004), 52–3.

25 Michael Denning, 'Wageless Life', *New Left Review* 66 (2010): 79–97 (85). Denning provides surveys of social ideas about unemployment, ranging from the mid-nineteenth-century emphasis on the idle, poor and dangerous to discussions of the informal sector and bare life.

26 For 'surplus population', see: Karl Marx, *Capital: I* (1867; Harmondsworth: Penguin, 1976), 794; Ambalavaner Sivanandan, *Communities of Resistance: Writings on Black Struggles for Socialism* (London: Verso, 2019).

According to some estimates, 40 per cent of the world population fitted the category.[27] Denning states: 'Bare life, wasted life, disposable life, precarious life, superfluous life . . . are among the terms used to describe the inhabitants of a planet of slums.'[28] These are not temporary aberrations generated by 'under-development' or blockages preventing the system from working efficiently. Rather, this is the way it works: capitalism sediments layer upon layer of distinct work relations, including: 'casualization, informalization and the proliferation of temporary and precarious jobs.'[29] Even the prefix in 'unemployment' normalises stable, waged work.[30] Many proletarians do not become workers.

Sekula emphasises that 'work exists in a fundamental condition of negativity', labour understood in its negative forms.[31] *This Ain't China* culminates with the workers facing unemployment. In *A Short Autobiography*, Sekula holds Fanon's *The Wretched of the Earth*, which was central to reclaiming the 'lumpenproletariat' as a revolutionary subject *in potentia*.[32] Later, Sekula noted how modernist photography found in the sailor the figure of the 'cancelled worker, an unemployed drifter or bum, literally "on the beach"'.[33] Capitalism is a permanent state of crisis where this position of 'cancelled worker' is always near at hand. If Sekula sometimes depicts people involved in waged labour, the depiction should not be confused with straightforward affirmation.

It is helpful to compare Sekula's position with the distinction that Gáspár Tamás made between the affirmative or 'angelic' and the negative or 'demonic' conceptions of social class. The first, 'angelic' account, associated with Rousseau, has shaped much socialist and Marxist politics; E. P. Thompson and Raymond Williams are included in the line of

27 Aaron Benanav, cited in Søren Mau, *Mute Compulsion: A Marxist Theory of the Economic Power of Capital* (London: Verso, 2023), 299.

28 Denning, 'Wageless Life', 79.

29 Ibid., 95.

30 A report of 2015 by the International Labour Organization suggests that only 20 per cent of people in Sub-Saharan Africa survive on wage labour. Cited in Gargi Bhattacharyya, *Rethinking Racial Capitalism: Questions of Reproduction and Survival* (London: Rowman & Littlefield, 2018), 24–5.

31 Sekula in Pascal Beausse: 'Allan Sekula réalisme critique/The Critical Realism of Allan Sekula', *Art Press* 240 (1998): 19–26 (22).

32 See the chapter 'Spontaneity: Its Strength and Weakness', in Frantz Fanon, *The Wretched of the Earth* (1961; Harmondsworth: Penguin, 1967), 85–118. Marx wrote of 'the great mob of porters etc. who render service in seaport cities etc.' as part of the working lumpenproletariat. See Karl Marx, *Grundrisse: Foundations of the Critique of Political Economy (Rough Draft)* (1857; Harmondsworth: Penguin, 1973), 272.

33 'Dismal Science', 127.

fire.[34] This 'angelic' understanding celebrates the working class in its existing empirical condition, affirming its distinct cultures, institutions and political practices and championing it as an ethically superior bastion of collective and egalitarian values – 'a separate culture and a separate morality inherent in the people'.[35] The 'angelic' account, Tamás argues, conflates class with the trappings of caste, estate or *Stände*. In contrast, Tamás finds a 'demonic' strain present in Marx's writings, where class is understood as a structural negativity; the working class is not external to capital, but a fundamental bearer of the capital relation, shaped by the abstract relations of value production – and, ultimately, the proletariat must become a self-abolishing class. Marx, he argues, does not advocate the substitution of proletariat for bourgeoisie, but the abolition of the logics of antagonism embodied in the value form.[36] Tamás's distinction possesses critical clarity. At the same time, it is charged with a powerful, but ultimately moralistic vocabulary of psychomachia ('angelic' versus 'demonic'). The distinction can easily become forced into an artificial opposition. Even if one wants to avoid romanticising lived experiences, they can still carry importance. 'Empirical' matters must be placed into relationship with Tamás's core insight, not expelled by it. This, it seems to us, is both a methodological issue and a political imperative. Sekula likewise steers away from the affirmative 'angelic' versions of class and labour found in many expressions of emancipatory politics, and, as we will explore shortly, he attends to the structural, abstract relations of value production. However, he does not advance so sharp a 'demonic' conception as Tamás. For Sekula, 'negativity' still conveys more of the physical and psychic distress and injury resulting from precarity, exploitation and expendability, arising from its manifestation as the commodity labour power. He also tries to have 'class' flex between an analytical focus and lived conditions. A cussed or dark proletarian humour is often highlighted, but without

34 Tamás argues that, faced with the remnants of the *ancien régime*, socialists shouldered the leadership of movements for reform: 'universal suffrage, socio-cultural egalitarianism, democratic parliamentarism and a more secular and tolerant, less militaristic society'. Those struggles frequently consigned it to functioning as the modernising wing of capital. Tamás summarises thus: 'we may rather confidently say that *the abolition of caste leads to equality; but the abolition of class leads to socialism*'. See G. M. Tamás, 'Telling the Truth About Class', *Socialist Register* (2006): 228–68 (238, 245).

35 Ibid., 234.

36 One strength of his argument is that he maintains a negative understanding of the proletariat without tipping into fashionable anti-work politics – a position untenable for actual proletarians.

romanticising or reifying it – and Sekula sometimes employs the 'self-erasing' spiral that such irony can entail.

The version of *This Ain't China* usually presented comprises forty-two photographs (thirteen colour, twenty-nine black and white, one of which is a diagram on the division of labour in the restaurant trade) and five text booklets in English and Mandarin (sometimes hung from a chain on the wall), with chairs for reading.[37] (The following year, Martha Rosler's *Semiotics of the Kitchen* plays out a related scenario, deadpan, in the domestic arena and with a tone of feminist sublimated vengeance.) Monika Szewczyk notes at least four types of photograph in play:

> Candid, black-and-white shots (of cooks at work in the restaurant kitchen and of all the employees goofing around outside); highly composed, full-color, 'editorial' photographs (of pizza, hotdogs, burgers, blended fruit drinks, and so on); dimly-lit, contre-jour, budget noir shots (taken partly in some kind of executive office and partly outside a suburban house with a gleaming Cadillac out front – this crime convention is reserved for the boss environment); and, finally, staged, frontal black-and-white frames of the protagonists (the cook and the waitress, and also Sekula himself) deadpanning bold gestures to the camera in a style that evokes the Brechtian cinema of Jean-Luc Godard.[38]

In fact, a further distinction could be added to her first category: the workgroup portraits suggest a more expansive framing, contrasting with those of labouring activities with their tighter cropping and higher contrast (recalling John Berger and Jean Mohr's *A Fortunate Man* of 1967). There is a conscious switching of genres in play, involving a foregrounding of representation and staging, to which the reference to the photo novel in the work's subtitle draws attention.

At the time Sekula made *This Ain't China*, 'the new communist movement', mainly Maoist in inspiration, was a central force within the US left. The mazey tangle of groupuscules amounted, in the estimations of

---

37 The performers in the photo novel are Sekula, his friends guitarist Gregg Arreguin, Helen Dresman and Ruth Krimmel, and, as the boss, Phil Steinmetz. An earlier version includes ninety photographs and five texts and has sometimes been shown as *This Ain't China: A Maquette*. There is a closely related video work, *Performances Under Working Conditions* (1974), that has Sekula, Arreguin and David Scholar preparing fast food without implements and ingredients, in a manner that suggests a time-and-motion study redone as anarchic slapstick comedy.

38 Monika Szewczyk, 'Negation Notes (while working on an exhibition with Allan Sekula featuring *This Ain't China: A Photonovel*)', *e-flux* #13, February 2010, e-flux.com.

participant Max Elbaum, to perhaps 10,000 activists. These groups looked to revolutions in the 'Third World' – China, Cuba, Vietnam, Angola and so on – and sought to build a base in the working class, particularly its racialised sections. In efforts at party-building, many activists from middle-class backgrounds attempted to 'proletarianise' themselves by entering industry.[39] Sekula would certainly have encountered activists from the new communist movement, but his relation to Maoism is mediated by Godard and the French theoretical journal *Tel Quel*. He played a part in arranging the visit by Godard and Jean-Pierre Gorin to UCSD during 1973, and Godard's militant films remained touchstones for him.[40] In the mid-1970s, Sekula was a member of the New American Movement (NAM), a multi-tendency revolutionary socialist-feminist organisation which contained Maoist trends. He would subsequently orientate towards the dissident Trotskyism of Max Shachtman and Hal Draper, embodied in the organisation Solidarity.[41] In an interview with Buchloh in 2003, Sekula notes that the Maoism of *This Ain't China* was intended to be 'overtly farcical', implying some critical distance, but this may be a later disidentification.[42] The work transposes a distant struggle, the Cultural Revolution, to the US. The AK-47 and portraits of Lenin and Mao involve what Szewczyk calls a 'joy', shared with Godard, that comes from 'piling on the revolutionary clichés'.

Szewczyk draws attention to the passage in the text where Sekula recounts an episode where Chinese Red Guards transform an expensive restaurant into a place offering nutritious food to workers. The cheap pizzas and fries photographed by Sekula are neither. Szewczyk notes that 'china' is also a common noun for porcelain, so the work's title can also be taken to mean: *This Ain't Porcelain* and 'negating china, with all its bourgeois associations, could mean affirming China'.[43] Sekula was attentive to the biopolitical and, from his *Meat Mass* onwards, he sustained an interest in the politics and class culture of food. *This Ain't China* involves a double address to the condition of precarious labour

---

39 Max Elbaum, *Revolution in the Air: Sixties Radicals Turn to Lenin, Mao and Che* (London: Verso, 2018).

40 Young, 'Sympathetic Materialism', 24 (for Maoism at UCSD, see 86–7). In Young's work, left-wing politics appears to be treated as external to the work and ironised.

41 Sekula notes that by 1977 or 1978 he had developed an anti-Stalinist 'skepticism' towards the cultural politics of the Communist Party USA (Sekula in 'Allan Sekula and Benjamin H. D. Buchloh Conversation', 33).

42 Ibid., 24.

43 Szewczyk, 'Negation Notes'.

and biopolitical reproduction; in this sense, its concerns are remarkably contemporary.

It is worth adding three further points to this discussion. First, the overtly performative aspect of *This Ain't China* is a way of dealing with the ethics of representation – resisting the tendency of humanist documentary to point the camera downwards at the poor and socially marginalised.[44] Acting, mimicking and clowning take precedence over picturing precarious labourers. There are strong parallels with Rosler's 'work of refusal', *The Bowery in two inadequate descriptive Systems.* Second, the reference to a photo novel should be taken seriously. The hammy character of some images is integral to the form. Sekula takes a trashy photographic genre and infuses it with union struggle and revolutionary politics. Did he know Lenin's democratic maxim: 'Every cook must learn to govern'? Had he read C. L. R. James's 1956 pamphlet *Every Cook Can Govern: A Study of Democracy in Ancient Greece*?[45] A Shklovskian 'knight's move' allows a fresh presentation of political themes, reinvigorating the realism. Third, the text also cycles through various modes, cancelling and revising itself as it moves. Given the early point in his development as a critical intellectual, this is not Sekula's best piece of writing. Nevertheless, the work's five fragments offer different perspectives on the restaurant trade: a short opening addresses the relation between fact and fiction (in class struggle); an account of the boss's transformation from theoretical chemist to planner aiming to 'revolutionize the restaurant industry' (incorporating reflections on the analogy between the restaurant and theatre); notes on union demands, Brecht and Chinese cuisine; workers' daydreams on the job; the boss's determination to resist unionisation, and his opinions of his employees (lazy, influenced by liberal arts education). The text ends with a warning, a meta-comment with ironic self-criticism: 'beware: a workers' defeat has been converted into an artwork'.

More than any other work, *This Ain't China* insists on its status as fictionalised performance. It is principally a work of genre switching, in image and text, a fragmentary collection of perspectives, made under the sign of Godardian Maoism. Arguably, as an assemblage of narrative fragments and pictorial episodes, *This Ain't China* emphasises its fictional status at the cost of coherence.

44 Martha Rosler, 'In, Around, and Afterthoughts (On Documentary Photography)', in *3 Works* (Halifax: Press of the Nova Scotia College of Art and Design, 1981), 59–86.

45 Sekula had a later edition: C. L. R. James, *A New Notion: Two Works by C.L.R. James*, ed. Noel Ignatiev (Oakland, CA: PM Press, 2010).

Negative Labour: Aerospace Folktales *(1973)*

Although made a year earlier, *Aerospace Folktales* is a highly formed photo-text work and probably the most accomplished of Sekula's performative documentaries. It again considers labour not as a 'thing' but in terms of its relational forms of negativity – dispossession, expropriation, (market) dependence, unemployment, various forms of unwaged existence (retirement, leisure time, social reproduction) – and as the commodity labour power. Class is a leitmotif of realism and social documentary – perhaps *the* prime one – but *Aerospace Folktales* is a negative form of the American Dream. The work was first shown in San Diego in 1973, although it had some precedents in *A Short Autobiography*. By the time it appeared in a print version in 1984, in *Photography Against the Grain*, it had been honed to fifty-one black-and-white photographs (including the seven intertitles) and three texts (two 'Interviews' and 'A Commentary').[46] Thirty-five of the photographs could be described as 'documentary' shots taken in and around the home of the Sekula family (his parents and some of his siblings); some pictures are casual, others more formally composed, including portraits and details from the apartment. Two images are rephotographed from a corporate relations magazine; two present written documents (a tenancy policy and curriculum vitae); three show page spreads from a book on the effects of nuclear weapons; one appears to be a pinboard with medical notes (with two names redacted); and one depicts a page from the family photo album, with two studio portraits of Sekula as a boy.

The work depicts the lives of a former Lockheed aerospace chemical engineer who is now unemployed (the artist's father), the engineer's wife (the artist's mother) and their children (Sekula's siblings). It avoids the downwardly directed, voyeuristic gaze of the 'observing outsider', attempting to explore the contradictions of those who work (or did) in the military-industrial complex from the inside with some critical

46 In a first version, *Aerospace Folktales* consisted of 142 black-and-white photographs (some of them photographed text); four taped interviews; and a written commentary. Sometimes the work is exhibited with large potted plants, probably Kentia or Parlour palms, and directors' chairs positioned for listening to the audio recordings. (Throughout this discussion, we reference citations to the work's written components: 'Introductory Note', 'Interview with the Engineer', 'Interview with the Engineer's Wife', and 'A Commentary'. Paginations refer to *Photography Against the Grain*.)

sympathy.[47] *Aerospace Folktales* gives us some idea of how crisis is experienced by what the engineer termed 'professional-technical personnel'.[48] The military-industrial complex underpinned economic prosperity in Southern California, providing decently paid unionised jobs, though, it is worth recalling, not without segregation. By 1964, the aerospace industry was the largest sector of US manufacturing, receiving 90 per cent of its research funding from government, above all from the US Air Force.[49] In the 1970s, Lockheed was the biggest employer in the San Fernando Valley, heavily dependent on defence contracts – although, as Benjamin Young informs us, the company 'was on the rocks for failed commercial airliner ventures; political controversy due to cost overruns, overbilling, and underperformance in its military contracts; a contentious government bailout to prevent its bankruptcy'.[50]

Sekula's family is pictured and their perceptions recorded in interviews. Portraits – so often taken as direct access to psychological 'selves' – proliferate throughout the work: both portraits of the characters and pictures that contain their portraits displayed around the house. We encounter 'my father' and 'my mother'. Nevertheless, what is presented is not unmediated experience, but a shaped and moulded representation that explores a particular tranche of US society. Sekula wrote in 1973: 'I use "autobiographical" material, but assume a certain fictional and sociological distance in order to achieve a degree of typicality'.[51] His reference to 'typicality' gestures towards Engels's and Lukács's accounts of realism – where a novel's character bridges their specific biography with wider social tendencies. Interpretations of *Aerospace Folktales* must navigate the tension between its fictive dimensions, sociological perspectives and documentary elements. That said, Sekula's comment primarily reminds us not to elide the artist's family straightforwardly with the folktales' characters. Sekula was conscious that personal

47 The classic criticisms of the tendency of photographers to 'aim their cameras downwards, toward those with little power or prestige' appear in: 'Dismantling Modernism, Reinventing Documentary', 53–76 (59); and Rosler, 'In, Around, and Afterthoughts'.

48 'Interview with the Engineer', 152.

49 David Noble, *Forces of Production: A Social History of Industrial Automation* (1984; Piscataway, NJ: Transaction Publishers, 2011), 7.

50 Young, 'Arresting Figures', 94. The 'engineer's wife' comments on the government withdrawal of contracts: 'Interview with the Engineer's Wife', 156. Sekula noted in a gallery talk that, by 2005, Lockheed's position as the major employer had probably been overtaken by Disney: 'Allan Sekula in conversation about Aerospace Folktales, 2005', YouTube video, posted by C Grimes Gallery, 1 May 2008.

51 'Dismantling Modernism, Reinventing Documentary', 70.

experience is always mediated by wider structural relations and requires the labour of form-giving. The approach is closer, therefore, to 'autofiction' or 'autoethnography' (indeed, autobiography and diary writing also entail such shaping and distancing). But resting easily on the prefix 'auto' – however critically framed – might still be too reductive. Although based on the materials of autobiography, this is a staged 'i/I'. Sekula works this 'inward' dimension alongside an 'outwardly' orientated view. *Aerospace Folktales* involves a certain reflexiveness – even more explicit in *A Short Autobiography* – in which the artist-subject addresses his own classed position as typified.

It is worth holding on to the word 'folktales', which steers us towards popular narrative forms, including perhaps the photo novel. It also suggests a diversion away from 'direct truth'. Vladimir Propp's *Morphology of the Folktale* became available in translation in 1968, although Sekula's approach is neither mimicking of Proppian 'functions' nor rigorously formalist in conception. The main figures are often presented as *dramatis personae*. The interviews are announced as 'Interview with the Engineer' and 'Interview with the Engineer's Wife'. Intertitles adopt the same distanced neutrality to refer to the parents, akin to types in a fairy story, or even suggestive of mythic archetypes. The designations 'my father' and 'my mother' are more typical of 'A Commentary', which is voiced by a narrator 'i' (jumping just once to the upper case). In the interviews, the interviewer is presented as 'I', but the interviewer's function is largely absent. His questions are implied through the words of the interviewees ('You are more or less interested in knowing . . .?' the engineer asks, sensing his son's purpose). Then, in the second half of these two (longish) interviews, a single question from the interviewer makes an unexpected appearance.

Signs of revealing the device are evident throughout, with the characters sometimes acting for the camera. Photographing in tight domestic spaces inevitably meant that family members were hyper-aware of the camera's presence. Even when not actively 'playing their part' (in the mode suggested by Erving Goffman), they might still be presenting themselves for the family photograph (a genre with its own modes) or part-relaxing for a 'candid' shot. In the age of mass media, even the private realm involves striking poses and self-consciousness in being photographed. Reinforcing this reflexivity, in one image the engineer handles the view camera. The opening has an image depicting the engineer and his friend, with an intertitle that draws attention to the ambivalence of the relations established by the camera: 'Unable to fathom my motives, they were uneasy.' 'A Commentary', with its repudiation of syntax (no punctuation, all lower case), further amplifies this fragmentary, staged character.

As we noted earlier, Sekula later characterised *Aerospace Folktales* as like 'a disassembled movie'.[52] The insertions, disruptions and narrative reframing attain, if not coherence – given the neo-Brechtian ambition of the work, that cannot be expected – then a narrative drift. This loose plot shifts from the public ('male') world of the engineer to the private, domestic interior ('female'). Young describes the work as a pendant portrait of two worlds, differentially gendered.[53] This insight is broadly accurate, we think – and, later, we will consider other examples of counterpointing and doubling in Sekula's work. Yet, if this is a pendant, there is an imbalance that must be acknowledged. The title, the establishing sequence and specific details (such as the CV, the manual on nuclear blasts, the décor): all this, we are told, centres the engineer. The engineer's wife certainly appears in the sequence in significant ways, but her husband's role remains primary: even her own interview is largely concerned with him. 'A Commentary' is still more lopsided than the image sequence.

The parental pendant is complicated by the third, and arguably key, role played by the narrator, who speaks as 'I' – the homodiegetic 'I'. Enunciative features are present throughout. The reflexive narrator bookends the image sequence: the first pairing of intertitle-and-image focuses attention on the first person; the concluding photograph incorporates portraits of Sekula. Other intertitles start 'I'. These intertitles and 'A Commentary' all provide an extradiegetic perspective that frames or brackets the rest, remarking on who or what we see and enabling us to make connections between the particular-in-itself and the particular as an instantiation of wider social forces. We learn that 'A Commentary' started out as compensation for research materials ('filling in for earlier omissions') and because 'one cannot photograph ideology'. Despite its title, however, it is not merely a conventional report, supplementing the two interviews and presenting itself as authoritative and transparent. It works more like a third character, who speaks from the perspective of 'i'.

There is an identifiable sequence in *Aerospace Folktales* that documents the social relations and crisis of the US military-industrial

52 'Introductory Note', 106.

53 Young, 'Sympathetic Materialism', 112.

complex as it encounters the sphere of social reproduction – the unpaid labour of women that is the basis of human life.[54] The opening group of photographs, all from 1969, consist of a text and two images. The first photograph is a quotation by the Lockheed chairman (taken from *Days of Trial and Triumph: A Pictorial History of Lockheed*).[55] This is followed by two rephotographed grainy images from the *Lockheed Star* (the bi-weekly newsletter of the corporation: in *The Salaried Masses*, Siegfried Kracauer cites 'sceptical employees' who referred to an equivalent publication as the 'Slime-Trumpet').[56] In the first rephotographed image, a group of men, some in business suits, others wearing military uniforms, converse in front of a helicopter. In the second, a larger group, mostly in shirtsleeves, give a 'thumbs up'. This second group is informal, yet most of the participants wear ties and they are probably managers or technical workers; it is probably a corporate portrait of a workgroup set in the military-industrial complex. This opening sequence represents the official, celebratory perspective of the company, and it is the first indication of Sekula's interest in company photographic archives, which he would later develop in 'Photography Between Labour and Capital' (1983). Given the focus on the engineer's unemployed situation, this triumphalist mood appears hollow and cast in ironic mode.

This initial cluster of images is followed by another set, opening with a depiction of the father and his friend in the empty parking lot of the Lockheed plant. The engineer (we will soon realise) is unemployed; his friend, in shorts and 'Hawaiian shirt', is either retired or on vacation. Both men embody two versions of non-work: as (utopian) leisure and as (tragic) insecurity. Next comes a photograph of the plant building, seen from below, in the mode of early-modernist photographs of factories. The third image is a close-up of the father at the wheel of his car. Sekula's work often uses this filmic expansion and contraction of framing.

---

54 An early wave of social reproduction theory was underway while Sekula was working on his performative documentaries, and he knew this work. The US edition of Mariarosa Dalla Costa's 'Women and the Subversion of the Community' (with an introduction by Selma James) appeared in *Radical America* 6:1 (1972): 62–102. For other significant work in this journal, see: the special double issue on Women's Labour, with essays by Lise Vogel, Selma James and others: *Radical America* 7:4 and 7:5 (1973); and for the essays on production and reproduction, *Radical America* 10:2 (1976). It was a journal that he read.

55 *Days of Trial and Triumph: A Pictorial History of Lockheed* (Burbank, CA: Lockheed Aircraft Corporation, 1969).

56 Siegfried Kracauer, *The Salaried Masses: Duty and Distraction in Weimar Germany* (1929/30; London: Verso, 1998), 42.

Introduced by another intertitle, the next grouping in the sequence begins with a picture presenting the engineer and his wife in front of their garage, with their daughter playing with a ball. The image after that is also set against the garage: a tightly framed portrait of the parents. The change of attire suggest that the photographs were made on separate occasions. An allusion to Walker Evans is evident. It is followed by a front-on photograph of the façade of a two-storey domestic building, akin to those used by sales or letting agencies. And after that, we see the 'Tenant Policies' for Marine View Apartments (the do's and don'ts of waste disposal, noise disturbance and pet ownership, and – laughable in its incongruous rhetorical shift from orders to faux-familiarity – a tip on child training). Another intertitle then announces the move indoors.

Paternal loss of social position is underscored by the shift to the interior; it might itself be initially read as a form of demasculinisation. As the engineer's wife observes in her interview, there is a prevailing attitude that 'if a man is out of work there is something wrong with him'.[57] Still, the interior will prove to be somewhat more complicated. It is worth noting how Sekula handled *A Short Autobiography* a year or two earlier, noting that both wife and husband are 'dressed for work': he for posting resumés to potential employers; she for domestic labour. In this earlier work, the father is described as 'unemployed' and the mother as 'employed' – the latter descriptor being a notable decision, emphasising the work of social reproduction. In *Aerospace Folktales*, the engineer's wife claims she has never worked (although she then reveals that she has), but her invisible daily housework is bought into sight and noted as 'unpaid labor'.[58] The dinner table with place settings for six, and the kitchen as the setting for her labour process, feature prominently. The kitchen especially is a sphere moulded by mass-produced commodities. As Ruth Schwartz Cowan reminds us, electrical goods transformed postwar domestic labour, without reducing it.[59] The images feature a prominent General Electric refrigerator, blender, toaster and kettle. Indeed, we soon realise that this kitchen is a stage for the collision of two worlds, or the consumption of one by the other: the *mise-en-scène* of the mother's work is shaped by the products of engineering labour.

57 'Interview with the Engineer's Wife', 156.

58 Ibid., 158. The 'unpaid labor' is in 'A Commentary', 164.

59 Ruth Schwartz Cowan, *More Work for Mother: The Ironies of Household Technology from the Open Hearth to the Microwave* (New York: Basic Books, 1983). For a recent study, see Helen Hester and Nick Srnicek, *After Work: A History of the Home and the Fight for Free Time* (London: Verso, 2023).

The home and the kitchen are not simply marked as 'feminine'. Rather, gendered worlds collide and overlap, destabilising the terms. In the preceding sequence, the father's nightly process of rearranging lamps is presented as a symptom of precision displaced from his professional identity into a neurosis in the domestic sphere.

Aerospace Folktales brings into sight the world of a technical professional. Many of the images detail neat, clean spaces where everything is in its place; the classics of literature in hardback editions, boxed, their spines embossed with gilt lettering; an armchair still wrapped in plastic; a crucifix. In one, science magazines are arranged in a neat row, covers visible as if for a public display, and on a shelf above them: a wedding portrait; a figurine with hands clasped in prayer; and another studio portrait of the father as a younger man in his Air Force uniform.[60] Similarly, there is one of a desk, arranged with clock radio, a vase of flowers and a display of family photographs. These are presented like formal still lifes, arrangements calling to mind Walker Evans's pictures of sharecropper interiors.

The Church and the military pervade this environment. Model aircraft are suspended from the ceiling, photographed from an oblique angle to ensure we take in the crucifix on the wall behind. Another photograph is taken from a low point of view, positioning the beholder beneath a US helicopter, as if menaced by a destructive power the engineer helped create. Then there is the small pamphlet, *The Effects of Nuclear Weapons*, first arranged at the front of the bookshelf next to the novels and volumes of 'great literature' which, as the intertitle announces, the engineer ordered fortnightly, encouraging his children to read for monetary reward. Three separate page spreads from this booklet are photographed: five of its illustrations show the effects of thermal radiation on bodies and objects, while two diagrams model the impact of the blast. Perhaps, also with a nod to the opening of Alain Resnais's *Hiroshima, mon Amour* (1959), all are further symptoms of a conjuncture of the domestic sphere with the US military-industrial complex.

The bookshelf holds clothback editions, each volume in its protective slip case: *Quo Vadis*, *Grimm's Fairy Tales*, Joseph Conrad's *The Nigger of the 'Narcissus'*, *Around the World in Eighty Days* by Jules Verne, a volume with both *Billy Budd* and *Benito Cereno* by Herman Melville. A prior photograph shows the bookshelf without the book on nuclear weapons, to reveal: *The Prisoner of Zenda*, *Lord Jim* by Conrad, Jonathan Swift's

60 It is another version of his work: *Meditations on a Triptych* (1973/8).

Gulliver's Travels, Nathaniel Hawthorne's *The Scarlet Letter*, Stevenson's *Travels with a Donkey*, H. G. Wells' *Tono-Bungay*. And, in a photograph before that, we glimpse other shelves of similar volumes, all cloth-bound and in their slipcases: *The Swiss Family Robinson*, *Leaves of Grass*, *Walden*, *Tales of the Gold Rush*, *Three Plays of Henrik Ibsen*, *Droll Stories*, *The Decline and Fall . . .*, *The Life of Samuel Johnson*. Notable, given Sekula's focus from the 1990s, is the prominence of maritime themes (including impressed labour, and the revolt of the enslaved) among this selection of classic Western, mainly Anglophone, literature. *Grimm's Fairy Tales* strikes a somewhat different note, but one that is surely important in the context of the current discussion. The two volumes are from a 1962 edition published by the Heritage Press, which ran the monthly subscription Heritage Club. The double volume had illustrations by Lucille Corcos. In German, the Grimm's collection was called *Kinder- und Hausmärchen*, literally, 'Children's and Household-Tales'. *Märchen* can be 'fairy stories' (as per the usual English translation), fables, myths, tall stories or, apropos Sekula's project, 'folktales'. Indeed, 'folktales' of various sources recurred in the Heritage list. In this context, Sekula's title is knowingly rich in connotations. It is also a further caution that we should not elide the work with 'autobiography' and, as we saw already, that we should be conscious of its emphasis on 'typicality' or 'performance' of roles. *Aerospace Folktales* presents a sociology of mythologised life.

Sekula calls the careful arrangements of domestic objects and furniture his father's 'art' – 'lower-level technocrat art'.[61] This 'art' implies not only an individual man's creative composing but also the way a social layer (re)presents itself. The engineer's resumé is a condensation of it; as his father says, 'a capsule description in writing of what your experience has been'.[62] The plastic cover, keeping the armchair looking its best should visitors call, reinscribes the private/public distinction at the heart of domestic privacy. The little library of literary classics signals the social aspirations for one's offspring. The term 'art' is just one of the means that allows Sekula to thread connections between his own creative activity and his father's world. The camera handled by his father in one image metonymically links them. The distance between the engineer and 'i/I' is significant. If the camera is shared, it also turns out – as we will see underscored by Sekula's essays – to be where clear

61 'A Commentary', 160.

62 'Interview with the Engineer', 152.

differences emerge. *Aerospace Folktales* is shaped by a fault line within a class, drawn along the generational axis – a *Buddenbrooks* moment – and, as we will soon see, it is one built on the distinction between the technical and the socio-cultural. The project constantly displays the critical reflexivity of the artist-homodiegetor, an upwardly mobile son of an unemployed engineer. The shocks of capitalist crisis on the technical-professional class and their reverberations through the microcosm of the nuclear family (note the doubling of 'nuclear') are registered through the layerings of semi-fiction, 'typicality' and '"autobiographical" materials'.[63] The mutual distancing of father and son occurs in the narrative, and also in the visual and verbal approaches to narrating: as both content and form.

Aerospace Folktales involves a series of reflections on the habitus and values of a particular social layer – the thought patterns, dispositions, gestures and speech patterns of a technical professional.[64] All the ordered details of living appear as ramparts against any recognition of (to use Althusser's formulation) the 'real conditions of existence':

> and so everything had its place everything had its order i mean it was his only defense[65]

In 'A Commentary', Sekula states, 'I wanted to chase my father's ideology out into the open'.[66] It is a story about, as Sekula put it elsewhere, 'people who have internalized a view of themselves as "professionals" and subsequently suffer the shock of being dumped into the reserve army of labor'.[67] 'A Commentary' tells us that 'getting laid off is no big deal': machinists, pizza cooks and secretaries are regularly jobless without it affecting their sense of self, 'but this was the first time experts were getting laid off'.[68] (One might observe that Reaganite California, 1967–75, saw the laying off of technical professionals and leftist professors like Marcuse.) Faced with the situation, the engineer works to sustain a system of belief in which unemployment is 'a dysfunction of a

63 'Dismantling Modernism, Reinventing Documentary', 70.

64 For habitus: Pierre Bourdieu, *Outline of a Theory of Practice* (1972; Cambridge: Cambridge University Press, 1977).

65 'A Commentary', 163 (formatting Sekula's).

66 Ibid., 161. Years later, he expressed regret at the hurt this harrying had caused his father.

67 'Dismantling Modernism, Reinventing Documentary', 70.

68 'A Commentary', 160.

perfectly equitable system'.[69] In his interview, the engineer sees a waste of expertise, or else failures to find solutions for redeployment, but never identifies systemic crisis. To imagine unemployment any other way might overturn an entire hierarchy of values, calling into question such middle-class pillars as merit, intelligence, opportunity, individual talent and hard work. When the father does speak about his situation, he sounds, we learn, like '*fortune* magazine' or the 'lockheed chairman of the board'.[70] When he complains of the government wasting tax dollars on foreign aid and 'I' asks about aid to the South Vietnamese, he can only point to 'mismanagement', despite the fact that the aerospace industry is a direct beneficiary of the Cold War.[71] Organisation, regularity and routine are not only significant to the engineer's professional identity; they are also the armour of a man 'caught in the middle'.

White-Collar Blues: The Professional-Managerial Class

Sekula paid particularly close attention to the debates on class that were circulating in the seventies, especially those addressing the recomposition of the US labour force, such as Stanley Aronowitz, James Boggs, Harry Braverman, Alvin Gouldner, C. Wright Mills and Erik Olin Wright. Similar discussions were conducted elsewhere in the Global North, by André Gorz, Serge Mallet and Nicos Poulantzas.[72] Of particular significance was the debate over the 'Professional-Managerial Class' (PMC) sparked by two essays published in *Radical America* by Barbara and John Ehrenreich.[73] Like the Ehrenreichs and several others engaged in these debates, Sekula was at this time a member of the NAM, which was critical of the New Left for ignoring the American working class.[74]

---

69 Ibid., 161.

70 Ibid., 163.

71 'Interview with the Engineer', 152–3. For aerospace industry and the Cold War, see Noble, *Forces of Production*, particularly 5–10. The engineer had a point, of course: there *was* capitalist 'mismanagement' in the crisis-ridden aerospace industry of southern California.

72 Sekula had books by all these figures, except for Boggs, whose work he would have read through journals such as *Monthly Review*.

73 Barbara Ehrenreich and John Ehrenreich, 'The Professional-Managerial Class', *Radical America* 11:2 (1977): 7–32; 'The New Left: A Study on Professional-Managerial Class Radicalism', *Radical America* 11:3 (1977): 7–22. In 1979, these essays were republished as a single study, along with responses, in *Between Labor and Capital*, ed. Pat Walker (Boston, MA: South End Press, 1979). See also Barbara Ehrenreich's extended survey of the PMC, *The Fear of Falling: The Inner Life of the Middle Class* (New York: Pantheon Books, 1989).

74 Barbara Ehrenreich notes that the thesis emerged from witnessing the class

Although independent, *Radical America* was closely allied to the NAM and in the 1970s it published translations of European debates on class.

The Ehrenreichs argued that the PMC was a layer of professionals, situated between the working class and capitalist class, estimated to be about 20 to 25 per cent of the US population at the time.[75] They list a diverse array of 'salaried mental workers'[76]: 'middle-level administrators and managers, engineers, and other technical workers', teachers, social workers, psychologists, and ' "culture producers", etc.'[77] The scare quotes on the final term are intended to emphasise 'culture' in its broadest sense, embracing the arts and the culture-industrial production of ideas and values (entertainers, scriptwriters for television, advertising copywriters). Others in the debate included architects, urban planners and doctors. The character of the PMC's 'betweenness' is important here. There was much uncertainty as to whether the older petite bourgeoisie could be considered a 'class' as such. The Ehrenreichs, however, claimed that the PMC 'must be understood as comprising a *distinct class* in monopoly capitalist society'.[78] Its location made the PMC antagonistic towards both labour and capital: while constantly forced to defend its autonomy from capitalist pressures, the PMC nonetheless occupied supervisory positions over the working class. It comprised workers 'who do not own the means of production and whose major function in the social division of labour may be described broadly as *the reproduction of capitalist culture and capitalist class relations*'.[79]

This situation 'between', the Ehrenreichs suggest, underpinned a specific ideology, based on the resources of specialist education and training, and emphasising the values of autonomy, professionalism, accuracy, rationality, efficiency, standardisation and objectivity.[80] This 'spontaneous philosophy of the engineers', to use a twist on Althusser, is of particular importance for understanding Sekula's project.[81] As the

---

contradictions while organising in the NAM: 'On the Origins of the Professional-Managerial Class: An Interview with Barbara Ehrenreich', 22 October 2019, dissentmagazine.org. Sekula resigned when the NAM entered the Democratic Party.

75 Barbara Ehrenreich and John Ehrenreich, 'The Professional-Managerial Class', 15.

76 Ibid., 13.

77 Ibid., 14, 11.

78 Ibid., 11 (our emphasis).

79 Ibid., 13 (our emphasis).

80 Ibid., 22.

81 This comes as no surprise, because the Ehrenreichs derive this part of their argument from the labour-process analysis of Braverman, Gorz and others central to Sekula's

engineer in *Aerospace Folktales* puts it: 'A good scientist and engineer, with his organizing ability, his preciseness, his ability to adapt to different situations, can be of great value in administrative positions and clerical tasks – checking procedures, and assisting in systems analyses.'[82]

The Ehrenreichs' account of the PMC, like the theories of the 'new working class', tended to homogenise the formation they described. Sekula attended to the cultural wing in *School Is a Factory* (1980/2), where he investigates the role of the PMC in reproducing class relations through ideology and training. Nonetheless, as some argued, engineers, research scientists and technical workers more typically play a direct role in the capitalist enterprise, unlike teachers and cultural professionals. On average, David Noble noted, the former wing of the PMC spend no more than ten years in technical work before advancing into management roles.[83] Thereafter, the control of labour – the so-called 'man problem' – and the attention to systems and rationalisation becomes their main activity.[84] The debates were often embroiled in demarcations between 'productive', 'unproductive' and 'reproductive' labour, distinctions that do not concern us for the present discussion.

The Ehrenreichs believed the PMC was undergoing proletarianisation, and might potentially boost future anti-capitalist forces.[85] Yet, the division within society's middle layer made it difficult to envisage a

---

own understanding. For a recent view, see Nick Chavez, 'Engineers, Materialism and the Communist Method', 30 May 2023, notesfrombelow.org.

82 'Interview with the Engineer', 153.

83 David Noble, 'The PMC: A Critique', in *Between Labor and Capital*, ed. Walker, 121–42 (132); David F. Noble, *America by Design: Science, Technology, and the Rise of Corporate Capitalism* (New York: Alfred A. Knopf, 1977), 41. One additional factor needs emphasising. The Ehrenreichs overlooked the importance of the military-industrial complex, of which aerospace was a key element. Alongside the contributions of David Noble, Sekula explored how the PMC are bound to state capital through the permanent arms economy. This is present in *Aerospace Folktales*, of course, but the military-industrial complex runs through much of Sekula's work, as a contiguous relationship to his experience as the son of an aerospace engineer.

84 Harry Braverman, *Labor and Monopoly Capital* (1974; New York: Monthly Review Press, 1998); Noble, *America by Design*, 262–3.

85 Barbara Ehrenreich and John Ehrenreich, 'The Professional-Managerial Class', 15. Other than his rediscovery of Marx on the labour process, it is Braverman's central claim that the capitalist degradation of work was being extended to the 'white-collar factory': *Labor and Monopoly Capital*, 351. See also Mike Cooley, *Architect or Bee? The Human Price of Technology* (London: Hogarth Press, 1987). For more critical assessments of this process, see: Noble, 'The PMC: A Critique'; Al Syzmanski, 'A Critique and Extension of the Professional-Managerial Class', in *Between Labor and Capital*, ed. Walker, 49–65; Stanley Aronowitz, 'The Professional Managerial Class or Middle Strata', in *Between Labor and Capital*, ed. Walker, 214–42; Erik Olin Wright, *Class, Crisis and the State* (London: New Left Books, 1978).

coherent class bloc that might be won for an anti-capitalist project.[86] Despite sinking down the social scale, the PMC remained fiercely attached to the ideologies of autonomy and professionalism. Viewing their own proletarianisation as a form of social death was an anxiety that Sekula highlights in *Aerospace Folktales*: 'my father built a middle class submarine because he was sailing in a blue collar ocean and he didn't want the sharks to eat his kids'.[87] The watery tropes are worth noting, given the part that they would occupy in Sekula's later work, but here it is the 'middle' and the danger of slipping out of it that matters.

Although *Aerospace Folktales* pre-dates the Ehrenreichs' intervention, it shares central elements pertinent to these broader debates. Sekula homed in on the class fraction that plays a technical role in manufacture.[88] His long essay 'Photography Between Labour and Capital' (1983) references and directly echoes the title of Pat Walker's collection on the PMC, *Between Labor and Capital*.[89] Walker identified five key themes to the debate, which reads like a compendium to Sekula's work of the 1970s and 1980s: 'the technical division of labor in the firm, the social division of labor in society, the educational system, the state and the family'.[90] Our claim is not that Sekula illustrated these arguments. His work makes a stronger contribution, elaborating, as it does, an analysis of shifting class relations in the US in dialogue with other socialists. Drawing on the unique resources and methods of art enabled him to explore the granularity of ideology and habitus. He does more than just add details or concrete examples: the particular lived experiences assembled for his projects had to be situated in historical and theoretical contexts, necessitating 'typification'.

As intimated above, the debates over 'the new working class', 'the white-collar factory', the 'PMC' and 'contradictory class locations' had consequences for socialist organising. Might this new wave of proletarianisation reinforce the political opposition to capital? Probably not. Other implications proved more 'troubling', in ways that sank deep into

86 Wright's suggestion that the PMC occupies a 'contradictory class location' merely defers the problem. See Wright, *Class, Crisis and the State*.

87 'A Commentary', 163. Thinking forwards to *Fish Story*, this is one of three nautical references; four, if you count the patterned shirt on both occasions.

88 For a treatment of Sekula and the PMC: Steve Edwards, 'White Collar Blues: Allan Sekula Casts an Eye Over the Professional-Managerial Class', 8 December 2021, nonsite.org.

89 The reference to Walker and the PMC is found in 'Photography Between Labour and Capital', n. 168.

90 Walker, 'Introduction', in *Between Labor and Capital*, xv. Like Sekula, Walker foregrounds how the 'educational system is structured like a factory' (xix).

the subjective and psychic intersections with the ostensible 'objectivity' of the political debates: many activists themselves came from the PMC, and they were often encountered with suspicion by manual workers, both within and without the movement.[91] As the son of an engineer, and himself an artist, photographer, educator and activist, Sekula inhabited this political tension in several ways. He and his father exemplified the much-debated contrasting wings of the PMC and he zoomed in on the tensions.

As far as Sekula was concerned, the 'middle view' of the PMC – 'the phantasmagoric middle ground' – offered a key to understanding the contradictions at the heart of photography's discourse.[92] Caught between the technical perspectives of the engineers and the romantic anti-capitalism of the cultural intelligentsia, capitalist image-culture is built from an understanding of the unstable configuration of the middle. It is Sekula's singular intervention to have perceived that any photo practice, politico-modernist or otherwise, cannot be separated from attitudes to technology, the division of labour and the subsumption of skill – which we will now explore in greater detail through Sekula's writing.

The View from the Middle: Critical Essays

In 'Photography Between Labour and Capital' (1983), Sekula discusses the position of the photographer within capitalism: 'the photographer mediates *between* capital and labour, acting as a kind of middle-man in the unequal traffic of representations'.[93] The essay is a study in the ideology of engineers articulated through accounts of the capitalist labour

91 The tensions are evident from branch meetings to prevalent factory entryism of the period. Barbara Ehrenreich notes that the PMC thesis emerged from witnessing the class contradictions while organising in the NAM. See Alex Press, 'On the Origins of the Professional-Managerial Class: An Interview with Barbara Ehrenreich', *Dissent*, 22 October 2019, dissentmagazine.org. Taxi driver John Welsh discussed some in: 'New Left Knots', in *Between Labor and Capital*, 173–90. See also Sandy Carter, 'Class Conflict: The Human Dimension', in *Between Labor and Capital*, 97–119. The example cited is attributed to Mary Gregor, a twenty-five-year-old print worker (98).

92 'Photography Between Labour and Capital', 251.

93 Ibid. As we will see, this conception is extended from a concern with the PMC in postwar America to interrogate earlier photographic debates. It is not a direct importation of the PMC to earlier periods; rather, the debates establish the relational dynamics for his analysis. The tensions of 'between' continue to be important for Sekula – most obviously in his later essay 'Between the Net and the Deep Blue Sea (Rethinking the Traffic in Photographs)', *October* 102 (2002): 3–34.

process. The text provides an in-depth analysis of one component of photographic ideology, associated with technical realism and objectivity. The essay stems from an engagement with the archive of the commercial photographer Leslie Shedden, who worked for two decades (1948–68) in Glace Bay (Cape Breton Island, Nova Scotia), producing portraits for miners and images for the public relations arm of the local mining company. Sekula's investigation of this archive opens onto a consideration of the tensions structuring photographic culture more broadly: historical document and aesthetic picture; empiricism and romanticism; 'optical truth' and 'visual pleasure', which he characterises as the opposition, evident in Shedden's archive, between 'the *instrumental realism* of the industrial photograph and the *sentimental realism* of the family photograph.'[94]

The core theme in the second part of the essay – titled 'The Emerging Picture-Language of Industrial Capitalism' – is the subordination of manual to mental labour. The 1970s saw an international debate on the labour process as socialist intellectuals including Braverman and Sohn-Rethel rediscovered this element of Marx's thought.[95] Sekula's original contribution to the debate involves thinking about labour-process analysis as *pictorial form*. Focusing on a range of examples, most importantly on the part 'played by scientific picture-making in the historical development of capitalism, in the construction of capitalist dominion over nature and human labour',[96] Sekula uses this material to explore the prehistory of photography found in the practices of 'technical', 'functional' or 'instrumental realism', and further considers the capitalist transformation of work by studying the ideology of the engineers.[97]

Each of Sekula's key examples of 'objective truth' involves a 'view from nowhere', to employ philosopher Thomas Nagel's phrase.[98] Historians of science have done important work in tracing this disembodied vision that lays claim to being above social interests. They see

94 'Photography Between Labour and Capital', 201. Sekula's italics.

95 Braverman, *Labor and Monopoly Capital*; Alfred Sohn-Rethel, *Intellectual and Manual Labour: A Critique of Epistemology*, trans. Martin Sohn-Rethel (London: Macmillan, 1978); and 'The dual economics of transition', in *The Labour Process & Class Strategies* (Brighton: Conference for Socialist Economics Pamphlet No. 1, Stage 1, 1976), 26–45.

96 'Photography Between Labour and Capital', 203. Sekula's italics.

97 Ibid., 203, 234, 201, 215. Cf. 'The Traffic in Photographs', in *Photography Against the Grain*, 79.

98 'Photography Between Labour and Capital', 200; Thomas Nagel, *The View from Nowhere* (Oxford: Oxford University Press, 1986).

'objectivity', which they distinguish from truth claims, as involving the subtraction of the observer's subjective experience: 'men of science' saw the observer as liable to error and partiality; attention might flag, and their senses were deemed unreliable. Rhetorically displacing the self from the scene of observation also helped mediate disagreements between gentlemen. Technical apparatus, cameras included, played an important role in this moralising of the self, through restraint and self-control.[99] The objective observer that emerged in this ideology was thought impersonal, almost automatic. One problem with this account is that, as a depoliticised version of Foucault, it gives insufficient weight to how claims to objectivity helped secure the authority of middle-class experts.[100] The 'assertion of neutrality' through which photography renders itself 'transparent' enables technical specialists to disavow 'tendentious rhetoric'.[101] This vision is not so much a 'view from nowhere' as one 'from the middle'. The middle view is a powerful location – a vanishing mediator – which secures a place for technical specialists as supposedly neutral arbiters between distinct social forces. As we saw with the discussion of the PMC, the spontaneous ideology of the engineers emerges from this position of authority within the production process.

In tying disembodied vision to labour-process analysis, Sekula argues that technical realism plays a significant role in the subsumption of labour power. Barthes's essay 'The Plates of the *Encyclopedia*' (1964) is important in his account, offering 'the essentials of a semiology of instrumental realism'.[102] Barthes presents these plates as an image of the 'Encyclopedic mind', the world viewed by a 'thinking machine'.[103] According to him, the plates offer an 'epic of substance' and constitute 'a *radical language*, consisting of pure concepts, with neither word tools nor syntax'.[104] Barthes is a regular presence in Sekula's work. For instance,

99 Lorraine Daston and Peter Galison, *Objectivity* (Boston, MA: MIT Press, 2007); Lorraine Daston, 'Objectivity and the Escape from Perspective', *Social Studies of Science* 22:4 (1992): 597–618; Lorraine Daston and Peter Galison, 'The Image of Objectivity', *Representations* 40 (Autumn, 1992): 81–128; M. Norton Wise, ed., *The Values of Precision* (Princeton, NJ: Princeton University Press, 1991); Jennifer Tucker, *Nature Exposed: Photography as Eyewitness in Victorian Science* (Baltimore, MD: Johns Hopkins, 2005).

100 Noble, *America by Design*, 42–7.

101 'On the Invention of Photographic Meaning', 6.

102 'Photography Between Labour and Capital', 115.

103 Roland Barthes, 'The Plates of the *Encyclopedia*' (1964), in *New Critical Essays* (Chicago, IL: Northwestern University Press, 1980), 23–40.

104 Ibid., 31, 32.

Sekula frequently cites the essay 'The Great Family of Man'. In this case, he notes that Barthes offers an excellent semiology of instrumental realism but is entirely silent on the structuring division of mental and manual labour. For Sekula, the plates rested on 'a hidden hierarchy', where the 'cyclopean eye' views the worker as 'the *object* but never the *subject* of knowledge'.[105] In this ideology, 'the line of sight assumes the privileged status of *supervision*', and the figure who embodies this ideational perspective is the surveyor or engineer.[106] In Sekula's view, technical realism in photography 'inherited and transformed the role assigned to illustration in the *Encyclopedia*', offering a 'global inventory or archive of appearances'.[107]

We see evidence of the new hierarchy of control in the photographic illustrations to F. W. Taylor's *On the Art of Cutting Metals* (1906), with skilled work subordinated to a rational vision that is 'essentially mathematical and abstract'.[108] Employing a modification of Étienne-Jules Marey's 'geometrical chronophotography', which the Gilbreths called a 'chronocyclegraph', photography was employed to further 'functionalise' work.[109] Using lights and an 'automicromotion' device, 'the worker's own capabilities' could be represented in photographs as simple actions, to be dissected, reconstructed and subordinated to managerial control and the regime of capitalist time.[110] The work of the Gilbreths, who made particular use of visual tools to record the gestus of work, plays a core role in Sekula's analysis, developed from Marx's account of the passage from formal to real subsumption of labour power.[111] Braverman had spotted the role of photography in deskilling: 'In *motion and time study* [of the Gilbreths], the elementary movements were visualized as the building blocks of every work activity'.[112] The mathematicisation of picture-making, Sekula suggests, contributed to an 'analytic geometry of work'.[113] Lillian Gilbreth sought to extend this rationalising of labour to the home, thus synthesising sentimental and instrumental realism, so that capitalist picture language 'speaks with three overlapping voices: the voice of

105 'Photography Between Labour and Capital', 213–14, 215, 217.

106 Ibid., 209.

107 Ibid., 217.

108 Ibid., 239.

109 Ibid., 247.

110 Ibid., 247.

111 Karl Marx, 'Results of the Immediate Process of Production' (1863–6), published as an appendix in *Capital: I*, 949–1084.

112 Braverman, *Labor and Monopoly Capital*, 173.

113 'Photography Between Labour and Capital', 246.

surveillance, the voice of advertising, and the voice of family photography.'[114]

Sekula follows Braverman in seeing Taylorism as the central logic of modern industry, arguably giving too much importance to this management trend. There was, in fact, a great deal of resistance to time-and-motion study, with many engineers and managers preferring incentives and welfare schemes to accommodate unionised labour (an approach that led to 'industrial relations' and the struggle for loyalty to the firm).[115] For Braverman, Taylorism contributed to standardising work practices and the shift of labour-process control from skilled artisan to capitalist or overseer; the proletarian was reduced to a mere 'detail worker', consigned to repetitive and fragmentary tasks. Sekula finds the same process in the photographic archive and in the exhibition *The Family of Man*. Here, shifting the class location, the photographer is positioned as a comparable detail worker, responsible for producing small lexical units within a larger ensemble, 'providing fragmentary images for an apparatus beyond his or her control.'[116] Across the seemingly diverse aspects of the

---

114 Ibid., 249. Overstepping the mark, Sekula associates Marey with supervisory vision. Anson Rabinbach has convincingly argued that Marey was part of a current of materialist thinking that counterposed labour power to vitalist conceptions of the body. The ideas might have been picked up by scientific managers, but Marey and others who inhabited this episteme were not primarily concerned with supervision or rationalisation. See Anson Rabinbach, *The Human Motor: Energy, Fatigue, and the Origins of Modernity* (Berkeley, CA: University of California Press, 1990).

115 Noble, *America by Design*, 264–78; 286–91. For a survey of the wide-ranging debates, see Paul Thompson, *The Nature of Work: an introduction to the labour process debates* (London: Macmillan, 1983). Responding to critics, Braverman argued that they were attending to mere epiphenomena; that fragmentation, deskilling and control of labour power remained the central logic of capitalism; and that these processes had been extended to office work: *Labor and Monopoly Capital*, 86–8. See also the exchange between the Ehrenreichs and Braverman: Barbara Ehrenreich and John Ehrenreich, 'Work & Consciousness', *Monthly Review* 28:3 (1976): 10–18; Braverman, 'Two Comments', *Monthly Review* 28:3 (1976): 119–24. Bill Schwarz suggested that the over-emphasis on Taylorism was alleviated because in Braverman's study of the separation of mental and manual precedes discussion of technology: Bill Schwarz, 'Reassessing Braverman: Socialisation and Dispossession in the History of Technology', in *Science, Technology and the Labour Process*, vol. 2, eds Les Levidow and Bob Young (London: Free Association Books, 1985), 189–205 (196).

116 'Photography Between Labour and Capital', 194, 251. The quotation here is from: Allan Sekula, 'Walker Evans and the Police', in Jean-Francois Chevrier, Benjamin H. D. Buchloh and Allan Sekula, *Walker Evans and Dan Graham* (Rotterdam: Witte de With, 1992), 194 (republished in *Art Isn't Fair*, 143). This aligns with Edelman's characterisation of the photographer: 'the *proletarian of creation*: he and his tool form one body'. Bernard Edelman, *Ownership of the Image: Elements for a Marxist Theory of Law* (1973; London: Routledge and Kegan Paul, 1979), 45. Edelman's emphasis.

representation of labour examined, Sekula considers how the activity of observing and transforming the labour process is presided over by equivalence, fragmentation, calculability, inter-changeability, measurability, detachment and rationalisation.

The invisible middle and its contradictions shape Sekula's wider thinking on photography. His earlier writings emphasise how practices with a more instrumental intent were aestheticised, and thus came to underpin a canon of photography. In 'On the Invention of Photographic Meaning' (1974), he considers the way that images by Lewis Hine, originally produced for charity campaigns, have been transformed into precious museum objects. In 'The Instrumental Image: Steichen at War' (1975), Sekula demonstrates that aerial reconnaissance photographs from World War I have been exhibited as aesthetic works, simply because Steichen was the commanding officer of the unit.[117] Sekula dwells on the contradictions inherent in photographic culture, with what he calls the 'hermeneutic pendulum' swinging between art and document; affect and objectivity; 'sentimental realism' and 'instrumental realism'; the 'honorific' and the 'repressive'.[118] Emphasising the role of the apparatus brings to the fore ideas of objectivity, whereas stressing the subjectivity of the maker generates the affective claims of art. As Sekula suggests in 'The Traffic in Photographs' (1981):

> In persistently arguing for the harmonious coexistence of optical truths and visual pleasures, in yoking a positivist scientism with a romantic metaphysics, photographic discourse has attempted to bridge the philosophical and institutional separation of scientific and artistic practices that has characterized bourgeois society from the late eighteenth century onward.[119]

Photographic history, in Sekula's hands, involves tracking this romantic subjectivisation of the camera-machine and its antipodal instrumentalisation. The power of his account stems from refusing to fix photographic meaning at any single point on the semantic horizon spanning from optical pleasure to objective truth, positivism to metaphysics. He focuses

117 'The Instrumental Image: Steichen at War' (1975), in *Photography Against the Grain*, 32–51.

118 For 'hermeneutic pendulum': 'Dismantling Modernism, Reinventing Documentary', 58.

119 'The Traffic in Photographs', 78.

instead on praxis, movement and process, while simultaneously refusing to cast polysemy as liberation.[120]

In this way, Sekula is concerned with how our understanding of photography is shaped by the larger gravitational forces of capitalist society, principally as conceptions of the medium rotate around the prevailing attitudes towards industrial society. Drawing together the hermeneutic pendulum of photography with a theory of labour and technics, Sekula casts photography as a synecdoche for capitalism, suggesting:

> Above all else, the ideological force of photographic art in modern society may lie in the apparent reconciliation of human creative energies with a scientifically guided process of mechanization, suggesting that despite the modern industrial division of labor, and specifically despite the industrialization of cultural work, despite the historical obsolescence, marginalization and degradation of artisanal and manual modes of representation, the category of the artist lives on in the exercise of a *purely mental*, imaginative command over the camera.[121]

As he put it in 'Photography Between Labour and Capital' (1983), his essay on mining photographs, 'The institutional promotion of photography as a fine art serves to redeem technology by suggesting that subjectivity and the machine are easily compatible.'[122] As far as Sekula was concerned, these swinging pendula are hardly matters of confusion or intellectual incoherence. Rather, they involve a particular kind of contradiction: that between discreet laws or reasonable, but incompatible, assumptions. This account of photography and the 'antinomies of bourgeois culture' draws heavily on passages from Marx's 'Economic and Philosophical Manuscripts' and *Grundrisse*, and from Lukács's 'Reification and the Consciousness of the Proletariat'.[123] Attention to these antinomies will recur in Sekula's thinking.[124]

120 'Dismantling Modernism, Reinventing Documentary', 74–5.

121 'The Traffic in Photographs', 78–9.

122 'Photography Between Labour and Capital', 201.

123 Marx, 'Economic and Philosophical Manuscripts', 354 (Sekula used a different translation when citing this passage, with 'antimony', in 'Dismantling Modernism, Reinventing Documentary'); Marx, *Grundrisse*, 162; Georg Lukács, 'Reification and the Consciousness of the Proletariat' (1923), in *History and Class Consciousness* (London: Merlin, 1971), 86–222.

124 'Dismantling Modernism, Reinventing Documentary', 74–5; 'Photography Between Labour and Capital', 227–8; Introduction, in *Photography Against the Grain*, xv

Value Form

It is often said that Sekula paid sustained attention to capital and labour and that he remained unfashionably attached to Marxism. It is less recognised that he adopted a specific Marxist approach to capitalist culture that emphasises the value form, drawing particularly on the readings of Marx by Lukács and Alfred Sohn-Rethel.[125] As Sekula notes when discussing the work of the Gilbreths, 'These images presented the worker's own capabilities as a "thing apart", and as an *abstraction*'; and in 'An Eternal Esthetics of Laborious Gestures' (1996) he notes: 'photography turns on a vexing puzzle of labor and value'.[126] His approach pays attention to the peculiar *forms* assumed when value is extracted from labour power in capitalist regimes of accumulation. Sekula's reading of Marx's *Capital* is attentive to the role of 'abstraction' and 'form determination'. In this analysis, *Capital* is not seen as a narrow economic account of capitalism (commodities, capital, money); rather, all aspects of society are constituted through the value relation, which not only exploits the worker but subjects the whole of society to abstract domination. In this sense, where capitalism involves impersonal power, the capital relation is not reducible

---

(xvii in MACK edition); 'Walker Evans and the Police', 193. It also occurs in a discussion on entropy and *informe* in Sekula Papers, S.1.07:01 [Canadian Notes/Misc. Notes], June 1995–October 1996.

125 In his library were: I. I. Rubin's *History of Economic Thought* (1929; London: Inklinks, 1979); Evgeny Pashukanis's *Law and Marxism: A General Theory* (1929; London: Pluto, 1987); Sohn-Rethel, *Intellectual and Manual Labour.* He did not have a copy of Rubin's *Essays on Marx's Theory of Value* (1923; Detroit, MI: Black & Red, 1972). In the later 1960s, students of Horkheimer and Adorno re-examined Marx's critique of political economy. This work, collectively known as the *Neue Marx-Lektüre*, or 'new reading of Marx', was conducted by Alfred Schmidt, Hans-Georg Backhaus, Helmut Reichelt and others. For a critical overview, see Riccardo Bellofiore and Tommaso Redolfi Riva, 'The *Neue Marx-Lektüre*: Putting the Critique of Political Economy Back into the Critique of Society', *Radical Philosophy* 189 (2015): 24–36. Other important contributions include Moishe Postone, *Time, Labor, and Social Domination: A Reinterpretation of Marx's Critical Theory* (Cambridge: Cambridge University Press, 1993); Arthur, *The New Dialectic and Marx's Capital.* Sekula did not engage directly with – and certainly was not a programmatic adherent to – value-form theory. To our knowledge, the only writer to observe the prominence of the value form and abstraction in Sekula is Alberto Toscano, 'The Mirror of Circulation: Allan Sekula and the Logistical Image', 31 July 2018, societyandspace.org.

126 'Photography Between Labour and Capital', 247; 'An Eternal Esthetics of Laborious Gestures', *Grey Room* 55 (2014): 16–27 (17). He cites Alain Lipietz's defence of Marx's theory of value, and notes that Gayatri Chakravorty Spivak is a 'lonely' voice in cultural studies who continues to argue for the 'relevance of the labor theory of value in the context of the internationalisation of the division of labour' (21, 27 n. 7).

to the personal power of the factory owner or the wider ruling class.[127] Accordingly, all social forms (economic, political, scientific, legal, ideological, philosophical, cultural, representational and so on) exemplify the logic of the commodity form, as their content is derived from the relations of value production, but they also take on an autonomous existence, exerting power over the entire social process.

Extending the discussion to photography, he emphasised the question of form. In 'The Traffic in Photographs' (1981), he finds the value relation (as fetishism) playing out in photographic ideology and across its antinomic wings. The second half of the essay is titled 'Universal Equivalent', where he effectively argues for a homology between the traffic in photographs and the circulation of money.[128] As with the relation of exchange value to use value, 'the photographic sign comes to eclipse its own referent.'[129] He highlights Oliver Wendell Holmes's dubbing of nineteenth-century *cartes de visite* as 'the sentimental "greenbacks" of civilization.'[130] This argument is developed at length in 'Photography Between Labour and Capital'. Marx's account of the money form is again the key to understanding the working of the photographic archive. The archive – 'the quantitative ensemble of images'[131] – appears as a space of rationality and equivalence: 'a kind of "clearing house of meaning"'.[132] According to Sekula, Holmes had already positioned photography as 'a global library of *exchangeable* images.'[133] In his essay of 1859, Holmes described photographs in monetary terms: 'a universal currency of these banknotes . . . which the sun has engraved for the great Bank of Nature.'[134]

In a distinct sense, the question of 'abstract visual equivalence' emerged simultaneously through another line of Sekula's research. *School Is a Factory* (a project which came into shape in 1979–80) includes, inter alia, a few arrangements of isotypes – compositions of pictographs designed (mostly) by Rudolf Modley in 1976. Isotypes date from Gerd Arntz's designs, produced in Red Vienna under the auspices

127 'Proletarians are subjected to capitalists by means of a mechanism of domination which simultaneously subjects everyone to the imperatives of capital'. Mau, *Mute Compulsion*, 211.

128 'The Traffic in Photographs', 96–100.

129 Ibid., 98.

130 Holmes cited in ibid., 100.

131 'Photography Between Labour and Capital', 194.

132 Ibid.

133 Ibid., 219. Sekula's emphasis.

134 Holmes cited in ibid.

of the left logical positivist Otto Neurath.[135] They were intended to visualise abstract 'social statistics', or biological, historical and social relations. Of course, the isotype is itself an 'abstracted' visual sign. One of Sekula's employments of the form uses a social hierarchy, with engineers and technical specialists in the middle. Another plate is titled 'The Fetishism of the Commodity and Its Secret' and tries to demonstrate how a seemingly equal exchange in the labour contract is anything but. It is worth observing that the cover image for *Photography Against the Grain* (1984), designed with Sally Stein, is not a photograph but another pictographic design. Here, photography features as part of a bureaucratic system, founded on the cash register, or the 'form of appearance of the value of commodities'.[136] Four pictographic types are arranged across four lines: at the top, there is a neoclassical building (x1); beneath that, a photographer stoops over a tripod (x4); on the next row, a woman opens a filing cabinet (x5); and, at the bottom, as the basis of the whole design, is a single cash register (not from Modley). With its schematised colonnade atop a two-storey podium, the building has close affinities with the historic frontage to the New York Stock Exchange (the museum often avails itself of the same architectural language, of course). However, we should not be overly lured by Peircean iconicity, and thereby lose sight of the fact that visual abstractions are necessarily involved with both the isotype *qua* isotype and European classicism as an architectural language.

In the 1982 postscript to *School Is a Factory* (1980/2), where he first cites Sohn-Rethel, Sekula notes how: 'abstraction . . . emerges from the triumph of exchange value over use value, from the triumph of abstract intellectual labor over manual labor, from the triumph of instrumental reason over critical reason'.[137] Here, Sekula 'doubles' this framework of abstraction so that it encompasses the cultural: modernism's claims to aesthetic autonomy, its separation from life and the free play of signifiers. In *Fish Story*, *The Lottery of the Sea* and *The Forgotten Space*, shipping containers will play this role of universal equivalent – their

135 The term derives from the (adapted) acronym for International System of Typographic Picture Education (ISOTYPE), also known as the *Wiener Methode der Bildstatistik*. Modley was assistant to Neurath in Vienna. He introduced the Vienna Method to the US in the 1930s, initially as curator of Social Science at Chicago's Museum of Science and Industry. In 1933, he founded Pictorial Statistics Incorporated in New York. The use of the isotypes was also picked up by Victor Burgin and later became central to the practice of Andreas Siekmann and Alice Creischer.

136 Marx, *Capital: I*, 184.

137 'Postscript' (1982), *School Is a Factory*, 234.

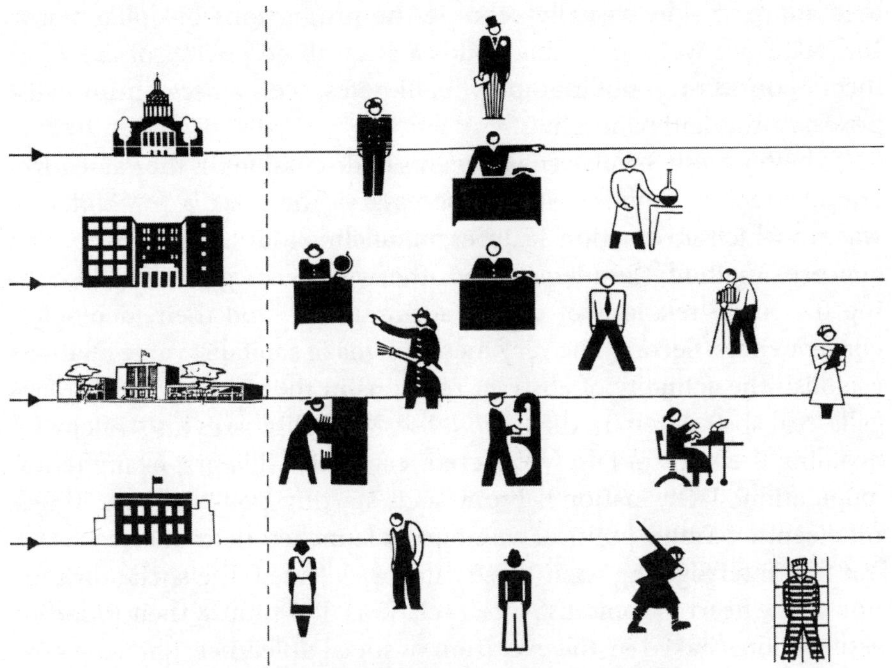

Figure 4: Rudolf Modley isotypes from School Is a Factory *(1980–2)*

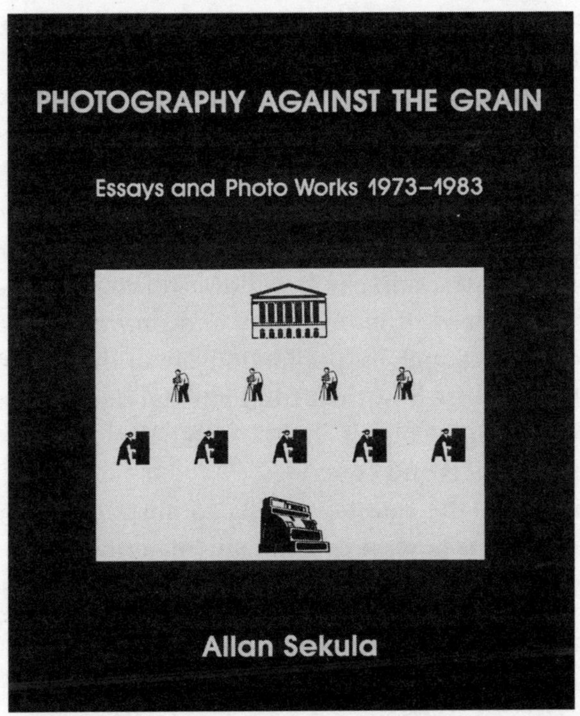

Figure 5: Cover to Photography Against the Grain *(1984)*

logo-adorned sides visually echoing the proportions of dollar notes. Indeed, as we will see, Sekula builds a generalised poetics of the value form, connecting photography, banknotes, containers, minimalist boxes, coffins and panoramas.

To better grasp Sekula's engagements in discussions of the value form and abstraction, another step is necessary. There are a few different ways in which 'abstraction' features, paralleling Marx. First, abstraction concerns method, the adequacy or otherwise of categories for describing the social relations of capital accumulation and their ideological consequences. Second, the very mechanisms of capitalist value relations establish the actuality of abstract relations in the world – which Marx calls 'real abstraction'. In the *Grundrisse*, Marx discusses his strategy for avoiding the traps of falsely 'concrete' categories (his first example was 'population'; later, 'nation'). From such starting points, Marx argues, nineteenth-century political economists launched their analyses without first interrogating what these categories elided: the social disjunction at the heart of capitalist social relations. Put simply, their founding assumptions 'baked in' the exclusion of social difference, ignoring how, for example, 'population' was riven by class. Thus, far from being the firm 'concrete' categories they appeared to be, they were already weak abstractions. (Marx also uses abstraction in this distinct but closely related sense: the 'abstract materialism of natural science' is 'abstract' because dehistoricised and thus rendered ideological.[138]) A caveat: it is important to recognise that these were not bad abstractions *because abstractions*. Abstraction, in Marx's account, is not set in stark opposition to the concrete but relates dynamically with it. When deployed appropriately in critical thinking (a logical universal, such as 'production in general'), abstraction can be a powerful route to understanding a phenomenon (indeed, it is necessary and unavoidable). Rather, the problem of categories such as 'population' lay in the failure of political economists to recognise how their fundamental categories were already super-diluted, setting in play a chain of analytical transitions between ever-thinning abstracts and concretes.

In Sekula's work, the question shifts to abstraction's relation with materiality. At stake is how we understand 'materialism'. As Marx put it: 'In the analysis of economic forms neither microscopes nor chemical reagents are of assistance. The power of abstraction must replace both.'[139]

---

138 Marx, *Capital: I*, 494 n. 4.

139 Marx, Preface to the First Edition (1867), *Capital: I*, 90.

To understand what is not obvious or immediately visible requires critical logic. Étienne Balibar has glossed this as Marx's 'strange "materialism without matter"'.[140] It is an important point (sometimes lost in 'new materialisms'). This returns us to the quotation from Brecht about photographing the factory – and what we referred to as the intractable problem facing the critical-realist photographer. Discussing this in 1997, Sekula writes:

> Reified social relations are in a sense invisible to ordinary empiricism, and can only be understood through recourse to abstraction, or as Marx put it in the introduction to the *Grundrisse*, through the movement upwards from the concrete to the abstract, and back down to the concrete. Thus the need for 'construction', a need in the end consistent for Brecht with the 'clumsy' motto: 'truth is concrete'.[141]

What is notable here is the way Sekula revises a key plank of political modernism – the neo-Brechtian (over)emphasis on 'something to construct' (or, better known from earlier translations, 'something must be constructed') – which was typically understood through the prism of an 'anti-naturalistic' impulse, and which championed montage or staged photography.[142] For Sekula, the 'construction' in question – *aufzubauen* in Brecht – shifts from the domain of politico-aesthetic choices (the artistic methods for disrupting a 'seamless reality') to Marx's method for approaching the social relations produced by the value form – that is, 'the movement upwards from the concrete to the abstract, and back down to the concrete'. Exploiting the everyday association of the word 'concrete' with building material, Sekula creates slippages (in turn, playful, cussed, knowingly ironic).

The neat formulation 'materialism without matter' has limitations if taken without critical diligence. In Balibar, this (philosophical) emphasis is meant to distinguish Marx's materialism from Engels's articulation of Marxism with the natural sciences. Clearly, materialism in

140 Étienne Balibar, *The Philosophy of Marx* (1993; London: Verso, 1995), 23. He writes: 'Marx's materialism has nothing to do with a reference to *matter*'. See also Alberto Toscano, 'Materialism without Matter: Abstraction, Absence and Social Form', *Textual Practice* 28:7 (2014): 1221–40.

141 'On *Fish Story*', 49. See Marx, *Grundrisse*, 100.

142 Bertolt Brecht, 'No Insight Through Photography' (1930), in *Bertolt Brecht on Film and Radio*, ed. Marc Silberman (London: Methuen, 2000), 144; 'The *Threepenny* Lawsuit' (1932), in ibid., 147–99 (164–5).

Marx's account of the value form is not reducible to matter-as-stuff, facticity, or empirically detectable physical observations involving microscopes or reagents. And, clearly, Marx was not disputing, say, empirical work in the natural sciences as such (which, in any case, would entail a whole set of arguments from the philosophy of science). The argument specifically concerned his critique of the theory of capitalism provided by political economists which started with 'population' and so on. Likewise, Marx was not arguing for abstraction understood as 'without materiality'; on the contrary, he was arguing for abstraction as *socially* material. This brings us to the second aspect of the discussion of abstraction. 'Real abstraction' refers not to 'abstraction' as 'separation from', as ideological dehistoricisation, or as ideational or methodological manoeuvre (although it has implications for them). Rather, it refers to the social actualisation of the value form 'as a force operative in the world'.[143] Third, for value-form theorists, value is not something existing 'inside' a commodity (the 'substantialist' argument, which is considered to underpin a 'pre-monetary theory') but is constituted by exchange relations. As Michael Heinrich put it: 'Commodities are values as "crystals" of their common substance, abstract labour.'[144] Abstraction, in this sense, involves the process by which concrete human activity is subordinated to forms of appearance and confronts its creatures as an 'alien force'. It is the point at which

143 Alberto Toscano, 'The Open Secret of Real Abstraction', *Rethinking Marxism: A Journal of Economics, Culture & Society* 20:2 (2008): 273–87 (274). Marx reflected in the *Grundrisse* on Adam Smith's category 'labour in general', a critical breakthrough in the history of political economy, albeit one Smith sometimes handled ahistorically. Marx intuited that Smith's insight was itself historically feasible only because 'abstract labour' was becoming prevalent, achieving 'practical truth as an abstraction' (*Grundrisse*, 105). See also Toscano, 'The Culture of Abstraction', *Theory, Culture & Society* 25:4 (2008): 57–75 (68); 'Beyond Abstraction: Marx and the Critique of the Critique of Religion', *Historical Materialism* 18 (2010): 3–29; Benjamin Noys, *The Persistence of the Negative: A Critique of Contemporary Continental Theory* (Edinburgh: Edinburgh University Press, 2010), and 'Art and Abstraction in the Present Moment', in *In the Mind but Not from There: Real Abstraction and Contemporary Art*, ed. Gean Moreno (2014; London: Verso, 2019), 219–39; Chris O'Kane, 'The Critique of Real Abstraction: From the Critical Theory of Society to the Critique of Political Economy and Back Again', in *Marx and Contemporary Critical Theory: The Philosophy of Real Abstraction*, eds Antonio Oliva, Ángel Oliva and Iván Novara (London: Palgrave Macmillan, 2020), 265–87.

144 Michael Heinrich, *An Introduction to the Three Volumes of Karl Marx's Capital* (2004; New York: Monthly Review Press, 2012), 64. Hence, value-form analysts reject the idea, held by some Marxist historians, that capitalism developed out of simple commodity production – that is, they oppose a reading of the stages of the form of value in Chapter 1 as historical progression.

capital mysteriously 'appears' as an 'automatic subject'; capital 'personified' as a 'self-moving substance'.[145]

Art is often seen as an enclave of liberated labour ('sensuous particularity') in a society dominated by abstraction, but, for Sekula, this underestimates the extent to which the forces of capital shape all social forms.[146] Continuing his discussion in 1997, he refers to capitalism's 'double veil of appearances and abstraction'[147] – the occlusions or distractions made by what we see, and the blockages caused by capital's accumulation processes. Sekula is attentive both to the 'matter-ness' of appearances and to the 'invisible' social materiality of 'real abstraction'; and he is attentive to the problems both present. Attuned as Sekula was to questions of representation in documentary photography, and to debates on the politics of representation, he also displayed a fine-tuned attentiveness to the complex dance of appearances and abstractions – their switching of characteristics, their exchange of energies and their metamorphosing.

Archives and Abstraction (Reading against the Grain)

'Photography Between Labour and Capital' focuses on engineering vision and technical realism, but it opens with a discussion of photographic archives. As Sekula notes, 'the model of the archive . . . is a powerful one in photographic discourse', and one that had been relatively unquestioned until that point.[148] He asks what it means for him 'to construct a pictorial history' of mining 'by using pictures from a company public relations archive without calling attention to the bias inherent in that source'.[149] Managers decide who or what is included, generating, as David Nye has put it, 'a managerial dream about life in the factory'.[150] 'Archives . . . constitute a *territory of images*' which is

145 Marx, *Capital: I*, 255, 256.

146 This is not to claim that art is a commodity like others. See: Dave Beech, *Art and Value: Art's Economic Exceptionalism in Classical, Neoclassical and Marxist Economics* (Leiden: Brill, 2015); Marina Vishmidt, *Speculation as a Mode of Production: Forms of Value Subjectivity in Art and Capital* (Leiden: Brill, 2019); Nizan Shaked, *Museums and Wealth: The Politics of Contemporary Art Collections* (London: Bloomsbury, 2022).

147 'On *Fish Story*', 49.

148 'Photography between Labour and Capital', 194. The best equivalent is David E. Nye, *Image Worlds: Corporate Identities at General Electric* (Cambridge, MA: MIT Press, 1985).

149 'Photography Between Labour and Capital', 199.

150 Nye, *Image Worlds*, 88.

'imposed by ownership'.[151] Sekula here extends his value-form approach to read the archive against the grain: 'archives establish a relation of *abstract visual equivalence* between pictures'.[152] In them, 'the possibility of meaning is "liberated" from the actual contingencies of use' and subordinated 'to the logic of exchange'.[153]

At first sight, 'The Body and the Archive' (1986) is a very different type of study. Probably Sekula's best-known historical analysis, it is viewed as one of the works that introduced Michel Foucault's work on 'power-knowledge' and 'regimes of truth' to the study of visual culture. Foucault's account of the emergence of a new conception of subjectification and the government of 'population' during the nineteenth century is well known.[154] Sekula concurs with the standard view that Foucault's panopticism provides the 'central optical metaphor' for modern disciplinary power but thinks it needs extending to include photography.[155] He develops his earlier account, expanding 'instrumental realism' to include 'the police' and 'biopower'. Again, he suggests that photography must be considered a 'dual system of representation': on the one hand, the 'honorific' or 'ceremonial presentation of the bourgeois *self*' and, on the other, the 'repressive' (the attempt 'to establish and delimit the terrain of the *other*').[156] Exaggerating for effect, Sekula suggests: 'every proper portrait has its lurking, objectifying inverse in

151 'Photography Between Labour and Capital', 194.

152 Ibid., 195.

153 Ibid., 194.

154 Michel Foucault, *Discipline and Punish: The Birth of the Prison* (1975; Harmondsworth: Penguin, 1979); Michel Foucault, *The History of Sexuality*, vol. 1 (1976; Harmondsworth: Penguin, 1981). For the impact of Foucault on photographic studies, see: John Tagg, *The Burden of Representation: Essays on Photographies and Histories* (London: Macmillan, 1988); Roberta McGrath, 'Medical Police', *Ten.8* 14 (1984): 13–18; David Green, 'A Map of Depravity', *Ten.8* 18 (1985): 36–43; Green, 'On Foucault: Disciplinary Power and Photography', *Camerawork* 32 (1985): 6–9; Green, 'Veins of Resemblance: Photography and Eugenics', in Patricia Holland et al., *Photography/Politics: Two* (London: Comedia/ Photography Workshop, 1986), 9–21.

155 'The Body and the Archive', 9 n. 13. Sekula rejects Tagg's claim that the camera would replace the carceral complex, observing, 'Once discourse turns on metaphor, it becomes a simple matter to substitute a photographic metaphor for an architectural one.' The central point was that 'any history of disciplinary institutions must recognize the multiplicity of material devices involved – some literally concrete – in tracing not only the importance of surveillance, but also the continued importance of confinement' ('The Body and the Archive', 9 n. 13; 36, n. 54). Cf. Tagg, *The Burden of Representation*, 87.

156 'The Body and the Archive', 6–7 (emphases Sekula's). In a later essay on modernist photography, he asserts: 'Roughly between 1885 and 1900, an institutional model of photographic meaning was invented: the model of the archive' ('Walker Evans and the Police', 193).

the files of the police. In other words, a covert Hobbesian logic links the terrain of the "National Gallery" with that of the "Police Act".'[157] The essay attends to this ignored '*shadow archive*' of 'juridical realism'.[158] It is 'extraordinary', Sekula observes, that media historians have ignored such archives, betraying 'a certain bourgeois scholarly discretion concerning the dirty work of modernization, especially when the status of photography as a fine art is at stake'.[159]

Sekula focuses on two pioneers of the criminal archive, Alphonse Bertillon and Francis Galton. Bertillon developed a system for identifying criminals that 'combined photographic portraiture, anthropometric description, and highly standardized and abbreviated written notes on a single *fiche*, or card'.[160] Galton produced composite portraits by superimposing photographs of multiple individuals within a single image to form 'blurred, fictitious apparitions'.[161] In this way, Galton believed, personal idiosyncrasies fell away and the image revealed the essential characteristics of different social types. These men occupied distinct positions in the attempt to 'define and regulate social deviance', although inattentive readers conflate their practices.[162] Bertillon found the criminal body inexpressive; ears or scars were just evidence for identification. In contrast, for Galton – protagonist of the pseudo-sciences of eugenics, physiognomy and phrenology – social pathologies were legible as signs on the body. His work belonged to the line of spurious 'racial' declinist theories and entailed a 'profoundly ideological *biologization* of existing class relations in England'.[163] Sekula notes in a pithy condensation: 'Where Bertillon was a compulsive systematizer, Galton was a compulsive quantifier.'[164]

Subsequent work in the history of photography has criticised the Foucauldian project of the 1970s and 1980s for both ignoring resistance to power-knowledge and failing to see that the schemes for governance were never straightforwardly realised. Critics sometimes collapse Sekula's work into this paradigm of total power.[165] It is true that much of

157 'The Body and the Archive', 7.
158 Ibid., 10 (emphasis Sekula's), 5.
159 Ibid., 56.
160 Ibid., 18.
161 Ibid., 46.
162 Ibid., 19.
163 Ibid., 42.
164 Ibid., 40.
165 Elizabeth Edwards positions Sekula this way in 'Tracing Photography', in *Made to be Seen: Perspectives on the History of Visual Anthropology*, eds Marcus Banks and Jay Ruby (Chicago, IL: University of Chicago Press, 2011), 159–89 (171–3).

the critical work of the time paid little attention to how ideas of social regulation were actually implemented. In practice, when these visions from above were rolled out, they encountered blockages of all sorts, from local bureaucratic inertia to subaltern subterfuge or outright resistance.[166] An important counterargument would be that these criticisms fail to account for the persistence of domination and hegemony. It is not wrong to see 'The Body and the Archive' as a biopolitical analysis, but it differs in significant ways.

Compared with most Foucauldian studies of the period, Sekula departs further from Foucault's Nietzschean-inspired universe of particulars.[167] He was also at pains to distance his account from the idea of a total machine of power that produced 'docile bodies'.[168] Indeed, many readers are inattentive to the intellectual traditions from which Sekula built his archival studies and unaware of how his model centres the functioning of money in capitalist exchange. This is evident from the outset of the essay, where Holmes's analogy of photography and banknotes serves as the essay's epigraph. On three occasions, Bertillon's system is compared with Taylor's rationalisation of work.[169] Reiterating the argument of his essay on mining photographs, Sekula suggests that the archive involves 'a vast substitution set, providing for a relation of general equivalence between images'.[170] Sekula's emphasis on abstraction in 'The Body and the Archive' can be further amplified. Like Foucault, Sekula sees the archive as a site defining the 'normal' and 'abnormal'. However, drawing on Ian Hacking, he also shows how

166 See as examples: Robin Kelsey, *Archive Style: Photographs and Illustrations for U.S. Surveys, 1850–1890* (Berkeley and Los Angeles, CA: University of California Press, 2007), 34; Elizabeth Edwards, 'Professor Huxley's Well Considered Plan', in *Raw Histories: Photographs, Anthropology and Museums* (London: Routledge, 2001), 131–55; Ann Laura Stoller, *Along the Archival Grain: Epistemic Anxieties and Colonial Common Sense* (Princeton, NJ: Princeton University Press, 2010). For an early criticism, see: Steve Edwards, 'The Machine's Dialogue', *Oxford Art Journal* 13:1 (1990): 63–76.

167 See Jacques Bidet, *Foucault with Marx* (London: Zed Books, 2016), 201–2.

168 Readers of 'The Body and the Archive' often overlook the concluding remarks on Ernest Cole's photo book *House of Bondage* (1967), where Sekula notes that South African pass laws were one instance in which the discourse of the racial type remained in play. In focusing on *tsotsis*, or Black urban petty criminals, 'Cole's documentation of the everyday flows of power, survival and criminal resistance got him into trouble with the law' (64).

169 Arguably, many Foucaldians overlook his attention to the regulation and disciplining of labour power in both *Discipline and Punish* and *The Punitive Society: Lectures at the Collège de France 1972–1973* (London: Palgrave Macmillan, 2015). See also: Didier Deleule and François Guéry, *The Productive Body* (London: Zero, 2014); Pierre Macherey, 'The Productive Subject', *Viewpoint*, 31 October 2015, viewpointmag.com; Bidet, *Foucault with Marx*.

170 'The Body and the Archive', 17.

notions of 'average' or 'social average' perform the brutal work of 'abstraction' and 'equivalence'.[171] Despite the differences between Bertillon and Galton, underpinning both was the work of Adolphe Quetelet, the Belgian astronomer and pioneer of sociology, who created a bell curve to plot 'social averages' and their 'deviations'. As Sekula puts it, 'In an extraordinary metaphoric conflation of individual difference with mathematical error, Quetelet defined the central portion of the curve, that large number of measurements clustered around the mean, as a zone of normality.'[172] This 'average man', he continues, exemplified 'an ideal, not only of social health, but of social stability and of beauty'.[173] Indeed, identifying the social average with European bourgeois men is extraordinarily violent in its implications.

'The Body and the Archive' is part of the late-twentieth-century trend that focused on the body as site of meaning. As Marina Vishmidt observes, for a range of intellectuals – Michel Foucault, Gilles Deleuze, Julia Kristeva and Elaine Scarry – the category of the body supplants the idea of 'the people'.[174] Recently, several thinkers have posited a different kind of politics for the body. Elaborating a left-Arendtian conception of the political, Judith Butler posits a coalition of vulnerable bodies 'appearing together' in assembly – a form for an ethical and democratic politics, where weakness or injury provides the common basis for improving conditions of life.[175] As Vishmidt convincingly argues, one problem with corporeal politics is that it conceives of the body as prior to, or independent of, capital's real abstractions.[176] The result is often politically demobilising, recognising and managing injury rather than envisaging social transformation. However, bodies exist in the mesh of real abstractions: shaped by the violence of 'abstract labour'; the

171 Ian Hacking, 'How Should We Do a History of Statistics?', *Ideology and Consciousness* 8 (1981): 14–26; 'Biopower and the Avalanche of Printed Numbers', *Humanities and Society* 5:3–4 (1982): 279–95.

172 'The Body and the Archive', 22.

173 Ibid.

174 Marina Vishmidt, 'Bodies in Space: On the Ends of Vulnerability', *Radical Philosophy* 208 (2020): 33–46.

175 Judith Butler, *Notes Towards a Performative Theory of Assembly* (Cambridge, MA: Harvard University Press, 2015).

176 Some Marxists, such as David McNally and Joseph Fracchia, suggest the body or 'corporeal organisation' – represents a grounding materialist category for experience and meaning. David McNally, *Bodies of Meaning: Studies on Language, Labor, and Liberation* (New York: State University of New York Press, 2001); Joseph Fracchia, *Bodies and Artefacts: Historical Materialism and Corporeal Semiotics*, 2 vols (Leiden: Brill, 2022). We will not engage within this debate here.

division of mental and manual labour; waged work and unpaid reproductive labour; and the sedimented geographical and racialised differences of bodies produced as an 'accumulation strategy'.[177] For Sekula, the body is not ontologically prior to abstraction.[178] He later noted that he read Foucault through Braverman and other studies of the labour process.[179] Sekula would go on to criticise the forms of materialism that go 'no farther than "the body" '.[180]

SECTION 2: 'IMAGINATIVE AND MATERIAL GEOGRAPHIES OF THE ADVANCED CAPITALIST WORLD'

Sekula's criticism of documentary empiricism and the illusions of a universal language in photography were made when these ideological claims possessed cultural weight. His emphasis shifted as the intellectual climate changed. As far as the would-be culturally savvy were concerned, he wrote in 1997, 'The old myth that photographs tell the truth has succumbed to the new myth that they don't'.[181] Noting the rise of theatricalised 'epistemological scepticism', he found that performative practice increasingly cut too easily with, rather than against, the grain.[182] Sekula distanced himself from the play of signs, quotations, appropriations and staging. A pervading anti-materialism meshed too closely with developments in capitalist culture. The associated rejection of social documentary by many media specialists contributed to the

177 David Harvey, 'The Body as Accumulation Strategy' (1998), in *Spaces of Hope* (Edinburgh: Edinburgh University Press, 2000), 97–116 (98).

178 Toscano notes that, rather uniquely, Sekula combines two (typically conflicting) critiques of abstraction: '(1) a materialist and corporeal, as well as partisan, practice of photography, practicing "purposeful immersion" into the social; (2) a "reduction" of phenomena of artistic form to social form' ('The Mirror of Circulation').

179 Sekula in 'Allan Sekula and Benjamin H. D. Buchloh Conversation', 45.

180 'Dismal Science', 50.

181 'On *Fish Story*', 52. Cf. 'Eleven Premises on Documentary and a Question'; 'Walker Evans and the Police', 193. Jeff Wall makes a comparable but more symmetrical statement on the 'two reigning myths of photography – the one that claims that photographs are true and the one that claims that they are not'. Jeff Wall, ' "Marks of Indifference": Aspects of Photography in, or as, Conceptual Art', in *Reconsidering the Object of Art: 1965–1975*, eds Ann Goldstein and Anne Rorimer (Los Angeles, CA: Museum of Contemporary Art, 1995), 247–67 (254). For a comparison of Sekula and Wall, see Steve Edwards, 'Photography Out of Conceptual Art', in *Themes in Contemporary Art*, eds Gill Perry and Paul Wood (New Haven: Yale University Press, 2004), 137–80.

182 For the opposing view, see Vishmidt, *Speculation as a Mode of Production*, 121.

persistent story of the time: 'The social is unknowable. The social doesn't exist.'[183] Sekula's practice increasingly drew much of its charge from this double negation of the two 'myths': on the one hand, refusing the transparency of the photograph; and, on the other, rejecting the scepticism associated with the staged image.[184] He explored an expanded model of documentary. To paraphrase David Bordwell, a staging-driven practice was displaced by a cutting-driven one.[185] At the same time, Sekula's free-standing 'academic' essays ceded to more associative and episodic prose writing, often integrated with his photowork.

School Is a Factory (1980/2) was the last of his performative documentaries. Sekula's 1982 postscript called for a project of 'political geography' to counter a variety of abstractions: on the one hand, the autonomy claims of older modernist aesthetics and the newer semioticians' 'disengaged play of signifiers'; and on the other, the bureaucratic 'realism' of commodity society.[186] He embarked on a series of works, billed as 'geography lessons': *Sketch for a Geography Lesson* (1983); *Geography Lesson: Canadian Notes* (1987); and *Fish Story* (1995), which, in early development in 1988, went under the designation *Geography Lesson: Fish Story*.[187] A precedent for this attention to 'geography' is already evidenced in his plans for *California Stories* in 1975: 'San Pedro Notes: A Geography'.[188] In part, this shift to an expanded version of documentary realism can be understood as a reorientation away from the narrative form of

---

183 'On *Fish Story*', 49.

184 In this regard, documentary is one of the central, if largely unacknowledged, forms of the avant-garde's attempt to sublate art and life in its effort to produce a new vision of the capitalist everyday, while remaining attentive to social division. Roberts, *Photography and Its Violations*; Jorge Ribalta, ed., *The Worker Photography Movement (1926–1939): Essays and Documents* (Madrid: Museo Nacional Centro De Arte Reina Sofia, 2011). See also the special issue of the *Oxford Art Journal* 38:1 (2015), edited by Stephanie Schwartz, particularly: Jorge Ribalta, 'The Strand Symptom: A Modernist Disease?', 55–71; cf. Stephanie Schwartz, *Walker Evans: No Politics* (Austin, TX: University of Texas Press, 2020).

185 David Bordwell, *Figures Traced in Light: On Cinematic Staging* (Berkeley, CA: California University Press, 2005), 8.

186 'Postscript' (1982), *School Is a Factory*, 252. He again acknowledges Sohn-Rethel.

187 *Geography Lesson: Canadian Notes* was prepared in 1985 and 1986; exhibited with a short brochure in 1987; published as a book in 1997. The earlier title *Geography Lesson: Fish Story* first appears on a page dated 27 October 1988 in: Sekula Papers, S.1.05:01 'UCLA seminar notes 1988–1991'; cf. S.1.05:02 [Fish Story/Misc.Notes & Contact Information] 1989 (entry dated 24 March 1989). He opened a new notebook in July 1989 with the title 'GEOGRAPHY LESSON: Fish Story – Notes'. See: S.1.05:04 Geography Lesson: Fish Story July 1989–March 1990.

188 Sekula Papers, S.1.02:01 [San Pedro notes and notes for a second Meditations on a Triptych] 1975 (page dated 6 June 1975).

autobiography associated with his earlier works, where the author (A) is equated with both narrator (N) and character (C). Instead, the geography lessons adopt a form that might ally author with narrator, but not with character; typically, this is the form of historical narrative, and, arguably, of other 'fact'-based narrative modes.[189]

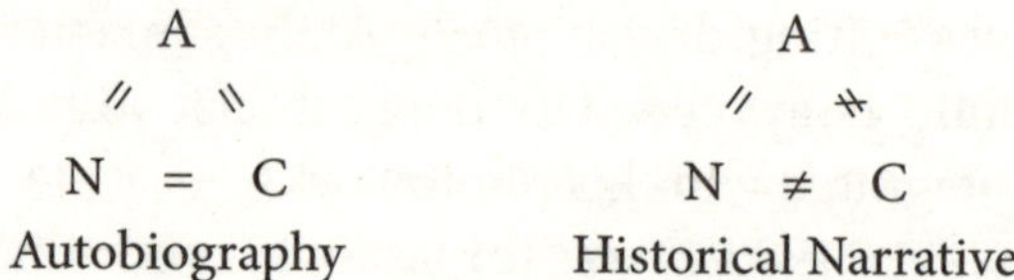

His works from all periods interrogate aspects of capitalist society, situating 'the simultaneous ideological and economic determinations of various spaces – small crowded apartments, border zones, the meticulously landscaped public spaces of central banks – within the larger system of postwar development'.[190] The geography lessons increase the reach and ambition of this project. *Sketch for a Geography Lesson* explores the geopolitics of a divided Europe, opening and closing with photographs of a television set: stills of a broadcast in which the audience is being engaged in a war game. Led by two US military officers, this mock-up presented the scene of a Russian invasion in Hesse, West Germany. The main sequence of nine colour photographs was made in the area around Fulde, in actual Hesse, close to the border with East Germany. Sekula imagines the hilly farming landscape through the prism of German Romanticism, while simultaneously drawing attention to the presence of the US military and the absence of any recognition of the site of a former Nazi labour camp. *Geography Lesson: Canadian Notes* is a larger project (in its exhibited form: forty-nine colour and thirty-nine black-and-white photographs, organised in eighteen subsets). Picking up threads from the Cape Breton project a couple of years earlier, it pairs the nickel (and uranium) mines of Sudbury with Ottawa's Bank of Canada to highlight their interlinking capital flows and their relationships to 'landscape'. We return to this project in a later chapter. Towards the end of the 1980s, plans appear for *Fish Story*, where the focus moves from the subterranean to the

189 Gérard Genette, *Fiction & Diction* (Ithaca, NY: Cornell University Press, 1993), 68–79. The pronoun 'I' or 'me' occurs three times in *Fish Story*.

190 'Imaginary Economies: An Interview with Allan Sekula', 238. Sekula favoured formulations of the 'simultaneously x and y', such as the 'simultaneously instrumental and heterotopic', discussed in Chapter 3.

maritime economy. The result – one of the first artworks in any medium to attend to neoliberal globalisation – is undoubtedly the most ambitious of all.

Fish Story *(1995)*

The photographs and essays for *Fish Story* consider the reorganisation of the global economy at the end of the twentieth century, taking on some of the assumptions associated with what came to be known as neoliberalism. During this period, the postwar gains of organised labour in the majority world were systematically rolled back in what David Harvey styled the 'restoration of class power'.[191] Trade union rights and labour protections were undercut; wealth redistributed upwards; the social state reduced to an 'anti-state state', and the burden of social reproduction turned over to women outside waged employment.[192] Stuart Hall pithily remarked, 'Globalization is how capital saved itself from the welfare state.'[193] In some of the major capitalist countries, investment in manufacturing was swapped for services, finance, insurance and real estate, with a concomitant loss of jobs in goods-producing industries.[194] As Gérard Duménil and Dominique Lévy argue, neoliberalism maximised income for the rich at the expense of industrial production, regardless of the impact on patterns of employment.[195]

In an important account from 1989 (with which, to our knowledge, Sekula was not engaged), Ambalavaner Sivanandan responded to those

191 David Harvey, *A Brief History of Neoliberalism* (Oxford: Oxford University Press, 2005); 'Neoliberalism and the Restoration of Class Power', in *Spaces of Global Capitalism: A Theory of Uneven Geographical Development* (London: Verso, 2006), 7–68.

192 Despite the rhetoric, the neoliberal state does not entail an eclipse of state provision, but acts to facilitate accumulation locally and globally, redirecting resources from 'welfare' towards security. Ruth Wilson Gilmore describes the process as a 'passive revolution' in *Abolition Geography: Essays Towards Liberation* (London: Verso, 2023), 27. On the role of the US state in creating conditions for globalisation, see Leo Panitch and Sam Gindin, *The Making of Global Capitalism: The Political Economy of American Empire* (London: Verso, 2012).

193 'At Home and Not at Home: Stuart Hall in Conversation with Les Back' in *Stuart Hall: Essential Essays Volume 2: Identity and Diaspora*, ed. David Morley (Durham, NC: Duke University Press, 2019), 263–300 (294).

194 This is a broad-brush account and emphasises the experiences of the US and the UK. Even across Western Europe, impacts varied considerably. A fuller account would need to consider the roles of the collapse of the Soviet bloc and China's opening to markets.

195 Gérard Duménil and Dominique Lévy, *The Crisis of Neoliberalism* (Cambridge, MA: Harvard University Press, 2011).

who saw these changes as resulting in 'deindustrialisation', 'the post-industrial society' and 'the end of the working class'; he argued that this characterisation was mistaken and deeply Eurocentric. He pointed to the respatialised economic geographies that were emerging as *Fish Story* was being prepared, highlighting the one-sided myths and discourses that Sekula would alight upon. High-value and high-skill activities, Sivanandan argued, were reserved by the old powers, while 'new circuits of imperialism' allowed 'capital to shift the burden of extracting surplus value from the workers at the centre to the workers at the (outer) periphery' of the global system.[196] Far from the 'end of the working class', this was its globalised recalibration, a re-siting of manufacturing to regimes with 'cheaper and cheaper labour, deunionised labour, captive labour, female labour and child labour'.[197] The free flow of capital was matched by immobility for workers, with increasingly draconian border controls.[198] Inequalities were exacerbated at varying scales – locally and globally, both for the majority world and within the minority one.[199] Within the majority world, the racialised poor, migrants and asylum seekers – Sivanandan's 'rightless, rootless, peripatetic and temporary, illegal even' – underpinned the operations of agribusiness, service industries, the securitisation of private property, healthcare provision and domestic labour.[200] The 'surplus population' that resulted

---

196 Ambalavaner Sivanandan, 'New Circuits of Imperialism' (1989), in *Communities of Resistance*, 169–95 (181). See also: John Narayan, 'New Times or New Circuits: Recovering Sivanandan's Political Economy', *Race and Class* 65:1 (2023), 14–33. The articles were interventions into the debate on Thatcherism and 'New Times'. With different theoretical emphasis, Nigel Harris tracked key global changes in *Of Bread and Guns: The World Economy in Crisis* (Harmondsworth: Penguin, 1983). More recently, US politicians fretted over their dependence on Taiwanese semiconductor production.

197 Sivanandan, 'New Circuits of Imperialism', 181. If, at the end of the nineteenth century, states stepped in to prevent the absolute immiseration of workers and ensure social reproduction, neoliberal capital is a return to the immiseration thesis but only for *certain* groups of people.

198 Kalyan Sanyal, *Rethinking Capitalist Development: Primitive Accumulation, Governmentality and Post-Colonial Capitalism* (London: Routledge, 2007).

199 Many of the standard accounts of neoliberalism focus on the majority world, ignoring the second prong of the neoliberal agenda as a response to anti-colonial movements in the majority world that levers open markets either by force or debt and structural readjustment. Kundnani emphasises the racist dimensions of neoliberalism, arguing that the 'oil crisis' of 1973 galvanised key policy makers in their attitude to the Middle East and the strategic commodity involved: Arun Kundnani, *What Is Anti-Racism? And Why it Means Anti-Capitalism* (London: Verso, 2023).

200 Sivanandan, 'New Circuits of Imperialism', 190. He distinguishes the more traditional 'civilisational racism' from global capitalism's new 'xeno-racism', which can also be targeted at 'white' migrants: 'Race, Terror and Civil Society', in *Catching History on the*

from systematic disinvestment was (and is) criminalisation.[201] In the US, Ruth Wilson Gilmore demonstrates, racialised mass incarceration (the 'prison fix') is a death-dealing response to these changes.[202] In 1996, Sekula condensed these issues in image for the work *Freeway to China*, which he titled 'One Thousand Trucks'. The caption describes the view:

> In a bold but unsuccessful effort to force cartage companies to recognize a truckers' union, the drivers, most of them recent immigrants from Mexico and Central America, removed their trucks from the waterfront. They parked a thousand tractors in a vacant lot between the derelict Kaiser steel mill and the new San Bernadino County Jail, more than seventy miles from the port.[203]

Addressing this photograph in a lecture, he referred to the 'growth industry' represented by this prison and the bail-bond office in the centre of the image.[204]

Capitalism – in both its historical and contemporary forms – cannot be understood without thinking about the sea. Indeed, as Liam Campling and Alex Colás underscore, 'Global capitalism is a seaborne phenomenon.'[205] Entrepôts, trading monopolies and colonial settlement; bonded labour and the trade in enslaved peoples; the merchant carrying trades; the early use of wage labour in deep-sea vessels and dockyards; privateering; the expansion of commodity frontiers; extraction of oil, minerals and fish; modern container shipping and oil tankers; the emergence of insurance and risk management; gun-boat diplomacy; spaces of 'exception' (tax havens, export processing zones, flags of convenience

---

Wing: Race, Culture & Globalisation (London: Pluto, 1982), 167–8. See also Sivanandan, 'Imperialism and Disorganic Development in the Silicon Age' (1979), in *Catching History on the Wing* (1982), 179–98. Cf. the idea of 'disarticulated development' in Samir Amin, *Imperialism and Unequal Development* (New York: Monthly Review Press, 1976).

201 Stuart Hall, Chas Critcher, Tony Jefferson, John Clarke and Brian Roberts, *Policing the Crisis: Mugging, the State and Law and Order* (London: Macmillan, 1978); Gilmore, *Abolition Geography*.

202 Ruth Wilson Gilmore, *Golden Gulag: Prisons, Surplus, Crisis, and Opposition in Globalizing California* (Berkeley, CA: University of California Press, 2007); *Abolition Geography*.

203 *Freeway to China*, in *Performance Under Working Conditions*, ed. Sabine Breitwieser (Vienna: Generali Foundation, 2003), 293.

204 'Globalism's Discontents and the Return of the Sea', AA School of Architecture, 10 November 1999, youtube.com.

205 Liam Campling and Alejandro Colás, *Capitalism and the Sea* (London: Verso, 2021), 1.

(FOCs)); vast underwater networks of pipelines, telegraph and digital cables; the list goes on. Sekula's attention to maritime industries and littoral spaces, central to his work from the late 1980s, evidences the structural changes underway.

However, *Fish Story* is not an illustration of social science. While the work attends to capital flows, it is not a project that tracks, say, commodity chains. The maritime world offers Sekula a unique point of reference for considering both the economic and representational layerings of capitalism. The maritime topos puts into play an unusually wide range of life metaphors. Sekula sometimes mobilises these, although it is not the existential metaphors associated with Herman Melville or Hans Blumenberg that preoccupy him; rather, his emphasis is on the cultural 'imaginary'. His central aim is to explore an image, a perspective, an ideology, an imaginative structure, a fantasy. The play between these terms matters: how image, thought and ideology intersect; how picture and word interact; how fantasy is manufactured, trafficked and circulated; how all these constitute relations of power.

As he makes clear in his essay 'Dismal Science' (1995) – Thomas Carlyle's term for political economy – his purpose in *Fish Story* was to explore 'this "dismal science" of the *image* of the ship and the sea and the sailor'.[206] The geography lesson trio addresses 'the imaginative and material geographies of the advanced capitalist world'.[207] The influence of Marxist geographers such as Neil Smith, Edward Soja and David Harvey is apparent, as is that of Sekula's co-teaching in 1990 with his friend Mike Davis.[208] Still, we should not lose sight of the word

206 'Dismal Science', 133 (emphasis Sekula's). He described his use of Carlyle's 'critical pessimism' as 'a bit of a joke'. 'Imaginary Economies: An Interview with Allan Sekula', 238.

207 'A Note on the Work', *Fish Story*, 202. It is, of course, compiled from a contingent geography, sometimes determined by funding, commissions and exhibition opportunities. North and Central America, Europe and East Asia feature prominently, but Africa, Australasia and South America are absent. Jeroen Verbeeck said that a planned trip to the African continent was scuppered by a back injury. Subsequent works enlarge this geographic scope, with images, or film and video sequences, made in Brazil, Japan, Laos, Panama and South Africa, and further trips to Europe.

208 Sekula and Davis co-taught the course 'Documentary Typographies' on the social landscape of Southern California at CalArts in 1990. They took students to a range of locations including the port and Fontana. At this point, Davis – already known for his role at *New Left Review* and for *Prisoners of the American Dream: Politics and Economy in the History of the US Working Class* (London: Verso, 1986) – had just completed the manuscript of *City of Quartz: Excavating the Future of Los Angeles* (London: Verso, 1990). See Andrew Witt, 'Allan Sekula: Photographic Work', *Getty Journal* 14 (2021): 151–79 (176 n. 12). Our thanks to Ina Steiner for drawing our attention to this essay.

'imaginative'. The formulation 'imaginative geographies' gestures to Edward Said's analysis of 'Orientalism' – a project drawing theoretically on Foucault, Gramsci and Williams.[209] One of Said's chapters is titled 'Imaginative Geography and Its Representations', and he often writes 'imaginative geography and history'. Said refuses the treatment of Orientalism as a false idea generated by Western colonialism. It was, in the proper sense of the word, a 'discourse' with tangible effects across civil institutions and political governance, whose imaginative horizons and habits of thought constituted actual world experiences. Emphasising this, Sekula adds the word 'material'.

Fish Story's first text panel (or short essay) gives a flavour of this multi-layered imaginary geography, at once material and ideological:

> Growing up in a harbor predisposes one to retain quaint ideas about matter and thought. I'm speaking only for myself here, although I suspect that a certain stubborn and pessimistic insistence on the primacy of material forces is part of a common culture of harbor residents. This crude materialism is underwritten by disaster. Ships explode, leak, sink, collide. Accidents happen everyday. Gravity is recognized as a force. By contrast, airline companies encourage the omnipotence of thought. This is the reason why the commissioner of airports for the city of Los Angeles is paid much more than the commissioner of harbors. The airport commissioner has to think very hard, day and night, to keep all the planes in the air.[210]

The fourth and last 'stanza' of this same panel condenses many of *Fish Story*'s themes. We include it in full to suggest the mode of thought in play and to highlight Sekula's distinctive rhetorical tone (to which we attend in Chapter 3):

> Space is transformed. The ocean floor is wired for sound. Fishing boats disappear in the Irish Sea, dragged to the bottom by submarines. Businessmen on airplanes read exciting novels about sonar. Waterfront brothels are demolished or remodeled as condominiums. Shipyards are converted into movie sets. Harbors are now less *havens* (as they were for the Dutch) than accelerated turning-basins for supertankers and container ships. The old harbor front, its links to a common culture

209 Edward W. Said, *Orientalism* (1978; London: Penguin, 1985).
210 *Fish Story*, 12.

> shattered by unemployment, is now reclaimed for a bourgeois reverie on the mercantilist past. Heavy metals accumulate in the silt. Busboys fight over scarce spoons in front of a plate-glass window overlooking the harbor. The backwater becomes a frontwater. Everyone wants a glimpse of the sea.[211]

Fish Story contrasts intractable material forces of gravity with a vision in which airplanes are, so to speak, levitated by the power of thought. This image – materialism versus idealism – is typical of the short texts written for the work that tend towards wry observations of ironies, sometimes courting absurdity or including a gruesome anecdote. He develops this contrast more polemically in the essay 'Dismal Science', emphasising how his work ran counter to:

> the commonly held view that the computer and telecommunications are the sole engines of the third industrial revolution. In effect, I am arguing for the continued importance of maritime space in order to counter the exaggerated importance attached to that largely metaphysical construct, 'cyberspace,' and the corollary myth of 'instantaneous' contact between distant spaces. I am often struck by the ignorance of intellectuals in this respect: the self-congratulating conceptual aggrandizement of 'information.'[212]

The idea that cyberspace, or what some now call 'cognitive capitalism', characterised the world economy, Sekula thought, revealed 'the blinkered narcissism of the information specialist' and the worldview catering for the needs of the 'managerial and intellectual classes'.[213] Inhabiting a fantasy world 'of wealth without workers, a world of uninhibited flows', this 'transnational bourgeoisie' imagine that goods are moved by air and that the world economy is encompassed by email.[214] In line with the arguments advanced by Sivanandan and others, Yann Moulier-Boutang emphasises that 'cognitive capitalism', far from eliminating 'the world of material industrial production', 're-arranges it, reorganises it and alters

211 Ibid., 12.

212 'Dismal Science', 50.

213 Ibid.

214 Ibid., 137, 50. Cf. caption to *Freeway to China (Version 2, for Liverpool)*, 297. At the time of writing, around 98 per cent of global finance transactions are made via underwater cables, not by satellite as many imagine.

the positioning of its nerve centres'.[215] It is in this sense that Sekula argues that 'a society of accelerated flows is also in certain key aspects a society of deliberately slow movement'.[216] In an interesting follow-through from his attention to the labour-process debates, this point echoes that of engineering activist Mike Cooley, who jibed that one could not 'fly the Atlantic on a [micro]chip'.[217] Sekula's essay 'On *Fish Story*' (1997) elaborates the scope of this discourse. Maritime industries, the subject of the economy; the working classes, the very category of labour, 'the figure of the sullen sailor'; documentary photography, Lewis Hine; realist aesthetic strategies, Brechtian epistemological realism: these were all being treated by the cognoscenti of the mid-1990s as quaintly awkward relics of earlier modes of life and thought.[218] The range of dismissals being made was not only extensive but also established overlapping 'bad-object' domains: economy, social class and realism (aesthetic and philosophical).

The photographs for *Fish Story* were made over several years, starting in the late 1980s, with elements being exhibited from 1990. In its full form – 'finished' is a word that sits uneasily with the mutability of Sekula's working methods, and the iterations of his projects – *Fish Story* was first exhibited in 1995 in Rotterdam, Europe's largest seaport, where it consisted of 105 colour photographs in 92 frames, organised in 7 sections, and 26 text panels (some are captions, two are devoted to quotations, and others present extended prose).[219] The bookwork, conceived alongside the exhibition, comprised ninety-six colour photographs – and this is now the project's most accessible version. Also included in the exhibition were: two slide projections, each a sequence of eighty transparencies, one based on photographs taken in Newcastle and Glasgow (1989/92, *Dismal Science*) and the other, in Warsaw and Gdansk (1990/5, *Walking on Water*); a booklet presented the captions and an accompanying text; vitrines with Sekula's publications; and a newspaper map of riots in Newcastle, which was screen-printed onto the wall.

215 Yann Moulier-Boutang, *Cognitive Capitalism* (2008; Cambridge: Polity, 2011), 48.

216 'Dismal Science', 50.

217 Mike Cooley, *Architect or Bee?*, 25.

218 'On *Fish Story*'. Robert Brenner's account of computer capital stock reinforces the point: Robert Brenner, 'The Economics of Global Turbulence', *New Left Review* I: 229 (1998): 248.

219 Sekula shot on colour transparency (Kodachrome and Fujichrome). He used three different 35mm cameras; and four for 120mm film (6x7, two 6x9 and a Cambo wide 6x12 for panoramas).

The photographs are organised into seven discrete sequences, each 'chapter' with its own short essay(s) or text panel(s). The opening chapter, 'Fish Story', consists of images taken between 1988 and 1993, primarily in port areas of Southern California, although also featuring New York, Minturno in Italy, Rotterdam and a location in Los Angeles far from the port (this section comprises eighteen plates in the book). It is followed by 'Loaves and Fishes' (eight photographs), which centres on Poland, bookended with San Diego, Rotterdam and Barcelona, the photographs mostly taken at the end of 1990. The next four chapters reflect specific trips: 'Middle Passage' (seventeen) is based on a transatlantic voyage in November 1993, from Port Elizabeth in South Africa to Rotterdam, onboard the container ship M/V *Sea-Land Quality*, clearly alluding to the transport of enslaved Africans; 'Seventy in Seven' (nineteen) is set in South Korean locations in September 1993, the title referring to a common idiom for the pace of East Asian economic development; 'Message in a Bottle' (six) was made in Vigo, Spain, in May 1992; 'True Cross' (thirteen), in Veracruz in Mexico, March 1994. The final chapter (fourteen photographs), 'Dictatorship of the Seven Seas' – the title from the Wobblies – returns to Southern California, with a couple of pictures from Hong Kong.[220]

The photographs depict cranes, trains, trucks, cars, a bus and vessels of all sorts, including model ships and things that resemble boats. There are people labouring, mostly men: fitting, welding, smelting, cutting, grinding, checking, steering, drilling, decontaminating, firefighting, fishing, trading, surveying and character acting. Others are idle, not necessarily by choice: pausing, dozing, waiting. Some actively protest. *Fish Story*'s emphasis continues to be on labour in the negative, recording the collapse of the older industrial powers and the relocation of shipbuilding and manufacture to South Korea and China.

---

220 The book includes an illustrated long-form essay called 'Dismal Science' (not to be confused with two other projects of the same name: the slide sequence displayed in the exhibition of *Fish Story*; and the 1999 retrospective exhibition at and catalogue for the University Galleries at the University of Illinois). Although clearly related, and included in the book, Sekula imagined the essay 'Dismal Science' as distinct from *Fish Story*. The essay is in five sections: 'Red Passenger' (Engels arriving in London), 'Forgetting the Sea', 'From the Panorama to the Detail', 'Phantom Mutiny', and 'Boxed In'. It contemplates the representations of the sea, from Netherlandish marine panoramas, through the unattached wandering vessel in Turner and Conrad, and the detail of the New Vision photographers, to the echoes and elisions of the shipping container in American art of the 1960s. In the process, Sekula considers how the sailor, the ship and mutiny figure in popular culture; in modernist film, photography and literature; in the cultural imaginary of left-wing writers; and in the thinking of military planners. Also included in the book *Fish Story* is an essay by the critic Benjamin H. D. Buchloh, with whom Sekula had worked in Nova Scotia.

The images vary in type and genre. They include formal portraits and candid shots; the depiction of human labours; landscapes, seascapes, harbour scenes; imagery one might associate with tourism or industrial photography; as well as images that demur from established aesthetic codes. There are several formalised straight-on compositions, sometimes occurring as diptychs and with a marginal adjustment to viewpoints. Carefully set-up centred single-point perspective occurs – most notably, the view towards the bow across the container stacks of *Sea-Land Quality*, the book's front-cover image (#28). Others in this same mode look down the corridor of an unemployment office or along train tracks (a classic film trope, #24). Still, more common are the off-centre obliques, glancing along the flanks of ships, buildings or objects. Other photographs appear to be caught on the hoof, skewed with barely a chance to align verticals (many, but not all, tilt the rising lines to the right, perhaps registering the photographer's dominant hand).

There is very little radical cropping and Sekula rarely bars visual access to subjects (in the manner associated with Robert Frank's *The Americans*). The photographs largely avoid the visual experiments of modernism, the radical distortions of both the early-twentieth-century avant-garde (László Moholy-Nagy, Alexandr Rodchenko, Germaine Krull) and American works of the 1950s and 1960s (Lee Friedlander, William Klein). In general, Sekula's photographs avoid the device of de-framing, a compositional form discussed in film theory and usually achieved by pushing the subject to the image's edges while hollowing out its centre. These factors signal commitment to the ethos of humanist photography: respect for the integrity of persons or things depicted. Nevertheless, there are anomalies. In a variation of the visual 'false attachment', a man is 'decapitated' by the trunk of a tree under which he dozes; three scientists are cropped by the photographic frame at chest-to-shoulder height. In 'Middle Passage', a vertical triptych depicting the discovery of the drifting yacht *Happy Ending* – notably, Sekula would later refer to this arrangement as a 'stack'[221] – starts with a more classic sea-and-skyscape (albeit a bit tipsy) before disorientating with views from above, producing abstract arrangements of shapes that suggest the tropes of early-twentieth-century photography – the New Vision (#32, #33, #34). In the South Korea chapter, a decorative pillar rises through the centre of the view, hinting at a pun on Friedlander's puns about amateurish 'bad photos' (#61). This is no mere nod to another

221 'Globalism's Discontents and the Return of the Sea'.

photographer, but an inversion with critical value. The pillar, it transpires, does not obstruct our view but is itself the subject: part of a memorial to the Hyundai workers killed during the building of the Seoul–Busan motorway.

The diptychs in *Fish Story* are not explicitly designated as such (as they are in other projects). Sekula later refers to them as 'implied diptychs'.[222] Nonetheless, their functioning *qua* diptychs can be deduced. Some share a caption. Some are obviously paired with the same or similar point of view. Some clearly play on a contrast or comparison. Yet it is their impact on our sense of time that most reveals their character. The diptych function decelerates how we proceed through a sequence or view the exhibited photographs. Diptychs have longstanding cultural associations with betrothal or marriage portraits, but the quality that seems to matter here is their 'open-book' form – which becomes most obvious in Sekula's book-works. (Sekula uses both horizontally and vertically arranged diptychs.) They can punctuate a sequence's tendency to 'filmic' propulsion, breaking up the flow, however unconventional the narrative. (The exhibited installation always troubles that forward motion, of course, enabling multi-directional and simultaneous viewing.) Time and viewing become more viscous, prompting the need to pause, to reflect, to check, to go back and forth – a thickening of time that impacts on the diptych itself but also on the entire sequence.[223]

Close-ups are untypical and occur in only a couple of places. There is a clipboard and a spanner near *Fish Story*'s opening (#3, #6). Most notably, there are several in 'Middle Passage', starting with a detail of an inclinometer (#27). A sequence of close-ups occupies the midpoint of

222 Ibid.

223 This viscosity or thickening of time is associated with Bakhtin's 'chronotope' (along with the temporal charging of space). While superficially similar to a 'motif' or 'theme' – famous examples include: sea, road, castle, threshold, border – the chronotope attends to how these interact as temporal and spatial forms (*chronos-topos*). Mikhail Bakhtin, 'Forms of Time and of the Chronotope in the Novel: Notes Towards a Historical Poetics' (1937–8/1973), in *The Dialogical Imagination* (Austin, TX: University of Texas Press, 1981), 84–258 (84). There is a fascinating (and sometimes highly technical) critical discussion of the chronotope and its effectivity. See, for example: Ken Hirschkop, *Mikhail Bakhtin: An Aesthetic for Democracy* (Oxford: Oxford University Press, 2002); Craig Brandist, *The Bakhtin Circle: Philosophy, Culture and Politics* (London: Pluto, 2002). Specifically on the sea chronotope, see Margaret Cohen, 'Chronotopes of the Sea', in *The Novel: Volume 2: Forms and Themes*, ed. Franco Moretti (Princeton, NJ: Princeton University Press, 2006), 647–66; and Cohen, *The Novel and the Sea* (Princeton, NJ: Princeton University Press, 2010).

this chapter, showing two museum objects: one, a model of an old harpoon boat, abandoned on an agitated sea and surrounded with debris; the other, a whale tooth incised with a 'pornographic' scene (#35, #36). Another pair follows, items found in the engine room of *Sea-Land Quality*: ear protectors; a model Star Trek character (#37, #38). These typically isolate the items from their surroundings, using a narrow focal depth to make the object of attention stand out crisply against out-of-focus backgrounds (or pick it out at near-mid distance). There are also a couple of examples where depth of field is pushed to the extreme. In a photograph of the chief mate inspecting containers, only the immediate foreground is in focus: flexible pipes as they bend around the edge of a deck (#29). Located some eighty feet or so away, the subject (as stated in the caption: 'Chief mate checking temperatures of refrigerated containters. Mid-Atlantic.') becomes a hominid smudge clambering the stack. (Sekula selected a close-up detail of this figure for the cover of his installation booklet for the Witte de With. He spoke of seeing the lonely actions of the chief mate as akin to the old practice of scaling masts on sail ships.)[224]

Some social theorists have observed that *Fish Story* is one of the earliest contributions to 'critical logistics' – an area of study that largely developed in the early 2000s (although dating back to the important worker co-investigations undertaken with Sergio Bologna for *Primo Maggio* in 1977).[225] Critical studies place containerisation at the heart of the 'logistics revolution', which configured the integrated system of globalised production and consumption.[226] Of course, containerisation has been a crucial technology for neoliberal globalisation. For Sekula, it is a methodological lens for focusing in on key aspects of the new economic geography and the role of the military-industrial complex. The US military made extensive use of container-shipped equipment during the Korean War and, as Deborah Cowen suggests, its

224 'Globalism's Discontents and the Return of the Sea.'

225 Laleh Khalili, Foreword to the 2018 Edition, in Allan Sekula, *Fish Story* (London: MACK Books, 2018), ii–ix; Bill Roberts, 'Production in View: Allan Sekula's Fish Story and the Thawing of Postmodernism', *Tate Papers* 18 (2012); Alberto Toscano, 'The Mirror of Circulation' and 'Seeing it Whole: Staging Totality in Social Theory and Art', *The Sociological Review* 60: S1 (2012): 64–83; Toscano, 'Logistics as Will and Representation', in Hamed Khosravi, Taneha Kuzniecow Bacchin, Filippo LaFleur, *Aesthetics and Politics of Logistics: Venice, Rotterdam* (Milan: Humboldt, 2019). There is also an extensive debate on 'chokepoints' and blockades as a strategy for halting capital in motion.

226 Edna Bonacich and Jake B. Wilson, *Getting the Goods: Ports, Labor, and the Logistics Revolution* (Ithaca, NY: Cornell University Press, 2008).

commercial application remains entangled with military power and social violence.[227] Laleh Khalili memorably metaphorises this connection when she refers to the modern practitioners of logistics as the 'quarter masters of capital'.[228]

First adapted to commercial shipping by Malcolm McLean in the US in 1956, transoceanic container shipment began in 1965.[229] Persistently low rates of profit inclined manufacturing capital to seek solutions, ranging from cost-cutting to financialisation. In a distinct but related process, the FOC registration – a 'lawyerly ruse' to conceal ownership of maritime vessels – undermined safety and environmental controls.[230] Combined with the deregulation of trucking and rail in the 1970s, the way was cleared for the expansion of containerisation.[231] Associated legal changes, such as the US Staggers Act of 1980, removed prohibitions on ownership across different transport modes and allowed corporations to establish 'backward linkages with component suppliers and forward linkages into distribution and retailing'.[232] Intermodal distribution systems, enabled by digital technologies, computer-driven transporters and stacking cranes, significantly reduced expenditure on variable capital and transport costs. Dispensing with the need to load and unload cargo from ships' holds, container shipping massively reduced turnaround time and accelerated the circulation of commodities through the world's ports.

From the perspective of capital, the great advantage of containerisation is geographically dispersed-but-integrated production ('the

227 Deborah Cowen, *The Deadly Life of Logistics: Mapping Violence in Global Trade* (Minneapolis, MN: University of Minnesota Press, 2014); Charmaine Chua, 'Logistical Violence, Logistical Vulnerabilities: A Review of *The Deadly Life of Logistics* by Deborah Cowen', *Historical Materialism* 25:4 (2017): 167–82. The military had been urging commercial shipping companies to adopt the technique since 1952. Stan Weir, 'New Technology: A Catalyst for Crises in Collective Bargaining, Industrial Discipline, and Labor Law' (1984), in *Single Jack Solidarity*, ed. George Lipsitz (Minneapolis, MN: University of Minnesota Press, 2004), 39–67 (45).

228 Laleh Khalili, *Sinews of War and Trade* (London: Verso, 2020), 265.

229 Marc Levinson, *The Box: How the Shipping Container Made the World Smaller and the World Economy Bigger* (Princeton, NJ: Princeton University Press, 2016). Compared with the critical accounts referenced, this history is rather boosterish, inspiring a 'BBC Box'.

230 'Between the Net and the Deep Blue Sea', 28. The FOC system was the target of the International Transport Workers' Federation's campaign ship *Global Mariner*.

231 Levinson, *The Box*, 372–4.

232 Charmaine Chua, 'Logistics', in *The Sage Critical Handbook to Marxism: Volume 3*, eds S. Farris, A. Toscano and B. Skeggs (London: Sage, 2022), 1442–60. On Stagger's Act, see Cowen, *The Deadly Life of Logistics*, 45.

stretched factory'), involving an international division of labour and the control of global labour arbitrage.[233] Firms relocated the production of components, and sometimes the entire production process, to low-wage economies, often with repressive employment legislation and large reserve armies of labour.[234] Respatialised production enables commodities to be 'manufactured *across logistics space* rather than in a singular place'.[235] Instead of stockpiling large inventories, with their associated handling and storage expenses, with the hope of 'pushing' commodities onto customers at some future point, companies could 'pull' as required ('just-in-time').[236] In such a system, absolute distance is less significant than overall costs, and between 1980 and 2009 US expenditure associated with transport and logistics was halved.[237] Global trade expanded exponentially, with a huge increase in container traffic.[238] By 1998 – three years after *Fish Story* – only a third of the twenty-foot containers moving through Southern California continued to hold fully formed consumer durables, as per the popular image of container contents; the growing share comprised components ('intermediate goods') in this expanding and complexly integrated global supply chain.[239] (The fragility of this integration has been exposed by the crises of the 2020 pandemic and the commencement of war in Ukraine in 2022.) Commodity-chain capitalism, with its economic niches, drives unevenness and difference throughout the world. 'Supply chains stimulate *both* global standardization and growing gaps between rich and poor, across lines of color and culture, and between North and South', Anna Tsing argues, underscoring how gender and racialisation

233 Cowen, *The Deadly Life of Logistics*, 102–5.

234 Toscano warns against seeing the process entirely from Long Beach. While the relocation of production to Asia might weaken workers in the Western capitalist states, collective strength and wages have risen for sections of the Chinese working class – a point underscored in *The Forgotten Space*. Alberto Toscano, 'Lineaments of the Logistical State', *Viewpoint*, 28 September 2014, viewpointmag.com.

235 Cowen, *The Deadly Life of Logistics*, 2; cf. Mau, *Mute Compulsion*, Chapter 12.

236 Martin Danyluk, 'Capital's Logistical Fix: Accumulation, Globalization, and the Survival of Capitalism', *Environment and Planning D: Society and Space* 36:4 (2018): 630–47; Chua, 'Logistics'.

237 Larkin cited in Danyluk, 'Capital's Logistical Fix', 637.

238 In the five years to 2014, of the top twenty world ports, eleven had no container traffic. By 2025, nine of the top ten container ports were located in Asia, seven in China. Levinson, *The Box*, 366–7. Cf. Khalili, *Sinews of War and Trade*, 64–5; World Shipping Council, 'The Top 50 Container Ports', worldshipping.org (2025).

239 Levinson, *The Box*, 360.

are sedimented and reproduced.[240] In a revealing anecdote, discussing his project *Dead Letter Office* (1996–7), Sekula notes how workers in northern Mexico in 1999 earned a daily wage less than that paid by Henry Ford in 1913.[241]

There are different ways to consider the uneven forms of the world economy (and not only that under neoliberalism) – among them, 'developed', 'newly industrialising', 'underdeveloped; or 'core', 'semi-periphery', 'periphery'. These accounts are much debated. Some thinkers stress the homogenising aspects of contemporary capitalism, while others emphasise its fragmentary drives. Here the theory of uneven and combined development (UCD, sometimes CUD) seems particularly helpful for its focus on the dialectic of integrative and differentiating tendencies under the violent synchronisations of value. This account was elaborated in the early twentieth century to understand the role of imperialism in the relations between local, regional, national and world economies. Leon Trotsky argued that the 'law of uneven development . . . operates not only in the relations of countries to each other, but also in the mutual relationships of the various processes within one and the same country'; and yet the 'reconciliation of the uneven processes of economics and politics can be attained only on a world scale'.[242] Put baldly, the modern world system involves a complex

---

240 Anna Tsing, 'Supply Chains and the Human Condition', *Rethinking Marxism: A Journal of Economics, Culture & Society* 21:2 (2009): 148–76 (150). Cf. Danyluk, 'Capital's Logistical Fix', 14.

241 'Working at the Light Table'.

242 Leon Trotsky, *The Permanent Revolution* and *Results and Prospects* (1906, 1930; London: New Park, 1962), 131. See also *The History of the Russian Revolution* (1930; New York: Sphere Books, 1967); *The Third International After Lenin* (1929, 1930; New York: Pathfinder, 1970); *1905* (1922; Harmondsworth: Penguin, 1973); 'A Serious Work on Russian Revolutionary History', in *Writings of Leon Trotsky: Supplement (1934–1940)*, ed. G. Breitman (New York: Pathfinder, 1979), 857–9. Commentaries include: George Novack, *Uneven and Combined Development in History* (New York: Merit Publishers, 1966); Michael Löwy, *The Politics of Combined and Uneven Development: The Theory of Permanent Revolution* (London: Verso, 1981); Bill Dunn and Hugo Radice, eds, *100 Years of Permanent Revolution: Results and Prospects* (London: Pluto, 2006); Marcel van der Linden, '"The "Law" of Uneven and Combined Development: Some Undeveloped Thoughts', *Historical Materialism* 15 (1) (2007): 145–65; and Neil Davidson, *How Revolutionary were the Bourgeois Revolutions?* (Chicago, IL: Haymarket, 2012). Cf. debates in the *Cambridge Review of International Affairs*. In its classic articulations, UCD continued to assume a developmentalist modernisation process; it now needs to be divested of this intellectual baggage and perhaps reformulated as 'uneven and combined accumulation'. For an account of Sekula drawing on UCD: Gail Day and Steve Edwards, 'Differential Time and Aesthetic Form: Uneven and Combined Capitalism in the Work of Allan Sekula', in *Cultures of Uneven and Combined Development*, eds James Christie and Nesrin Değirmencioğlu (Brill: Leiden, 2019), 253–88.

division of labour with spades and wheelbarrows as significant as precision-engineering tools and micro-processors. This account gets to something important about the current phase of capitalism that is both uneven and integrated, with violence very much to the fore. One of Sekula's short essays for 'Middle Passage' describes 'The Korean Workers' Museum' onboard *Sea-Land Quality*: a collection of abandoned 'crude' tools, fashioned by hand by the vessel's builders – 'an improvisatory iron-age approach to shipbuilding' from the centre of advanced construction discovered on the latest model of container ship.[243]

The integrating connections are not always easy to trace, and contradictions abound. Writing in the mid-1990s, Sekula employed deliberate repetition to weave some linking threads:

> There is no longer 'a city' at the centre of the system, but rather a fluctuating web of connections between metropolitan regions and exploitable peripheries. Thus the lines of exploitation today may run, for example, from London to Hong Kong, from Hong Kong to Shenzhen, from Taipei to Shenzhen, from Taipei to Hong Kong and Taipei to Beijing, from Beijing to Hong Kong and from Beijing to Shenzhen, and perhaps ultimately from a dispersed and fluid transnational block of capitalist power, located simultaneously in London, New York, Vancouver, Hong Kong, Singapore, Taipei, and Beijing, drawing ravenously on the rock-bottom labor costs of the new factories in the border city of Shenzhen and in the surrounding cities and countryside of Guangdong province in southern China.[244]

The repeats are themselves worked simultaneously in two registers: as content (the place names); and as form (the vortex of figures and the rhetorical employment of anaphora: 'from . . . , from . . . , from . . . , from . . . , from . . . and from . . .'). Sekula's geography of the world, the placemaking of capitalism, includes the legacies of imperialism and settler colonialism, extractivism, urban industrialisation and deindustrialisation, regional development and disinvestment, stretched factories, population displacement and migration, pollution, 'rust belts' and postcolonial wastelands. Frequently, this 'landscape' is viewed imaginatively from a perspective that is seaborne.

---

243 'Workers' Museum', *Fish Story*, 74.

244 'Dismal Science', 48–9. 'Dismal Science' opens with a note on unevenness. Discussing Friedrich Engels' recollection of his arrival in London on a sailing ship, Sekula foregrounds how the German writer dramatises his awe at the sight of the growing English metropole by staging the 'backwardness' of his homeland. Ibid., 45–6.

For labour in the majority world, containerisation was part of a new global system that drastically reduced the numbers of workers required to handle cargo, and undermined dockers' control of hiring and the labour process. (In the US and Europe, employment levels, wages and union density also fell sharply in the associated industries of rail and trucking, and manufacturing jobs followed this downward spiral.)[245] Sekula drew on the knowledge and experiences of local worker activists on the US West Coast, notably Stan Weir – one of the five people to whom *Fish Story* is dedicated. Longshore worker, seafarer and Trotskyist activist, Weir played a major role in contesting the transformation of the waterfront, as embodied in the 1960 agreement of the International Longshore and Warehouse Union (ILWU), 'Mechanization and Modernization'.[246] At the outset, Weir grasped that the union leadership was prepared to give up worker control in exchange for bonuses, retirement packages and increased security for 'A men'.[247]

Containerisation transformed the maritime infrastructure, entailing an entirely new *dispositif*: deep-water ports; giant cranes; autonomous vehicles; new designs for ships and vehicle chassis; large off-dock storage facilities – a description that reads like an index to *Fish Story*. The first chapter includes photographs of former shipyards, containers being unloaded with a hammerhead crane in San Pedro and a robot truck in Rotterdam's then-new container port. The third chapter, 'Middle Passage', includes a properly pelagic leg onboard the container ship *Sea-Land Quality*. The vessel – at the time, among the largest in the world – belonged to the company that the aforementioned McLean founded and was one of the first container ships built at the Daewoo shipyards (on South Korea's island of Keoje).[248]

However, the largest concentration of containers occurs in 'True Cross', the sixth chapter, set on Mexico's Gulf Coast, pointing to the example of a port in an economy subjected to the hegemonising force of another. Here, we see: the container storage facility at the Port of Veracruz, where some boxes serve as temporary homes for street vendors (#70, #79, #80);

245 Cowen, *The Deadly Life of Logistics*, 45.

246 Weir, *Single Jack Solidarity*. For a very different argument, see: David Wellman, *The Union Makes Us Strong: Radical Unionism on the San Francisco Waterfront* (Cambridge: Cambridge University Press, 1995).

247 'A men' were regular employees and ILWU members; 'B men' were day labourers and were not union members but worked under its jurisdiction. With collusion from the union, Weir and eighty-one other 'B' workers were deregistered by the Pacific Maritime Association, disqualifying them from work.

248 'Dismal Science', 54, 74, 101.

surveying for an extension to a container field (#73, #74); container stacks arrayed behind a car transporter (#77); containers forming barriers to encroaching sands (#78). The sixteenth-century Fort of San Juan de Ulúa – part of which Sekula also shows us with photographs of drilling for coral samples – was built by the arriving Spanish colonisers on an outcrop of La Gallega reef (Culúa to indigenous communities). As part of the modernisation programme initiated by Porfirio Díaz, a narrow breakwater was built to enclose the harbour in 1902, hooking the fort to the mainland. By the middle of the twentieth century, the breakwater had widened into a land bridge, while the areas around the fort had grown into a substantial island, consuming about half of the reef. Just two years before Sekula visited Veracruz, the reefs had received protected status, although Vergara Bay to the north was excluded and earmarked for port expansion.[249] In Sekula's photographs, the containers being used as unofficial abodes appear to be located at the furthest reaches of the original container terminal (itself neighbouring the fort), on the Gulf-facing northern edge of the reef-cum-island. The earth in these photographs is likely a mix of sand, rubble and pulverised coral. The surveyor stands on similar ground, and the open sea can be glimpsed; he is almost certainly at the western end of the island where it converges with the land bridge. His surveying was perhaps preparation for the takeover of the container terminal in 1995 by ICAVE (in turn absorbed in 2001 by the global logistics company Hutchison Port Holdings). The car transporter and metal-box barriers indicate much sandier contexts, and these photographs were most likely taken where the artificial land bridge merges with the mainland at the southern end of Vergara Bay. The holding area for trucks is here (still is at the time of writing), with close access to the car-exporting lots and terminals. The coast northwards around Vergara Bay and beyond is dominated by dunes, which are blown relentlessly southwards by northerly winds. In the past, these sand-blowing winds were thought to carry disease – a belief that has metaphorised in the language of urban planners to describe unofficial settlements.[250] Holding back drifting dunes

249 Phase 1 of the New Port of Veracruz was 2014–18, with phase 2 scheduled for 2019–30. The container terminal relocated in 2019. Environmentalists challenged the lifting of fragile corals from the excluded area to be 'rehomed' in the reserve. The Supreme Court temporarily halted works in February 2022. A key argument was that the development had failed to consider environmental damage holistically, but instead relied on (and hid behind) 'fragmented' research.

250 Alfred H. Siemens, Patricia Moreno-Casasola and Clorinda Sarabia Bueno, 'The Metabolization of Dunes and Wetlands by the City of Veracruz', *Journal of Latin American Geography* 5:1 (2006): 7–29.

with containers highlights: the physical barrier against encroaching sand; an Anthropocenic 'battle with nature' and 'Sisyphean' task; the repurposing of damaged containers and a terminus in their 'demotion' as use values; and a social metaphor prevailing in the local polity for spreading 'infection'. The shifts here between literal and figural point to the 'imaginative and material geographies', which we will return to shortly.

'Why', Sekula asks rhetorically in 'Dismal Science', 'would anyone be foolish enough to argue today that the world economy might be intelligently viewed from the deck of a ship?'[251] An answer can be found in the *Grundrisse*, where Marx wrote:

> Circulation, because a totality of the social process, is also the first form in which the social relation appears as something independent of the individuals, but not only as, say, in a coin or in exchange value, but extending to the whole of the social movement itself . . . Circulation as the first totality among the economic categories is well suited to bring this to light.[252]

Following the maritime trade, attending to connections, allows Sekula to illuminate the process of neoliberal globalisation. In the third stanza of the essay for the opening sequence, Sekula notes that the movement of goods 'can be explained in its totality only through recourse to abstraction'.[253]

It is worth underlining what is at stake. Sekula works with and questions oppositions that are often oversimplified. That between concrete and abstract is typically figured in the contrast between the material maritime economy (use values in transit, 'gravity', 'crude materialism') and the stock market (the movements of value). Nonetheless, with the container port, as Sekula observes, 'the harbor comes to resemble the stock market'.[254] As presented, 'abstraction' in the port is explicitly associated with the rationalised methods of logistics and the anonymised contents of containers. What is perhaps more important to note, however, is the combination of 'concrete' and 'abstract' qualities. Sekula argues that there was once the impression that ports offered tangible insights into

251 'Dismal Science', 48.

252 Marx, *Grundrisse*, 197.

253 *Fish Story*, 12.

254 Ibid.

worldwide commerce: 'In the past, harbor residents were deluded by their senses into thinking that a global economy could be seen and heard and smelled.'[255] Today the rank odours of commodities have disappeared, wrapped and sealed in containers. Sekula also describes how we are misled by the sounds of national anthems, traditionally played to announce a ship's arrival; these are largely empty gestures in the era of the flag of convenience. But the earlier 'materialism' could also be deceptive, the apparent security of sense data luring people into a materialist complacency (a version of 'the occlusion of appearances'). Sekula shows how containerisation scuppers older empiricist illusions by bringing abstraction to the fore. Ironically, then, 'abstraction' is now made more 'visible', even though its social nature remains occluded.[256]

Sekula understands container boxes and their associated apparatus not as 'things'; nor are they reducible to 'processes involving things' (multi-modal logistics, integrative systems).[257] These are manifestations of capital as a social relation, a process existing in and driving a global circuit of accumulation. In late-twentieth-century debates, Marx's analytic abstractions were often confused with his description of the role of capital. His focus in *Capital I* on the productive process, and the creation of value therein, was isolated from the total circuit of capital.[258] Production can be methodologically 'abstracted' from that circuit for analytical purposes, but it cannot be divorced 'in actuality' from the cycles of production-circulation-consumption (and reproduction).

255 Ibid.

256 David Cunningham has advanced closely related arguments. He follows Adorno, in downplaying the phenomenological, and in emphasising objective or real abstraction) loses Sekula's critical interplay: his oscillations – intellectual, rhetorical and poetic – between abstract and concrete, between real abstracts and faux concretes, and between empty abstractions and the crude matter-ness of stuff. David Cunningham, 'Renouncing the Single Image: Photography and the Realism of Abstraction', *Photographies* 9:2 (2016): 147–65.

257 According to Marx, 'capital is not a thing, it is a definite social relation of production pertaining to a particular historical social formation, which simply takes the form of a thing and gives this thing a specific social character': Marx, *Capital: III* (1894; Harmondsworth: Penguin, 1981), 953.

258 Tombazos argues that the volumes of *Capital* are written under distinct temporal logics, following the rhythm of capital itself: in Volume I, production is conceived as linear; in Volume II, circulation is cyclical; Volume III offers a mixed conception of 'organic' time, 'the unity of the time of production and the time of circulation': Stavros Tombazos, *Time in Marx: The Categories of Time in Marx's Capital* (1994; Leiden: Brill, 2014), 3. In less Hegelian mode, Stefano Bracaletti also describes the mode of Volume III as 'mixed': 'Temporality in Capital' in *The Government of Time: Theories of Plural Temporality in the Marxist Tradition*, eds Vittorio Morfino and Peter Thomas (Leiden: Brill, 2018), 80.

One consequence of the critique of logistics has been that *Capital II*, where the circuit of capital is emphasised, has begun to receive more attention. (The circuit itself must also be studied through another abstraction – this time, a type of abstraction that isolates and focuses on one simple cycle.) When Sekula was writing, debates typically pitted 'consumption' against 'production', so it is notable that he elects to focus on the 'intervening' stage in the circuit. It is only in the circuit M-C-M' (money1-commodity-money2) that capital is realised in the money form and enabled to expand in a fresh cycle. By increasing the rapidity of the circuit of valorisation (the speed of goods to market or of turnover), greater surplus value is accrued and more is squeezed from fixed capital (even when *fixed* capital is *mobile*, as it is with ships and trucks).[259] Transportation plays a vital role as a 'continuation of a production process *within* the circulation process and *for* the circulation process'.[260] As Marx suggests in a now-famous passage from the *Grundrisse*: 'the creation of the physical conditions of exchange – of the means of communication and transport – the annihilation of space by time – becomes an extraordinary necessity'.[261] Because valorisation is only realised when commodities reach their market, contemporary commentators increasingly argue that surplus value is produced not only during production, but also while moving commodities through space.[262]

Of the eighteen photographs in 'Middle Passage', half are situated at sea; of the others, one is taken at the departing Port Elizabeth (New Jersey) and eight at the transit stopover at Rotterdam (three of these in the city's Maritiem Museum Prins Hendrik). We have already noted how this chapter includes an unusual number of close-ups and plays with depth of field. Notably, the sequence – announced as a 'passage' (it is, after all, a journey of sorts) – is not organised chronologically. The opening pairing of photographs is set in the mid-Atlantic, contrasting the inclinometer with *Sea-Land Quality* sailing into an expansive seascape.[263] There is negligible depth in the first photograph, just a straight-on, flat detail of the device's gauge. The maritime panorama

259 Karl Marx, *Capital: II* (1885; Harmondsworth: Penguin, 1978), 233–6.

260 Ibid., 229. Cf. 'Economically considered, the spatial condition, the bringing of the product to the market, belongs to the production process itself. The product is only really finished when it is on the market' (Marx, *Grundrisse*, 533–4).

261 Marx, *Grundrisse*, 524.

262 Cowen, *The Deadly Life of Logistics*, 100; Toscano, 'Lineaments of the Logistical State'; Chua, 'Logistics'.

263 The comparison between 'panorama' and 'detail' is explored in the 'Dismal Science' essay.

looks across the tops of the container stacks, towards the bow and, beyond that, to the horizon. A skyscape of storm clouds with shafts of sun breaking through cites Romantic painting and endows the image with an iconic quality rare in Sekula. The space is deep, and everything is in focus. It would be easy to let things rest here. Yet, the view of the containers isolates them from the ship, making them appear as self-moving capital. Furthermore, the centred recession formed by the boxes suggests the single-point perspective of late Quattrocento or Cinquecento art – typically terrestrial scenes and architectural settings, such as *La città ideale*. Sekula sees the pattern as a 'ground-plan', and the tops of the containers take on the appearance of gridded paving in *Architectural Veduta*.[264] This panel, dated to c.1490 and once attributed to Francesco di Giorgio Martini, ultimately finds its vanishing point at the far side of a distant imaginary harbour, at the point of transition to open seas. Its moment is significant in the history of European colonial expansion and, shortly after, the inauguration of the transatlantic trade in enslaved people – which the title of Sekula's chapter explicitly invokes. That said, the actual route travelled by *Sea-Land Quality* does not retrace the historical Middle Passage (the segment of the 'triangular trade' from Africa to the Americas) but takes us from the Americas to Europe. Photographed from a high position in the vessel's control tower, Sekula's image literally adopts the implied command of the visual field associated with perspective. Ironically, though, the contrasting detail of the inclinometer is the more 'panoramic' in format (their physical sizes, both in the book and the exhibition, are similar). Its calibrations show how the deck level veers from the horizontal. Reinforced by its pairing with the panorama, these calibrations also invoke the history of techniques for visual measurement. Sekula is repeatedly attentive to rationalising techniques, and specifically to the ways these are often visualised: Quetelet's 'average'; the Gilbreths' time-and-motion studies; and even his own interest in the isotype. This attention extends into Sekula's production of metaphors and similes: stereoscopic images seen as banknotes (Oliver Wendell Holmes); containers as dollar bills; the archive as clearing house. Further on in the sequence, there is a second photograph of model ships from the Maritiem Museum Prins Hendrik, which again brings to the fore the question of measure. A hyper-localised focus – comparable in this regard to that used in the photograph of the chief mate checking refrigerated containers – alights not on any of

264 'Globalism's Discontents and the Return of the Sea'.

the three model vessels displayed but on the very near corner of the vitrine containing them. Specifically, it alights on the near tip of a long red-and-white scale ruler receding the length of the glass case. Its form and colours are soon repeated on the safety barriers of a Rotterdam berth.

It should be apparent that *Fish Story* is not reducible to a story about containerisation and global logistics.[265] Sekula says that the project triangulates the decline of shipbuilding in the West and Poland with its rise in South Korea.[266] But it is more than that. We are back with 'the imaginary and material geographies of the advanced capitalist world'.[267] Sekula's photographs made in Veracruz trace a geographic and social locus of modern containerisation, and the longer-term plans for securing the conditions for capital circuits. But, as already intimated, they do so through more than the mere facticity of metal boxes and their associated apparatus. The scope of the photographs for 'True Cross' is wider ranging and includes: a monument to Mexico's defenders against the US invasion in April 1914 (#72); drilling for samples of coral stone from the fort's walls (#75, #76); a child begging outside a city café (#81). In the accompanying four-part essay, containerisation is woven with other threads: the fort's history as colonial stronghold for gold and prisoners; the Nahuas' surprise at the Spanish obsessive fetish for gold (they 'fingered it like monkeys; they seemed to be transported by joy'); the material characteristics and resilience of coral and gold; the undermining of the fort by dredgers for the container terminal; scientist-conservators attempting to use an electric current to regenerate the coral stone (*piedra muca*); the Zapatistas; the supply of 'Mayan' coffee to trendy outlets in Los Angeles; the role of Japanese investment in this circuit (specifically in Pacific-coast port development and sea-freight companies); the launch, in 1994, of the North American Free Trade Agreement (NAFTA), a trilateral trade bloc; the wholesale replacement of Veracruz's dockworkers in 1991; and histories of worker militancy and anarchist rebellion, real and fictional, connecting Peru, Germany, Los Angeles, Tijuana, Tampico and Chiapas. Even a list as comprehensive as this can convey only the raw bones; the essay

265 There is a brief discussion of containers in the postscript to 'Dismal Science', and even this discussion becomes a reflection on the box's limited manifestation in art.

266 'Imaginary Economies: An Interview with Allan Sekula', 247.

267 'A Note on the Work', *Fish Story*, 202.

traverses time and space, from merciless colonial rampage to merciless neoliberal 'modernisation'.

The written components (the captions and short essays) clearly amplify the images. Without them, we might not know that cars were on the transporter's trailer; or that the wall being drilled belongs to a fort composed of ancient coral; or that the begging child is shrouded by the election poster of a would-be president who had been assassinated only the day before. The supplementing or anchoring of images by text is established practice in the traditions of documentary photography, of course. At other moments, image–text relations are more ambivalent. The photograph of the monument to the heroes who fought against the US occupation in 1914 is a case in point. The caption announces the nature of the monument. Yet, the short essay actively demotes it, highlighting instead a plain obelisk commemorating 'all the world's mariners who lost their lives at sea'. Indeed, Sekula contrasts the obelisk with three nationalist memorials – and even in that list, the monument pictured is last to be mentioned. When considered alongside the essay, then, the photograph emphasises not so much the presence of this monument to 1914 but rather the visual (and political) absence of the internationalist monument. The latter remains unseen. Here, the work of the essay is not to 'supplement' or 'anchor' the photograph, to ground its meaning, but instead to produce a hole. Having read the essay, we return to the photograph with different 'eyes', questioning what we have before us. Sekula had scope to include a photograph of (or incorporate) the internationalist obelisk. Maybe he did not take a picture of the obelisk; although this is highly unlikely, given how many photographs he made (as much for diarising his travels as for active picture-making). Or maybe he did, and the results were not felt to be successful. Interesting as they might be, such questions miss the point. Even if the essay sought to compensate retrospectively for an oversight or mistake in the image-making process, a considered choice has nonetheless been made to show an image of the 1914 monument and to write about the obelisk. The interplay of presence and absence is notable. Affirmative representations (whether textual or visual) cede to negative ones.

The caption for the photograph of the monument to 1914 records its commemoration of an anti-imperial and nationalist struggle. At first, the photograph strikes one as a pictorial memorialisation of a historical memorialisation. It is, moreover, a temporal marker in another sense, running counter to the ideology celebrated by the monument. Indirectly, it alludes to NAFTA, signalling the closure to the geopolitical era established by the Mexican Revolution eighty years earlier, auguring a new phase in Mexican–US relations. When Sekula made the image in March 1994, NAFTA and the Zapatistas' uprising against it were just weeks old. In the photograph, the monument appears to be 'fenced off', although a closer look reveals that the barriers do not prevent access to the monument but protect the adjacent lawns. Had the photographer been seeking a standard photo-of-monument, this extraneous clutter would have been an unwanted distraction. Nonetheless, the 'mistiming' of Sekula's visit was serendipitous, offering a visual suggestiveness that could be actively mobilised. The temporary fencing, comprising simple wooden stakes and old sugar sacks, hints at NAFTA's part in 'the new enclosures'. We return to 'True Cross' with yet other eyes in Chapter 4.

As the above examples start to show, seeing is a thematic within the photographs: watching, gazing, looking, inspecting, showing, pointing, making visible, occluding, disappearing. The two opening photographs, both taken on the Staten Island Ferry, reinforce this, establishing an allegorical pretext for the project. (In the book, but not the exhibition, all the photographs are preceded by a plate – we mentioned it earlier – showing a technique for fabricating fishing nets, from Diderot and d'Alembert's *Encyclopédie*, with a disembodied human hand and self-moving shuttle.) The first photograph shows a coin-operated long-range binocular viewer, of the type often encountered on promenades, at scenic locations or at other tourist attractions, and designed to magnify distant views (#1). The apparatus (the object in focus) is sited next to the panoramic window flanking the ferry's interior deck. This ferry is famous for connecting the south-westernmost borough of New York State to Lower Manhattan's financial district. The route is also well known for offering an affordable way to enjoy seaborne views of the Statue of Liberty and Ellis Island – views shared by ships and immigrants arriving at port in the early twentieth century. In the second photograph, a boy holds the binocular device – or rather, hangs from it, using his weight to swing the viewer around on its axis (#2). Our viewpoint shifts slightly to include the ferry's seating area.

Much could be said about these two photographs: the apparatus's anthropomorphism; that its manufacturer, Bausch & Lomb, had close ties to wartime innovation in lenses and optical equipment; that the boy wears a military-style flight jacket; that C. L. R. James wrote his study of Melville's *Moby Dick* while interned on Ellis Island; that Sekula discussed images of the immigrant arrivals in New York by Alfred Stieglitz and Lewis Hine in his 1974 essay 'On the Invention of Photographic

Meaning' (we will look at this in Chapter 3); and that he returned to Stieglitz in 'Dismal Science' and called this opening to *Fish Story* a 'Stieglitzian prologue'.[268] But let us stay with the question of sight. Out of focus – and behind the window's glass screen – are a harbour, a trawler and Liberty (who, let us not forget, is specifically 'Liberty Enlightening the World'). They visually 'de-realise' or evaporate into the winter haze of distance. A little plaque on the device draws attention to a red knob. Marked 'TURN TO CLEAR VISION', the knob is for focusing the lens, but (as a glance online quickly reveals) the instruction has also acquired metaphorical associations, from life coaching to spiritual revelation; Sekula alludes to other connotations, political and epistemic. The boy does not look through the binoculars but back over his shoulder towards his mother (as the caption clarifies). Maybe he never had the quarter needed to make the machine function (a common enough seaside frustration for children who nonetheless look into the darkened space of the blinded binoculars)? Maybe his viewing time was up (this paid-for pleasure lasts for just 1.5 to 2.5 minutes) and he wanted another coin? Maybe his mother summoned him; or maybe he just turned his gaze away from the magnified view and towards the parental authority off-frame? Does he turn away from Liberty? We do not know – and there are many permutations to the possible apparatus-boy-mother-Liberty scenario – but the act of looking and the blocking or aversion of sight are involved. Both photographs share the caption: *Boy looking at his mother. Staten Island Ferry. New York harbor. February 1990.* Yet, to state the obvious, there is no mother. Indeed, there is no boy in the first image, only a locus for his possibility, which needs the retroactive confirmation of the second image; unless, of course, we are to surmise an identification of binoculars with boy, with the optical apparatus as his stead, double or premonition.

268 'On *Fish Story*', 55. Alfred Stieglitz's *The Steerage* and Lewis Hine's *Immigrants Going Down Gangplank, New York* – canonical images of this immigration – figure large in Sekula's thinking and signify the poles of the 'hermeneutic pendulum'. See Allan Sekula, 'On the Invention of Photographic Meaning', in *Photography Against the Grain*, 3–21. Ellis Island now has a museum which animates the space with large blow-ups of Lewis Hine's photographs of arriving migrants arriving in the period 1904 to 1909.

2

'A horizontal sort of beast'

SECTION 1: 'AGAINST THE ABSTRACTION OF GLOBAL CAPITAL'

Mourning and Left-Wing Melancholia

Fish Story could appear, Sekula notes, to be 'performing a grotesque juggling act at a triple funeral: a memorial service for painting, socialism, and the sea' – a formulation that binds together the typically separated worlds of aesthetics, politics and the maritime economy.[1] Sekula clearly wants to distance himself from this (later referring to it as self-mockery), but 'funeral' is a powerful metaphor, and he returns to it:[2] the essay concludes with a 'provisional funeral' and the 'coffin of remote labor-power'.[3] Once more, this is labour in a negative mode – in this instance, 'dead labour', both with its everyday resonances and in the specialist sense used by Marx (as stored past labour power). In part, then, *Fish Story* is a work of mourning that examines the effects of respatialised production, the ruins of industry and the defeat of working-class solidarity.[4] The sense of defeat is underscored by an aside about Marx, to whom, Sekula notes, 'no one is listening anymore'.[5]

1 'Dismal Science', 48.

2 'Imaginary Economies: An Interview with Allan Sekula', 247.

3 'Dismal Science', 137.

4 It is worth noting that one of the most famous examples of lament or elegy is the Old English poem *The Seafarer*.

5 *Fish Story*, 12. The context is a methodological reflection on how to understand capitalism: 'Marx tells us this [that we have to use abstraction to grasp totality], even if no one is listening anymore'.

This mood is not merely a pessimistic predilection on the part of Sekula. Made during the high period of neoliberal restructuring, his response to this landscape of abandonment is a work of 'mourning and melancholia' – and this, as we will see, must be approached with critical care.

The images in *Fish Story* repeatedly figure a sense of loss and devastation. Its opening chapter details the transformation of the waterfront. Two years after the closure of the Todd Shipyard in San Pedro, a clipboard remains, charting the very last round of tasks to be undertaken by a welder (#3). In the same establishment, a spanner is displaced to reveal a 'shadow' appearing in the accumulated dust, a ghostly doppelgänger (#6). In a former Los Angeles shipyard, we see the interior of an abandoned building (#7). Other photographs in the sequence approach devastation collaterally, linking to the maritime industries environmentally, militarily, politically and so forth. In the working port of San Diego in 1990, we see the *Exxon Mediterranean* at dock (#8). Now renamed and refurbished, this is the *Exxon Valdez*, the supertanker responsible for spilling about 41,000 cubic metres of crude oil into Prince William Sound in 1989. A pair of images show a mid-century wooden home, of the type built for San Pedro's shipyard workers during the wartime boom, now being relocated by truck to South-Central Los Angeles (#12, #13). Helmeted workers in protective clothing attend local calamities: dousing a fire that has ravaged shops in Koreatown (#14); clearing a chemical spillage from a refinery explosion (#15). A one-time shipyard sandblaster scavenges copper from industrial debris (#17). This is an element of uneven and combined accumulation sometimes called 'organized abandonment' (Harvey).[6]

The theme of decline continues in the other chapters. The second, 'Loaves and Fishes' includes photographs showing: a man salvaging bricks from a demolished warehouse in Rotterdam (#26); the interior of a Gdańsk unemployment office (#24); a detail from the façade of the 'Queen's Casino', formerly the Palace of Culture and Science in Warsaw (#23). The latter centres on a niche containing a socialist-realist sculpture of a male worker holding a book inscribed 'Marx Engels Lenin' (a fourth name redacted by chisel is still readable as 'Stalin'). Ironies abound. The optimistic (if bombastic) representation of 'Worker' is paired with a deflationary representation of those without work. The images from Poland were made in the year Solidarność candidate Lech Wałęsa superseded General Jaruzelski, heralding the

6 David Harvey, *The Limits to Capital* (Oxford: Blackwell, 1982), 397.

end of Polish Stalinism. The third chapter, 'Middle Passage', includes the short essay ('Workers' Museum'), which ends by describing the mood onboard *Sea-Land Quality* as a 'mournful and weary anticipation of unemployment'.[7]

'Dictatorship of the Seven Seas', the final sequence, reinforces the displacements of manufacture from the US to China or South America. An unemployed American couple survive by scavenging and sleeping in containers (#93). A chair that was originally designed for the homes of San Pedro's shipyard workers is now de-functioned and retired to a museum storeroom (#94). Six photographs record the dismantling of the Kaiser steel mill in Fontana ready to be shipped to China in 1993 (#85–89). A picture of the Wilmington tracks documents the transporting inland of Brazilian slab steel, the shortage of which Kaiser was founded to overcome (#92).[8] The sense of destruction is not restricted to the old industrial economies. In the South Korea chapter, two photographs share the same ominous caption: 'Doomed fishing village of Ilsan' (#54, #55). The sense of explicit foreboding feels at odds with Sekula's approach to his captions, which generally favour the flatly descriptive and factual mode. Two views from the beach contrast an idyllic cove scene of small boats with the expanding industrial hub of Ulsan in the distance. The views show changing uses of the coast – underscored by the chapter title 'Seventy Years in Seven' (what took seventy years in Europe, takes only seven in East Asia).

Sekula often builds patterns of association or comparison between his images through visual links. For example, in the first chapter, an attractive cove takes us by surprise. It is Minturno's ancient Roman harbour (#10), which Sekula juxtaposes with a San Pedro hammerhead unloading containers from Asia (#11). The harbour walls in Minturno have strong horizontals, which are replicated by the crane's beam. There is also a visual interplay between the boxiness of the containers and the

---

7 *Fish Story*, 74.

8 Mike Davis details how Henry J. Kaiser, an industrialist favoured for New Deal contracts, recognised that 'a Pacific War would make unprecedented demands on the under-industrialized California economy' and with government support 'proposed to adapt Detroit's assembly-line methods to revolutionize the construction of merchant shipping'. Kaiser expanded in the 1950s and 1960s to become the 'flagship of the West's postwar smokestack economy'. Preferring a stable bargaining relationship, Kaiser favoured unionisation and the plant provided thousands of decently paid unionised jobs. From the 1970s, fortunes turned: restructuring and modernisation efforts preceded the closure in 1983, and then the assett strippers arrived. Mike Davis, *City of Quartz: Excavating the Future of Los Angeles* (London: Verso, 1990), 347, 357.

negative rectilinear space suggested by the ancient basin. Sekula establishes a similar relation between #17 and #18, where the robotic container truck duplicates the shape of the old electricity locker from which the scavenger extracts copper – and in these partnered photographs, the box forms also share an identical orientation to the picture plane. These are examples of formal mirroring. But they are also more than that. Formal similarities and juxtapositions – within individual images and between adjacent or nearby photographs – are used to deepen and develop connections. The Italian scene reinforces the sense that the sequence explores an archaeology of ruins. Adjacencies in the sequence highlight similarities between what seem to be distinct qualities, drawing out continuities: across centuries; between trading empires; between economic success and collapse; or between the wealth of official accumulation and the marginal 'economy'.

The photograph of *Exxon Mediterranean* (#8) is paired with another of *Lead Fish* – a variant of a conference room designed by Frank Gehry, as it was exhibited at the Los Angeles Museum of Contemporary Art in 1988, built of timber with lead-shingle 'scales' (#9). Both images present comparable dark bulging forms, which have a similar angle to the picture plane. As with the Minturno scene, the photograph of *Lead Fish* seems anomalous. Though it obviously picks up the 'fish story' metatheme, it is seemingly at odds with the scenes of economic decline. Indeed, the Gehry exhibition marked the architect's rise, although some saw it as exemplifying a collapse of architectural integrity.[9] This photograph can be read, then, as a cultural equivalent of the economic thread: 'the cultural logic of late capitalism', to use Jameson's famous coinage. The quality of light on the lead shingles hints at the oil being denied by Exxon's refurbished vessel, and the 'fish' recalls the damage to marine life. Despite its renaming, the shadow cast by the tanker ship on the water's surface also triggers memories of the spill in Alaska. This is further underscored by the prominence of the vessel's gauge for determining onboard loads: indicating its currently empty hold while docked

9 This 1988 design by Gehry was part of a retrospective for, as a reviewer put it, 'architecture's aging *enfant terrible*', but still at a point before he had designed a major building. 'Gehry's preoccupation with form' was seen as sculptural rather than architectural (there were no plans, projections or spatial studies in the show). It risked being neither art nor architecture, but simply 'low-grade and high-style kitsch'. Gehry was criticised for turning the responsiveness to site – the contextual situating of a structure's form and materials – into mere 'whimsical metaphor' and 'fish fetish' or 'fish shticks'. Inside was a lamp in the form of a fish. Sam Hall Kaplan, 'The Undisputed Arrival of Frank Gehry: The Experience of Architecture as Art', *Los Angeles Times*, 21 February 1988.

in San Diego but also figuring the previous year's discharge of raw crude. Sekula's formal comparisons, montage and relays serve to elaborate linkages and trace patterns of thought.

As an extended example of this process, we return to the photographs of the spanner and the interior of a former Los Angeles shipyard (#6, #7). These two images share a 'found aesthetic' of accidental abstraction: textured surfaces, scratches, stains and paint daubs. They repeat the same strong geometry of diagonals: one through a tight close-up with a shallow depth of field, looking down onto a workbench top; the other by framing a larger space into which recedes an oblique plywood wall. They also share colourways, dominated by gold and red with a bronze segment; and each includes glimpses of contrasting colder light. These visual parallels are formal in the most conventional sense, but they are also connotative. Arguably, this is photography itself among the ruins. The spanner's 'shadow' alludes at once to the photographic negative, to 'light-writing' and to the index. It is reminiscent of the photogram and the compositions of photo-modernism. Two moments of 'abandonment' are involved: the ex-shipyard building is also an ex-film set. Hanging on the curving wall, and holding the centre of attention, there is a reproduction genre painting in faux-gilt frame, presumably left behind by the moviemakers. It depicts two wealthy young women, dressed in the fine laces and swagged silks of the mid-nineteenth century, practising 'feminine accomplishment'. The paired photographs are haunted by two types of non-work – unemployment and leisure (in another iteration of Sekula's father and friend standing in the parking lot from *Aerospace Folktales*).

With the 'charming' genre scene, we are meant to appreciate the depicted moment synaesthetically. The pianist turns a page of music, while her companion sets down her violin to exchange a few words. The piano's strings may still be resonating but they are fading out; conversation might replace instrumental music. Juxtaposed with twentieth-century dereliction, this cessation in music-making takes on resonances that go beyond the intention of its genre. What seems to prevail now is the absence of sound: instrumental, conversational, industrial, filmic. Time and persistent exposure to light have bleached the reproduction's cheap inks; so far, only the darkest tones have resisted California's glare. This faded twentieth-century image of nineteenth-century domestic culture underscores the waning of the classic bourgeoisie and, with it, the disappearance of the economic world that this class brought into being. If the evident warm glow seems 'magical', it is not to suggest anything 'enchanting', but, rather, to draw together changing functions, distinct historical moments, different levels of transience and odd absurdities. These photographs launch a *mise-en-abyme* with their layers of history: residues of the maritime industry; the movie-making industry; nineteenth-century bourgeois life. Another cascade alludes to different types of human performance: shipyard workers; actors, camera operators, sound engineers; amateur musicians; and two artist's models posing. We will come to realise, through a caption later in the sequence, that the symbolic pause is sometimes filled with shouting, crashing, firing, exploding and ricocheting. At the time of the photograph, the site was being used by marines to rehearse 'counter-terrorist' scenarios (#16).

This is not the only intrusion by the film industry in the spaces of other industries. This thread surfaces in Sekula's sequence depicting the dismantling of the Kaiser crucibles ten years after the plant's closure in 1983. The plant had already been used as a setting for *A Nightmare on Elm Street 2* (1985), and by James Cameron for the final scenes of *Terminator 2: Judgment Day* (1991). Mike Davis characterises Fontana as 'the junkyard of dreams'.[10] End of Fontana's dreams; wind-up of Kaiser; demise of industrial unionism; movie finale; termination of Schwarzenegger's 'Terminator' (sort of); conclusion of *City of Quartz*; *Fish Story*'s last chapter. The scrapheap is piled high.

Enzo Traverso argues that the experience of the left since 1848 has been one long history of setbacks, further entrenched after socialist optimism was 'buried under the debris of the Berlin Wall'.[11] Employing a Benjaminian figure, he suggests that, from the current perspective, 'history itself appears as a landscape of ruins'.[12] The images summoned by this simile may vary: at one moment, architectural ruins (ancient or

---

10 Davis, *City of Quartz*, 394. He suggests amphetamine, not steel, became Fontana's major product, 391.

11 Enzo Traverso, *Left-Wing Melancholia: Marxism, History, and Memory* (New York: Columbia University Press, 2016), 2. His account probably places too much emphasis on 1989. Well before that point, the radical right was resurgent and neoliberalism a newly hegemonic force. For socialists who did not believe the grey monolith of Stalinism offered any alternative to the neon-and-plastic utopias of capitalism, the shock has been less intense. The same moment, remember, witnessed the collapse of South African apartheid. Still, deindustrialisation was in full flow in capitalist America and Europe, in the former Eastern Bloc, and also in the north-eastern regions of China itself. As Naomi Klein and others highlighted, industries initially displaced to China and the western Pacific soon took flight anew as the 'swallows' were lured to different shores by higher rates of extraction and laxer regulatory regimes.

12 Ibid., 7.

modern); at another, cyberpunk's post-apocalyptic backdrop of scrapped vehicles and the remains of a society bloated from its own waste. There is, of course, a maritime version of the ruination motif. Sekula used photographs of a shipwreck – a scene near Istanbul – in the sequence for *TITANIC's wake* and in *Shipwreck and Workers* (2005–7); in *Fish Story*, he notes Marcel Proust's parallel of mental instability with maritime calamity, 'the shipwreck of my nervous storms'.[13] 'Left-wing melancholy', Traverso writes, 'is what remains after the shipwreck.'[14]

The motif clearly recalls the historical destruction famously observed by Walter Benjamin in his discussion of Paul Klee's *Angelus Novus* in his essay 'On the Concept of History'. In Thesis IX of this essay, Benjamin imagined the angel being blown backwards by the storms of history: 'Where a chain of events appears before *us*, *he* sees one single catastrophe, which keeps piling wreckage upon wreckage and hurls it at his feet . . . the pile of debris before him grows towards the sky.'[15] This figure is already seeded in Thesis VII, which invokes the ancient Roman *triumphus*, where, to celebrate victory over an enemy, the spoils of war were publicly paraded: armour, weapons, standards, enslaved enemy prisoners and prized objects (Benjamin scare quotes 'cultural treasures'). Although initially seeming to be the very opposite, such assemblages of booty are 'wreckage' or 'junkyards' of sorts.[16] Benjamin alludes to these processions only in general terms, but his account resonates with specific examples. Among the most spectacular was the procession for the Roman success in reasserting the power of the Imperium in 70 CE: the quelling of revolt by and massacre of the Jewish people in the eastern Mediterranean provinces. The triumphal march is depicted by the reliefs on the inside of the Arch of Titus on the Via Sacra, showing the plunder of sacred trumpets, tables of precious metals and the large solid-gold Menorah sacked from the Temple of Herod before its destruction. In commemoration, coins in all denominations were minted. Marked 'Ivdea Capta', 'Ivdea Devicta' or 'De Ivdaeis' ('Judea Conquered', 'Judea Defeated', 'booty of the Judeans'), they show

13 'Dismal Science', 52. The words cited are those of Proust's narrator.

14 Traverso, *Left-Wing Melancholia*, 25. He develops the thoughts of Hans Blumenberg, *Shipwreck with Spectator: Paradigms of a Metaphor for Existence* (1979; Cambridge, MA: MIT Press, 1996).

15 Benjamin, 'On the Concept of History' (1940), in *Selected Writings Volume 4, 1938–1940* (Cambridge, MA: The Belknap Press, 2003), 389–400 (392).

16 Ibid., 391. Cf. Braudel's tripartite – *longue durée:* repetition, time of the vanquished, time of the victors – in Fernand Braudel, *Capitalism and Material Life 1400–1800* (1967; London: Weidenfeld and Nicolson, 1973), xv.

allegories of submission: a captive kneeling before a trophy of arms, or a woman weeping beneath a palm tree. As these coins circulated through many hands, they warned of the futility of resistance to Rome acting as an ongoing *triumphus*.

The term 'left-wing melancholy' is best known from a 1931 review of that title by Benjamin. In that essay, he chastises the poet Erich Kästner for succumbing to a defeatism – 'negativistic quiet' – born of the left-radical intelligentsia's separation from practical political action and proletarian collectivity.[17] 'Tortured stupidity: this is the latest of two millennia of metamorphoses of melancholy', Benjamin complained.[18] Franz Mehring, Kurt Tucholsky, expressionism, Neue Sachlichkeit and Aktivismus are all caught in the line of fire, while Brecht is considered to have found a 'political lyricism' that avoided the 'complacency and fatalism' of petit-bourgeois radicals.[19] Traverso advances a more sympathetic conception of 'left-wing melancholia' – one that is not reducible to political resignation and nostalgia.[20] This too draws on Benjamin, particularly his call 'to organize pessimism' from his essay 'Surrealism' (1929) and his accounts of allegory and the ragpicker.[21] This left melancholia is quite different to the 'indolence of the heart, that *acedia* which despairs'.[22] 'Articulating the past historically', Benjamin writes in Thesis VI, 'means appropriating a memory as it flashes up in a moment of danger'; it means 'fanning the spark of hope in the past'.[23] Traverso emphasises the need to summon fortitude from defeat and the importance of reaffirming commitment, drawing on Reinhart Koselleck, Daniel Bensaïd and Michael Löwy. According to Koselleck, 'If history is made in the short run by the victors', then 'historical gains in knowledge stem in the

---

17 Walter Benjamin, 'Left-Wing Melancholy' (1931), in *Selected Writings Volume 2, 1927–1934* (Cambridge, MA: The Belknap Press, 1999), 423–7 (425); from sumer 1974, an English translation circulated in *Screen* from Summer 1974. In 'The Author as Producer' (1934), Kästner appears as a representative of 'Neue Sachlichkeit'. Benjamin, in *Selected Writings Volume 2, 1927–1934*, 768–82 (776).

18 Benjamin, 'Left-Wing Melancholy', 426.

19 Ibid., 426.

20 Traverso, *Left-Wing Melancholia*, 84.

21 Walter Benjamin, 'Surrealism' (1929), in *Selected Writings Volume 2, 1927–1934*, 207–21 (217).

22 Benjamin, 'On the Concept of History', 391. Benjamin's use of *acedia* (listlessness or torpor) here relates back to his Trauerspiel study – a type of 'melancholy' that submits to destiny shaped by the victor.

23 Ibid.

long run from the vanquished'.[24] Löwy suggests that what is at stake in Benjamin's Theses is a socialist '*apokatastasis* in the sense that every past victim, every attempt at emancipation, however humble and "minor", will be rescued from oblivion . . . recognized, honoured and remembered'.[25] Thus, as Traverso puts it, while deploying the tragic key, left melancholia is 'a kind of epistemological posture' that binds mourning to hope.[26]

Given Sekula's long-held interest in the ideas of Benjamin, Traverso's account holds an evident appeal. Still, the left's melancholic adherence to past forms of struggle and self-defeating attachment to failure must be acknowledged. Furthermore, Freud distinguished between mourning and melancholia, which he took to be different psychic processes.[27] It is noteworthy that Traverso refers to Freud's important essay only once and in passing. To briefly summarise, for Freud, mourning involves a process through which the subject decathects from a lost object, so that the libido can be attached anew; melancholy, in contrast, entails a transposition of the lost object onto the self in a process he calls 'anti-cathexis'. Whereas mourning allows the subject to process loss and move on, 'the black bile' spirals in self-destructiveness. The characteristics of melancholy are, Freud suggests:

> a profoundly painful dejection, cessation of interest in the outside world, loss of capacity to love, inhibition of all activity, and a lowering of the self-regarding feelings to a degree that finds utterance in

---

24 Reinhardt Koselleck, 'Transformations of Experience and Methodological Change: A Historical-Anthropological Essay', cited in Traverso, *Left-Wing Melancholia*, 25.

25 Michael Löwy, *Fire Alarm: Reading Walter Benjamin's 'On the Concept of History'* (2001; London: Verso, 2016), 35. Löwy is commenting on Benjamin's Thesis III regarding Judgement Day. *Apokatastasis* is from the Greek for restoration or reintegration to a primary state, as theorised by the Stoics and Aristotle. It appears in the Christian Bible in Acts 3:21, *Apok*, the entry of all souls into heaven was rejected by the Catholic Church. It is also discussed by Benjamin in 'The Storyteller' (1936), *Apok* the *Selected Writings Volume 3, 1935–1938* (Cambridge, MA: The Belknap Press, 2002), 143–66 (158).

26 Traverso, *Left-Wing Melancholia*, 48. This is a Marxism coded in the tragic, rather than romantic, mode. Fredric Jameson, *The Political Unconscious: Narrative as a Socially Symbolic Act* (London: Methuen, 1981), 110–19.

27 Wendy Brown, 'Resisting Left Melancholy', *boundary 2* 26:3 (1999): 19–27; Sigmund Freud, 'Mourning and Melancholia', in *On Metapsychology* (1917; Harmondsworth: Penguin, 1991), 245–68. Jodi Dean argues that Brown misunderstands Benjamin's account of Kästner, she suggests that Brown finds the problem in fidelity to an ideal, rather than in the political compromise that is Benjamin's target: Jodi Dean, *The Communist Horizon* (London: Verso, 2012), 160–3. See also: Bruno Bosteels, 'The Melancholy Left', in *Marx and Freud in Latin America: Politics, Psychoanalysis and Religion in Times of Terror* (London: Verso, 2012), 159–93.

> self-reproaches and self-revilings, and culminates in a delusional expectation of punishment.[28]

In melancholia, the death drive latches onto mourning. Moreover, Freud suggests that mourning can apply to abstract notions, such as 'one's country, liberty, an ideal'.[29] While there is an honourable tradition of defending lost causes and crying in the wilderness, it is difficult to see how the left can hold to melancholy and, importantly, Sekula's reference is not quite to the left's defeatist attitude but specifically to the 'mournful and weary anticipation of unemployment'.[30] Perhaps the differences expressed here are merely terminological: one has to understand the historical defeat without, as Jodi Dean argues, averting our gaze from the 'communist horizon' or the 'communist hypothesis'.[31]

In this vein, Lucien Goldmann and Daniel Bensaïd present the secular wager on socialism as a 'strategic hypothesis and regulating horizon'; while accepting frailty, error and even catastrophe, an openness to the future is maintained.[32] The task is to refuse pessimism and blind optimism alike, facing historical actualities while building towards advances in social justice. Although focused on the economic rather than political processes, *Fish Story* could be considered alongside Chris Marker's *Le fond de l'air est rouge* as 'a sort of epitaph of the last revolutionary hopes of the twentieth century' (to use Traverso's words).[33] Marker's reflective essay film offers a negative practice of refusal 'from the standpoint of the defeated' and their disidentification with narratives of capitalist triumphalism. While funerals are a central motif in *Le fond de l'air est rouge*, and although history piles up ruling-class victories over the popular classes (Benjamin's 'barbarism'), the film steps out of linear time and employs horizontal montage to suggest a continuum of revolt. Similarly,

28 Freud, 'Mourning and Melancholia', 252.

29 Ibid.

30 *Fish Story*, 74.

31 Dean, *The Communist Horizon*, 169–79; for the 'communist horizon', see: Bruno Bosteels, *The Actuality of Communism* (London: Verso, 2011); for the 'communist hypothesis': Alain Badiou, *The Communist Hypothesis* (London: Verso, 2010). For Dean, and for us, it is those who reject social transformation ('the common') who are truly melancholic.

32 Daniel Bensaïd, *Le pari mélancholique: Métamorphoses de la politique, politique des metamorphoses* (Paris: Feyard, 1997), 343, Traverso cites this passage in *Left-Wing Melancholia*, 234. Lucien Goldmann, *The Hidden God: A Study of the Tragic Vision in the Pensées of Pascal and the Tragedies of Racine* (1955; London: Routledge and Kegan Paul, 1964). Badiou reminds us that Mallarmé's 'casting of the dice' takes place from 'the bottom of a shipwreck': Alain Badiou, *Being and Event* (1988; London: Continuum, 2005), 193.

33 Traverso, *Left-Wing Melancholia*, 105.

Fish Story contemplates defeats without capitulating to defeatism. Class is not an identity, and the abolition of the cultural forms and modes of existence of the old industrial working class does not mean the end of class, and certainly not the end of opposition to capitalist abstraction.[34]

Another way of understanding this dialectical vision of mourning and left melancholy is through a consideration of agency. Although the histories of the left are scattered through the work, *Fish Story* pays more attention to the demise of radical working-class cultures than to the questions of political strategy. The overarching, determinate form of agency in *Fish Story* is that of capital; the roving search for valorisation that reconstructed the postwar social-democratic consensus is everywhere visible in the project.[35] Jeroen Verbeeck elaborates on how *Fish Story* presents 'a phenomenology of defeat', contrasting it with Sekula's subsequent focus on 'the praxis and lived experiences of social resistance' in works such as *Waiting for Tear Gas*, *Freeway to China*, *Ship of Fools* and *Black Tide/Marea Negra*.[36] But Verbeeck also alights on three images that punctuate *Fish Story* with resources of hope, drawing attention to distinct forms of worker agency: 'occupation, strike, and riot'.[37] Verbeeck underscores that all three involve 'the negative presence of labor'.[38]

Two such images occur in the chapter set in Vigo, Spain, in 1992: a shop window of an establishment occupied by women clerks in a dispute over pay (#65); and a rally at the end of a half-day general strike opposing cuts to unemployment benefits (#68). The benefit cuts were being made by the socialist government in a bid to join the European Community's monetary union. This photograph depicts a spirited gathering and conveys the optimism of solidarity and the cheery energy that can be sustained during brief moments of symbolic action. The women, however, had already been in occupation for eighteen months, and the photograph conveys a suspended temporality: commerce stands still;

34 G. M. Tamás, 'Telling the Truth About Class', *Socialist Register* (2006): 228–68.

35 The primacy given to the agency of capital aligns *Fish Story* with Marx's *Capital*, where the capitalist is 'capital personified and endowed with consciousness and a will': Karl Marx, *Capital: I* (1867; Harmondsworth: Penguin, 1976), 254. Marx makes similar observations throughout the three volumes of *Capital*.

36 Jeroen Verbeeck, 'A Modest Gesture: Modalities of Protest in Allan Sekula's *Fish Story* (1989–1995)', in *Allan Sekula: Collective Sisyphus*, eds Carles Guerra, Anja Isabel Schneider and Hilde Van Gelder (London: Koenig Books, 2013), 42–57 (44).

37 Ibid., 48.

38 Ibid. He refers to Sekula's note on the 'semiotics' of the general strike and riot (Sekula Papers, S.1.05:07, Fish Story Notebook 3, 1992–3: 20 February 1993).

the mannequin holds a frozen pose; there is a faded advertisement for *Vogue*; the glass is cracked and reinforced with tape. Notably, the chapter is titled 'Message in a Bottle', a metaphor implying hope that the despatch will be found across distant maritime space and time – as, in fact, we do with Sekula's photograph. The vitrine window, itself like a fish tank, displays not only its shop dummies but also the signs and press cuttings posted by the striking clerks: 'NOS DEBEN 18 SUELDOS' ('They owe us 18 months' wages'). On the outer edges of the image, in the two entrances, are two women 'caught on camera' and in movement. Here, there is a *mise-en-abyme* of 'messages in bottles'. The idiom repeats elsewhere. Later, for instance, David Jones, a crew member of *Sea-Land Quality*, calls home to Jacksonville from a Rotterdam phone booth. The photograph preceding the fashion shop, the first in the Vigo sequence, shows another glass 'bottle', a jeweller's display (#64), where a man arranges a model galleon, probably made of silver. Notably, in the occupation picture, the arrangement of repair tape holding together the window corner looks as if an artist had sketched the historic sail in broad strokes. The suggestion intended by the jeweller almost certainly relates to the sunken Spanish fleet in Vigo Bay, attacked by the British on its return from Havana in 1702. Sekula's allusion steers towards Jules Verne's fictional account of Nemo's underwater search for its gold.

Verbeeck's third example is one we already encountered in Chapter 1: the firefighter in Koreatown (#14), directing water at a blazing store, torched during the multicultural uprising that followed the acquittal of four Los Angeles Police Department officers tried for beating Rodney King who had apparently committed a number of misdemeanours. This incident points to the limitations of documentary. A videotape of the beating, recorded by neighbour George Holliday, provided incontrovertible visual evidence of police brutality, but the acquittal of the four officers shows how the document is limited by evidential dispute and institutional racism.[39] Sekula's photograph connects police, courts and photographic evidence in a way that calls to mind 'The Body and the Archive'. A sign of compounded instances of state terror and exclusion, this image also represents a riotous refusal of the racist consensus.

There are other moments in *Fish Story* where the traces of unbroken political radicalism surface. There is the image of equitable allocation of work by Barcelona's dockers' union, 'La Coordinadora'. The

39 *Reading Rodney King/Reading Urban Uprising*, ed. Robert Gooding-Williams (London: Routledge, 1993).

slide sequence *Dismal Science* includes posters advertising a Trotskyist meeting. At the end of *Fish Story*, Sekula also includes a newspaper illustration that maps the 1991 riots in north-east England, on an estate built in the 1930s for Tyneside's shipyard workers. If strike, riot, occupation, resistance and worker autonomy punctuate the photographic sequences, the essays excavate a history of rebellion more consistently. *Fish Story* is haunted by revolutionary sailors and port workers, anarchists, syndicalists, Wobblies, Bolsheviks and Trotskyists – figures systematically overlooked in the academic accounts of the work. We should note how Sekula considers the prominence of mutiny in the first four decades of the twentieth century, reflecting on the role of the Kronstadt sailors in the Russian Revolution and their 1921 rebellion against the Bolsheviks. A roster of anti-capitalists appears: Karl Marx, Friedrich Engels, the anarchist Flores Magón brothers, Bill Haywood, Emma Goldman, Rosa Luxemburg, Leon Trotsky, Victor Serge, Hermann Remmele, C. L. R. James, Stan Weir, Subcomandante Marcos, Thomas Müntzer. The essay discusses revolutionary novels and films: Eisenstein's *Battleship Potemkin*; Theodor Plievier's *The Kaiser's Coolies*; B. Traven's *The Death Ship*; Victor Serge's *Birth of Our Power*. The rhetoric of resistance is addressed: Trotsky's account of the Tsarist fleet as synecdoche for social contradictions; Eisenstein's 'Bolshevized vitalism of revolt'; the 'eroticized Bolshevism' of the sailor and the queer imagination; the 'three distinct but often overlapping visions of mutiny' that circulated after 1921 'encompassing fading anarchist dreams, Bolshevik legends, and enduring bourgeois nightmares'.[40] The 'insurgent waterfront'; the syndicalist idea of an 'industrial republic of the ocean'; 'the dictatorship of the seven seas': this collective 'proletarian cosmopolitanism of the waterfront' is both recalled and imagined as an international, which joins port workers and mariners in a global federated republic of terraqueous toilers – ultimately as a synecdoche for subalterns of all types.[41]

Communist Figurations

In 'An Eternal Esthetics of Laborious Gestures' (1997/2014), Sekula proffered a reading of Louis-Jacques-Mandé Daguerre's *Boulevard du Temple.*

40 'Dismal Science', 126, 122, 118.
41 Ibid., 118.

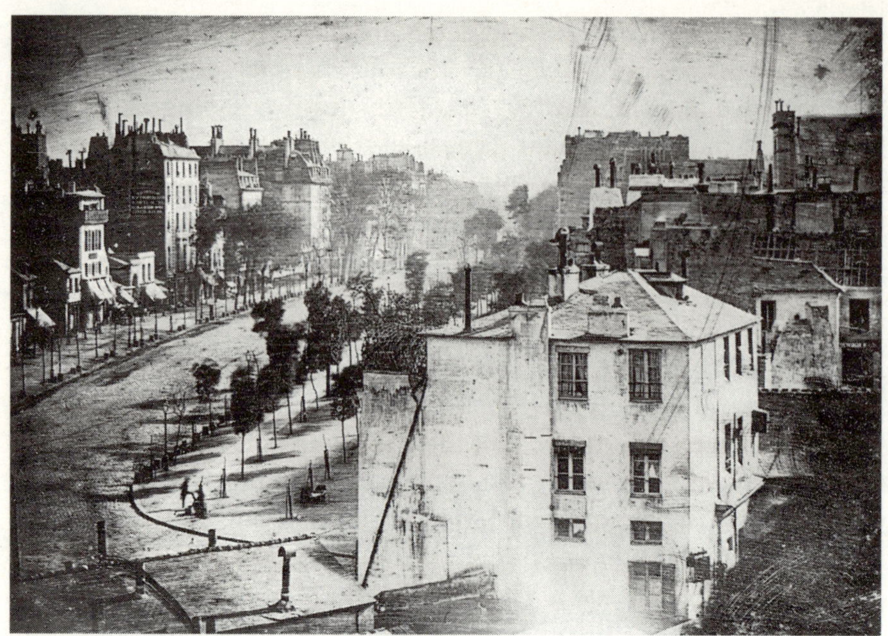

Figure 6: Louis-Jacques-Mandé Daguerre, Boulevard du Temple (c.1838) Daguerreotype. Whereabouts unknown (believed destroyed)

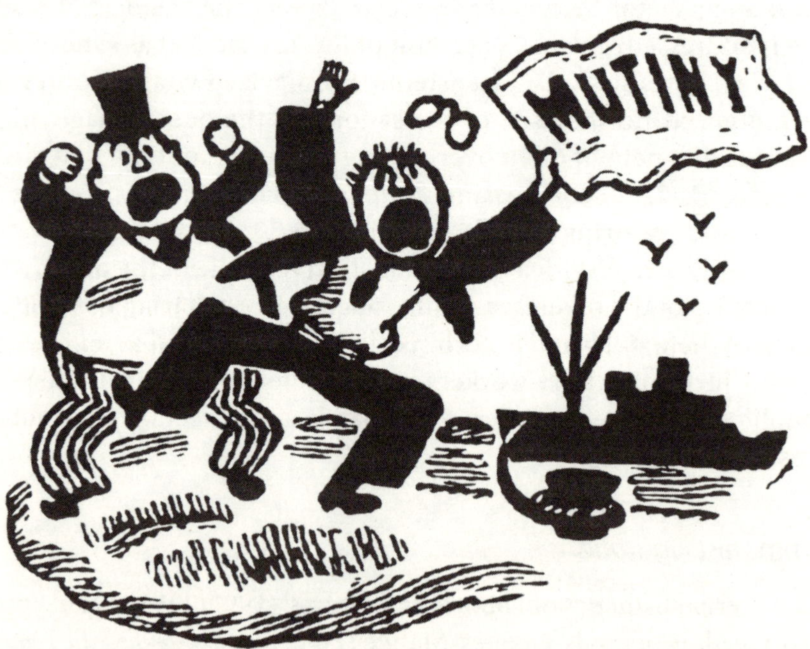

Figure 7: Item from The Dockers' Museum *(2010–13): Mutiny. Titled by Sekula Cartoon (artist unknown) believed to be from* The Labor Defender, *c.1920)*

Made from the roof of Daguerre's Diorama in c.1838, at around eight o'clock in the morning, this famous 'daguerreotype' (as the process would come to be known) is often treated as 'originary' for the medium: the first photograph to record the human body.[42] From an elevated position, we gaze over neighbouring properties to the rear; beyond, a wide, tree-lined street recedes into the distance. As is well known, the slow exposures required at this time made it difficult to capture movement. If motion registered at all, it appeared as ghost-like smudges. The street is empty of people and vehicles, but, on a corner of the boulevard, a man has remained stationary long enough to register as a silhouette. He stands with one foot raised onto a shoe-shiner's box and, with long legs astride and his arms perhaps held behind his back, he conveys not only balance but also a certain class command. However, the bootblack working at his feet is barely distinguishable from shadows and a staked sapling. Some commentators claim that the shoeblack's feet are identifiable, but the worker is deduced rather than seen. Sekula homes in on this photographic rendition of 'the first humans': a silhouette of a bourgeois and a blur of a worker. He reads the bourgeois *bon homme* as a dandy – not unreasonably given his swaggering pose and the location (the street was then known as 'Boulevard du Crime', a base for theatres and night-time entertainment). This figure is, in the syntax of some commentators, 'having his boots brushed'. Sekula enlarges on the critics' use of this grammatical construction. The gerund is sometimes valued for its quality of 'activation', but in this instance, it surreptitiously attributes agency to the dandy while robbing it from the bootblack. This discursive evaporation of subaltern labour, Sekula says, is an instance of the 'brutalism that blames the poor for the mud on the boots of the rich'.[43] He is especially interested in the interplay of the dandy and the bootblack, which he reads as an instance of fetishism: a process that places capital, not labour, as the force that sets production in motion. In contrast, Sekula emphasises the role of a lowly social actor in making history. Considering *Boulevard du Temple* and the approach of its

42 'An Eternal Esthetics of Laborious Gestures', *Grey Room* 55 (2014): 15–27 (23–5). The essay is included in Allan Sekula, *Art Isn't Fair: Further Essays on the Traffic in Photographs and Related Media*, eds Sally Stein and Ina Steiner (London: MACK Books, 2020), 151–60. The gestation of this essay was long: published in 2014, Sekula shared a draft with Steve Edwards in 1997. The Daguerre image we now have is a reconstruction based on photographic reproductions made before the plate was ruined, sometime in the mid-twentieth century, during cleaning.

43 'An Eternal Esthetics of Laborious Gestures', 26.

commentators, he is concerned with recovering a figure 'hidden from history' – the labourer erased in the time of exposure stands in for a broader social purview.

Sekula's reading of *Boulevard du Temple* points towards one important coordinate of his work. He writes: 'the practice of photography allows for the possibility of a radical consciousness *from below* of the relation between esthetic servitude and esthetic mastery'.[44] Sekula drew on diverse thinkers concerned with low-plane practices: the witticisms and stories of labourers and social activists; the Russian Formalists' attention to excluded popular forms; Mikhail Bakhtin's focus on the lower body and Rabelaisian scatology; Bertolt Brecht's celebration of 'crude thinking' as a plebian riposte to 'fine thought'; Benjamin's opposition to history 'empathizing with the victors'. He also engaged with the oral history of Studs Terkel; Raymond Williams's insistence that 'culture is ordinary'; the interest in popular culture developed by Stuart Hall and others at the Birmingham Centre for Contemporary Cultural Studies; and even Jacques Rancière's politics of recognition in a subaltern key. We consider some of their metaphoric patterns in the following chapters. Here we focus on the consideration of history from below. As Theodor Adorno suggested, with a nod to Gorky's bleak 1902 play: 'Anyone who has allowed the lower depths to enter into composition composes from the bottom up.'[45]

'Below' is a spatial location, of course. It also signals lowly *topoi*. Foremost, however, this 'bottom up' for Sekula is a methodological approach that orientates practice – in his critical studies as much as his photo and video works. Thus, whether dealing with subaltern subjects or elite forms, archives must 'be read from below'; the historian should 'brush history against the grain'.[46] In this conception, the

44 'On *Fish Story*', 51. Sekula draws on Hegel's master–slave dialectic. The phrase 'history from below' is attributed to various thinkers; possibly it comes from the radical historian Jesse Lemisch, 'The American Revolution Seen from the Bottom Up', in *Towards a New Past: Dissenting Essays in American History*, ed. Barton J. Bernstein (New York: Vintage, 1968), 3–43, but it seems likely that it was Georges Lefebvre who coined the term. See Harvey J. Kaye, *The British Marxist Historians* (Cambridge: Polity, 1984), 227.

45 Theodor W. Adorno, 'Mahler' (1961), in *Quasi una Fantasia: Essays on Modern Music* (1963; London: Verso, 1992), 81–110 (87). In thinking about Mahler, Adorno refers to Maxim Gorky's play *The Lower Depths* (1902).

46 'Photography Between Labour and Capital', 202. 'Against the grain', which Sekula uses for his 1984 collection of writings and photo works, is from Benjamin's Thesis VII. Two years later, Terry Eagleton used the same title for his collection of essays.

labour of reading and looking is a partisan endeavour, infused with a perspective of negation from a position of situated subjectification – a form of methodological regicide. Sekula was particularly interested in the work of historians who rejected the stories of the victors and adopted the subaltern view. Several threads could be followed here, from the work of the Annales historians Lucien Febvre and Georges Lefebvre to that of Ranajit Guha and the group around *Subaltern Studies*. Centrally, Sekula attended to writing by English Marxist historians who focused on the experiences of neglected 'common people' and the desire to recover their agency as makers of their own history – primarily: Eric Hobsbawm, A. L. Morton, E. P. Thompson, Christopher Hill and George Rudé. He also read C. L. R. James's pioneering *The Black Jacobins*, a parallel work that the communist historians were somewhat suspicious of because 'of the author's known Trotskyism'.[47] This historiographic orientation has sometimes meant studying not only 'wages, labor markets, apprenticeship systems, workshop regimes, mechanization and de-skilling', but also the political forms of trade unions and parties, strikes, mutinies, riots and revolutions.[48] In an expanded sense, it refers to the lifeworld of ordinary people and the universes they forged. These oppositional historians drew on sources that were, in their moment, atypical: from chapbooks and sermons to threatening letters. In his well-known programmatic statement of this approach, Thompson spoke of attempting to 'rescue the poor stockinger, the Luddite cropper, the "obsolete" hand-loom weaver, the "utopian" artisan, and even the deluded follower of Joanna Southcott from the enormous condescension of posterity'.[49] This tradition values subaltern lives and actions as a corrective to elite histories, but also – and this would be an example of Tamás's 'angelic' – as moral exemplars for subjectification: 'enriching historical analysis and providing self-consciously generative accounts designed to inspire a politics

---

47 C. L. R. James, *The Black Jacobins* (1938; London: Penguin, 2001); Eric Hobsbawm, 'The Historians' Group of the Communist Party', in *Rebels and their Causes: Essays in Honour of A.L. Morton*, ed. Maurice Cornforth (London: Lawrence and Wishart, 1978), 21–47 (23). He also read American representatives of this trend, including Staughton Lynd, Eric Foner, David Montgomery and Howard Zinn.

48 Geoff Eley, *A Crooked Line: From Cultural History to the History of Society* (Ann Arbor, MI: University of Michigan Press, 2005), 184.

49 E. P. Thompson, *The Making of the English Working Class* (1963; Harmondsworth: Penguin, 1980), 12. In 1995, we accompanied Sekula to see sites of Luddism in the English East Midland's.

precisely by attacking the exclusionary narratives of conventional historiography'.[50]

In one dimension, this historiography concerned itself centrally with social class and revolutionary upheavals, but its focus existed in some tension with the tradition of a 'People's History': a communist historiography shaped during the Popular Front.[51] This vision of the 'national popular' identified democratic currents and forces *within* a national formation. There are distinct variants of people's history, but in this version 'the people' excludes 'the elite'. For the members of the influential British Communist Party Historians' Group, the 'national popular' came to be identified with forms of Protestant dissent: the radical sects of the English Revolution; the writings of Milton, Bunyan and Blake; the concept of the 'Norman Yoke'; the recovery of lost common-law rights; and the ideal of the 'freeborn Englishman'.[52] This was an archaeology of ideas drawn from: revolting peasants, millenarians, antinomians, outlaws, Regicides, Levellers, Diggers, Ranters, Jacobin conspirators, Luddites, Owenites, trade unionists and Chartists. Whether espousing 'free justification' of the saints, or the gamut of ideas from 'mystical pantheism to a robust plebian materialism', all opposed established power relations and practised plebian solidarity.[53] To this lineage, Morton and Thompson added the romantic anti-capitalism of John Ruskin and William Morris.

Much was gained from this overhaul of the historical perspective, but the approach is not unproblematic. Some criticisms belong to highly specialised historical engagements concerning interpretations of events; others involve methodological considerations (economism or culturalism, structure or agency, 'experience' or representation). The impact of poststructuralist thought, particularly that of Foucault, challenged the

---

50 Geoff Eley and Keith Nield, *The Future of Class in History: What's Left of the Social?* (Ann Arbor, MI: University of Michigan Press, 2007), 164–5.

51 A. L. Morton, *A People's History of England* (London: Lawrence and Wishart, 1938); *People's History and Socialist Theory*, ed. Raphael Samuel (London: Routledge and Kegan Paul, 1981).

52 For an account of some of these themes in British communist historiography, see Raphael Samuel, 'British Marxist Historians 1880–1980 (Part One)', *New Left Review* I:120 (1980): 21–96. There was no Part Two. See also: Bill Schwarz, '"The People" in History: The Communist Party Historians' Group, 1946–56', in *Making Histories: Studies in History Writing and Politics*, eds Richard Johnson et al. (Minneapolis, MN: University of Minnesota Press, 1982), 44–95; David Parker, 'The Communist Party and its Historians, 1946–89', Socialist History 12 (1997): 33–58.

53 A. L. Morton, *The World of the Ranters: Religious Radicalism in the English Revolution* (London: Lawrence and Wishart, 1970), 17, 74–5.

underpinning humanism of this project and emphasised the importance of language and subjectification for history. Feminists stress the role of gender and the family in shaping class formation and the limitations of a radicalism centred on male wageworkers. Queer historians point to the heteronormativity of people's history. Postcolonial thinkers, some influenced by Communist Party historians, underline the significance of racialisation, colonialism and global history. These debates still shape and reshape history writing. Their shifts in emphases have redrawn the boundaries of history from below, challenging us to consider those who were, for example, neither English, nor male, nor dissenting Protestants. As Paul Gilroy notes, the national focus and the theme of the 'freeborn Englishman' exclude, inter alia, the Irish and people of colour.[54] All this needs fundamental revision for a new socialist politics. Gilroy's own suggestion is particularly helpful: using the Atlantic 'to produce an explicitly transnational and intercultural perspective', treating a maritime body 'as one single, complex unit of analysis'.[55] A figure–ground reversal flips conceptual-political priorities, breaking with methodological nationalism to refocus attention on transnational connections and exchanges across pelagic space.[56]

The critiques are important, but even commentators as intelligently sympathetic as Geoff Eley and Keith Nield fail to recognise the reconstruction of Marx and Marxism that has taken place in recent work, and which has responded to these criticisms.[57] We propose to take one example of how this communist figuration can be reimagined for contemporary anti-capitalist politics: *The Many-Headed Hydra* (2000) by Peter Linebaugh and Marcus Rediker. This book – greatly admired by Sekula – is particularly significant because, while it cleaves to a militant view 'from below', it recasts the communist historians' account of class formation in the seventeenth and eighteenth centuries as

54 Paul Gilroy, *The Black Atlantic: Modernity and Double Consciousness* (London: Verso, 1993), 14. While this dimension constrains the thought of these internationalists, Gilroy is careful not to suggest that the result is straightforwardly racist.

55 Gilroy, *The Black Atlantic*, 15. Fernand Braudel's study of the Mediterranean is the pioneering work in this vein. In addition to Gilroy's study: Marcus Rediker, *Between the Devil and the Deep Blue Sea: Merchant Seamen, Pirates, and the Anglo-American Maritime World 1700–1750* (Cambridge: Cambridge University Press, 1987); Peter Linebaugh and Marcus Rediker, *The Many-Headed Hydra: Sailors, Slaves, Commoners and the Hidden History of the Revolutionary Atlantic* (London: Verso, 2000).

56 In a similar move, recent studies have also flipped attention from the continental to the archipelagic.

57 Eley, *A Crooked Line*; Eley and Nield, *The Future of Class in History*.

multi-ethnic, transnational and gendered. As the authors subsequently note, 'To the traditional *subjects* of labour-history – the minority of mostly white, male, waged, skilled, artisanal or industrial workers – we wished to add the majority who were variously motley, female, unwaged, and located in other settings within a capitalist economy.'[58] For Linebaugh and Rediker, this 'motley proletariat' includes all those who perform dependent labour under capitalism as a condition for their reproduction.[59] They build their account from multiple individual lives across the 'Revolutionary Atlantic'.

To understand Linebaugh and Rediker's intervention, it is helpful to begin with Christopher Hill's important essay 'The Many-Headed Monster' (1965), where he argued that the elite in Britain before 1640 almost universally shared a 'hatred of democracy' (to adopt Rancière's terms).[60] For them, democracy would have constituted a tyranny against authority and property. Hill assembles an extraordinary array of early-modern metaphors for the propertyless 'multitude' – here not a neo-Spinozist category but a damning conception 'from above', ranging from 'ungodly' to 'wild' and 'bloody'.[61] The multitude was said by the gentlemen to be prey to violence and tumult, as well as servile and mechanical. It was described variously as: the 'many-headed multitude'; the 'base multitude'; 'that wild beast multitude'; 'the many-headed monster'; 'a giddy, hot-headed, bloody multitude'; the 'headless multitude'. The Levellers were said to be a 'motley hundred-headed faction'. In a series of demonising tropes, the figuration of the multitude collects all of those positioned outside of the dominant relations of power and property. That said, Hill himself overlooked the transnational and racialised motifs: 'motley', 'heap of fools' and 'pied chameleon'. The chameleon, like the Hydra, is a reptilian allusion, and it also changes its colours. The terms also imply vari-hued and ragged attire, suggesting poverty and clowning, but they also point to the differentially racialised

58 Peter Linebaugh and Marcus Rediker, '*The Many-Headed Hydra*: Reflections on History from Below', in *Beyond Marx: Theorising Global Labour Relations in the Twenty-First Century*, eds Marcel van der Linden and Karl Heinz Roth, with Max Menninger (Leiden: Brill, 2014), 34–5.

59 Linebaugh and Rediker, *The Many-Headed Hydra*, 6. This is to say, they refuse the identification of the working class with 'doubly free labour'.

60 Christopher Hill, 'The Many-Headed Monster' (1965), in *Change and Continuity in Seventeenth-Century England* (New Haven, CT: Yale University Press, 1991), 181–204. Jacques Rancière, *Hatred of Democracy* (London: Verso, 2007).

61 The key neo-Spinozist account is Michael Hardt and Antonio Negri, *Multitude: War and Democracy in the Age of Empire* (New York: Penguin, 2004).

image of multitude. We can identify three key features in this phantasmic vision 'from above', which continue to inform the anti-communist imagination. First, it is thought to be not only plural but also singular. Second, it is not human, but a beast or monster. Third, it is seen simultaneously as many-headed and acephalous. In the view from above, the propertyless multitude may be active, but it is not conscious; it lacks reason. Driven by base urges, frenzied passions, envy and lust, its agency is cast as riotousness. Linebaugh and Rediker add to this account of the many-headed Hydra the gentleman's favourite hero, Hercules – 'a symbol of power and order' – who destroys this monstrous assembly by lopping off heads.[62]

In the face of the gentlemen as a property-owning class, the multitude could be demonised precisely because of their lack of property. If Hill delineates how the Hydra is seen from above, Linebaugh and Rediker take the perspective from below. They consider the interconnections set in motion by Atlantic capitalism, a new economy that uprooted, transplanted and threw together enslaved peoples from Africa; indigenous Americans exiled from the commons; dispossessed English labourers and Scots from the highland clearances; those Irish who refused to submit to their colonisers' schemes; dissidents, antinomian radicals, impoverished artisans, dislocated sailors and rabble from everyplace. Linebaugh and Rediker take the Hydra as a means of 'exploring multiplicity, movement, and connection, the long waves and planetary currents of humanity'.[63] They suggest that if the gentlemen totalise 'from above', the motley proletariat engages in 'universalism from below'.[64] This is a process of conscious identification and revolutionary agency where, in collective self-making, subalterns struggle together against murderous capitalist rule despite divisions based on gender, ethnicity or religion. *The Many-Headed Hydra* argues that the motley proletariat, brought into being by the propertied class, responded to the deathly view from above with rebellious practices

62 Linebaugh and Rediker, *The Many-Headed Hydra*, 2.

63 Ibid., 6.

64 Universalisation from below is an example of what Étienne Balibar calls *l'égaliberté*. According to Balibar, the central concepts of freedom and equality, which arose with the French Revolution, are not bound by time and place but are capable of infinite extension. Balibar argues that equality and freedom imply one another, and any demand for the extension of one is likely to entail the other. Étienne Balibar, '"Rights of Man" and "Rights of the Citizen": The Modern Dialectic of Equality and Freedom' (1990), in *Masses, Classes, Ideas: Studies on Politics and Philosophy Before and After Marx* (London: Routledge, 1994), 39–60.

and ideas of solidarity. Employing a term from Hill's *The World Turned Upside Down*, we can describe this lowly perspective as one of 'teeming freedom'.[65]

In a related argument, Thompson made a theoretical distinction between horizontal and vertical social forms. On the horizontal axis, the central distinction is that between above and below. Here, collective belonging is shaped primarily in relation to an external force (the gentlemen or 'patricians') and the multitude's internal variations do not result in fragmentation. The consequence is a class understanding of society and struggle. On the vertical axis, internal distinctions split apart the multitude, as with the divisions of nationalism or racism, and the topological distinction becomes vague. In moments of active class confrontation, Thompson suggests, the plebeian crowd should be viewed as 'a horizontal sort of beast'.[66] These figurative patterns – drawn from Hill, Thompson, Gilroy, Linebaugh and Rediker – illuminate important aspects of Sekula's practice.

Waiting for Tear Gas [white globe to black] *(1999–2000): Take 1*

As we saw, *Fish Story* took shape at the high-water mark of the neoliberal assault on the postwar consensus. Its mournful tenor testifies to that dismal time. In contrast, *Waiting for Tear Gas [white globe to black]* assumes the militant tone of the anti-capitalist protest against the Third Ministerial Conference of the World Trade Organization (WTO), held in Seattle between 28 November and 3 December 1999. Co-edited with Sally Stein, *Waiting for Tear Gas* is a sixteen-minute slide cycle, composed of eighty-one 35mm colour diapositives, projected consecutively in a darkened space. The work has also featured in several publications, sometimes edited down.[67]

---

65 Christopher Hill, *The World Turned Upside Down: Radical Ideas During the English Revolution* (London: Penguin, 1972), 361–6.

66 E. P. Thompson, 'The Patricians and the Plebs', in *Customs in Common* (London: Penguin, 1993), 16–96 (64). The argument has strong echoes of Sartre's *Critique of Dialectical Reason* (1960).

67 Sekula credits Sally Stein for collaborating on the sequence design in *TITANIC's wake*. A particularly memorable installation was curated with Jürgen Bock inside the Salazarist *Monument to the Discoveries* in Belém, Lisbon, in 2001, adding a historical layer to the WTO's 'globalisation' agenda. Thirty-two of the images conclude Alexander Cockburn, Geoffrey St. Clair and Allan Sekula, *5 Days That Shook the World: Seattle and Beyond* (London: Verso, 2000). The full cycle is published in *TITANIC's wake* and in *Art Isn't Fair*.

A number of commentators have suggested that the mass protest in Seattle in 1999 effectively marked the end of the postmodern consensus, because, for the first time in over a decade, partial claims for recognition gave way to universal demands for global equality, liberation and solidarity.[68] Around this point, the term 'capitalism' returned firmly to the social lexicon and, with it, the challenge of thinking about collective struggle. Sekula's representation of the events in Seattle is a significant marker of anti-capitalist collectivity emerging under these changed conditions.[69] As Cockburn and St. Clair describe, 'foundation careerists, NGO bureaucrats, policy wonks' and the big union organisations conducted a sideshow, while those committed to direct action took to the streets.[70] The 'motley' alliance formed 'a carnival with an ominous edge' that 'abandoned the respectable, police-sanctioned official AFL-CIO parade' – and attempted to disrupt the 'star chamber for the global capitalists'.[71] They were met with the material force of the repressive state apparatus: police in full body armour, the National Guard and some special military forces, all wielding batons and dispensing pepper spray, tear gas, rubber bullets and concussion grenades.

Much of the current theoretical debate on democratic assembly emphasises 'appearance', 'recognition' and 'the count' as conditions of democratic inclusion. Judith Butler's discussion of the 'performative assembly' is directly relevant here, both because she attempts to theorise the Occupy movement and because she claims that photography and video are incapable of representing the assembly of bodies. Camera framings (literal and metaphoric) 'function as a potentially exclusionary designation', she argues, establishing a 'zone of the uncapturable', so that 'no picture of the crowd can represent the people'.[72] Democratic frames must, Butler believes, be more porous and exceed representation. Her

---

68 For discussions of the Seattle events: Cockburn, St. Clair and Sekula, *5 Days*; *The Battle for Seattle: The New Challenge to Capitalist Globalization*, eds Eddie Yuan et al. (New York: Soft Skull Press, 2001); *The Battle of the Story of the Battle of Seattle*, eds Rebecca Solnit and David Solnit (Oakland, CA: AK Press, 2009). Michael Denning makes these events the basis for a suggestive cultural analysis in *Culture in the Age of Three Worlds* (London: Verso, 2004), 35–50.

69 None of this is intended to claim that this was entirely unprecedented, but these protests represent the point at which the movement against neoliberal globalisation gained a hold in a wider public imagination.

70 Cockburn, St. Clair and Sekula, *5 Days*, 29.

71 Ibid. 23, 59, 7. They attribute the star chamber point to environmental organiser Michael Donnelly.

72 Judith Butler, *Notes Towards a Performative Theory of Assembly* (Cambridge, MA: Harvard University Press, 2015), 164–5.

sense of the photographic frame is clearly inadequate, because, as a cut in space, it can be employed to suggest a limitless extension of the assembled, implying that *l'égaliberté* is capable of infinite expansion. There is a slippage in this account, as distinct forms of framing become laminated. As Marina Vishmidt notes (and as touched on in the previous chapter), in much post-Marxist thinking the body displaces people or class. Sekula's depiction of the crowd makes the sovereign power of international capital and state repression too apparent to fit with ideas of the political as 'recognition' or 'enactment'. There really is nothing to be 'included in' when the antagonist is the WTO and its guard dogs. This was a period of intense discussion around the meaning of and possible strategies for contemporary socialism.[73]

In recent debates, various categories and concepts have been suggested for naming the anti-capitalist collective: the '99%', 'horde' or 'pack', 'multitude', 'part-of-no-part', the 'plebs'. Our preference is for 'motley proletariat' as a characterisation of diverse subjects drawn together by dependent labour under capital.[74] It is not entirely clear the extent to which Linebaugh and Rediker intend this term to point to empirical referents, or if it is being used allegorically to enunciate or call into being a more transient set of possibilities; perhaps the 'motley proletariat' exists in the space between these options. For us, the motley proletariat is a knowing abstraction; a political form that allows 'the accumulation of differences, inequalities, hierarchies, divisions'.[75] Capitalism involves dispossession and exploitation, not simply exclusion or recognition, and antagonism is ineradicable from the logic of value production. In both history and social theory, there is a long-running debate over the terms 'people', 'working-class' and 'proletariat'. None of these categories can be reduced to simple positivity, because they are at once real and imaginary, turning on the gap between empirical bodies of people who occupy objective positions in social relations

73 For a sample of the debates: Michael Hardt and Antonio Negri, *Empire* (Cambridge, MA: Harvard University Press, 2002); John Holloway, *Change the World Without Taking Power* (London: Pluto Press, 2003); *Debating Empire*, ed. Gopal Balakrishnan (London: Verso, 2003); *Take the Power to Change the World: Globalisation and the Debate on Power*, ed. Phil Hearse (London: Socialist Resistance Books, 2007).

74 Bosteels notes that the category is used by García Linera and that the Spanish translation of Lenin in his pamphlet on left-wing communism employs 'motley' as a way of describing the relation between proletarian and semi-proletarian elements: *The Actuality of Communism*, 225–6.

75 Silvia Federici, *Caliban and the Witch: Women, the Body and Primitive Accumulation* (New York: Autonomedia, 2004), 115.

and forms of representation.[76] As such, the depiction of the crowd is itself a site of struggle over definitions of politics: for the right, it is a mob or unruly mass, prone to irrational violence; for the left, the crowd is a placeholder for the sovereign power of the people as 'the revolutionary alliance of all the oppressed'.[77] As Jodi Dean notes, whereas reactionary crowd theory from Gustave Le Bon onwards suggests that crowds are an irrational, de-individualised mass acting under 'imitation', 'suggestion' or 'contagion', in contrast, according to Elias Canetti, the density and direction of the crowd generates an egalitarian 'discharge'.[78] In Canetti's view, the crowd names an anti-individualist social body – a collective – that is capable of infinite expansion.[79] Dean writes: 'Equality in the crowd is de-differentiation, de-individuation, the momentary release from hierarchy, closure, and separation.'[80] We would add that it is important that it involves an *appearance* (both a public manifestation and an image) of a common form that fills the political void. The motley proletariat names a constitutive anti-capitalist politics.

There are too many positions and platforms in the Seattle crowd for it to be described as a class formation, but *Waiting for Tear Gas* attempts to give form to a 'horizontal beast'. Standing in opposition to the neoliberal globalisation agenda that is indifferent to anything but the relentless pursuit of profit, the anti-capitalist crowd emerges as united rather than separated in its differences. The crowd is like but also unlike the motley proletariat. History from below, we suggest, offers a productive way of understanding the horizontal counterpower that emerges in *Waiting for Tear Gas*. Sekula's private notes acknowledge the alliance's unusual strangeness, variety and inspired character; make sharp comments about the speeches (and apparel) of union leaders; and trace how rank-and-file trade unionists joined the direct action.[81] Punk hair

76 Jacques Rancière, *Staging the People: The Proletarian and His Double* (London: Verso, 2011).

77 Georg Lukács, *Lenin: A Study on the Unity of His Thought* (1924; London: New Left Books, 1970), 23.

78 Jodi Dean, *Crowds and Party* (London: Verso, 2016). Unfortunately, Freud's *Group Psychology and the Ego* follows Le Bon.

79 Elias Canetti, *Crowds and Power* (1960; Harmondsworth: Penguin, 1984), 18–19.

80 Dean, *Crowds and Party*, 215.

81 Sekula Papers S.1.09:02, No.2 [Global Mariner Seattle WTO], October 1999–2000. A large proportion of the notes focus on trade union politics, starting with the speeches by trade union leaders. A repeating target is James Hoffa, Jnr, son of the former General President of the Teamsters, who had just become GP himself after internal scandals had

and militant *trabajadores*, bohos and feminists, rock musicians and African American longshore workers all associate freely. Some protesters wear a suit and tie. A shop or restaurant worker steps onto the street with refreshments. 'Turtles' cross the road. And the devil himself appears, complete with cardboard chainsaw, pointing to the destructive business of logging. (In fact, there are two devils – are they Moloch and Belial?) To employ a distinction from Jameson, Sekula translates this utopian impulse into a utopian representation; the proviso is that in his hands it remains an allegorical form.[82]

The sequence opens with an image of a white globe and closes with a black one. In between, three discrete social groups are depicted. They are far from equally weighted. In just four images we see WTO delegates or their aides; they are mostly pushed towards the background, behind glass, emphasising their inaccessibility and political distance. (One image brings the delegates unusually close, and perhaps summons paparazzi tropes. Outside their hotel, a man gestures that his team do not want to be photographed, while another's necktie blows wayward, appearing to reject him.) The police are prominent in thirteen photographs, either as the dominant subject or as a menacing force in the background. Nevertheless, most of the images attend to the protesters.

The sequence of photographs shows gestures and fragments of action, collective joy and fatigue. Sekula described his approach to the Seattle protest as attempting – counter to the media stereotypes – 'a simple descriptive physiognomy'.[83] It is tempting to relate this evocation of comparative anatomy to the analysis of power-knowledge in 'The Body and the Archive'. Yet, the pictures do not follow the conventions of the document required for case histories; rather, his portraits are made askance with bodies in motion. It seems more pertinent to connect Sekula's 'simple descriptive physiognomy' of Seattle to Benjamin's analysis of the crowd in his Baudelaire studies, or to August Sander's capacious portrayal of the German people in *Antlitz der Zeit* (1929). Perhaps most significantly, *Waiting for Tear Gas* has much in common with that trend in history from below that is concerned with discovering 'the

---

rocked the union. Sekula writes about the chanting of his name and the cult of personality, noting the alternative chant of 'I-L-W-U'. Even Hoffa's choice of footwear is mentioned: tasselled loafers that Sekula wished he had photographed. Sekula later discusses rank-and-file militants and their decision to join with the direct action, and points to allegiances of some locals to Trotskyism and the TDU.

82 Fredric Jameson, *Valences of the Dialectic* (London: Verso, 2009).

83 *Waiting for Tear Gas [white globe to black]*, in *Art Isn't Fair*, 170.

faces in the crowd'. The reference here is to the work of George Rudé and his efforts to escape the anonymous presentation of eighteenth- and nineteenth-century protesters as a mindless mob.[84] In a series of studies, Rudé examines the records of those arrested and tried, whom he has traced through rate books and other local sources. (As Arlette Farge notes, these 'prudently mute protagonists' had good reason to remain silent.[85]) Rudé certainly intends a humanist act of individualisation, a return of agency to those occluded in established narratives, but the approach also enables him to delineate the crowd's configuration, identifying trades, connecting elementary life stories and discerning the patterns of solidarity within communities. In this way, the approach proffers a study of class composition. In contrast to other approaches in contemporary photography, which pick out individuals from the crowd, isolating them and pushing collectives into the background, like Rudé, *Waiting for Tear Gas* employs symptomatic detail to build up the collective life of the motley assembly.

Raymond Williams observed that 'there are in fact no masses; there are only ways of seeing people as masses.'[86] Sekula understood the point and eschewed the standard figurations of the crowd. He breaks down false universals and abstractions. Obviously, he avoids the reactionary tropes often associated with 'mob', 'pack', 'herd' or 'horde'. *Waiting for Tear Gas* also avoids metaphors drawn from elemental forces that have dominated the revolutionary imagination: deluge, flood, wave, tide, surge, storm, eruption, spark, fire, earthquake (for example, *Storm Over Asia*; *Ten Days That Shook the World*; *The Fire Next Time*). Some of these metaphors have acquired racist inflections in the context of the politics of migration. Like Andy Warhol's *Race Riot*, *Waiting for Tear Gas* depicts an image of police violence against peaceful demonstrators; it is the police that are rioting against the motley crew.[87] Sekula's work

84 The term is from Asa Briggs and was used as the title of Chapter 13 of Rudé's *The Crowd in History 1730–1848*, revised second edition (London: Lawrence and Wishart, 1981). See also *The Crowd in the French Revolution 1730–1848* (London: Lawrence and Wishart, 1984); and with E. J. Hobsbawm, *Captain Swing* (London: Lawrence and Wishart, 1969).

85 Arlette Farge, *The Allure of the Archives* (1989; New Haven, CT: Yale University Press, 2015), 86; Rudé, *The Crowd in History*, 7.

86 Raymond Williams, *Culture and Society 1780–1950* (1958; Harmondsworth: Penguin, 1963), 289.

87 As Gilmore notes, before the 1960s, virtually all riots in the US were attacks on people of colour, but with the LA Watts uprising in 1965, black and other protesters held the streets against police brutality. Ruth Wilson Gilmore, *Abolition Geography: Essays Towards Liberation* (London: Verso, 2023), 206.

does not depict the protesters as the violent pack presented by the mainstream media – but neither do we overtly see the police clubbing protesters or directly unleashing toxic sprays. On a couple of occasions, the police are seen grabbing a demonstrator but, for the most part, actual moments of violence precede or are displaced from the frame. Nonetheless, police weaponry is in plain sight and bursts of gas are evident. Protesters cover their noses and mouths, or rub their eyes; two hold discharged rubber bullets.

Waiting for Tear Gas is usually accompanied by a short text explaining Sekula's idea of 'anti-photojournalism: no flash, no telephoto zoom lens, no gas mask, no auto-focus, no press pass and no pressure to grab at all costs the one defining image of dramatic violence'.[88] Under these self-prescribed conditions, detached vision is unavailable: the photographer is likely to be clubbed or gassed along with everyone else. The negative protocols are central to *Waiting for Tear Gas*. The absence of auto-focus and lack of flash provide a different form for the experience of the crowd; for the sensations aroused by the police charge; and for the chaos and confusion that attends the moment of gas or percussive explosion. 'Bad photography' has been central to the claims of critical realism: in this work, Sekula found a new way to employ this strategy of 'deskilling', the consequence of which is to give us a perspective internal to the dynamic of the crowd, moving with its ebbs and flows.[89] This is a work of movement, which Jean Mitry characterises as the 'being-with' of the camera.[90] As we have seen, Sekula disclaimed a 'personal style', and *Waiting for Tear Gas* combined different techniques. Almost all images involve a mid-distance subject typical of a standard lens. There are no close-ups and only one example of conspicuous cropping. In some images, bodies fill the frame; other pictures feature one or two figures. Points of view change according to available opportunities. In

---

88 *Waiting for Tear Gas [white globe to black]*, in *Art Isn't Fair*, 170.

89 Jeff Wall, '"Marks of Indifference": Aspects of Photography in, or as, Conceptual Art', in *Reconsidering the Object of Art: 1965–1975*, eds Ann Goldstein and Anne Rorimer (Los Angeles, CA: Museum of Contemporary Art, 1995), 247–67; John Roberts, *The Art of Interruption: Realism, Photography and the Everyday* (Manchester: Manchester University Press, 1998); *The Impossible Document: Photography and Conceptual Art in Britain 1966–1976* (London: Camerawork, 1997); and *The Intangibilities of Form: Skill and Deskilling in Art After the Readymade* (London: Verso, 2007).

90 Jean Mitry cited in Gilles Deleuze, *Cinema 1: The Movement Image* (London: The Athlone Press, 1986), 72. The best account of photography in these terms is Sally Stein, '"Peculiar Grace": Dorothea Lange and the Testimony of the Body', in *Dorothea Lange: A Visual Life*, ed. Elizabeth Partridge (Washington, D.C.: Smithsonian, 1994), 57–89.

some instances, Sekula is positioned above his subjects; in others, lower. In his other works, he sometimes depicts the same object, person or event twice, marking a time lapse, so it is noteworthy that *Waiting for Tear Gas* rarely proceeds through continuity editing. It generally consists of discrete photographs. Disjunctures between the images are more apparent – further underscored in the slide presentation with the momentary breaks. Nonetheless, the absence of matched shots adds to the sense of fluidity.

Multitude and crowd; motley proletariat; class: all are relational categories that take on existence in situations of antagonism, formed in opposition to those who stand counter to them – whether in 'equilibrium' or 'reciprocity', or as 'field of force'. The terms here come from Thompson's great account of the relation between the gentry and the plebs in the eighteenth century: 'There is a sense in which rulers and crowd needed each other, watched each other, performed theatre and counter-theatre to each other's auditorium, moderated each other's political behaviour.'[91] The crowd and the forces of order defined reciprocal subject positions; they constituted each other. The relation could involve physical confrontations that were also a symbology of revolt. On the gentry side, this involved interventions ranging from charitable works to the bench and the gallows; for the plebian part, threatening letters, burning effigies, maiming livestock or food riots. This account is not so distant from the idea of 'performative assembly', but, at certain points, this reciprocity can snap – as Thompson claims it did in the 1790s, when it gave way to class-conscious, even revolutionary, perspectives.[92] Although Thompson warned against the over-extension of this analysis to all crowd situations, his account seems pertinent to the formations in *Waiting for Tear Gas*.[93] Here, the crowd and the police confront one another, playing out roles of opposition, force and repression. The slide sequence establishes multi-layered and interchangeable points of detail, where the oppositions to capital are totalised by their contrast to 'vertical' external social power.[94] An important caveat would

91 Thompson, 'The Patricians and the Plebs', 57. Reference could be made to Charles Tilly's 'repertoires of contention', but Sekula does not seem to have known that body of work.

92 Thompson, 'Eighteenth-Century English Society: Class Struggle Without Class?', *Social History* 3:2 (1978): 133–65 (165).

93 Thompson, 'The Moral Economy Reviewed', *Customs in Common*, 259–351 (260).

94 The discussion of crowd 'symbolism' is a significant aspect of Canetti's *Crowds and Power*.

be that counter-theatre involves more than just representation or performance; it is a trial of strength, a testing of resolve. In counter-theatre, the multitude pits its collective will against the state's determination to hold out. In this space, new collective identities are shaped and Sekula offers some possible figurations for that motley collective, both playful and earnest.

Sekula's sequence pays attention to the territorialisation of the crowd by the state. His project documents 'the attitudes of people waiting, unarmed, sometimes deliberately naked in the winter chill, for the gas and the rubber bullets and the concussion grenades'.[95] The act of waiting for tear gas is a dangerous (and, in some ways, heroic) strategy that is calculated to draw the state's latent violence into the open. These protesters taunt power: they deflate it with humour and vulnerability. The 'bare breasted ladies' – their name – explicitly play out the reciprocal bonds of authority and opposition: contrasting their flesh to the armoured bodies of the police. Larne Abse Gogarty notes that women in this work proclaim their agency and effectively 'sneer towards a male gaze, rather than seeking to seduce'.[96] Sekula observed that the media's litany of standard crowd tropes missed the key thing: how 'the human body asserts itself in the city streets, against the abstraction of global capital'.[97] In this instance, he does present the human body as concrete and vulnerable, and the crowd as a tentatively emergent political force for human survival.

SECTION 2: HISTORY IN THE ALLEGORICAL MODE

As a photographer, filmmaker, essayist and storyteller, Sekula took an expanded sense of history from below. Although his work is usually framed by the discourses of art, it makes as much sense to think about the context of the new social history. Certainly, his writings on photography in the 1970s and 1980s make important and still fecund contributions to the social history of art. He later observed how, as a creative practitioner, he 'increasingly tried to dissolve the boundary between essay-writing, a "poetics" of sequenced descriptive photographs, and

95 *Waiting for Tear Gas [white globe to black]*, in *Art Isn't Fair*, 170.

96 Larne Abse Gogarty, 'State Violence, Mirrors and the Perspective of Infinity', *Waiting for Tear Gas 1999–2000 by Allan Sekula*, 2016, tate.org.uk.

97 *Waiting for Tear Gas [white globe to black]*, in *Art Isn't Fair*, 170.

the practices of research in cultural, economic and social history'.[98] It is worth recalling the experimental social history films of the 1970s and '80s, such as Sue Clayton and Jonathan Curling's *The Song of the Shirt* (1979), Laura Mulvey and Peter Wollen's *Amy!* (1979) and Mick Eaton's *Darkest England* (1984). Now largely ignored outside specialist circles, these films combined neo-avant-garde narrative modes with social history, seeking novel forms for the presentation of the past. Comparison could also be made with radical social history films in the documentary register – films such as *Harlan County, USA* (1976, dir. Barbara Kopple) and *Union Maids* (1976, dir. Jim Klein, Julia Reichert and Miles Mogulescu).[99]

These are filmmakers who engaged with history, but pressures to attend to representation also came from the historians' side. Our discussion of history from below has been straying into questions of representation – the use of metaphors, figurations, narrative and visual media. This wave of social history was often attentive to such matters. In 1991, Raphael Samuel argued for 'enlarging the vocation of the historian to take in perceptions of the past, arguing that the novelist and the story teller, the film maker and the caricaturist are at least as worthy of our attention as the professional scholar'.[100] But as the 'linguistic turn' and cultural history developed through the 1990s, there was a stand-off between social historians committed to history from below and those who, drawing on poststructuralism, emphasised history as textual effect.[101] The debate rapidly became sterile. The historians' account of language often dissolved into a reheated history of ideas or political history, rather than, as claimed, an engagement with representation.[102] Both wings of this debate – those arguing for 'postmodern history' and those who wanted to defend class and social history – often lacked critical nuance, caricaturing their opponents. For those working in

98 'On *Fish Story*', 52.

99 An example of this criticism would be Noel King, 'Recent "Political" Documentary: Notes on "Union Maids" and "Harlan County, USA"', *Screen* 22:2 (1981): 7–18.

100 Raphael Samuel, Editorial, *History Workshop: A Collectanea, 1967–1991: Documents, Memoirs, Critique and Cumulative Index to History Workshop Journal* (Oxford: History Workshop, 1991), iv–v.

101 For a thoughtful assessment, see Eley and Nield, *The Future of Class*, though we envisage a more robust defence of Marxism than their plea for 'a generous and pluralist historical practice', in which class remains a 'useful' category.

102 John Foster, 'The Declassing of Language', *New Left Review* I: 50 (1985): 29–45 and Robert Grey, 'The Deconstructing of the English Working Class', *Social History* 11:3 (1986): 363–73. The subsequent literature is vast, some of it summarised in Eley, *A Crooked Line*.

'disciplines of representation' or aware of the historical avant-gardes, there is no necessary contradiction between militant commitment and attention to signification. Indeed, Sekula's work amply demonstrates the falsity of the opposition: it emphasises, at once, a partisan commitment to the social histories of subaltern experience, awareness of the representation of politics and a close attention to the politics of representation.

One element of this debate that surfaced in the late 1980s considered history in film. Prompted by movies such as *Reds* or *The Return of Martin Guerre*, and by the growing involvement of historians in advising film directors and scriptwriters, historians became concerned with the erosion of serious scholarship and the way filmic narratives distorted history. It struck some that there was a deficit of complexity that could be included in film compared with a scholarly book, but also, contrariwise, that film's superfluity of detail overwhelmed the proper focus of history. In *The American Historical Review*, Robert A. Rosenstone convened a forum on the subject in 1988. Exploring the issue with greater sympathy than most, and traversing mainstream feature film and documentary, Rosenstone acknowledges film's advantages (visual and aural) with respect to summoning verisimilitude and emotive effects.[103] Leaving aside the type of crass revisions that directors might make for the sake of spectacle or dramatic resolution, the question of 'accuracy' is never straightforward: fidelity to detail (say, the physical appearance of a protagonist) might be far less important than truth to the historical essence of the event or process depicted. Rosenstone goes as far as to wonder if the rise of celluloid history might be akin to the earlier displacement of Homerian epic by Herodotus and Thucydides.

Contributing to the forum, Hayden White unpicked some contradictions in the historians' debates, noting a replay of discussions over the historical novel. The easy binary of fiction/non-fiction rests, he argues, on an impossible foundation of 'representational literalness' which is unachievable in historical scholarship as much as in film. The anxiety

---

103 Robert A. Rosenstone, 'History in Images/History in Words: Reflections on the Possibility of Really Putting History on to Film', *The American Historical Review* 93:5 (1988): 1173–85. Rosenstone's essay also brings to attention works that stretch the documentary conventions: the film essay *Sans Soleil* (1982) by Chris Marker; Jill Godmilow's part-re-enacted reflexive documentary *Far from Poland* (1984) (she called it a 'drama-tary'); Brecht's epic theatre; Ousmane Sembène's *Ceddo* (1977); and *Quilombo* (1984/86) by Carlos Diegues, a Brazilian historical drama-meets-irrealism.

Short Autobiography (1971)

1

These pictures represent a contradiction between the art world and the third world.

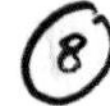

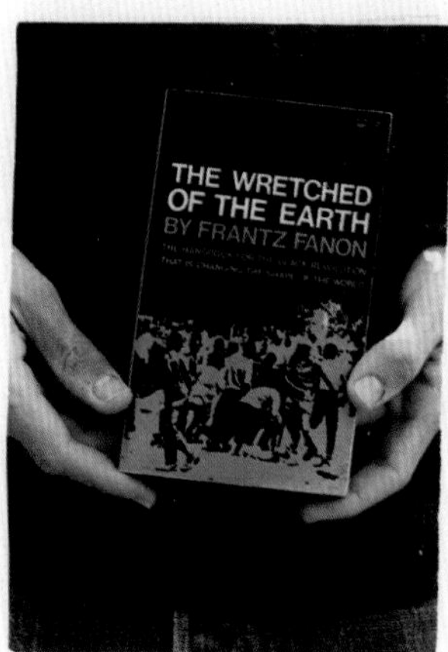

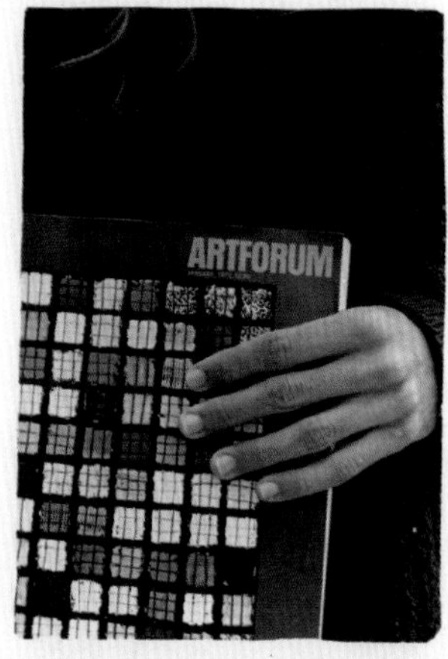

2

10

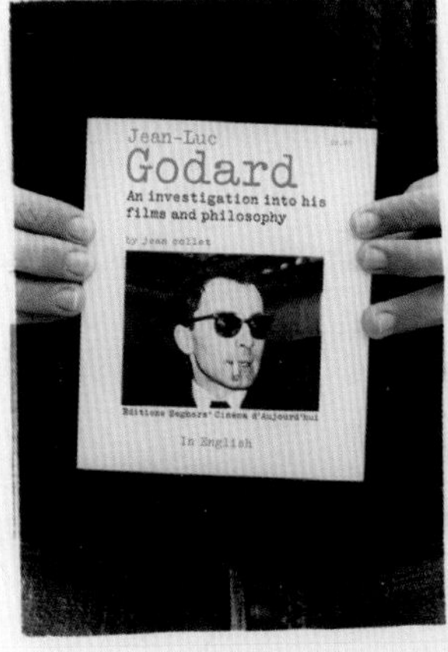

Godard and Mao in San Diego.

We're going to make a movie about the Republican National Convention. We're looking at Godard and reading Mao. I've got enough money to buy a camera.

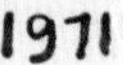

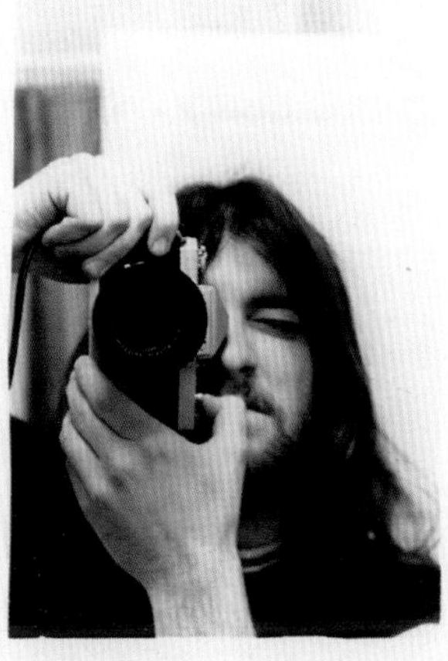

Box Car (1971)

3

<u>Box Car</u>

During a journey by freight train
from Santa Barbara to Los Angeles,
I made a photograph from an open
box car of a chemical company where
I had worked two years earlier.

December 1971

4

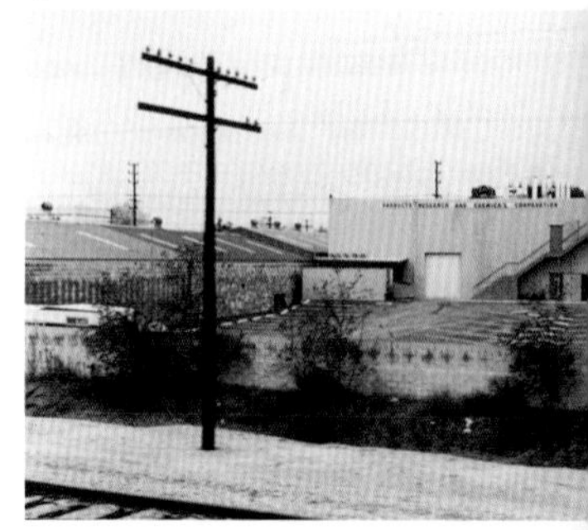

Meat Mass (1972)

5

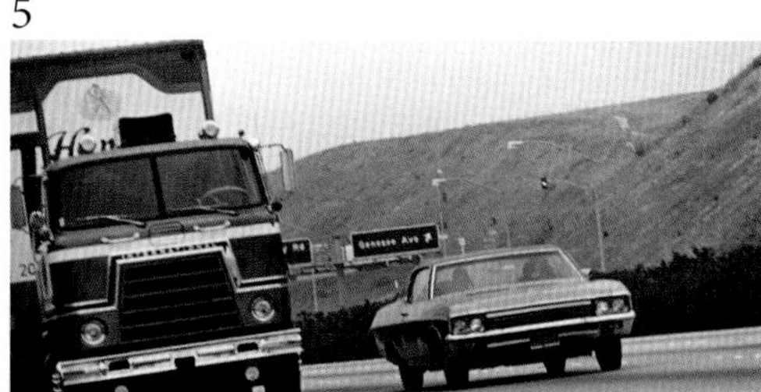

6

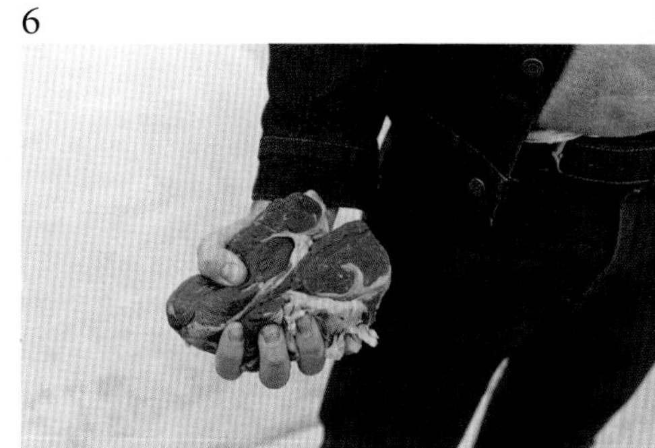

Two, three, many . . . (terrorism) (1972)

7

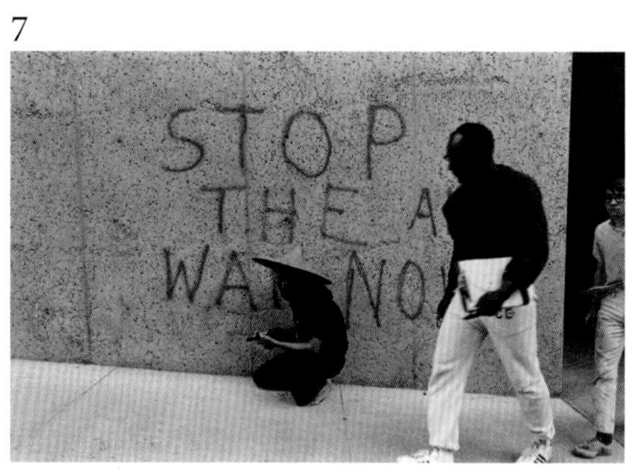

8

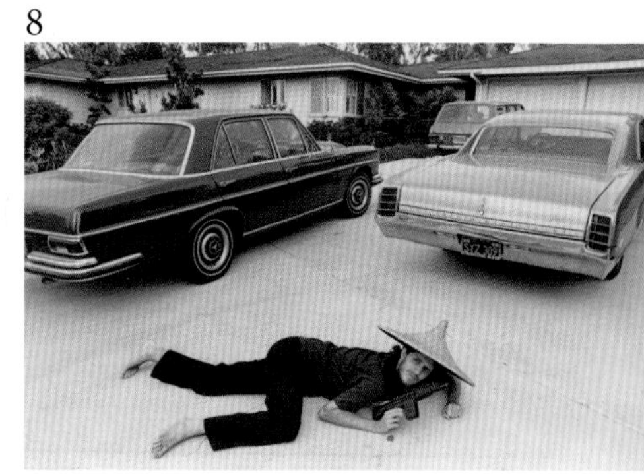

9

Lockheed today is a broadly based industrial complex, adding constantly to our skills in translating discoveries of science into advanced products, systems, and services for human progress and national defense. Our productive abilities are rooted in decades of experience. In the words of chairman Dan Haughton: "We'd rather be advancing the state of the art than standing still. Our competence has kept us in the forefront of the industry.... I know that at Lockheed our own eyes are on the future, and our efforts are in large part directed toward realizing it fully."

Days of Trial and Triumph: A Pictorial History of Lockheed, 1969

10

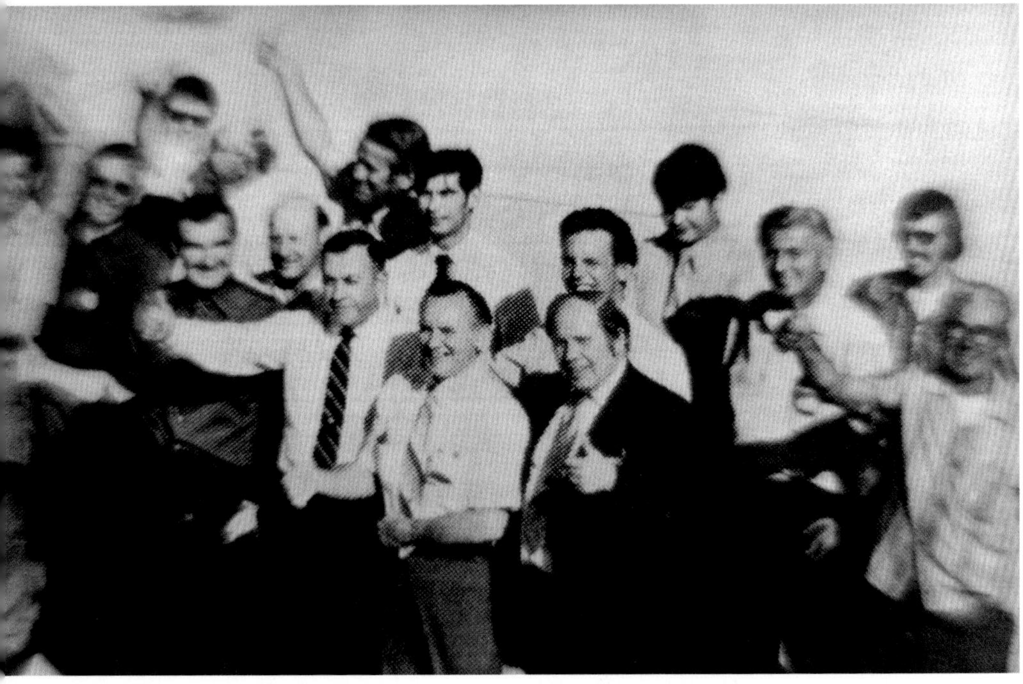

11

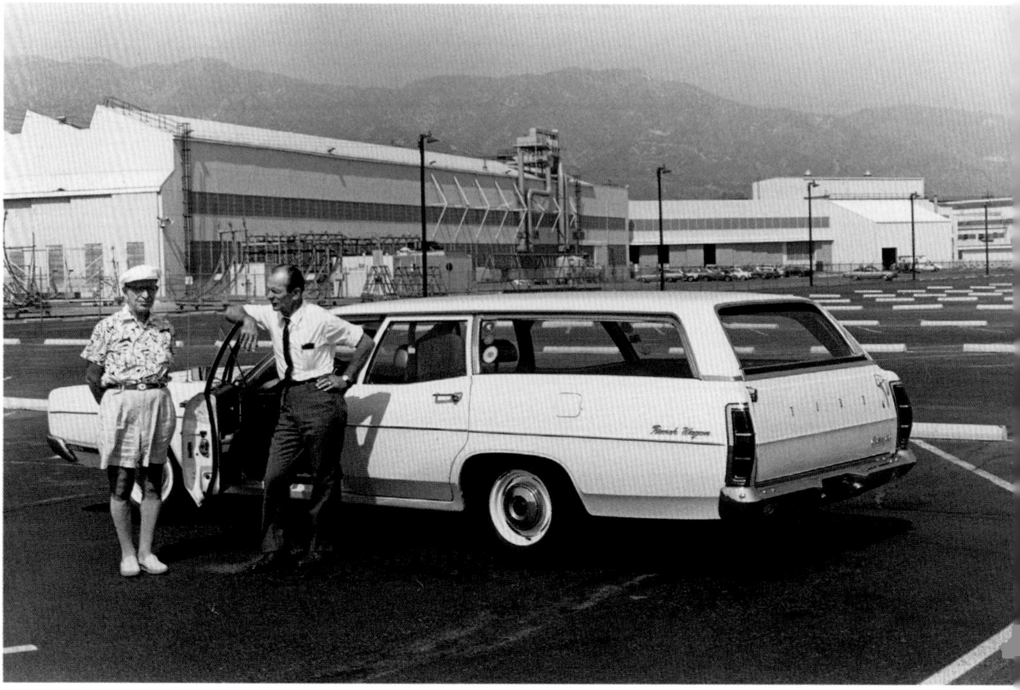

12

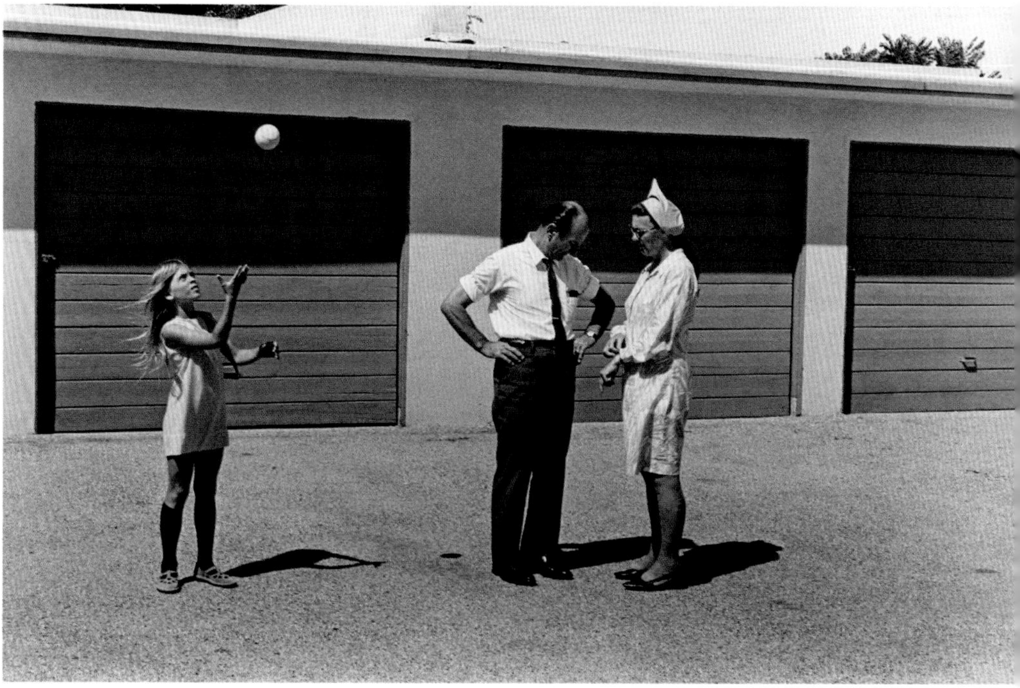

3

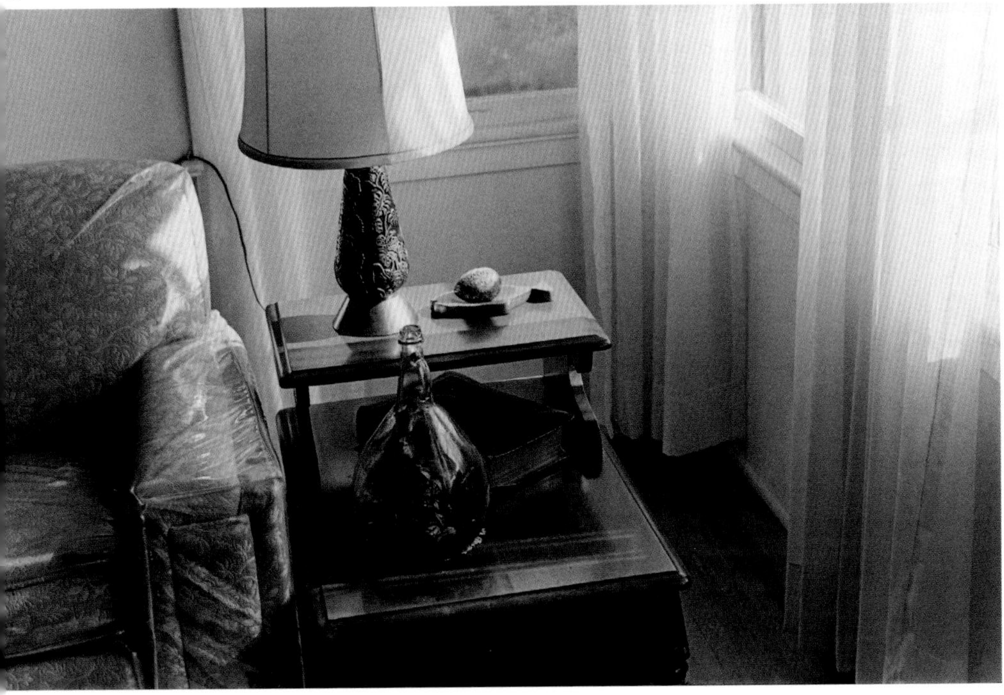

14

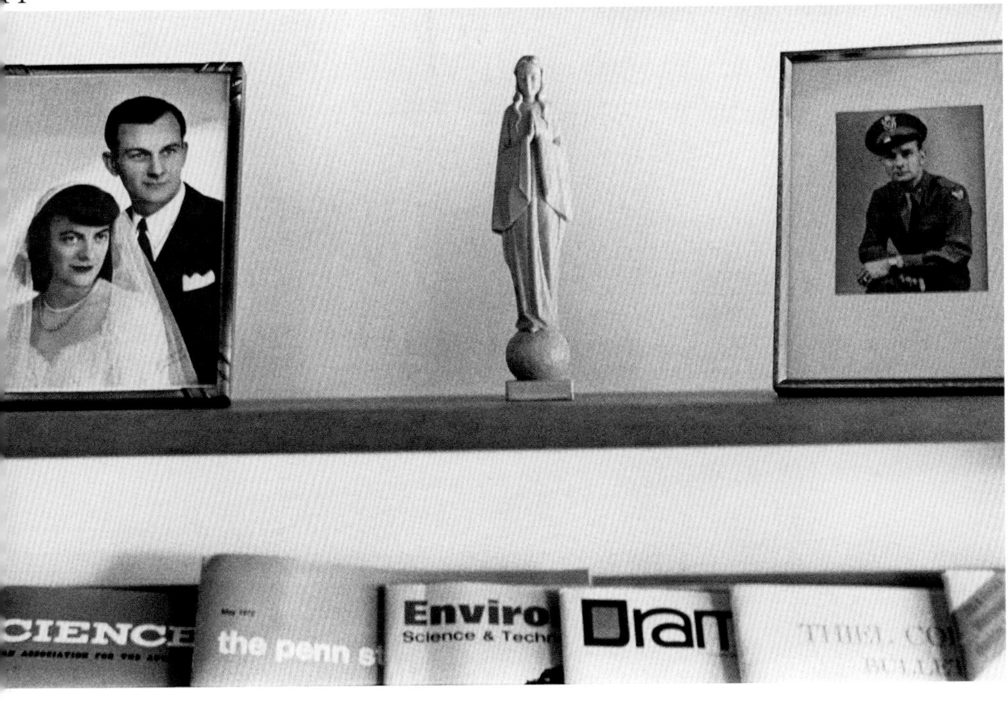

Aerospace Folktales (cont.)

15

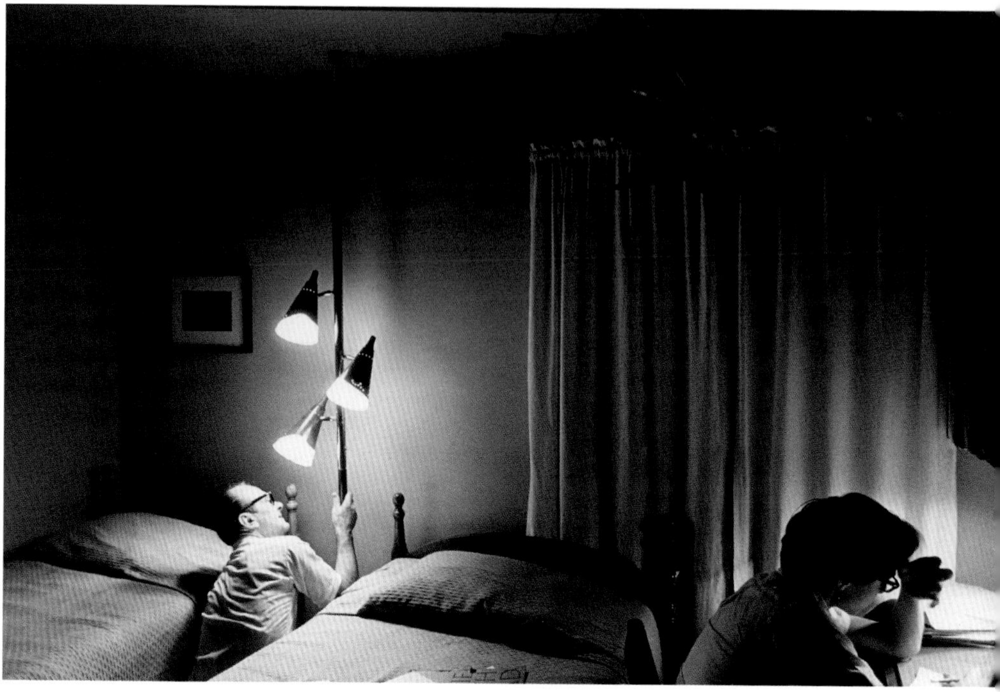

16

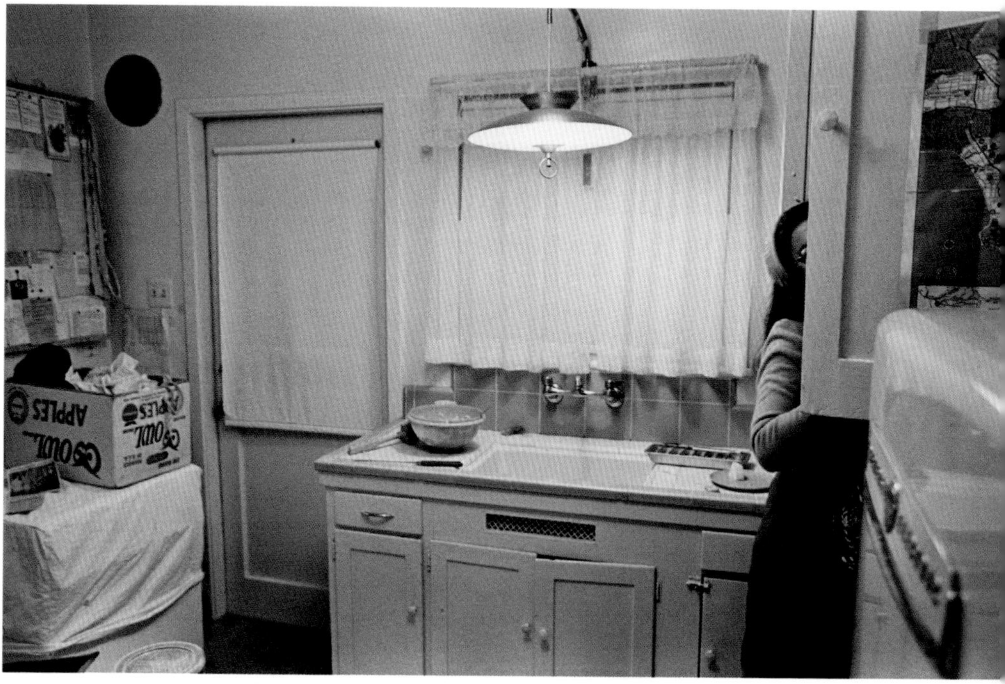

17

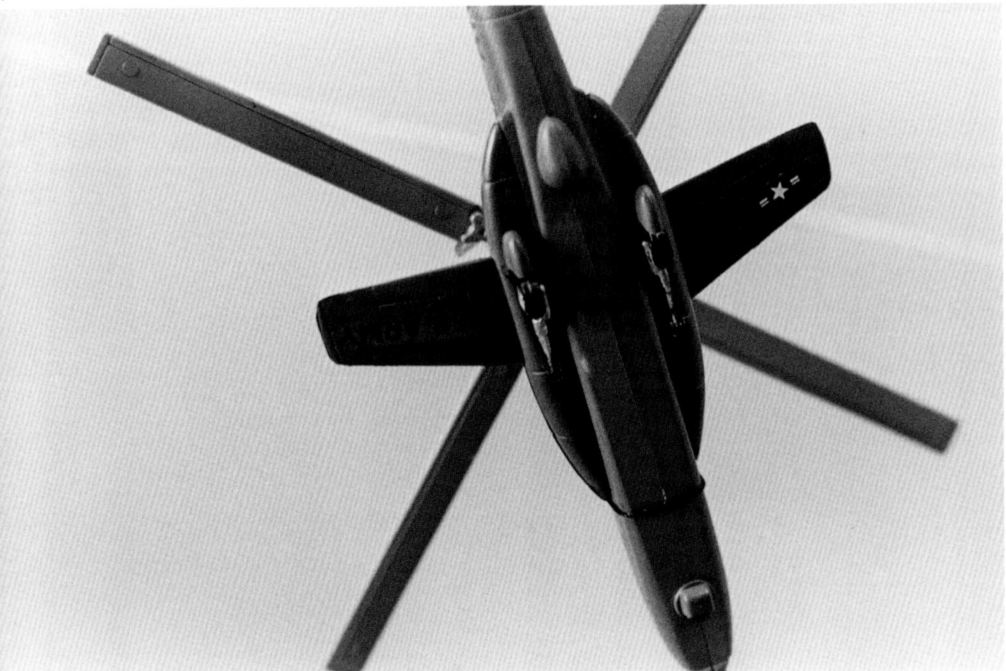

18

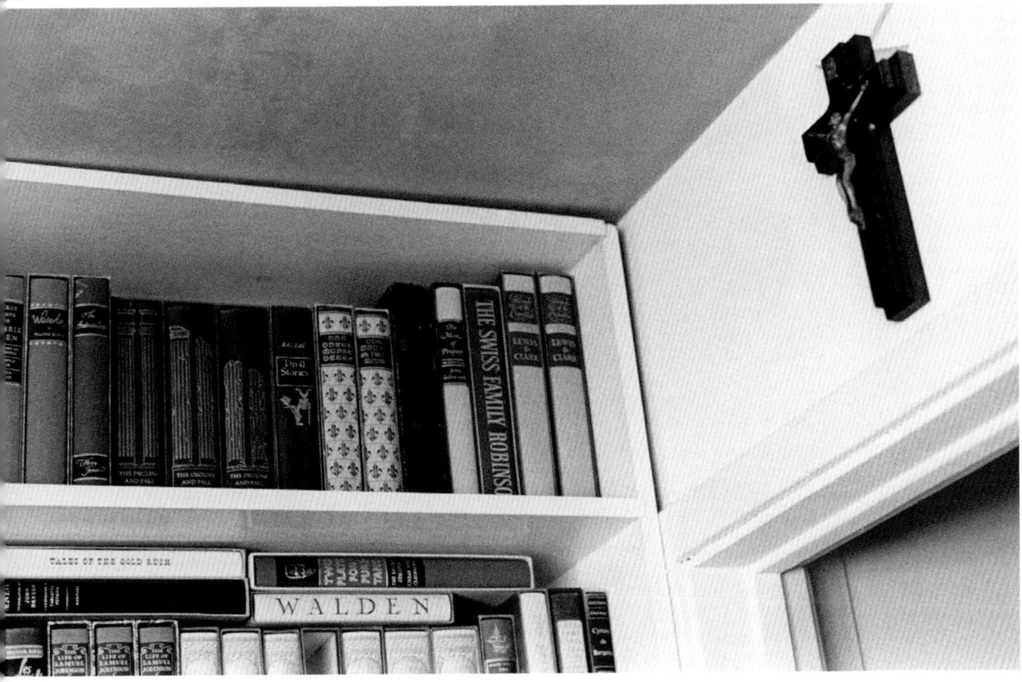

19

QUO VADIS?
Grimm's FAIRY TALES
Grimm's FAIRY TALES
JOSEPH CONRAD · THE NIGGER OF THE NARCISSUS
The Effects of NUCLEAR WEAPONS
Benito Cereno
Billy Budd

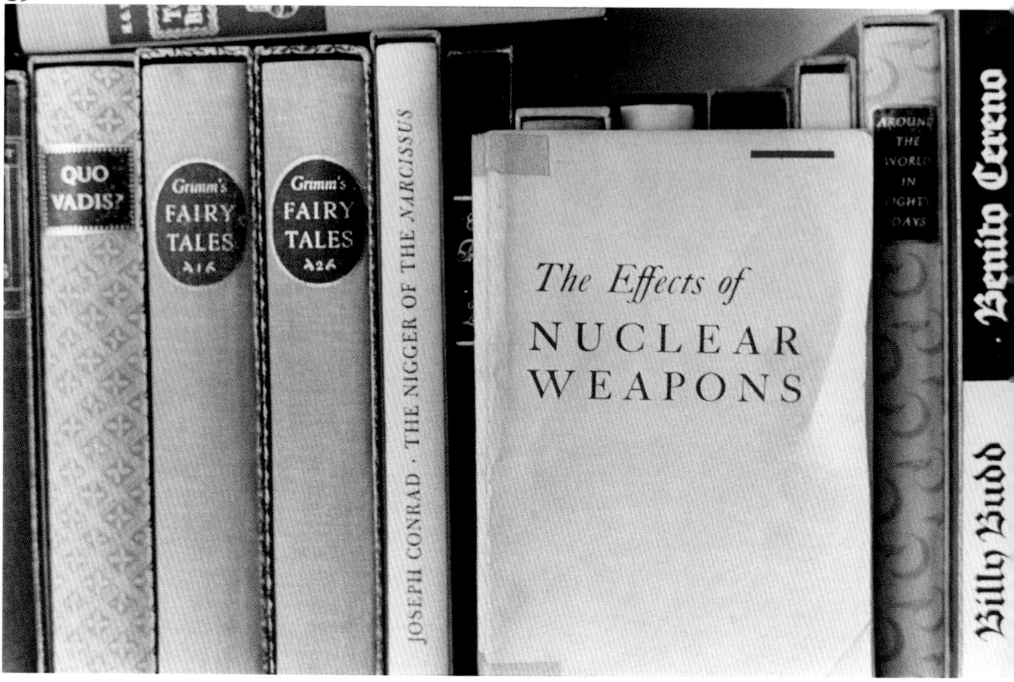

20

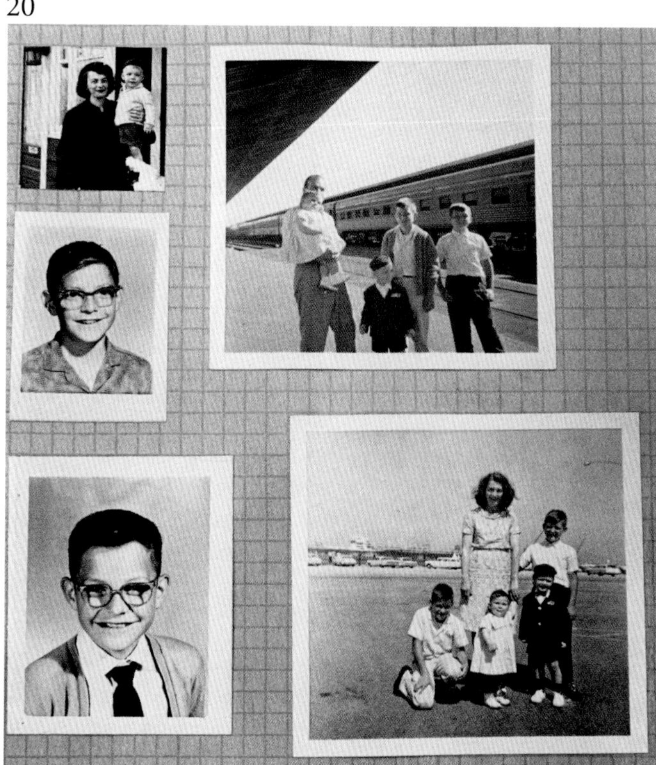

This Ain't China: A Photonovel (1974)

21

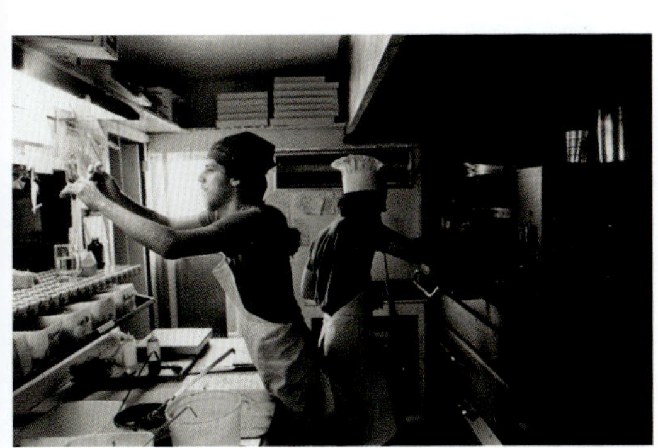

22

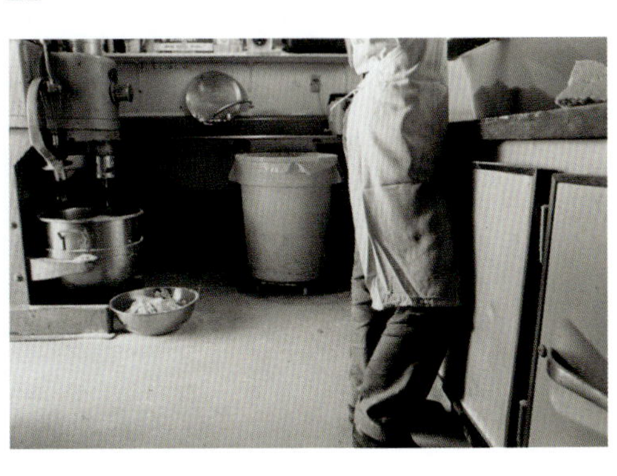

23

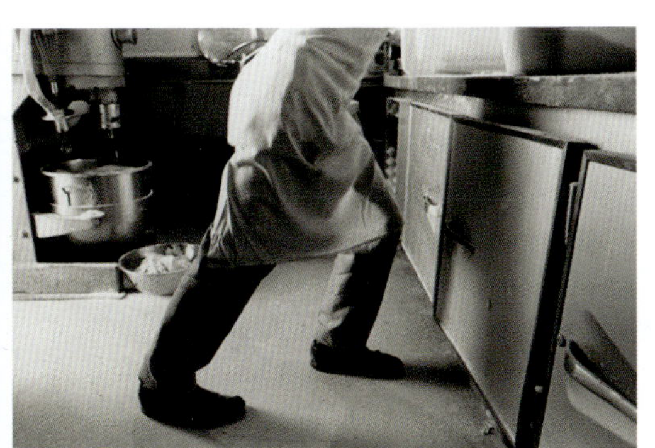

24

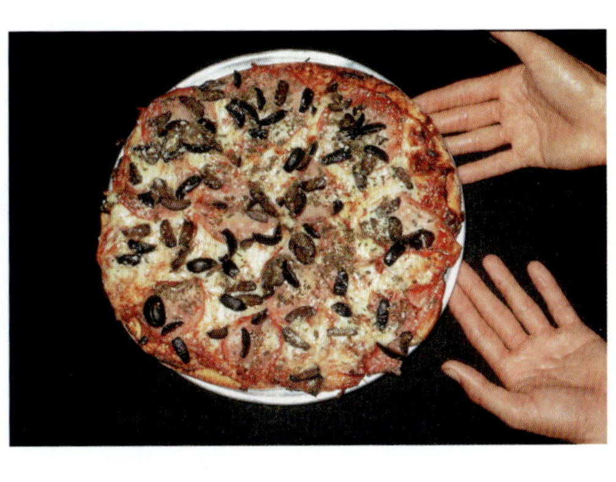

25

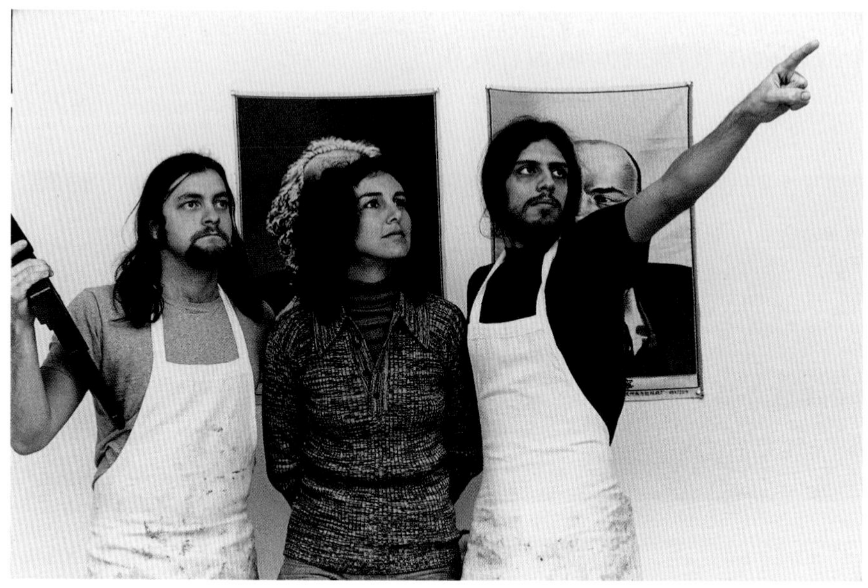

26

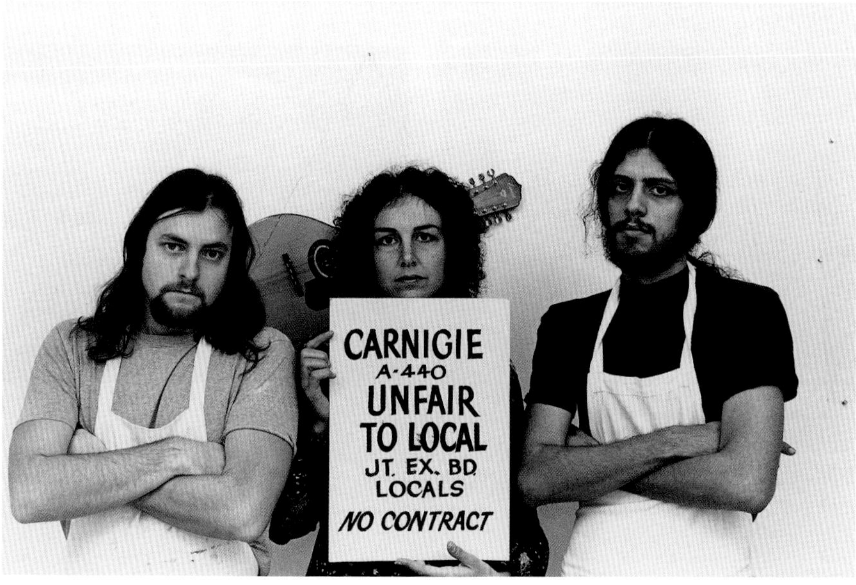

California Stories: Attempts to correlate class with the elevation of the main harbor channel (San Pedro, July 1975) (1975/2011)

27

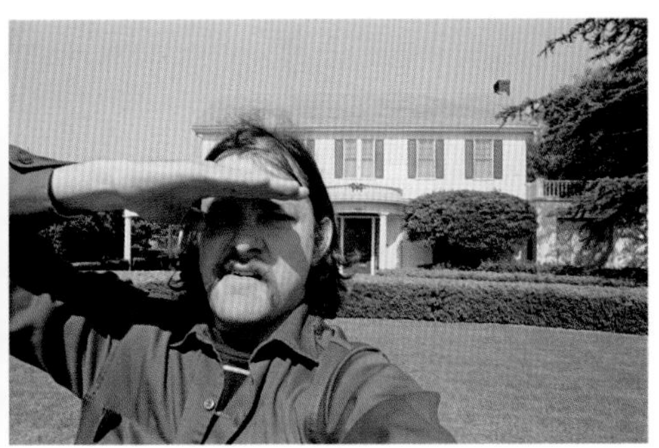

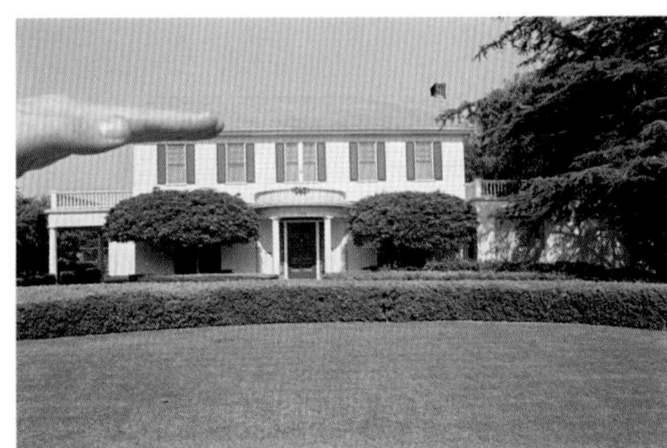

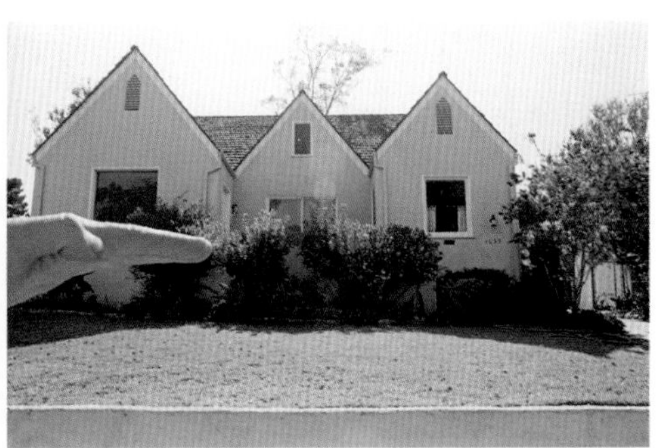

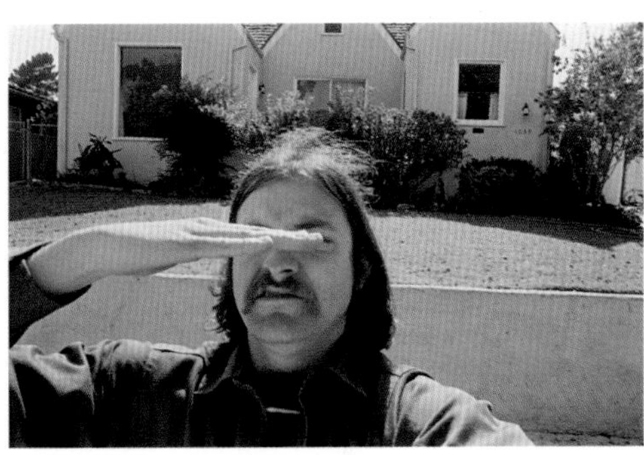

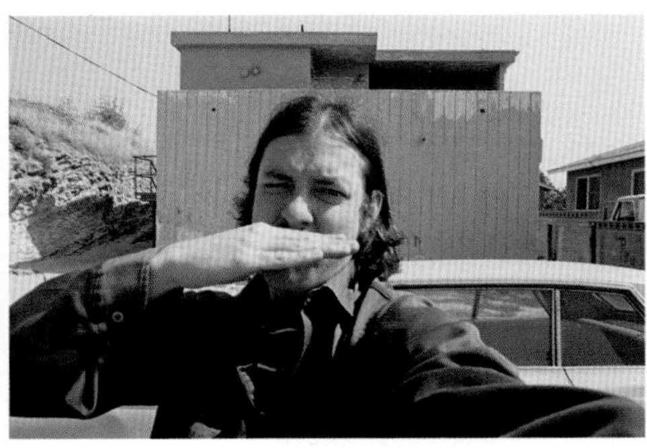

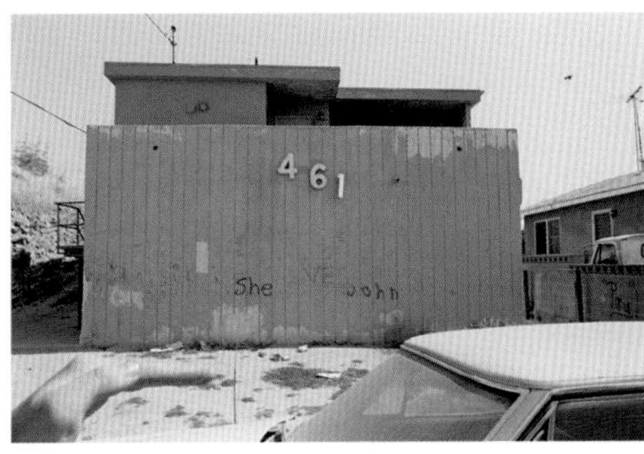

Sketch for a Geography Lesson (1983)

28

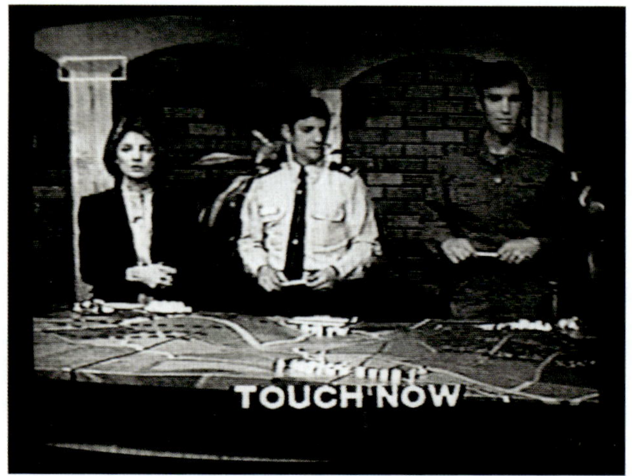

29

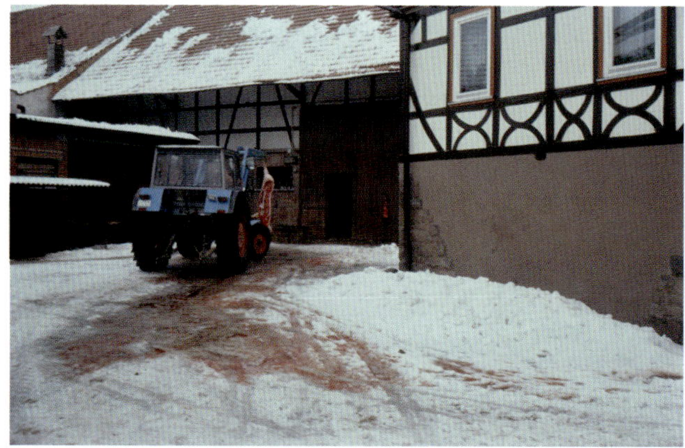

30

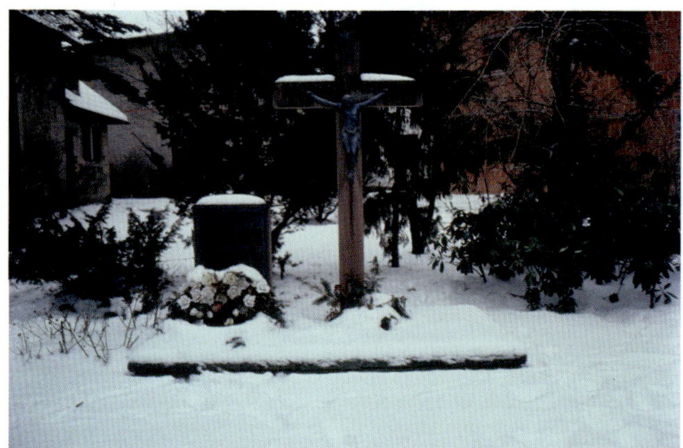

31

icht am Metallgitter oder Drahtzau
egt die Landesgrenze

32

U.S. ARMY
KEEP OUT
U.S. ARMEE
ZUTRITT VERBOTEN

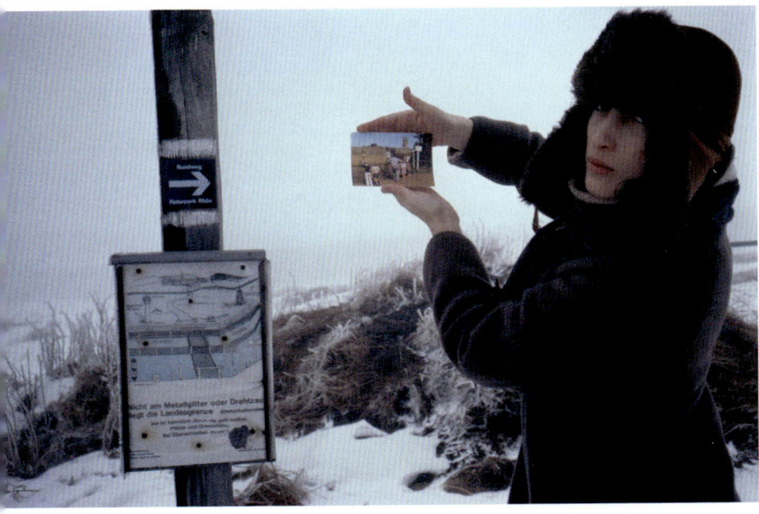

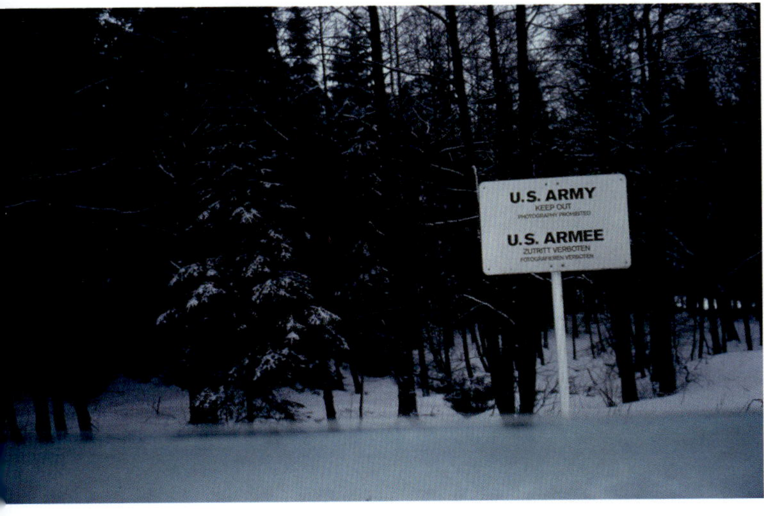

33

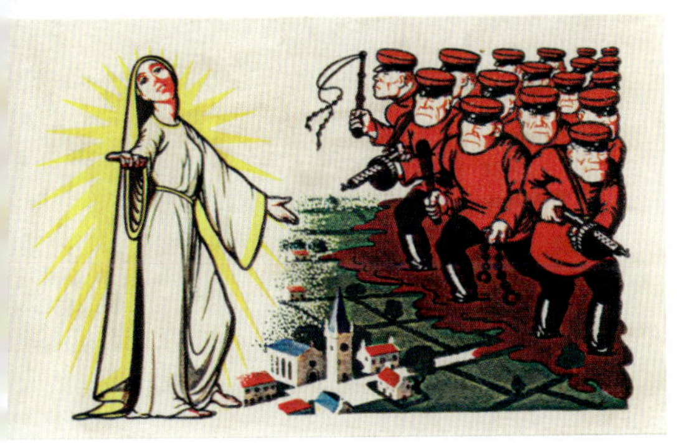

34

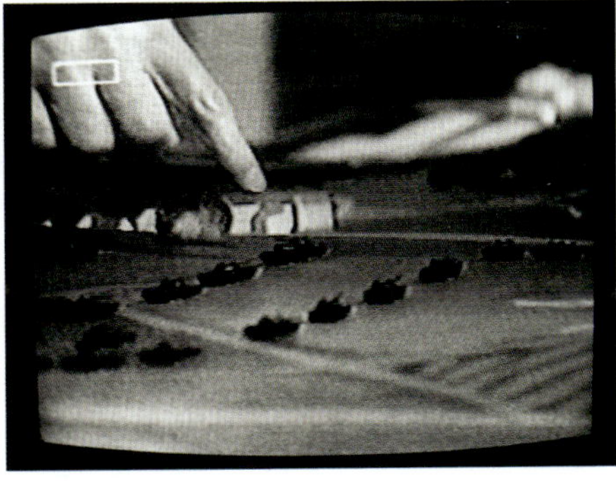

Geography Lesson: Canadian Notes (1987)

35

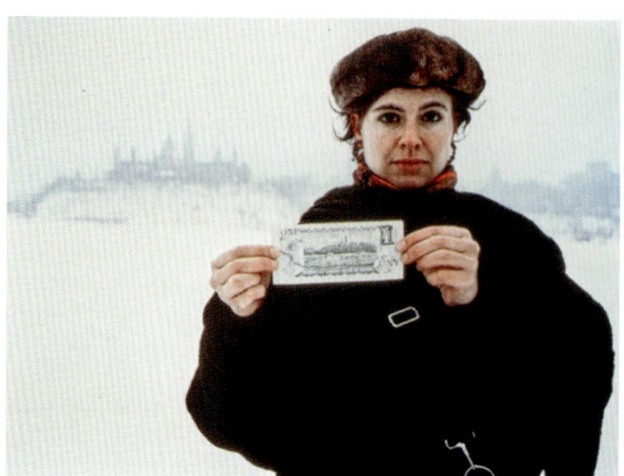

36

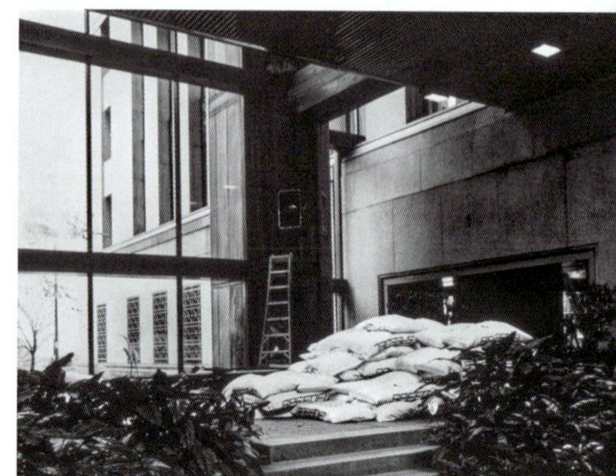

37

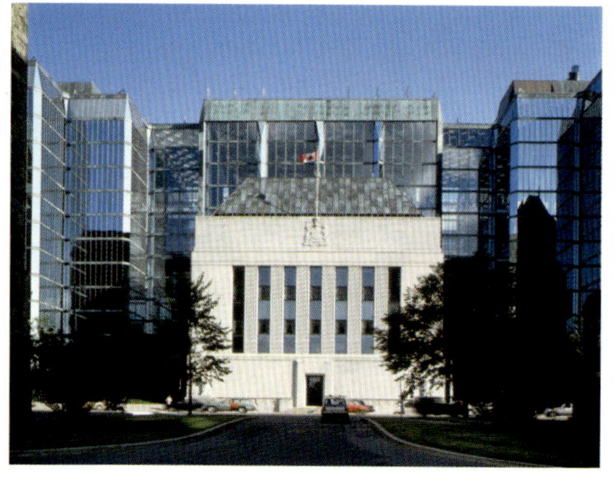

38

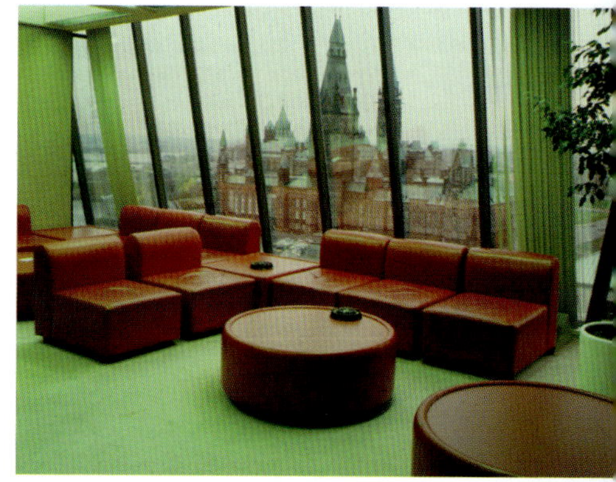

39

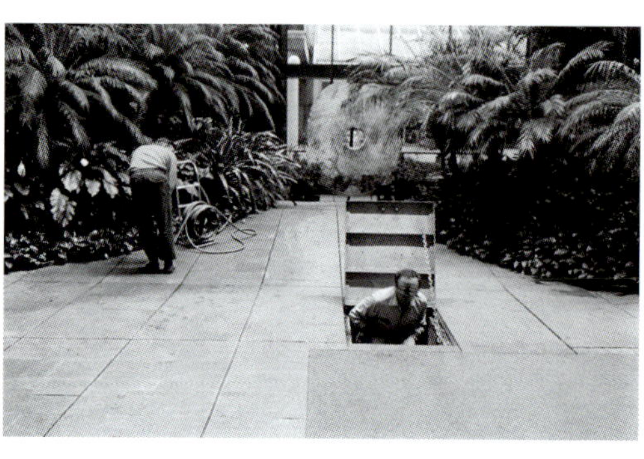

40

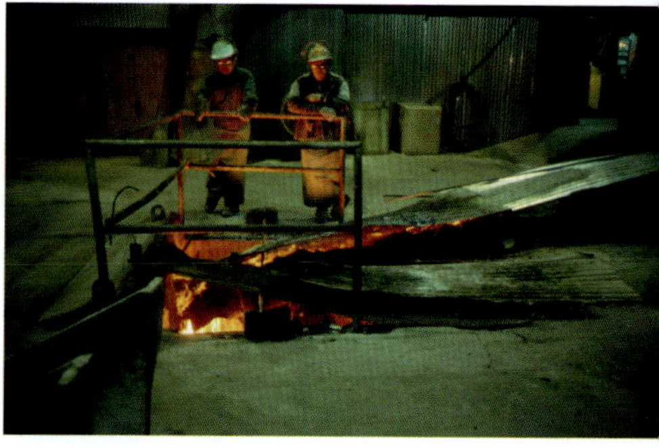

41

42

HANDS OFF
BRITISH
NATIONAL UNION
OF MINEWORKERS!
PRESIDENT

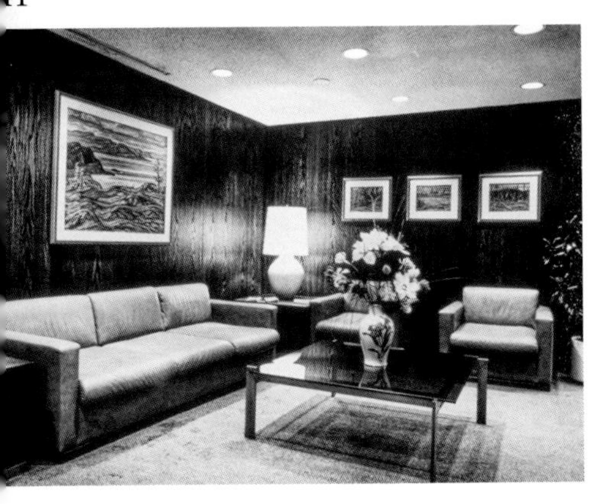

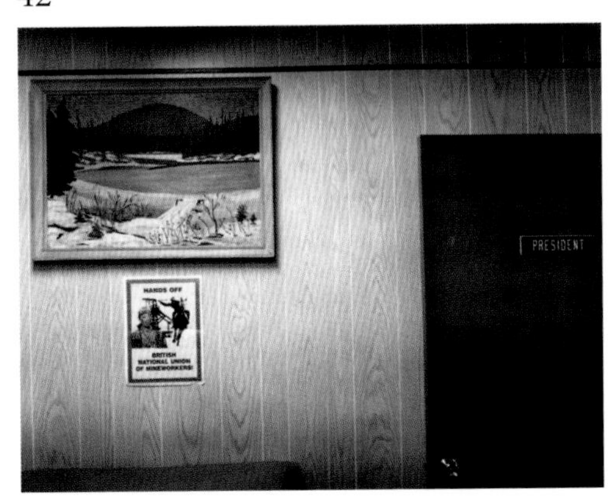

43

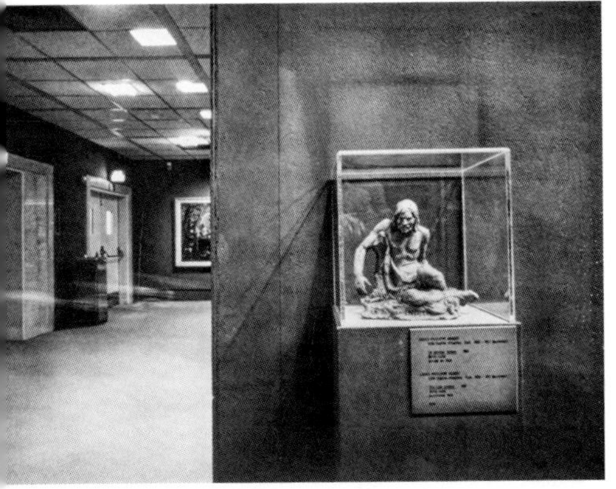

44

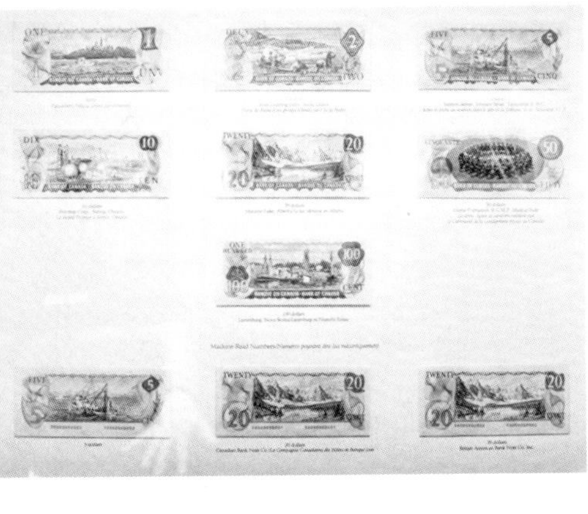

Geography Lesson: Canadian Notes (cont.)

45

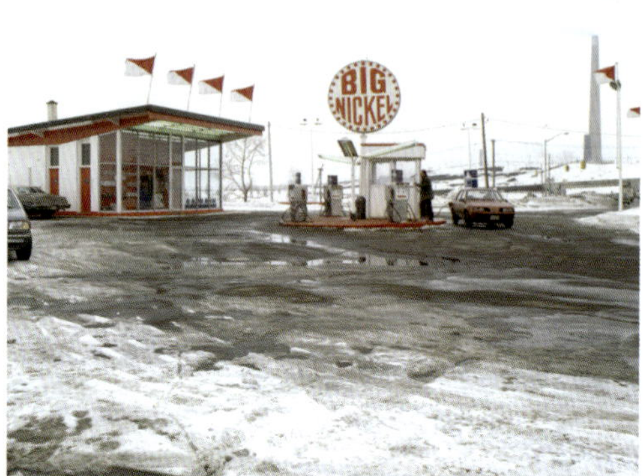

46

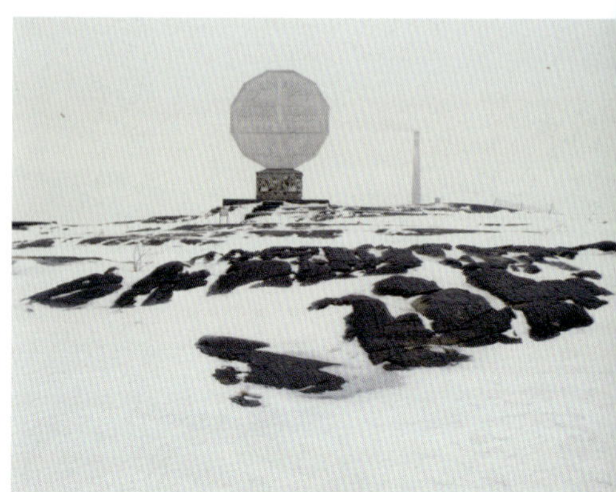

47

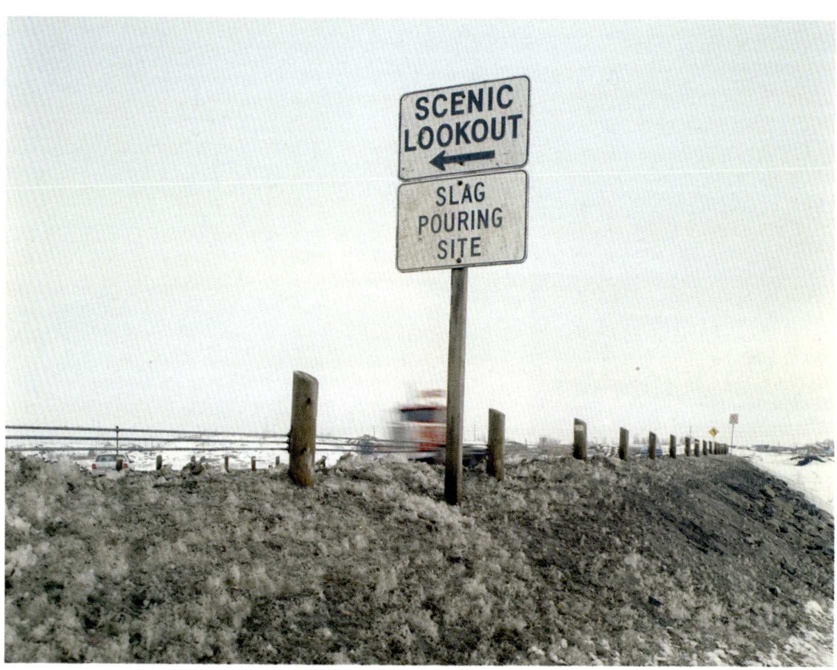

Fish Story (1995)

48

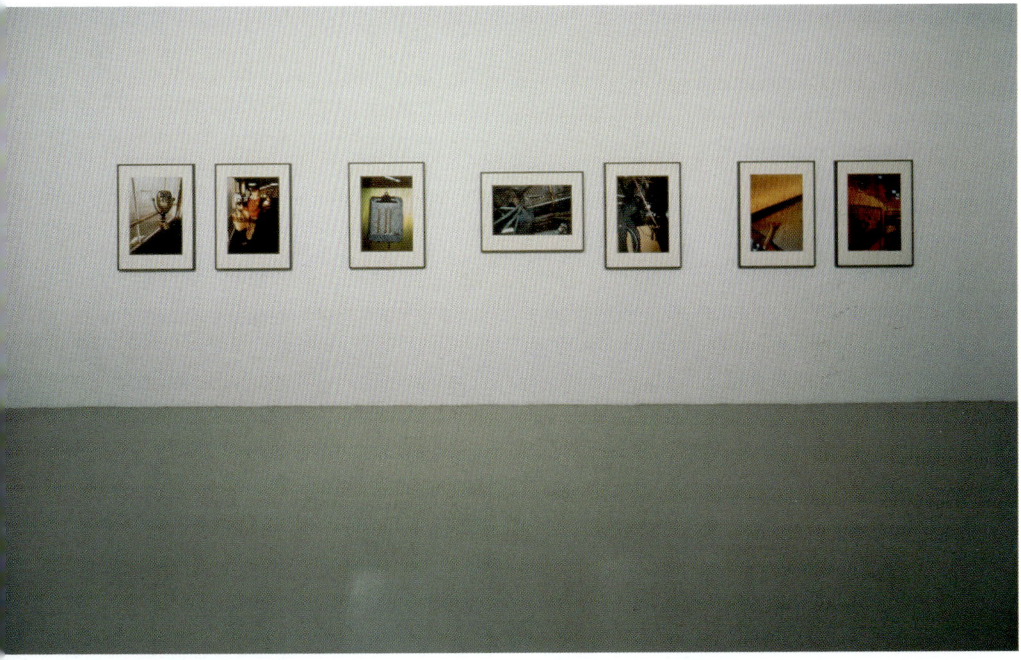

49

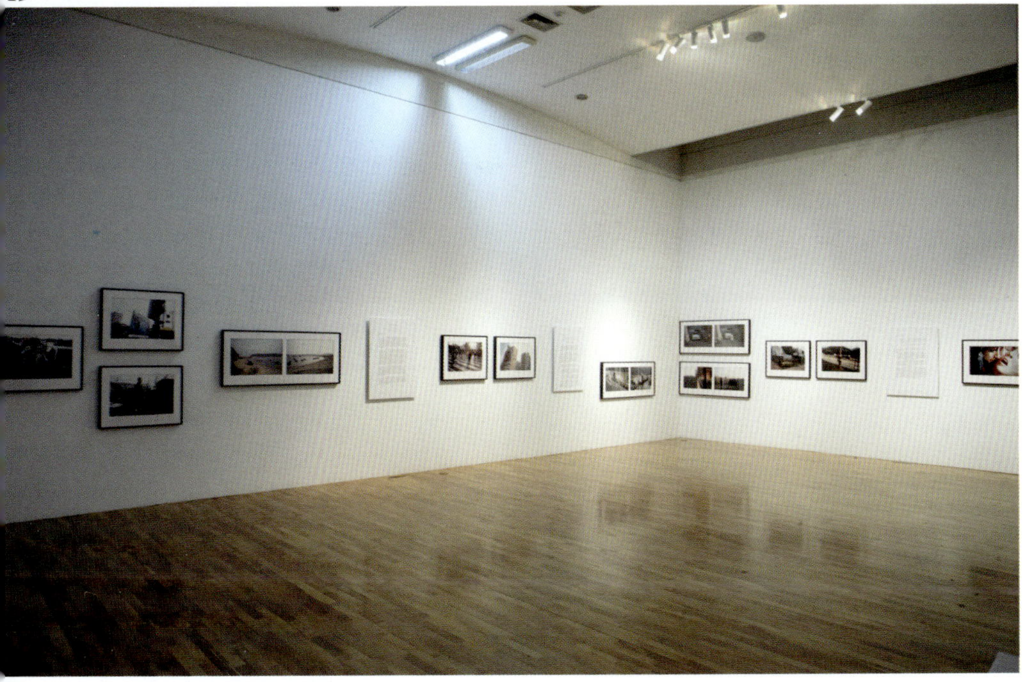

Fish Story (cont.)

50 (*Fish Story* plate #1)

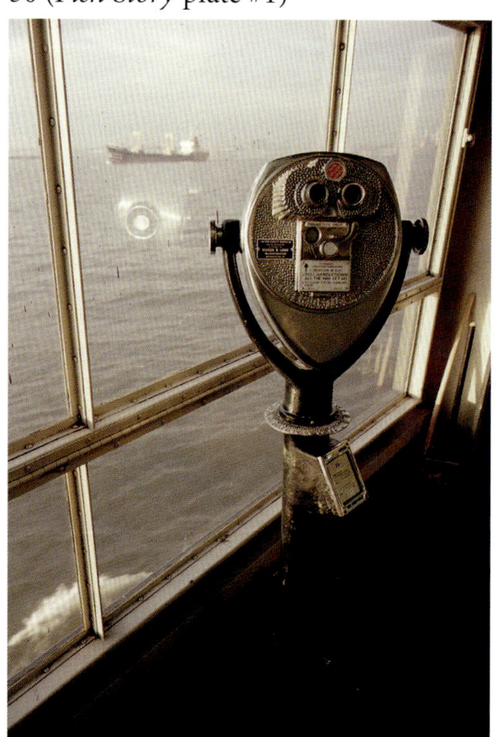

51 (#2)

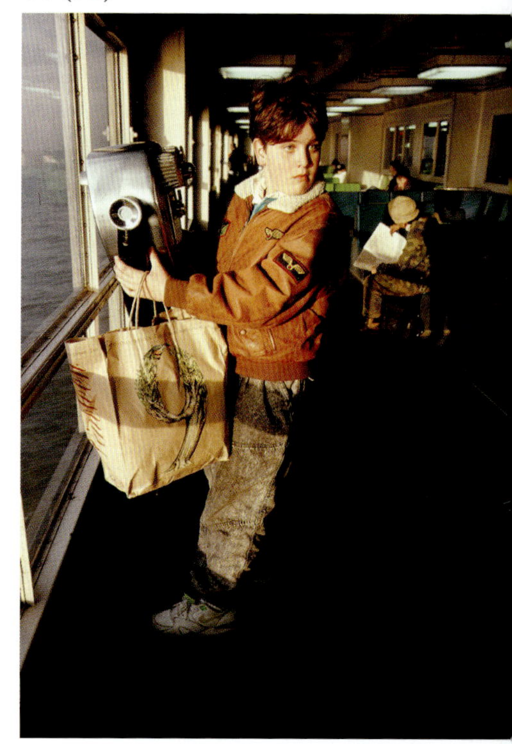

52 (#3)

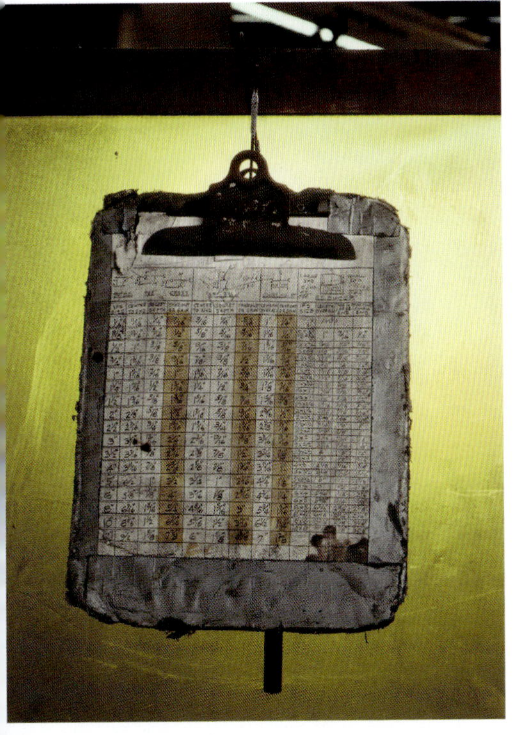

53 (#5)

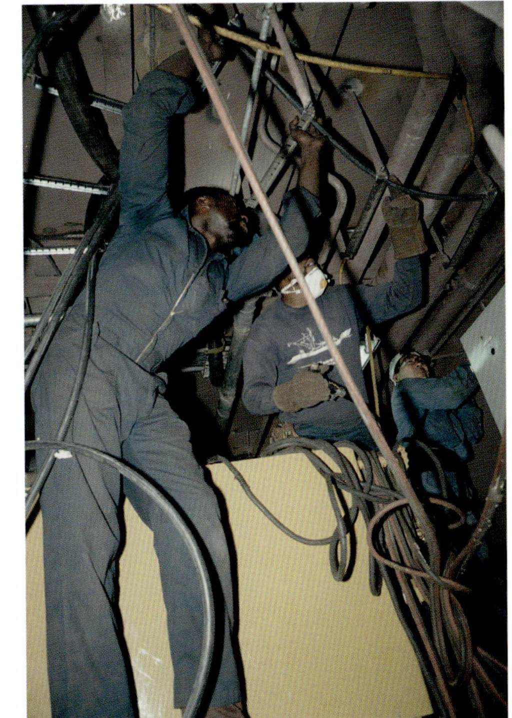

54 (#6)

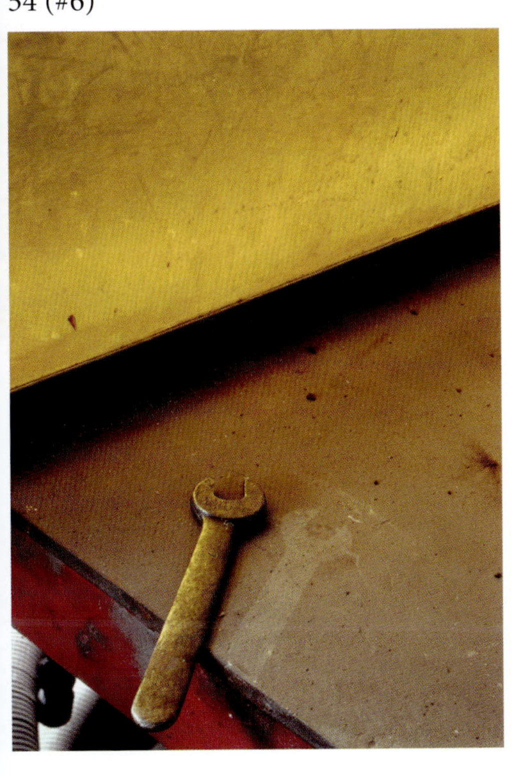

55 (#7)

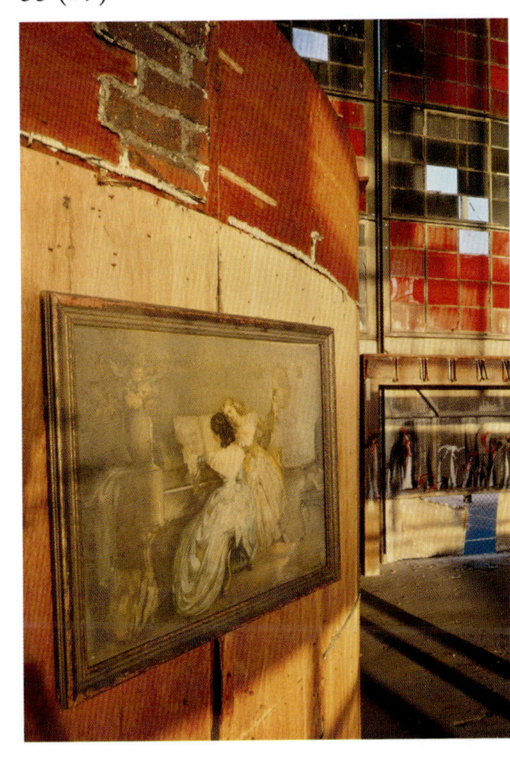

Fish Story (cont.)

56 (#8)

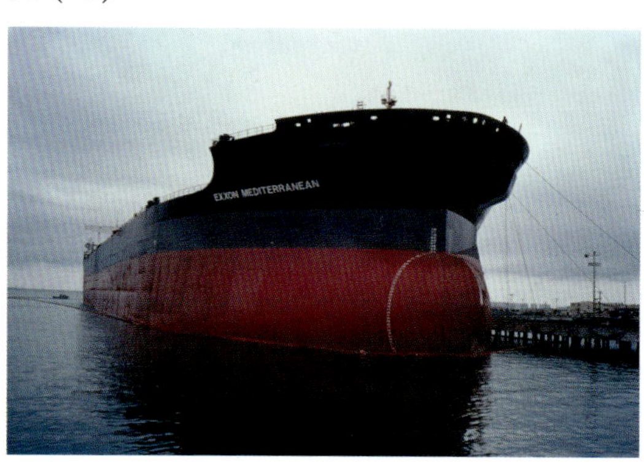

57 (#9)

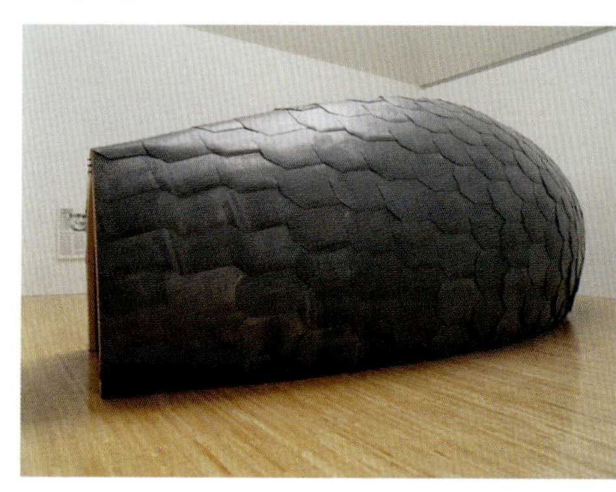

58 (#10)

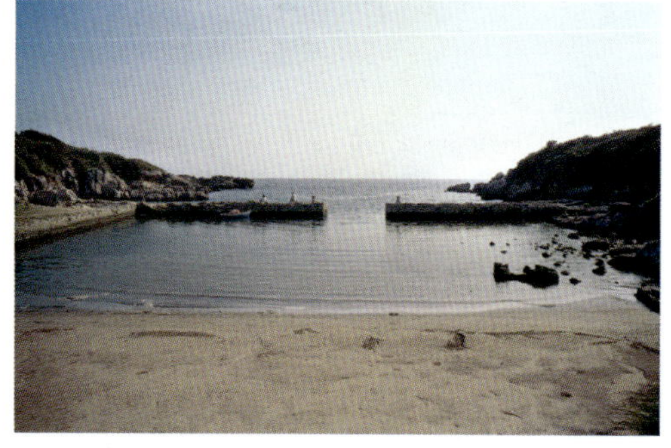

59 (#11)

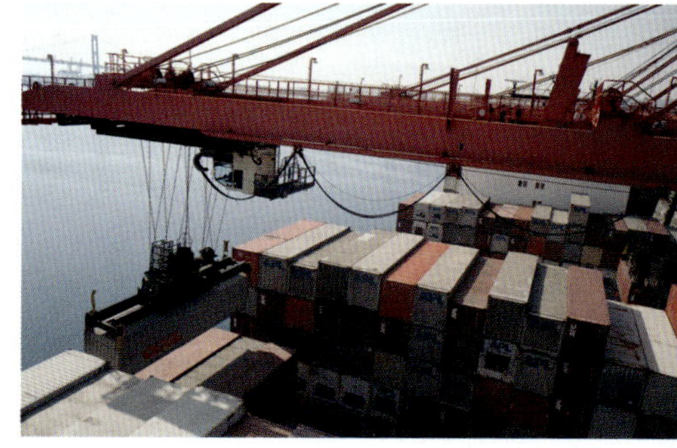

0 (#12)

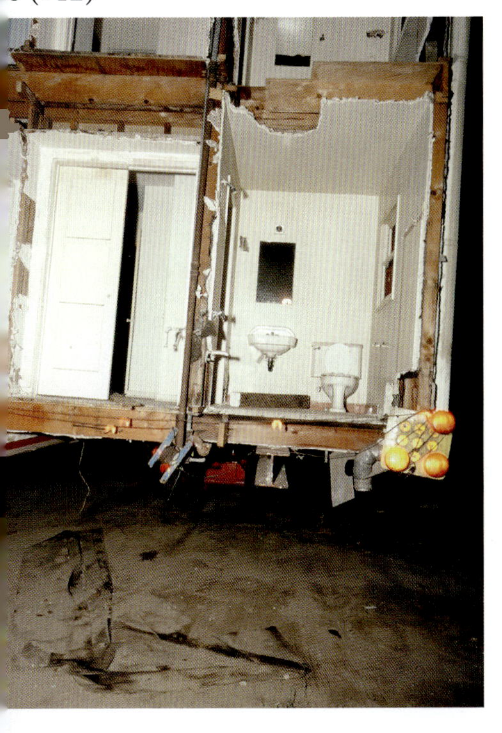

61 (#14)

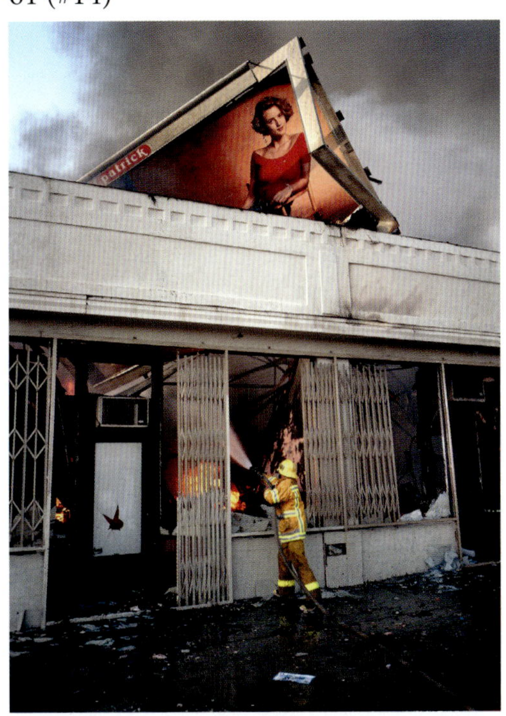

2 (#15)

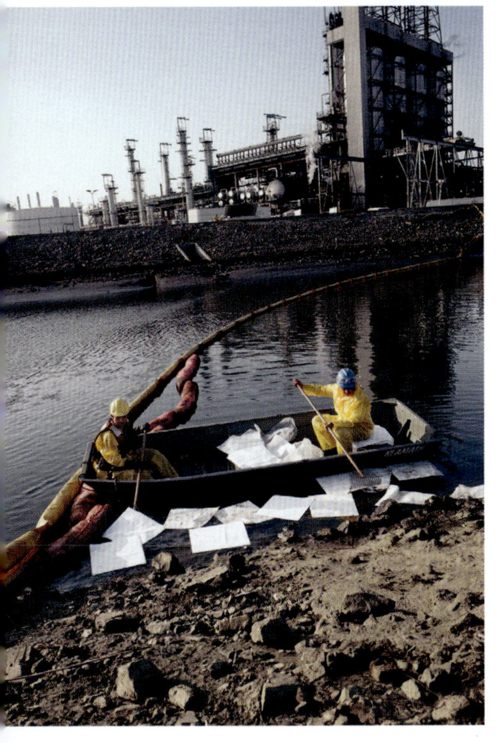

63 (#17)

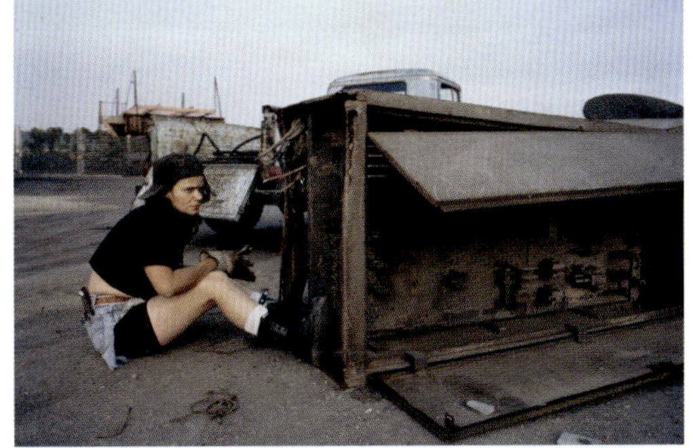

Fish Story (cont.)

Loaves and Fishes

64 (#23)

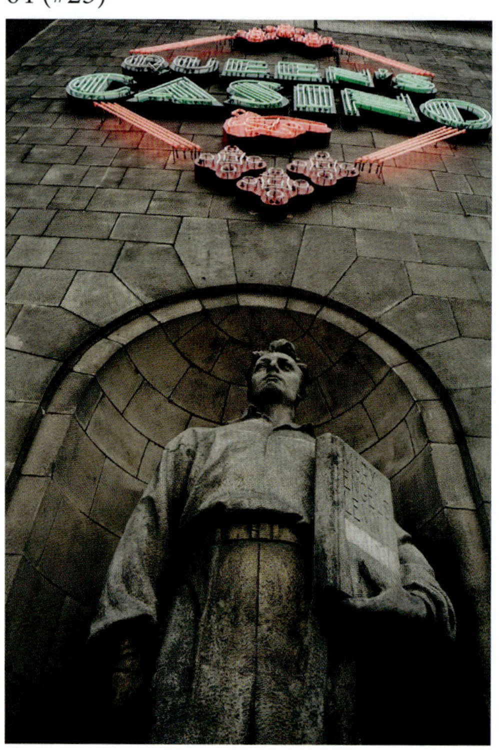

65 (#24)

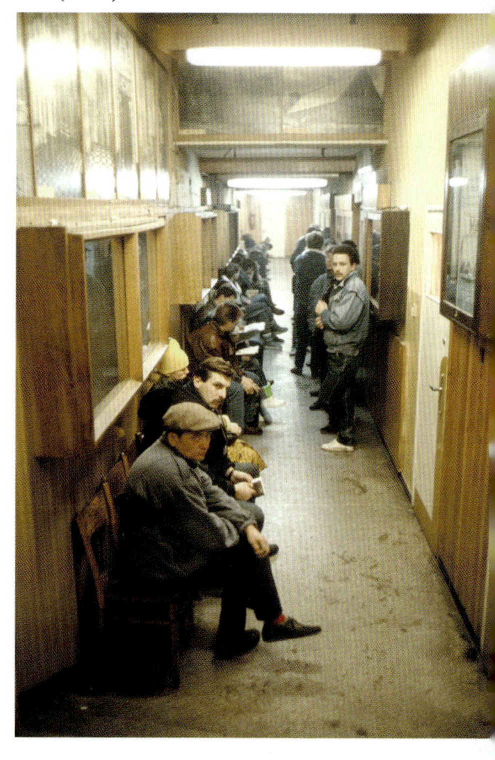

Middle Passage

6 (#27)

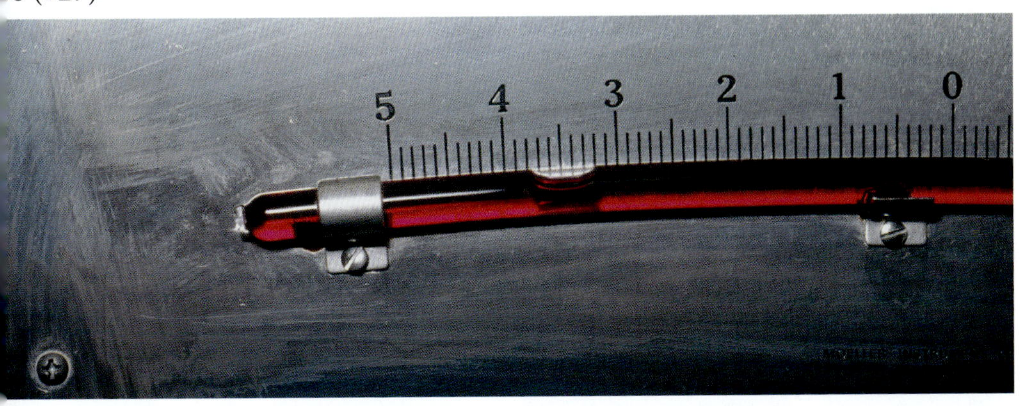

7 (#28)

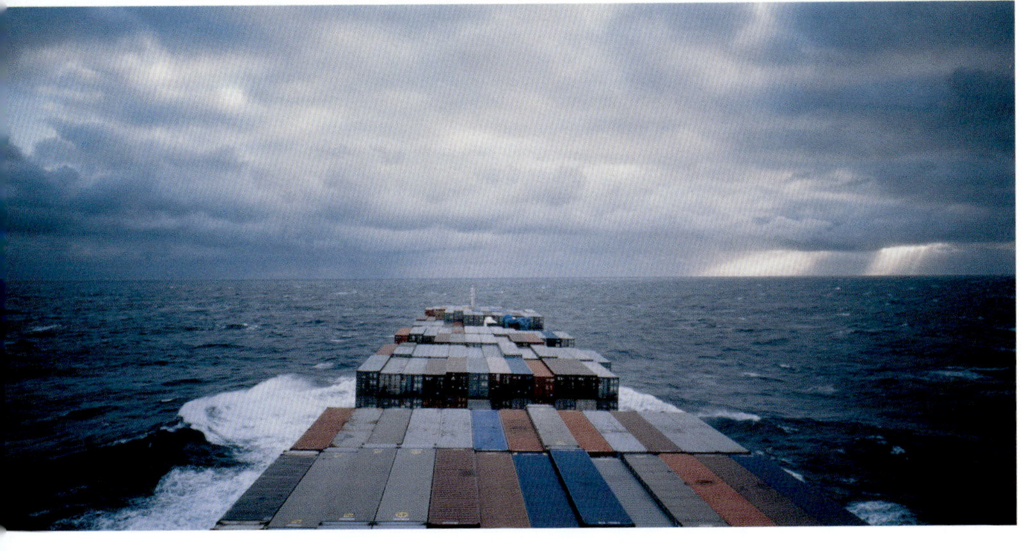

Fish Story (cont.)

Middle Passage (cont.)

68 (#29)

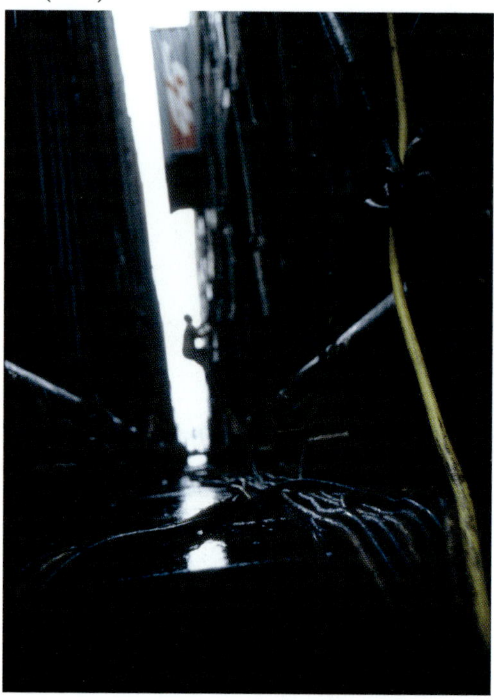

69 (#30)

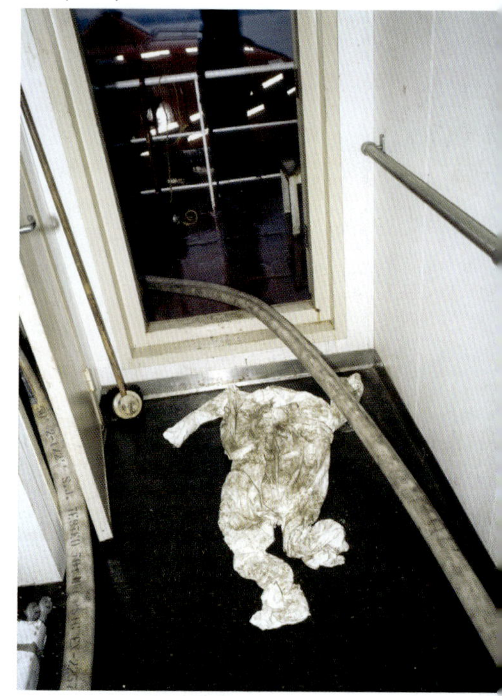

70 (#31)

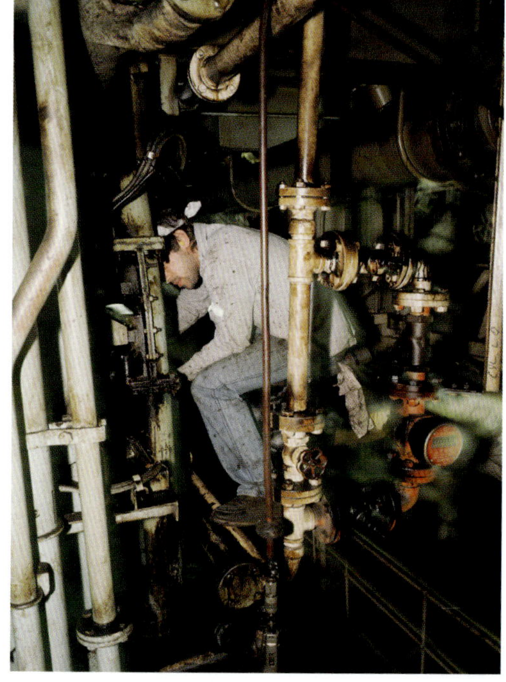

Fish Story (cont.)

Middle Passage (cont.)

71 (#37)

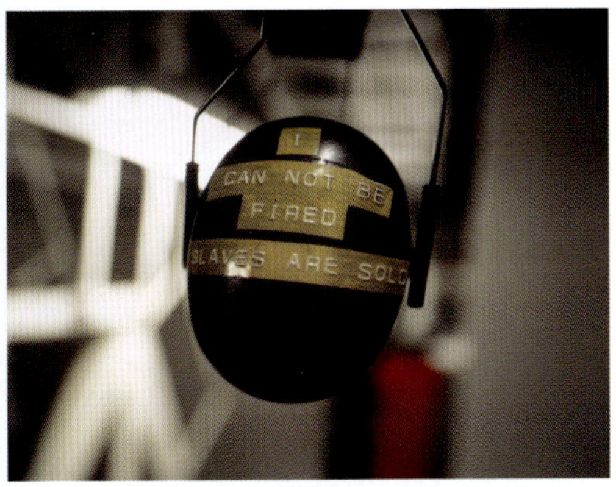

72 (#38)

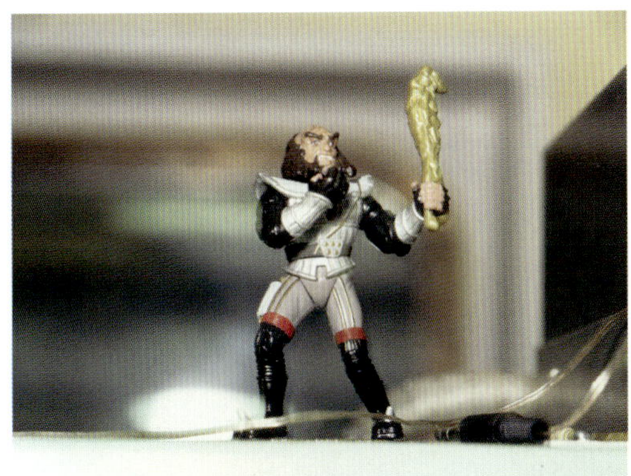

73 (#42)

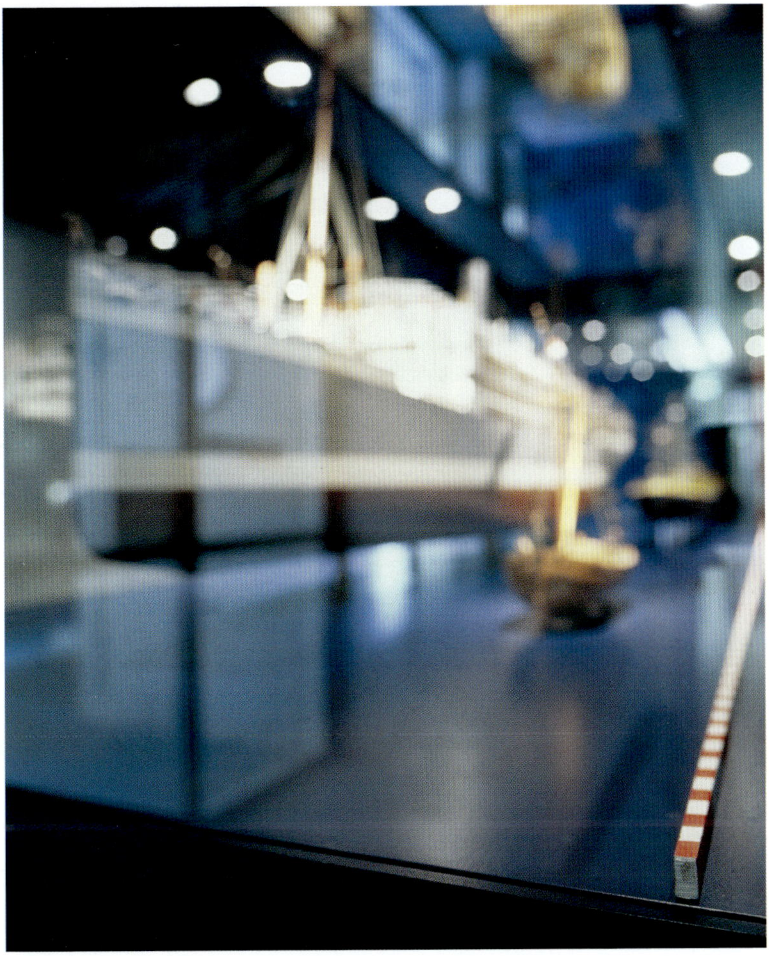

Fish Story (cont.)

Seventy in Seven

74 (#54)

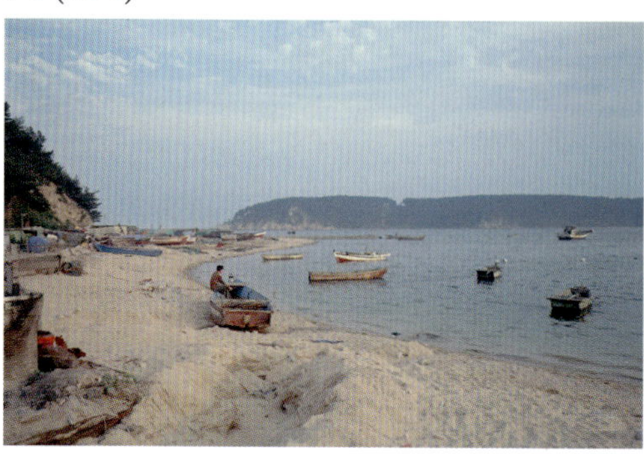

75 (#55)

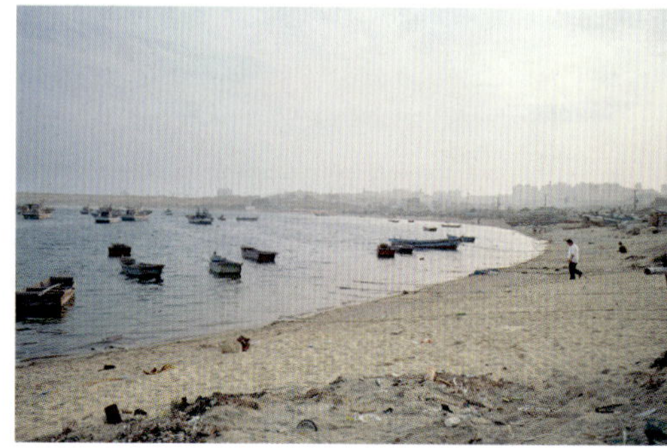

76 (#61)

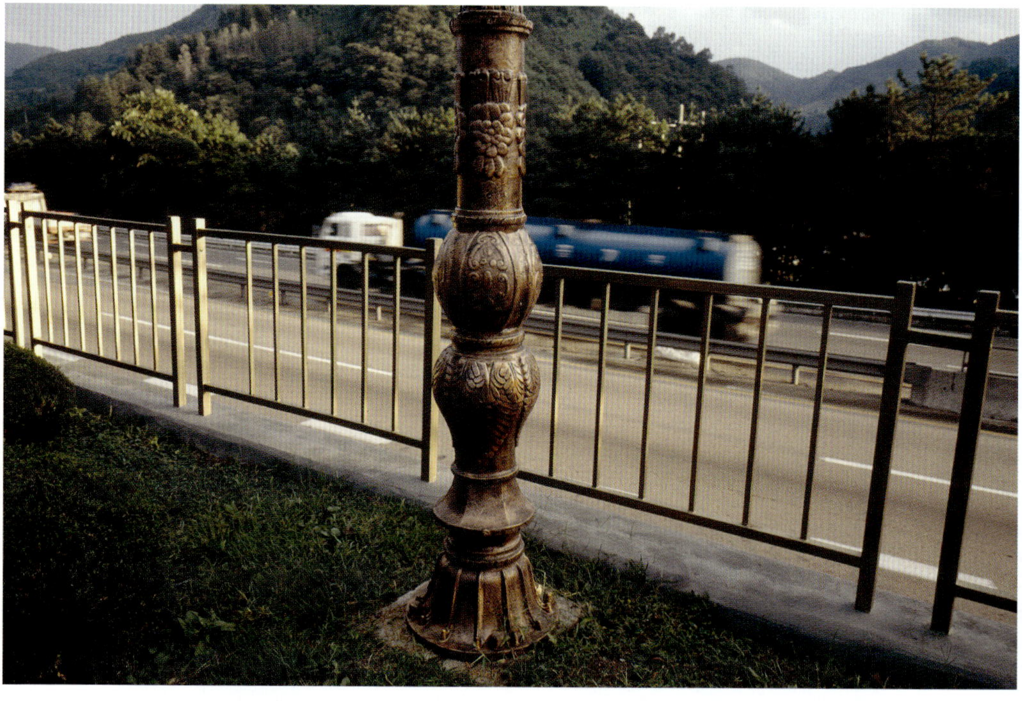

Message in a Bottle

77 (#64)

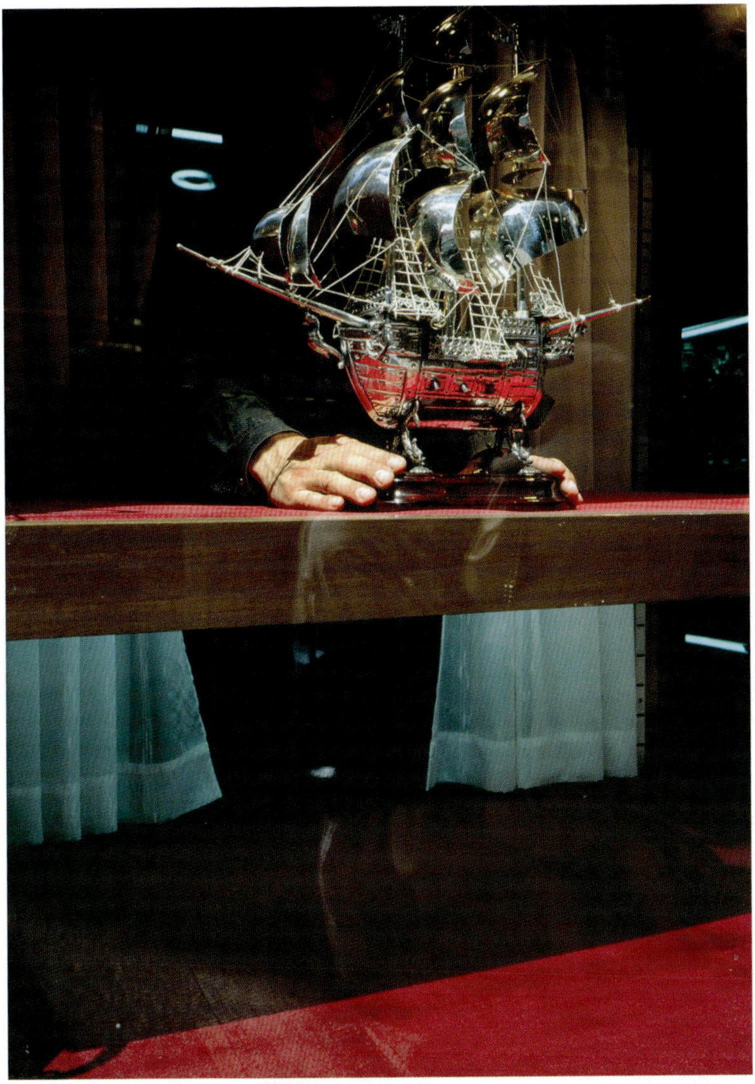

78 (#65)

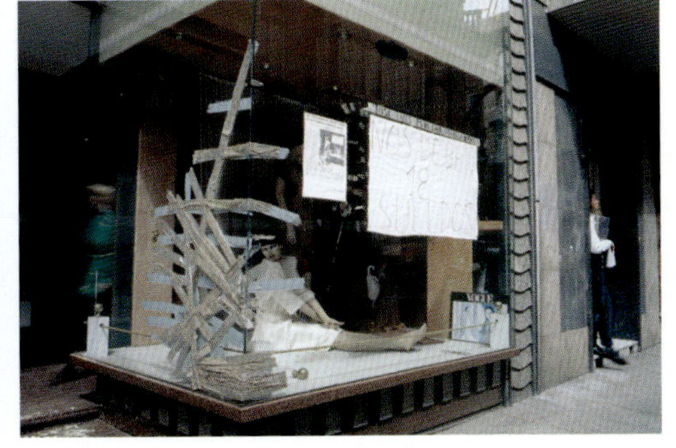

79 (#68)

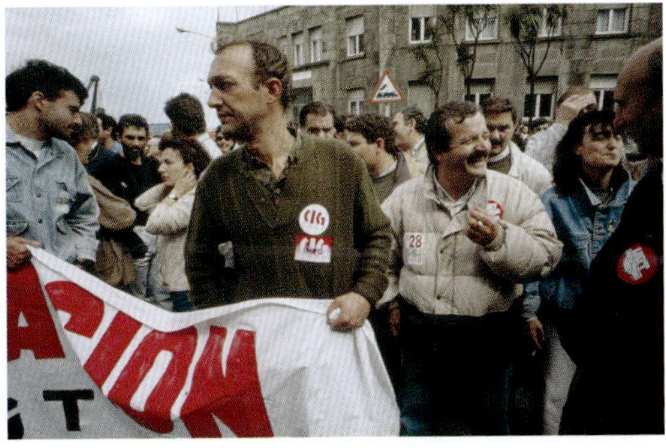

Fish Story (cont.)

True Cross

80 (#70)

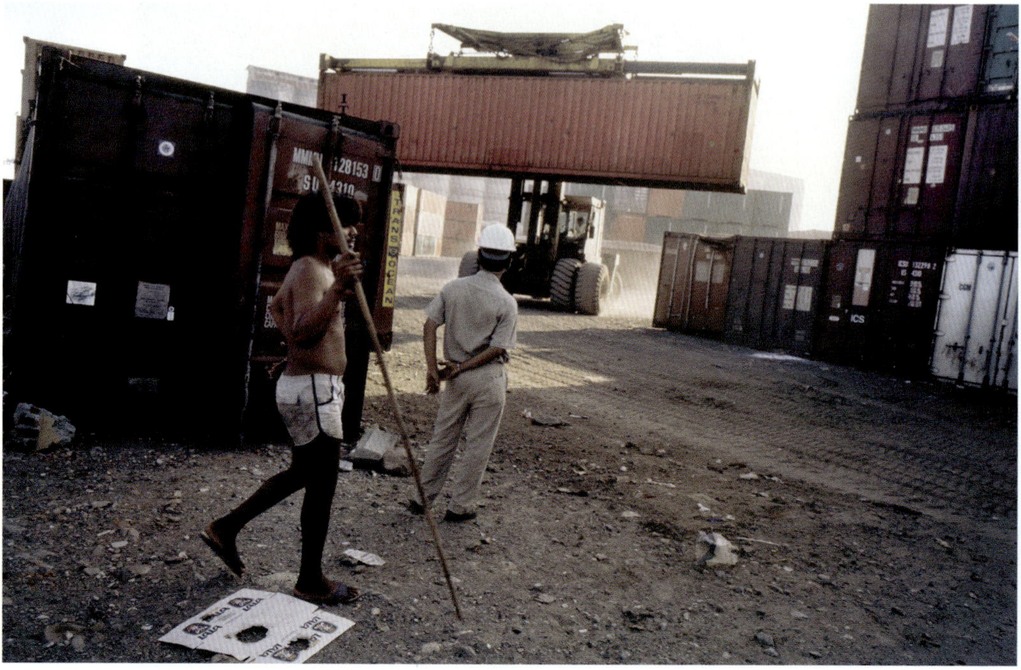

81 (#72)

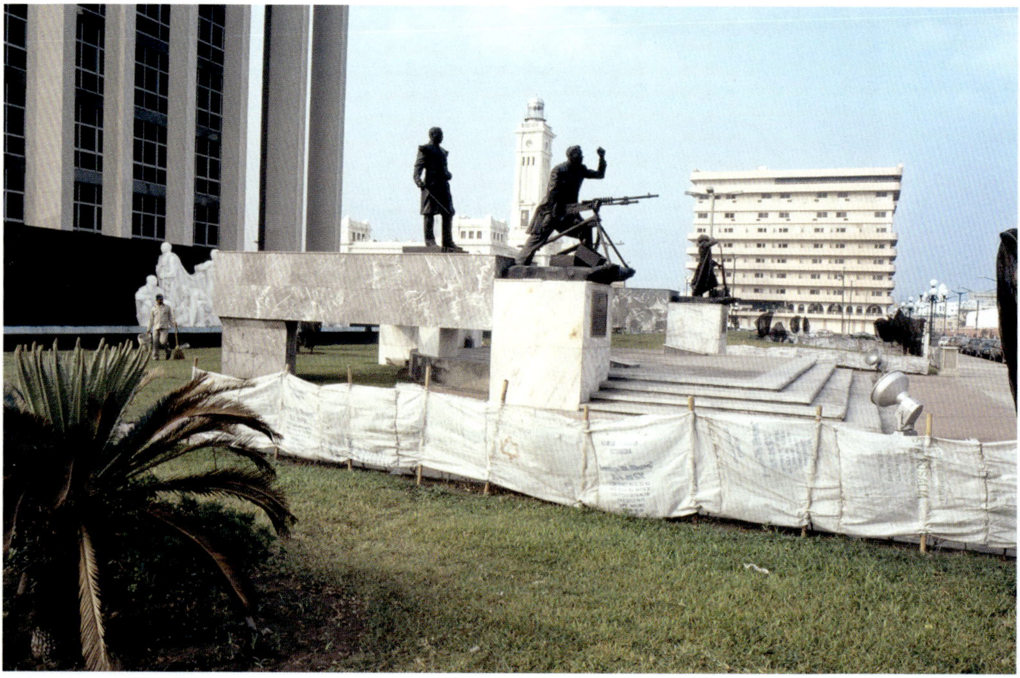

82 (#73)

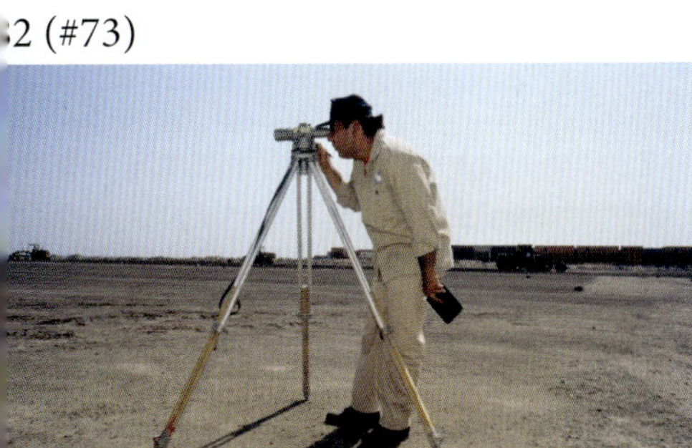

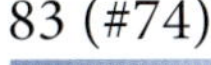

83 (#74)

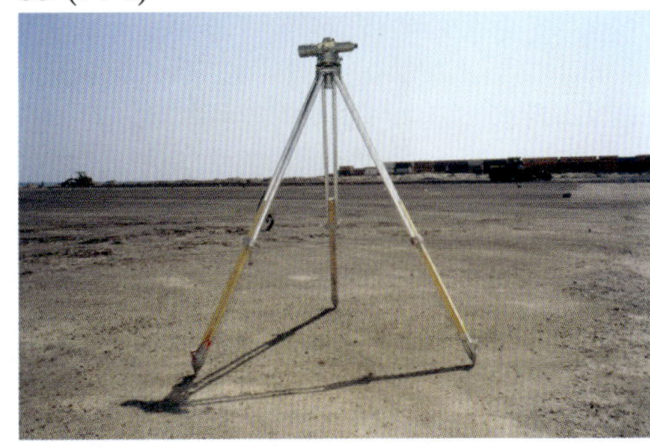

84 (#75)

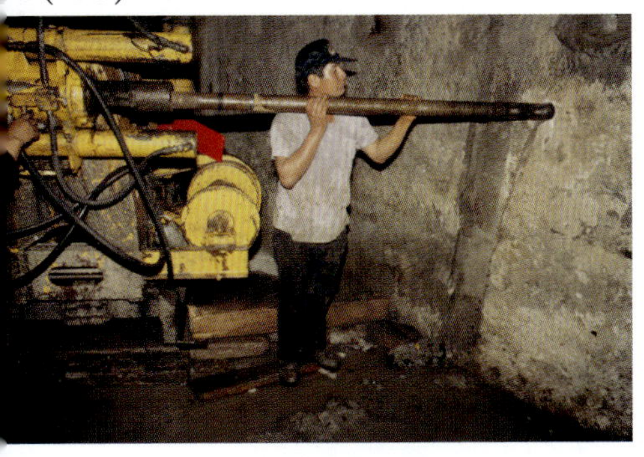

85 (#76)

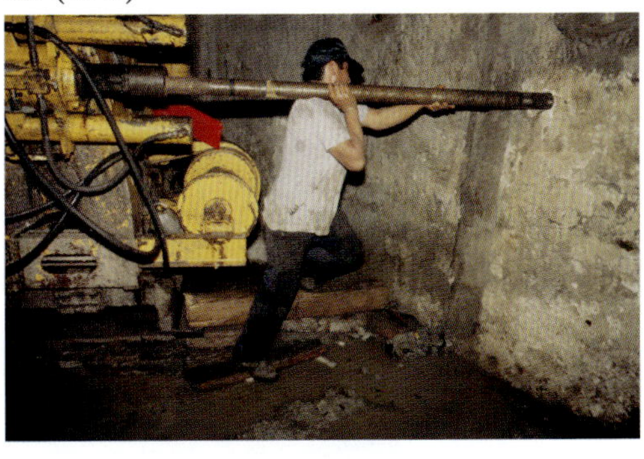

86 (#77)

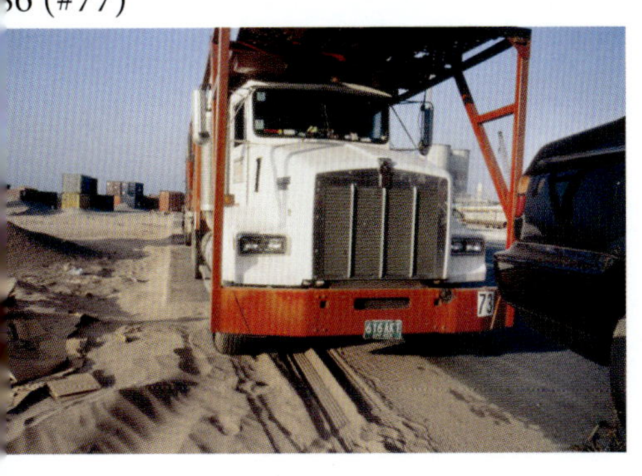

87 (#78)

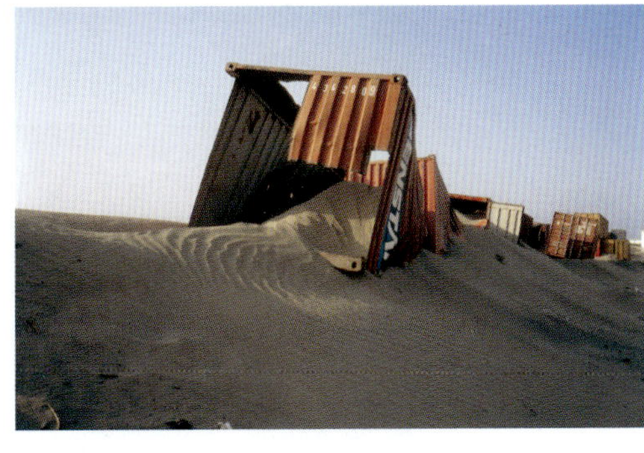

Fish Story (cont.)

True Cross (cont.)

88 (#79)

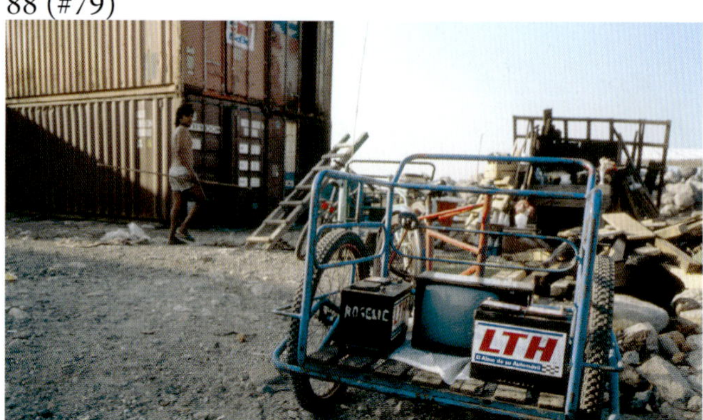

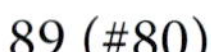

89 (#80)

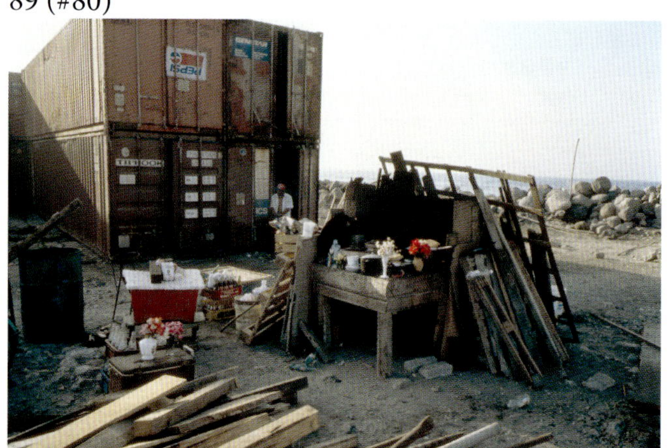

90 (#82)

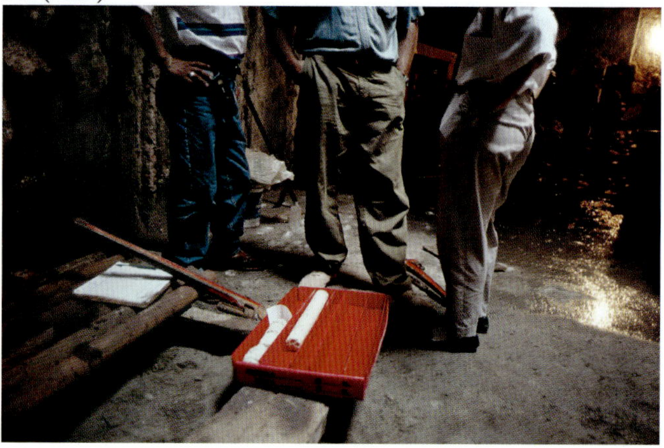

91 (#85)

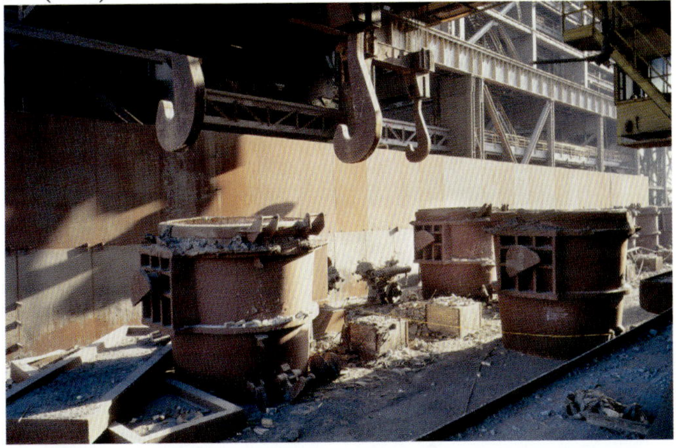

92 (#86)

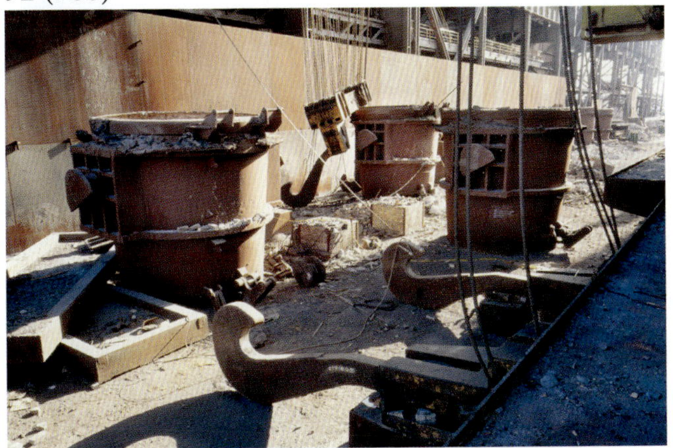

93 (#87)

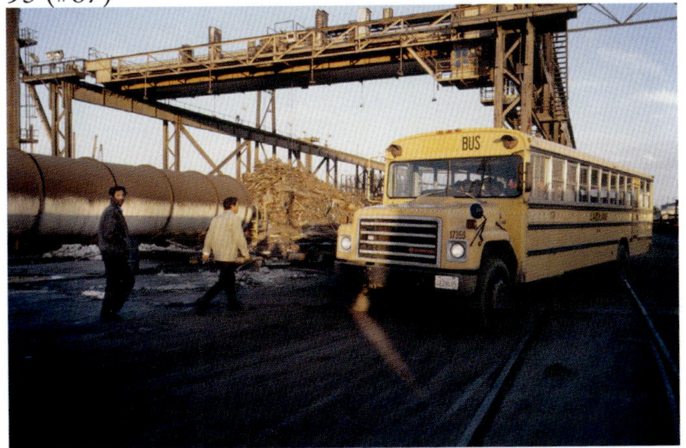

Fish Story (cont.)

Dictatorship of the Seven Seas (cont.)

94 (#91)

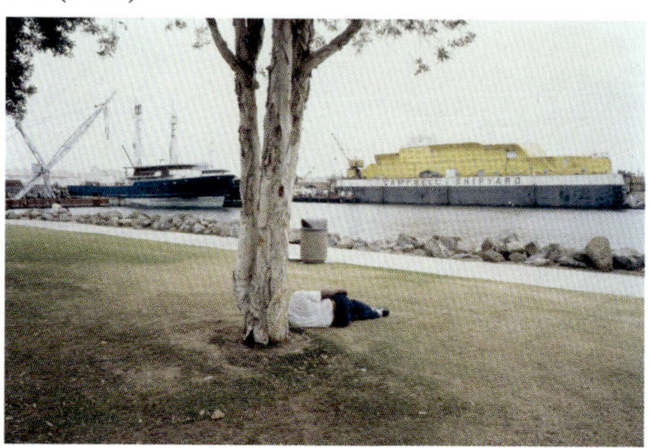

95 (#92)

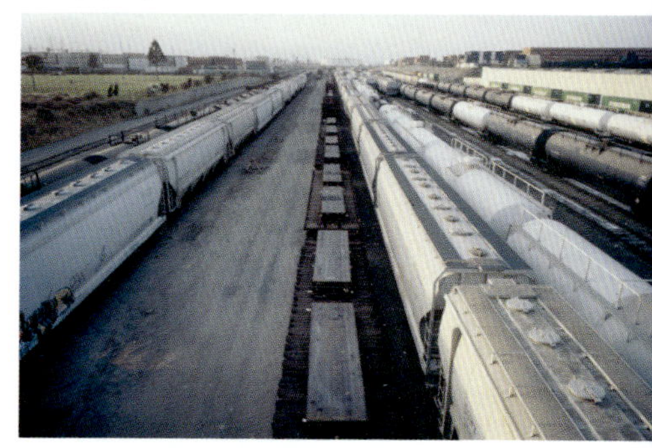

96 (#93)

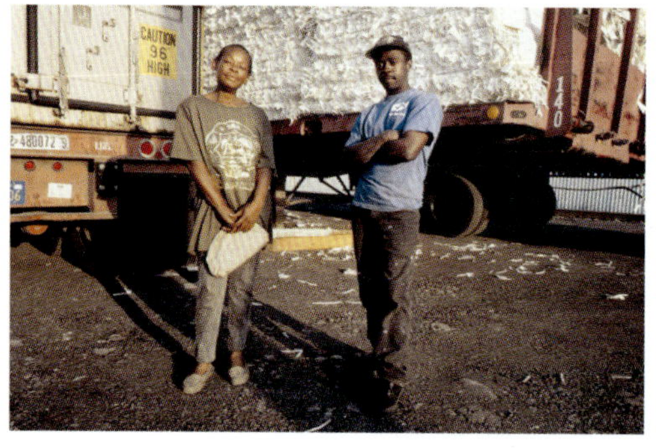

97 (#94)

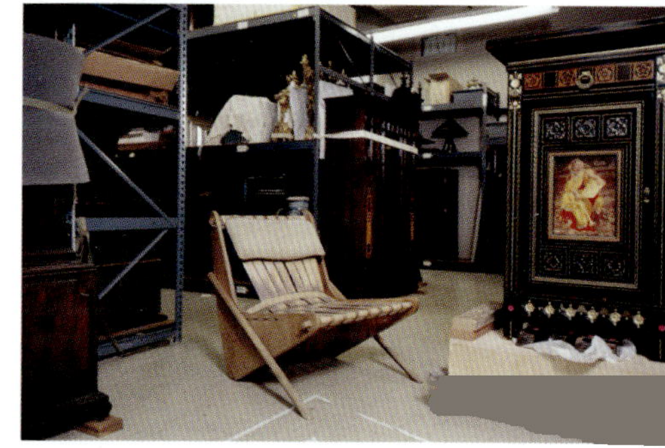

Dead Letter Office (1997–98)

98

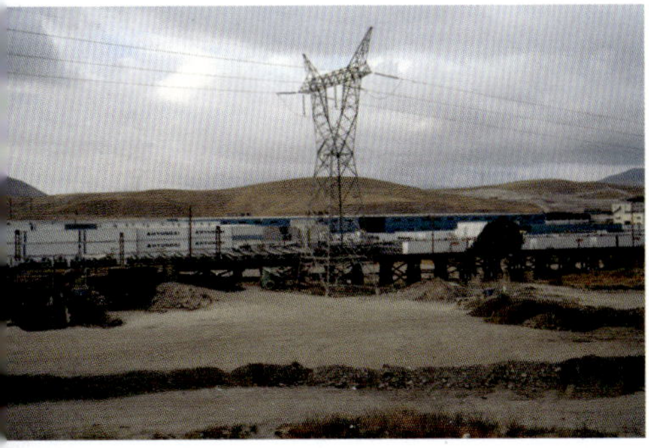

99

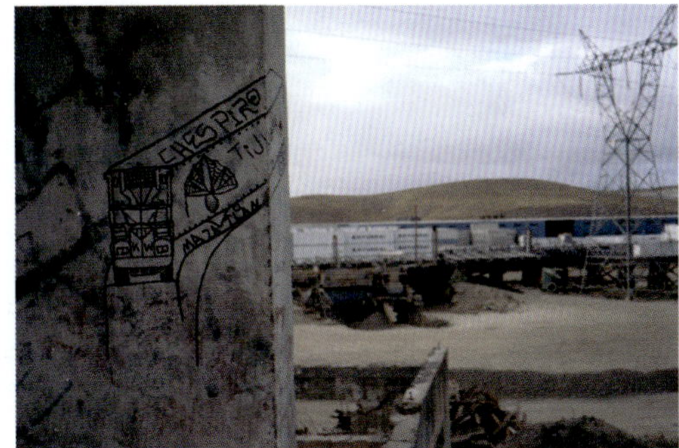

100

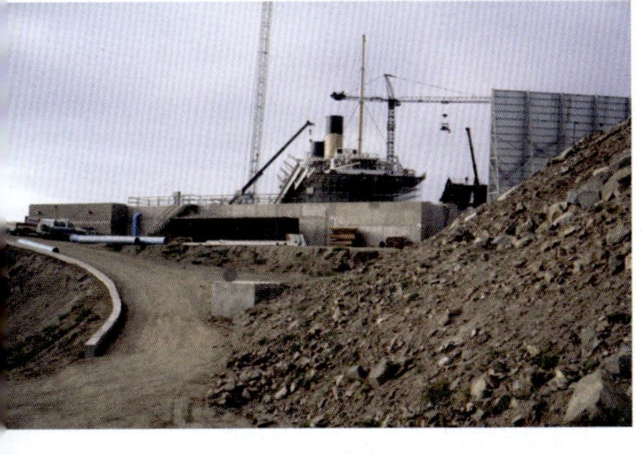

101

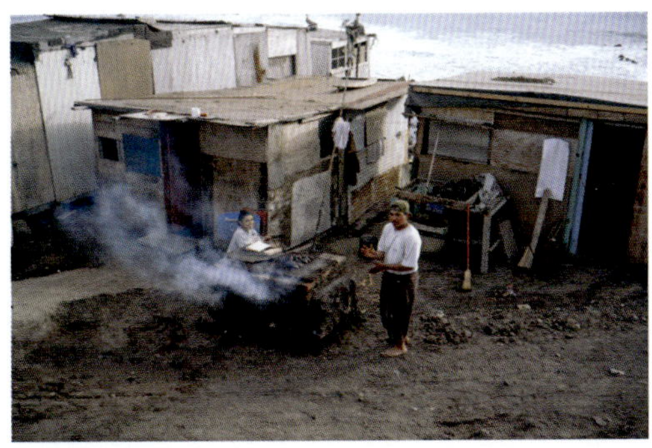

102

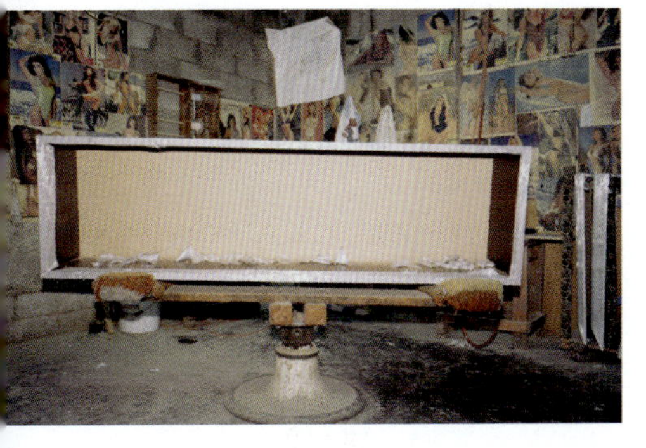

103

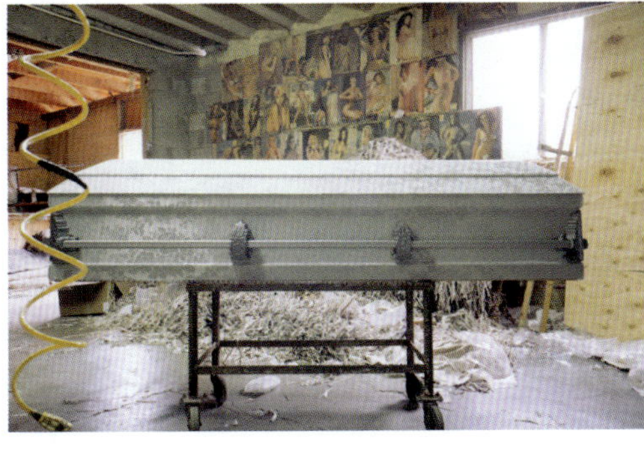

Freeway to China (Version 3 for Liverpool) (1998–99)

104

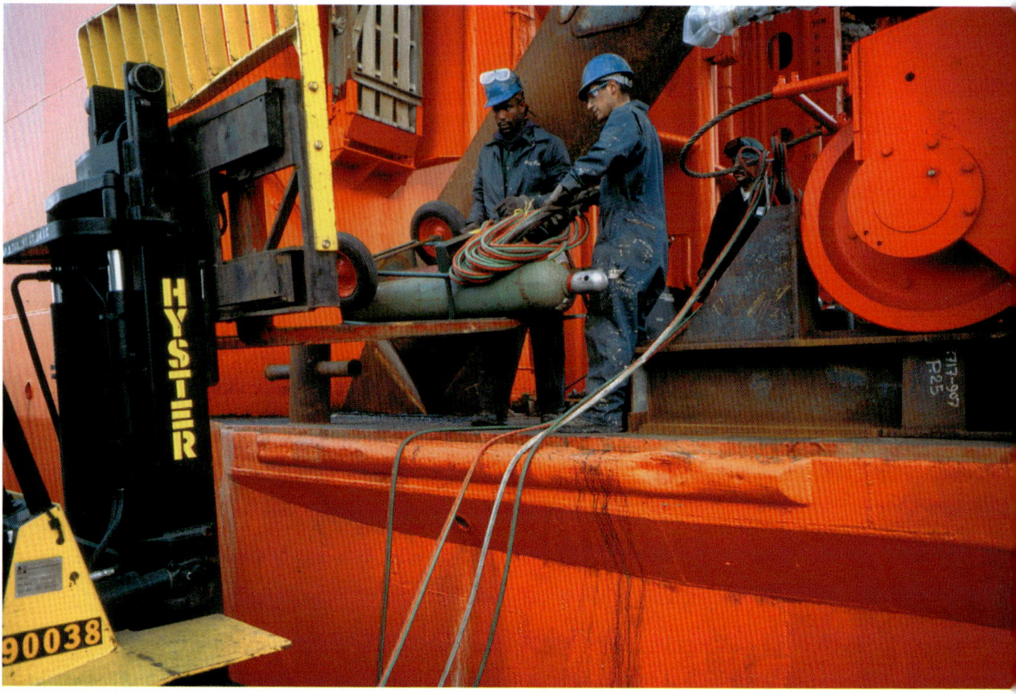

105

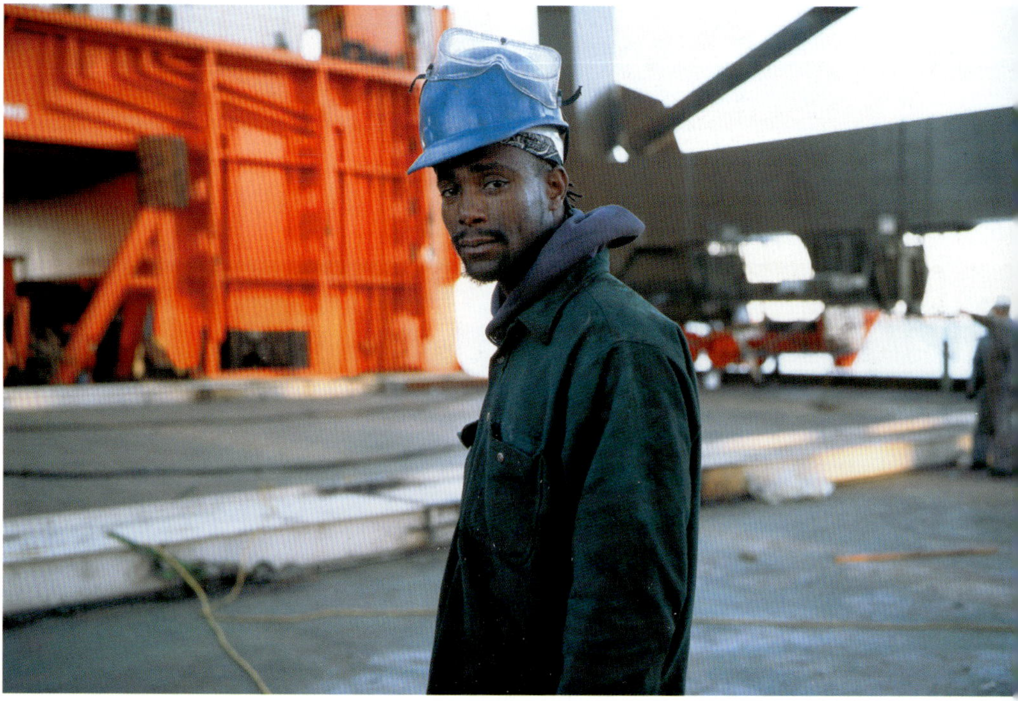

106

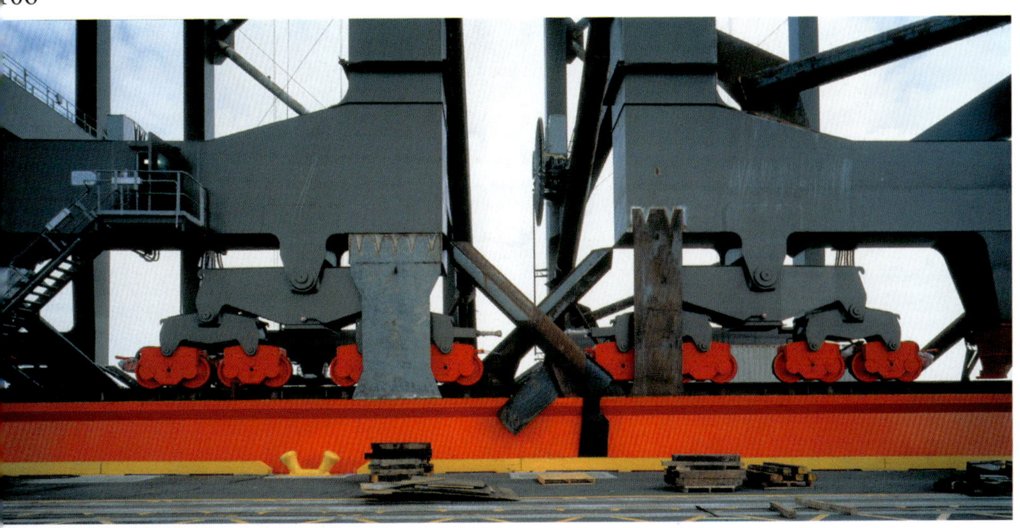

107

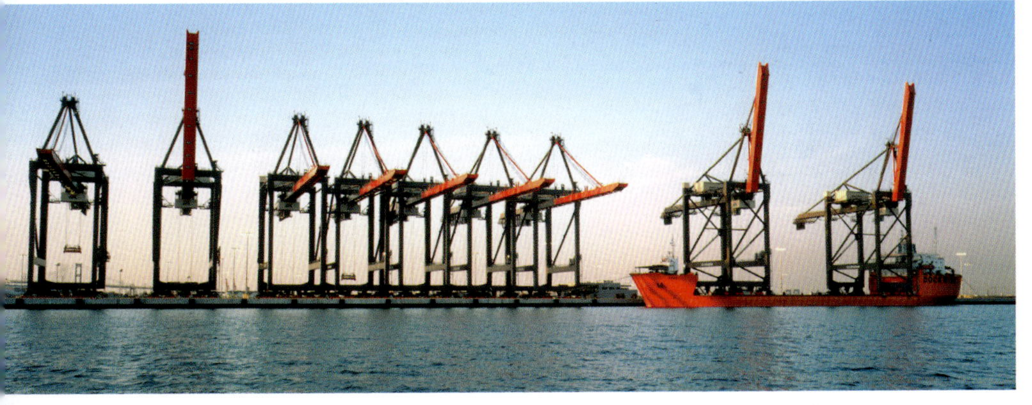

Freeway to China (cont.)

108

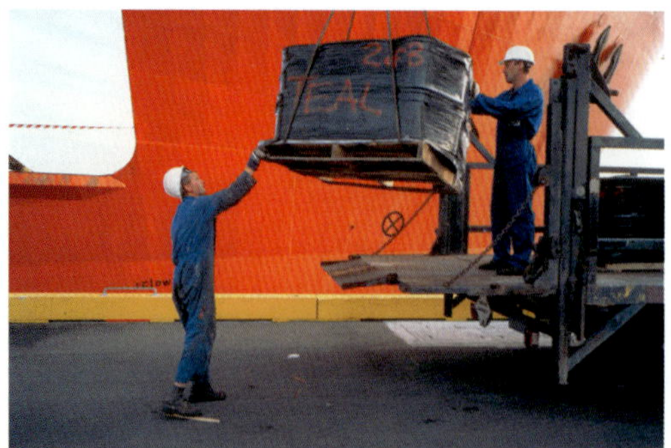

109

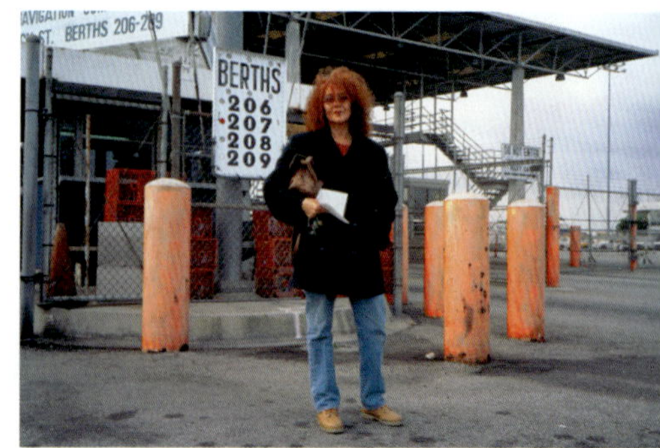

110

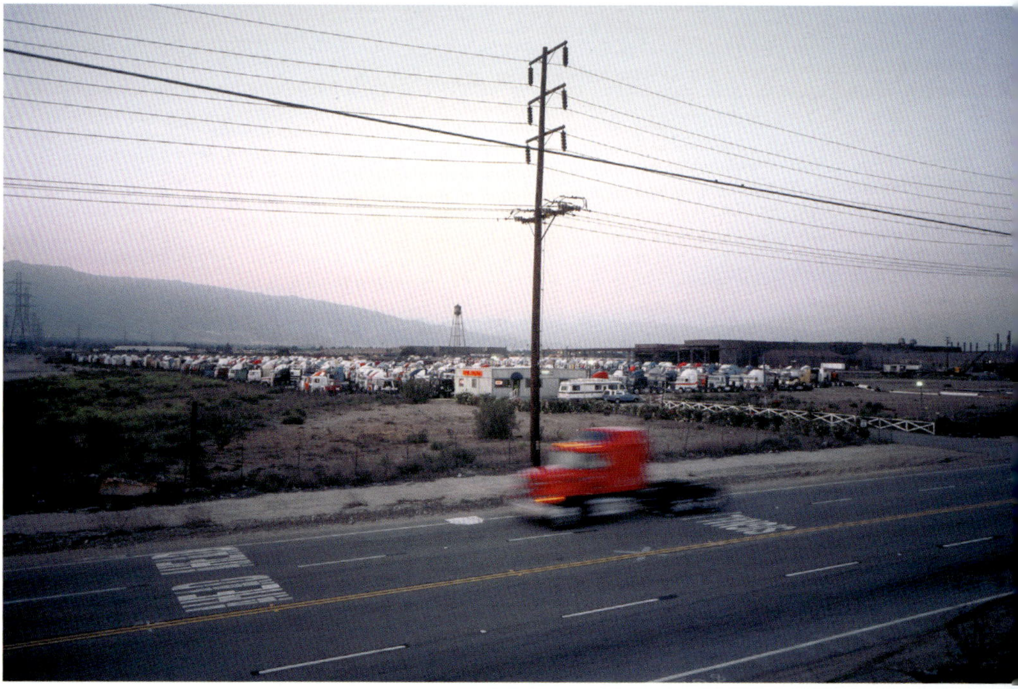

111

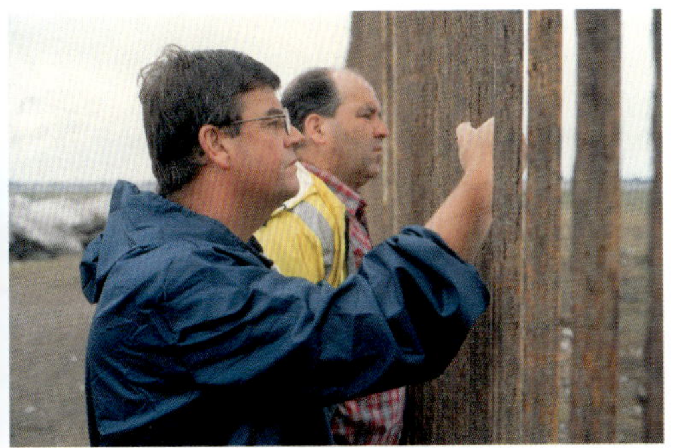

112

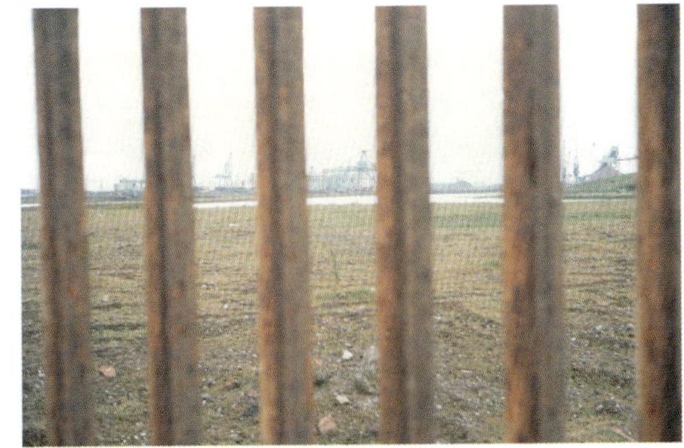

113

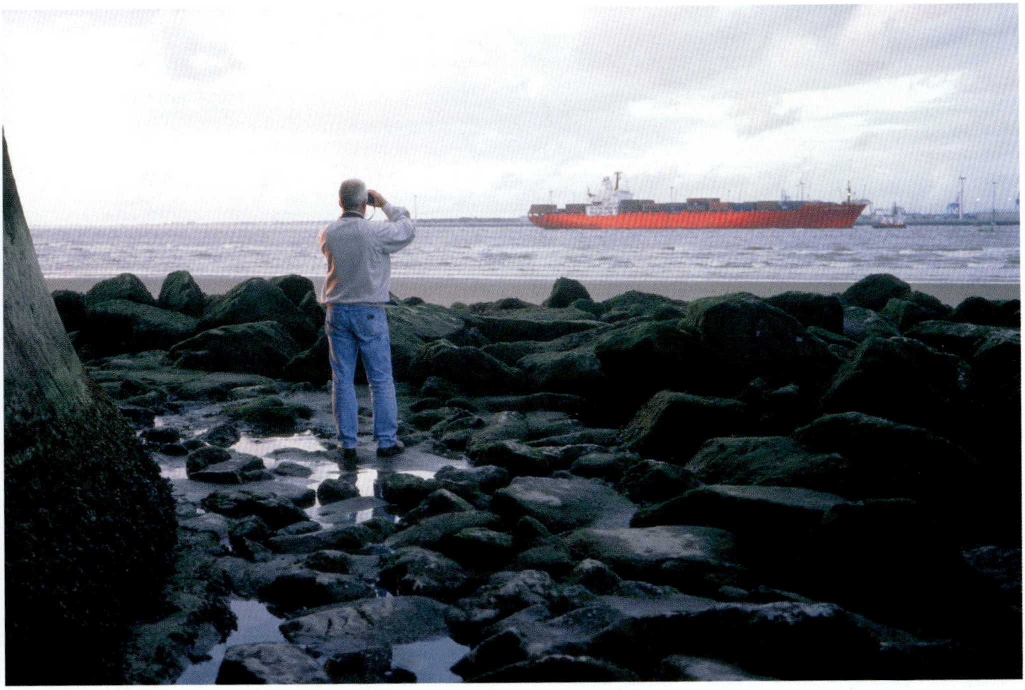

114

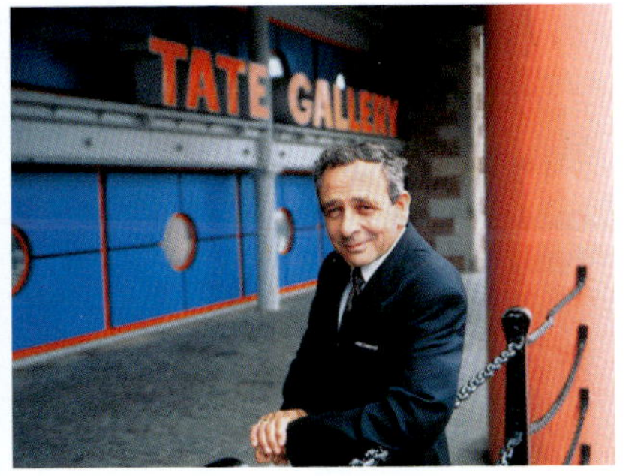

115

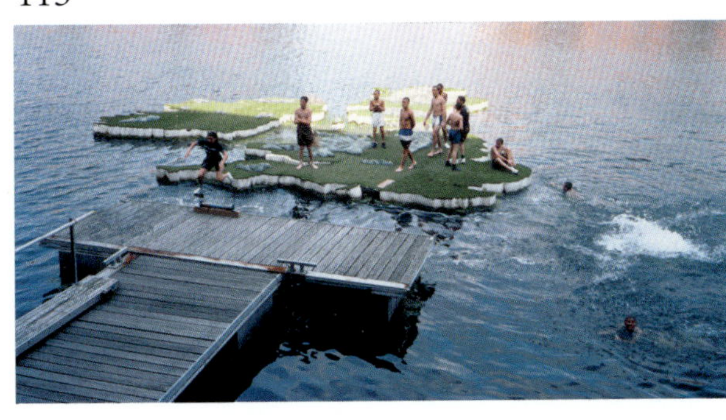

Waiting for Tear Gas [white globe to black] (1999–2000)

116

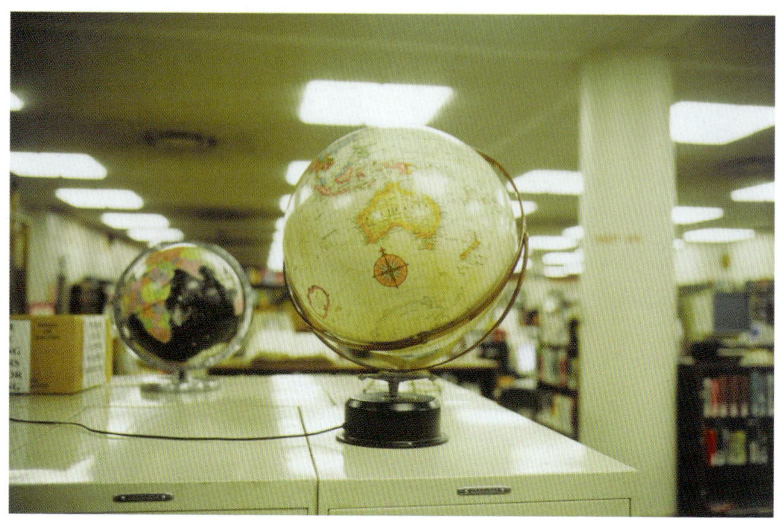

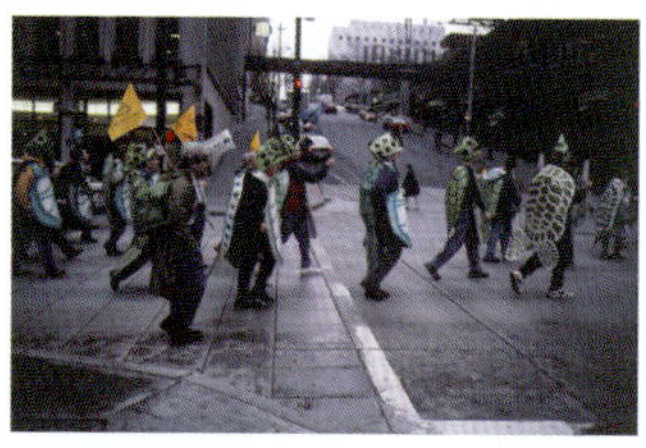

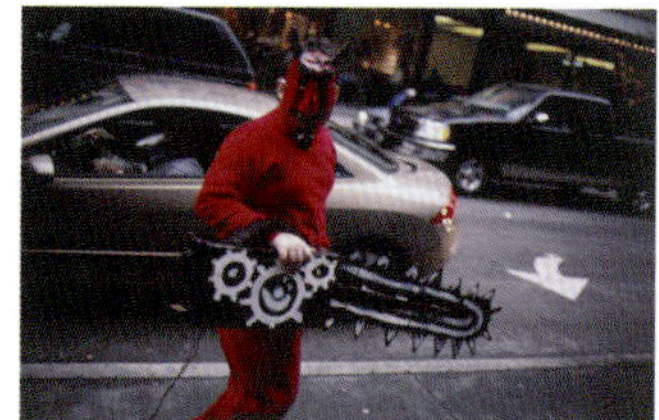

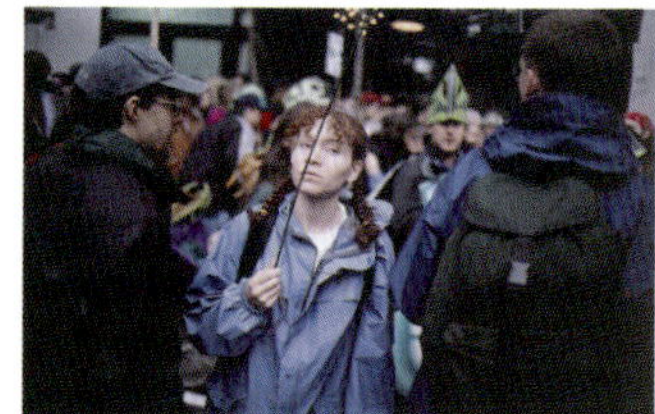

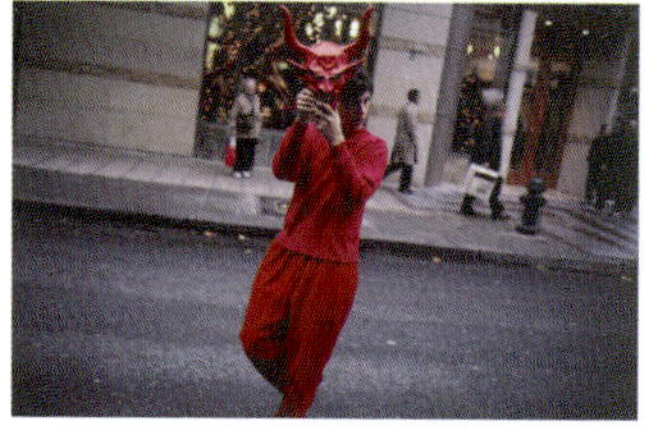

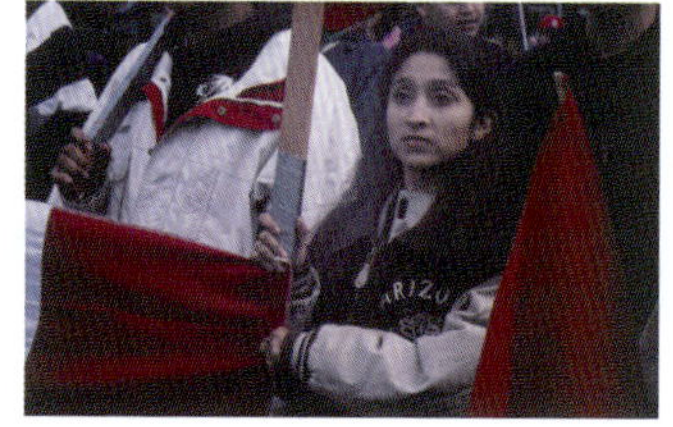

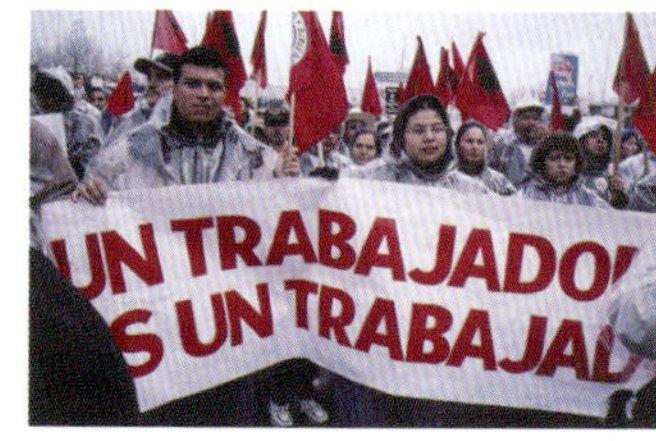

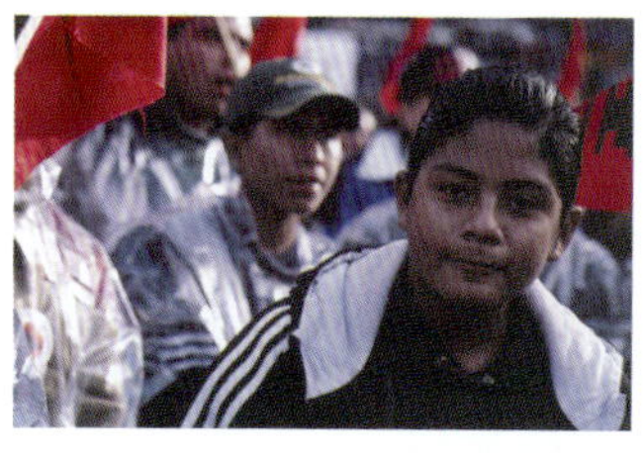

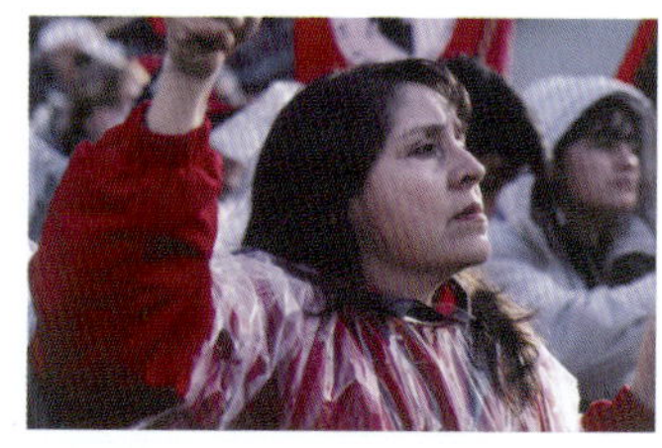

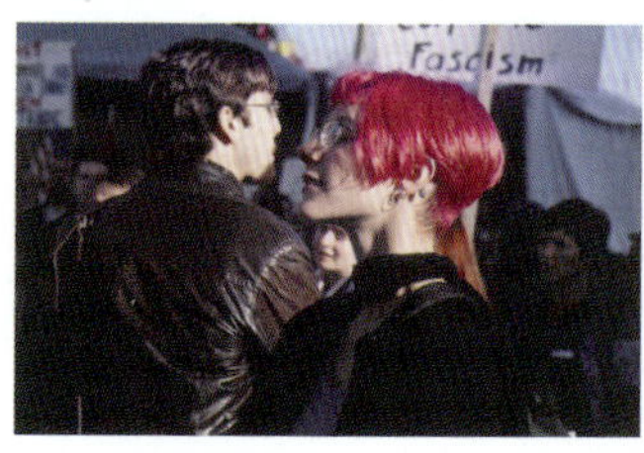

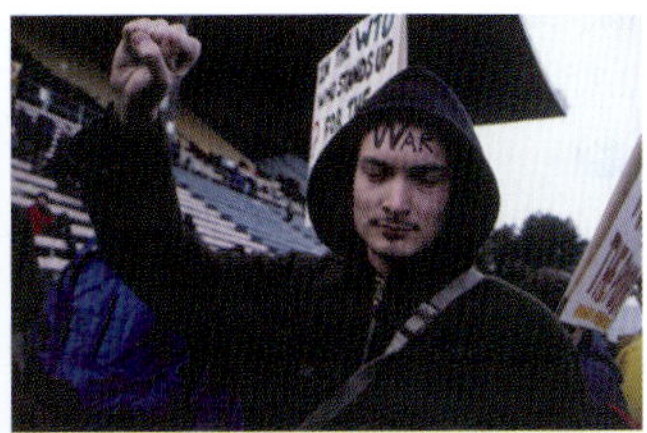
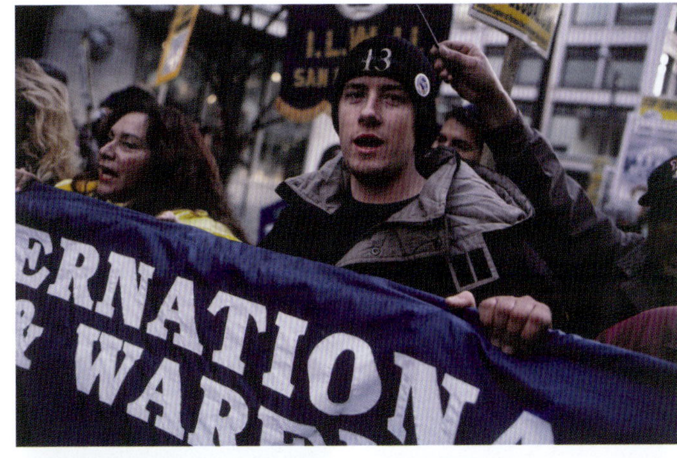
ERNATION
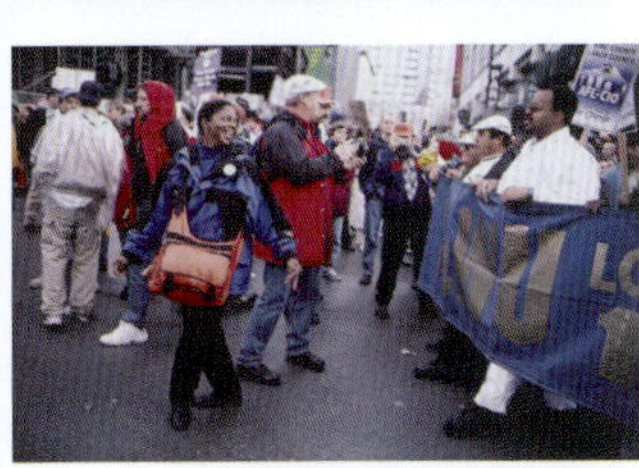
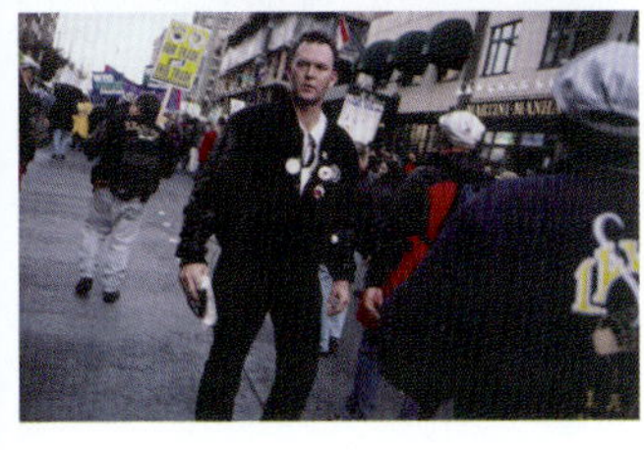
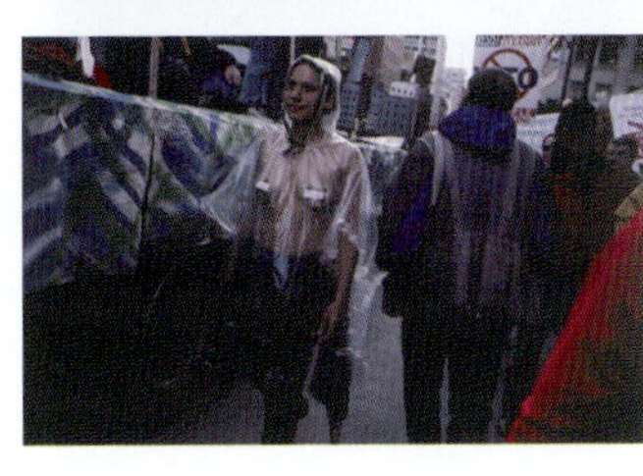
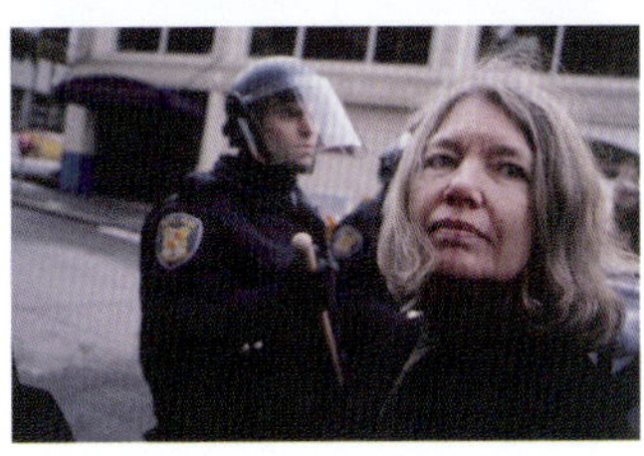
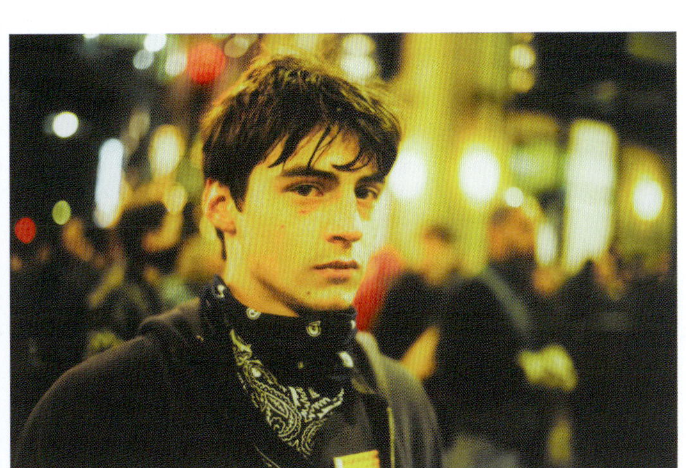
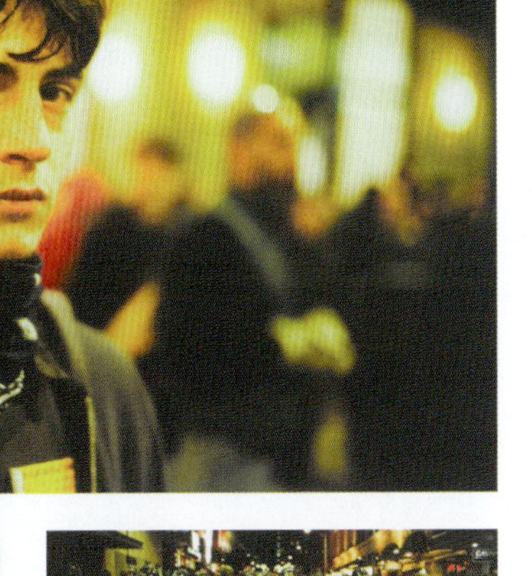
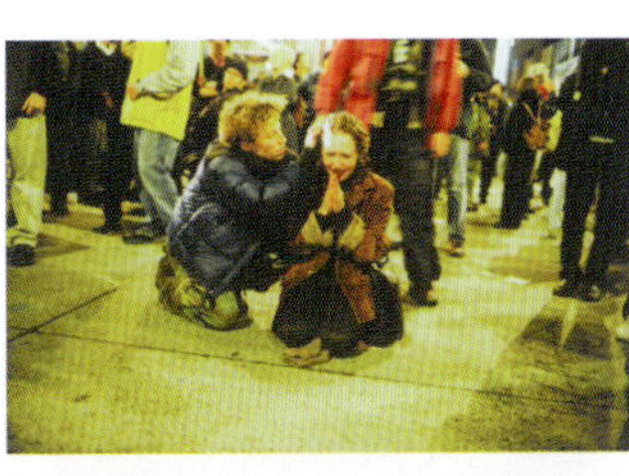
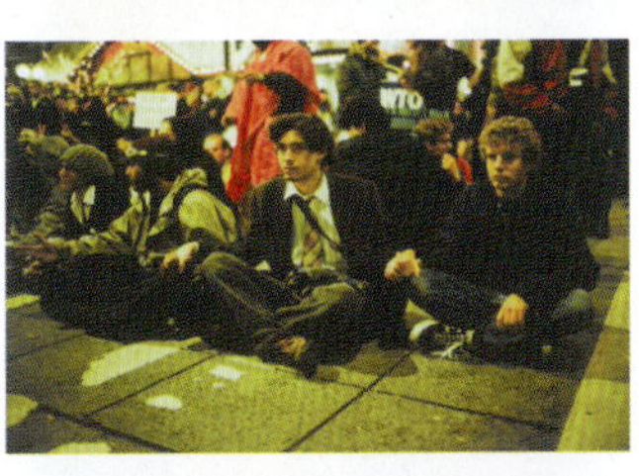
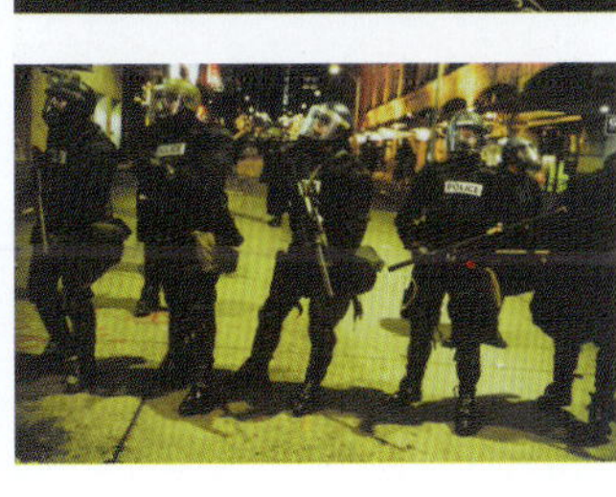
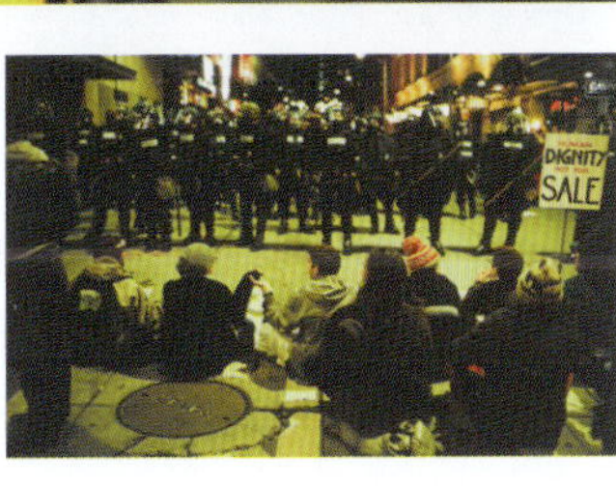
DIGNITY
SALE
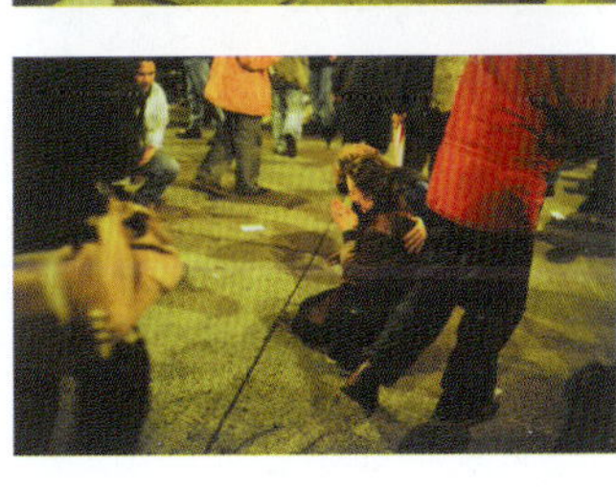

Waiting for Tear Gas (cont.)

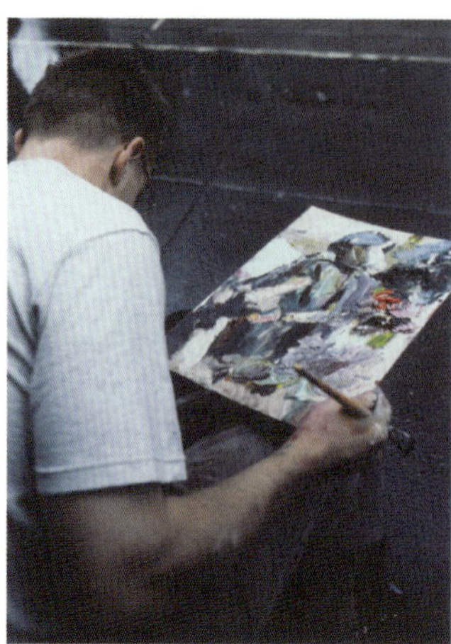

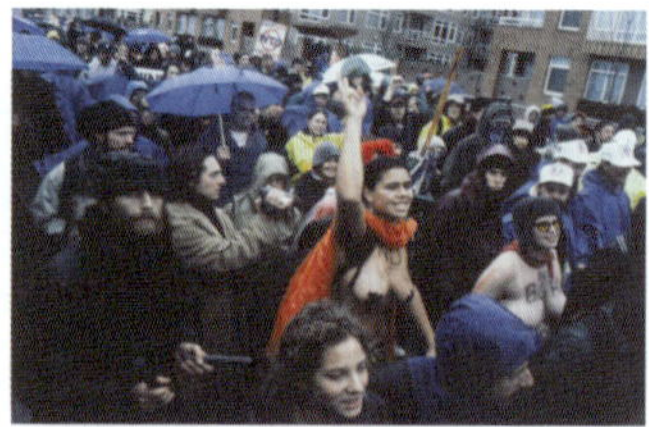

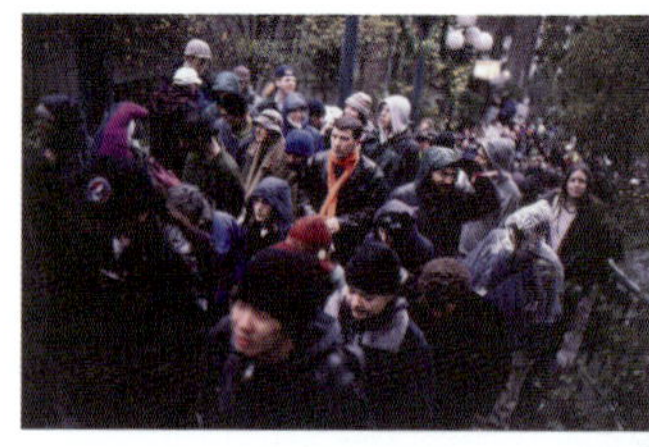

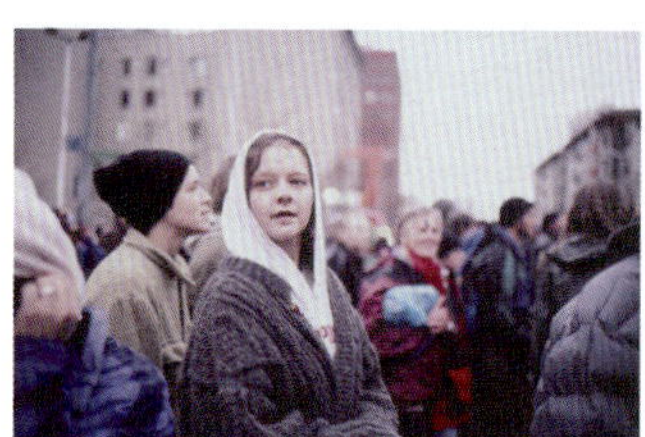

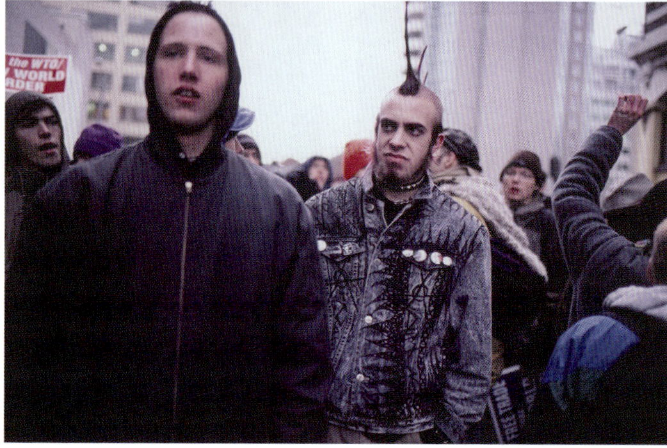

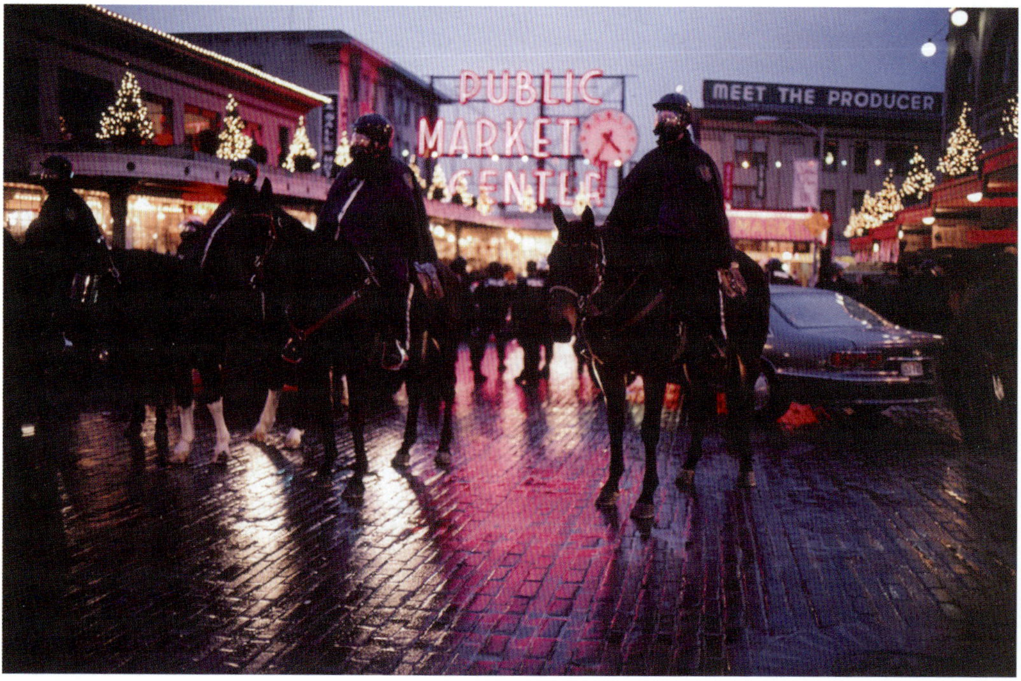

Waiting for Tear Gas (cont.)

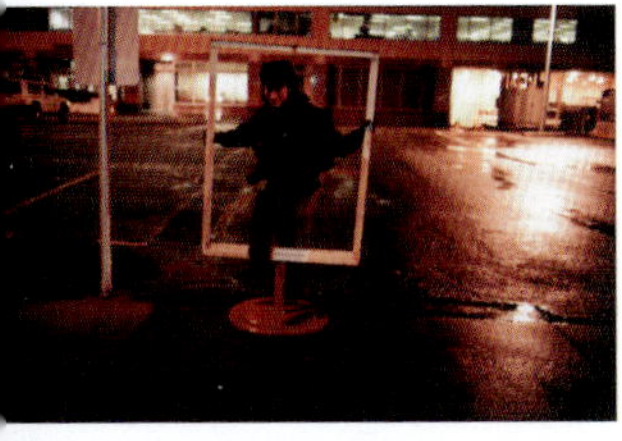

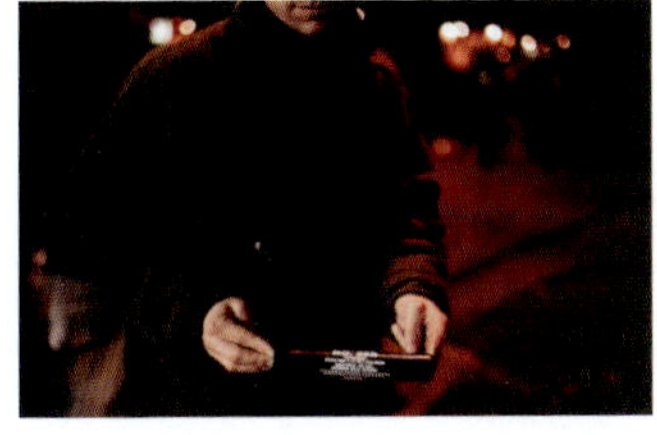

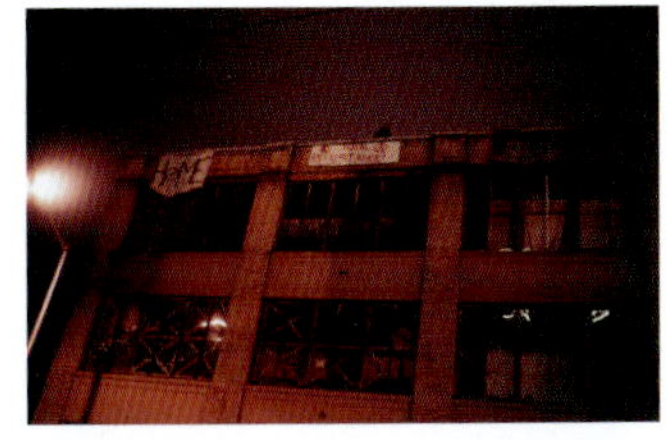

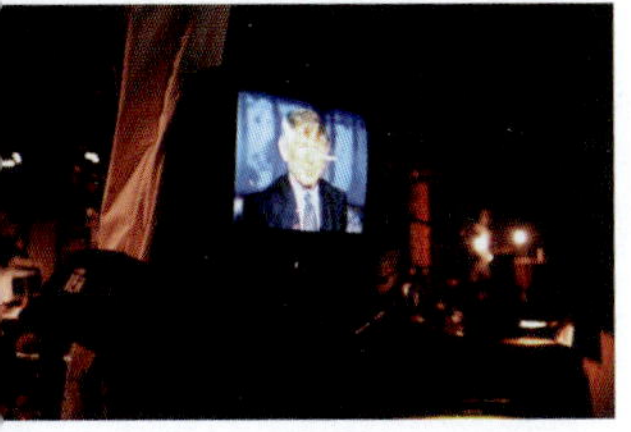

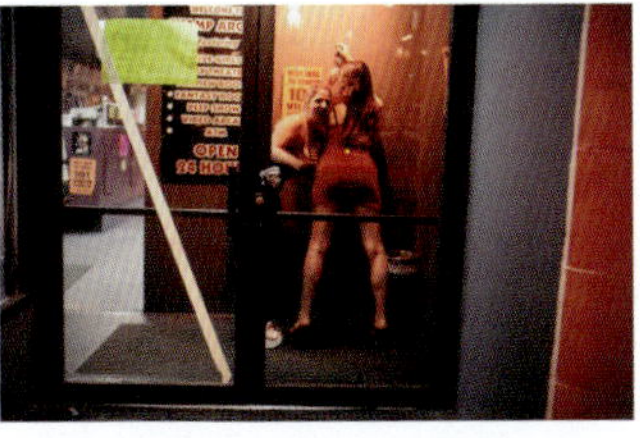

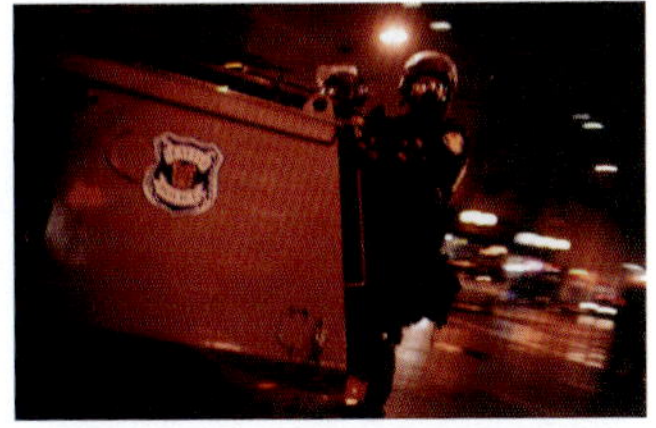

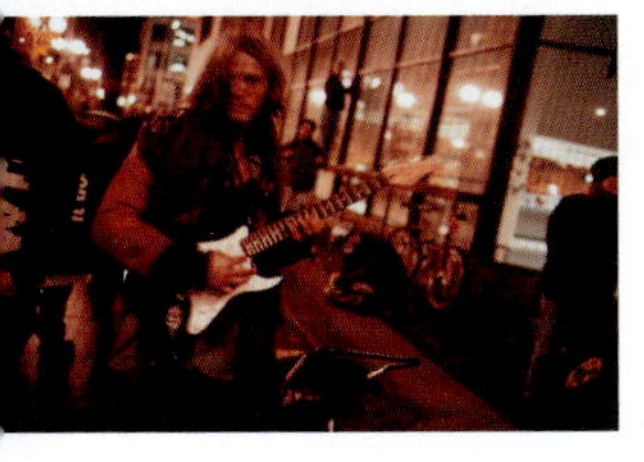

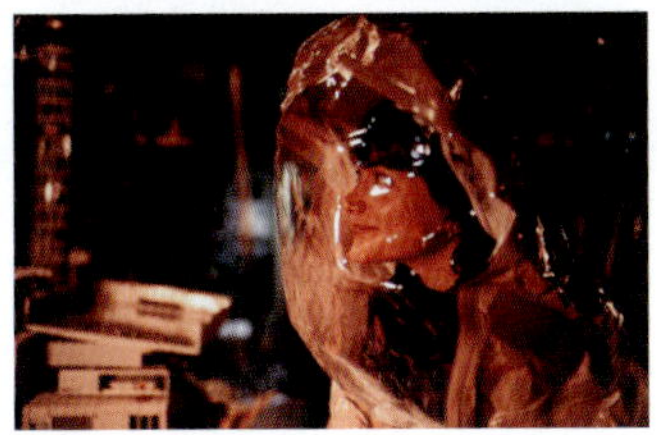

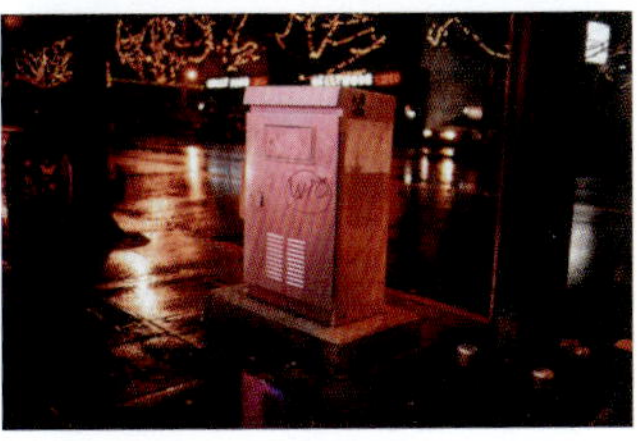

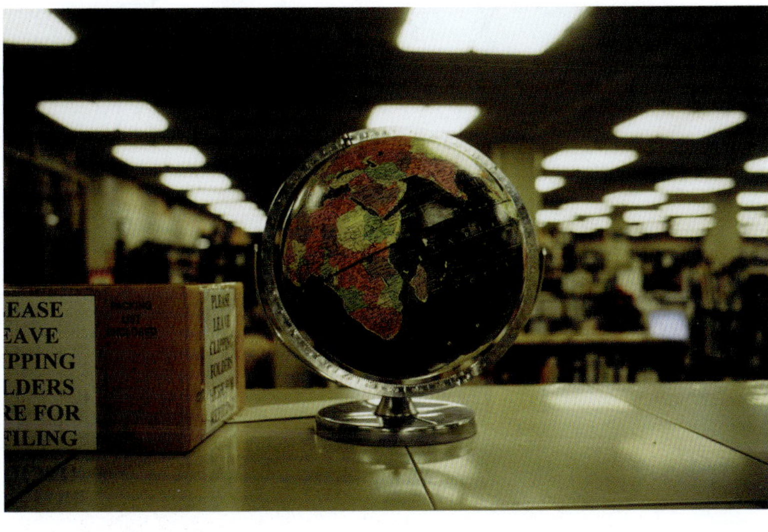

TITANIC's wake (1998–2000)

117

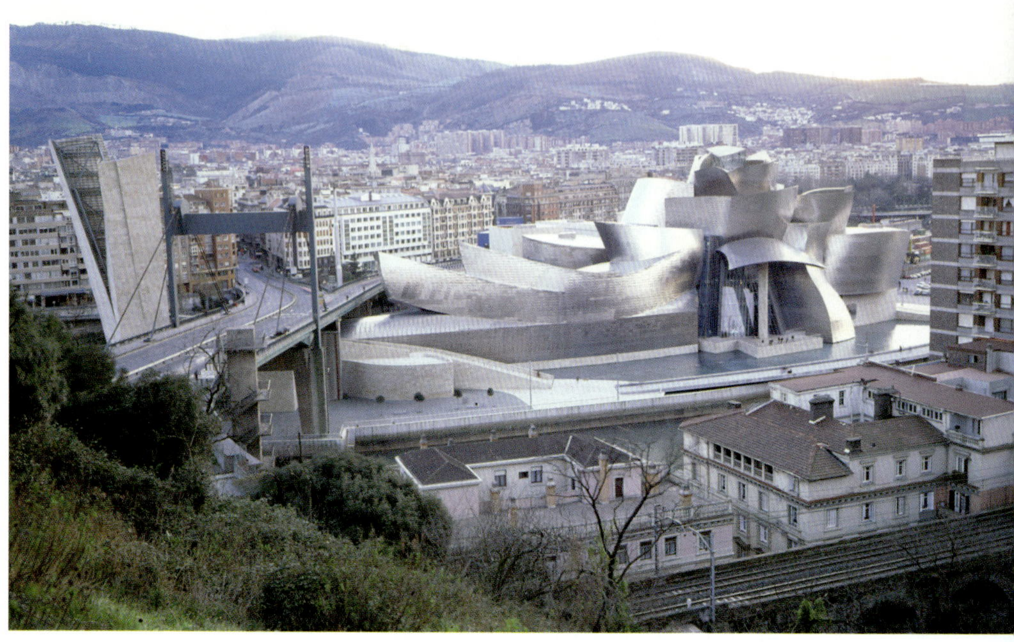

118

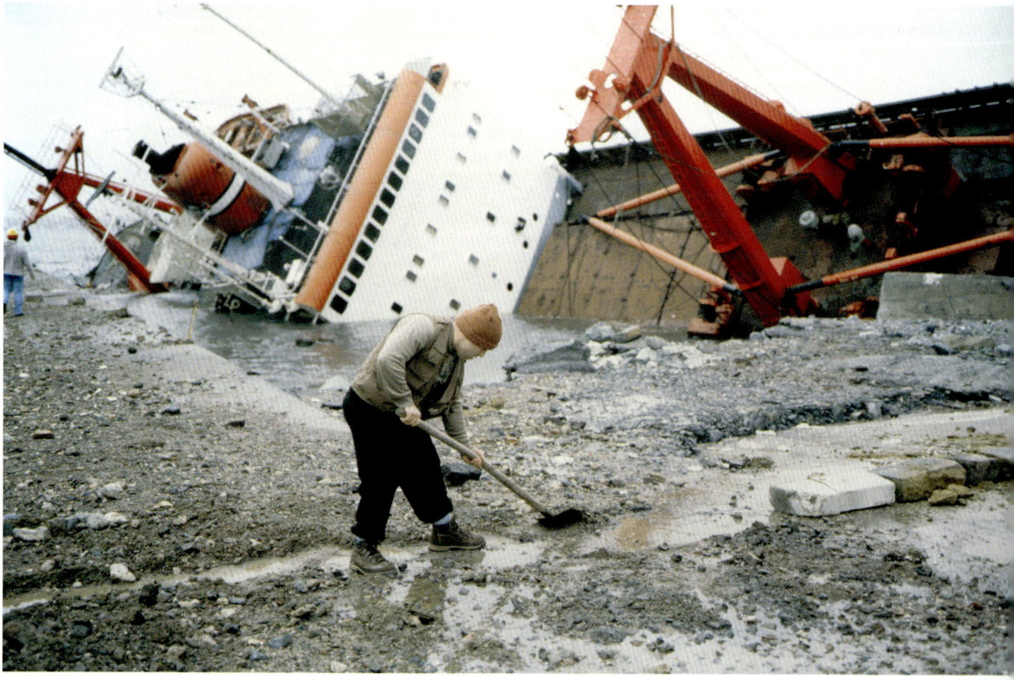

19

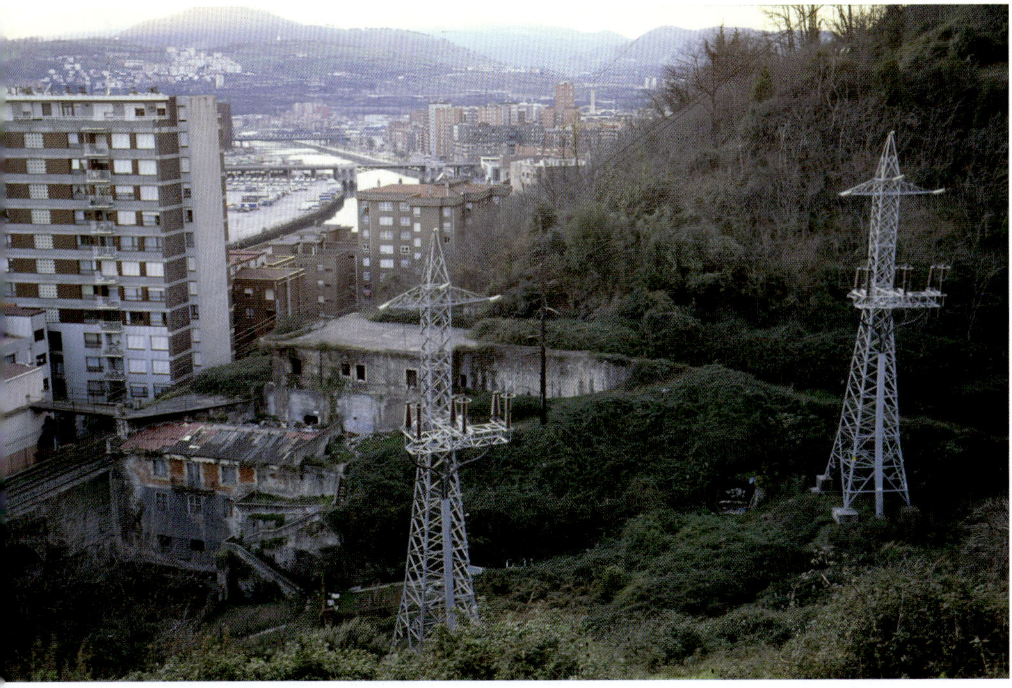

Black Tide/Marea Negra (2002–3)

20

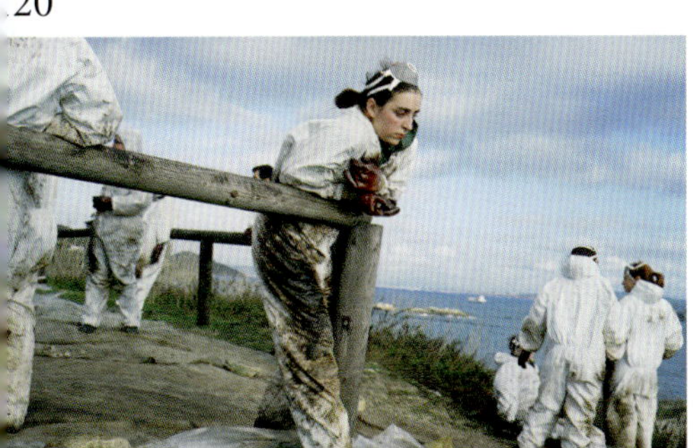

21

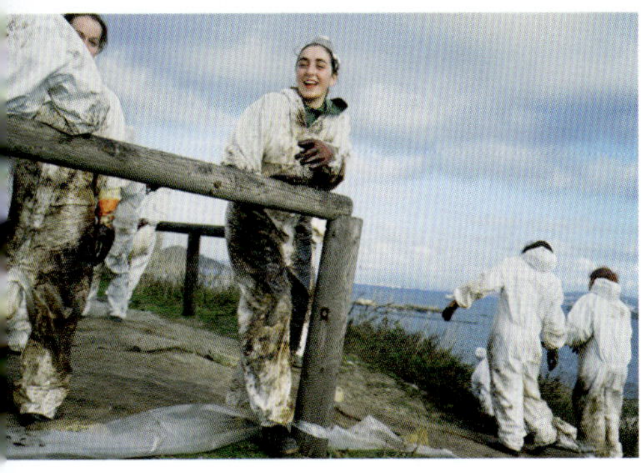

122

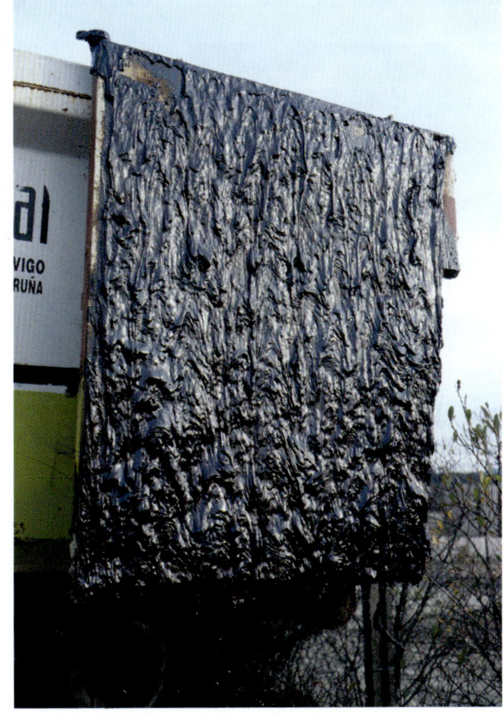

The Lottery of the Sea (2006)

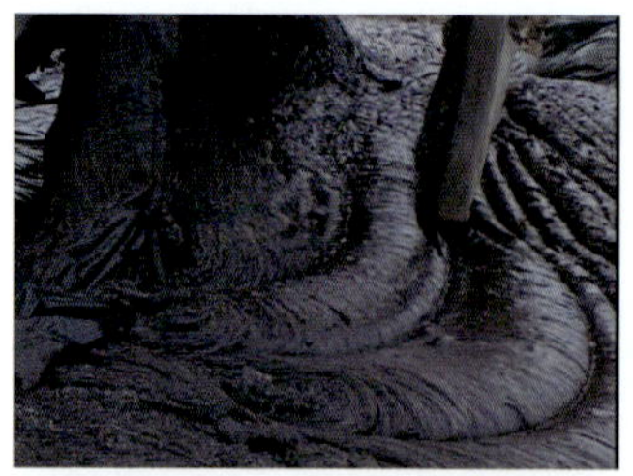

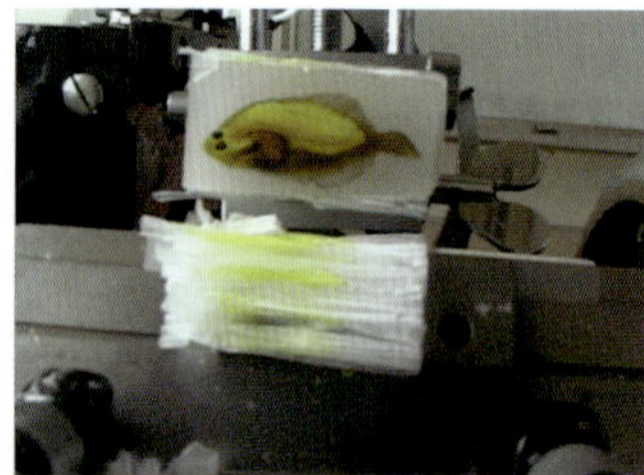

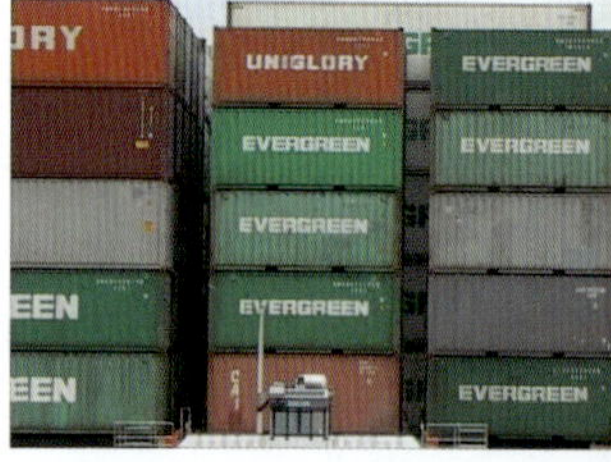

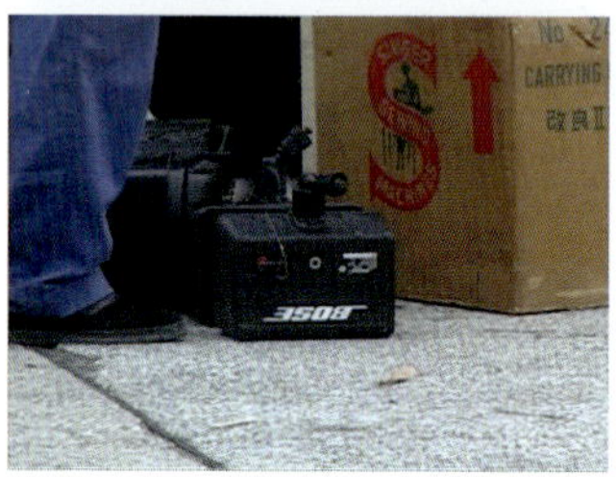

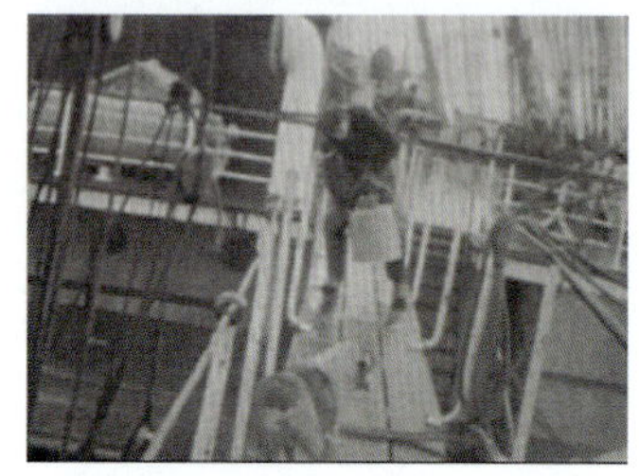

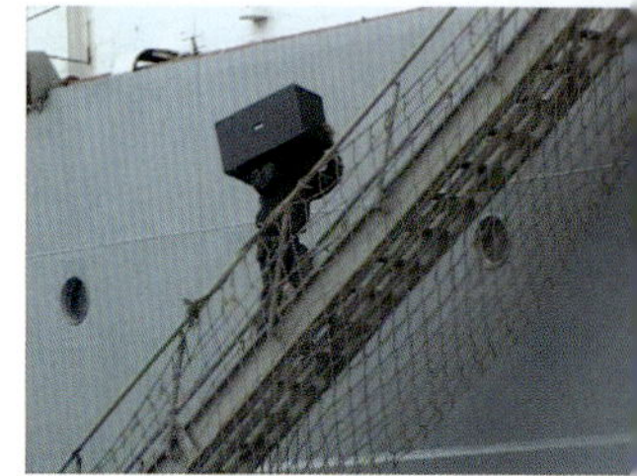

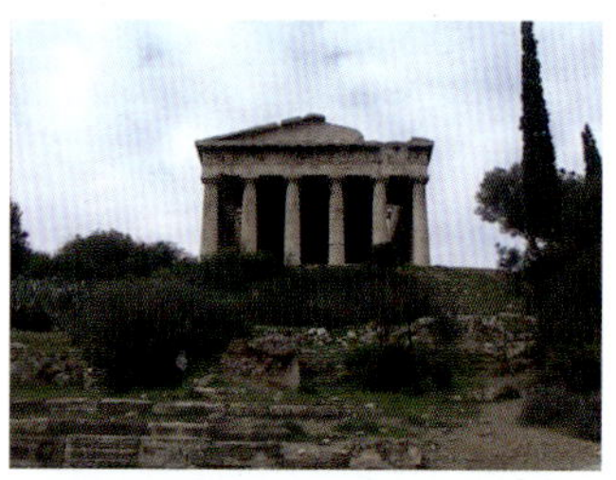

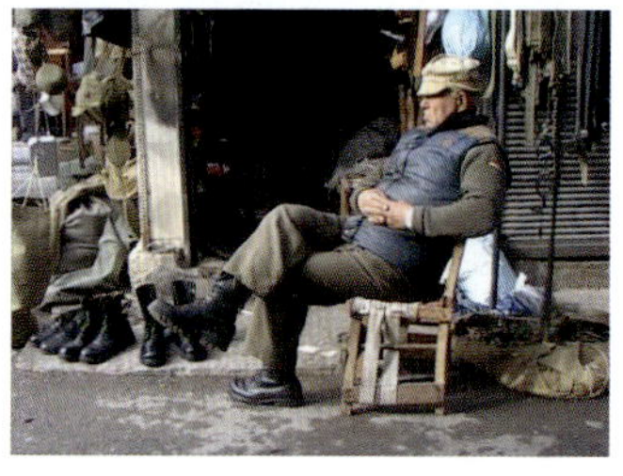

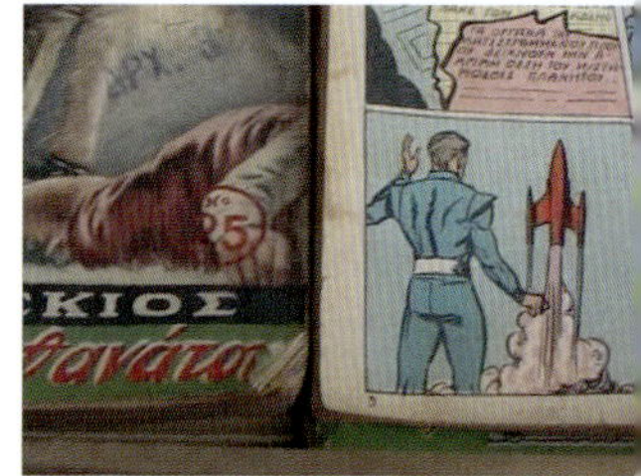

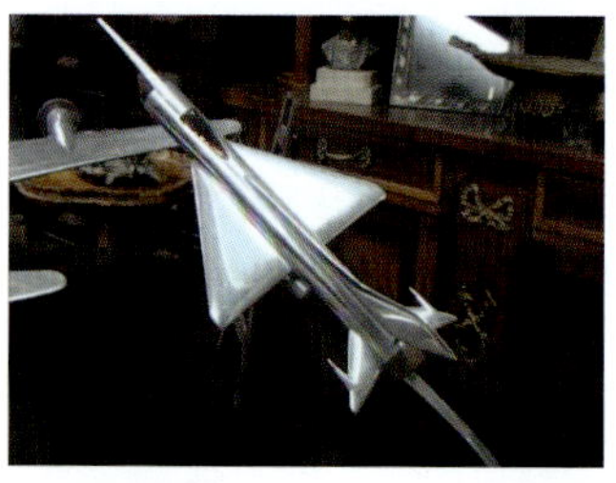

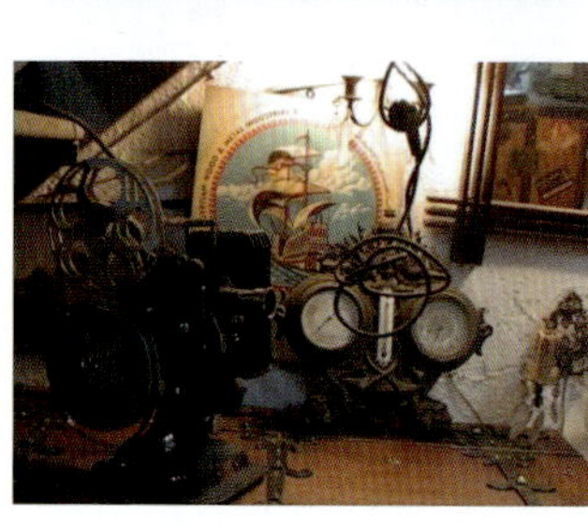

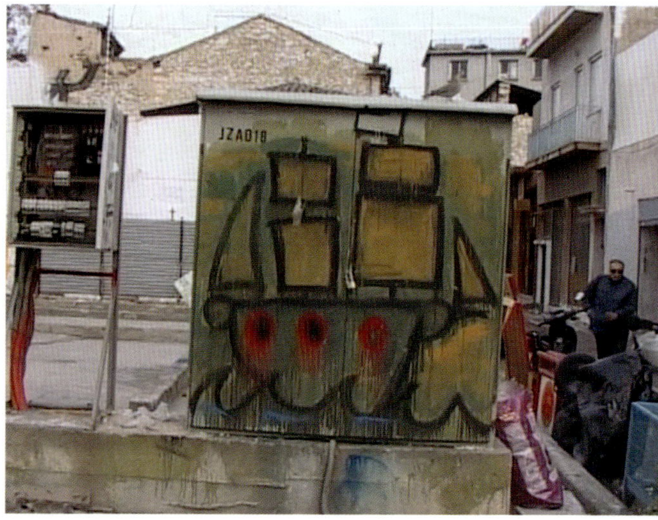

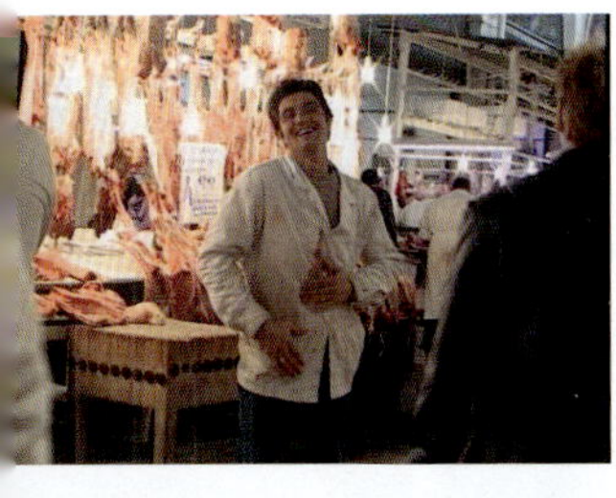

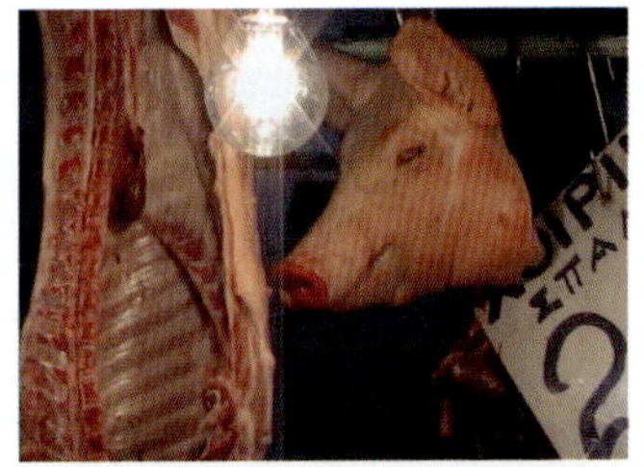

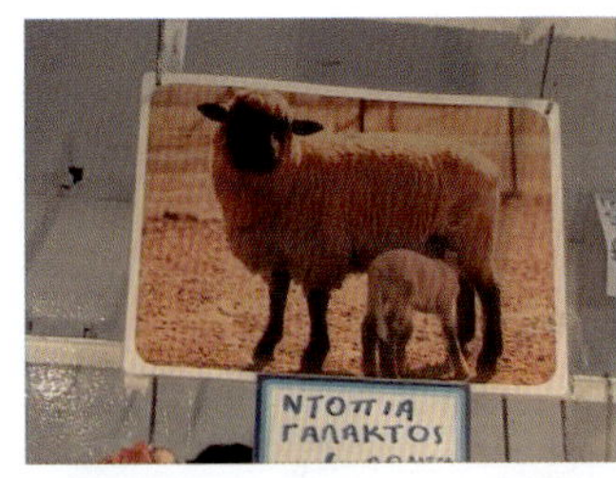
ΝΤΟΠΙΑ
ΓΑΛΑΚΤΟΣ

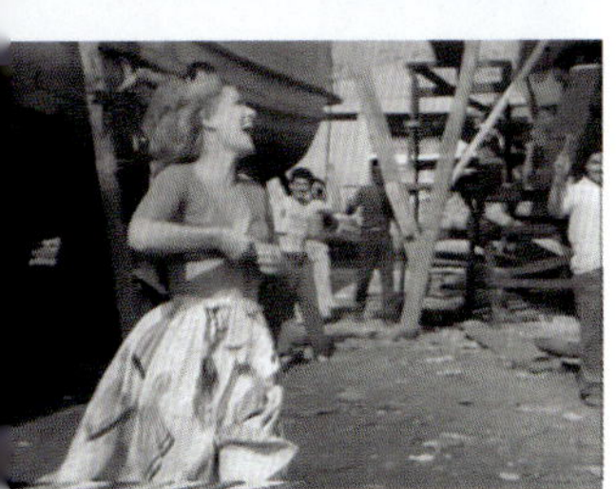

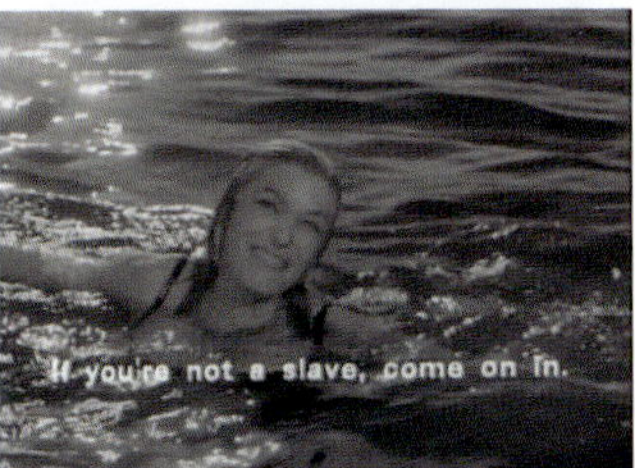
If you're not a slave, come on in.

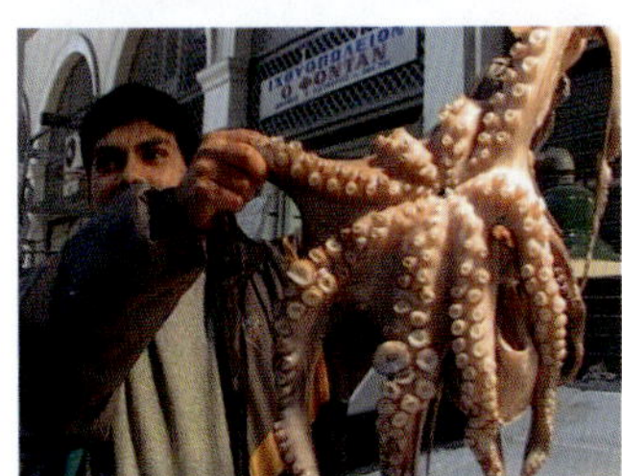

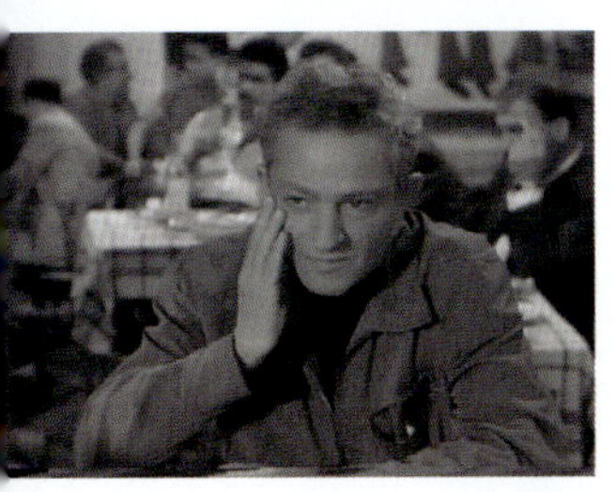

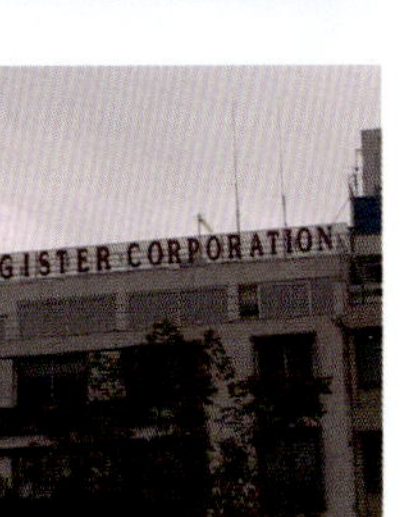
PANAMA REGISTER CORPORATION

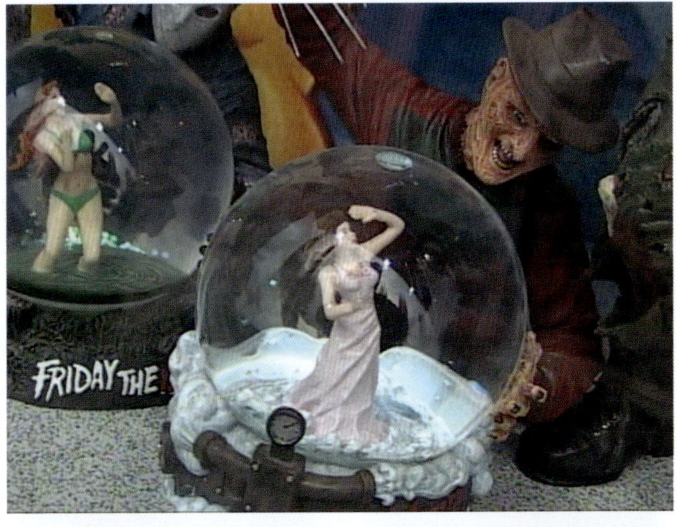
FRIDAY THE

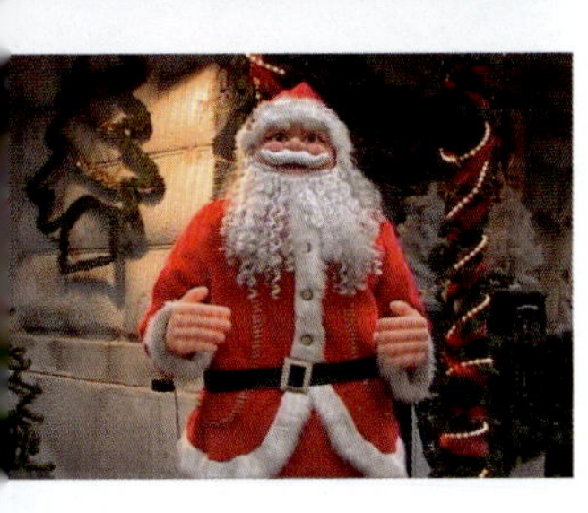

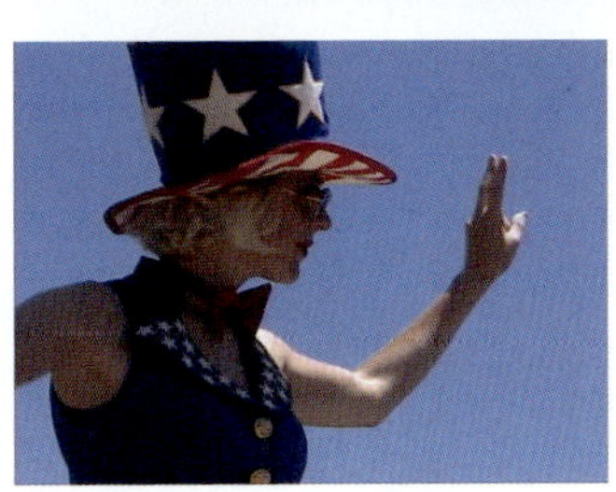

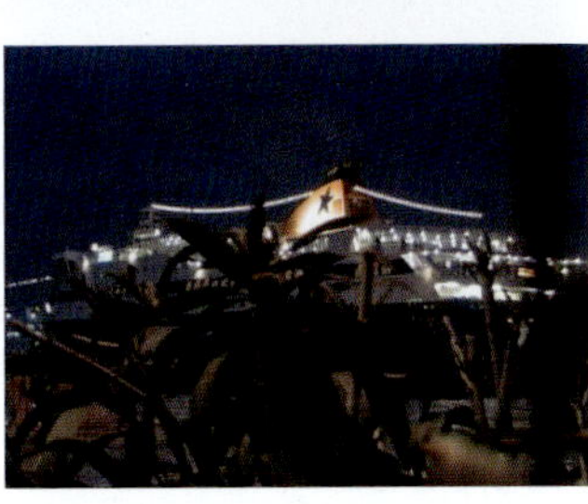

Ship of Fools (2010)

124 125 126

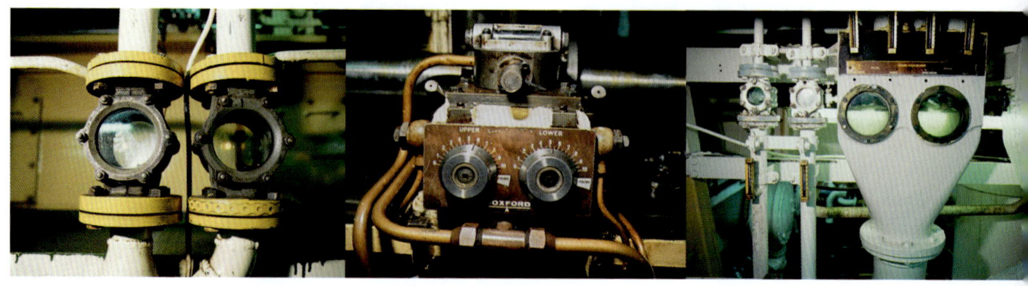

127

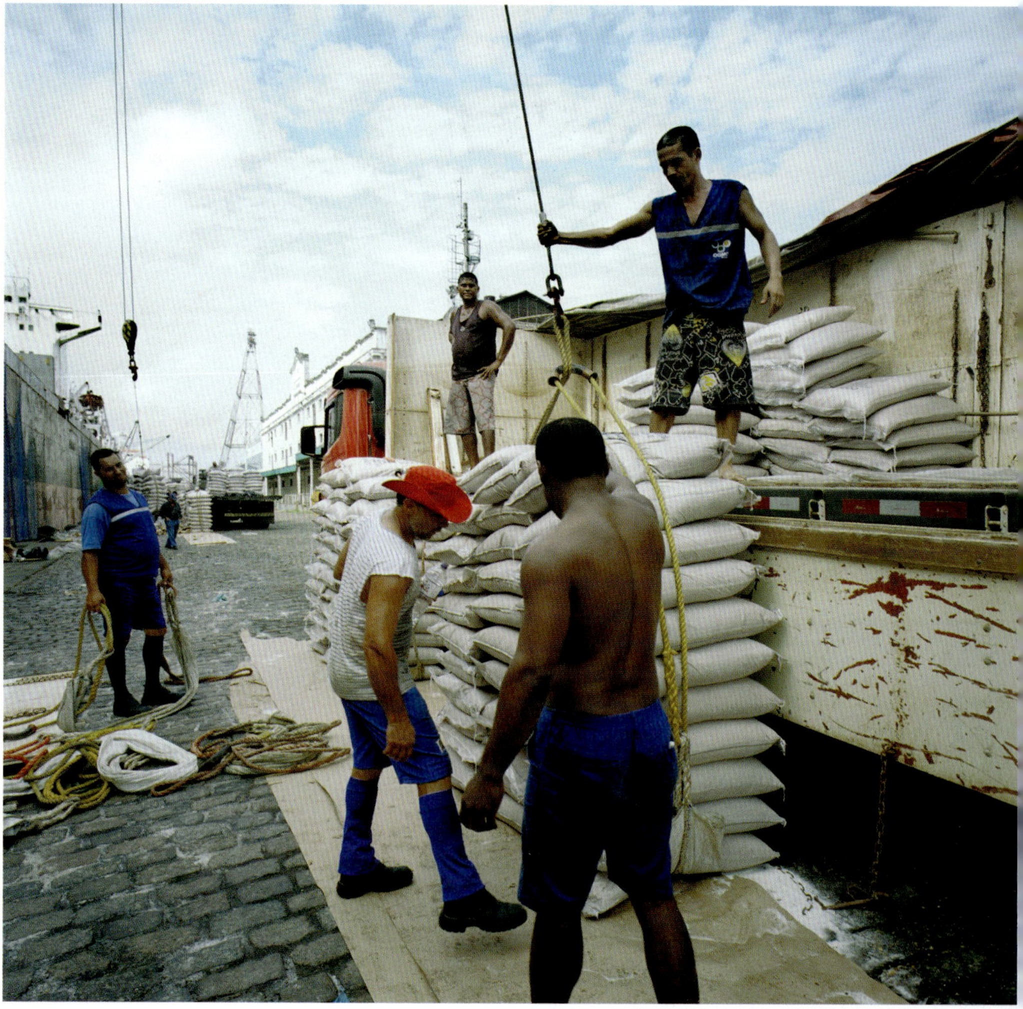

128

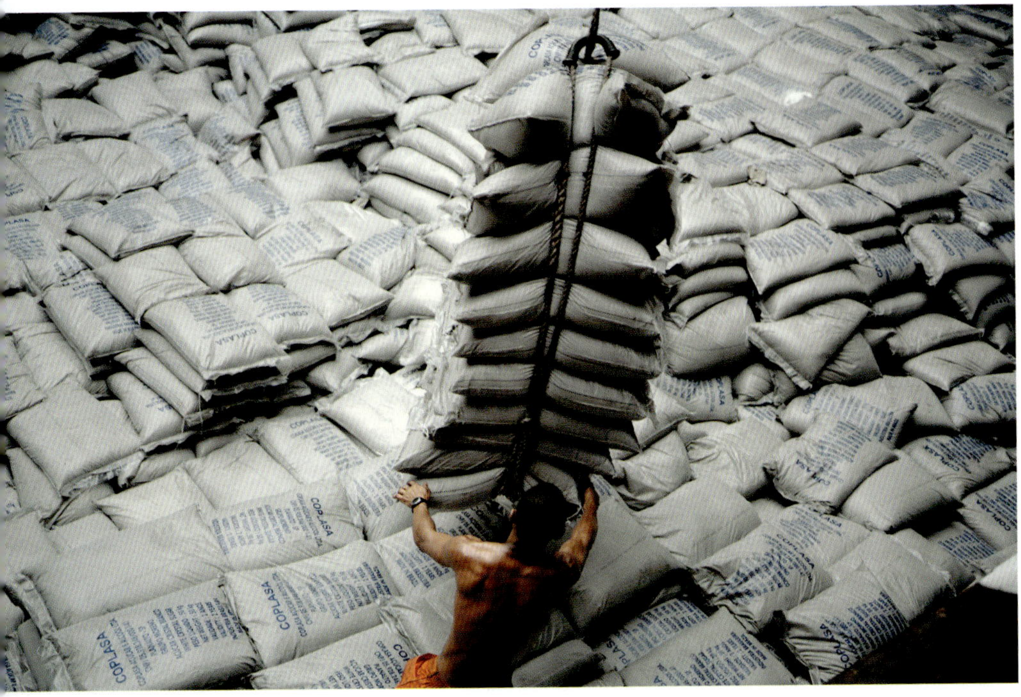

The Dockers' Museum (2010–13)

129

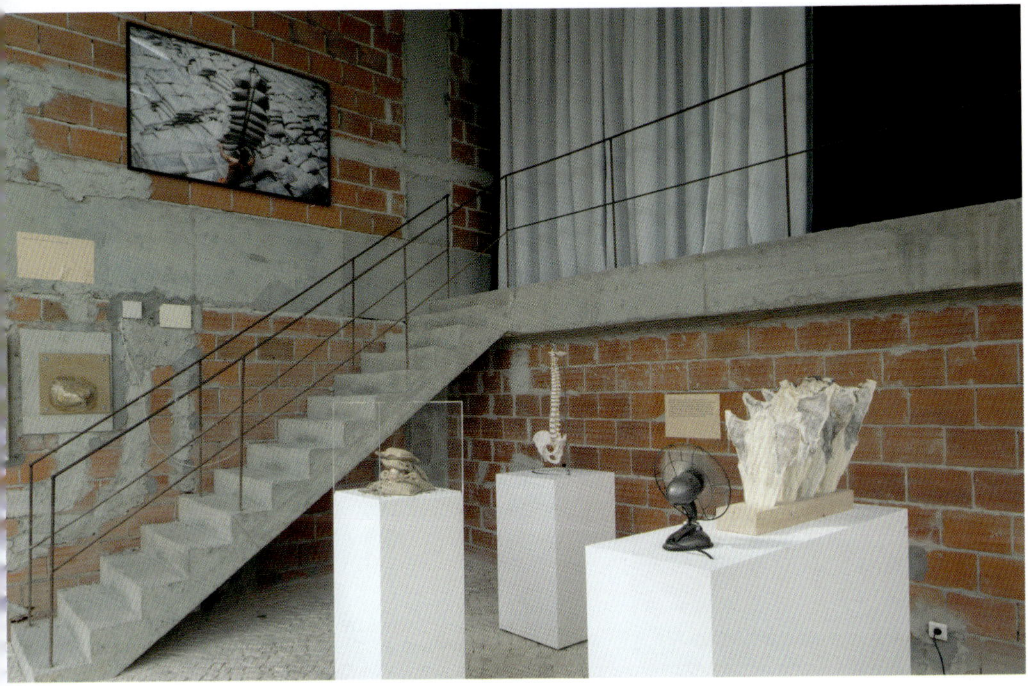

The Dockers' Museum (cont.)

130

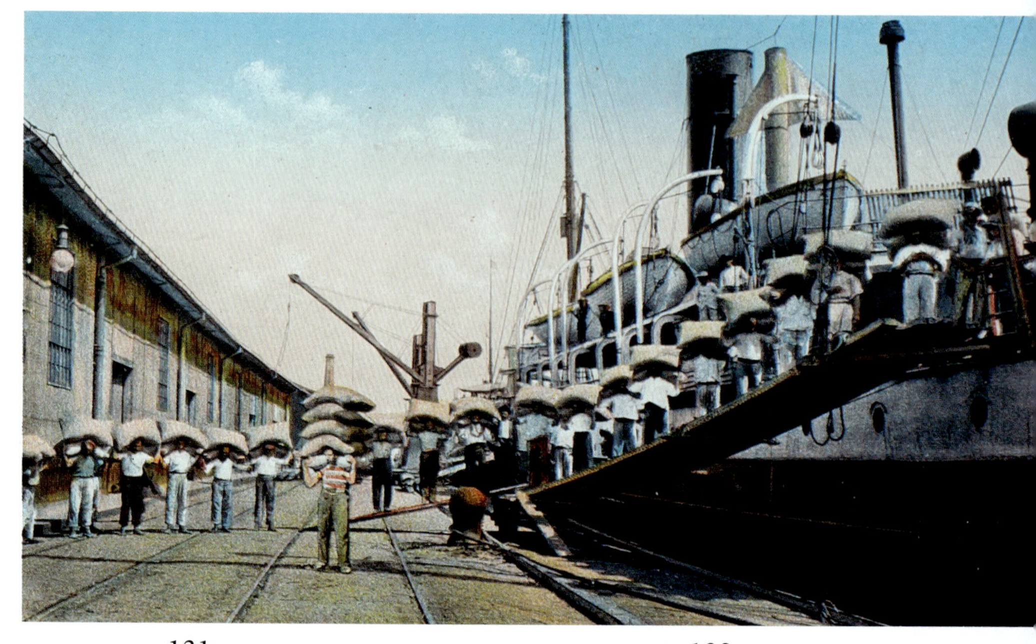

131

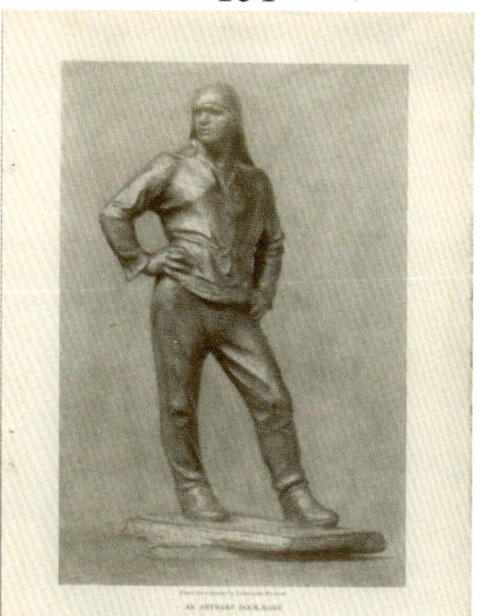

132

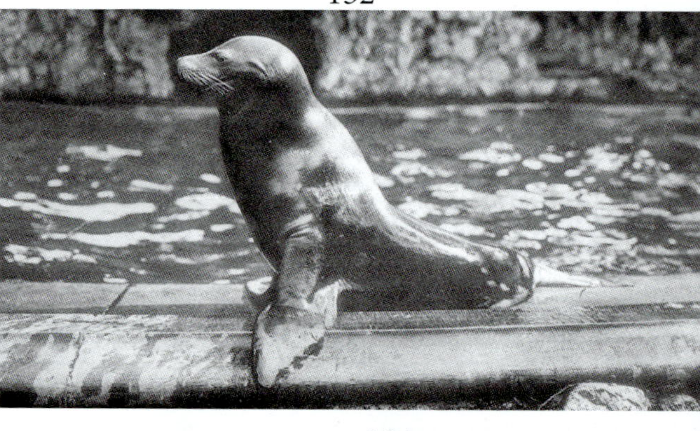

133

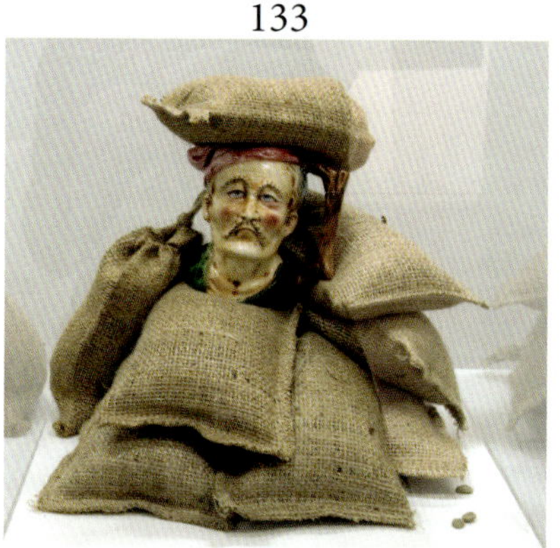

134

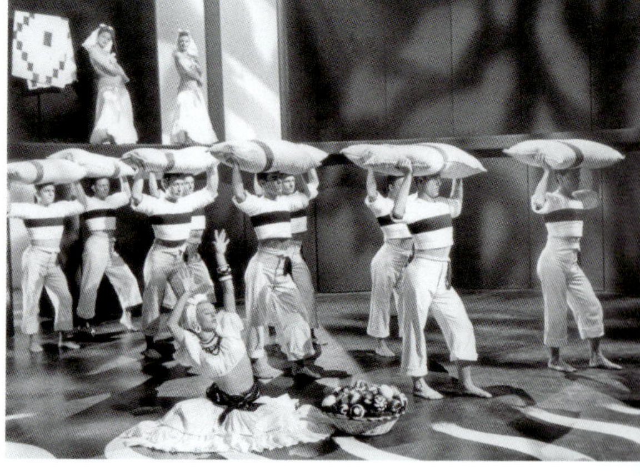

over informational detail, he continues, should be reframed as a question of the relation of detail to historical generalisation ('typification' or levels of representation). 'Narrative' per se is not the problem with film; it is an inescapable structural condition of representation.[104] Ultimately, White thinks that the representation of historical events and persons in film troubles historians, not because of its inaccuracies or the degree of its adequacy to representing the past, but because 'it raises the specter of the "fictionality" of the historian's own discourse'.[105] For White, historiography should be complemented by 'historiophoty': 'the representation of history and our thought about it in visual images and filmic discourse'.[106] His essay – like the forum – is centred on the filmic, but it touches briefly on the wider question of visual or aural representation. As with Samuel's point above, White acknowledges that visual materials – often ignored or treated as illustration – ought to be as central to historians' research as written documents, and that distinct skills of 'reading' are required.

Attending to history as reading and representation means thinking about forms and narrative modes, but we see no reason that this should entail a loss of commitment to subaltern politics. To take just one example, as well as its lack of 'motleyness', Thompson's history was also criticised for its 'partisanship' and 'anachronism'. As cultural anthropologist Renato Rosaldo observes, 'Thompson takes sides. He refuses to stand outside his history because its antagonisms live on into the present. Often writing in the first person, Thompson positions himself more as a partisan than as an omniscient narrator.'[107] Thompson clearly understood that he was taking sides; he wrote, if we are to discover what subaltern subjects thought about authority, documents 'must be held up to a Satanic light and read backwards'.[108] In Rosaldo's sympathetic critique, Thompson nonetheless elides the issue of whether 'the central concepts belong to the author [the historian] or to the agents of historical change [that the historian writes about]'.[109] Thompson,

104 Jameson, *The Political Unconscious*.

105 Hayden White, 'Historiography and Historiophoty', *The American Historical Review* 93:5 (1988): 1193–9 (1195).

106 Ibid., 1193.

107 Renato Rosaldo, 'Celebrating Thompson's Heroes: Social Analysis in History & Anthropology', in *E.P. Thompson, Critical Perspectives*, eds Harvey J. Kaye and Keith McClelland (Cambridge: Polity, 1990), 103–24 (118).

108 Thompson, *The Making of the English Working Class*, 62.

109 Rosaldo, 'Celebrating Thompson's Heroes', 104.

Rosaldo argues, also draws on the melodramatic mode to stage a Manichean struggle, where 'the past and the present become contemporaneous within a single field of conflict'.[110] Some of this criticism is astute, but Thompson's project can be stated more positively: 'as a class-conscious aeolian harp', to use Catherine Gallagher and Stephen Greenblatt's metaphor.[111] With its extended figurative patterns, Thompson's history can be understood as a form of allegory. It is an approach based on rigorous archival research but one that is not narrowly historicist (in the sense of 'how it really was'); rather, it is an engaged history that can be made usable to later generations. As Fred Inglis put it, 'this was a new past to live by', one that in changing 'social memory' enabled agents to think 'forward to a new set of possibilities'.[112] By weaving narratives composed of specific incidents and individual radical lives, history from below projects a collective vision across time; it involves the creation of radical traditions and narratives capable of countering the constant appeals to the past by established ideologues.

As conventionally defined, allegory is an extended trope, one that 'twice tells' (deriving from *allos agoreuein* or 'other-speaking').[113] Seeing history from below in this light would also pick up, in a more constructive vein, Rosaldo's identification of Thompson's 'anachronisms' and 'Manichean' structures (think: the psychomachia of Virtues and Vices). In history from below, we suggest, there is a doubling of time: both historical investigation into past events and a tale pertinent for contemporary readers of that study.[114] It is worth noting that Thompson, C. L. R. James and Christopher Hill all actively engaged with allegorical literature. Linebaugh and Rediker's writing itself takes on an explicit allegorical form. In *The Many-Headed Hydra*, the struggles of the present guide the stories to be found in the archives. Rediker's *The Fearless Benjamin Lay* presents an exemplary life, one well lived, and with *The Magna Carta Manifesto* and *Red Round Globe Hot Burning*, Linebaugh's work further accumulates incidents, anecdotes and parables, forming

110 Ibid., 117.

111 Catherine Gallagher and Stephen Greenblatt, *Practicing New Historicism* (Chicago, IL: University of Chicago Press, 1997), 57.

112 Fred Inglis, *Radical Earnestness* (Oxford: Oxford University Press, 1984), 199.

113 *Allos agoreuein*, 'other-speaking', is more precisely 'other-to-public-speech', highlighting the connection to the politics and marketplace of the ancient agora. More on this in Chapter 3.

114 Eley, *A Crooked Line*, 56.

an assembly of fragmentary insights for the present.[115] Positioned between John Bunyan and Walter Benjamin, writers like Thompson, Hill, James, Linebaugh and Rediker employ an allegorical temporality. Fusing the radical antinomian past with Benjaminian 'now time', they refuse the narrative closures of political defeat to enrich the current communist imagination.[116]

Sekula described *Fish Story* as 'an "art historical" allegory of the sea as an object of representation' – an allegory of 'disappearance' of the maritime world.[117] Identification with the exploited and those on the wrong side of history is central to his view of the world, but rather than referring to Thompson's cast of characters, he retrieves another group from 'enormous condescension': precarious fast-food workers, seafarers, striking dockers, scavengers, informal traders, fishing communities, union organisers and protesters. Thompson's 'foolhardy' practitioners of insurrection resurface explicitly in *Ship of Fools* (2010), Sekula's photo sequence of the campaigning activists of *Global Mariner*, the ship of the International Transport Workers' Federation. This work's title is a direct acknowledgement of a late fifteenth-century allegory: Sebastian Brant's *Das Narrenschiff* (1494), an early product of print technology, illustrated with woodcuts by Albrecht Dürer. The 'ship of fools' subsequently became a popular theme – one painted by Hieronymus Bosch (1490–1500), for example. Centuries later, Foucault alighted on it. Brandt mixed high and vulgar voices with that of the 'fool', enabling criticism that would not otherwise have been possible.[118]

In allegorical literature, the journey is a classic device – as in *The Faerie Queen* – enacting a spiritual (or, later, existential) voyage. Bakhtin identified the road as a major chronotope in earlier literature. However,

---

115 Marcus Rediker, *The Fearless Benjamin Lay: The Quaker Dwarf Who Became the First Revolutionary Abolitionist* (London: Verso, 2017); Peter Linebaugh, *The Magna Carta Manifesto: Liberties and Commons for All* (Berkeley, CA: University of California Press, 2009); *Red Round Globe Hot Burning: A Tale at the Crossroads of Commons and Closure, of Love and Terror, of Race and Class, and of Kate and Ned Despard* (Berkeley, CA: University of California Press, 2019).

116 For an important use of avant-garde narrative against political closure, see: Laura Mulvey, 'Changes: Thoughts on Myth, Narrative and Historical Experience', in *Visual and Other Pleasures* (London: Macmillan, 1989), 159–76.

117 'On *Fish Story*', 53.

118 Sekula in Hou Hanru, 'Allan Sekula and Bruno Serralongue', *Flash Art*, 14 November 2014, flash-art.com (first published as 'In Conversation with Bruno Serralongue and Allan Sekula', *Art Practical*, 15 February 2012).

it is worth noting that it continues to be prominent in modern paraliterature – to which Sekula was attentive – and it plays a key role in the canon of modern American photography (Walker Evans, Dorothea Lange, Robert Frank, Stephen Shore, Ed Ruscha). The 'road' can include the sea-lanes between ports. And, as is made explicit in Sekula's *Freeway to China* (1998–9), it sometimes involves metaphorical extension: encompassing both neoliberal trade roots and the organisational pathways of international solidarity connecting maritime workers.[119] On occasion, Sekula's journey is relatively localised; at other times, it becomes global. In the conventions of literary allegory, a series of encounters shape these voyaging narratives; the characters met by the protagonist present him (nearly always 'him') with tests or trials. Sometimes, the characters that Sekula encounters are identified by name, and *Freeway to China* is structured around a number of formal 'portraits'. Elsewhere, his characters are embodiments of roles, such as in the 'Machinist and apprentice' in *TITANIC's wake*. *Ship of Fools* includes a cycle of portraits, the titles for which explicitly suggest allegory. Once again, the example of August Sander seems foremost in the handling of the portraits, which suggest a contemporary *Face of Our Time* – although, here, it involves an activist world onboard one ship, rather than the physiognomic effort to map the German people.[120]

That said, the comparison with classic allegorical narrative only goes so far. Sekula does not present the sequences through a guiding protagonist. The individuals encountered do not pose challenges and temptations. Furthermore, while conventional allegorical heroes might be lured from their paths, their journeys ultimately have direction and destination; problems emerge so that they can be resolved en route to narrative epiphany. Sekula's sequences do not share these qualities. Historians of allegory identify a break between its traditional and modern modes, where the affirmation of spiritual discovery and resolution in earlier allegory is contrasted with its modern characteristics: negative, sceptical, doubting, ironic, unresolved; selfhood that is

119 Despite the overarching motif of the sea, what Sekula mostly presents is the juncture with solid ground, hinterlands and infrastructural networks. Only occasionally do his captions give properly maritime locations: 'Mid-Atlantic' (*Fish Story*, 1995); or 'Off the Albanian Coast' (*TITANIC's wake*, 2000).

120 Alfred Döblin's short accompanying essay to Sander's book sees Sander's project as an assembly of representative 'social types', highlighting a measure of affinity between allegory and realism.

alienated, unheroic, diminished, declined, debased.[121] Yet, even this thread of negativity remains channelled through a guiding character in literary allegory and is absent from Sekula's work.

The sequences do not present the succession of events or retrace the steps of his journeys. Sekula's projects are accumulative and retroactive; their narratives interrupt as much as carry the journeys; they cross-pollinate, both internally and exogenously. This could be put down to the difference between literature and the visual-plastic arts – but that explanation is too easy, because Sekula challenges this very opposition, actively exploiting their mutual inflection. Insofar as a 'destination' can be discerned, it is acquired through extended reflection ('the road of critical research'). Sekula's approach to allegory is less about presenting 'vertical' translations between literal and figural levels. On the whole, it is not a practice of 'allegoresis' (that is, the exegetical interpretation of a text's 'hidden' layers, and often a text that was not intentionally written as an allegory). Rather, allegory is approached as a complex skein of associations spreading with a 'horizontal pressure', and prioritises the process of engagement by the perceiver.[122] Allegory's *allos* is not, Maureen Quilligan insists, 'some other hovering above [below, behind, inside] the words of the text, but the possibility of an otherness, a polysemy, inherent in the very words on the page'; allegory, in this sense, attends to 'the radical significance of . . . literal surface'.[123] Although this is not to be confused with formalism, there are still risks of over-internalisation.[124] With these caveats in mind, the distinction between allegoresis and allegory underscores how Sekula's approach poses epistemological and representational conundrums. His works offer the possibility of allegorical explorations of the problems in understanding modern capitalism, the difficulties of representing that understanding, and the challenges of comprehending its representational elisions and paradoxes.

121 Edwin Honig, *Dark Conceit: The Making of Allegory* (1959; New York: Oxford University Press, 1966); Angus Fletcher, *Allegory: The Theory of a Symbolic Mode* (Ithaca, NY: Cornell University Press, 1964); Gay Clifford, *The Transformations of Allegory* (London: Routledge and Kegan Paul, 1974); Maureen Quilligan, *The Language of Allegory: Defining the Genre* (Ithaca, NY: Cornell University Press, 1979).

122 Quilligan, *The Language of Allegory*, 33, 235. She sees structuralism as the return of allegoresis and favours poststructural methods.

123 Ibid., 26, 29.

124 This is seen as an internalisation where the text interrogates its own (in)adequacies; its self-reflexivity becomes a vortex of auto-consuming infinite regressions. Quilligan tries to sidestep this exegetical danger – or rather, mobilises it – centring how, by retarding reading with 'the labour of language', allegorical narratives pose ethical choices.

A focus on classic literary allegory, then, overly restricts our understanding of the mode. Another vector may be more apposite: the distinction between 'allegory' and 'symbol' – between the 'other-speaking' (allegory's *allos agoreuein*) and the 'throwing-together' of the symbol's *sum ballein*. (Everyday usage tends to collapse together allegorical and symbolic representation: an allegorical figure with its attributes is often said to 'symbolise' a quality; and even the specialist Angus Fletcher titled his book *Allegory: The Theory of a Symbolic Mode*.) The approach to allegory we have in mind draws on literary discussions, albeit of a more aesthetic-philosophical bent. At the core of this interpretation are engagements with Benjamin's early study on the German 'mourning play' (*Trauerspiel*), along with some of his later writing on Paris and Central Park, and with Paul de Man's essay 'The Rhetoric of Temporality', an intervention that drew on Benjamin.[125]

This line of discussion became important for strands of critical art practice at the time when high modernism was under fire for its seeming detached autonomy and claims to universalism. Played out on the pages of the journal *October* in 1980, and sparked by two essays by Craig Owens, the modernist (and Romantic) 'symbol' was rejected in favour of 'allegorical procedures'.[126] Allegorical qualities were discerned in the work of contemporary artists, many associated with Douglas

125 Walter Benjamin, *The Origin of German Tragic Drama* (1928; London: New Left Books, 1977). Benjamin, 'Paris, Capital of the Nineteenth Century' (1955), *New Left Review* I: 48 (1968): 77–88; retranslated as 'Paris, the Capital of the Nineteenth Century', in *Selected Writings Volume 3, 1935–1938*, 32–49. Paul de Man, 'The Rhetoric of Temporality' (1969), in *Blindness and Insight: Essays in the Rhetoric of Contemporary Criticism*, revised second edition (London: Routledge, 1983), 187–228; *Allegories of Reading: Figural Language in Rousseau, Nietzsche, Rilke, and Proust* (New Haven, CT: Yale University Press, 1979); 'Sign and Symbol in Hegel's Aesthetics', *Critical Inquiry* 8 (1982): 761–75. Originally from 1928, the English translation of Benjamin's *Trauerspiel* sparked Anglophone interest in allegory. Jameson engaged with the subject in *Marxism and Form* (1971). German interest dates from the mid-1970s.

126 The journal *October* was a platform for this discussion. Craig Owens, 'The Allegorical Impulse: Towards a Theory of Postmodernism', *October* 12 (1980): 67–86; 'The Allegorical Impulse: Towards a Theory of Postmodernism Part 2' Part 2, *October* 13 (1980): 58–80 (59–80); cf. 'Photography *en abyme*', *October* 5 (Summer 1978): 73–88 and 'Earthwords', *October* 10 (1979): 120–30. See also Joel Fineman, 'The Structure of Allegorical Desire', *October* 12 (1980): 46–66. Stephen Melville, 'Notes of the Re-emergence of Allegory, the Forgetting of Modernism, the Necessity of Rhetoric, and the Conditions of Publicity in Art Criticism', *October* 19 (1981): 55–92; Benjamin H. D. Buchloh, 'Allegorical Procedures: Appropriation and Montage in Contemporary Art', *Artforum* 21:1 (1982): 43–56.

Crimp's *Pictures* exhibition of 1977.[127] Photography played a central role – less in terms of working out of photographic history (although Sherrie Levine – one of Owens's allegorical artists – used Walker Evans) and more from the perspective of artists engaging with the role of photography as a reproductive technology in media and commercial advertising. While many of the artists listed as 'allegorical' would be associated with 'postmodernism' (Owens), or specifically 'critical postmodernism' (Hal Foster), others (Crimp, Buchloh) remained suspicious of even critical postmodernism's tendency towards ironic detachment and depoliticisation. This latter position was hinted at by Buchloh, who distinguished between the ironised strategies of Levine and the more political work of Martha Rosler.[128] As a practice opposing high-modernist claims, Sekula's work was certainly implied, even if his name did not feature. What is important to understand here is both his relation to and his departures from 'allegorical procedures' as they were being formulated around 1980. We saw earlier that Sekula was moving away from obviously constructed or staged artwork, which characterised many of the celebrated examples of 'allegorical procedures'; he was highly critical of 'postmodernism', scepticism, easy irony and the 'oh, look, "reality" is just fiction' school of thought. However, instead of throwing out the baby of allegory with the bathwater, he recovered allegory for his 'imaginative geographies'.

The dominant strands of modernist criticism were associated with the late-Romantic idea of the artistic symbol: organic, transcendental, instantaneous, fully present and offering a plenitude of meaning – the inspired manifestation of the artist-genius. It was viewed as timeless and self-contained; requiring no interpretation, it 'speaks for itself'. For critical thinkers, the aesthetic ideology of the symbol offers an illusory whole – a false reconciliation of subject and object, sign and signified – as compensation for a dirempt world.[129] In contrast, in the allegorical

127 Douglas Crimp, 'Pictures', *October* 8 (1979): 75–88; 'On the Museum's Ruins', *October* 13 (1980) and *On the Museum's Ruins* (Cambridge MA: MIT Press, 1993), which includes other essays from the early 1980s. The artists listed are Cindy Sherman, Jack Goldstein, Robert Longo, Troy Brauntuch and Sherrie Levine.

128 Doubts were also expressed by Crimp in *Pictures*.

129 On aesthetic ideology: Paul de Man, 'The Rhetoric of Temporality' and *Aesthetic Ideology* (Minneapolis, MN: University of Minnesota Press, 1996); Terry Eagleton, *The Ideology of the Aesthetic* (Oxford: Blackwell, 1990). Gail Day interrogates these debates in *Dialectical Passions: Negation in Postwar Art Theory* (New York: Columbia University Press, 2011). See also Fred Orton, *Figuring Jasper Johns* (London: Reaktion, 1994) and his *Aesthetic Thinking: Essays on Intention, Painting, Action and Ideology* (Leiden: Brill, 2022).

consciousness, the symbol's transcendental inspiration is replaced by fragmentation, temporal extensions and disjuncture, and meditations on worldly ruin and death. Allegory – disillusioned and based on non-identity, ruptures and gaps – is closely associated with the practice of montage, a method that tears, and thus questions, any sense of a seamless continuum. Montage contains all the elements of allegory: 'appropriation and depletion of meaning, fragmentation and dialectical juxtaposition of fragments, and separation of signifier and signified'.[130] Like photographic framing, allegory rips portions of the world from their 'naturalised' contexts.

Many of these ideas run throughout Sekula's work. He rejected the modernist fetish of the single print and preferred the impure forms or mixed presentational modes that polluted photographs with words. The photobook and picture story employ the montage method, juxtaposing images and allowing the viewer or reader to compose 'third meanings'. In his work, narrative extensions and detours prevail over the idea of or belief in a timeless aesthetic. As we have seen, *Fish Story* is made from photographic sequences (switching genres and styles), slide sequences, textual reflections and detailed captions for the photographs which are spatially displaced from the pictures; none of this coheres smoothly or without the labour of attention. In place of large images that ape the scales of advertising or history painting (Jeff Wall's approach), *Fish Story* – even when presented for gallery exhibition – reworks the more intimate models of the photobook.[131] Individual photographs rarely clamour for attention, but collectively they stack up, their significance accumulating over time. As a portrayal of capitalism, this is the antithesis of Edward Burtynsky's huge construction sites, or Andreas Gursky's images of stock markets and large banks, with their frenzied traders, electronic transactions and display of instantaneity. Despite their economic subject matter, these large-scale gallery photographs shadow the Romantic symbol, with diminutive human figures overpowered by their spectacular(ised) contexts.[132] *Fish Story* offers nothing so eye-catching; the pictures are deliberately modest and seem quite ordinary. Sekula's low-plane vision made him one of the first to rework the 'bad

130 Buchloh, 'Allegorical Procedures', 44.

131 Buchloh, 'Allan Sekula: Photography Between Discourse and Document', 190.

132 Steve Edwards, 'Crowds and Commons: Figuring Photography from Above and Below', *Third Text* 23:4 (2009): 447–64. For Sekula on Gursky: 'Epilogue: A Debate on Critical Realism Today', in *Critical Realism: Around Allan Sekula's Art*, eds Hilde Van Gelder and Jan Baetens (Leuven: Leuven University Press, 2006), 121–37 (124).

object of contemporary art'.[133] But this reworking is important. Through his politicised allegorical procedures, Sekula's works prise open the symbolic joins, revise realism and documentary against aesthetic ideology, and encourage viewers to wend their way through each sequence's extended horizontal components.

De Man contrasts the symbol's rhetoric of (a)temporality with allegory's temporal character. Allegory constantly shuttles from literal to figural dimensions, doubling and deferring meaning, and involves the '*repetition* . . . of a previous sign with which it can never coincide'.[134] Temporality is central to understanding allegory, underlining its historical layering. Allegory's delays and stretched temporalities replace the symbol's immediacy of impression. De Man pursues a deconstructive version of this idea, but it is, once more, Benjamin that is most relevant to Sekula. Returning to the subject of our opening discussion, Benjamin emphasises the defining mood of allegory as melancholic, joining times, 'over-ripeness and decay', death and ruins.[135] Temporal vectors momentarily intersect, folding, constellating and re-constellating, allowing alternative scenarios to be weighed. Various forms of imagery and writing combine, both accelerating and slowing our attention. We find the 'irregular rhythm of the constant pause, the sudden change of direction' and 'dialectics at a standstill'.[136] In the work of totalisation, finality is displaced and deferred. Sekula's additive and digressive method, with its layerings of material, similarly holds off historical closure.

Photography, Space and Time

The temporal condition at the heart of allegory has its counterpart in the debate over the 'photographic paradox', prominent during the late 1970s and 1980s, which drew on the earlier work of Roland Barthes, André Bazin and (for some) Siegfried Kracauer. In discussions of photography, that debate has been set aside – the analogue form central to considerations of the ontology of the medium has been displaced, or at least stretched, by digital code; and other intellectual approaches

133 'Imaginary Economies: An Interview with Allan Sekula', 237. For all its emphasis on low-key subjects, we need to recognise that even the tradition of photographic realism often laid claim to immediacy and a spurious organic unity.

134 De Man, 'The Rhetoric of Temporality', 207.

135 Benjamin, *The Origin of German Tragic Drama*, 179.

136 Ibid., 197; 'Paris, the Capital of the Nineteenth Century', 40.

have come to seem more pressing.[137] We return to the peculiar temporal qualities of photography because time is central to Sekula's projects, to his conception of photography, to allegory and, of course, to history from below.

The photographic paradox is charged by the gap between the click of the shutter and the moment of viewing the image created. The account of it is, at heart, a phenomenological interpretation where the ontology of the medium has death as its ultimate horizon. Bazin, for instance, speaks of photography as being akin to the embalming of the dead, or a fly caught in amber; opting for a more sci-fi ring, Peter Wollen points to its cryogenic qualities.[138] But all of these thinkers, including Kracauer and Benjamin, view photographs as time-space packages that allow glimpses of the past in the present.[139] The central version of the photographic paradox is to be found in the work of Barthes, both in his early essays 'The Photographic Message' (1961) and 'The Rhetoric of the Image' (1964) and in his final book *Camera Lucida: Reflections on Photography* (1980).[140] These works have been the topic of much discussion, though commentators seem to have missed Barthes's strangely utopian account of 'denotation'.[141] In 'The Rhetoric of the Image', discussing a Panzani food advertisement, Barthes distinguishes three levels of the semiotic 'message': linguistic (the advertisement's slogan); connotative (the way the imagery conveys symbolic content, in this case 'Italianicity'); and denotative (the image's literal content). Attending

---

137 We mention only two of these methodological innovations, both with implications for concerns with postcolonial ideas. First, anthropologists – Elizabeth Edwards, Deborah Poole and others – have emphasised networks of photographic use, rather than the semiotics of the image; second, Ariella Aïsha Azoulay's contractualist decisionism has offered a politicised account of photographic agency, which has struck many as an urgent necessity in response to language-centred models. (Arguably, both approaches are problematised by Sekula's value critique of photographic exchange or 'traffic'.)

138 André Bazin, 'The Ontology of the Photographic Image' (1945), in *What is Cinema? Volume I* (1967; Berkeley, CA: University of California Press, 2005), 9–16. Peter Wollen, 'Fire and Ice' (1984), in *Other Than Itself*, eds John X. Berger and Olivier Richon (Manchester: Cornerhouse, 1989), *Other Than Itself* centred on photography and allegory.

139 Siegfried Kracauer, 'Photograph' (1927), in *The Mass Ornament: Weimar Essays* (Cambridge, MA: Harvard University Press, 1995), 47–63.

140 Roland Barthes, 'The Photographic Message' (1961) and 'The Rhetoric of the Image' (1964), in *Image/Music/Text*, ed. Stephen Heath (London: Fontana, 1977), 15–31 and 32–51; *Camera Lucida: Reflections on Photography* (New York: Hill & Wang, 1981).

141 For responses, see: *Writing the Image After Roland Barthes*, ed. Jean-Michel Rabaté (Philadelphia, PA: University of Pennsylvania Press, 1997); and *Photography Degree Zero: Reflections on Roland Barthes's Camera Lucida*, ed. Geoffrey Batchen (Cambridge, MA: MIT Press, 2011).

specifically to the denotative aspect, he argues, photography introduces 'a decisive mutation' in the history of images, which involves for the first time '*messages without a code*'.[142] The 'paradox' specifically concerns a split within this denotative level. He writes: 'What we have is a new space-time category: spatial immediacy and temporal anteriority, the photograph being an illogical conjunction between the *here-now* and the *there-then* . . . Its unreality is that of the *here-now* . . . its reality that of the *having-been-there*.'[143]

At some point around 1970, Barthes abandoned the structuralist 'science of the text' for interpretations of 'obtuse' or excessive meanings that involved subjective, affective or erotic responses by the reader. With regard to photography, this shift is evident in his essay on Eisenstein's film stills and the 'third meaning'.[144] *Camera Lucida* rejects semiotics, and the presentation of denotation shifts markedly from the earlier essays: the photograph is not a copy of, but an emanation from, an object. Nonetheless, the temporal paradox remains central. *Camera Lucida*, even more than the earlier essays, has a phenomenological underpinning (and is dedicated to the Sartre of *L'imaginaire*).[145] The book presents photographs as forms of memento mori, which ultimately remind beholders of their time-bound, mortal existence; the 'there-then' points to what is inevitably to come.[146] This argument is elucidated with reference to (or reinforced by) a photograph of his recently deceased mother, taken before he was born, which he

142 Barthes, 'The Rhetoric of the Image', 45.

143 Ibid., 44.

144 In his study of Eisenstein's stills, Barthes discusses 'The obtuse meaning', suggesting that the 'third meaning' transcends (or is a remainder of) symbolic meaning in photographs. He returns to 'obtuseness' in *Camera Lucida*, where it suggests being outside or beyond culture. Barthes, 'The Third Meaning: Some Research Notes on Eisenstein Stills' (1970), in *Image/Music/Text*, 52–68.

145 Jean-Paul Sartre, *The Imaginary: A Phenomenological Psychology of the Imagination* (1940; London: Routledge, 2004). Sartre contrasts the total apprehension of imagination to the partiality of perception. Interestingly, he discusses kinds of apprehension: the mental image of memory; the photograph and the sketch or cartoon. Barthes takes the term *analagon* from this work, as he takes *noeme* from Husserl.

146 In a remarkable essay, Thierry de Duve offers a nuanced reading and extension of this paradox, combining semiotics, phenomenology and psychoanalysis. Distinguishing two ideal types of photograph – the 'snapshot' and the 'time-exposure' – he explores distinct forms of time in the image. However, both forms are written under the sign of death. Drawing on Freud's psychopathology, the two forms are identified, respectively, with mania and depression. Thierry de Duve, 'Time Exposure and Snapshot: The Photograph as Paradox', *October* 5 (1978): 113–25. This issue of *October* was devoted to theorising photography.

withholds from view; and another by Alexander Gardner of Lewis Payne in his cell awaiting execution. For Barthes, the photograph is a mournful sign of absence, rather than presence; its trace entails or evokes a kind of absolute loss. 'Death is the *eidos*' of a photograph.[147]

Much debate has centred on Barthes's contrasting ideas of the *studium* (the social world of codes and conventions to which the image belongs) and the *punctum* (the detail which touches the viewer privately, 'that accident which pricks me').[148] Barthes presents the *punctum* as involving a naïve or 'primitive' instance – 'I dismiss all knowledge, all culture' – but, here, phenomenological *epoché* does not lead to objectivity or universal judgement; rather, it initiates a wholly personal response involving a suspensive moment of time.[149] Central to this argument is the future anterior tense: 'it will have been'. Barthes writes of Gardner's photograph of Payne: 'the *punctum* is: *he is going to die*. I read at the same time: *This will be* and *this has been*; I observe with horror an anterior future of which death is at stake.'[150] A positive reading might suggest that, by subjectively suturing the viewer, the *punctum* draws the reader into the *studium*. Certainly, the book shares with the author's earlier essays a distaste for the role of the photography in political manipulation, but if previously his response entailed demythification, now it is one of personal withdrawal. *Camera Lucida* is an inventive account of photography and time, but its enthusiastic reception is symptomatic of a desire to flee from the radical critique of the preceding period. As we have seen, Sekula was most drawn to the early writing of Barthes.

There is, though, a way other than Barthes's of thinking about photography's future anterior and temporal paradox, one associated with Benjamin.[151] Benjamin's dialectical images conjoin fragments of the past to possible futures, in imaginative flashes or sparks. This allows for a very different conception of the future anterior, attributing the image with an active role in the present. There are two significant differences between these approaches. First, Benjamin's dialectic, unlike that of Barthes, is collectivist rather than focused on the individual. Second,

---

147 *Camera Lucida*, 15.

148 Ibid., 27.

149 Ibid., 51.

150 Ibid., 96. His italics. Barthes's argument appears to be the exact inverse of his earlier criticism of Steichen's empty humanism in *The Family of Man* exhibition: Barthes, 'The Great Family of Man', *Mythologies* (1957; London: Vintage, 1993), 100–2.

151 Our thinking here is informed by Peter Osborne's essay 'Sign and Image' in his *Philosophy and Cultural Theory* (London: Routledge, 2000), 20–52.

Benjamin shatters the historical continuum that underpins Barthes's subjectivist reading, so that it becomes possible to look back from a future imagined to other possible pasts. Here the future anterior is an instance of the not-yet, a futural positionality that reads the past for usable histories and, like Thompson, rescues the defeated from the condescension of the present. This is an approach associated with left Benjaminian thought as it was formed in Paris by: Bensaïd, Löwy, Traverso, Stathis Kouvelakis and the wider milieu around the journal *Futur Antérieur* (1989–98). As Toni Negri put it in his postface to that journal:

> Socialism had been defeated in the conjuncture, but it left us a heritage of organisation, of struggles, of a biopolitical sense of the existing world, which could – to the extent that we were able to detach ourselves from it – be proposed as the basis for a reappropriation and/or a construction of new political means of transformation.[152]

Fusing the senses of historical time to be found in Benjamin and Thompson, Sekula summons sidelined hopes. With the resources of language, he is readily able to move between tenses. Yet, for photographs, the same ease and precision in flexing time is more difficult to effect, if not impossible. In ways available to them *qua* photographs (sequencing being just one method), photographs can also laminate temporalities to stave off both melancholic and presentist dangers. Ways can even be found to predicate or adopt anticipatory perspectives.[153] We conclude this chapter by considering two works that foreground allegory's temporal questions.

---

152 Toni Negri, Postface to the complete text of the journal *Futur Antérieur* (1989–98) as published on the *Multitudes* website: geocities.ws.

153 This is contra Hayden White, who (in passing, and alluding to Barthes) suggests that, unlike film or literature, still photographs cannot predicate (White, 'Historiography and Historiophoty', 1196). Peter Wollen tries to depart from Barthes's account, but still argues that an individual photograph cannot narrate, although a sequence of photographs can. We cannot open up the question, but it is noticeable how often the discussion is generated from film scholars or from photographers fascinated with filmic conventions. Attention is often given to the film still, actual or staged; to stillness per se; to Marey or Muybridge; or to Marker's *La Jetée*. See, for example, *Stillness and Time: Photography and the Moving Image*, eds David Green and Joanna Lowry (Brighton: Photoforum, 2006).

Freeway To China (Version 2, for Liverpool) *(1998–9)*

Freeway to China (Version 2, for Liverpool) (1998–9) is built from port-related scenes from Southern California and Merseyside. The thematic continuities with *Fish Story* are apparent, although the project has a tighter internationalist perspective and a focus on union activism (and what happens when workers are let down by their unions, as happened to the Liverpool dockers). The project contains twenty-three colour photographs (nine organised into three diptychs and a triptych) with paragraph-long captions. Included in the printed version is an additional black-and-white image by Dave Sinclair, a local photographer who was working closely with the striking Liverpool dockers and their families, with whom Sekula co-exhibited at Liverpool's Open Eye. Speaking in 1999, Sekula explained how this was the first project in which he had used titles that referred to genre (portrait) or that were allegorical ('Queen of the Pirates'). Hitherto, his titling practice had striven for the descriptive (he also understood that very descriptiveness as heightened attentiveness to the lexical or – and we come back to this in the next chapter – as prose poems). Underscoring this unleashing of allegorical allusions, the captions too grew in length: starting out as descriptions, they went 'somewhere else'.[154] One sequence taken on Los Angeles' Terminal Island (a sort of reverse effect of *Fish Story*'s Fontana sequence) highlights the integration of a global workforce as well as the national masks of the flag of convenience:

> The *Teal* berthed at Pier 300 after unloading two of four German cranes transported across the Indian and Pacific Oceans from a construction site in Abu Dhabi on the Persian Gulf, where they were manufactured by Filipino and other South Asian migrant laborers. Belgian-owned, the *Teal* is registered in the Netherlands Antilles, a pervasive legal ruse that permits the hiring of cheaper foreign crews.[155]

From a photograph of the harbour, our vision is propelled outwards, expanding geographically, and back through this moment's prehistories, helping us to grasp how the immediately given instantiates the impact of wider space-time conjunctures.

---

154 'Globalism's Discontents and the Return of the Sea', AA School of Architecture, 10 November 1999, youtube.com.

155 Sekula, 'Freeway to China (Version 2, for Liverpool), 1988–99', 278–305 (287).

The sequence of port scenes is punctuated by portraits.[156] The captions to the portraits detail experiences of struggle, defeat and defiance. Included are portraits of Ray Familathe, the Los Angeles longshore worker who travels to Merseyside on six occasions in solidarity; Liverpool strikers Mickey Tighe and Marty Size, watching scabs at work in their yard; and John Stanson, a former merchant seafarer and dock clerk, who left the industry to work as a guard for Tate Liverpool. Importantly, such portraits do not merely embody social processes; even in defeat, the agency of subjects is foregrounded. Below, we will look in detail at two of these portraits, one of Mason Davis, the other of Louisa Gratz. Sekula's engagement adheres to the best traditions of respect for the subject in humanist documentary and committed photojournalism. It is, however, more dialogical in conception: he is a witness, but also a medium channelling these people's stories, critical insights or sassy observations. Asked by Sekula why the history of the docks is absent from the Maritime Museum, Stanson responds, 'Are you familiar with Gramsci's idea of cultural hegemony?'[157] Stanson is an 'organic intellectual', Sekula later remarks, and stands outside the Tate in the sort of confident and debonair pose in which the museum's director might expect to be photographed.[158]

There seems to be something critical about the temporal registers enabled by these encounters. Note how, in the examples mentioned above, the individual vignettes cross-reference and condense socio-historical transformations. 'Liverpool', for example, coalesces the geographical toing and froing created by the present and by a history of past disputes. Another image, as we will see, folds in the earlier international solidarity with the boycotting of *Neptune Jade*. The captions describe and name what is photographed, but they also include testimonies from the activists and workers featured, bringing together recollections and anticipations. There are examples of prosopopoeia, the personification of an abstract idea, or the 'speaking from beyond the grave'; prolepsis, or anticipation; and, arguably, analepsis, where a past event is narrated later than its chronological point in a story (although chronology is fugitive in Sekula's work).[159]

156 Only the images of Davis, Gratz and Stanson are formally titled as 'Portrait'.

157 'Freeway to China (Version 2, for Liverpool), 304.

158 'Globalism's Discontents and the Return of the Sea'.

159 Prosopopoeia from *prosopon* + *poein*, person + to make; prolepsis from *pro* + *lambanein*, before + take; and analepsis from *ana* + *lambanein*, up + take.

There are stories set in the past that have no known end. Mason Davis, shop steward and former shipyard employee, goes on to work in the shipyard as a welder on temporary contracts before disappearing, reputedly to New York in search of work. He appears in two photographs, first unloading a gas cannister in a mid-distance shot, and then in a half-length portrait close to the camera, standing side-on with his head turned towards us. He is just off-centre in the frame, the front of his torso more or less marking the photograph's vertical midline. These images are woven into a sequence where the colours orange and blue are prominent. The photograph of Davis is arresting by the standards of any portrait, holding in tension the deep tangerine of the ship with the range of blues on his safety helmet, overalls and hoodie. His head is highlighted by the composition and by the handling of depth of field: the out-of-focus, orange-painted wall (a component of the ship's architecture); the directional 'pointing' towards Davis that is achieved by this wall and, from the other side, by the metal girders of a massive container crane (the ship's cargo). The container crane's blue-grey beams form an arrow that visually 'rests' on Davis's shoulders and even carries through to the tilt on his cheekbones. On the picture's right, out of focus, there is someone's arm and pointing hand; this gesture, surely made by another working docker, is presumably directed towards a work task, though here it also reinforces the flow of deictic forces converging on Davis's head. In a further emphasis, and entering the otherwise shaded area, the overexposure of a patch of sunlight glows beneath his chin. Davis's presence remains keenly felt, despite his whereabouts now being unknown; and yet his expression – thoughtful and wistful – reads, 'there-then', at the moment Sekula pressed the button, as if he were already imagining himself elsewhere.

Another example involves second-guessing decisions whose outcomes cannot be predicted. This photograph depicts the local union negotiator Louisa Gratz (Sekula mis-transcribes her name; she should be 'Luisa'). It is a full-length and centred portrait, but much more informal than that of Davis. As we saw, *Freeway*'s opening photo sequence is characterised by bold oranges and blues, but this image shifts to a more subdued culmination. Bollards, once fluorescent-orange warnings to stop trucks scraping the security entrance, are now faded and scuffed. The sequence's earlier deep blues have ceded to cool-grey concrete and dull cloud; cobalt hues survive only in Gratz's denim jeans. This is, almost certainly, a highly practised and resilient activist, but, as the caption emphasises, she is clearly exhausted from the toll of negotiations – even a bit traumatised, knowing that a future of precarity for her members lies in the balance. Reflecting on her experience of a series of disputes, Gratz warns that, if the bosses are allowed to get their way, 'pretty soon we are all going to end up on the damned freeway homeless'.[160] The weight of this possibility is present in Gratz's very bearing, a slightly off-balance stance, wind-dishevelled red hair and her slim build overwhelmed by a peacoat. Within Sekula's frame, her position is visually boxed by the structures of the worksite: chain-link fences, metal stairways, signage and bollards. At one level, these are typical elements of a berth's landside gate; the image could be seen as merely documenting what was behind Gratz. Yet, it also registers figural layers of hemming-in and of contingency. This is not only a female figure standing in a port environment, but, re-scaling, also the situation confining workers and union – their futures held in the balance of forces between management and strikers. The caption notes that Gratz's discussions with management that day were over the potential illegality of secondary action, and that these were especially difficult because the employers were already suing the ILWU over secondary boycotting of *Neptune Jade*.[161] Contrasting with the melancholic suspending and languid stretching of time in Davis's portrait, the temporalities of Gratz's feel tensile and brittle. Still, the constricting qualities provoked by securitised berths also have an opposing force in the sequence's opening: the longshore workers' blockade of the scab-loaded container ship *Columbus Canada*.

Colour is central to this sequence and plays a structural-allegorical role in marking time. In the long caption to the photograph of the berthed *Teal*, Sekula meditates on the ideological significance of the colours blue and orange. In Southern California, they summon connotations of ocean, sky, citrus orchards, with the associated sunshine and optimism. In the context of Liverpool – a British city heavily scarred by the politics of Ireland's partition – orange is associated with Protestant loyalism, dating from that community's allegiance to King William of Orange. As another Dutch lineage, these were the colours of the old South African flag, contested by anti-apartheid protesters. Sekula further amplifies the colour orange allegorically to apparently unrelated phenomena: the Day-Glo in Pop Art and the hellfire in John Milton's *Paradise Lost*.

160 'Freeway to China (Version 2, for Liverpool), 291.

161 The case of *Neptune Jade* became a *cause célèbre*. The first picket against this scab-loaded vessel took place in Oakland in September 1997 and then spread internationally. The lawsuit launched by the global shipowners, the Pacific Maritime Association, ran from October 1997 to November 1998.

We can push this discussion of colour further. As already mentioned, orange appears on the architecture of *Teal* and on the beams of the container cranes it carries, and a washed-out fluorescent orange shows up on the bollards. A paler mango marks the edges of berths. In a triptych of images from the Port of San Pedro, it is sported by shipping containers and by a worker's safety gilet. Rusty hues are on other containers, as well as on a vessel that transports them and the cranes that lift them. Orange and blue are also the colours of Liverpool's Tate Gallery, as well as appearing in the Albert Dock's reflections of a clear summer sky, the terracotta brickwork of historic warehouses and the ferric-red of their cyclopean Doric columns. As we saw, the valence of orange is unstable, its Californian resonances being at odds with those in Liverpool. Even in Merseyside, its stability is in question, albeit in a different sense: it is as if its vibrancy shades over into the dourness of Presbyterian sectarianism; or into the unionist 'red-white-and-blue'. The long caption for the photograph of Ray Familathe reports how, after he buys a Union Jack to take home as a gift, he is challenged by his Republican trade union associates: 'What is this shite? You're a citizen, we're subjects!'[162] Sekula intended to riff on the inflections of colour, noting in a lecture how the high chroma used on modern ships contrasted with the monochrome palette of the ages of sail and steam (where colour mainly appeared on ensigns), and how the orange paint was itself an anti-rust treatment (orange to stop orange); and we learn that a photograph showing two dockers manoeuvring a paletted crate are in fact loading the same rust-inhibiting paint.[163]

Kaja Silverman has also puzzled over Sekula's use of colour in *Freeway to China*. As she sees it, the reddish orange detaches itself from industrial surfaces, abandoning its corporate associations and refusing its role as a celebration of capital. It seizes agency, switches political sides, casting its lot with the dockworkers. Self-emancipated, it seizes the hue's joy and warmth, becoming an ally and anti-capitalist subject.[164] In her account, we could say, colour appears as comrade. Silverman does not enumerate how this works in *Freeway* (she elucidates further with *Waiting for Tear Gas*, as we will see) but, returning again to the photographic sequence with her remarks in mind, we can see how orange

162 'Freeway to China (Version 2, for Liverpool), 282.

163 'Globalism's Discontents and the Return of the Sea'

164 Kaja Silverman, 'Disassembled Movie', in *Synopsis 3: Testimonies Between Fact and Fiction* (Athens: National Museum of Contemporary Art, 2003), 191–5 (194).

hues also turn up as Gratz's auburn locks, and as the interior glow of a room where striking Liverpool dockers listen to a radio phone-in on a film they co-wrote (*Dockers* for Channel 4). In the long shot of *Teal* and the giant cranes, the sky blushes from cool blue into warm pinks and oranges closer to the horizon, while the bright paintwork of the industrial structures is reflected across the seawater's agitated dark-blue surface. Bearing in mind Silverman's suggestive reading, this sunset might be less a figure of finality ('end of the day', 'setting of the sun', 'twilight' – widely used metaphors for the closure of eras) and more a harbinger of better times ahead (as per the popular saying 'red sky at night is shepherds' delight'; perhaps even a hint at the retrospective insights and wisdom of Minerva's owl which 'takes flight at dusk').

The same hues show up again in a photograph towards the end of the sequence. Standing among the dark blacks and algae-emeralds of a rocky shoreline on a midsummer's evening, a man with binoculars observes a ship entering the Mersey. (The ship is called *Cast Performance*, as if by some designed irony.[165]) In addition to the brand colours on the vessel and its containers, and further to the pink-lilac washes across estuary and skyscape, Sekula's photograph picks out the intense burning hues on the west-facing silhouette of the shipspotter. The back of his head and sides of his body glower; his sweatshirt even ruches in such a way to form flame-like shapes licking his flank. Once noticed, the earlier Milton allusion comes back to mind. Sekula's caption here ponders what could have been if Liverpool's tugboat crews had felt confident to come out in solidarity with its dockers. The 'what could have been' of the caption segues into the image of a man looking out through binoculars to 'what is' or, arguably, 'what could be'.

Colour as Comrade: Waiting for Tear Gas [white globe to black]*: Take 2*

Some commentators have suggested that *Waiting for Tear Gas* (1999/2000) resists standard narrative form. According to Stephanie Schwartz, there is 'neither an obvious nor a single narrative line', 'no crescendo' and 'no movement from dawn to dusk or from peace to violence'. There is no beginning and, she suggests, Sekula denies the

165 Sekula happens on these vessels, but they are highlighted as found objects. In another example, *Teal* – the ship we see in Los Angeles – also suggests a colour, named for the plumage of the waterfowl; *Neptune Jade* offers yet another.

viewer a conclusion because the sequence starts again.[166] Zanny Begg similarly argues that *Waiting for Tear Gas* 'unfolds like a rhizome'. The images 'revolve continuously in a slide carousel with no beginning or end. Each image appears before the viewer before being slowly replaced by another flowing between night and day, intensity and quietude'.[167] Although it is difficult to see how a loop can be rhizomatic, there is a point to these readings. Perhaps *Waiting* does grow in a way that sends out photographs from nodes, and viewers might encounter and leave the sequence at any point. In one important sense, the continuous cycle could be problematic; it risks implying that resistance and repression are eternally recurring phenomena, an endless stand-off in which everything seems to remain unchanged. Alternatively, the reiterating rhythm can remind us that *this happened* and that *it would happen again*. Here, we focus on how Sekula's carousel loop internally organises time.

However much there is, or is not, a passage 'from a to z', however anti-linear the looping of the slide reel, there is, above all, a chromalogical form to *Waiting for Tear Gas*. Eisenstein and Silverman give us a way of understanding it. Eisenstein suggests that colour should be treated as a structural element in polyphonic montage, with colours as 'independent expressive themes'.[168] As we saw with *Freeway to China*, Silverman sees colour as liberating itself from its initial role as a signifier of capital. Her argument is developed for *Waiting for Tear Gas*, where the role of affect and structure are brought to the fore. She argues that, far from being an apolitical or politically suspect matter, affect can be politically relevant for the left. The 'artificial tears' typically elicited by emotive news coverage are contrasted with an alternative affective response shared by the Seattle protesters: they produce 'artificial tears' provoked by tear gas. Sekula's use of colour, Silverman continues, is structured to mobilise this affect, and reverberates for the socialist project.[169] Red, she argues, is an obvious manifestation of agency: it is a choice made by

166 Stephanie Schwartz, 'Waiting: Loops in Time', *Waiting for Tear Gas 1999–2000 by Allan Sekula*, 2016, tate.org.uk.

167 Zanny Begg, 'Recasting Subjectivity: Globalisation and the Photography of Andreas Gursky and Allan Sekula', *Third Text* 19:6 (2005): 625–36 (627).

168 Sergei Eisenstein, 'From Lectures on Music and Colour in *Ivan the Terrible*' (1947), in *The Eisenstein Reader*, ed. Richard Taylor (London: British Film Institute, 1998), 167–86 (172).

169 Silverman, 'Disassembled Movie', 191–5; see also: Colin Gardner, '"It's Not Blood, It's Red": Color as Category, Color as Sensation in Jean-Luc Godard's *Le Mépris*, *Pierrot Le Fou*, *Weekend*, and *Passion*', *Criticism* 61:2 (2019): 245–70.

many protesters for their clothes, hair or banners. Its bright countering symbolism, however, is overwhelmed and weakened by the visual weight of the black ranks of police. Meanwhile, the yellowish sodium light cast by streetlamps, and sometimes amplified through the clouds of tear gas, is said to do something unexpected. Like the corporate orange in *Freeway*, this yellowness 'from above' revolts and takes the side of the protesters. Highlighting the power of radical affect, yellow, Silverman argues, unites protesters with one another and with the ground. It 'affirms their presence in the world' and 'permits them to do what they have come to do: show exactly how globalization makes them feel'.[170] Silverman discerns the translation of the poisoned atmosphere into an at-one-ness with the earth. Although sympathetic to Silverman's intent, we remain unconvinced by this aspect of her argument – but we can still build on Silverman's insights to bring colour's structural role to bear on the sense of time.

That colour is important is underscored by the single anomalous vertical image (#46).[171] Over the shoulder of an artist at work, we see the painting on his lap: a composition of brushstrokes and splotches, mostly in a range of blues, and possibly depicting helmeted police. Silverman reads the move from landscape to portrait format as Sekula's way of interrupting, breaking the sense of 'industrial' predictability – and we can imagine him saying this. Nevertheless, an emphasis on the art of colour seems equally viable – and here, there is a built-in collision between colour as paint pigment (used by the artist photographed) and colour as light (projected through Sekula's slide transparency). Sekula's personal notes emphasise colour: 'red dragon', 'red faced girls', 'devil-painted kids', 'red kids' (from Nova, an alternative school devoted to social justice); 'splotches of iridescent violet cladding' (on a Gehry museum); 'the slowly gathering crowd of color-coded trade unionists'. That colour matters is further underscored by his strike-through: 'Unions in color-coded rain ponchos: SEIUL purple, Teamster yellow, machinist blue. The most striking color is that of the farmworkers . . .'

170 Ibid., 195.

171 Sekula Papers, S.1.09:02 No. 2 [Global Mariner Seattle WTO] October 1999–2000. The WTO pages are yellow-highlighted and given their own pagination, which shows the missing sections (1–20, 26–7, and in the subsequent notebook, 36: S.1.09:03, No. 3 [Novorossysk InSite 2000 Seattle WTO], December 1999–March 2000). Sekula's opening title dates this set of notes '11/29–12/3'. Events recorded are dated Monday 29 November 1999 (protests and rallies preceding), Tues 30 November ('N30'), and (in the later notes) the non-existent Wednesday 31 November.

The farmworkers' colour is never stated; presumably the 'most striking' quality was unforgettable. But the ponchos of SEIU (the Service Employees International Union; Sekula's 'SEIUL' is a mistake) have to be 'purple', not 'violet' – perhaps because the former was felt to be more accurate (although colour naming is notoriously fugitive); maybe because it just rolled better; perhaps because the word was already used to describe the Gehry museum. Lost in the crowd, Sekula finds beacons: he mentions the 'red hair, tinted glasses' of Luisa Gratz (her name here transcribed 'Louisa Coratz'); he meets 'Andrew, a ruddy British-born shipwright'; and there is 'a red illuminated sign . . .: "Closed"'. An Inlandboatmen's Union militant holds a 'placard with the blue octopus threatening a yellow globe'. A woman is kneeling, praying and bleeding from the mouth, but Sekula specifically alights on the 'blue down jacket' worn by her friend and how 'Press photographers shot [them] from 3–4 meters back, flashs obliterating the strange yellow street light . . .'. 'A group of Teamsters from Local 174, a local with TDU affiliated – or at least sympathetic leadership, stand around in their blue jacket'.[172] He also mentions a 'secretserviceman, tell-tale coil of white wire behind his ear . . .'. In his notebooks, these recollections are presented (mostly) in the present tense, as are the correcting annotations added later.[173] They are written in a voice that suggests free-form prose – an exercise in stream of consciousness. These are not simply notes or aides-memoires; they are drafts anticipating a more formal presentation, potentially as text for a wall panel or essay.

That there is a structural intent to Sekula's composition is indicated by a key shift occurring at exactly the midpoint in the cycle. Chromasigns shape a double cycle, each with two sub-phases. Twice over, there is a passage from day to night. First, we have the rally, giving way to scenes of protesters encountering tear gas. In the clarity of daylight, red and blue primaries dominate. Colour hues adhere to objects. Things and people retain their independence, even as they unite in solidarity. The evening scenes show the sit-down protest and the scenes of tear gas.

---

172 TDU (Teamsters for a Democratic Union) is the rank-and-file group, the longest running in the US.

173 The notes are made retrospectively (some dated 7 December, some as late as the end of the following March) and contain annotations correcting his recollections of the sequence of events (these tend to allude to social arrangements, or who he dined with): '[NB: Bad memory. This happens Tu. night'; '[correction re. Monday night: . . .]'; '[this occurs before showing, correct sequence of events]'. The retrospective nature of the notes is also emphasised in his in-prose metacommentary: '[I learn this later from reading . . .]'.

Here, colour is encountered as a quality of light, spreading through hazes, fog and smoke, where the jaundiced hues of streetlamps dominate. Rather than sticking to the surfaces of objects, or even emanating from the dispersing nebula, colour defines sets of relations. Police and delegates are, for the most part, metonymically aligned through black body armour and business suits, although some protesters also wear black; either way, as Silverman observes, black provides the main contrast to yellow. Her discussion pertains to this phase of the cycle. Exactly halfway through the reel, a second cycle starts: commencing in daylight at the delegates' hotel, it moves to the anti-capitalist marches.[174] Again, billows of white gas are released before nightfall. This night-time is different to the first: full of quirky observations, it has a much warmer colourway of tawny russets, rose golds and burnished bronzes.

The importance of Sekula's negation of photojournalistic protocols is revealed by colour. Disavowing the use of flash means losing the jarring colour casts it produces. Instead, he works with natural light (even where the 'natural light' available is, strictly speaking, 'artificial light', such as that produced by streetlamps). The chromatic cast alters as twilight advances and the world becomes illuminated by streetlamps, commercial lights (signage, window displays, advertising) and seasonal decorations. While blues are largely subdued under the sulphureous glow, with a few notable exceptions, reds survive to punctuate the scenes. In many of the images, 'cheery' festive lights add a connotative incongruity, but they also work at a level affected by the protocols. Heightened by the sharper light-dark contrasts, the night-time illumination burns out details; overexposed, these lights halo, streak, blur and flare; they reflect on glass and objects, and sometimes replicate inside the lens's optics. Slide transparency film is one of the trickiest mediums to use for night scenes; taking successful slide transparencies requires the use of a tripod, light meter and long exposures – none of which Sekula employed here.

Although the slide projector has a long history and continues to be used as a 'legacy technology', its use as an art medium belongs to the late twentieth century.[175] The popular Kodak Eastman rotary tray or carousel

174 The images of the WTO delegates are clustered in this first temporal cycle, with only one such photograph in the second one.

175 Much is made of the social ritual for sharing holiday snaps with friends and relatives. Maybe it was more widely used in the US, but in our experience, its domestic use in the UK was restricted to middle-class consumers. Moreover, this sharing of 'what we did' possessed a different modality to the automated slide reel used for *Waiting for Tear Gas*.

projectors were launched in 1961, ceasing production in 2004 under the commercial pressure from digital technologies.[176] Sekula had used slide-carousel technology before – for *Untitled Slide Sequence* (1972, black and white) and for the two colour-slide cycles incorporated into the exhibition version of *Fish Story*; he would use it again for *Prayer for the Americans* (1999–2004) and the planned, but never completed, *Reverse Magellan* (2010). It is worth recalling how these devices work. Small diapositive transparencies, mounted in card or plastic frames, are projected enlarged onto a wall or screen. Slide projectors are industrialised versions of the sixteenth-century magic lantern. The first Kodaslide machines of 1937 lowered single slides into the gate; before long, Kodak employed a slide-to-slide straight-tray mechanism, which allowed successive images to be projected. In 1939, Kodak introduced Ready Mounts, standardising the format for slides. Carousel projectors replaced straight trays in 1961. In the forty years of manufacture, Kodak made nineteen million slide projectors and, during the 1980s, its revenue from projectors and slide developing rivalled that of Hollywood.[177]

The challenges of night shooting notwithstanding, slide film is notable for its superior qualities of saturation, contrast and detail. Further, coloured translucence behaves differently from the coloured ink of print. Projected colours transmit with added intensity (assuming, of course, that the transparencies have not faded) – all of which is heightened by the darkened viewing context. A standard carousel tray carries slides in numbered slots, #1–80, with an addition slit, the home #0, which is sometimes used – as it was for *Waiting for Tear Gas* – to maintain an uninterrupted loop of eighty-one images. The projection can be set to a timer and Sekula's sequence was programmed to show each slide for ten seconds. That is around the midpoint in the timer range (three to twenty-two seconds for Kodak Eastman), yet, for most viewers, this ten-second projection feels prolonged and time seems to stretch. Between each slide there is a moment where the absence of light reigns, contrasting with the periods of luminance. The shift from bright light to near-total darkness can sometimes cause viewers to sense after-images. Sound accompanies the experience, but in a different way to that of film-cinema, to which slide projection is often compared. Noise

176 The carousel was widely used in education and for corporate presentations. It was replaced by PowerPoint (launched in 1987).

177 Page Sarlin, 'The Work of Ending: Eastman Kodak's Carousel Slide Projector', *Photoresearcher* 24 (2015): 10–19 (14–15) 14–15; and her documentary *The Last Slide Projector* (2004, 0:59:22).

is generated by the apparatus: the motor whirs (more so as it overheats), overlaid by the meditative rhythm of the slide changeover's 'click-click-SNAP'.

We should not ignore the photographs of the globes that figure in *Waiting for Tear Gas* (#1 and #81). These objects are of the type that can be plugged in to an electricity supply and illuminated from within. Although they are unlit in Sekula's photographs, their forms allow light to pass through the transparent plastic, which gives them an affinity with the acetate diapositives (and more generally with his editing at a light table, to which he alludes in his text). The globes sit on top of a double bank of filing cabinets in Seattle Public Library.[178] The cabinets are the taller ones (probably four drawers high, or approximately Sekula's shoulder height), so the globes are shot from a low vantage. This gives the ceiling a strong role: fluorescent lights recede in perspectival recession and burn-out (the form of these fixtures is also reminiscent of light boxes used to preview transparencies). The arrangement emphasises the contrast between the room's spatial void and the spherical forms set forth in the foreground. In the first image, the black globe can already be seen behind the white one, out of focus. Together the two views reveal that Sekula has refocused and zoomed in from almost the same standpoint. The static viewing here contrasts with the dynamics of shooting the demonstration, moving 'with the flow of the protest', as Sekula describes.[179]

These are specifically political globes and, as is the cartographic convention for depicting national geography, they are rather colourful. 'White' and 'black' pertain to the representation of oceans. In both cases, our view is from the southern hemisphere, with Europe and North America invisible. The white globe is just off-centre in the frame, with the out-of-focus black globe a couple of feet behind to its left. The arrangement gestures to an orbital representation or an orrery, and a movement of the orbs is implied. Australia is most prominent in the white globe, with the Indonesian archipelago retreating northwards around the curvature, and, going southwards, part of

178 This is the Bindon and Wright-designed Seattle Public Library (1960) that preceded the building by OMA/LMN (2004). Sekula took a break from the protests of 30 November, to escape the rain and to read up for his forthcoming trip through the Black Sea with *Global Mariner*. Sekula Papers S.1.09:02, No. 2 [Global Mariner Seattle WTO], October 1999–2000.

179 The filing box, along with the filing cabinets, perhaps, links back to the issues raised in 'The Body and the Archive'.

Wilkes Land and the pole are visible. The earth's axis tilts away from us and slightly leftwards, presenting the nearest point to the viewer as the Great Australian Bight. There are two symbols laid over the maritime whiteness: a baroque cartouche and a colourful compass symbol with fleur-de-lys ordinates. Contrary to this archaic intrusion, landforms are depicted according to modern mapping conventions. The black globe is fully centred. The axis is parallel to the picture plane. Here, the equator is closer to the viewer, its nearest junction on the Somali coast. The African continent and the countries surrounding the Arabian Sea are prominent. This is – and was at the time of photographing – an outdated geography: Rhodesia with its capital Salisbury (from 1980, Zimbabwe and Harare); South West Africa (Namibia from 1990); the Malagasy Republic (existed 1958–75); Muscat and Oman (a designation that ended in 1970); and Egypt identified as Nasser's United Arab Republic (1958–71). The USSR is visible. The historical period suggested by this representation is roughly 1958–70 – a high point in decolonisation. This insight into the time of geopolitics – admittedly, one that might be harder to spot in the slide projection – propels us to re-examine the white globe. Initially, it reveals less information, but on closer examination Timor-Leste appears to be part of Indonesia (annexed from 1976 to 1999). Meanwhile, the eastern half of the island of New Guinea looks to be in its post-Pacific War incarnation as a Territory of Papua and New Guinea (1949–75), which united regions colonised by Germany and Britain, and was once administered by Australia. The white globe seems to show geopolitical arrangements in non-coinciding periods: 1949–75 and 1976–99 – a lag and contradiction in the space-time of Western cartography, perhaps?

It is reasonably assumed that the subtitle alludes to the two globes. But the formulation 'white globe to black' is ambiguous. The alternative formulations – 'white globe to black globe' or 'white to black globe' – sound less elegant, and that would be good enough as an explanation. Still, 'white globe to black' could suggest not 'to black globe' but simply 'to black'; perhaps to the darkness between slides or daylight to night. Indeed, the words are not placed after a colon but given in square brackets: '[white globe to black]' – strictly, Sekula used them only for the printed version of *Waiting for Tear Gas*. Square brackets are diacritical marks that add modifications to a quoted passage, clarifying information or context; in mathematics, they shape specific intervals in an equation; in photography, 'bracketing' is a technique for taking photographic exposures either side of the main one, but with different aperture settings (which cameras sometimes automate as a 'burst').

The full rotation of the slide tray could be allied to the turn of the earth – and with this in mind, the entire slide cycle, with its two phases, might be seen as prefigured by the globes. The circuit named in the subtitle is suggestive of the diurnal cycle, although not identical to it. The black globe in focus (#81) casts a retrospective glance back across the cycle, but it too is prefigured by being included in the background to the white one. An auto-controlled carousel is unidirectional.[180] On an automated loop, the black globe is adjacent and prior to the white. As slide #81 switches to #1, we experience something akin to the twist of Sekula's lens: the black globe moves from foreground to background, from in focus to out of focus.[181]

Let us try another way of reading the internal doubling apparent in *Waiting for Tear Gas*. Note how, in its sequential structure, the development of suspended chemical dyes generates tropes for the gaseous vision associated with the police curfew – the time of somnambulance and nightmares. Drawing on the fascinating account of the *Spartakusbund* revolt of 1919 by symbologist Furio Jesi, we suggest that, in *Waiting for Tear Gas*, Sekula uses colour to map two temporal modes. Jesi suggests that, in conditions of revolt, time is suspended: 'everything that is done has a value in itself, independently of its consequences and of its relation with the transitory or perennial complex that constitutes history'.[182] In this moment, a battle for symbols arises.[183] A second kind of time is narrative time, where repression re-emerges against the revolt. (Revolution is something different again.) 'Every revolt', Jesi argues, 'is circumscribed by precise borders in historical time and historical space.'[184] He writes:

> Every revolt is a battle, but a battle in which one has deliberately chosen to participate. The instant of revolt determines one's sudden self-realization and self-objectification as part of a collectivity. The battle between

180 Controlled manually (say in a lecture hall), they can also be reversed.

181 We imagine the actual shooting process to have been in the reverse direction, zooming in on the black globe after an establishing shot containing both orbs.

182 Furio Jesi, *Spartakus: The Symbology of Revolt* (2000; Calcutta: Seagull, 2014), 46.

183 'Symbol' has a specific technical meaning for Jesi, not to be confused with the aesthetic debates summarised earlier.

184 Ibid., 53. On Revolution and time, see: Reinhart Koselleck, 'Historical Criteria of the Modern Concept of Revolution' (1969), in *Futures Past: On the Semantics of Historical Time* (1979; New York: Columbia University Press, 2004), 43–57.

> good and evil, between survival and death, between success and failure . . . is identified with the battle of the whole collectivity – everyone has the same weapons, everyone faces the same obstacles, the same enemy. Everyone experiences the epiphany of the same symbols.[185]

Individual space, Jesi suggests, 'expands, becoming the symbolic space common to an entire collective, the shelter from historical time in which the collective finds safety'.[186] We suggest that Sekula employs colour as a chromasign to code both the collective suspended time of revolt (and the anticipation of tear gas) and the point at which state repression reimposes historical time.

With the doubling cycle in mind, it is also possible to imagine the structure of *Waiting for Tear Gas* as akin to the rhythms of the semi-diurnal tide. (Perhaps, then, Sekula does not entirely skip the 'natural' metaphors of protest?) The sequence's 'day–night and day–night' mimics the 'in–out and in–out' of the tides – four phases regulated by the forces of lunar gravitation.[187] If tear gas dominates the 'first night', an air of growing otherworldliness takes hold on the second – even a certain enweirding. The difference between the 'two nights' is not absolute, but a matter of tenor. The 'second night' also contains repression – police lines; a van racing past with two cops standing on the rear fender; the arrest of an isolated protester – but its overall atmosphere shifts from the more hellish scenes of the 'first night' towards an idiosyncratic dreamscape. Sekula explicitly comments on this mood in the final paragraph of the project's short text: 'One fleeting hallucination could not be photographed', he writes, of a boom box playing Jimi Hendrix's take on the US national anthem.[188] And he imagines the long-dead musician alive among the protesters debunking 'pumped-up sovereignty'.

The oddness of these scenes is also a matter of chroma. Writing about director Vincente Minnelli, Deleuze suggests: 'Colour is dream, not because the dream is in colour, but because colours in Minnelli are given a highly absorbent, almost devouring, value'.[189] Although the technical context and degree of formal control are very different for *Waiting for Tear Gas*, something similar is at work in the way the

---

185 Jesi, *Spartakus*, 53.

186 Ibid.

187 Like the images projected onto a screen or wall, the moon is a light reflector not a light emitter.

188 '*Waiting for Tear Gas [white globe to black]*', 170.

189 Gilles Deleuze, *Cinema 2: The Time-Image* (London: The Athlone Press, 1989), 63.

red-amber-bronze radiance pervades this phase of the sequence. It starts, however, with a transitioning interplay of pink and blue, their coolness akin to daytime chroma combining with the diffusions characterising the night scenes. Outside the market hall, a line of mounted police in gas masks is echoed by the rows of triangular Christmas trees perched on architectural canopies. The market's pink-neon signage imparts much of the scene with a lurid cast; a fuchsia pool spreads across the wet pavement, visually burning out detail at its most intense point. The sky's twilight cerulean plays a supporting role, reflecting on a passing car and knitting a pink-blue modulation across the paviours. Another sign reads 'MEET THE PRODUCER', adding layers of irony: the historic market is a popular hub for independents and its very existence represents a stand against corporate redevelopment; it looms behind the official cavalry (Cossacks) that tries to occupy the public space – a figurative reminder of the protesters' counterpower.

Other images share this ambience. A man holding up the US flag at its centre, a giant spiral of glittering material is formed on the ground in front of a police line – striking in itself, but also invoking not only the form of Robert Smithson's *Spiral Jetty* but, perhaps, by extension, his concern with environmental entropy. One protester is draped in a silvery survival blanket, an abstract dazzle of lavender, lilac and gold facets. Others wear blue rain capes, the colour shifting under the lights from ink to plum to crimson to silver. A group stare forwards and upwards in unison, evoking the scene in *Close Encounters* where humans welcome extra-terrestrials, awestruck by their vibrant *son et lumière*. A woman with SLR camera hanging around her neck steps playfully through a street signboard's empty frame. We see the entrance to a twenty-four-hour 'red light' establishment, appealing to potential clients with 'best deal in town', 'live girls', 'sex theatre', 'peep show', 'fantasy booth', 'video arcade' and 'ATM'. Front-of-house, in the vestibule-vitrine, are two of its employees. One sex worker in a red mini-dress throws her arms up the wall and thrusts out her rear in a sexualised gesture that redoubles – and in the context of the sequence is re-inflected to parody – the position demanded by the police when frisking suspects. Elsewhere, on the street, an electric-guitar player with portable power source picks up Sekula's hallucinatory Hendrix reference. He is followed by a woman in a hazmat suit. She looks up and smiles blissfully through her astronaut helmet. There are few 'serene' moments in the cycle – earlier, a woman with a pink-dyed bob pauses, closes her eyes and inhales the collective air – but this figure in protective gear enters the realm of the fantastic. She seems to be standing on another planet, in another world, transported by a cosmological vision. Or she is herself an angelic apparition: the plastic she wears catches the lights, framing and decorating her face, the fabulous reflections morphing between the appearance of rock crystal, lava lamp and moiré. This 'second night' presents 'an unreal real' (which we will return to in more detail later). We not only mean 'real' in the sense of sheer facticity. The transformed atmosphere is an experience familiar to many who have found themselves in conditions where hegemonic 'normality' breaks down. Other worlds are momentarily glimpsed, and new social realities temporarily lived.

Waiting. There is a suspended time and a certainty to the imminent release of lacrimator. As Sekula records in his notes, the protesters knew the violence would come: 'In the crowd, people start to prepare for tear gas. "Do you have water?" "Don't rub your eyes"'; 'People fill the intersection, expectant. Waiting for gas.' *Waiting for Tear Gas* generates images of collective suspension in another sense.[190] The colour cycles suggest alternative visions, alternative temporalities, shading between utopia and dystopia, closures and openings. As viewers of the slide cycle, we also pause, literally. We tarry for ten seconds while each slide is visible, and are momentarily suspended in the dark ('click-click'), before ('SNAP') the revelation of the next image. Maybe we also expect and hope? Like the protesters photographed, we await the outcome of the present, on unknown political contingencies. Which elements have endured or will endure? Which have changed or will change individual perspectives or the world? Whichever: there will be tears.

Waiting for Tear Gas is encountered under distinct orders of aftermath and anticipation – and these unfold further temporal facets: one that passes before our eyes (the now-past present of N30; the present of viewing); and another where everything is determined by times to come (and now informed by our knowledge of what happened between 1999 and our own moment). The horizon of 'death' here (if that designation is even to be retained) is far from the subjectivist melancholy of the Barthesian memento mori. Co-eval temporalities present the choice between domination by the insect–human–machine RoboCops and collective agency. Different futures; different relations to the past. As we saw in the previous chapter, Sekula's photographic sequences and essays point to other places and times. They break the 'relentless

190 As we will see in Chapter 4, he would later describe the demonstrators in terms of another type of suspension: 'liquid immersion'.

"synchronicity" of modernity'.[191] They challenge its prehistories, legacies and historicist history of the victors, or the reimposition of 'historical time'.[192] They refuse synchronicity with the destinies projected by capital. Sekula's work invokes a complex of temporal forces: reaching back to recover lost threads and reaching back to us from a time that is 'not-yet'. We could call this manifesting in our present a 'materialised anticipation'; that is, not just a hopeful anticipation, but the active, albeit tentative, presence of a possible future. *Waiting* helps make this tangible. Like the handling of time sometimes encountered in speculative fiction and film, this is a peculiar conundrum where the future is a constitutive aspect of the present. It is not simply us waiting for a future, but a future already 'waiting' for us to catch up – and which, therefore, casts the present as retrospection, where the present is revised as a structure of recollection, at once occurring now and yet having already happened.[193] *Waiting for Tear Gas* embodies another wager, a cast of the dice.

---

191 'Dismal Science', 130. Sekula is referring to Bloch.

192 Jesi, *Spartakus.*

193 Gérard Genette, *Narrative Discourse: An Essay in Method* (1972; Ithaca, NY: Cornell University Press, 1983); Tzvetan Todorov, 'The Typology of Detective Fiction' (1966), in *Modern Criticism and Theory: A Reader*, eds David Lodge and Nigel Wood, second edition (London: Longman, 2000), 137–44; Mark Currie, 'The Expansion of Tense', *Narrative* 17:3 (2009): 353–67.

3

A poetics in realist language

SECTION 1: METONYMY AND METAPHOR REVISITED

Discussion of Sekula's work has largely focused on aspects of its content; indeed, some commentators are of the opinion that he paid insufficient attention to the image *qua* image. We disagree; and, in this chapter, we explore how Sekula's 'critical realism' entails an interplay between the literal and the figural, subject and form.[1] We consider his relations with political modernism, and with linguistics, especially with formalism and structuralism, and their critiques. Along the way, we will encounter multiple figural modes. Focusing primarily on several of his essays and a section of the long video work *The Lottery of the Sea* (2006), we consider Sekula's project as a 'poetics of prose'. Sekula sustained an active interest in theories of language. As a student, he took a course in linguistics at UCSD, when the 'linguistic turn' in the Humanities and Social Sciences was in full flow. From his earliest artworks, Sekula was interested in the intersections of images with words. His knowledge of linguistics, from Saussure and Benveniste to Whorf and Chomsky, was far from tokenistic.[2] He was particularly interested in the work of

1 We use 'figural', not 'figurative', to avoid the latter's established discursive contrast in the visual-plastic arts with 'abstraction'.

2 Sekula was familiar with key contributors to structuralism (Levi-Strauss, Barthes, Lacan, Greimas, Kristeva, Todorov, Genette, Lotman); the linguistics associated with Russian and Czech formalism (Shklovsky, Jakobson, Tynjanov, Propp, Mukarovsky). He read key contributions to sociolinguistics (Labov, Hymes) and from the early 1970s engaged the foundational literature of cognitive linguistics (Lakoff, Johnson, Turner). In addition, he

Jakobson and in the 'sociological poetics' or 'sociological method' of Vološinov, Medvedev and Bakhtin, as well as contemporary Marxist critical engagements with formalism, such as the work of Fredric Jameson and Raymond Williams.[3] He saw the Bakhtin Circle and the recent Marxist work that built on it as the basis for a social theory of language. This familiarity with theories of language also attuned him to questions of rhetoric and the critical debates around tropes.

The Cult of Metaphor and Metonymic Turn

In the 1970s, Sekula was among those who objected to the prevailing 'cult of metaphor' – a tendency prominent in discussions of symbolist and modernist poetry, and a highly aestheticising trend privileged in American literary formalism. Metaphor in this context was not limited to a figure of speech; rather, it was an edifice of institutionalised values, defining (and policing) what constitutes 'art' (that is, 'Art', 'good art', 'pure art', 'true art'). Championed as the highest vehicle for metaphor, the genre of poetry was positioned as superior to prose, because it was deemed 'more literary'. (The hierarchy is still conveyed by the adjectives 'poetic' and 'prosaic': the latter does far more than suggest 'prose-like', conveying a sense of dull commonplaces.) The 'cult of metaphor' overlaps with the debate over 'symbol and allegory' discussed in the previous chapter. Similar hierarchies – Michael Fried's 'art' and objecthood', Clement Greenberg's 'avant-garde' and 'kitsch' – were operative in the visual arts, distinguishing 'high' or 'autonomous art' from 'non-art' (documentary, propaganda, pedagogy, moralism, instrumental or other

---

read philosophies of language (Carnap, Wittgenstein, Russell, Peirce, Searle and Goodman, along with Adam Schaff's Soviet-Marxist variant and its Althusserian critique by Michel Pêcheux).

3 From the mid-1970s, Sekula paid close attention to the 'Bakhtin Circle'. He first mentioned this work in 1984, in his introduction to *Photography Against the Grain*, indicating 1975 as the year when he started to engage with their work. At that point, very little was available in translation, so especially important for him would have been V.N. Vološinov's *Marxism and the Philosophy of Language* (1929), which was first translated into English by Seminar Press in 1973, the Harvard edition following in 1986. Sekula had both editions. He directly acknowledges the importance of Raymond Williams's *Marxism and Literature* (Oxford: Oxford University Press, 1977), which devotes several pages to Vološinov. (Introduction, *Photography Against the Grain*, xiii). It would be easy to forget what it meant to read this material in the early 1970s. The very purpose of Jameson's *The Prison-House of Language* (Princeton, NJ: Princeton University Press, 1972) was to develop an immanent critique of Russian formalism and structuralism, yet it contains no reference to the Bakhtin Circle.

heteronomous practices). Such judgements became embedded in the distinction between 'modernism' and 'realism', which not only rested upon Kantian aesthetic categories but was increasingly overdetermined by global geopolitics and Cold War ideology.

Both modernist formalism and liberal humanism shaped the discourses of art and photography. Sekula's formation in the politicised orbit of San Diego in the early 1970s heightened his awareness of – and distance from – art's 'high-modernist' critics. A distinction needs underlining. Hardcore 'high-modernist' formalism in the visual-plastic arts was generally critical of metaphor along with anything deemed to be 'literary' or 'narratival'. Greenberg's core argument identified the specific characteristics of distinct media (painting, sculpture and so on), so any muddying of the waters with 'literary' metaphors was anathema to him. (It is also worth recalling that he defined photography – and not unsympathetically – as a narrative art.) As the official spokesperson for photography at MoMA, John Szarkowski emphasised, in contrast, the medium's non-narrative dimension, emphasising instead five categories: 'the thing itself', 'the detail', 'frame', 'time' and 'vantage point'.[4] Nonetheless, the fundamental aesthetic values represented by the 'cult of metaphor' continued to underpin these distinct versions of modernist theory.

The values embedded in this ideology extended through liberal humanism, which was especially powerful in photographic criticism. (In practice, there was overlap between these two approaches. However, the high modernists – and it was they who held critical sway – differed sharply, their more rigorous proponents shirking humanism's 'moralistic' aspects.) Addressing the criticism and history of photography, Sekula repeatedly encountered the cult of metaphor in its liberal-humanist variant. From the perspective of the presiding aesthetic ideology, photography was inherently compromised by its 'mechanical' nature, as well as by its instrumental uses and representational codes. Yet, at the same time, photography's 'underling' status resulted in an exaggerated 'aestheticising' mission, making its compensatory claims to be 'art' all the shriller. While self-conscious 'art photography' – the symbolist mysticism of Minor White and *Aperture* – would be easily identifiable with this trend, ironically, this liberal humanism was primarily promoted via documentary and street photography, with origins reaching back to the Popular Front and Photo League.

4 John Szarkowski, *The Photographer's Eye* (New York: Museum of Modern Art, 1969).

Sekula provided some canonical statements criticising the cult of metaphor as it appeared in art and photographic criticism. His opposition to this tendency meant attending to the contrasting trope of metonymy, along with another figure of contiguity known as synecdoche, emphasising part–whole relations. Metonymy plays out on several levels in his work: as a preference for specific mediums or aesthetic modes (realism, photography, documentary, prose, essayism) and, more locally, as specific figures within his photo sequences and writing. As we have already seen, metonymy could signal opposition to the dominant strands of modernism and a commitment to exploring alternative aesthetic lineages. As far as Sekula was concerned, this meant reconsidering 'realism' (other artists pursued assemblage, performance, pop, post-minimal or conceptual art). Of all the plastic-visual arts, photography has been deeply entwined with discussions of a broadly 'metonymic' type – and this is further emphasised in the case of documentary – having close affinities with photography's 'indexicality' (to use Peirce's term). Sekula underscores the social angle of contiguity, emphasising photography's power of 'unavoidable social referentiality'.[5]

Sekula's essayistic practices are allied to metonymy. It would be a mistake to identify 'essayistic' qualities solely with the most obvious written elements: the text panels, the essays and the voiced-over ruminations in video and film. It is equally relevant to the visual and visual-aural constructions of Sekula's works: the narrative organisation or sequencing of photographs (on walls, in books, as projections), drawing on the methods of picture prose, photo story and other paraliterary models. *Fish Story*, as we saw, interleaves written essays with the photographs, organising them as 'chapters'. 'Essayistic' aspects can also be discerned in works without the obvious addition of 'words': the silent slide installations or the video works without voice-over. *Photography Against the Grain* is subdivided into two sections: 'Essays' and 'Photo Works'. The 'Essays' assume the form of classic illustrated essays of the sort that could appear in academic journals of art theory. Yet, the most cursory glance at the section on 'Photo Works' underscores Sekula's experimentation in combining photographic images with essays or creative writing; and he invokes multiple narrative forms, such as, 'folktale', 'photonovel', 'meditations', 'sketch'. With a nod and a wink, *This Ain't China* also appeals to the 'psychological novel', 'political novel', 'parable', 'story' (alongside 'dramaturgy', 'theatre', 'opera', 'script', 'the

5 Introduction, *Photography Against the Grain*, ix–xv (ix).

show'). Later, he turns to the video and film essay *The Lottery of the Sea* (2006), and, collaborating with Noël Burch, *The Forgotten Space* (2010) – a form celebrated for its 'associative logic', its metonymic chains, its digressive sidetracks, and its meditative linking of thoughts and observations. The nature of the written essay form was addressed by both Lukács and Adorno, where the 'essayistic' method is seen as particularly suited to exploring a theme in detail. Moreover, these qualities have made the essay especially adept at considering social complexities and contradictions, combining an immediately given scene with mediated reflections on its place in a larger social totality.

Finally, Sekula's writings and artworks employ metonyms, synecdoche and relays. We might see pictured an object that is contiguous with a person. As we have discussed, photographs throughout *Fish Story* set up chains of reference and association. Sekula's images, which can appear banal or uneventful in themselves, provide jumping-off points for connotative relays. *The Dockers' Museum* (2010–13) works this same approach artefactually – an extensive installation composed of maritime industry-themed objects sourced through eBay. Here, Sekula works with the objects themselves, and their mutual adjacencies and combinations, to unleash metonymic connections from the items by activating their idiosyncratic histories and capacity to pique recollections.

Thinking with Jakobson

Sekula appealed to Jakobson's writings throughout his career. There are several factors that perhaps made Jakobson especially significant for Sekula. We have already encountered Jakobson's approach to realism. We might also note his attention to the serious study of popular speech and song, which allies with Sekula's alertness to workers' jokes and quips. Jakobson's concern with folklore and myth links with those aspects of Barthes (and Levi-Strauss) that fired some of Sekula's thinking on photographic ideology and opens onto a broader theory of capitalist cognition. Jakobson may have been a linguist, but his discussions often considered visual as well as verbal examples, complementing Sekula's work arguing against a rigid divide between the realms of word and image. This expansiveness also underlines Jakobson's critical connections with the radical avant-gardes – and the challenges they made to the separation not only of visual and verbal modes, but also of discrete cultural forms, and of 'art' and 'life'. Jakobson bridged the intellectual formations of formalism and structuralism. His presence in US academic life was significant, moving to the New School in New York in 1941 and taking up a post at Harvard in 1949. Jakobson's work was 'in the air', becoming a point of reference for French intellectuals (Lacan, Barthes and so on) and for emerging critical approaches to art history.[6] More importantly for Sekula, Jakobson also bridged Russian and Czech formalism and sociological poetics.

In 1974, in 'On the Invention of Photographic Meaning', Sekula drew on the distinction between metaphor and metonymy from Jakobson's 'Two Aspects of Language and Two Types of Aphasic Disturbances' (1956).[7] The terms of the distinction were clearly at work throughout 'Dismantling Modernism, Reinventing Documentary' (1976, 1978), which also touched on Jakobson's 1960 essay 'Linguistics and Poetics'.[8] In 'Photography Between Labour and Capital' (1983), Sekula returned to 'Two Aspects'. In the mid-1990s, Jakobson appeared once more in the 'Dismal Science' essay, although this reference is to an early piece on Dada (1921) where the figure of the sailor is described as inherently 'revolutionary'.[9] In a 2005 interview, Sekula applauded Jakobson's 'On Realism in Art' (1921). To recall (and this is Sekula's précis), far from being static, 'realism is actually engaged in a complex discursive play, pitting newer realisms against older and seemingly exhausted or over-conventionalized forms of depiction'.[10] To Sekula's eyes, Jakobson's relational and historical subtlety underscored the intellectual poverty prevailing in discussions of realism and documentary in the visual arts

---

6 For example, Rosalind Krauss, 'Notes on the Index: Seventies Art in America', *October* 3 (1977): 68–81.

7 'On the Invention of Photographic Meaning', 21. (It was originally published in January 1975: *Artforum* 13:5 (1975): 37–45; note that Sekula lists the date of the work as 1974.)

8 Jakobson, 'Linguistics and Poetics' (1960), in *Language in Literature*, eds Krystyna Pomorska and Stephen Rudy (Cambridge, MA: The Belknap Press, 1987), 62–94.

9 Jakobson, 'Dada' (1921); first English translation in 1987 in Jakobson, *Language in Literature*, 34–40. Discussion of the figure of the sailor appears on page 34. The sailor is revolutionary because at home everywhere, or, more precisely, because sailors were free of the petit-bourgeois bias: they were detached from the 'homeliness' of a particular place (sailors were free of *byt*). It is interesting to note how, in *The Lottery of the Sea*, the motif of risk shifts from the sailor to Adam Smith's *The Wealth of Nations*. Smith's book is the harbinger of capitalism's levelling down – and ultimately of neoliberal globalisation.

10 Sekula, in Katarzyna Ruchel-Stockmans, 'Interview with Allan Sekula', in *Critical Realism in Contemporary Art: Around Allan Sekula's Photography*, eds Jan Baetens and Hilde Van Gelder (Leuven: Leuven University Press, 2006), 138–51 (149).

and photography.[11] 'Eleven Premises on Documentary and a Question' (2006) also opened with this same Jakobson essay.

The contrast between metaphor and metonymy (like that between poetry and prose) was already established in mid-twentieth-century literary criticism – and already recognised as a terrain of 'ideological battles', as Victor Erlich observed in the mid-1950s.[12] Jakobson had broached the subject in his earlier writing, but it was 'Two Aspects of Language and Two Types of Aphasic Disturbances' that proved to be especially central.[13] Jakobson's main purpose in this essay is to make a case for the importance of linguistics in the study of 'speech disorders', hitherto dominated by medical and educational approaches (and focused on diagnosing aphasia as either emissive or receptive). Parsing Kurt Goldstein's clinical records with the eye of a structural linguist (and with Saussure's distinction of paradigm and syntagm), Jakobson re-describes the two types of aphasia – today they would be understood as forms of neurodivergence – as 'disorders' of similarity or contiguity. Posed in the *clinical* frame of that period, 'similarity disorders' demonstrate a patient's difficulties in: making sense of a word isolated from extended utterances; nomination; identifying synonyms (such as 'unmarried man' for 'bachelor'); or finding words to identify pictured objects. (The problem is also one of understanding the linguistic code, system or metalanguage.) In extremis, such patients err towards the condition of the idiolect (the contradictory state of a 'private language'). Metaphors, which rely on relations of sameness or similarity, are lost on these patients. They compensate by developing the opposite skill, where context is all, readily making links through contiguity and metonymic connections. Things are reversed with 'contiguity disorders', which amount to difficulties in proposition and contexture. These aphasics struggle to combine simple linguistic elements into more complex units (words into sentences, or phonemes into morphemes). They tend towards agrammaticism and find difficulties with words that have a purely grammatical role (conjunctions, prepositions). Their speech

11 As we saw earlier, studies of documentary *film* were seen as an exception to this. Sekula also commented that, compared with film, he thought photography was more constrained by genre (ibid., 145).

12 Viktor Erlich, *Russian Formalism: History – Doctrine* (The Hague: Mouton, 1955), 206. Erlich notes how Jakobson used metaphor and metonymy as 'a basis for still more fundamental distinctions'.

13 Roman Jakobson, 'Two Aspects of Language and Two Types of Aphasic Disturbances' (1956), in *Language in Literature*, 95–114.

lacks inflection, taking the form of the one-word sentence (or single-phoneme utterance), resulting in a 'telegraphic style' and the production of 'word heaps'. In extremis, this condition results in the total loss of language (*aphasia universalis*). Compensating for contexture-deficiency, this type of aphasia can lead to proficiency with metaphoric substitutions, often inflating the role of homonyms.

Although metaphor and metonymy are evident through the discussion of clinical aphasia, their explicit consideration comes to the fore in the final section of Jakobson's essay. On the one hand, metaphor's substitutive principle – transposing a quality from one word entity to another to highlight similarities or correspondences – shares affinities with the 'contiguity disorder'. On the other, and as with the 'similarity disorder', metonymy works with contextual principles; it exploits contiguities and associative relations: proximate adjacencies (spatial), concurrences (temporal), predicative (syntactic, narratival).[14] Here the argument expands well beyond Jakobson's opening claim to offer a linguistic reinterpretation of then-existing clinical descriptions. He calls for comparative studies across a gamut of disciplines – psychopathology, psychology, linguistics, poetics, semiotics and so on – to understand not only clinical aphasia, but also personal predilections, stylistic preferences and modalities of thought. Freud's accounts of dreams, Jakobson points out, identify similar processes: on the one hand, the symbolism, similarity-substitutions and identifications of the objects or persons featuring in his patients' dreams (metaphor); on the other, the displacements (metonymy) and condensations (synecdoche). Likewise, James Frazer's description of 'magic rites' contrasts the use of imitative and homeopathic charms (metaphoric) with forms of magic that work through contagion (metonymic). The contrast between metaphor and metonymy can exemplify entire literary genres, such as poetry and prose. As we have already noted, Jakobson suggests that the same can be said for artistic movements. He cites the examples of Romanticism and symbolism (metaphoric) as compared to realism and the Russian heroic epics (metonymic); surrealism (metaphoric) as compared to cubism (metonymic). Drawing on observations by Eisenstein and Béla Balázs, Jakobson notes that film deploys the 'two aspects' within its very techniques: the metaphoric operations of montage and lap dissolves are compared with the metonymic

14 Jakobson, 'Two Aspects', 110.

work of the *mise-en-scène* or the synecdochic function of close-ups.[15]

As his conclusion expands the range of reflection, Jakobson complains of a reduction that is especially prominent in the cultural context. Here, metaphor has come to dominate: 'The actual bipolarity has been artificially replaced . . . by an amputated, unipolar scheme which, strikingly enough, coincides with one of the two aphasic patterns, namely with the contiguity disorder.'[16] Put simply, he observes that metaphor and similarity are overvalued in studies of culture – this is the 'cult of metaphor' to which Sekula objects. Accordingly, Jakobson calls for more attention to be given to metonymy.[17] Where Jakobson's essay commences by considering how the terms of language might illuminate clinical studies, it ends by reversing the dynamic: at the close, the clinical 'extreme' of the 'contiguity disorder' provides insights into cultural logics. Sekula's work can, in part, be understood as an effort to pursue Jakobson's project: to rectify the discursive imbalance that privileges metaphor and to attend the ignored axis of metonymy.

With 'On the Invention of Photographic Meaning', Sekula aimed to develop 'a historical understanding of the emergence of photographic sign systems' and to challenge the powerful discourse of photographic transparency by demonstrating its conventional character.[18] The essay centres on the contrast between two photographs of migration: Alfred Stieglitz's *The Steerage* from 1907 and *Immigrants Going Down Gangplank, New York* by Lewis Hine from 1905. As suggested in Sekula's conclusion, Jakobson's 'poles of discourse' – metaphor and metonymy – supplied the terms for this critical analysis of photographic ideology. This discourse had, Sekula argued, privileged art photography over documentary, and this contrast echoed through the terms used to discuss the two photographers: Stieglitz/Hine; symbolist/realist; seer/

15 Ibid., 111.

16 Ibid., 114.

17 Jakobson alludes to his own remarks on the 'metonymical turn' of the 1920s–30s, citing four essays ('Two Aspects', 512 n. 25): 'Futurism' (1919), 28–33; 'On Realism in Art' (1927), 19–27; 'Is the Film in Decline?' (1933), 458–65; and 'Marginal Notes on the Prose of the Poet Pasternak' (1935), 301–17 – all paginations to *Language in Literature* (Cambridge, MA: Harvard University Press, 1987). For example, Jakobson notes Pasternak's liking for figures of contiguity (metonymy and synecdoche), he deduces a thematology ranging across formal devices and structure, and ultimately uses this to demonstrate the passive quality of Pasternak's poetic world.

18 'On the Invention of Photographic Meaning', 21.

witness; expression/reportage; inner truth/empirical truth; affective value/empirical value. Importantly, however, Sekula presses beyond these schematic polarities. He objects to the 'binary folklore' of photographic discourse: challenging both the '"symbolist" folk-myth' (associated with metaphor) and the '"realist" folk-myth' (associated with metonymy).[19] Hine's status was a case in point. Get beyond the superficial view, Sekula suggests, and Hine does not occupy one polarity (documentary) but breaks down the rigidity of the art–documentary opposition. First, Sekula emphasises, Hine could be located within the established tradition of the 'realist mystic' or seer, an authorial status associated with modernism and symbolism.[20] Similarly, he notes that 'even the most deadpan reporter's career is embroiled in an expressionist structure'.[21] Indeed, the example of Hine showed how readily one 'pole' of the 'hermeneutic pendulum' can switch to its opposite; how the liberal humanism of photographic discourse could treat reportage as aesthetic products, subsuming their metonymic work into the cult of metaphor.[22]

Although Jakobson's 'Two Aspects' is not directly mentioned, its framework shapes Sekula's 'Dismantling Modernism, Reinventing Documentary'. Here, to diagnose problems in photographic discourse, Sekula reaches for Jakobson's 1960 'Linguistics and Poetics'. Sekula again emphasises the appropriation of the utilitarian or instrumental image for the canon of art photography and its cult of authorship:

> Documentary is thought to be art when it transcends its reference to the world, when the work can be regarded, first and foremost, as an act of self-expression on the part of the artist. To use Roman Jakobson's categories, the referential function collapses into the expressive function. A cult of authorship, an auteurism, takes hold of the image, separating it from the social conditions of its making and elevating it above the multitude of lowly and mundane uses to which photography is commonly put.[23]

---

19 Ibid.

20 Ibid., 20. (In his introduction to *Photography Against the Grain*, Sekula expresses embarrassment at this earlier formulation.)

21 Ibid., 21.

22 For the 'hermeneutic pendulum', see Chapter 1 and 'Dismantling Modernism, Reinventing Documentary', 58.

23 Ibid.

With reference to two of Jakobson's categories – the 'emotive' and 'referential' functions of language – Sekula tries to show how the discourse of photography elevates the former over the latter. Jakobson had outlined six key functions of communication: 'emotive' (emphasising the addresser); 'conative' (emphasising the addressee, aiming at achieving an effect on the addressee); 'referential' (pointing to the context); 'phatic' (emphasising the moment of contact between addresser and addressee); 'poetic' (the message 'for its own sake'[24]); and 'metalinguistic' (where discussants address the extent of their mutual comprehension; speech that is about the linguistic code). For Jakobson, these functions necessarily interact, overlaying one another in different combinations and to varying degrees. While, in any specific instance, one function might be 'dominant', this priority does not mean that it acts in isolation from the other functions. Thus, the 'for its own sake' of the poetic function is not, despite initial appearance, the same as *l'art pour l'art*. Likewise, Jakobson's acknowledgement of a single function's 'dominance' does not imply its absolute autonomy from other functions. In his essays, Sekula actively employs Jakobson's categories to help describe assumptions common to the history of photography, enabling him to propose an aesthetic-ideological diagnosis of cultural repression, as well as suggesting avenues beyond it.

In 'Photography Between Labour and Capital', Sekula returns to Jakobson's essay on aphasia.[25] Sekula again explores the binary that haunts photography: on the one hand, the myth of science and objective truth, and on the other, the myths of art and their cult of subjective experience.[26] In Sekula's view, the mere fact of this art–science duality is a commonplace of photographic history. Instead, the point is to grasp 'that photography is neither art nor science, but is suspended between both the *discourse* of science and that of art'.[27] Again, we can see that his emphasis is on the ideological function of this dichotomy. It is here that he presents the oscillation between objectivism and subjectivism as one of the 'antinomies of bourgeois thought'.[28] (Indeed, Sekula goes on to argue that realism, one pole of the leading binary, is itself riven by yet another opposition, that between instrumental and sentimental modes

24 Jakobson, 'Linguistics and Poetics', 69.

25 'Photography Between Labour and Capital', 266 n. 101.

26 Ibid., 200.

27 Ibid., 201. Selula's emphasis.

28 Ibid., 227. Cf. Introduction, *Photography Against the Grain*, xv (xvii in MACK edition).

– industrial publicity and the family album. And, once more, for Sekula, these contrasting modes coexist; they are not mutually exclusive.[29])

The immediate context for Sekula's return to Jakobson in 'Photography Between Labour and Capital' occurs in the section 'The Emerging Picture-Language of Industrial Capitalism', wherein he explores the 'transitional' status of *De re metallica* and the rationalised vision of the *Encyclopaedia*, interpreting them as preludes to the role later played by photography. A footnote on Jakobson's 'poles of meaning' (also called 'poles of discourse') summarises Rosalind Krauss on Timothy O'Sullivan (1840–82). Krauss had criticised the art-historical appropriation of O'Sullivan's geological survey photographs, resulting in their decontextualisation and transformation into aestheticised 'landscapes' – that is, a metaphoric appropriation of the survey's 'metonymic fragments'.[30] The Jakobsonian frame is already at work in Sekula's preceding pages, in his discussion of Nadar's photographs of worker mannequins in the Paris catacombs (1861):

> Nadar's underground project generated photographic meaning along both the metonymic and metaphoric axes of linguistic expression. This rhetorical dualism was intentional. Nadar's metonymic ambition, his essential *realism*, led him to technologically extend the limits of photographic representation, to discover new vantage points, new illuminating powers. On the other hand, Nadar sought to metaphorize his underground excursions; that much is clear from his autobiographical account. The world underground and especially the catacombs were conducive to allegorical suggestion, even without the overt theatricality of his staging, which further impels our reading in that direction.[31]

Instead of addressing the discursive production of the history and criticism of photography, our attention is here turned to the photographer Nadar. It was Nadar who rhetorically worked the two aspects of photographic meaning. Nonetheless, perhaps the key thing to underline is how Nadar's catacomb project is seen by Sekula as playing along both metaphoric and metonymic axes *simultaneously*. As Sekula presents it, if this is a 'dualism', then it is one where both metaphor and metonymy

29 Ibid., 201.

30 Ibid., 227. Sekula refers to a paper by Krauss that became 'Photography's Discursive Spaces: Landscape/View', *Art Journal* 42:4 (1982): 311–19. He both applauds her account and is critical of its limits.

31 'Photography Between Labour and Capital', 226.

play strong parts. Moreover, Sekula discerns that: 'The allegory involved a contradictory ideological movement: toward a materialist *demystification* of religion and aristocratic class privilege, and toward the *mystification* of material science. In this, the essentially bourgeois character of Nadar's republicanism and materialism is evident.'[32] Thus, Sekula also shifts from the dual rhetoric of metaphor and metonymy – that is, the metaphoric suggestiveness of the underworld and the metonymic realism of Nadar's efforts – to their co-presence within Nadar's materialist attitude. The simultaneity of Nadar's secularism and deification of science is understood as constituting an ideological *contradiction*. Here, we are back with the 'antinomies of bourgeois thought'. However, instead of cultural discourse's 'amputated, unipolar scheme' (to recall Jakobson's formulation), Sekula's account suggests a more fluid conception of the relations generated by the antinomy.

Jakobson, as we saw, suggested a broadened applicability of the metaphor–metonymy distinction, which was soon picked up by others.[33] Structuralism offered especially fertile ground. For example, Lacan's treatment of the psychoanalytic 'symptom' as metaphoric and 'desire' as metonymic influenced thinkers gathered around the journals *Cahiers pour l'Analyse* (1966–9) and *Screen*.[34] The treatment of metaphor and metonymy as a general theory of cognition – as 'modes of thought'[35] or as 'mental strategies of conceptualisation'[36] – was underscored by the emergence of cognitive linguistics in the 1980s, launched by Lakoff and Johnson's *Metaphors We Live By* (1980). Here, metaphor maps correspondences across different conceptual 'domains' or 'knowledge frames', while metonymy finds physical or causal correspondences within them.

32 Ibid.

33 Jakobson credits Levi-Strauss for opening linguistics to wider cultural applications. ('Linguistics and Poetics', 89).

34 For example, Luce Irigaray used the metaphor–metonymy distinction to demarcate psychosis and neurosis respectively.

35 Charting the relations between different disciplinary and theoretical approaches, Gerard Steen credits Jakobson. Gerard Steen, 'Metonymy Goes Cognitive-Linguistic', *Style* 39:1 (Spring 2005): 1–11 (2).

36 René Dirven, 'Metaphor and Metonymy: Different Mental Strategies of Conceptualisation', *Leuvense Bijdragen* 82 (1993): 1–28; revised version in *Metaphor and Metonymy in Comparison and Contrast*, eds René Dirven and Ralf Pörings (Berlin and New York: De Gruyter Mouton, 2002), 75–111. For a recent summary of debates in cognitive linguistics, Adeline Terry, 'Metaphtonymies We Die By: The Influence of the Interactions between Metaphor and Metonymy on Semantic Change in X-phemistic Conceptualisations of Death', *Lexis* 16 (2020).

Sekula's thinking had already developed within a context that linked language use to ideology, from Marx to Vološinov to Barthes and Pêcheux. Yet, as we have seen, from early on, he challenged the metaphor–metonymy opposition itself, identifying their antinomic presentation as a discursive construct of capitalism.[37] If, in the face of the dominant aesthetic ideology, metonymy needed to be emphasised, this was no call to establish a counter-cult of metonymy. Likewise, the attributing of tropes to specific genres or media is problematic: prose is never 'all metonym', but often employs metaphor freely. There are also problems with the mapping of tropes onto moral-political values ('good metonymy', 'bad metaphor'). Indeed, the role of metonymy in advertising and politics has been subject to increasing scrutiny. 'Post-truth' disinformation campaigns and conspiracy theories often use principles of contiguousness (the power of 'guilt by association') to establish fallacious metonymic chains. Once in play, they are hard to dispel; a simple trigger readily unleashes the full cascade of groundless associations.

Rigid dichotomising of metaphor and metonymy is a fool's errand. In practice, figures of association (such as metaphor) and those of contiguity (metonymy, synecdoche) overlay or blend into one another. With a slight shift in emphasis, the same figure can be read on both metaphoric and metonymic axes – as would be the case with Sekula's use of the word 'traffic' in his essay 'The Traffic in Photographs'. Other locutions possess similar motility: from everyday expressions such as 'commodity chains' or 'container fields', through to the specialist semiotic or philosophical employments of 'vehicle', 'freight', 'carrier', 'bearer' (think of Marx's use of *Träger*).[38] The distinction between metaphor and metonymy, then, can sometimes be a matter of subtle re-inflection, historical changes in language use or controversial points of interpretation. In cognitive linguistics, 'conceptual metaphor' and 'conceptual metonymy' are understood as being on a continuum, as distinct-yet-*interacting* cognitive processes. There are 'metonymy-based metaphors', and vice versa.[39] Metaphors can be motivated by metonymies,

---

37 Notably, Barthes criticised the opposition (for which he found Jakobson culpable) and found metonymy to be a species of metaphor. Roland Barthes, 'The Rhetoric of the Image' (1964), in *Image/Music/Text*, ed. Stephen Heath (London: Fontana, 1977), 32–51 (50 n. 2).

38 Marx, preface to first edition of *Capital: I*, presents the capitalist as 'bearer' of economic or class relations and as character-mask. Elsewhere, the commodity is the 'bearer' of value. See Kyle Baasch, 'The Theatre of Economic Categories: Rediscovering *Capital* in the Late 1960s', *Radical Philosophy* 208 (2020): 18–32.

39 Louis Goossens, 'Metaphtonymy: The interaction of metaphor and metonymy in expressions for linguistic action', in *Metaphor and Metonymy in Comparison and Contrast*,

and metonymies by metaphors. In his essay on allegory and literary theory for *October*, Joel Fineman explored 'metonymic metaphors' and 'metaphoric metonyms'.[40] Jameson referred to metaphor and metonymy's 'ceaseless metamorphosis from the one into the other'.[41] The mutations can matter in ways that go beyond debates over interpretation (as with *Träger*). In 1968, in *Cahiers pour l'Analyse*, Thomas Herbert (a pseudonym for Michel Pêcheux) advanced a theory of ideology – drawing on Lacan, Althusser and Poulantzas – in which metonymic processes are first rendered metaphoric, so that transferences are enabled to scale between distinct aspects of the social. He summarised a formula for the mutations between metonymy (m) and metaphor (M), through the domains of the economic (1), political (2) and ideological (3): m1 ➔ M1 ➔ m2 ➔ M2 ➔ m3 ➔ M3.[42] Here, Herbert/Pêcheux transcodes the linguistic debate into a politico-methodological point about the determination of social 'levels'. Although not referring to Pêcheux, an excellent illustration of this process is *Policing the Crisis*, where Stuart Hall and his co-authors show how a series of unrelated phenomena (sex education, long hair, militant trade unionism, immigration, drug use, squatting, the anti-Apartheid movement and the new crime of 'mugging') became metonymically linked by the media and politicians. In the process, the 'moral panic' focused on West Indian youth, and the empty signifier of 'the silent majority', facilitated an authoritarian move to the right by state agencies and the wider polity.[43]

349–77 (a revised version of Goossens's essay from 1990); Gunter Radden, 'How Metonymic are Metaphors?' (a revised version of Radden's essay from 2000), in *Metaphor and Metonymy in Comparison and Contrast*, 407–34.

40 Joel Fineman, 'The Structure of Allegorical Desire', *October* 12 (1980): 46–66.

41 Jameson, *Prison-House*, 123.

42 Thomas Herbert, 'Remarques pour une théorie générale des idéologies', *Cahiers pour l'Analyse* 9.5 (1968): 74–92.

43 Stuart Hall, Chas Critcher, Tony Jefferson, John Clarke and Brian Roberts, *Policing the Crisis: Mugging, the State and Law and Order* (London: Macmillan, 1978). 'Race', Hall suggests in another essay, 'is the prism through which British people are called upon to "live through", to understand, and then to deal with crisis conditions'. Stuart Hall, 'Race and "Moral Panics" in Postwar Britain', in *Stuart Hall: Selected Writings on Race and Difference*, eds Paul Gilroy and Ruth Wilson Gilmore (Durham, NC: Duke University Press, 2021), 56–70 (63). The analysis has been applied to Nixon's 1968 'law and order' campaign by Ruth Wilson Gilmore in *Abolition Geography: Essays Towards Liberation* (London: Verso, 2023).

In 1975, Pêcheux would subject this essay to critique because of its idealism and 'structuralist pseudo-solution'[44] – and, in turn, he subjected that revision to critique in his 1982 postscript for the English translation (for its idealism and Platonic logic, and for ignoring 'the oscillation between sense and nonsense in the divided subject').[45] Nonetheless, through these self-critiques and revisions, he retained his understanding of the roles of metaphor and metonymy as socio-historical and ideological processes. Meaning is constituted in discourse formation, as the subject form is ideologically interpellated ('put into place') by, and 'stabilised' in, the relevant 'domains of thought'.[46] Metaphor imports and translates preconstructed materials between different domains of thought (*inter*discourse).[47] Metonymy works within a domain (*intra*discourse), absorbing those imported materials through metonymic 'articulation', by making selections or substitutions from the elements of its particular discursive formation. By threading these materials into a 'sustaining process', the procedures of interdiscourse and subjectification are forgotten, naturalised and occluded.[48] Thus, discourses conceal their dependence on the 'complex whole in dominance' – a contradictory material 'law of unevenness-contradiction-subordination'.[49] Drawing on psychoanalysis, Pêcheux hoped to break capitalism's 'imaginary identifications' and to engineer 'interpellation in reverse' by seeking faultlines, jars, flashes, 'fleeting forms of appearance' or absurd eruptions (unconscious slips, jokes, faltering speech, parapraxis).[50]

Sociological Poetics

In his introduction to *Photography Against the Grain*, Sekula credits Vološinov with helping him go beyond the double closure presented by two formations: individual subjectivism and abstract objectivism (the second section of *Marxism and the Philosophy of Language* contained a critique of the 'two trends of thought in philosophy of language').[51] For

44 Michel Pêcheux, *Language, Semantics and Ideology: Stating the Obvious* (1975; London: Macmillan, 1982), 92.

45 Ibid., 217.

46 Ibid., 112.

47 Ibid., 117. 'Transdiscourse' attends to the intersection of inter- and intradiscourse.

48 Ibid.

49 Ibid., 113.

50 Ibid., 216–18.

51 Introduction, *Photography Against the Grain*, xiii (xv in MACK edition). Vološinov, *Marxism and the Philosophy of Language*, 45–63.

Sekula, there was, first, the 'individualistic subjectivism' manifest in modernist formalism through its authorially shaped stylistic tendencies and expressivist interpretation of artwork (based on the Humboldtian account of language). Second, structuralism exemplified 'abstract objectivism'. Sekula describes how the Bakhtin Circle enabled him to develop a critique of structuralism:

> while I was clearly indebted to structuralism, and particularly to Roland Barthes' early essays on photography, the isolation of an abstract language system from social language, from language use, seemed to have produced a related kind of closure [to that of individualistic subjectivism], more 'scientific' perhaps than that effected by modernist criticism, but closure nonetheless.[52]

This abstract objectivism was taken to underpin both structuralism and the earlier formalism of the Slavic linguists.

Sekula stresses that the contributions of the Bakhtin Circle (along with Walter Benjamin's writing on technical reproducibility) provided ways for him to understand 'the *socially*-created character of language'.[53] Vološinov's *Marxism and the Philosophy of Language* was one of the key texts that revised the reflectionist understanding of knowledge and consciousness. As far as he was concerned, the sign is a locus of class struggle – always socially embedded and saturated, and thus ideological. This meant that language and consciousness do not simply 'reflect' social existence; rather, language operates as a 'refracting and distorting medium'.[54] The metaphors of refraction and distortion might be inadequate, but Sekula understood that language is riven by social antagonism. This endows the sign with 'social *multiaccentuality*'.[55] Existing 'in the dialectical flux of the social generative process', the sign is 'vital and mutable'.[56] Influenced by Raymond Williams's account of Vološinov in *Marxism and Literature* (1977), Sekula resets structuralism's oppositions in social, historical and materialist terms. This entailed avoiding the 'overly synchronic or ahistorical' approach, to acknowledge 'the importance of

52 Introduction, *Photography Against the Grain*, xiii (xv in MACK edition).

53 Ibid.

54 Vološinov, *Marxism and the Philosophy of Language*, 23.

55 Ibid.

56 Ibid., 24, 23.

historical shifts in the meaning, function and cultural status of photographic representation'.[57]

According to Vološinov, the sign itself is best understood not in terms of the fixities of 'form' and 'content' derived from traditional idealist aesthetics, but instead as a dynamic fusion of form and content.[58] Pavel Medvedev, a fellow member of the Circle, grasped the intersection of form and content (or recognised the limitations of the form–content dyad itself):

> This terminology [form and content] can only be accepted under the condition that form and content are thought of as limits between which all the elements of the poetic construction are situated. Then content will correspond to thematic unity, and form to the actual realization of the work. But it is necessary to bear in mind here that every element of the work is a chemical combination of form and content. There is no formless content and there is no contentless form. Social evaluation is the common denominator of the content and form of every element of the construction.[59]

In a sense, the tradition of sociological poetics displaces the form–content distinction. In an interview in 2005, Sekula affirmed: 'I take seriously the sociological model of Bakhtin and Vološinov, for whom it was ultimately impossible to separate form from content, the word from usage and meaning, and the sign from the universe of living human dialogue.'[60] As he put it in *Photography Against the Grain*, the writing of the Bakhtin Circle opened the possibility of – and here the terms of Bakhtin's *Dialogical Imagination* come to the fore – 'a sociology of literature based on a recognition of the "heteroglossia" of "living language," on a recognition of discourse as an arena of ideological and social difference and conflict'.[61] Sekula developed his understanding of photographic culture from this position, along with his thinking about realism and the visual–verbal nexus of his own artistic practice.

---

57 Introduction, *Photography Against the Grain*, xiii (xv in MACK edition).

58 Williams, *Marxism and Literature*, 39.

59 M. M. Bakhtin/P. N. Medvedev, *The Formal Method in Literary Scholarship: A Critical Introduction to Sociological Poetics* (1928; Cambridge, MA: Harvard University Press, 1985), 140. Erlich was broadly sympathetic to Medvedev's attempt to '[go] beyond the a-social poetics of pure Formalism and the a-literary sociologism of crude Marxists' (Erlich, *Russian Formalism*, 115).

60 Sekula in Ruchel-Stockmans, 'Interview with Allan Sekula', 149.

61 Introduction, *Photography Against the Grain*, xiii.

A number of thinkers – Jameson, Williams, Eagleton – identify affinities between sociological poetics and the formalism of Jakobson and Tynjanov.[62] Jakobson and Tynjanov were seen as drawing closer to Vološinov.[63] They evidenced a more dialectical relation between synchrony and diachrony, where the one projects onto or through the other; and an emerging model of historical change or 'mutations'.[64] Later, in 'Linguistics and Poetics', Jakobson speaks of the 'projections' and 'promotions' between these axes (selection/combination or syntagma/paradigm).[65] Nonetheless, Jameson suggests that the project to reintegrate diachrony would be necessarily stymied until the synchrony–diachrony opposition inherited from structuralism was fundamentally recast. As Williams argues, Tynjanov and Jakobson's attempt to make the diachronic more 'functional' was itself ultimately limited by 'the familiar reification of objective idealism' and lacked 'the full emphasis of social process'.[66] Approaching from the other direction, Wlad Godzich sees the Bakhtin Circle as thinkers engaging in an immanent critique of the Russian Formalists, seeking 'the fundamental instruments for a sociological poetics yet to come'.[67] Marxist poetics would be premised on the achievements of Jakobson and Tynjanov's work, while also pushing beyond its limits. This is what Sekula attempts.

62 Jameson, *The Prison-House of Language*, 20–1. Williams, *Marxism and Literature*, 42. Terry Eagleton, *Literary Theory: An Introduction* (Oxford: Blackwell, 1983), 111. Jameson compares Jakobson's account of 'mutations' to Althusser's 'epistemological break' and to the moment when the superstructure feels the 'geological shifts' of historical change (*The Prison-House of Language*, 136).

63 Jakobson especially admired Vološinov's section on indirect speech. Ladislav Matejka and I. R. Titunik, 'Translators' Preface, 1986', in Vološinov, *Marxism and the Philosophy of Language*, vii–xii (vii–viii). See also Titunik, 'The Formal Method and the Sociological Method (M. M. Baxtin, P. N. Medvedev, V. N. Vološinov) in Russian Theory and Study of Literature', in ibid., 175–200 (187).

64 Jakobson and Tynjanov, 'Problems in the Study of Language and Literature' (1928), in *Language in Literature*, 47–9; Jakobson, 'The Dominant' (1935), ibid., 41–6.

65 In poetry, he wrote, 'The poetic function projects the principle of equivalence from the axis of selection into the axis of combination. Equivalence is promoted to the constitutive device of the sequence' ('Linguistics and Poetics', 71; first sentence italicised in original).

66 Williams, *Marxism and Literature*, 42.

67 Wlad Godzich, 'Foreword', in Medvedev, *The Formal Method in Literary Scholarship*, vii–xiv (vii).

Metonymic Breaks

Given the stakes of 'documentary', which is often seen as a mimetic copy, it is worth considering the literal and figural aspects of Sekula's work. Literally, a key tranche of it is 'about' maritime industries: logistics, FOCs, labour conditions and so on. The works can also be 'about' how the maritime world is figured (its representation in paintings, photography, films and novels); or how it is deployed rhetorically (signifying outdatedness, in the economic sense, or, less pejoratively, nostalgia-inducing reference for the leisure industries). In these ways, figuration is what Sekula explicitly discusses. In addition, Sekula works or poses his presentations figuratively. These same discussions can provide Sekula with the means to say something figuratively 'about' late capitalism. At times, they also shade into critiques of the art world and its favoured cultural theories, or of urban redevelopment and its associated rhetoric. It is not a matter of choosing whether the figural or literal is the dominant or subsidiary aspect; they clearly work together in Sekula's practice. As we have seen, he rejected the postmodern claim that social referentiality in photography was a ruse or fiction and held both literal and figural in dialectical tension. 'Figural' work can heighten a 'literal' point, of course. For example, we mentioned earlier the locution 'container field', where the metaphor suggests that the terminal's storage expanses are akin to agricultural land, contrasting farm with port. Moreover, it can point to actual processes of supplantation, as farmland is sold to the logistics industry. As we saw in Chapter 1, 'logistics' is a military metaphor; but it is also, in literal terms, the expansion of military techniques into the domain of commerce.

While Sekula's engagement with the tropes of metonymy, metaphor and synecdoche is readily apparent in his writing, it might be harder to understand how he employs these ideas in his visual studies. Before moving on, let us explore his photographic figurations by returning to some examples from *Fish Story*. The chair depicted in the final chapter was designed by architect Richard Neutra for Channel Heights in San Pedro, an estate built in 1943 (#94). The opening chapter of *Fish Story* includes two photographs registering the relocation of another San Pedro house from this period: a night-time scene of the sawn-through wooden structure being transported by truck, exposing the privacy of its bathroom and toilet to public view. The chair's worldly usefulness is 'museum-ified'. Moreover, it is not only displaced from its initial functionality into a museological object; it also finds itself relegated from the light of display to the museum's storage facilities. Twice over, the chair's 'life' – its place in a social process – is 'stilled'. This 'stilling' adds social valences. Channel Heights was a wartime project commissioned by the Federal Works Agency to house employees of the harbour and shipyards. The chair and the house in transit recollect an era when – provoked by the exigencies of the war economy – a politics of public housing was possible. Facilitated by the permanent arms economy and high taxation, military Keynesianism created a 'welfare-warfare' state that sought to resolve social antagonism by offering some protections to the US working class, though always with the differential gendered conditions and the unequal access enshrined in American apartheid (lower wages and ghettos for African Americans and the deportation of Mexicans). Even these social schemes would soon fall victim to policies of privatisation and tax cutting allied to the Cold War.[68] Through these contiguities, the photographs of house and chair assert a social and political point, the one that underpins *Fish Story* as a whole: deindustrialisation, and the conservative and neoliberal values behind that transformation. Although they are not spatially adjacent, the images of the chair and the house are connected, and their positions in the opening and closing chapters frame the work. The photographs are metonyms for the historical repression of labour and its organisations, and the impact of this on public policy. Such mid-century housing schemes were denounced by lobbies of developers and right-wing Republicans as evidence of 'creeping socialism', generating yet another figurative line with the 'invasive-vegetal' metonym for a politics of social cooperation.[69] These three photographs also project us into domestic space. Although *Fish Story* is focused on the maritime industries, with their primarily masculine workforce, allusions to social reproduction recur throughout. Connections with the mid-century San Pedro estates, direct or indirect, might be traced through these public-political and private-domestic vectors. They also point to the imbrication of social reproduction in military Keynesianism.[70] To reinforce the military and historical link, in the final chapter, shortly before we encounter the

68 Gregory Hooks, *Forging the Military-Industrial Complex* (Urbana, IL: University of Illinois Press, 1991); Gilmore, *Abolition Geography*, 117–18, 140–1, 199–223, 318–34.

69 Ehrhard Bahr, *Weimar on the Pacific: German Exile Culture in Los Angeles and the Crisis of Modernism* (Berkeley, CA: University of California Press, 2007), 165. There are surely also allusions to Mike Davis's history of real-estate politics in *City of Quartz: Excavating the Future of Los Angeles* (London: Verso, 1990).

70 Cf. 'Dismal Science', 133.

chair image, we see a man standing on the deck of a restored cargo ship on the San Pedro waterfront, cradling in his arms three old rifles: he is an actor dressed as a World War II soldier.

To take another example, the port works as a synecdoche for 'labour' and the 'forgotten space' signals the forgetting, occlusion and disavowal of the labour associated with such sites. This synecdoche takes us from the spaces of maritime trade and its labour to the functions of global capital. Here, it matters how we imagine the part–whole relation that characterises synecdoche. This is not the part–whole relation that might be encountered, for example, in the sectoral subdivisions of an OECD report, delineating component parts of a national economy. Rather, in Sekula's handling, the 'parts' are better understood as *qualitative* 'condensers' of larger social totalities, as exemplary intensified figures; qualities pertaining to smaller elements can be expanded ('de-condensed') at ever-widening scales to perceive the larger entity. As a figure of contiguity, synecdoche relays in both directions – part-to-whole or whole-to-part. Here, rather than the contexts of economic statistics and facts, it is linguistic and literary contexts of thought that are most apt, establishing relations through their tropes. Another useful framework would be the Freudian psychoanalytical process of condensation, to which Jakobson has already pointed in his discussion of synecdoche. Yet another appropriate framework would be Marx's appeal, in his efforts to explain the critique of political economy, to chemical terminology (affinity, distillate, precipitate, crystallise and, once again, condense and reagents, and so on). None of these examples – literary, psychoanalytic, Marx's use of the chemical – is amenable to a quantitative relation of part-to-whole. Understood in the qualitative manner, the synecdochic expansions – contractions can be spatial (revealing how one locality sits within the global); temporal (relating the present to its pasts); conceptual (the relations of general condition and particular instance). Thus, we are directed to links between different places, different points in history, different industries and different societal aspects, and their varying distributions of the sensible.

In a series of important studies, William Pietz argues that fethishism – in all three of its theoretical articulations: Freudianism, Marxism and anthropology – is a process of metonymy, linking occluded or repressed instances to their moments of generation.[71] It could be argued, though,

71 William Pietz, 'The Problem of the Fetish I', *Res* 9 (1985): 5–17; 'The Problem of the Fetish II: The Origin of the Fetish', *Res* 13 (1987): 23–45; 'The Problem of the Fetish IIIa: Bosman's Guinea and the Enlightenment Theory of Fetishism', *Res* 16 (1988): 105–23.

that fetishism is more like a broken chain of connections. Sekula explores the cognitive and ideological power conveyed by capitalism's picture language, its semiotic debris, material cultures and tokens of social practice. He argues that connections between appearances and their social constitution are weakened or ruptured. He imagined capitalism as generating not only 'antinomies', but also something akin to a social 'contiguity disorder', lacking contexture.[72] As Sekula underscored, his aim was to counter capitalism's 'attenuated or broken metonymy'; he sought to make those connections 'metonymically accessible'.[73]

A principal example of the break in contiguity is the ways modern container ports displace old ports' urban 'visibility'. Sekula repeatedly returns to figures of concealment. In *The Lottery of the Sea*, his voice-over observes that – and the words scripted are telling – 'the port retreats into enforced invisibility'. The film made with Noël Burch dubs the occlusion as '*forgotten* space'. This occlusion plays out at other levels: containers secrete their contents; ships' ensigns conceal the ownership of vessels. As these examples highlight, the question of 'visibility' and 'invisibility' applies equally to its literal meaning ('in sight', 'out of sight'); to figural extensions of cognitive awareness ('out of sight, out of mind', to cite the opening of *The Forgotten Space*); and simultaneously to their political, discursive, ideological and psychoanalytic implications.

Tropes certainly occur in Sekula's work as 'figures of speech' but, like Jakobson and others, they are also understood in their expanded sense so that the epistemic and political implications of metaphoric and metonymic practices are recognised. Still, Sekula resists the schematising that beset some readers of Jakobson. Attentive to their interrelations and blendings, his work suggests a more fluid handling of antinomies, tropes and linguistic functions. Tropes, in his works, are heuristics for probing how meaning is produced, distributed, trafficked and circulated through language, images, objects and the social institutions that support or use them.

It is interesting to compare the handling of metonymy in Pêcheux and Sekula, who locate metaphoric – metonymic relations differently, while both understanding them in terms of capitalist social relations (and not only as literary tropes). For Sekula, the metonymic connections are 'broken or attenuated' by capitalism: by its abstractions; by the

72 Jakobson, 'Two Aspects', 109.

73 Sekula in Pascal Beausse, 'Allan Sekula réalisme critique/The Critical Realism of Allan Sekula', *Art Press* 240 (1998): 20–26 (26).

exploitation of geographic distances and the unevenness of global labour regimes; or by legal frameworks like the FOC. In Pêcheux's account, metonymy is one of the means by which social relations are 'naturalised', as part of the interpellative process. Accordingly, whereas Sekula wants to 'make accessible' again the metonymic linkages destroyed by capitalism (an effort of cognitive mapping), Pêcheux hopes to find, exaggerate and exploit them (an effort to disrupt the subject form and its identification or cathexis with the discourses established). The distinction here is more one of emphasis than substance. They share a political vision to counter the ideologies and imaginary identifications of capitalism.[74] This also parallels, as we discussed in our Introduction, the distinction between realism as a mode for charting social networks and dependencies, and modernism as a critical work on ideological suture. Again, we have before us the 'torn halves of a dialectic'.

SECTION 2: *THE LOTTERY OF THE SEA* (2006)

Readers may be familiar with the shorter film *The Forgotten Space* that Sekula made in 2010 with Noël Burch, but to understand better how Sekula achieves ideological relays, condensing and expanding in multiple dimensions, we want to attend to *The Lottery of the Sea* (2006). This video essay is almost three hours in length, organised around a prologue (arguably, two) and eleven chapters, each of which focuses on a location, some of which are visited twice (Athens, Japan, Barcelona, Panama, Los Angeles, Spanish Galicia, Lisbon, Amsterdam). While picking up examples from across the work's chapters, we focus especially on the

74 Pêcheux's account impinged on the question of ideological forgetting: that is intradiscourse's use of metonymy to occlude the metaphoric translation of interdiscourse. Drawing on Freud's essay on 'Negation', Pêcheux developed an argument with Catherine Fuchs in 1975, which elaborated two stages of 'forgetting': first, a forgetting akin to unconscious repression; second, a forgetting that works over that first process (preconscious, conscious and/or ideological) (126). He revised this account in 1982 to avoid the suggestion of there being two (Platonic) logical steps, proposing instead a non-sequential simultaneity of production and product, and stressing the impossibility of erasing or forgetting: 'the unconscious traces of the Signifier are never "erased" or "forgotten" but work without intermission in the oscillation between sense and nonsense in the divided subject' (Pêcheux, *Language, Semantics and Ideology*, 217). Traces of the forgetting process always remain and the ideological breaks can erupt. Although Pêcheux's work is rooted in Lacanian-Althusserian theory, his account has sometimes been compared with Vološinov's work.

prologue(s) and the first chapter on Athens. Without dwelling on technical questions of linguistic tropes, our detailed (and decelerated) discussion can show how ideas transcode between levels. *The Lottery of the Sea* spans history, political economy, commerce, the military and the environment (among other things), threading between aspects of the military-industrial complex (to which compound Sekula added a third adjective: '-entertainment').[75] The scalar shifts not only connect the literal wholeness and constituent parts of Athens' Piraeus port as an entity (or indeed, that of the global economy); they also bring together capital's social 'domains'.

The film opens with blank tape, the equivalent of black leader in film, directing us to focus on the opening bars of Phil Ochs's haunting lyrics – 'Sailors climb the tree, Up the terrible tree'. With Ochs's song continuing ('Where are my shipmates? Have they sunk beneath the sea?'), we see shots of oil and black plastic bags pouring onto the earth in slow, thick folds; a machine rhythmically slicing through a histological sample of flat fish encased in a cryogel embedding medium. Stacked containers pass by, emblazoned 'Evergreen' and 'Uniglory'. Ochs's composition *The Scorpion Departs but Never Returns* was itself prompted by the destruction of the American nuclear-powered submarine *Scorpion* while it was monitoring Soviet activity south of the Azores in 1968 – an event still unexplained, but which is wrapped up with the militarisation of the oceans during the Cold War. A significant anti-war activist, Ochs adopted an approach that was nonetheless empathetic, taking the bewildered perspective of a crew member. The lyrics are close to episodic hallucinatory poetry, an individual voice – isolated and alienated – calling out to comrades and family with the trope of prosopopoeia, from beyond the grave, somewhere from the sedimental ooze on the sea floor. The song readily serves as eulogy not only for *Scorpion*'s crew but also for maritime disasters in general. As Sekula's video essay progresses, we come to realise that the lyrics resonate for working mariners risking their existence on the rust buckets or 'death ships' enabled by the 'open registry' or 'flag of convenience', an American

75 Others have sought to extend in new directions the category introduced by Eisenhower in his 1961 address to the nation. For the prison-industrial complex, see: Mike Davis, 'Hell Factories: The Prison Industrial Complex', *The Nation* 260:7 (1995): 229–34; Ruth Wilson Gilmore, *Golden Gulag: Prisons, Surplus, Crisis, and Opposition in Globalizing California* (Berkeley, CA: University of California Press, 2007) and *Abolition Geography*. In the latter volume, Gilmore also points to a 'nonprofit industrial complex' (224–41). Sekula offers another insight.

invention. Reputedly, *Scorpion*'s crew dubbed the vessel *Scrapiron* due to its dire state of repair. *The Lottery of the Sea* opens, then, with the American role in establishing the postwar world order – geopolitical and economic. It opens in the D-minor key of sadness, anxiety and loss – or, arguably, more: Ochs's poetry sears utter despair and devastation.

The song gives way to the burring engines of the passing container barge, and in turn to scenes on a quay in Yokohama. 'The informal economy', Sekula announces, alongside his video recording of a band of workers inspecting and buying used consumer goods from the back of a van (Bose speakers, a camera).[76] We discern that they are a mix of 'petty traders' from Yokohama's Chinatown and 'the latest volunteers for the bottom of the global market in maritime wages'. Leading up to the title – *The Lottery of the Sea* – Sekula establishes the idea of risk via Adam Smith: asking about the affinity between maritime risk and aesthetic sublimity. Inserts of early black-and-white film show mariners handling a lifeboat and rigging, battling rough seas and posing cheerfully for the camera. The footage was taken from *Around Cape Horn* (1929), a silent film made by Irving Johnson (and on which he often lectured). It records his journey from Hamburg to Chile (Talcahuano) onboard *Peking*, a vessel belonging to the company F. Laeisz, one of the last generation of freight sail ships. This voyage outward transported wheat and general cargo, returning with nitrates (primarily used for fertiliser and explosives). 'Every seafarer was a gambler, a subscriber to the "lottery of the sea".' The voice-over expounds on Smith's account: on the one side, sailors, whose mobility and cosmopolitanism sank their wages; on the other, the interests of merchant shipping, which, by combining into larger fleets, could insure against the fortunes of maritime trade. Both sides, Sekula tells us, suggested prototypes for the present day: low-wage economies, deregulation of the labour market and the 'triumph of big business'. The contemporary scenes on a Japanese dock drive home the developed realisation of those eighteenth-century beginnings, albeit with 'big business' (ironically) retained simply through brand names, displaced by the informal second-life trade.[77]

---

76 The transcript for the voice-over (presumably Sekula's) is given in *Art Isn't Fair*, 241–70. Comparing this transcript with the one we initially made has been interesting for the different choices of punctuation (and thus pace) and syntactic form.

77 The motif of the lottery also plays as the physical dangers faced by sailors battling the elements and the financial gambles taken by capital. The theme of gambling recurs through *The Lottery of the Sea*: maritime workers risk their health on the gas and chemical ships; retired seamen play dominos; the lights of a fruit machine shine the word *SUERTE*

The video's title is from *The Wealth of Nations*. Published in 1776, Smith's study became the central work of the period of classical political economy. By the late twentieth century, it had become distorted into an ideological bludgeon by neoliberal theorists promoting 'freedom' (individual liberty linked to free trade, deregulation and so on). In his tenth chapter, Smith noted the peculiarity of sailors' wages in his day: compared with the remuneration of port workers, mariners' pay was suppressed; and, unlike land-based labourers, their wages were relatively equalised across widely dispersed geographical locations.[78] As Sekula notes, the 'generalised' condition of sailors in the mid-eighteenth century anticipated the telos for all labour, the passage of time to the present in turn realising a wider process of generalisation. Put another way, the condition Smith described foreshadowed globalisation: remuneration for work is pushed downwards as the labour arbitrage broadens, while reforming specific customs and practices.

Sekula's words oscillate between the historical description of Smith's eighteenth-century analysis and allusion to Smith's twentieth-century neoliberal epigones. The essayistic voice and the imagery can pull in different directions. The video footage does not simply 'illustrate' the words, although we certainly intuit connections. In the final stanza, however, the two elements come together when Sekula's camera follows one mariner carrying onboard a large black box that he has purchased. In a gesture reminiscent of traditional methods of port work, the item is balanced on his shoulder. 'The followers of Adam Smith can take

('luck'); the Spanish government unsuccessfully gambles on hiding behind a pack of lies; Texan property developers take on a venture in Catalonia; and to stem the loss of traffic to northern routes opened by global warming, the Panamanian Government stakes the Canal's future on expansion.

78 Adam Smith, *The Wealth of Nations*, Part 1, Chapter 10: 'Of Wages and Profit in the Different Employments of Labour and Stock', paragraph 34. Hegel made a related point contrasting land and sea:

> The principle of family life is dependence on the soil, on land, *terra firma*. Similarly, the natural element for industry, animating its outward movement, is the sea. Since the passion for gain involves risk, industry though bent on gain yet lifts itself above it; instead of remaining rooted to the soil and the limited circle of civil life with its pleasures and desires, it embraces the element of flux, danger, and destruction.

G. W. F. Hegel, *The Philosophy of Right* (1821; Oxford: Oxford University Press, 1967), trans. T. M. Knox, 151. Discussions of this passage – including its recognition of global trade and colonialism, and the degree of importance of the affective relations of the home – often coincide with those on the 'amphibious animal'.

heart. Inside every seafarer, a merchant is struggling to break free', Sekula notes – a maritime riff on the much-repeated Smithian mantra that it is the 'natural propensity' of humans to 'truck and barter'; the ideology implies that markets form (and by extension and abstraction, 'the market' forms) the natural basis for society.

The first chapter of *The Lottery of the Sea* is introduced with the intertitle 'Athens. December 2003'. We will attempt a scene-by-scene overview, exploring some lexical elements in greater depth, though this analysis can be no more than a maquette. The chapter includes footage of Athens' ancient monuments; low-key commerce and the port of Piraeus; and a couple of clips set in the latter from the 1960 black-and-white film *Never on Sunday*. Together, Sekula's montage of film and voice-over builds a narrative comprising interlocking economic, political, historical and philosophical reflections. He expands from the Smithian theme of the prologue to meditate on the ancient Athenian Agora. Our entry point is a shot of the Hephaisteion, the ancient temple perched atop Agoraios Kolonos (Market Hill). Initially, it is seen at a distance from the south, looking over the Agora, and then more closely, looking up directly to its portico from the perspective of the Agora itself. Sekula's tone is both factual and ironic, seriously critical and tongue-in-cheek: 'The ancient *agora*, legendary birthplace of democracy. Stepping-stones of philosophy, market stalls of small traders, political platforms'. He invokes, in other words, the discourse on the cradle of Western civilisation, its status in the quest for truth and democracy, while we sense that these same values are called into question. The Agora provides an important hinge for this section. As a marketplace and a site of public debate, it drew together economic and political activities – combining both lowly and elevated values, everyday actualities and lofty ideals, the rhetoric of traders and that of politicians. Sekula's statement elaborates on the description of the Agora in its varying aspects of politics, philosophy and economy. These resonances are picked up in subsequent scenes of contemporary petty commerce (and return later in the video, in scenes shot in Barcelona's Diagonal Mar, at a development known as 'El Fòrum', named after the Classical Roman equivalent, and a site of commoditised 'democracy').

We move to the modern city, to the Monastiraki flea market five minutes away, where a trader sits outside a small army-surplus store. Dressed in his wares, he is surrounded by military boots, khaki knapsacks, duffle bags and canteens. Sekula takes us inside another second-hand outlet, presumably nearby, where his camera alights on old comic books. A faded cover depicts two men with a searchlight and large dog as they discover a woman's dead body. A story page shows men and women getting intimate at a jazz dance. Wearing fancy blue overalls (they have the pointy shoulder extensions of mid-century sci-fi uniforms), one man watches a jet rocket rise vertically. Recall how model planes and a helicopter also featured in *Aerospace Folktales*, where they added menace to the domestic life, bringing the war back home. Here, in Athens, the video cuts to a three-dimensional model of another jet ascending diagonally from its stand. With the local sound of the shop's radio, we hear Sekula's overlaid account of the city's foundation myth: an encounter between Athena and Hephaestus. The virgin goddess of war, wisdom, weaving and craft, Athena is an allegorical figure in Western art for freedom and democracy, and a patron and namesake for the city. The 'midwife' to Athena's 'birth', Hephaestus is the artisan god of craft, metalwork, forges and fire, to whom the Hephaisteion was dedicated. As the story goes: Athena visits Hephaestus' forge to commission weapons, but he attempts to rape her. Athena successfully fights off her assailant, and Hephaestus ejaculates on her leg. Athena wipes away the semen from her thigh using wool, and from this discarded swab a child is conceived by the earth. Erichthonius is raised secretly by Athena (she keeps the infant in a box!) and becomes Athens' originary citizen hero and basis for its myth of autochthony.

Sekula read feminist classicist Nicole Loraux, who studied the ideological role of autochthony and 'the mythic overdetermination of masculine values in the name of the Athenian citizen' (the assertion of a purely male lineage).[79] Existing studies already recognised the exclusions of Athenian citizenship (on grounds of gender, ethnicity, status and species), but Loraux also emphasised how the repressed 'feminine' returned to haunt the political, social and civic imaginary. Official discourse polarised the masculine and feminine, but here she discerned precisely its repressed gender ambivalences. Loraux took poetics and rhetoric as starting points for unfolding the 'political, social and ideological history of the collective', describing her project as that of a 'historian of the intimate relations of Athens with the words of its myths'.[80] The playfulness,

79 Nicole Loraux, *The Children of Athena: Athenian Ideas about Citizenship and the Division between the Sexes* (1981; Princeton, NJ: Princeton University Press, 1993), 142. See also *Born of the Earth: Myth and Politics in Athens* (1996; Ithaca, NY: Cornell University Press, 2000) and *The Experiences of Tiresias: The Feminine and the Greek Man* (1990; Princeton, NJ: Princeton University Press, 1995).

80 Loraux, *The Children of Athena*, 37, 16.

flexibility and reflexiveness that infused Loraux's methods might have been attractive to Sekula, combined as they were with bold historiographical quips and trenchant political interventions. Navigating between simple historicism and mere symbolic reading, Loraux made non-reductive connections between myth and history, mythos and polis, fiction and social practice, cultural symbology and Athenian topography.[81] 'There is something real in imaginary formations', she insisted.[82] Her use of psychoanalysis was likewise unorthodox, rejecting the focus on the family, and seeing psychoanalytic methods instead as relevant for understanding politics and war.[83] 'Expansions' across 'domains' were also central: how myth was mobilised to ground law in nature, placing autochthony as the source of the Athenian politico-military framework and of the principle of democracy itself.[84]

Sekula's presentation of the myth is more declarative and paratactical than narratival, delivered in clipped, direct sentences and clauses:

The god of the forge
chases the virgin goddess.
The patroness of the city
eludes his grasp.
His ejaculate fertilizes the earth.
A city of men springs forth
from the soil:
citizens without mothers.

A race of ship-owners,
venturing forth onto the sea,
Slaves bending at the oars.

Ancient Athens and its port:
walled-in, a continuous fortress
against invaders.

---

81 Loraux drew on Levi-Strauss's work on myth and the idea of the 'imaginary' (*L'imaginaire*) that came from Sartre and Lacan. As she emphasised, the 'imaginary' was not about binding single meanings to cultural expressions but attending to the interplay between words and meanings (Loraux, *The Children of Athena*, 15).

82 Loraux, *The Children of Athena*, 20.

83 Ibid., 17 n. 28.

84 Loraux, *Born of the Earth*, 34. This study ultimately expands to reflect on the false appeals to the classical Athenian precedent by the anti-immigrant rhetoric of France's Front National: 'democracy in the face of strangers' (127).

Women laughing and wailing
inside the white walls.

Unless already familiar with this myth, Sekula's rendition is elliptical, almost inner speech – a disorientation reinforced by the video of idiosyncratic junkshop finds. When Sekula refers to 'ejaculate', it pertains to Hephaestus, of course, but also figuratively sticks to the two unmistakably erectile jets. An oscillation is established, with potential repercussions: are the aircraft also destined to flop? They end their days in a lowly second-hand outlet, their displays of strength turned to nought. Do the ancient world and the jet age resonate as 'spent' civilisations and signifiers of military and colonial hubris?

In relating the foundation myth, Sekula opts for the present tense, in both its simple and continuous forms. In part, this conforms to grammatical guidance for fiction, but it also confounds the historic present tense – collapsing the duality of historical and narratival purposes, as well as its inner rhetorical tensions of mediacy and immediacy. This choice – further emphasised by Sekula's image track – blurs the mythical story with historical developments and also alternates between classical and modern periods. The autochthonic claim – 'A city of men springs forth from the soil' – speaks thrice over: Erichthonius's (mythic) progeny founded the city state; 'a race of ship-owners' was begot (historical past); mythicised, that 'race' continues today (historical present). This blurring, however, is not for the sake of ambiguity, but to expose the elision of nature and society (the modern myth). Sekula reports the ancient legend but also parodies the age-old tale by relating it to the historical mythicisation of Greek shipping – a point reinforced by the visual array of second-hand objects.[85] The 'heroic' entrepreneurial endeavours of ship-owners, Sekula reminds us, depended on unfree labour.[86] In turn, this observation oscillates between, on the one hand, the constitutive role of enslaved people in the ancient economy (and, thus, for the 'foundations' of 'civilisation' and 'democracy') and, on the

85 Many of these objects rework, in low-key, older impresa, visual-verbal emblems that in some of their exemplary cases allegorised the Roman goddess Fortuna in maritime representations. These emblems and stamps – typically visual-verbal mottos, such as those used in heraldry or on *ex libris* – were explored by Aby Warburg in one of his most socially astute early essays on Sassetti in the fifteenth century.

86 There are some glitches in Sekula's associations. First, oars were used on warships, the triremes, but not on merchant vessels. Second, Charles M. Reed argued that both ship-owners (*naukleroi*) and maritime traders (*emperoi*) were typically not Athenian (and thus not citizens).

other, the contemporary globalised merchant marine's exploitation of waged and indentured labour – 'slaves' in the figurative sense.

Several themes flow and converge through this sequence: military, sexual fantasy, metalwork, enslavement, finance and shipping. The military topic is explicit and implicit: the shop selling surplus army kit; Athena's warrior aspect and her very purpose for visiting Hephaestus; the aerodynamic jets, which certainly do not suggest civilian aviation; the man in his smart blue overalls, probably a pilot in uniform. (Recall also how, at the very outset, Ochs's eulogy was to the crew of a nuclear submarine.) Sexual violence and erotic fantasy manifest in the ancient myth, in the graphic novels and, as we will see, through other elements. Metalworking links Hephaestus to an array of pre-used vernacular objects. Following the shot of the jet, we are shown a scaled-down replica of a harbour-patrol boat. The following scene features items sitting on a wooden trunk with heavy metal hinges: an old cine projector; a sign for the Egyptian Wood and Metal Industrial Company with a galleon pictured at its centre (a modern impresa); and a combination of barometer, thermometer and clock set, anthropomorphically, into an elaborate piece of ironwork. Next, we see an oval enamel of a mermaid; breasts semi-concealed by wavy locks, she holds a ship in her left hand and, in her right, an anchor. This enamel is set among the curlicues of blackened metal, perhaps a headboard for a marital bed. An old calculating machine's argentic body and shiny brass components simulate the 'silver' and 'gold' it was once employed to reckon – the shot coinciding with the voice-over's reference to 'race of ship-owners' and 'slaves bending at the oars'.

We next move to an exterior shot of a back street with two modern utility boxes, again of metal: one is open, exposing an electrical board that is surely best kept concealed; a larger one remains padlocked, upon whose doors is painted a crude, if cute, representation of a sail ship, green and yellow with three big red portholes – improbably balanced on blue shark-fin waves. The metal doors lack the absorbency of typical paint surfaces, and the paint has dribbled. There is at once a 'high' reference to American modern art and, in a 'high' reference debased, to the Athenian citizens-cum-race-of-shipping magnates sired by Hephaestus's premature ejaculation. The camera homes in on the portholes, which appear to bleed.

Notably, the image of portholes adjoins one of beef being ground by hand through a traditional metal mincer. There is, so to speak, a red thread: the blood red of the painted portholes is picked up by the raw meat and by the protective rubber gloves worn by the machine's operative. With this edit, we are relocated to Piraeus's covered market. From behind a hanging meat joint, a little Greek flag staked into its flesh, a stallholder suspiciously observes Sekula watching him. Two young butchers lark about, performing 'dancing together', dispersing and laughing in a show of homosocial embarrassment. Meat is chopped. Lit by strip lights and incandescent bulbs, the latter flaring in Sekula's camera, we see, in turn, the display of dangling tongues, draped tripes, entire carcasses and a pig's head. Customers flow along the market's aisles, while traders entice them to spend. Over one stall, there is a photograph of a ewe and suckling lamb, the image itself hanging – literally and symbolically – from two meat hooks. The passage from the dancing butchers to the tripe display is overlaid with Sekula's unforgettable comment:

> Two kinds of agoraphobe:
> those who fear the market in the abstract,
> but love it in close proximity.
> And those who see it
> the other way around,
> from the corner office
> high above the street, or from behind
> the bullet-proof window of the
> speeding limousine.
> Confident in the numbers . . .

In this incisive observation, Sekula concertinas 'market' between the concrete sites of everyday plebeian life (a specific market in Piraeus, but also all such markets) and the fetish of neoliberal mantra. The first comes with all its rumbustiousness, raucous banter and sexual innuendos; with blood and guts visible and smellable, and – if not actually touchable, certainly a haptic world of wetness, liquids and stains. The second neutralises these sensory characteristics. Immunised from the display and olfactory overload, its 'desiccated' world comprises spreadsheets and the calculation of profit (although the acts of separation and self-protection – 'behind the bullet-proof window' – surely hint at both visceral fears and fears of viscerality). There is an obvious connection in all this to Sekula's earliest works: *Meat Piece* and *Meat Mass*.

'An unlikely pastoral among the red carvings, our sister mammals', Sekula remarks of the photograph of the sheep, as if picking up two of

Athens' three autochthonic exclusions as set out by Loraux (gender, race, species). At this point, Sekula inserts the first clip from the movie *Never on Sunday* and the mood vaults to the comic-erotic. To a jaunty balalaika, a laughing Melina Mercouri runs through a boatyard, stripping off her clothes as she goes, teasing the gawping and cheering shipwrights. Having jumped into the sea from a jetty, she shouts back her challenge: 'If you're not a slave, come on in.' Responding to her taunt, the men all leave their work and plunge into the water. The edit suggests that we are clearly meant to intuit Mercouri as a manifestation of 'sister mammal'. Her jibe reprises the reminder that unfreedom underpinned the freedoms of the ancient polis – and its mode is an echo of 'women's speech', which was officially denigrated there. By way of conceptual expansions, semantic slippage and the old film's intent, we recognise this unfreedom as also the labour discipline underpinning the modern maritime industries. Here, though, unfreedom is rebuffed: an erotic carnivalesque is liberating, a feminine-provoked dive into the oceanic; Marcuse's Eros liberated from 'civilisation'.

The segment stops as sharply as it started, and we return to the gentle hubbub of the market: crowds stroll through its interior alleys. The huge number of bulbs over the meat stalls form a sparkling tunnel of light. Sekula remarks: 'The pseudo-disclosure of the *agora*: everything is fresh, but dead . . .' Cuts of meat are flipped and sliced. A stallholder peels a green fruit and pretends to stab Sekula's observing lens. An array of small carcasses hang heads down, white 'bracelets' still attached to their heels. A small child looks up at us. Younger butchers hustle for trade, while an older one sits picking his nose. Outside the market hall, an Asian man holds up an octopus, asking, 'You like?' 'It's beautiful,' we hear Sekula reply. 'It's beautiful,' the man echoes. Another episode with Mercouri intervenes, this time set inside a taverna, where an outsider explains that his reason for visiting Greece is 'to find the truth' (we return to this scene shortly). Back in Piraeus's market hall, the end-of-sale scrub of the fish-display tables transfers us, with an edit, to the sea and a close-up of creaking tether ropes. Sekula's camera scans flags flying from a ship, both Panamanian and Greek. Shots taken from the passenger seat of a moving car depict a cement ship, cement works and heaps of loose materials: 'The commodities we don't think about. Heavy, omnipresent, uniform in composition, but largely invisible.' These 'unacknowledged goods' are carried by Greek ships, 'but their Greekness is attenuated or disguised'. We mentioned the open-registry or flag-of-convenience (FOC) system in Chapter 1. At this moment in *The Lottery of the Sea*, Sekula explains the open-registry system with footage of the buildings of the Panama Register Corporation (with Greek flag flying on its roof) and the Mediterranean Shipping Co., Greece, SA. Panama (1919) and Liberia (1948) were the first open registries established by the USA, a system that expanded to include other FOCs such as the Marshall Islands, Cambodia and (ironically) 'land-locked Bolivia'. Sekula also points to the US's postwar investment in Greek shipping – while not an FOC, Greece's maritime status was subjected to significant economic and geopolitical influence from across the North Atlantic. Here, with offset or disguised nationalities, we have central examples of 'attenuated or broken metonymy'. The theme also points back to the 'pseudo-disclosure of the *agora*' and the carcass in Piraeus's market adorned with the little flag of Greece.

A sequence of anthropomorphs continues the elaborating of the FOC. Mannequins wear maritime uniforms. A close-up of breast badge 'A/T *Kimon*' references the fifth-century general, an aristocrat known for destroying the Persian fleet, creating the Athenian maritime empire and opposing Periclean democracy. Next – and, it would seem, back inside a second-hand shop, like those we toured earlier – Sekula shows models of horror-film villains. Freddy Krueger and Jason Voorhees loom over their anonymous female victims, the latter set inside glass balls in frozen recoil from the imminent male violence as stand-ins for US imperial brutality. The Terminator points an automatic rifle from his waist. Jason wields a machete overhead. A rather sinister Santa Claus automaton grins at us, waggling his hips. We segue to a bright sunny day: against a clear blue sky, an 'Uncle Sam' stilt-woman in dark glasses twirls a streamer, overlaid by the 1940 patriotic tune (*Shout! Wherever You May Be*) *I am an American*.[87] Although the US flag features, the sequence has no direct bearing on the FOC narrative; yet Sekula's point is obvious enough. The music and the performer, dressed in the stars and stripes, with her elevated height and bountiful smile, directs us to the machinations in the world order – the geopolitical and economic conditions for the FOC. At the same time, her Marilyn Monroe looks and teetering stick feet imply a certain vulnerability. The flag of convenience, then, becomes an

87 Schuster, Cunningham and Whitcup's composition was performed by Gray Gordon and his Tic Toc Rhythm Band for war-bond rallies. The version we hear in *The Lottery of the Sea* is by Gene Krupa and His Orchestra. It was revived for the Vietnam War in 1966 by Paul Lavalle's Band of America.

emblem in distinct senses. First, there is its everyday sense as a diversionary ensign of ownership. In Sekula's hands it also becomes a motif revealing the very machinations of the entire global economic system; a synecdoche, or a portal through which we can reflect on its social and political underpinnings.

We return from America's glaring sun to the contrast of a murky Piraeus winter: a distant sea view of container ships; a close-up of rain dripping from a blue-painted metal banister; a mid-distance scene of a small trawler returning to harbour, pursued by a flock of gulls. In the twilight, a young, bearded man hurries through wet streets, wearing khaki cagoule and legionnaire-style kepi, bag on shoulder and stuffed bin liner in hand – his headwear suggestive of an older Hellenic army uniform, most likely surplus clothing. He is perhaps a seafarer. Over these scenes, Sekula's voice reminds us that we are 'three years into "the war on terror"'. Looking for weapons of mass destruction, the US navy 'asserts its right' over the Panamanian and Liberian open registries the US had founded, searching thousands of vessels. Sekula caustically deploys the absurd, bathetically descaling from the war conducted as an abstract and idealising term down to tangible commodities piled in the ships' holds: the imagined weapons of mass destruction are sought 'amidst the bags of tapioca and the giant rolls of newsprint'. He continues, 'Anxiety and fear take charge, and the port retreats into enforced invisibility, no longer a theater of the world's connectedness.' Concluding with scenes around Piraeus's terminal for Blue Star Ferries, Sekula shares an anecdote about the 2004 Olympic Games, hosted by Athens. The police beat up Mexican journalists for photographing the port – the very activity that, just eight months earlier, as proven by the footage we have been watching, Sekula had engaged in surreptitiously from behind the yuccas. Filming a departing night ferry from behind the spiky planters of a restaurant terrace, he wraps the chapter with sarcastic tricolon: 'wrong place, wrong time, wrong sport . . .'.

Metonymic breaks do not solely involve actual absences: even when they enter our field of vision, bulk goods (ores, minerals, cement, scrap) remain invisible, slipping beneath the bar of recognition. Here, invisibility is taken beyond literal absence – and even beyond 'out of sight, out of mind' to the condition of 'hidden in plain sight'. It is unlikely that these heaps of loose minerals would be 'seen' without Sekula explicitly referring to them; more likely, viewers would register the photographed scene at a different scale, as generic views of a port. Of course, such 'aspect blindness' is selectively distributed; it is unlikely to be shared, for instance, by those workers who are involved in loading and unloading these primary commodities.

Further associations unfold from this one motif, which might be highlighted by contrasting it with that of the container. Containers are largely associated with the conveying of higher-value manufactured goods destined for either consumer retail or industry (as components). Although, in principle, ores can be containerised (if bagged and palleted), with their low value-to-weight ratio they are typically transported loose – a practice that continues even decades after Sekula made *The Lottery of the Sea*. Compared with containerised commodities, then, the qualities of these materials signify (by extension) a broader set of subaltern values, such as: crudeness (unprocessed, raw, rude, plebeian humour); lowliness (monetary value, perceptual presence, social recognition). The contrast between the box container and loose minerals also has an aesthetic resonance: the contrast of form and formlessness. The implied superiority of form is closely tied to an aesthetic discourse on Periclean Athens. The allusions also invoke a number of late-twentieth-century debates in art: the 'simple gestalts' or 'unitary forms' in minimalism, famously dismissed by Michael Fried as 'literalist'; the turn to 'antiform', which sought to de-hierarchise ocular centrism and figure-ground distinctions, championing peripheral seeing. Robert Smithson's gallery-based *Non-Sites* used angular metal boxes to contain broken rocks or coal sourced from dispersed locations. His *Partially Buried Woodshed* deployed a large pile of tumbling earth; *Asphalt Rundown* spilled mineral pitch down a slope. He wrote a word piece called a 'heap of language'. A couple of decades later, Rosalind Krauss and Yve-Alain Bois took up the antiform impetus to challenge the high-modernist privileging of 'form'. Their exhibition *L'informe: mode d'emploi* traced an alternative lineage of the 'unformed'.[88] For anyone schooled in post-1960s art, such suggestions are hard to ignore. Sekula made these analogies explicit with reference to the container: his 'Dismal Science' essay ends by playfully comparing the shipping container with Andy Warhol's Brillo boxes and with the serial logic of Dan Graham's *Homes for America*, this new art of the 1960s appearing as the shipping industry was undergoing transformation. Smithson's *A Tour of the Monuments of Passaic, New Jersey* (1967), exceptionally, looked to industrialised landscapes, yet, to Sekula's mind, even Smithson

88 Yve-Alain Bois and Rosalind Krauss, *L'informe: mode d'emploi* (Paris: Éditions Centre Georges Pompidou, 1996).

failed to engage with capital's practicalities and working dynamics, wandering the shores of the Passaic in search of 'monuments' (pipes and so on) yet not noticing the activity at New Jersey's Port Elizabeth. He was, Sekula notes, too 'enamored of a science-fiction scenarios [*sic*] of entropic heat-death and sought only evidence of stasis and decay'.[89] In Sekula's assessment, Smithson focused on revisiting his childhood haunts, entertaining nostalgic reveries prompted by the banal industrial residues he photographed, rather than on the signs of the economy in transformation.

Nonetheless, Sekula would also have been aware of the dangers of simply aestheticising the lowly and the formless; recall Walter Benjamin's complaint about the way some Weimar photographers could 'no longer record a tenement block or a refuse heap without transfiguring it', turning 'abject poverty' into an 'object of enjoyment'.[90] Once we accede to the aesthetic realm, both forms and formless antiforms can readily be treated as 'objects' of sensuous meditation, irrespective of the theories that might privilege one over the other. At this point, however, have we lost the link (the interplay) between allusions and the literal bulk ores stashed on a dockside in Piraeus? Or, perhaps better, might we instead surmise that, with the very recognition of the limit of the figural–literal interplay, we touch on an important point about the aesthetic, about realism and about documentary form? Certainly, Sekula's account of the spaces of maritime labour strays into allegories of art.

The romantic comedy *Never on Sunday* was a blockbuster of its day, written and directed by Jules Dassin, who also starred alongside Mercouri. The film loosely follows the storyline of the 1956 play *My Fair Lady* – itself based on Bernard Shaw's *Pygmalion*, which in turn was based on the ancient story – with an educated man attempting to reshape a working-class woman into his ideal. Dassin's variant adds to the gender and class dynamics a cultural and geopolitical twist: the man is an American classicist and Hellenophile called Homer Thrace; Mercouri's Illia is a sex worker in Piraeus. *Never on Sunday* is parodic of American values and the way fantasies of a Greek past serve to occlude its present reality. Homer tries to reign in Illia, seeing her behaviour and spirit as the degradation of the Greek ideal. Having the female role as a sex worker plays further on the classicist's imaginary: Greece as 'pure',

89 'Dismal Science', 136.

90 Walter Benjamin, 'The Author as Producer' (1934), in *Selected Writings, Volume 2: 1927–1934* (Boston, MA: Harvard University Press, 1999), 768–82 (775).

'ideal', and as humanity's 'childhood' – but the female character being anything but. As the life and soul of the port, Illia works the established trope of 'tart with a heart'. (She also coordinates a sex-worker strike.) Predictably, Thrace's effort to domesticate, educate and 'civilise' her backfires, making her miserable. The film already allegorises the imposition of US values on other societies and, in Sekula's hands, this is further intensified to include economic and military hegemony. Dassin and Mercouri (who later became a real-life couple) were both prominent left wingers in the postwar period.[91] The excerpts used by Sekula can only hint at this fuller context, but it resonates from the choice. Recall the scene in the taverna. Asked if he is staying long, he replies haltingly and awkwardly: 'Maybe. I'm looking for something in Greece.' The 'something' he seeks is cast as embarrassing: 'You won't laugh?' When Illia presses, 'Why? You look for something funny?', he responds nervously, 'I came to Greece to . . . to find the truth.' The amusement of this scene works on multiple levels. First, in the film itself, in the relation between two characters, both played humorously by the actors. Second, as noted above, in the parody of modern American fantasies of the cradle of Western civilisation. Simultaneously, it is a jibe, on Sekula's part, at the postmodern prohibition on commitment or realism. Fail to comply with the new code of ironic relativism (marshalled, as Sekula once caustically put it, by the 'fun police') and you risk becoming a social outcast.[92] Like Dassin's character, you risk being interpellated as unhinged, developing strange bodily ticks, speech fragmenting into inchoate stammer; becoming almost aphasic. Themes of veracity–deceit, even when ironised, evidence Sekula's effort to restitch capitalism's 'attenuated or broken metonymy'. Finally (and this connection emerges as this chapter of *The Lottery of the Sea* unfolds), we have Sekula himself, an American in Greece, employing a documentary mode and trying to get behind the FOC to show the connections.

Broken metonymies and the effort to mend them recur through the video. The sixth chapter – made alongside Sekula's photo work *Black Tide/Marea Negra* – follows the aftermath of an oil spill off the northern

91 Dassin was a former member of the Communist Party USA (he left after the Nazi–Soviet pact); with the 'Hollywood blacklist' he moved to Europe. Mercouri was supporter of the Greek resistance to the Occupation. The two later married and were prominent opponents of the Greek junta from 1967. Dassin was himself a Hellenophile, so there is already an auto-referential joke in the film, however compromised by the primitivising sense of an authentic and libidinal Greece as opposed to a phony, buttoned-up America.

92 'On *Fish Story*', 58.

coast of Spain. (The sea, as the prologue to *The Forgotten Space* notes, is 'remembered only when maritime disaster strikes, when the black tide rolls in'.) In these scenes, we watch the painstaking labour of volunteers as they try to clear oil from Galician shorelines. Equipped with nothing but their own manual labour and basic tools, residents, military personnel and an influx of environmentalists try to clean up the mess: raking the sea and the beaches; digging into rock crevices with their fingers; and trying to exploit oil's capacity to self-adhere by rolling it into balls. The considerable slowing of the pace (in sharp contrast to the snappy editing of the prologue and first chapter) and the scarcity of voice-over and dialogue help convey the frustrations of the near-impossible task. The shift in filmic temporality also allows us to detect other levels of metonymic transfer. We witness social cooperation as the volunteers pass trugs along human chains in a 'Labor of Sisyphus' (which is the title of a subsection of *Black Tide/Marea Negra*). We come to recognise a grotesque homeopathy (metonymic) involved in the cure. Nearly everything involved in the clean-up is a product of oil: the fuel to run the tractors; the plastic sheets laid across the ground; the bin bags and containers used to collect the oil; the protective white hazmat overalls and safety masks worn by the volunteers; the brown parcel tape used to seal gaps between their footwear and clothing. Nothing that we see in these scenes just is what it appears to be. Although relevant in its own terms (a bin liner is a bin liner), the items signify beyond their mere facticity. Towards the end of the Galicia sequences, Sekula notes that the Christmas mass ignores the disaster that is consuming everyone's lives. The priest 'discovers no link to the gospels'. This ideological non-representation signals a failure to draw out theological abstractions by means of a didactic sermon or a religious allegory. Noting an irony of transcendental timing, albeit in secular tone, Sekula's voice-over spotlights the missing connections between a local environmental tragedy and its global maritime-economic context:

> On Christmas eve
> The Swiss company
> that chartered the ship
> is dissolved
> and reconstituted under a new name
> breaking the link
> to its Russian parent company TNK.

Metonymic chains are strained and snapped; connections of causality, property or responsibility are actively hidden. Sometimes, however, their reconstructions require the power of metaphor; it can take a 'metaphoric vault' to re-establish contiguities across the broken-metonymic 'chasm'. As Sekula notes, it is often by way of 'some great imaginative geographical leap' or 'jump in the imagination' – echoes of Benjamin, again – that we ever grasp the connections.[93]

In *The Lottery of the Sea*, things constantly emerge 'from below'. Submarines break the surface of the ocean; Captain Nemo, Sekula notes, funded his ventures by lifting gold from sunken galleons. The surface of the sea, among other things, appears as a metaphor for consciousness. Interconnections between consciousness, cognition, recognition and recollection, and the reflection on political praxis and popular insurrection, recur throughout. Sekula once quoted Benjamin's comment that culture remains reified so long as we fail to experience things and events politically; so long as the residues of these things and events do not break 'the surface of human consciousness'.[94] Sometimes, his topography can be playful. In *Lottery*'s chapter on Panama, Sekula reminds us of the battles waged against Noriega and his US backers by resistance movements; we sense a subaltern 'underground' secreted metaphorically in a popular song about fireflies that 'come down from the mountain'. Later, in the chapter 'Los Angeles March 2003', we see the La Brea Tar Pits adjacent to LACMA, a black pond oozing through the ground. The sequence reflects on Upton Sinclair's novel *Oil!*, in 'which oil was detected and blasted upward from the caverns of the underworld'. The chapter concludes with scenes protesting the Iraq War – perceived by many as a campaign by Anglo-American interests for control of Gulf reserves and to stabilise global oil prices. Later in the film, in the long Galicia sequence, a local man notes of the oil from the tanker spillage 'But it comes back, and comes back'. Towed out of Spanish waters, it sinks two miles down, but the tide returns oily cargo:

> Oil seeps upwards, drifting
> toward the unwelcoming shore
> as if cursing it
> for its inhospitality.

---

93 Sekula in Beausse, 'Allan Sekula réalisme critique/The Critical Realism of Allan Sekula', 26.

94 Sekula cites Benjamin's 'Eduard Fuchs, Collector and Historian' (1937) in the Introduction, *Photography Against the Grain*, xiv (xvi in MACK edition).

Sometimes, we are transferred from the cognitive and interpretative plane onto a political and organisational one. A dockers' organiser from Barcelona's 'La Coordinadora' notes that his members 'are the last link in the global chain commerce'. He goes on to describe the development of a transnational trade union from its start in one locale and tells how it is committed to the collective and the syndicalist model of the assembly. The multiplication of metonymic 'associations' and 'assemblies' (which occur at the levels of both content and form), alongside the metaphorics of 'from below', implies models of social transformation. Metonyms combine with metaphors, overlapping; one tropic modality feeds into or yields to the other. Looked at in this way, the slower accumulative temporalities of metonymic connections (the building of a movement or alternative models of social cooperation) both contrast *and* interweave with sudden 'metaphoric' transpositions, the 'evental' sparks, and Benjaminian 'tiger's leap', the unanticipated insurrections, mutinies and 'the threat of revolt from below decks'.[95]

SECTION 3: POIESIS AND PRAXIS

Chiasmus and Dialectical Image

If, at first sight, Sekula seems to be an artist interested in flows and processes (of maritime logistics, commodity circulation) rather than in static structures, we soon discover that these opposing qualities connect. In 1997, he wrote:

> The relationship between ships and the land is increasingly the opposite of what it was in the nineteenth century. That is, sites of production become mobile, while routes of distribution become fixed and routinized. Factories are now like ships: they can sail away in the night. And cargo ships now resemble buildings, giant floating warehouses shuttling back and forth between fixed points on an unrelenting schedule.[96]

95 'On *Fish Story*', 54.

96 Ibid. Cf. *Fish Story*, 184 (short essay 'Big and Even Bigger' for the final chapter). Note another close variant by Sekula and Burch: 'As ships become more like buildings – the giant, floating warehouses of the 'just-in-time' system of distribution – factories begin to resemble ships, stealing away stealthily in the night, restlessly searching for ever cheaper labour' (Allan Sekula and Noël Burch, '*The Forgotten Space*: Notes for a Film', *New Left Review* 69 (2011): 78). In yet another example, Sekula discerns historical turnarounds in the

The 'mobilising of the static' (so to speak) is captured in *Fish Story*'s sequence depicting the dismantling for shipment of Kaiser steelworks. Contrariwise, 'freezing of movement' is exemplified by the 'Russian Factory Ship' in *TITANIC's wake*, one of those super vessels with facilities for processing onboard.

The formulation employed by Sekula is *chiasmus* – a type of parallelism or parataxis, where a clause or phrase is repeated in inverted form, as in: 'Fair is foul and foul is fair'.[97] (It is often rendered in shorthand as 'ABBA' – or, to emphasise its crossing or folding point, AB:BA.) That said, chiasmus should be understood as more than a palindrome. The inversion or mirroring in the second iteration can take the form of a direct reversal of words, as the shorthand suggests, or else a more indirect construction that is similar syntactically or propositionally. The form is widespread and longstanding, often deployed in political oratory.[98] As with the other tropes, chiasmi are now regarded as more than narrow figures of speech, and as more than stylistic ornamentations associated with classic rhetoric. They are often understood as modes of thought, or as cognitive (re)shapers.[99] Chiasmi can be discerned not only at the micro-structural level but also at the macro-structural: as an extended thematic or as conceptual devices organising arguments across entire texts (including non-linguistic forms).

Chiastic formulations are frequently employed in dialectical thought. Because they work with similar conceptual patterns, some have argued that chiasmus is *the* figure of dialectics.[100] Marx infamously criticised Proudhon by inverting *The Philosophy of Poverty* into 'the poverty of philosophy'. His metaphor of the camera obscura to explain

---

inner nature of the terraqueous: 'Today the relationship between the sea and the land is increasingly the opposite of what it was in the nineteenth century. Sites of production become mobile, while paths of distribution become fixed and routine.' See *Freeway to China (Version 2, for Liverpool)*, 1998–99, in *Performance Under Working Conditions*, 278–305 (279).

97 Parataxis is where two propositions are made without indicating their relation or subordination.

98 Thought to date back to early Semitic peoples, the form is prominent in Biblical texts. Chiasmic effects were cultivated at the Elizabethan court, later in *belles lettres*, and have been widely used by dramaturges and poets.

99 A key text in this extension is: Max Nänny, 'Chiasmus in Literature: Ornament or Function?', *Word & Image: A Journal of Verbal/Visual Enquiry* 4:1 (1988): 51–9.

100 Gillian Rose, *The Melancholy Science: An Introduction to the Thought of Theodor W. Adorno* (London: Macmillan, 1978); Maxwell Kennel, 'Plato, Adorno, and the Dialectic', *Identities* 18:1–2 (2021): 84–97.

ideology, his mention of Feuerbach's god-man and his image of standing Hegel's dialectic on its head: all show something of this pattern. Chiasmus is not identical to dialectic – certainly not if one takes the dialectic in its more orthodox sense (as destined to synthesis, a 'stabilised' or 'closed' 'unity'). However, dialectic in its negative traditions shares with chiasmus the exchanging interplays (fusions and separations) of opposites that avoid a closing, superseding or sublating *Aufhebung*. Insofar as there is a totality posited, it is deferred. Moreover, instead of establishing a linear temporality, '*chiasmus* begins by already doubling back on itself'.[101] Working both first-order and second-order layers of association–dissociation, its diagonal or crisscross exchange of qualities can bring seemingly sharp contrasts into an underlying interrelation – an entwining or cross-contamination – highlighting relational asymmetries.

For example, Gillian Rose notes how chiasmus informs much of Theodor Adorno's writing – comparing it with his paratactical approach, immanent critique and 'logic of aporias' (Adorno).[102] She discerns chiasmi at various operative scales, from the level of the clause (posing two antitheses, AB:BA) to his overarching thought process. Indeed, she characterises his work as existing in the space between argument and trope.[103] Parataxis sidesteps the norms of logical argument, removing the explicatory connectors of a sentence or argument. Chiasmus enables the presentation of the orthodoxy before transforming its terms into social criticism.[104] Superficially, chiasmi can *appear* to be antinomic (more precisely, an antinomy of antinomic pairs), but their function is to go beyond antinomy (two equally valid but mutually irreconcilable doctrines).

We were discussing earlier the transferences of dynamic and static qualities between actual objects in the world:

[factories-become-shiplike]:[ships-become-factory-like]

Or:

[static->mobile]:[mobile->static]

---

101 Kennel, 'Plato, Adorno, and the Dialectic', 97 (his italics). Kennel's conclusion suggests that chiasmus is best placed for pushing the limits of dialectical thought.

102 Rose, *The Melancholy Science*, 13; Adorno is cited at 54.

103 Ibid., 13.

104 Ibid., 66.

But the point is as relevant to thought or the effort to grasp the world in thought, and especially to questions of fetishism (static-becomes-dynamic) and reification (dynamic-becomes-static). 'The use of chiasmus stresses the transmutation [in conventional thinking] of processes into entities', Rose writes, while it methodologically avoids falling into that same reificatory trap with the formulation of one's own critique.[105] As an immanent method of critique, Rose argues, Adorno first states or shows a bourgeois antinomy and then, with the chiasmic inversion, removes the antinomic quality, foregrounding its social constitution and proposing a dialectical approach.[106] Hegel's philosophy of mind is a key site (especially his account of domination and self-consciousness in the dialectic of lordship and bondage). Adorno dismisses the ideologically compromised nature of Hegel's articulation while simultaneously distilling its kernel of intuited truth: the aspect of Hegel's method that corresponds to a real social process. Another example, Rose observes, would be Marx's account of value and real abstraction: 'The relation between the antinomy [bourgeois, Hegel] and the chiasmus [critique, Marx] is established by showing that Hegel's thinking proceeds in a manner analogous to the model of social processes explicated by the theory of value.'[107] Rose's discussion of Adorno takes us back to 'the antinomies of bourgeois thought' that preoccupied Sekula. His chiasmus of ship-and-factory (and static-dynamic) at first appears as a relatively straightforward inversion (effectively producing 'static ships' and 'dynamic factories'). Yet, closer attention enables us to see that the shift is more nuanced. More is at stake than a mere adjectival exchange. Rather, the chiastic reversal points to the social transformations of neoliberal globalisation. Nonetheless, Sekula's chiasmus here is primarily observational, a description of capitalist transformation. The examples of Adorno and Marx that Rose offers treat the chiastic inversion as critique, as a 'corrective' to the established bourgeois or capitalist view. However, parallels might be found with the chiastic structure of the most well-known passages of the *Manifesto of the Communist Party*, where Marx and Engels contrast the spatio-temporal conditions of capitalist and pre-capitalist societies. It plays, inter alia, on qualities such as static/dynamic, tangible/intangible, near/distant, local/global and so on. Notably, there is a

105 Ibid., 13

106 Ibid., 54, 59.

107 Ibid., 59.

long tradition of discussing the *Manifesto* (and the handling of these qualities) in terms of its poetic character.[108] Elsewhere, Sekula employs chiasmus in other ways, although it is still closer to a diagnostic of bourgeois thought's antinomies. Recall the passage we encountered earlier. With Nadar's nineteenth-century materialism, the impulse of demystification (its anti-secular undermining of established traditions of social privilege) is paralleled by a contrary movement: the mystification of materialism (the deification of science).[109] Here, developing the point made briefly in an earlier essay, Sekula not only challenges the binaries of materialism–anti-materialism or demystification–mystification – those would be expressions *of* 'the antinomies of bourgeois thought' – he also analyses how the terms of the antinomies cross over.

Across three works – *TITANIC's wake* (1998–2000), his essay 'Between the Net and the Deep Blue Sea' (2002) and *The Forgotten Space* (2010) – Sekula focuses directly on the interplay of figures of corrosivity, economic relevance and life status. *TITANIC's wake* includes *Bilbao diptych*, two photographs depicting the city seen from the hillside. The bipartite structure presents a single-and-continuous-but-ruptured panorama to capture the urban transformation of the late 1990s. Looming large is Frank Gehry's newly built, titanium-clad Guggenheim Museum, on the site of a former industrial wharf, while other industrial areas can be traced along the river as it heads seawards. The rail yards of Renfe-Operadora – Spain's state-owned national rail company – can be seen neighbouring the museum (before their closure and the area's landscaping). The Guggenheim, poster child for the 'Bilbao miracle', contrasts with the activities of the city's older industries. In the left image, Sekula mimics the hillside viewpoint favoured by most photographers of the museum, while, in the right-hand one, he dwells on an assembly of old workshop buildings adjacent to the railway. There is more than the contrast of unevenness at work here. This visual archaeology of the city fabric evidences the ideology of the new urban policy, with its strategies of deliberate disinvestment from and investment skewed towards prized sites and accompanied by the siphoning of public resources to subsidise international private capital. In a twist on Neil Smith's formulation, Arantxa

108 See, for example, contributions from Margaret A. Rose, Marshall Berman, Martin Puchner.

109 'Photography Between Labour and Capital', 226.

Rodríguez calls this process 'uneven redevelopment'.[110] Neoliberal urban discourse also employs rhetorical contrasts and hyperbole to advance its case. 'Rust' in this discourse is a sign for the 'outdated' (deindustrialisation, death), criticising any 'left nostalgia' for 'rust belt' communities. In contrast, 'titanium' signals the hypermodernity of the modern service economy (cutting-edge vitality, immunity to corrosion).

In the essay 'Between the Net and the Deep Blue Sea' – and earlier still in lectures – Sekula challenged the much-vaunted 'immortality' of titanium, pointing to the tarnished cladding that is wrapped around the museum and to a tank of hydrofluoric acid in the neighbouring rail yard.[111] The contiguity of titanium and acid here is primarily figural, although it draws much of its force from the actual adjacency of the museum and the Renfe facility. The Guggenheim's then–Director General felt the need to respond. Oblivious to Sekula's play with the terms of neoliberal rhetoric – and, as Sekula says in a lecture, his *imagining* of an industrial accident – the Director General took the argument on its most literal of levels and reasserted that titanium cannot corrode. Sekula replied, and both the essay and correspondence appeared in *October*. A further riposte was made a few years later in the film *The Forgotten Space*, utilising footage of the acid container made by Sekula on his earlier visit. In the film's closing section, pointedly subtitled 'Rust', an inversion of value is undertaken. Although rust is treated (figurally) as lowly and as a signifier of an industrial 'past', it nonetheless remains (literally) useful. The film depicts a pile of rusty chains, which are being produced for the contemporary shipping industry. 'Rust', then, is essential to the present and future. Sekula and Burch push the point further. Inside the Guggenheim, they film Richard Serra's permanent installation: a series of huge, tilting Corten steel plates configure over-bearing and oppressive corridors and dead-end spirals. Here, the

110 Rodríguez also appears in *The Forgotten Space*, interviewed from a prospect close to the one Sekula gives in his *Bilbao diptych*. In *The Forgotten Space*, this same view is handled through a pan. Arantxa Rodríguez, Elena Martínez and Galder Guenaga, 'Uneven Redevelopment: New Urban Policies and Socio-Spatial Fragmentation in Metropolitan Bilbao', *European Urban and Regional Studies* 8:2 (2001): 161–78; Rodríguez and Martínez, 'Restructuring Cities: Miracles and Mirages in Urban Revitalization in Bilbao', in *The Globalized City: Economic Restructuring and Social Polarization in European Cities*, eds Frank Moulaert, Arantxa Rodríguez and Erik Swyngedouw (Oxford: Oxford University Press, 2005), 181–207.

111 Sekula drew on his youthful experience as a chemical technician engraving titanium with acid ('Globalism's Discontents and the Return of the Sea').

deliberate rusting of steel is celebrated in the centrepiece of the museum's display – translated into an urban picturesque of heavy industry. It is an aesthetic actively sought out by artists and designers for whom this oxidation is the 'patina' of 'controlled corrosion'. Played through the gallery audio guide, Sekula and Burch highlight Serra's personal nostalgia (his father worked as a pipefitter in the shipyards). On exposure to air or water, a layer of cohered rust forms on Corten – a steel originally used for coal wagons on the US railways. Switching between figural and literal levels, chiastic turns establish relations – direct, critical, ironic – between urban policy, architecture, art and economic history. Titanium's economic fragility also soon became apparent: the metal became affordable for architectural usage when, after the collapse of the USSR, Soviet-mined metal flooded onto the global market. Gehry had to revert to stainless steel for his Walt Disney Concert Hall in Los Angeles – the opening of which became the subject of Sekula's short video *Gala*.

Arguably, Sekula's diptychs and horizontal montage – when taken not simply as contrasts – attempt a type of chiastic labour. As work with both text and image, and attentive to both their interrelations and relative autonomy, Sekula's projects highlight another aspect of chiasmus, appealing to both word and image, and linguistic and non-linguistic qualities. Chiasmus, writes Max Nänny, is 'experienced only verbally in time but its chiastic arrangement must be seen as a simultaneous, quasi-spatial pattern'.[112] Chiasmus is known as the 'crisscross' or 'diagonal' figure. Specialists sometimes use the visual-spatial mark 'χ' – the Greek *chi* – replacing the standard keyboard 'X' with its iconic equivalent to emphasise: its non-linguistic aspects; the moment of transformation at the crossing point; and the twin inclining-declining rhythm of the intersecting lines.

It is, then, perhaps unsurprising that an intimate association is often posited between chiasmus and the dialectical image discussed by Benjamin and Adorno. 'Dialectical image' captures all the ambiguities and tensions of the word 'image' in Critical Theory – put broadly, the tensions between picture and perception. The word slides between a reference to actual pictures (prints, collages, photomontages and so on); quasi-'images' belonging to the linguistic realm (such as metaphor, metonym, analogy, correspondences); literary 'thought-image' (*Denkbild*); Wittgensteinian 'images'.[113] Benjamin's discussions of the

112 Max Nänny, 'Chiasmus in Literature: Ornament or Function?', 51.

113 Anthony Auerbach, 'Imagine no Metaphors: the Dialectical Image of Walter Benjamin', *Image[&]Narrative* 18 (2007).

dialectical image are scattered and inconsistent. From the archives of nineteenth-century Paris, Benjamin assembled the self-representations and phantasmagorias of capitalist commodity culture, seeing himself as an 'allegorist of commodity fetishism'.[114] It is an apt way to see Sekula's project. Making the twist or switch, the 'dialectical' moment reveals reified images *as* reified. If, as Benjamin writes, 'image is dialectics at a standstill',[115] the dialectical image 'flashes up' or is 'suddenly emergent'; prompting an 'awakening' from the capitalist dreamworld.

Readers may realise that we are at the nexus of a thorny problem, addressed in the correspondence between Benjamin and Adorno in the 1930s. Were Benjamin's dialectical images 'dialectical', as intended, or, as Adorno charged, had they become 'undialectical', too fixed in their reified state? Adorno accused Benjamin of being 'at the crossroads of magic and positivism'.[116] It could be a formulation for photography itself, and, with more precise coordinates, one invoked by Sekula's consideration of Nadar. Adorno's judgement is far from final. Despite his aspiration to critique, Rose notes that Adorno's method of chiasmus and analogy itself can be unconvincing. The terms of her point are worth noting. A gap remains, she writes, 'between Adorno's critique of philosophy and his social critique which is only filled by his aesthetics or sociology of art'.[117] Art has the capacity to structure meaning in alternative ways, but in doing so it does not fulfil the functions of philosophy and social critique. Put otherwise, the chiasmus's 'crossroad' is less a point replete with the presence of an intersection, but rather more like a fissure or absence.

For Sekula, as we saw, photography was 'suspended between' the discourses of art and science. We might pause to note how this 'suspended between' departs from a conception of a liberal 'middle ground' based on the affirmative and additive principle of 'both . . . and . . .'. Sekula's conception is based on a very different formulation: the 'neither . . . nor . . .'. The latter puts into play dynamic forces, and

114 Rose, *The Melancholy Science*, 42.

115 Benjamin, 'On the Theory of Knowledge, Theory of Progress', in *The Arcades Project* (Cambridge, MA: Harvard University Press, 1999), 456–88 (462, N2a,3). Rolf Tiedemann said the meaning of dialectical image and dialectics at a standstill 'remained iridescent': Rolf Tiedemann, 'Dialectics at a Standstill: Approaches to the *Passagen-Werk*' (1988), Ibid., 942.

116 Theodor W. Adorno, 'Letters to Walter Benjamin III (10 November 1938)', *Aesthetics and Politics* (1977; London: Verso, 1980), 126–33 (129).

117 Rose, *The Melancholy Science*, 76.

so the ideological 'contradiction' entails both static and mobile moments. Yet even this account needs further clarification. Sekula was surely aware of Barthes's withering essay on 'Neither-Nor Criticism' (1955): a denunciation of the petit-bourgeois 'adepts of a bi-partite universe', who believe they are moral arbiters transcending sordid partisan squabbles.[118] Informed by the humanist values ascendent in the mid-twentieth century, these critics appeal to the superiority of 'culture' (Typically they might have used the upper case 'Culture'). The 'neither . . . nor . . .' is not inherently exempted from a middling bourgeois liberalism. The middle in Sekula – the 'between' – is not so much a resolving mediation as a structuring absence for an invisible power. Sekula never abandoned partisanship, so we need to grasp his negationary conceptualisation of 'suspended between' as fully tensile. Perhaps, then, there remain inescapable limits on the employment of chiasmi and dialectical images in repairing 'broken metonyms' or making visible fetish forms?

Moving-image works like *The Lottery of the Sea* can shape our exposure to the temporal rhythms of the voiced observation in ways that are different to the photo-text works, where the viewer has more latitude to skip or retrace steps. In the video essay, the viewer is propelled forward, often before having digested a scene – the density of the essayistic rumination can be difficult to absorb. Sekula was conflicted about the respective strengths of still photo-text and time-based work. He complained, as mentioned earlier, of the dictatorial rhythm of time-based media, which removes the viewer's freedom to backtrack and check. The photo sequence can be dissolved back into its constituent parts. Nonetheless, it seems that the temporal plasticity of video and film allowed for the timing of delivery, heightening the ironies and absurdities he found in global capitalism and its representations. His openness to the format coincides with a wider resurgence of the video and film essay. The extended combinations of visual, aural and sonic materials allowed for complex, polyvalent and intensified dialectical images to be constellated. The video and film essay is known for its capacity to exploit the correlations and disjunctions between the various elements that we see; between those we hear (local sound, music or the narrator's prose); between what we see and what we hear; and between all these dimensions and what we remember we have already seen or heard. Eisenstein called this type of assemblage 'vertical montage'. As we tried to show

118 Roland Barthes, *Mythologies* (1957; London: Vintage, 1972), 81–3.

with *The Lottery of the Sea*, this visual-aural essay conveys both what can and cannot be seen; both what is and what is not said. With its visual-aural-recollective entwinement, and by combining elements from varying spatio-temporal registers, it can recover what is subject to the amnesias of capitalism.

Even though it moves relentlessly forward, the format nonetheless varies our sense of time, switching between, on the one hand, more 'dramatic' collisions and, on the other, 'digressive' trajectories. Aesthetically, these temporal modalities both contrast and cross over – as does the narrative with the descriptive elements; the realist devices with those of montage; the literal and figural; and the figures of similarity and contiguity. While these tensions occur throughout *The Lottery of the Sea*, as features of specific local editing and sequencing choices, they also unfold as a macro-trend across the entire video. We previously noted the contrast between the tightly choreographed and energetic edits of the opening (prologue and the Athens chapter), and the more expansive sequences set in Galicia, with their long-held shots, where the momentum slackens considerably. Structurally, *The Lottery of the Sea* expands by means of accumulations, aggregations and overlays. Even within the tighter montage, there are passages that have the capacity to 'wander' and take on a life of their own (think of the clips from *Never on Sunday*). Another layering of tension suspends between the in-process viewing experience and the post-viewing reflection.

The digressive mode was explicitly how *Fish Story* was imagined, highlighted by Sekula's lead-in to the chiasmus of factories and ships: '*Fish Story* follows a meandering path among spaces that are simultaneously instrumental and heterotopic. The task of framing and sequencing is to reveal this double character'.[119] Detours can counter rigid separation of instrumental and heterotopic spaces, enabling viewers to move between them. But they also draw attention to that 'double character' as such. This wandering is not simply between different locations (although there is that, of course). It is also between different conceptualisations of any one locale – between its facticity and its imaginative, figural or allegorical charge. 'Heterotopia' is often mentioned by Sekula. In Foucault's account, the ship is heterotopia *par excellence*. Heterotopias are social condensers or congealers of multiple and often incompatible elements. They are actual places that are also imaginative spaces (figurally replete

119 'On *Fish Story*', 54.

with, and generating, representations, both illusory and compensatory). They are, therefore, counter-sites, entailing contradictory 'mirrorings'. As we saw with objects – for example, the bin liners in Galicia – the spaces, too, are what they are and are yet otherwise. Arguably, Sekula doubles over his own formulation, since 'heterotopic' already includes 'instrumental' as one of its conflicting registers. Nonetheless, the double character in question touches on problems undergirding Sekula's practice: at its most bald, the tensions between 'documentary' and 'art', but also, or more precisely, documentary-as-literal and documentary-as-figural. With lens-based media, these issues become acute: particularly prone to being perceived along the heteronomous axis alone. We are not so far from the problem Adorno perceived with dialectical images: the crossing between 'positivism' and 'magic'.

Poetics of Prose

From the mid-1990s, Sekula insisted on the importance of 'poetics'. As we saw, he describes *Fish Story* as 'a "poetics" of sequenced descriptive photographs' and he also compares his short essays, wall texts and caption lists to 'prose-poems'.[120] Challenging the instrumentalised casting and denigration of documentary and realism by critics and practitioners, he later re-emphasised that it remains vital to recognise that 'there is a poetic play within realist language'.[121] The inverted commas around 'poetics' in the first of these quotations is worth noting: it is both a heightening and a cautioning. It should be obvious that Sekula's formulations seem, by some standards, oxymoronic: a *poetics* of *prose*, of *realist* language or of *descriptive* photos (and, remarkably, the perspective he criticises has remained stubbornly intact despite decades of postmodern hybridisation and genre-bending). Understanding Sekula's idea of 'poetics' will take some effort to fine-tune. Note that he speaks of 'poetics', not 'poetic'; and 'poetics' is treated as singular ('a/the poetics of').

Prose poetry is now an established form – albeit, like most mixed modes, often deemed 'paradoxical'.[122] With precedents in the writings of

120 'On *Fish Story*', 52, 58; 'Globalism's Discontents and the Return of the Sea'.

121 Sekula in Hou Hanru, 'Allan Sekula and Bruno Serralongue', *Flash Art*, 14 November 2014, flash---art.com (first published as 'In Conversation with Bruno Serralongue and Allan Sekula', *Art Practical*, 15 February 2012).

122 Paul Hetherington and Cassandra Atherton, *Prose Poetry: An Introduction* (Princeton: Princeton University Press, 2020) provides a comprehensive overview.

Baudelaire and Rimbaud, the prose poem is often associated with imagistic commentaries on the experience of urban modernity, suggesting affinities with Sekula's projects, and further reinforced by his long engagement with Benjamin. This said, there are no examples of text blocking in Sekula. He does not, as is often claimed for prose poetry, elevate connotation over denotation; rather, he mobilises both at once; the modest value of denotative description remains crucially important for him, even if his work is irreducible to merely documenting.[123] Nor does his writing simply push 'inconclusive' qualities. While the prose poem is often said to 'resist closure' at the semantic, narratival or expositional levels, it nonetheless coheres at the level of its tight form. If it becomes too long, its energy is felt to dissipate; a crafted concision aims at semantic and formal tensility. It would be hard to compare the sprawling nature of *Fish Story* or *The Lottery of the Sea* with this sort of terse form, and even Sekula's short essays are lengthy by the standards of most prose poems. His writing also has less of the pitch of the micro-story, and less of its voicing through a narrator's experience ('A strange thing happened to me today . . .'). Even though Sekula's writing is clearly distinct from the conventions of discursive prose, he never takes leave of the discursive form. Approaching similar expressive possibilities from the perspective of prose, the 'lyric essay':

> partakes of the poem in its density and shapeliness, its distillation of ideas and musicality of language. It partakes of the essay in its weight, in its overt desire to engage with facts, melding its allegiance to the actual with its passion for imaginative form . . . It might move by association, leaping from one path of thought to another by way of imagery or connotation, advancing by juxtaposition or sidewinding poetic logic . . . it may meander, making use of other genres when they serve its purpose: recombinant, it samples the techniques of fiction, drama, journalism, song, and film.[124]

While some feel that 'lyric essay' sounds too staid, its practitioners are keen to distinguish it from 'poetic prose', which they fear endows prose with an overwrought, cloying character. Sekula touched on a similar point: although he greatly admired the work of Jean Vigo, he

123 In *Aerospace Folktales*, Sekula experimented with the use of blank space in the presentation of the written textual elements. His later notebooks are full of calligrammatic sketches.

124 Deborah Tall and John D'Agata, 'New Terrain: The Lyric Essay', *Seneca Review* 27:2 (Fall 1997): 7–8 (7).

believed the 'poetic realism' or 'lyrical documentary' of 1930s French film succumbed to fatalist themes; injecting the individualised emotive voice into the 'social' modes could have unhelpfully elegiac side effects.

And, yet, despite the patent differences and difficulties in associating these forms with Sekula, there is still something to be said for the comparisons. Much is shared with the techniques often employed in prose poems: truncated expression, syntactic condensations, parataxis; fragments, punctuated metre; rhythmic listing or prosody; mixing of genres, modalities and registers (such as combining elevated abstract vocabulary with demotic or pedestrian language); an attention to the colloquial and quotidian; the use of humour; heteroglossia (whether via citations, reported speech, direct speech or intertextuality); density of vivid imagery and implied meanings; affinities with the folktale, fable or parable; a project of social criticism; a heightened artistic handling of spatial and temporal qualities.[125] As with the prose poem and lyric essay, Sekula's writing heightens the associative with extended metaphors and through the weird suggestiveness of his imagery.[126] It 'accretes by fragments, taking shape mosaically'.[127] Wandering and 'tensing between the presentational and the representational' sounds not too far from Sekula's 'meandering path among spaces that are simultaneously instrumental and heterotopic'.[128] However, Sekula's writing tends not to 'spiral in on itself', but rather spins outwards, its figural density and TARDIS-like qualities ballooning connections, connotations or metonymic cascades, and drawing in meanings from external conceptual domains.[129] Earlier, we touched on the type of deliberately clipped prose used in the retelling of the Athena-Hephaestus myth – and this is a feature that can often be found in Sekula's delivery. In the next chapter, we will discuss a paragraph from *Dead Letter Office* in which parataxis, unexpected connections and weird imagery are unleashed.

125 Michael Benedikt, *The Prose Poem: An International Anthology* (New York: Dell, 1976). Apropos colloquial speech, it is worth recalling David Antin's 'talk poetry'. Antin taught Sekula at UCSD.

126 Ibid., 7.

127 Ibid.

128 Martha Aldrich, 'The Boarding School', *Seneca Review* 37:2 (2007) cited by Hetherington and Atherton, *Prose Poetry*, 25.

129 Tall and D'Agata, 7. The TARDIS (an old police box that is 'bigger on the inside'), from the BBC's sci-fi series *Dr Who*, is an acronym for 'Time and Relative Dimensions in Space'.

Sekula's prose might be related to other 'mixed modes' such as 'lyric(al) research' or 'documentary poetics'.[130] Mark Nowak points to the latter's expansive character, encompassing auto-ethnography and 'objectivist' documenting. While some of these works still lodge firmly within 'poetry', others draw on American Depression-era photo-text documentary projects (such as were funded under the Works Progress Administration and Farm Security Administration).[131] Indeed, Nowak believes that 'documentary poetics . . . is currently more widely and . . . fully leveraged in visual culture (film, photography) than the language arts'.[132] Among others, he perhaps has Sekula in mind. The point is not to establish the correct definitional box into which to shoehorn Sekula's writing. We have limited this discussion to the qualities of his written (or spoken) elements, but 'poetics' for Sekula is also a question of image work ('a poetics of . . . photographs'). Theorisations of 'hybrid' forms gained momentum in the 1980s and 1990s; two-column lists contrasting 'modernism' and 'postmodernism' (the latter supposedly 'hybrid') were ten-a-penny. The delineations of the qualities of the prose poem or lyric essay closely parallel those of the video and film essay. The claims made often challenged straw targets, forgetting the many 'modern' (and even premodern) precedents, both practical and critical. Traversing boundaries and sounding the major key as 'ambivalence' were celebrated and affirmed as 'new'. What again needs to be underscored with Sekula is the importance of tensility and negativity (even the splenetic), of purposefulness and partisanship; and his dismissal, as he incisively put it, of contemporary culture's 'requisite praise for semantic indeterminacy

130 Alissa Quart cited by Dana Isokawa, 'Where Poetry Meets Journalism', *Poets & Writers* (November/December 2019); cf. Joseph Harrington, 'Docupoetry and Archive Desire', *Jacket2* (October 2011); Philip Metres, 'From Reznikoff to Public Enemy: The poet as journalist, historian, agitator', *Poetry Foundation*, 4 November 2007; Metres, '(More) News from Poems: Investigative / Documentary / Social Poetics On the Tenth Anniversary of the Publication of "From Reznikoff to Public Enemy"', *Kenyon Review*, March/April 2018; Mark Nowak, 'Documentary Poetics', *Poetry Foundation*, 17 April 2010; Nowak, *Social Poetics* (Minneapolis, MN: Coffee House Press, 2020); Kathryn Nuernberger, 'Docupoetics and the Art of Lyrical Research', 14 February 2020, kathrynnuernberger .com.

131 Notably, Barbara Ehrenreich reappears. Acknowledging the precedent of New Deal projects, she founded the Economic Hardship Reporting Project in 2012, which supported the production of creative forms of independent journalism – often combining the work of writers and photographers – to be co-published via established outlets such as the *New York Times* and the *Guardian*: economichardship.org.

132 Nowak, 'Documentary Poetics'.

and epistemological scepticism, as if ambiguity were not a general condition of meaning, but a virtue'.[133]

Sekula's 'poetics of prose' takes us back to Jakobson and the Bakhtin Circle, whose understanding of 'poetics' was rooted in Russian formalism's (and constructivism's) rejection of symbolism's subjectivist aesthetic. As we have seen, the aversion to content departs from Jakobson's account, which presents the 'poetic function' as one of six interrelating functions. 'Poetics' is 'that part of linguistics which treats the poetic function in its relationship to the other functions of language'. Further: 'Any attempt to reduce the sphere of the poetic function to poetry or to confine poetry to the poetic function would be a delusive oversimplification.'[134] In short, 'poetics' belongs as much to prose as to poetry (the latter just wears the poetic function on its sleeve). In its more precise meaning, 'poetics' became a central concern for structuralist approaches to literature and for the writers around *Tel Quel*, although, as many complained, structuralism still too often demonstrated 'repugnance before content as such'.[135] Nevertheless, 'the poetics of prose' was the title for a book by Todorov.[136] Still, nowhere in Sekula's writing do we find anything like Todorov's dense technical analyses. Nor does his work seem to invite such a reading; indeed, recalling his

---

133 'On *Fish Story*', 52. Sekula's use of 'poetics' is also akin to Jacques Rancière's attempt to define a 'poetics of knowledge'. Rancière advances a study of history attentive to its 'literary' dimensions (including rhetoric and historiography): history's ways of naming, framing, constituting and identifying the objects of study; its way of establishing truth: 'literary procedures by which a discourse escapes literature, gives itself the status of a science'. See Jacques Rancière, *The Names of History: On the Poetics of Knowledge* (1992; Minneapolis, MN: University of Minnesota Press, 1994), 8. Rancière's literary and political sensitivity did not seek to reduce history to discursive effects or demean its ambitions to 'science'. Sekula's 'imaginative geographies' and 'imaginative economies', his handling of 'heterotopias', could be seen in a similar light: confronting the contradictions and paradoxes that are thrown up. Hayden White describes Rancière as working in 'the liminal zone between any given present and any possible past . . . His own speech is to be taken neither literally nor figuratively; his own mode of address is to be taken as neither active nor passive; and his assertions are to be taken as neither denotative nor connotative'. Hayden White, 'Foreword: Rancière's Revisionism', in Rancière, *The Names of History*, vii–xix (xix). Note also that 'Poetics' here is translated from the French singular '*La Poetique*' (alluding to Gaston Bachelard's *The Poetics of Space*).

134 Jakobson, 'Linguistics and Poetics', 72–3, 69.

135 Jameson, *The Prison-House of Language*, 196. *Tel Quel* (1960–82) was a French journal devoted to avant-garde literature and theory, which advocated for Maoism from 1971 to 1976. It is associated with several prominent names in the development of post-structuralism, including Philippe Sollers, Julia Kristeva, Marcelin Pleynet, Michel Foucault, Jacques Derrida, Roland Barthes and Jean-Louis Baudry.

136 Tzvetan Todorov, *The Poetics of Prose* (1971; Ithaca, NY: Cornell University Press, 1978).

critique of technicism and his reach for popular modes, to do so would seem inappropriate. Sekula's commitment to the poetics of prose, then, is best understood as a working principle framed by certain critical concerns: to challenge the widespread aesthetic prejudice that would see documentary as transparent and lacking in form; to counter the argument that only certain approaches ('metaphoric' modes, such as those of Stieglitz or staged photography) pay attention to the complexities specific to form or representation; and instead to explore the poetic function of prose, and consider its expansion beyond the linguistic register. It is useful to recall the distinction between *aesthesis*, emphasising sensory experience, and *poiesis*, stressing the active transforming of materials – the doing, making or bringing into being.[137] The connection between *poiesis* and the constructivist *Technē* is relevant – pointing to concerns with the material qualities of language and image-making, and also pointing to 'critical realism' with the emphasis on social materiality, and the allying of *poiesis* and *praxis*.

The challenge Jakobson bequeathed was never going to be straightforward. Discussing structuralism's efforts, Terence Hawkes noted that 'the poetics of prose' had proven an 'elusive' project.[138] The alternative of sociological poetics was also seen to be 'precarious', as Erlich put it (and was intimated by Godzich's projective 'sociological poetics yet to come').[139] Thus, 'elusivity' and 'precarity' framed the poetics of prose from both critical directions. As we saw, Jakobson's 'Two Aspects of Language and Two Types of Aphasic Disturbance' (1956) was a call to rebalance studies that have been skewed towards metaphor, with its 'manifest' foregrounding of figural language. In contrast, the figural work of metonymy and the figural qualities of prose tend to be 'unostentatious', their tropes 'latent' and thus overlooked.[140] The figural work of metonymy tends to be overshadowed or smothered by the work of reference. But Jakobson argues that the privileging of metaphor and the concomitant undervaluing of metonymy need to be understood as more than a mere cultural prejudice. Certainly, there was cultural bias at work (call it 'the cult of metaphor' or 'aesthetic ideology'), but

137 Jacques Rancière, *Aisthesis: Scenes from the Aesthetic Regime of Art* (2011; London: Verso, 2019).

138 Terence Hawkes, *Structuralism and Semiotics* (London: Methuen, 1977), 87. Discussing Jakobson's 'Linguistics and Poetics', Joel Fineman identifies 'a real difficulty in structuralist poetics' itself. Fineman, 'The Structure of Allegorical Desire', 52.

139 Erlich, *Russian Formalism*, 115.

140 Jakobson, 'Linguistics and Poetics', 89, 87.

Jakobson suggests that the hierarchy has another basis: 'when constructing a metalanguage to interpret tropes, the researcher possesses more homogenous means to handle metaphor, whereas metonymy, based on a different principle, easily defies interpretation'.[141] He repeats the point in 'Linguistics and Poetics': 'so-called realistic literature, intimately tied to the metonymic principle, still defies interpretation'.[142] This unevenness is explained in terms of Rudolf Carnap's distinction between object language and metalanguage, and the extent to which these two levels of language share the same linguistic code[143] – or, as Jakobson puts it, of their homogeneity, consonance or 'kinship'. With a consonance between the two levels, metaphor, he argues, lends itself to metalinguistic commentary and already entails self-conscious reflection upon the signs of the object language. In contrast, metonymy is largely subsumed at the level of object language (its operation is not paralleled by the metalanguage and has little kinship with it). Sekula's efforts, therefore, were never going to be simply a matter of rectifying the 'cult of metaphor' and pursuing the project posed by Jakobson as if it were a leftover research thread.

In Sekula's work, centrifugal and centripetal dynamics escalate, extending and intensifying, accumulating significance as they overlap, elaborating further contradictions of capitalist globalisation. Metonyms cascade – generatively, but also unpredictably, perhaps even sometimes leading nowhere. Metaphors can enrich and vault, but also impoverish, overreach and fall flat. Though these multiple strands and registers can develop their own momenta, they nonetheless 'add up' in ways that are provisional and productively motile. In a sense, Sekula's work offers an alternative to the dioramas and the large-scale models in museums and visitors' centres (such as one of the Panama Canal in *The Lottery of the Sea*) – those aesthetic-cognitive machines that purport to give their viewers a commanding prospect of the whole. The connections generated by his projects can be especially unruly where words play a minor part, and where the signifying capacities of images or artefacts are unbound (such as in long passages of *Lottery*, *Tsukiji* (2001) and *Gala* (2005) in the slide sequences; and in the object-photo installation of *Ship of Fools/The Dockers' Museum*). But, as we also saw, words themselves can sometimes be the primary source of this unruliness. Chains

141 Jakobson, 'Two Aspects', 113.

142 Jakobson, 'Linguistics and Poetics', 90.

143 Jakobson, 'Two Aspects', 103–4.

– where 'this leads to that' and 'that prompts thoughts of this' – proliferate, taking on varying inflections: sometimes historical, at others, economic. In one moment, we detect the flow of goods in the global distribution chain; then 'umbilical cords of gold'; and in another the flows of desire. As viewer-readers, we can find ourselves tracking Sekula's travels, or roughly retracing the outline of his research, sometimes following the ever more profligate concatenations of internet searches. We may be tempted into reading the photographs transparently and at speed, and then – on the basis of an unexpected friction – find ourselves slowed to puzzle something strange. Yet, although we might follow, track and retrace, the temporality is as much anticipatory as it is recollective; its purpose as much a matter of praxis as it is a reminder not to forget or a matter simply of encouraging us to recognise.[144] This projective sense is Sekula's, but it is equally a temporality that we are invited to adopt. The works 'seed' clues whose leads might only emerge for us at later junctures. These themselves are wagers and possibilities, with no guarantee that anything will come of them.

144 Compare also Sekula's comment that 'perhaps to go forward, we must take several steps backward and recover abandoned paths' ('On *Fish Story*', 50).

4

Amphibious (ir)realities and capitalism's dreamworlds

SECTION 1: THE RETURN OF THE SEA

In the wide-ranging essay 'Between the Net and the Deep Blue Sea (Rethinking the Traffic in Photographs)' (2002), Sekula addressed the projects he had undertaken in the years following *Fish Story: Dead Letter Office* (1996/97), *Dear Bill Gates* (1999), *Waiting for Tear Gas* (1999/2000) and *TITANIC's wake* (1998/2000). The essay title implied the common saying 'caught between the devil and the deep blue sea.' There is some debate about the origins of this expression, probably dating from the 1600s, where there are recorded versions with either 'dead sea' or 'deep sea', without the colour (the 'deep blue sea' version is thought to be of late-nineteenth-century origin). Some think that the 'devil' refers to the caulking line around the hull, a critical seam on timber-built vessels that needed to be kept watertight: repairing it was dangerous; not repairing it was dangerous. Others have noted that the nautical term 'devil' only emerged into usage in later centuries. Whatever the etymology, this widely used expression alludes to facing a dilemma, an impossible choice between two equally bad options (comparable to other expressions, such as 'between a rock and a hard place' or, based on Greek mythology, 'between Scylla and Charybdis'). In Sekula's case, there's also a bibliographic angle, with an allusion to Marcus Rediker's *Between the Devil and the Deep Blue Sea: Merchant Seamen, Pirates and the Anglo-American Maritime World, 1700–1750,* which had been published in 1987. As an activist-scholar in the tradition of 'history from below', Rediker has paid close attention to the maritime world and Sekula read his work. As the subtitle to the essay makes clear, there is another point of reference: this time to Sekula's own 1981 essay 'The Traffic in Photographs' – and with it, as we have already seen, its critique of the liberal humanism of Ed Steichen's exhibition *The Family of Man*. The latter plays a role in the 2002 essay both as direct topic of discussion and as metaphor for the *Global Mariner*'s campaigning exhibition on maritime labour conditions (Part 4 is called 'Refloating *The Family of Man*'). Meanwhile, Bill Gates's Corbis picture agency serves as the updated archive and thus as the (then still) relatively new digital 'traffic in photographs'.

As we saw in the previous chapter, Sekula draws on Jakobson's account of metonymic expansion. Returning to the valences of Sekula's lead title, 'Between the Net and the Deep Blue Sea', we can see how he pursues chains of contiguity, how allusions rapidly multiply and how the register of the word 'net' alters. At its most basic, the 'net' suggests a fishing net, relaying us, at different moments, to: Winslow Homer's painting *Lost on the Grand Banks* (a reproduction of which forms part of *Dear Bill Gates*); the trawler-meets-disaster in the film *The Perfect Storm*; the motif of nets in Bilbao's fish market; the fishermen in *The Family of Man*. The discussion of the latter invokes reflections on a project by Anita Conti, a photographer omitted from Steichen's exhibition – who Sekula admired for prioritising the visual perspective of marine creatures over that of the marine-extractive industry. Writing in 'Dismal Science' in the mid-1990s, Sekula also employed the word in the sense of an act of visual possession – especially so in the case of Dutch maritime panoramas whose 'open' character he describes as 'a net cast outward upon a world that yields property but that in its idealized totality is irreducible to property'[1] – and suggesting discussions of the cone of vision in perspective and the psychoanalytic gaze.

In the essay 'Between the Net and the Deep Blue Sea', 'the net' also manifests prominently as the internet; Sekula embraces the rise of the digital platform (and cultural and social claims made for it); the dominance of Microsoft, Corbis and how Gates's wealth enabled him to buy Winslow Homer's *Lost on the Grand Banks* for a record price of more than thirty million dollars; and the role of computer-generated imagery (CGI) in blockbuster films and in the design and construction of the Bilbao Guggenheim. It is worth recalling that, when Sekula was writing this essay at the turn of the century, the internet as a widely used feature

1 'Dismal Science', 44.

of everyday life was still in its relative infancy, even in the more privileged echelons of the majority world. Although it began to enter wider use around 1993–4, it was the early 2000s before broadband connections supplanted dial-up. This moment preceded the arrival of 'Web 2.0' (2004–5) and, beyond that, the deeper transformations prompted by smartphones, social media, algorithmic acceleration and AI. Nonetheless – and significantly, we suggest, early as this was – Sekula was writing immediately in the wake of the first speculative 'dot.com' bubble of 1997–2001.

In 'Dismal Science', he writes that the 'incomprehension' of the role of maritime economy 'is the product of forgetting and disavowal', the shipping container being its principle sign.[2] In 'On *Fish Story*', capital's fantasy of self-reproducing value 'exists within a fog of disavowal'.[3] The metaphor brings to mind maritime atmosphere, both in its aestheticized sense (a misty seascape) and in the threatening disorientation of a thick fog bank.[4] The inflections of Sekula's writing are insistent: 'the return of the sea' clearly implies Freud's 'return of the repressed'; there is a repeated use of 'denial' and 'disavowal' (*Verneinung* and *Verleugnung*); and there is a pointed highlighting with inverted commas around the terms 'disappear' and 'forgetting', and, twice over, around 'returns'. In his 1997 essay, with the post-apocalyptic film *Waterworld* (dir. Kevin Reynolds, 1995) in mind, he notes that 'When the sea "returns" in contemporary mass culture, it does so in bizarrely de-realized fashion.'[5] The same emphasis recurs in the 2002 essay with reference to *The Perfect Storm* (dir. Wolfgang Petersen, 2000): 'it [the sea] "returns" as pure media simulation.'[6]

Initially, it might appear that Sekula resorts to 'false consciousness', and there is little doubt that he wants to skewer these Hollywood creations. However, we want to tease out a rather different reading. The neoliberal culture's 'recollection' or 'return' of the sea entails distortions, overlays, masks, deflections, layers of wrenching violence upon violence. Yet, these qualities are simultaneously 'un-real' and 'real'. This doubling can be seen in the films' narrative themes and tropes (sci-fi, horror), as well

2 'Dismal Science', 54, 137.

3 'On *Fish Story*', 53.

4 Cf. 'fog of teargas' ("Between the Net and the Deep Blue Sea', 34). The 'fog of war', with its sense of violence and concealment, might also be suggested.

5 'On *Fish Story*', 56.

6 'Between the Net and the Deep Blue Sea', 15. Based on an actual event and the non-fiction book of the same name, the film addressed the disappearance of the fishing boat *Andrea Gail* in an unusually powerful cyclone in October 1991.

as in the technologies of their realisation (as with the film *Titanic*, these blockbusters were achieved with colossal sets, animations and CGI, the use of which ramped up during the 1990s).

Freudian concepts acquire social and ideological valences for Sekula. The (social and cultural) whole becomes (psychically) freighted. Of course, there are many precedents for taking accounts originally designed to analyse individual psychic afflictions and expanding their application onto the social level – such as scaling up neurosis onto the cultural plane – but as methodology it is questionable and contested. Posed thus, Sekula would likely concur.

It is remarkable that the presence of psychoanalysis in Sekula's writing is rarely noted. Yet, from the time he studied with Marcuse at UCSD, Sekula was alert to combining Marx and Freud.[7] In *Eros and Civilisation* (1955), Marcuse reinterpreted Freud's account of repression from *Civilization and Its Discontents*.[8] Freud had argued that 'civilisation' (or socialisation) was achieved through the repression of the libidinal drives. Marcuse understood socialisation as itself repression – conforming specifically to the modes and mentalities of capitalist social relations. Capitalism, he suggested, had learned to incorporate disruptive forms of desire through 'repressive desublimation' – a kind of controlled release of repressed forces. Accordingly, for Marcuse, 'liberation' was equated with the release of those repressed drives, through art, imagination and Eros.[9] Sekula seems to have been attentive to the role of the aesthetic.[10]

There is already plenty here to make psychoanalytic specialists tense up. A range of distinct psychic modalities are in play. As we proceed, there will be more muddying of the waters. Yet, to highlight this

7 On Marcuse's controversial period at UCSD (which overlapped with Sekula's first undergraduate years from Fall 1968), see Judith Moore, 'Angel of the Apocalypse: Marxist Professor Herbert Marcuse's Years at UCSD', *San Diego Reader*, 11 September 1986.

8 Herbert Marcuse, *Eros and Civilisation* (1955; London: Abacus, 1972); Sigmund Freud, *Civilisation and Its Discontents*, in *Civilization, Society and Religion* (1930; Harmondsworth: Penguin, 1985), 243–340.

9 Herbert Marcuse, *One-Dimensional Man*; *Eros and Civilisation* (1969; London: Abacus/Sphere Books, 1972); *The Aesthetic Dimension: Toward a Critique of Marxist Aesthetics* (1977; Basingstoke: Macmillan, 1979).

10 Sekula said he found the 1930s essay on art 'The Aesthetic Dimension' (incorporated into *Eros and Civilisation*) much better than *The Aesthetic Dimension*. See: Sekula, in Katarzyna Ruchel-Stockmans, 'Interview with Allan Sekula', *Critical Realism in Contemporary Art: Around Allan Sekula's Photography*, eds Jan Baetens and Hilde Van Gelder (Leuven: Leuven University Press, 2006), 138–151 (148). Elsewhere, he notes that Marcuse's aesthetics were out of step with the prevailing Duchampian mood at UCSD.

overlooked aspect of Sekula's work, we alight on and assemble further traces. What is at issue for us is not the (in)adequacy of his use of psychanalytic theory; that would be a different project. Rather, we want to hint at a type of aesthetic thinking and doing. To be clear, we now refer not so much to Sekula's object of attention (the role of sea in neoliberal culture and economy, although discussions of this will be unavoidable) but to Sekula's own *poiesis*. Our focus is on how he mobilises the resources of psychoanalysis (inter alia) to imaginatively array figures and to establish relations – in ways that are, in turn, serious and playful, controlled and unruly.[11]

A Return to the Sea

Like 'net', 'the deep blue sea' provokes multiple associations, signalling the maritime world in general, or, to give an example with Titanic specificity, the chasm into which the doomed 1912 ocean liner sank. In Sekula's essay, 'deep blue sea' also suggests the 'deep digital blue' of a film-studio screen used to project a simulated storm. Although not mentioned by Sekula, it is likely relevant that 'Deep Blue' was the name of the IBM computer that beat chess champion Garry Kasparov in 1996 and 1997, which was compared with the 'Mechanical Turk' that features in the first of Benjamin's Theses.[12] 'Deep blue sea' also plays out as wateriness or fluidity: the liquidity of financial markets; the 'abyss' or 'liquid immersion' entailed in searching the internet or the Corbis picture archive.[13] It also signifies the resistive and carnivalesque 'liquid circus' of Seattle's anti-WTO protesters; or the 'exaggerated liquid symptoms of human empathy and grief' chemically induced from their eyes by tear gas.[14] 'Deep blue sea' is the sheer material conditions on which the *Global Mariner* sails, but also the conditions exhibited on board (how the international shipping industry violates labour safety, and

11 Buck-Morss describes Walter Benjamin's 'dreamworld' as both analytic category and a poetic manifestation of a collective mental state. Her book was published just before Sekula's essay. See Susan Buck-Morss, *Dreamworld and Catastrophe: The Passing of Mass Utopia in East and West* (Cambridge, MA: MIT Press, 2000), x.

12 Kasparov suspected that there had been surreptitious human interventions in the game – as with the 'Mechanical Turk' – a claim denied by the Deep Blue team. 'Big Blue' was the nickname for IBM; 'Deep Thought', the name given to the computer in 1988 (said to allude to the pornographic film *Deep Throat* from 1972).

13 'Between the Net and the Deep Blue Sea', 13, 12. Elsewhere, 'abyss' refers to the Atlantic chasm and to a discussion between Freud and Roman Rolland. Ibid., 17, 25.

14 Ibid., 6, 7.

which 'refloats' *The Family of Man*). It would include Sekula's *Dear Bill Gates*, with his own immersion in the bay outside the entrepreneur's home. Thus, the idiom 'deep blue sea' is mobilised both for and against capitalism. As we suggested with *Waiting for Tear Gas*, a colour – here, blue – can both adhere to capital and, in a process we called 'colour as comrade', free itself from it.

Alongside his argument about the return of the sea – the late twentieth century's forgetting and fitful recollection of the maritime world – Sekula develops a line of thought that emphasises a return to the sea. Here, he discusses Freud, Freud's correspondence with Romain Rolland, and Sándor Ferenczi's *Thalassa: A Theory of Genitality*.

The immediate context for Sekula's discussion of psychoanalysis and the oceanic is his consideration of *The Family of Man* (and it is worth noting that his attention was not, as was then more common, on Lacan's mirror phase).The 'hidden *telos*' of Steichen's exhibition, he suggests, is 'an erotic and utopian return to the sea, a solitary quest conducted in the name of humanity'.[15] The idea of an 'oceanic feeling' was raised by Rolland in a letter to Freud in 1927 to describe the spiritual ecstasies of the nineteenth-century mystic Ramakrishna and the sensation of being indistinguishable from (at one with) the world. Freud adopted the idea to describe a vestigial consciousness of very early infancy: the 'primitive ego-feeling' where the child's sense of 'self' is still unformed and undifferentiated from the mother's body (the removal of the breast constituting a significant moment for ego formation).[16]

Sekula traverses the ambivalence of Eros and Thanatos in the oceanic. On the one hand, the oceanic implies the vital liquid requirements of many organisms (more poetically, the aquatic element of life); it is a vitalistic, energising 'joyful splash';' the "female" life instinct'; the 'infantile, pre-Oedipal bliss' of prenatal intrauterine experience; or the coital

---

15 'Between the Net and the Deep Blue Sea', 24.

16 In the late 1960s, influenced by the writing of Anton Ehrenzweig, 'the oceanic' was of great interest to artists such as Robert Smithson and Robert Morris. In the mid-1990s, its qualities resurfaced as an aspect of Bois and Krauss's *L'informe: mode d'emploi*. The idea has been important to many subsequent debates: Julia Kristeva, *Black Sun: Depression and Melancholia* (1987; New York: Columbia University Press, 1992); Luce Irigaray, *Marine Lover of Friedrich Nietzsche* (1981; New York: Columbia University Press, 1991). For a recent reclamation of the oceanic as communistic, drawing on Fred Moten's account of the Middle Passage, see Jackie Wang, 'Oceanic Feeling and Communist Affect', rigabiennial .com.

'regressive longing for immersion'.[17] On the other hand, the oceanic suggests destructive and entropic aspects: the threat of asphyxiation through drowning and other dangers at sea; the ever-present mortal risks faced by those working in the maritime economy, or, as a privileged corollary, the frisson of danger actively enjoyed by wealthy leisure sailors. It is also the psychoanalytic 'immersion and dissolution of the self' and 'death instinct'.[18] The 'ecstatic bathers' in *The Family of Man* seem to enjoy 'infant bliss' and momentarily escape patriarchal authority; but Thanatos also lies in wait.

Ferenczi's study *Thalassa: A Theory of Genitality* (1924) preceded the Rolland–Freud correspondence. 'Thalassa' means 'sea' and is also the name for the Mediterranean's divine personification. Ferenczi's book is key to understanding the 'ecstatic bathers' in Steichen's exhibit – and it refines Sekula's own earlier assessment of *The Family of Man* (in 'The Traffic in Photographs').[19] These images of bathers appealed to contemporary advertisers for beer and menthol cigarettes, Sekula tells us, harnessing libidinal drives and 'imaginary utopia'.[20] Sekula's argument becomes somewhat compressed, and its implications dispersed, so it is worth backing up a bit.

In *Thalassa*, Ferenczi advanced the idea of a 'perigenetic parallel' or 'phylogenetic parallel': a perceived echoing between ontogenetic processes (the development of the individual human from birth to adulthood) and phylogenetic ones (the development of the various species across millennia: of humans from other mammals, from amphibians and from fish). Ferenczi thought that a 'biological unconscious' survived in modern individuals: deep bodily (and cellular) memories of traumas dating from primordial cataclysms. The prime example would be an ancient environmental desiccation prompting the transformation from gill- to lung-breathing (and also impelling changes

---

17 'Between the Net and the Deep Blue Sea', 24, 27, 26, 25. The 'infantile, pre-Oedipal bliss' was in Sekula's 'The Traffic in Photographs', 89.

18 'Between the Net and the Deep Blue Sea', 25. The point resurfaces in Sekula's discussion of Condé and Beveridge in 2009.

19 'Between the Net and the Deep Blue Sea', 26. Sándor Ferenczi, *Thalassa: A Theory of Genitality* (1924; New York: The Norton Library, 1968). Ferenczi's writings and correspondence with Freud became available in translation in the 1980s and 1990s. Ferenczi increasingly departed from the phallocentrism, rationalism and narrative of Oedipal aggression at the heart of the Freudian account. Post-*Thalassa*, he developed instead a more wombcentric argument, which spoke more of the quest for empathic relations.

20 'Between the Net and the Deep Blue Sea', 26 (originally 'The Traffic in Photographs', 89).

in the arrangement of reproductive organs and thus the mode of coitus). Expressed through eroticism, genitality, sleep and other states, 'the thalassal regressive trend' manifests an urge to make 'a return to the maternal womb.'[21] Yet, as far as Ferenczi was concerned, it is not, as might commonly be suggested, that the sea metaphorises the maternal body, but, rather, the other way around: amniotic fluid is a symbol and partial substitute for the lost primordial sea. Glossing Ferenczi, Sekula writes: 'For male mammals, coitus is the expression of a regressive longing for an entropic return not only to the inert floating passivity of the prenatal state, but to the liquid origins of the species.'[22] Sekula questions the methodological legitimacy of Ferenczi's phylo- and ontogenetic parallels (based on the highly questionable 'recapitulation theory' of biologist and naturalist Ernst Haeckel).[23] Ferenczi himself expressed concern with his own unscientific methods – his analogies and homologies across disciplines (and 'reciprocal analogizing').[24] He described his method as 'utraquistic': viewing a phenomenon from two opposing perspectives.[25] However, after some opening caveats, he became increasingly emboldened, revelling in hypotheses, digressions and leaps of imagination, and indulging methodological excess. He argued that the bigger the imaginative leap – the further apart the disciplines or topics compared – the better the interpretative value could be. Later in the book, he described advancing his theory 'in the form of a kind of fairy tale', and he even mobilised his readers with the words 'we shall once again have to allow our fantasies free rein.'[26] Nonetheless, despite Sekula's criticism of Ferenczi's logic, he remains attracted to this 'remarkable book.'[27] Sekula, it seems, admires its speculative and imaginative force, its slippages between registers. Indeed, Sekula soon invites us to 'Just for

21 Ferenczi, *Thalassa*, 53.

22 'Between the Net and the Deep Blue Sea', 26. Note how Gehry's motif for the Bilbao Guggenheim is also described as 'primal'. *Dead Letter Office* alludes to how Baja is figured as 'the vestigial organ, a primeval reptilian tail'; and has 'the primordial abyss' encountered by the transatlantic liner.

23 Infamously, Haeckel promoted scientific racism, Social Darwinism and eugenics. Recapitulation theory was based on comparative morphology of embryos by Étienne Serres and Johann Friedrich Meckel (dating from the 1790s, and systematised in the 1820s). An influence on Freud, it was already disproven by the early twentieth century. In 2001–2002, Sekula records in his notebooks 'Ferenczi's basic argument erroneous' (Sekula Papers, S.1.10:01).

24 Ferenczi, *Thalassa*, 3.

25 Ibid.. From Latin *uterque*, 'both of them'.

26 Ibid., 99, 53–4.

27 'Between the Net and the Deep Blue Sea', 25. Ferenczi appears as a bibliographic reference in a notebook from 2000–1 (Sekula Papers, S.1.09:06).

a moment, imagine . . .', a seaborne alternative to *The Family of Man*.[28] The reverie, it transpires, is itself fictional. Meanwhile, its content is actual: the 're-floating' on *Global Mariner* of another exhibition of the 'family' of hominids.

Several years later, Sekula returned to Ferenczi. Added to *The Dockers' Museum* was an appropriated cartoon, *Mermaid Honeymoon*, depicting a fish woman being carried to the marriage bed by her mariner husband. The room's wallpaper has welcoming fish motifs, and cut into the mattress is a rectilinear pool with water plants, and, surrounded by shells and starfish – an inescapable allusion to *The Flooded Grave*, Jeff Wall's large-scale tableau, a transparency in lightbox, of 1998–2000. Sekula added the subtitle *(The Frenzy of Ferenczi)*. In a notebook from 2010, along with a reference to the Freud–Ferenczi correspondence, he wrote in a carefully drawn script: 'amphimixis . . . thalassal regression.'[29]

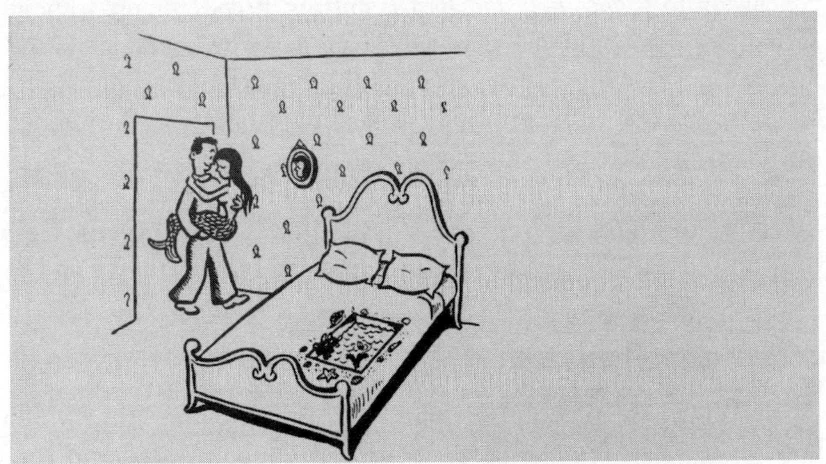

Figure 8: Item from The Dockers' Museum *(2010–13):* Mermaid Honeymoon (The Frenzy of Ferenczi). *Subtitled by Sekula. Cartoon (artist unknown), circa early 1960s (or according to M KHA: 1920s from* Labor Defender, *which we doubt). Graphic sometimes digitally rendered as vinyl cut-outs (to be applied to a wall or window).*

28 'Between the Net and the Deep Blue Sea', 27.

29 Sekula Papers, S.1.15:01 2010–11. 'Amphimixis' is a biological term (mostly employed in the late nineteenth and early twentieth centuries), used in embryology for the fusion of male and female gametes to form the zygote through sexual reproduction. A chapter of Thalassa focused on amphimixis. Following Ferenczi, it was extrapolated to refer to the fusing of eroticisms (usually, but not always, anal and genital) into an amorphous unity during coitus. The idea has been revived to challenge transphobic assumptions in psychoanalysis (for example, that transgender experience merely 'confuses' sexual dimorphism; the primacy of genital – especially, phallic – eroticism).

The oceanic, and Ferenczi's version especially, suggests a further inflection to the understanding of a 'fish story'.[30] The Ferenczian digression ultimately helps Sekula underscore the depth of ideology and the restructuring of the subject (hollowing out the political subject for the consumer subject). From Madison Avenue's advertisers in the 1950s and 1960s to Corbis.com: these are only the most blatant carry-overs from the oceanic bliss staged by Steichen. In the film genre of sea-going catastrophes – in *Waterworld*, *Titanic* and *The Perfect Storm* – a traditional sexual division of labour is re-established and a cathexis with military violence mobilised. Despite some pseudo-feminism in the latter two films:

> These melodramas pretend that the 'male' death instinct serves the 'female' life instinct, as if in optimistic rejoinder to Freud's pessimistic conclusion to *Civilization and Its Discontents*. It goes almost without saying that this traditional view, which can never be honest about the fact that its 'morality' instrumentalizes the instinctual level of psyche, has served as one of the principal ideological justifications for war, for organized aggression on a grand scale.[31]

In a version of Marcuse's 'repressive desublimation', the oceanic feeling is weaponised and the psyche instrumentalised for commerce and war.

Anal Capitalism, Anal Vision

In 'Left-Wing Melancholy', Benjamin compared the three-volume collection of Kästner's poems unfavourably ('too crowded and somewhat stifling') with their original mass media publication, where they:

> dart through the daily papers *like fish in water*. If this water is not always the cleanest and has quite a lot of *refuse floating* in it, all the better for the author, whose poetic minnows can fatten themselves thereon.[32]

30 In his early conceptualisation of *Fish Story*, Sekula toys with three key elements: Freud's 'uncanny'; the story of his mother's attempted suicide by drowning; and Frank Gehry's anecdote about his architecture being influenced by seeing a carp in his grandmother's bathtub. Some of these elements survive in the finished version, but he seems to have been unable to find a form to handle the maternal incident.

31 'Between the Net and the Deep Blue Sea', 27.

32 Benjamin, 'Left-Wing Melancholy' (1931), in *Selected Writings Volume 2, 1927–1934* (Cambridge, MA: The Belknap Press, 1999), 423–7 (423, our emphases).

The essay ends on a note of digestive waste and its failure to pass: 'Constipation and melancholy have always gone together.'[33] Excreta and waste flows regularly occur in Sekula's work and are a recurring motif in the notebooks. As already seen, Sekula often works with the valences of the terms he uses, and the anal or faecal motif is no exception. Sometimes 'shit' is an accusatory charge against the prevailing social system, but it could also be an identification with counter-capitalist or anti-idealist values, signalling an act of solidarity with the socially marginalised, the lowly; or an expression of a Rabelaisian scatology to affirm 'base' corporality.[34] Sekula recorded a found ditty:

> bathroom graffiti – L.A. Hilton 5 Feb 77
> here I sit and try to shit
> the boss outside is having a fit
> no time to waste
> no time to linger
> watch out ass here come the finger[35]

The anonymous worker-poet – maybe without realising – harked back to *Modern Times*, although Chaplin's temporary escape from a relentless production line to the restroom was handled more delicately as a

33 Ibid., 426.

34 Other examples include: a diagram of a shitting dummy from Harun Farocki's film *Leben – BRD* of 1990 (Sekula Papers, S.1.05:06 Fish Story, Notebook 2, July 1991–1992); in 1996 he records Peter Wollen's discussion of the Channel Tunnel ingesting UK passengers and excreting them in France, with reference to cinema and the endoscope: S.1.07:01 [Canadian Notes/Misc. Notes], June 1995–October 1996; a meeting with Panamanian environmental lawyer Felix Wing Solis of 26 July 2002 where Sekula notes of pollution and habitat degradation that 'shit runs downhill!!' (S.1.10:05 Notes and Interviews Panama #1, 2002); a discussion of Jeff Wall's *Morning Cleaning, Mies van der Rohe Pavilion, Barcelona* (1999), where he observes an 'anal-compulsion/informe' (S.1.11:01 Vienna/[Lottery of the Sea], 16 May 2003–2004, not dated 18 May 2003). Later examples likely refer, in part, to his experiences of hospital treatment: Sekula's Gut-o-rama plumbers' diagram (S.1.16:03 2011); his calligrammatic wordplay 'what flies . . . and what sinks/what smells . . . and what stinks', with sketch of a steaming turd (S.1.17:02 2012).

Sekula recalls an occasion in 2000 at a fundraiser on Santa Monica Pier for right-wing Democrats: the high heels of female delegates had to tread through the shit left by the police horses. Sekula in Hou Hanru, 'Allan Sekula and Bruno Serralongue', *Flash Art*, 14 November 2014, flash---art.com (first published as 'In Conversation with Bruno Serralongue and Allan Sekula', *Art Practical*, 15 February 2012).

35 Sekula Papers, S.1.02:05 [Misc. Notes 1977]. Sekula initially wrote '76' before overwriting a correction to '77'. This notebook, comprising a few quotations on pasted paper, would appear to have been compiled later.

cigarette break. What is remarkable is that this crude doggerel was carefully pasted into a notebook, inscribed in proper ink, in Sekula's finest hand, on heavy-gauge watercolour paper.[36]

As we have seen, the cut-through house in *Fish Story* exposes the bathroom to public view. Sanitation pipes and toilets are a focus for his essay on Michael Asher (1999), which works the idiom 'down to earth'.[37] These motifs also return us to political economy, and in Sekula's reading of Asher, the pipes ultimately transmute from mere utilitarian conveyors of bodily waste into flows of money. In *The Lottery of the Sea*, Sekula's camera dwells on faecal matter floating in a Barcelona hotel pool. His edit segues directly from the bobbing faecal matter to a shot of himself emerging from the water. It is not clear if it really is the same pool, but the edit is deliberate, and we are meant to read it as the same body of water – or, at least, to read a contiguous contamination. As he exits the pool, he holds his camera to his eye, pointing it directly towards the filming lens (and towards us as the viewers). The retail-hotel complex he is filming – part of The Forum at Diagonal Mar (thus picking up the Agora theme of the video work's opening) – is unwisely built near to the city's sewage plant and is subjected to wafting odours. In a long, slow pan of the cityscape, Sekula lingers on this proximity of privatised commercial luxury and social muck.

Sometimes the analysis drifts into psychoanalytic terms. In his 1989 essay 'Gay Bashing as an Art Form', Sekula points to the conservatives' homophobic culture war directed against the queer motifs in Robert Mapplethorpe's photographs. Sekula conjoins the economy and politics with the libidinal drives of psychoanalysis: 'conservatives project their own fears of both unfettered desire and an impotent economy onto gay and lesbian people'.[38] He makes impolite reference to the 'parsimonious

36 Sekula once told us an anecdote – and this is one to keep in mind, given the direction of intellectual travel – about an intemperate exchange with Marcuse at UCSD while debating the 'art' status of Martha Rosler's *Garage Sale*. Feeling frustrated and defensive, an inarticulate young Sekula resorted to expletives: 'What's all this fucking shit about the dialectic?' In response, Marcuse, who objected to sexual profanities, replied – and, in the retelling, Sekula mimicked the philosopher in cod-German accent – 'For you, my boy, zie dialektik comes between zie fuck und zie shit.' Something does not add up about this story and the timelines of Marcuse at UCSD (and Rosler has disputed the accuracy of Sekula's memory). Nonetheless, our point is that, true or not, Sekula's imagination held to the anecdote (which, incidentally, reprises the psychoanalytic angle of 'amphimixis'.

37 'Michael Asher – Down to Earth' (1999), *Art Isn't Fair*, 163–8.

38 'Gay Bashing as an Art Form' (1989), *Art Isn't Fair*, 137.

effort to control the orifices of government spending'.[39] The government's refusal to fund art such as Mapplethorpe's is positioned as anally retentive, as a reaction formation attempting to control a repressed wish.

Another striking example is Sekula's 'Foreword to *Manhole Covers*', an introduction he wrote to the photobook published in 1994 by Mimi Melnick and Robert A. Melnick.[40] Sekula discusses this project alongside the Melnicks' earlier *Manhole Covers of Los Angeles* (1974). Scaled to accommodate the typical width of human shoulders, the covers are access points to the city's drainage infrastructure for water and sewerage (and he nods to Duchamp's interest in 'American plumbing'). Sekula's initial purpose in this short text is to challenge the commonplace idea of Los Angeles as a world of surfaces, 'the myth of the depthless city'.[41] He especially has in mind the writing of Reyner Banham and the early work of Ed Ruscha, to which he suggests the Melnicks' earlier book is 'an unrecognized companion piece'.[42] Unsaid, but surely implicated, is Fredric Jameson's famous account of postmodernism, which asserts the increasing ascendancy of flat surfaces and depthlessness.[43] Sekula proposes four ways to re-envision Los Angeles based on a depth model: the tectonic instability of California; the city's figuring as psychically unstable and irrational (Nathanael West and *film noir*); novelistic attention to its sexual underworlds; and the rebellion of subaltern and racialised 'underclasses' in Watts in 1965. Highlighting an awareness of the problem posed, he acknowledges:

> These are different and incommensurate registers of depth, ranging from the geological to the social. One could argue that the recessionary early 1970s was a period, like the present, predisposed to a dystopian metaphoric slippage from one register to another.[44]

As we have seen in Pêcheux's account, metaphoric slippage between domains or levels – metalepses, where figures of speech from one

39 Ibid., 138.

40 Foreword to *Manhole Covers* by Mimi Melnick with photographs by Robert A. Melnick (1994), *Art Isn't Fair*, 149–50.

41 Ibid., 149.

42 Ibid.

43 Fredric Jameson, 'Postmodernism, or The Cultural Logic of Late Capitalism', *New Left Review* I: 146 (1984): 53–92; Mike Davis, 'Urban Renaissance and the Spirit of Postmodernism', *New Left Review* I: 151 (1985): 106–13.

44 Foreword to *Manhole Covers*, 150.

context transgress into others – is a key feature of the suturing of the subject in ideology.

The Melnicks' projects entailed a systematic exercise in cataloguing, but Sekula discerns the excessive preoccupation of the collector – and one growing ever 'madder'.[45] There is, he notes, 'a definite American surrealist edge to their deadpan scholarly obsession with these anthropomorphic cast iron disks that mark the entryways into the subterranean world of conduits, water mains, and sewage'.[46] The ostensible organised rationality of the projects cedes to irrational inclinations. This is not the pattern of *Dialectic of Enlightenment*; rather, for Sekula, the crazier aspects are what open new critical space. Approving of this 'surrealist' aspect – even the 'nervous sweat of the insatiable collector' – he amplifies his interpretation.[47] Sekula notes how the manhole covers have closed forms which both 'satisfy a certain organicist longing' and are similar to coins. Having established this analogy of sewage and money, he extends the line of thinking:

> manhole covers are the secret cousins of coins. If coins make the abstraction of commodity exchange seem concrete, manhole covers imitate coins at a level of much more material flows. They are the very image of the discrete ceremonial opening to the urban cloaca.[48]

The manhole covers take on other characteristics of money: they are simultaneously abstract and concrete; as with Marx's account of the commodity with its use value and exchange value, they have a dual character. They are the openings to the 'sewer' or 'drain'; the 'urban cloaca' is the city's equivalent of the excretory orifice in amphibians, reptiles and birds (and a few non-placental mammals), which is sometimes also used for scent-marking, for copulation ('cloacal kiss') and, in some sea turtles, for 'cloacal respiration' underwater. Sekula's description suggests that excremental flows are doubled with, or as, the circulation of money. Hands in exchange are very messy.

Sekula had addressed these themes in *Geography Lesson: Canadian Notes* (1986). The state capital Ottawa and the provincial mining town

45 Ibid. The Melnicks' projects linked to Ed Ruscha and Pop Art, but the Bechers seem closer in spirit. Sekula finds the Melnicks more 'modest' and 'naïve'.

46 Ibid.

47 Ibid.

48 Ibid. Cf. 'Between the Net and the Deep Blue Sea', 23. Metallic inks on *The Family of Man's* luxury cover are like neocolonial 'coinage' on a blue sea.

of Sudbury contrast the world of high finance with the activities of digging and furnace work. The abstract architectural spaces of the Bank of Canada meet the abstraction of the commodity.[49] Sekula here, in part, reprises Sohn-Rethel's account of mental and manual labour by counterposing 'brain' to 'the asshole of Canada':

> Realizing that all physiological metaphors are suspect, I'll propose a provisional anatomy of the Canadian body politic: The brain, in Ottawa, is worrying about its asshole, forgetting its asshole, thinking about warming and fattening its ass in the tropics. This brain could be American. But perhaps the asshole has a mind of its own.[50]

In a reversal of values, the architecture of the Bank of Canada in Ottawa is described both as 'retentive' and as a 'turd in a vitrine'. Ottawa and Sudbury are also related by the creation and distribution of wealth, and by the integration of financial capital with that of the extractive industries.[51] Although this is rarely acknowledged, the cerebrum depends on the anus. Sudbury's mines effectively shit metal-money. Sekula's visual play with the sign 'Big Nickel' – the name of a mine museum in Sudbury – provides one of the keys for establishing this connection to the state vaults, while simultaneously employing bathos. As he underscores, by definition, nickel as coinage is far from 'big'. Money is presented as both abstract, symbolic process and as physical, material production. It is a work concerned with two kinds of 'subterranean' space and two kinds of invisibility – and with the feigning, disguise, obscurity, displacement and secrecy in economic processes (the work turns on the 'disavowal' central to fetishism). Red fake leather sofas in the bank's rest area retain the circular bum imprints (and cigarette burns) of office staff who have returned to their terminals.[52] Corporate offices in Ottawa present themselves as at one with the landscape, as if to illustrate Barthes's claim that ideology naturalises history; banknotes bear landscape imagery; paintings by Group of Seven member A. Y. Jackson hang in the reception room of a uranium-mining company called 'Eldorado'; the walls on which they hang sport prominently grained wood. In an abandoned Sudbury mine, there are experiments with

49 'Globalism's Discontents and the Return of the Sea'. (Note how Sekula's 1999 lecture title plays on Freud's *Civilisation and Its Discontents*.)

50 *Geography Lesson: Canadian Notes*, 59.

51 Ibid.

52 'Globalism's Discontents and the Return of the Sea'.

underground plant cultivation, and even the office of the mining union's president has a framed picture by the 'Captain Ahab of Canadian painting' (Jackson) displayed on cheaper-looking wood panelling.[53] It is tempting to see the immensity of the landscapes painted as displaced versions of the financial sublime. In the imaginary geography sketched by Sekula, the pristine landscape and 'commercial society' are seemingly the products of invisible hands. In both, the First Nations are occluded – underscored by a photograph of a small statue from 1901 called *The Last Indian*, by Louis-Philippe Hébert (Sekula writes: Louis-Phillipe Herbert). There is a topological switch. In Ottawa, money is hidden in bank vaults beneath the ground, mythologised in the Bank's Currency Collection and overlaid with its Garden Court of staged 'nature'.[54] Meanwhile, in Sudbury – 'not a landscape' because 'defoliated by years of roasting nickel ore over open fires'[55] – ore is disgorged from underground, its slag photographed by Sekula. A road sign points simultaneously to a 'Scenic Lookout' and a 'Slag Pouring Site'. The slag heap chiasmically renders visible the hidden horde while figuring it as a pile of shit. One photograph shows bags of fertiliser waiting to be spread onto the plant beds of the Bank of Canada. While shit-as-compost can be seen as organically regenerative, Sekula's emphasis seems to offer us a double irony where muck has been supplanted by industrial products.

In popular idiom, shit (or its substitutes and metonyms) often expresses money or economy. The economy is sometimes said to be 'going down the pan' – that is, flushed down the toilet. There is also the common saying 'where there's muck, there's brass', which signals that there is money to be made by getting one's hands dirty – or, with a slightly different valence, that with effort dirt can be turned into (poor-person's) gold. Effectively, Sekula inverts the usual dynamic of this expression to suggest that where there is 'brass' (money or gold), we can find muck (labour). In this switch, there are obvious echoes of Marx – and probably also of Piero Manzoni's tinned *Merda d'artista* (1961) – but let us, instead, follow a descending pathway of psychoanalysis.

---

53 John O'Brian, 'Memory Flash Points', in *Geography Lesson: Canadian Notes*, 74–91 (84).

54 Sekula cites a Canadian friend speaking of the bank: 'It's nice to eat your lunch there in the garden in the winter, sitting above all the gold in Canada' (*Geography Lesson: Canadian Notes*, 62).

55 Ibid.

One point of reference for Sekula – in his bibliography for *Geography Lessons: Canadian Notes* – is Ernest Borneman's collection *The Psychoanalysis of Money*, which collected the key literature on money and its associated anal character.[56] In 1908, in the essay 'Character and Anal Eroticism', Freud wrote:

> Wherever archaic modes of thought have predominated or persist – in the ancient civilizations, in myths, fairy tales and superstitions, in unconscious thinking, in dreams and in neuroses – money is brought into the most intimate relationship with dirt. We know that the gold which the devil gives his paramours turns into excrement after his departure.[57]

Freud points to other cultural associations, past and present, involving 'identification of gold with faeces'.[58] He connects childhood anal-erogenous fascination with the character traits of parsimony (remember those conservatives railing against Mapplethorpe), obstinacy and obsessive tidiness. He discerns affinities between the seemingly distant complexes associated with the defecation of intestinal waste and the fascination with money.

Ferenczi expanded Freud's argument in his 1914 essay 'The Ontogenesis of the Interest in Money'.[59] His argument boils down to this: behind the money symbol lies the turd: gold is 'nothing other than odourless, dehydrated filth that has been made to shine'.[60] Building upon Freud's point, Ferenczi suggests that the repression of infant anal eroticism is sublimated as an obsession with money and hoarding, with

56 Ernest Borneman, *The Psychoanalysis of Money* (1973; New York: Urizen Books, 1976). Borneman was a Marxist activist, jazz critic, film director and producer, and sexologist. He rejected those psychoanalytic accounts that derived the nature of capitalism from the anal character, arguing that it is the conjuncture that matters: capitalism does not cause but amplifies the anal character and its relation to money (cf. 67–70). Sekula would also have approved of Borneman's opposition to the instrumentalisation of psychoanalysis in the US.

57 Sigmund Freud, 'Character and Anal Eroticism' (1908), in *On Sexuality*, vol. 7 (1905; Harmondsworth: Penguin, 1977), 209–15 (214).

58 Ibid. Freud cites the expression for a wealthy spendthrift *Dukatenscheisser* ('shitter of ducats'). Observe the fairy tale preserved by the Grimm brothers, 'The Wishing-Table, the Gold-Ass, and the Cudgel in the Sack', which includes a magical gold-shitting and -spitting donkey.

59 Sándor Ferenczi, 'The Ontogenesis of the Interest in Money' (1914), in *First Contributions to Psycho-Analysis* (1916; London: Karnac, 2002), 319–31.

60 Ibid., 327.

the activity of collecting and with aesthetic pleasure.[61] Children's early love of manipulating, smelling and tasting their own excrement (copraphilia and copraphagia) is progressively substituted by 'more hygienic' options as social prohibitions are learned: shit gives way to mud, to sand, to art materials; to collecting objects (pebbles, glass marbles, buttons, apple pips, 'primitive coins'); and, eventually, to gold or money.[62] There is an identification of faeces with gold and other money forms. Playground swaps are already 'an enthusiastic money exchange'; their collecting betrays the 'character of capitalism'.[63] The shit substitutes (rather like the money form itself in Marx's account of value) lose their intrinsic value and come to serve another purpose. Ferenczi also challenges the narrow 'economistic' understanding of capitalism, arguing that economists and sociologists have failed to take account of its 'libidinous and irrational' dynamic.[64] 'Capitalistic interest' in money responds not only to the reality principle (the realm of ego, the 'practical and utilitarian') but also to the pleasure principle and repressed anal eroticism.[65] While the interest in all forms of money (including paper) is implicated in this argument, gold holds a special place, given its lustre. Shine or sheen often figures in fetishism, but gold's attractive appearance reveals how the aesthetic is also implicated in the chain of distortions and substitutions. Fostered by the childhood enjoyment of shit-substitutes-as-art-materials – paint and clay, and their manipulation and moulding into new forms – Ferenczi insists that 'there can be no question that aesthetics in general has its principal root in repressed anal-eroticism'.[66]

As Kaja Silverman notes: 'according to Freud, the unconscious treats shit, money, gift, penis, and child as interchangeable terms. Capital has only tipped the balance in favor of the first of these terms.'[67] Silverman's account (in dialogue with Harun Farocki) is focused on anal substitutions in Godard's *Weekend* (1967). It involves responding to two prominent theorisations of the phallus as a 'despotic signifier' by Jean-Joseph

61 Ibid., 320.

62 Ibid., 326.

63 Ibid.

64 Ibid., 328, 326.

65 Ibid., 331, 326..

66 Ibid., 325.

67 Kaja Silverman and Harun Farocki, *Speaking about Godard* (New York: New York University Press, 1998), 90. The book consists of exchanges between Silverman and Farocki, but the arguments presented here are drawn from Silverman's role in the exchange.

Goux and by Guy Hocquenghem.[68] As Lacan famously wrote: the phallus is identified with 'the *name of the father*' that supports the 'symbolic function which, from the dawn of history, has identified his person with the figure of the law'.[69] Despite their differences, both Hocquenghem and Goux share the central idea that, in the words of the former, the phallus 'plays the same role in our society's sexuality as money does in the capitalist economy: the fetish, the true universal reference-point for all activity'.[70] In *Symbolic Economies: After Marx and Freud*, Goux positions the phallus as a universal equivalent in capitalist culture, part of an interchangeable set of transpositions: gold/father/phallus/language; the phallus and gold are both 'figurative standards'.[71] Beginning from a similar equation, and drawing on Deleuze and Guattari's *Anti-Oedipus*, Hocquenghem refuses 'Oedipal Imperialism', including Freud's oedipalisation of homosexuality. In *Homosexual Desire*, Hocquenghem argues for anal sexuality as a non-binary site for unravelling the phallocentric law of gender and, with it, other hierarchies of signification and value.[72] The anus, an organ without gender distinction, is a sexual 'commons' that is privatised by capital (and becomes a signifier for privatisation in general). In Hocquenghem, the structuring of politics, desire and representation around the sign of the anus points to a horizon beyond oedipalised gender relations.

Acknowledging Hocquenghem's intervention, while departing from his claim for utopian liberation through the sign of the anus, Silverman proposes that, rather than the phallus, the anus is 'the "truth" of late capitalism'; excrement, the counterpart of the universal equivalent.[73] The polymorphous character of late capitalism – which she calls 'Anal Capitalism' – integrates all flows of desire into the circuit of commodity cathexis ('repressive desublimation'). Where 'commodification reigns

---

68 Guy Hocquenghem, *Homosexual Desire* (1972; Durham, NC: Duke University Press, 1993), 95. Hocquenghem draws from Gilles Deleuze and Felix Guattari, *Anti-Oedipus: Capitalism and Schizophrenia* (1972; London: The Athlone Press, 2000).

69 Jacques Lacan, *Écrits: A Selection* (1966; London: Tavistock, 1977), 67.

70 Hocquenghem, *Homosexual Desire*, 95.

71 Jean-Joseph Goux, *Symbolic Economies: After Marx and Freud* (1973; Ithaca, NY: Cornell University Press, 1990), 112–21. Arguably, a third reference is Georges Bataille, *Visions of Excess: Selected Writings, 1927–1939* (Minneapolis, MN: University of Minnesota Press, 1984).

72 Hocquenghem, *Homosexual Desire*; *The Screwball Asses* (1973; Los Angeles, CA: Semiotext(e), 2010); and Bill Marshall, *Guy Hocquenghem: Theorising the Gay Nation* (London: Pluto, 1996).

73 Silverman and Farocki, *Speaking about Godard*, 90.

supreme', Silverman argues, the reign of the phallus (its 'erotic colonization') is displaced by the anus; and all forms of singularity (such as male/female) are replaced by shit.[74] According to Freud, unlike physiological needs, desire for a lost object cannot be satisfied.[75] Desire manifests through the partial drives where the propulsion of (unfulfilled) striving for the lost object is sublimated and finds enjoyment in moments of repetition, failure, misprision and metonymic slippage.[76] The drive revels in the excess or surplus of desire, and always leaves a supplement, enabling 'serial' consumption to recommence – with more packaged enjoyment, as commodities and commodity images momentarily plug the gap or hole in desire.[77] Silverman suggests that, in anal capitalism, 'the enjoyment of each new commodity' is increasingly brief and unfulfilling, passing quickly 'into the category of "shit"'.[78] In Godard's *Weekend*, the circuit of libidinal substitutions only stops with the drawn-out scene of a traffic jam, culminating in a 'cosmic scrap heap' of wrecked vehicles and strewn bodies.[79]

In 1998, Sekula jotted down in his notebook: 'darkroom/bathroom', '"notorious pleasure in seeing image appear"', 'Jones: love of tunnels', '"there would be no photography without the anus"', 'The anal stage of

74 Ibid., 111, 90.

75 See, for instance, Freud, 'Three Essays on Sexuality' (1905), in *On Sexuality* 33–169; 'Instincts and their Vicissitudes' (1915), in *On Metapsychology* (Harmondsworth: Penguin, 1991), 105–38.

76 For this account, see Slavoj Žižek, *The Ticklish Subject* (London: Verso, 2000). According to Jacques Lacan, Holbein's use of anamorphosis disrupts the 'transparency' of representation and makes the viewer conscious of their own gaze. In Lacan's essay, Holbein's anamorph exemplifies *objet petit a*: the unattainable object-cause of desire sought in the other (Lacan, 'Of the Gaze as *Objet Petit a*', *The Four Fundamental Concepts of Psychoanalysis* (1964; London: Penguin, 1994), 67–119). *Objet Petit a* is a retrospective illusion that masks the gap, an elusive paradox that, the moment it manifests, is already being lost. It is best understood not as an actual object that has been lost (although its substitutive processes might alight on objects) but as a supra-sensible reified one. Žizek refers to it as a 'formal frame of consistency' in *The Plague of Fantasies* (London: Verso, 1997), 39. *Objet Petit a* is, simultaneously, a surfeit of meaning and a lack at the core of the symbolic order into which infants are socialised by language, law and custom – all that remains of *das Ding* after the process of symbolisation (a process that shifts from breast, to anal gift-object, to genital castration and other metonymic displacements). Some readers take Lacan's discussion of Holbein's anamorph further as 'making aware', so that by seeing the resolved anamorph the viewer is explicitly put into the role of voyeur or Peeping Tom.

77 Kevin Floyd suggests that capitalism disassociates desire from the gendered body, producing a 'reification of sexual desire as such': *The Reification of Desire: Toward a Queer Marxism* (Minneapolis, MN: University of Minnesota Press, 2009), 46.

78 Silverman and Farocki, *Speaking about Godard*, 90.

79 Ibid., 111.

photography', 'documentary as a "stain"/Sekula – living dead'.[80] He had been in conversation with photographer Olivier Richon, one of his hosts on a trip to Europe. Richon's ideas were circulating at conferences, and developed for 'The Place of Darkness', one of his 'Three Essays on Photography'.[81] The exact formulations in Sekula's notebook do not appear in Richon's essay, but there are clear echoes. Richon pursued a comparison between camera lens and anus (the eye being a common analogy, the mouth less so). The 'diaphragm' controls the passage of light into the camera and depth of field.[82] Meanwhile, the darkroom was compared with the domestic bathroom (both spaces of privacy, of attentiveness to a process, and for creative production); indeed, bathrooms were often used by those without access to a darkroom for developing film. The faeces are a part of us that is externalised, making our own shit analogous to photography, 'a sign caused by its referent'.[83]

Richon's account follows the uptake of Freud not by Ferenczi in 1914, but by his contemporaries Lou Andreas-Salomé in 1915, Ernest Jones in 1918 and Karl Abraham in 1922. Richon compares this moment in the history of psychoanalysis with the photography of Blossfeldt, Atget and Sander, and with Eisenstein's films. He explores the education of the sphincter as a double apprenticeship in cleanliness and disgust; the ambivalence and morose 'sniffy' physiognomy of the anal character. Central again are the questions of value and creativity (artistic or intellectual) as sublimations of infant anality: the 'first production' being a 'template' for later aesthetic pleasures, where, for example, a soiled and smelly reality can be made over into a pristine and odourless image. Notably, Richon explores the being 'out of sight' – a theme shared with Sekula's account of maritime industries, bulk ores and so on.[84] And he picks up on the questions of time and rhetoric in Jones's work: his concern with the interplay of literal and figural, the role of hidden tunnels, reverse sides and

80 Sekula Papers, S.1.08:02 1998. In 'Walker Evans and the Police', Sekula discusses photography's 'adolescent stage'.

81 Olivier Richon, 'The Place of Darkness', in *Allegories* (London: Royal College of Art, 2000), 15–20.

82 Ferenczi, incidentally, described the linguistic gaps between the vowels and consonants – and specifically their impeded vocalisation in stuttering – in terms of the dilations of the sphincter. Amphimixing urethral and anal eroticisms, he conceives 'disturbances of ejaculation as a kind of genital stuttering' (Ferenczi, *Thalassa*, 9).

83 Richon, 'The Place of Darkness', 16.

84 Ibid., 18.

opposites; and his suggestion that the 'excretory product' primed 'the concept of time' (specifically the value attributed by humans to a slower expenditure).[85]

The excremental, we should recall, is always also regenerative – nutrients added from a cycle of decomposition are a prelude to new life. Sekula's photograph 'Fertilizer, Garden Court, Bank of Canada' from *Canadian Notes* (1987) gestures to this process. But this is not merely to recoup an affirmative and organic dialectic. The humus, of course, is not simply organic matter, but a product of the chemical industry (in this case, supplied by Swiss firm Speedel Pharma AG). In Sekula's sequence depicting workers tending to the bank's atrium planting, we are presented with a gardener's descent, via a trapdoor, into an underworld (and connecting with tropes of vaults and mines). Framed by the image's perspectival recession lines, a large stone 'sphincter-eye-coin' is given central prominence. Once mistaken by Europeans for a millstone, and reminding many today of abstract sculpture, this is the bank's prized 'Yap stone' or *rai/fei*, a traditional form of money used on the Island of Yap in Micronesia. Origin stories of these prized quartz-sparkling stones recount a legend of fishermen substituting *rai* for the fish they failed to catch for their king. In another account, the *rai*'s 'full moon' shape was said to have been preceded by other forms: fish, lizards or turtles. They also appear in another origin genre: those narrated, with primitivising assumptions, by political economy on the genesis of money and the magic of value. Was Sekula aware of the film *His Majesty O'Keefe* (dir. Byron Haskin, 1954) – based on the 1950 novel by Lawrence Klingman and Gerald Green – with Burt Lancaster playing the role of David Dean O'Keefe, settler and colonial adventurer who was shipwrecked on Yap in 1871? We have here another Robinsonade. Sekula's sequence points to the fantasy of economic relations arising spontaneously and mysteriously as if from nature: 'the Ur-token of an emerging culture of exchange'.[86] The Bank's atrium of lush foliage conjures a tropical environment. As we have seen, throughout *Canadian Notes* he finds capitalist extractivism constantly being overlaid with naturalising tropes that occlude history, whether through planting or painting. Organic and inorganic; above and below; shit and money; eye and anus; life and death: all are combined in Sekula's image work as a practice of condensation.

85 Jones cited by Richon, ibid., 16.
86 *Geography Lesson: Canadian Notes*, 61.

The psychoanalytic dimension of Sekula's work adds fresh perspectives on the well-established association of art with money and social privilege. Of course, it is not unusual to highlight what Clement Greenberg called art's 'umbilical cord of gold', and Sekula was a constant critic of the commodification of art. Given the widespread redevelopment of ports, where some of the most well-known contemporary museums have been located once the ports have been displaced, the concern with art and money threads through many of his maritime projects: the Liverpool wharfs transformed into Tate (*Freeway to China*); the Guggenheim Bilbao (*TITANIC's wake*, *The Forgotten Space*). The link between art and money is also central to *Gala* (2005), a short video focusing on the labour of catering and hospitality workers underpinning the grand opening of the Gehry-designed Walt Disney Concert Hall in Los Angeles. It is the topic of his final project, *Art Isn't Fair* (2012), which addressed the art industry. Interviewed in 2006, shortly after he shot the footage at Miami's new satellite of the for-profit Art Basel, he spoke of the art world's 'reliance on the new pseudo-agora of the art fair'.[87] As with the oceanic, Sekula draws on psychoanalysis to put anal vision to work in order to explore the culture and politics of capitalism.

SECTION 2: CRITICAL IRREALISM

Recalling Sekula's formulation on the return of the sea, let us note its fuller context: 'The sea returns, often in gothic guise, remembered and forgotten at the same time, always linked to death, but in a strangely disembodied way.'[88] He insists on the connectedness of seemingly disparate phenomena revisiting late modernity, and doing so 'in both romantic and gothic guise'.[89] We have already discussed *Fish Story*'s relation to the 'triple funeral' in Chapter 2. In 'Between the Net and the Deep Blue Sea', there are more themes on death: those that perished when the iceberg or megastorm struck in Hollywood fictionalisations, such as *Titanic* and *The Perfect Storm*, and, by implication, the historical events upon which these were based. It is suggested as the immanent

87 Sekula, in Ruchel-Stockmans, 'Interview with Allan Sekula', 150. He also uses the phase 'pseudo-agora' in the opening to *The Lottery of the Sea*, although here to signal the market per se.

88 'Between the Net and the Deep Blue Sea', 18.

89 Ibid., 14.

outcome for Winslow Homer's desperate fishermen; as the displacement of Bilbao's traditional industries; as eco-disaster and economic death in Baja California.

Also resurrected (so to speak) is Marx's penchant for gothic figurations. Capital as a blood-sucking vampire; phantasms of the market haunting their creators: spectres, alchemists, werewolves, vampires, gravediggers and hobgoblins all occur in his writing.[90] Notably, Sekula casts Bill Gates as 'the Disembodied Industrialist'.[91] Describing *Fish Story*'s 'Middle Passage', he calls the *Happy Ending* incident as 'odd, macabre, Disney-esque', Sekula refers to the 'ghostly boiler suit' and remarks how 'every vessel is a ghost ship'.[92] Elsewhere, he connects the art fair to 'necrophilia', 'mausoleums and the 'séance': 'The auctioneers [sic] gavel', he writes, 'is just another form of spirit-rapping'.[93] The shipping container, as we have seen, is a 'coffin' – literally, the metal chamber in which migrant workers might suffocate. We also have the Marxist category of 'dead labour' embodied in commodities, externalised from their creative agents and acting back on them. These levels of referentiality are brought together rhetorically when Sekula presents the cargo container as 'the very coffin of remote labor power'.[94] The subtitle to Sekula's *Camera Austria* essay, 'The Coffin Learns to Dance', directly alludes to the séance and 'table-turning' in *Capital* – the discussion of 'the fetishism which attaches itself to the products of labour as soon as they are produced as commodities'.[95] Here, Marx speaks to the 'mystical character' or 'mysterious character of the commodity': the way it 'transcends sensuousness' and generates 'grotesque ideas far more wonderful than if it were to begin dancing of its own free will'; its 'magic and

90 Franco Moretti, 'The Dialectic of Fear' (1978), in *Signs Taken for Wonders: On the Sociology of Literary Forms* (London: Verso, 1983), 83–108; Chris Baldick, *In Frankenstein's Shadow: Myth, Monstrosity, and Nineteenth-Century Writing* (Oxford: Clarendon, 1987); David McNally, *Monsters of the Market: Zombies, Vampires and Global Capitalism* (Leiden: Brill, 2011); Warwick Research Collective, *Combined and Uneven Development: Towards a New Theory of World-Literature* (Liverpool: Liverpool University Press, 2015).

91 'Between the Net and the Deep Blue Sea', 15.

92 'Globalism's Discontents and the Return of the Sea'.

93 Sekula, in Ruchel-Stockmans, 'Interview with Allan Sekula', 150.

94 'On *Fish Story*', 55.

95 Karl Marx, *Capital: I* (1967; Harmondsworth: Penguin, 1976), 165. 'Table-turning' is used in the first English translation by Samuel Moore and Edward Aveling; in Fowkes's 1976 translation, this is 'dancing of its own free will'. In 'The Traffic Photographs' and 'Dismal Science', Sekula references from the Ben Fowkes translation. His book collection included editions from Vintage (Fowkes), International Publishers and its imprint New World Paperbacks (both Moore and Aveling).

necromancy'; the 'fantastic form of a relation between things'; its 'enigmatic character' and appearance as a 'social hieroglyphic'.[96]

The gothic and supernatural – but also the weird, fantastic, sci-fi, speculative, uncanny, magic, numinous – are all representational modes that are 'un-real', 'non-real' or sometimes 'surreal'. Better, we think, is the term 'irreal'; better still, to imagine Sekula's practice through the lens of 'critical irrealism'. Coined in 2001 by Michael Löwy, 'critical irrealism' was meant as an ironic provocation to the 'adepts of the realist canon'.[97] Löwy's aim was to broaden out from the limited model of aesthetic realism bequeathed by Lukács. Cannot irrealist tendencies, Löwy asks, be just as capable of 'criticality' as 'critical realism'? Allegorical art, supernatural tales, 'gothic novels, fairy tales, fantastic stories, oneiric narratives, utopian or dystopian novels, surrealist art': cannot these be vehicles for social critique, which 'help us understand and transform reality'?[98]

There is very little 'irrealism' that is not also in large part 'realist' in classic terms: fidelity to scenic details and credible descriptions, for example, often accompany with an incredible narrative, or vice versa.[99] The divide between 'real' and 'irreal' can be blurred, and Löwy specifically mentions Kafka in this regard. Lukács, Löwy argues, advanced a rather inflexible account of 'realism', opposing it to modernism's 'anti-realism'. Here, the distinction between real and irreal has yet another dimension: for Lukács, in modernist 'anti-realist' writing, the 'truthful reflection of reality' was diminished by its 'exalting [of] man's subjectivity, at the expense of the objective reality of his environment'.[100] Löwy counter-argues that subjective perspectives can 'illuminate social reality from the inside'.[101] As far as he is concerned, 'critical irrealism' should be understood not as an antithesis to 'critical realism' but rather as its complement; the two modes simply employ different methods to

96 Marx, *Capital: I*, 163–9.

97 Michael Löwy, 'The Current of Critical Irrealism: "A Moonlit Enchanted Night"', in *Adventures in Realism*, ed. Matthew Beaumont (Oxford: Blackwell, 2007), 193–206 (206). Cf. Löwy and Robert Sayre, *Romanticism Against the Tide of Modernity* (Durham, NC: Duke University Press, 2001). See also Löwy's earlier work on Romantic anti-capitalism: *Georg Lukács – From Romanticism to Bolshevism* (London: New Left Books, 1979).

98 Löwy, 'Critical Irrealism', 194, 206.

99 Ibid., 202.

100 Lukács, 'The Ideology of Modernism' (1957), in *The Meaning of Contemporary Realism* (London: Merlin, 1963), 17–46 (23, 24). Discussed by Löwy, 'Critical Irrealism', 195.

101 Löwy, 'Critical Irrealism', 196. Recall Hayden White's paralleling of debates on history film and the historical novel (Chapter 2).

critically illuminate the world.[102] He discerns a shared commitment – an 'elective affinity' – to a 'social, political, and philosophical outlook', which he traces to the revolutionary wings of anti-capitalist Romanticism, and continuing through symbolism and surrealism.[103] Löwy distinguishes between a revolutionary-Romantic nostalgia and a conservative nostalgia for premodern life; the former's purpose being – and, here, there is a reprise of the left melancholy discussed in Chapter 2 – to make 'a *detour* through the past to a utopian future'.[104]

Löwy's insistence on the relational complementarity of critical realism and critical irrealism is important, but there remain some limitations to his articulation – especially as we consider Sekula's practice. The first limitation concerns how Löwy establishes 'critical realism', which is understood through the reflective model – realism as 'reflection on reality'. However, Sekula's conception of 'critical realism', as we saw earlier, is conceived on a processual and praxial research programme. He draws on the less dogmatic aspects of Lukács's account and his version of critical realism is more shaped by Brecht and the philosophy advanced by Roy Bhaskar and his colleagues. The second limitation is Löwy's over-equating of the 'everyday' with the bourgeois quotidian – that is, as boring convention, banality and so on: ideas drawn from Romanticism and, later, associated with the Russian-formalist turn against *byt*. Once again, this conception of the everyday determines how Löwy shapes the countertendency: the dreams of the critical-irrealist imagination echo Surrealism's 'marvellous', with its 're-enchantment' of the lowly. This conception parts ways with Sekula's approach to the everyday, which is closer to Henri Lefebvre's critique: 'The [Surrealist's] marvellous is supposed to turn everyday life inside out, to discover its other, infinitely more interesting side.'[105] But, Lefebvre argued, the everyday could be construed as marvellous only because the things or processes envisaged in this way lay outside the lived experience of bourgeois viewers. This magical thinking amounted to exoticisms based on race and social class.

This distinction is particularly significant in the context of photography. Surrealism in photography became most influential not so much for explicitly 'Surrealist effects' but rather for its legacy in documentary

102 'It describes the absence of realism rather than an opposition to it' (ibid., 195).

103 Ibid., 197, 196.

104 Ibid., 197.

105 Henri Lefebvre, *Critique of Everyday Life*, Vol. 1 (1947, 1958; London: Verso, 1997), 110–18 (115).

street photography. Stretching from Brassaï and Mass Observation onwards, this lineage – another form of bourgeois social tourism – celebrates a poetics of the ordinary (the 'marvellous'). It appeals for the commonplace to be transfigured to a higher status. Often cloaking transcendental reverie in a low-plane vision, it favours personal lyricism over the social. It should be evident that we are here in the presence of one of those bourgeois antinomies criticised by Sekula. Re-enchantment is not what Sekula discerns as he looks at photographic culture. Sekula's own camera often picks up on everyday items, yet his practice '*within* concrete life situations'[106] – although at once a realism and a carefully crafted rhetorical representation – does not mobilise 're-enchantment'. If anything, it is the opposite. Insofar as there is a 'magic' recovered, it is of a specific type. The lowly in Sekula is often empowered with plebeian wit and guile – wryness, quips, scatology and gallows humour.

Fish Story's 'Middle Passage' introduces the personal effects at a workstation onboard *Sea-Land Quality*. Ear protectors belonging to an engine-room wiper are isolated for our attention (#37). Presented side-on, we see just one earpiece, a viewpoint that defamiliarises: without clear visual referents or context, the ear-cup initially appears as a shiny black egg-like form; it is an occasion where the caption, not the image, identifies what we see. There is a reason for choosing this viewpoint: the protectors have been subject to *détournement*: stuck to the cup is a Dymo label with the words 'I CAN NOT BE FIRED SLAVES ARE SOLD'. The tape actively declares the object's synecdochic contiguity with the recalcitrant worker, while highlighting that belongings often serve as tropes for those who own them. The following photograph in the sequence shows a model Klingon standing on the control console (#38).[107] Snarling, the *Star Trek* character Gowron wields his war club menacingly. In one sense, the two photographs are 'found objects'. But, in Sekula's edit, they connect, and not simply by dint of being incidental curios from the same location. This character was a member of a militaristic caste whose society was based on enslaved labour, so the two photographs highlight social power and the feeling of being compelled to work. Strictly speaking, the engine-room wiper was not enslaved;

106 *Photography Against the Grain*, x (Sekula's emphasis). (MACK edition, xii).

107 Klingons were at first the villainous antagonists of the Federation but became its ally in *The Next Generation* (1987–1994). Sekula's journey on *Sea-Land Quality* occurred during the final series.

their statement is a metaphoric association of two forms of labour 'unfreedom': one that is both objective and subjective, and one that is only subjective (and aiming to voice the perceived harm caused by, and resistance to, a captain's or company's control). The individual gesture also escalates in scale (certainly in Sekula's employment, and maybe also for the engine-room wiper): in the wider economy of seafaring, there can be fine lines between formally 'free' wage labour and contracts that amount to modern indenture. Even without the contractual abuse that has become commonplace in contemporary global shipping, and simply due to geographical isolation, a seafarer is rarely able to walk out of a job mid-voyage.

Sekula represents the Klingon from the level of the console top, and its white surface fills the lower parts of the photograph, receding sharply away from us. This worm's-eye viewpoint exaggerates the figurine's size and status. Nevertheless, we immediately grasp the ironies of this photographic amplification of both his height and power. The very narrow depth of field reveals that the Klingon shares focal range with (and thus immediate proximity to) an audio-jack; from head to toe, he is about three or four jacks in stature. The Klingon's aggressive gesture is ineffective, even comic; his club-wielding turned to futile flailing. More precisely, the model reads as an image of authority debunked. (Arguably, it is also a nod to the comedic aspect intended for Gowron.) We intuit the Klingon's diminution from the cheap plastic manufacture: the schematic detailing of his uniform, the crude painting of his facial features, beard and hair, and the unconvincing articulation of his joints. To connect legs to body, and perhaps to allow for repositioning of his limbs, he has been inadvertently endowed with a codpiece – once a European fashion symbol of virility, but also a target for ribald derision since Rabelais and Montaigne. His outer left foot failing to make firm contact with the console, and his stance barely balanced, he also looks to be about to trip over the thin semi-transparent audio wire. We already saw how figurines of various sorts play roles in *The Lottery of the Sea* (Terminator, Jason, anonymous women terrorised by villainous aggressors, Santa, shop mannequins) – triggering 'uncanniness' but also serving important deictic gestures, allegorically pointing beyond themselves.

Another lineage of the everyday – a low-plane 'uncanniness' – can be found where an anthropomorphic vision appears in Sekula's work: with non-human animals or with inanimate objects; sometimes more implicit, at other times direct. In *Fish Story*, there is a remarkable degree of association of the human body with plumbing and tubes: three pipe fitters work on a tuna boat in San Diego (#4, #5); a fireman in Koreatown has a hose, as do the workers cleaning the Wilmington chemical spill (#14, #15). Industrial activities often 'cyborg-ise' human and machine. They do so with the tools they hold (and which often name their trade) and also with the conduits of electricity, gases or fluids that drive these tools: welders in Gdansk (#22); the man grinding and woman cutting steel in Hyundai's shipyard (#47, #49, #50); the drilling for samples of coral stone in Veracruz (#75, #76). As we saw earlier, the chief mate checks containers, visually set in a blurred distance with the focus on the tubes conveying refrigerants or power (#29). One step removed, on the floor next to the hose used to test the lifeboats, a pair of overalls – a body-sub – is like the sloughed-off skin of a reptile (#30). Across the project, conduits, ducts, pipes and tubes – details normally taken as incidental – very much come to the fore, threatening to take on lives of their own. Making photographs in the confined spaces of engine rooms determines their emphatic presence, but only in part: Sekula mobilises the contingencies of the context to highlight an imbrication of workers with metal, plastic and rubber ducts. A mere setting is transformed into an active *mise-en-scène*. The tuna-boat pipe fitters, for example, and the third assistant engineer at work (#31), are striking for the way space almost flattens into an intertwining surface pattern of the sort we might associate with designs by William Morris.[108]

Earlier, we discussed the opening photographs from *Fish Story* on the Staten Island Ferry (#1, #2). The binocular machine resembles an abstracted face or mask: a head, two eyes and eyebrows, two ears, pock-marked skin, chin, neck. The device figures a moment of 'seeing as'. In *Ship of Fools*, there is a triptych of photographs with four pieces of technical equipment. Here, the *Global Mariner*'s calibration dials and pipework 'look like' four weird characters, a point emphasised by their repetition and by the triptych's title, 'Engine Room Eyes'. The large scale of the 'eyes' (or, at one step removed, 'glasses') make them into the 'baby faces' favoured by cartoons, manga, toys, puppets or the 'cuter' characters in sci-fi films, such as ET. These images allude to the machine-human (or machine-enhanced human) analogy prominent in modernist photography – for example, Franz Roh's *Foto-Auge* (1929); Dziga Vertov's 'I am kino-eye, I am a mechanical eye' (1923); Christopher

108 Caroline Arscott, *William Morris and Edward Burne-Jones: Interlacings* (New Haven, CT: Yale University Press, 2008).

Isherwood's 'I am a camera with its shutter open . . .' (1939). Sekula toys with the discourse of machine–human parallels. There is certainly a simple delight involved. As well as 'looking like' eyes, all entail optics – or optical translations of pressure. Moreover, the 'Engine Room Eyes' are part of – and monitor – the ship's 'innards': like an endoscope, they 'look into' and probe the 'bowels' of the vessel. Sekula mobilises these classic tropes of twentieth-century visual representation not simply as citations, but to highlight social mystification, criticising the 'futuristic' fantasies of the machine. These images also suggest the 'ethnographic objects' that fascinated Western avant-garde artists in the early twentieth century and their exoticising, primitivising and archaicising of African and Oceanic art. These images may share the qualities of surprise or destabilisation to which the 'marvellous' aspired; but here the 'irreal' undertakes rather different work. Sekula's approach is not about 'convulsive beauty'. If there are ambiguous resonances, these are not there to be valued for the sake of the indefinite or elusive but to sharpen our recognition of social contradictions. If – in his photographic sequences and films, or for the assembly of small objects in *The Dockers' Museum* – Sekula forms a *Wunderkammer*, it is not to serve as a repository of the weird and arcane, to be admired by privileged voyeurs at once 'objectively' and 'magically'. Rather, it is an effort to amplify low-plane insights and to reveal absurdities in capital's social actuality. These anthropomorphs can also suggest the fetishes of so-called advanced civilisation, or what Soweto Kinch calls 'White Juju'.[109] This gambit is not unlike Marx's returning the charge of 'fetishism' to the colonisers, who were considerably more 'fetishistic' than the pre-Columbian cultures accused of being attached to idols. The Nahua, recall, were shocked by how newly arrived Europeans obsessed over golden objects; later, Western economists similarly attributed to money a mystical moving power.[110]

We will return to further examples of Sekula's critical irrealism shortly. First, we want to consider the extensions to Löwy's account

109 *White JuJu* is Soweto Kinch's collaboration with the London Symphony Orchestra (released 2022 from a live recording in 2021) – a musical homage to Black British history and Black Lives Matter. Kinch says that while 'juju' is typically imagined in terms of an African woman holding a chicken, it is visible as the statues, gargoyles, heraldry and allegorical figures of British architecture.

110 Marx, *Grundrisse: Foundations of the Critique of Political Economy (Rough Draft)* (1857; Harmondsworth: Penguin, 1973), 239. Marx initially drew his conception of fetishism from Charles de Brosses' *The Cult of Fetish Goods* (1760).

made by the Warwick Research Collective (WReC). Like Löwy, WReC also focus on literary examples, and criticise the opposition of 'ideal-type' realism and modernism.[111] Here, however, 'realism' is firmly distinguished from any trace of passive objectivism.[112] Instead, it is understood as a shapeshifter. It is 'an always mutating mode' (Joseph Cleary) – an understanding that is akin to Jakobson's dynamic and relational account – and is allied with Frantz Fanon's 'fighting realism'.[113] This conception feels very proximate to Sekula. Moreover, for WReC, critical irrealism is 'a refinement of [critical realism], under the specific circumstances of combined and uneven development'.[114]

Temporally, 'modernity' is not taken by WReC as a chronological category to be contrasted with 'tradition' or the 'archaic';[115] spatially, it is not simply a force of Westernisation emanating from an established 'core'. Instead, modernity is something reimagined whenever and wherever social transformations occur; whenever and wherever the cultural and experiential shocks of capitalist violence are encountered.[116] Too often, a rather fixed and ideal model of 'capitalism' (with its own internal stages) threads through left accounts of modernity – and especially those that have been important for thinking about art and aesthetics:

111 WReC, Combined and Uneven Development. WReC's project is an intervention into the debates on 'world literature' and postcolonial theory, the aim being to produce a literary comparativism revived with materialist underpinnings. Their account draws on Immanuel Wallerstein's world-system's theory, Fredric Jameson's 'singular modernity', and the writings of Franco Moretti, Pascale Casanova, and Roberto Schwarz. In WReC's study, 'world-literature' and 'world-system' (with hyphens) point to capitalism's sustained production of inequalities, to be distinguished from the non-hyphenated 'world literature', which simply signals geographical breadth or diversity (WReC, *Combined and Uneven Development*, 8, 12). Other relevant works include: *Marxism, Modernity and Postcolonial Studies*, eds Crystal Bartolovich and Neil Lazarus (Cambridge: Cambridge University Press, 2002): this includes Lazarus's important essay 'The Fetish of the West in Postcolonial Studies', 43–64; Lazarus, *The Postcolonial Unconscious* (Cambridge: Cambridge University Press, 2011); Benita Parry, *Postcolonial Studies: A Materialist Critique* (London: Routledge, 2004).

112 WReC, *Combined and Uneven Development*, 78 (following Schwarz and Swanson).

113 Cleary and Fanon, cited WReC, *Combined and Uneven Development*, 77. We might recall how the *locus classicus* of Lukács's critical realism, Balzac, was prone to include the most bizarre character transformations: man become demon, and the like.

114 WReC, *Combined and Uneven Development*, 70. On Sekula's engagement with unevenness and anomaly, see Day and Edwards, 'Differential Time and Aesthetic Form', in *Cultures of Uneven and Combined Development*, eds James Christie and Nesrin Değirmencioğlu (Leiden: Brill, 2019), 253–88.

115 WReC, *Combined and Uneven Development*, 66–7.

116 Ibid., 15.

Lukács, the Frankfurt School, Kracauer and Marcuse (for whom a 'technological veil' lies at the heart of capitalist domination).[117] Critical Theory and Cultural Studies sometimes hold to a schematised and metropolitan-centric understanding, which merges Max Weber's theme of bureaucratic rationality with ideas about the 'total commodification' of the lifeworld. Despite the important insights developed, *the account of the commodity form* at the heart of the argument is vague and based on a temporal vision of inevitability. This emphasis has proved remarkably resilient in the face of the challenge to teleologies of progress and Westernised assumptions from both postcolonial and ecological theories. Such ideas continue to underpin even some of the best accounts of capitalism and culture.[118] Societal actualities are messier than most theories allow.

Yet, if the generalities of ideal-model capitalism (or ideal-model history) are one tendency, another swings towards particularisation with 'multiple modernities'.[119] Debates can stall in these opposing camps, but what matters is how (to pick up the terms) the 'singular' and the 'multiple' (and their interrelation) are conceived – how to think the differential registers of integrative and dispersive trends. Uneven and combined development (UCD) is one way of doing this, but other intellectual currents – such as the Spinozism of post-Althusserian thought, or the anti-historicism of neo-Benjaminian philosophy – offer rich insights that could be worked through; all are

---

117 Marcuse, *One-Dimensional Man*, 41.

118 In *A Singular Modernity*, Fredric Jameson argued that modernism might best be understood as 'a mode in which [the] transitional economic structure of incomplete capitalism can be registered and identified as such'. Fredric Jameson, *A Singular Modernity: Essay on the Ontology of the Present* (London: Verso, 2002), 142. With the modernist culture of the early twentieth century in mind, Jameson notes how intellectuals and writers lived in two worlds simultaneously. In this account, 'modernism' is the outcome of the collision of older and newer social formations. While Jameson here acknowledges the importance of unevenness, the implication of his statement still suggests that the world progressively moves towards 'completed' capitalism. Indeed, this is a recurring theme in Jameson's periodisation, where cultural forms are presented as symptoms of successive stages of capitalism. Our problem is not Jameson's taste for periodisation, but the resulting closed totalities that do not allow for alternative practices or longer continuities. The locus classicus (or an issue running through his work) is *Postmodernism: Or, the Cultural Logic of Late Capitalism* (London: Verso, 1992).

119 Arguably, Marx's logical-historical distinction is elaborated by Dipesh Chakrabarty as 'History 1' (logical) and 'History 2' (actual lived situations). Dipesh Chakrabarty, *Provincializing Europe: Postcolonial Thought and Historical Difference* (Boston, MA: Princeton University Press, 2007). Many subsequent commentators in postcolonial theory, and sometimes Chakrabarty, too, have privileged 'History 2' as the only valid approach.

conjunctural conceptions predicated on ideas of plural or discordant temporalities.[120]

Even in the late twentieth century, critical debates based on the ideal model often elided distinctions between theoretical categories and historical actualities.[121] Marx explained how his analysis in *Capital* commenced as 'only an approximation' – a 'theoretical simplification' that assumed 'that the laws of the capitalist mode of production develop in their pure form' – developing greater concretion by the third volume, which considers how 'practical frictions' and forms 'adulterated by survivals' produce 'significant local differences'.[122] Jairus Banaji's work is especially significant for his keen attention both to Marx's analytic categories and to the historical details of differing regimes of labour exploitation. In his account, 'modes of production' should not be conceptually confused with the specific 'forms of exploitation' (such as capitalism associated with free-wage labour, or feudalism with peasant).[123] Capital

---

120 Louis Althusser and Étienne Balibar, *Reading Capital* (1965; London: New Left Books, 1978); Etienne Balibar and Warren Montag, *Spinoza and Politics* (1985; London: Verso, 2008); Pierre Macherey, *In a Materialist Way: Selected Essays* (London: Verso, 1998); Antonio Negri, *The Savage Anomaly: The Power of Spinoza's Metaphysics and Politics* (1981; Minneapolis, MN: University of Minnesota Press, 2000); and Negri, *Spinoza for Our Time: Politics and Postmodernity* (2010; New York: Columbia University Press, 2013); Vittorio Morfino, *Plural Temporality: Transindividuality and the Aleatory Between Spinoza and Althusser* (Leiden: Brill, 2014); Jason Read, *The Politics of Transindividuality* (Leiden: Brill, 2015); *The Government of Time: Theories of Plural Temporality in the Marxist Tradition*, eds Vittorio Morfino and Peter Thomas (Leiden: Brill, 2018). Walter Benjamin, 'On the Concept of History', in *Selected Writings Volume 4, 1938–1940* (1940; Cambridge, MA: The Belknap Press, 2003), 389–400. Ernst Bloch also recognised the importance of things being 'out of time', in 'Non-Contemporaneity and Obligation to its Dialectic', in *Heritage of Our Times* (1935; Cambridge: Polity Press, 1991). Recent works building on Benjamin and Bloch include: Michael Löwy, *Fire Alarm: Reading Walter Benjamin's 'On the Concept of History'* (2001; London: Verso, 2016); Daniel Bensaïd, *Marx for Our Times: Adventures and Misadventures of a Critique* (1995; London: Verso, 2002); Massimiliano Tomba, *Marx's Temporalities* (Leiden: Brill, 2013); and Enzo Traverso, *Left-Wing Melancholia: Marxism, History, and Memory* (New York: Columbia University Press, 2016). See also Peter Osborne, *The Politics of Time: Modernity and Avant-Garde* (London: Verso, 1995).

121 For this argument, see: Harry Harootunian, *Marx After Marx: History and Time in the Expansion of Capitalism* (New York: Columbia University Press, 2015).

122 Karl Marx, *Capital: III* (1894; Harmondsworth: Penguin, 1981), 275

123 In particular, see Jairus Banaji, 'Trajectories of Accumulation or "Transitions" to Capitalism?' in *Theory as History: Essays on Modes of Production and Exploitation* (Leiden: Brill, 2010), 333–48; and *A Brief History of Commercial Capitalism* (Chicago, IL: Haymarket, 2020); Andrea Komlosy, *Work: The Last 1,000 Years* (London: Verso, 2018); Andrew B. Liu, *Tea War: A History of Capitalism in China and India* (New Haven, CT: Yale University Press, 2020); Sven Beckert, *Empire of Cotton: A New History of Global Capitalism*

subordinates forms of labour associated with 'non-capitalist' modes of production alongside 'newer' ones, in ever-morphing combinations.[124] What were once taken to be dying features, old 'remainders', 'residues' or 'survivals' of earlier societies, are integrated into contemporary capital circuits – and integrated not as adjunct inflections to capitalism but as forms essential to it. In the light of these accounts, capitalism's 'integrations' of 'residual' and 'modern' forms must be grasped in terms of the ongoing brutality of its social synchronising. Unevennesses may be inherited, but, through the value form, these can be made over into the structural social configurations of the present. The violence simultaneously fuses and fractures, both synchronising and discording.

In contrast to an understanding of globalisation as a process of homogenisation, as discussed earlier, critical irrealism draws attention to the aesthetic registrations of capitalism's systemic production and integration of unevenness.[125] As we learn from Roberto Schwarz (a key figure for WReC), something strange occurs when the European realist novel with its celebration of bourgeois individualism encounters the social conditions and slave economy of nineteenth-century Brazil.[126] The mix of imaginary and factual elements is a literary response to the all-too-real 'irrealities' of capitalist-colonial, -postcolonial and -neocolonial experiences.[127] The abstractions of capital can elude representation – which is why Marx complemented his detailed economic evidence with gothic tropes.[128] The fantastic is required to make fuller sense of statistics, sociological facts and political reports. As emphasised by Isaak Rubin, in his early theory of the value form, Marx's account of the fetishism of commodities is not a mere dialectical adornment or 'interesting literary-cultural digression' tacked onto 'serious' economic analysis; rather, it is 'a propaedeutic to political economy',

(London: Penguin, 2015); Marcel van der Linden, *Workers of the World: Essays Towards a Global Labour History* (Leiden: Brill, 2011). There are important differences among these thinkers, but they all reject teleologies of progress that identify industrial capitalism and consumerism as the 'end of history'.

124 There is a debate to be had about 'formal' and 'real' subsumption as fixed phases – or whether that received picture should be rethought, just as many have rethought 'so-called primitive accumulation' as an ongoing process of 'accumulation by dispossession' continuing to this day.

125 WReC, *Combined and Uneven Development*, 10–14. This is compared with Ernst Bloch's notion of the 'simultaneity of the nonsimultaneous'.

126 Roberto Schwarz, *Misplaced Ideas: Essays on Brazilian Culture* (London: Verso, 1992); *Two Girls and Other Essays* (London: Verso, 2012).

127 WReC, *Combined and Uneven Development*, 70

128 Ibid., 75–7.

articulating the full exemplification of the theory of value.[129] Similarly, the tropes and figures employed are more than entertaining embellishments; they provide an artistic mode through which to capture the value form and the mystifications of capitalist social relations. Gothic, fantasy, magic realism, 'varieties of numinous narration',[130] 'modernist' and 'expressionist' tropes: these become increasingly important – indeed, they are necessary complements to 'naturalistic' or 'realist' ones. To reread 'modernist' literature through the lens of combined and uneven development is, WReC suggests, to discern its 'realism' (and the inverted commas in the last few sentences indicate the limitations and calcification of these categorial conventions).[131] Largely unnoticed, bizarre and irreal elements pulse through Sekula's imagination and – far from being superficial flourishes – are essential to understanding the mutating presentations of the social system, even simply to describing its inherent contortions. Echoing his point about 'broken or attenuated metonymy', Sekula argues that, in the stretched spatialised production of neoliberal globalisation:

> Labor is no longer proximate or contiguous – that is, no longer accessible through the realist rhetorical device of metonymy – except through some great imaginative geographical leap, the uncanny ability to wear Nike sneakers and jump in the imagination to an assembly line in Indonesia.[132]

Like the (often metaphoric) 'leaps', irrealist strategies become increasingly prominent in his work as a way to grasp the systemic integrations that occur across this 'uncanny' gap. This work of imagination is central: imagining the industrial accident next door to the Bilbao Guggenheim (as we saw); imagining, in *Freeway to China*, connections between Los Angeles and Liverpool.[133]

Sekula's debt to Critical Theory in 'Photography Between Labour and Capital' – with its focus on Taylorism and large-scale industry – might seem to hold to an ideal-type capitalism. Titling a work *Freeway to*

129 Rubin, *Essays on Marx's Theory of Value* (1928; Detroit, MI: Black & Red, 1972), 5, 6.

130 WReC, *Combined and Uneven Development*, 57.

131 Ibid., 67.

132 Allan Sekula in Debra Risberg, 'Imaginary Economies: An Interview with Allan Sekula', in Allan Sekula, *Dismal Science: Photo Works 1972–1996* (Normal, IL: University Galleries, 1999), 235–51 (248).

133 'Globalism's Discontents and the Return of the Sea'.

China might also suggest a direction of travel, although the word 'freeway' also skewers neoliberal rhetoric (and in capitalism, there is no such thing as a 'free way'). That would, however, focus on just one aspect of Sekula's work, which invariably proves to be more complex. As seen already, his attention to unemployment and reproductive labour in his earlier projects is pertinent to recent debates on precarity. An attention to uneven labour practices in the capitalist world system gained traction in Sekula's work as he developed his imaginative geographies – above all in *Geography Lesson: Canadian Notes* and *Fish Story*. His *Shipwreck and Workers* (2005–7) offers a variety of forms of labour, including small craft production, forestry, grape harvesting and, notably, childbirth. *The Forgotten Space* (2010, with Noël Burch) draws attention to Filipina domestic workers in Hong Kong, whose employment can approach indenture; and to Mexican American truckers, whose pitiful income is concealed by their formal status as 'independent' entrepreneurs.

It is quite routine for photographers to expose the 'uneven' character of modern capitalism – for example, via the established motif of wealth versus poverty. There are many images that set an informal low-lying shantytown against a distant conglomeration of vertical high-rises, exploiting the lens's capacity for visual compression – riffs on classic photographs by Andreas Feininger and Walker Evans. The point we underscore is twofold. First, 'unevenness' is readily pictured. Second – and key – although Sekula's work utilises the comparative trope, it also aspires to capture the world system's *combined* character. Thus, as we saw with *Geography Lesson: Canadian Notes*, Ottawa and Sudbury do not just contrast; they are also mutual articulations of one another, as well as of US capital. We will soon encounter similar entwinements centred on Mexico.

Sekula juxtaposes images of places and people across regions, borders or oceans, assembling incidents from different moments and locations into larger configurations. His practice of realism – a critical realism – is attuned to the challenges and contradictions presented by the global economy.[134] Photography's descriptive power allowed him to record these spaces as socially constituted sites: to explore the way places are ideologically and economically located within wider circuits. In this way he drew on social documentary's established tropes of capturing

134 André Bazin, *What Is Cinema*, Vol. 1 (1967; Berkeley, CA: University of California Press, 2005), 23–52.

'spaces of more idiosyncratic psychic investment, of actions and materialized memories'.[135] The terraqueous economy, with its international mediations and alternative connectivity – Marx's 'Circulation as the first totality' – condenses or synchronises the uneven relations between dispersed nodes and temporal contradictions of the global economy. The sea's centrality for global supply chains holds in play radically divergent experiences: high-tech terminals combine with older-style docks; robot trucks one day, the next, repainting the ship by dangling over the side on ropes with paintbrush in hand; the systemic nature of near-indentured conditions for seafarers; workers finding themselves as unpaid hostages on vessels abandoned by their owners, their distant families carrying the financial can.[136] (Perhaps the internationalised labour markets in construction, agricultural or domestic work could compare, although they do not share the figural density of imaginative maritime geography. Indeed, as highlighted by *The Forgotten Space*, families are often dispersed among these geographically far-flung sectors.)

Anamorphosis, Anachronism

Crucially, WReC not only consider the fantastic themes addressed by writers but extend their attention to literary forms. An 'aesthetics of anamorphosis' – of distortion, deformation, disfigurement, warping, re-shaping, trans-forming – characterises UCD.[137] The most famous anamorph in the visual arts is Hans Holbein the Younger's panel *The Ambassadors* (c.1533). In front of two sixteenth-century diplomats, with their array of global goods and devices for colonial exploration, a weird monochrome diagonal splodge hovers just above the floor. Only from a certain oblique angle of viewing does the mark foreshorten to reveal itself as a skull and thus as a memento mori. As the viewer moves in relation to the physical canvas, the image of the skull alters between its distorted and undistorted shapes. As does, of course, the rest of

135 'Imaginary Economies: An Interview with Allan Sekula', 238.

136 Abandoned Seafarer Map: abandonedseafarermap.cargo.site (updated quarterly: Eliza Ader, Jacob Bolton, Miriam Matthiessen). From 2000 to early 2022, 500 cases of these 'floating prisons' were reported to the ILO alone (indicating just the tip of the iceberg). The authors describe abandonment as 'routine' and a 'systemic issue', exacerbated by FOC, and based on the owners' 'calculated economic decision'.

137 WReC, *Combined and Uneven Development*, 72. From the Greek *ana*: 'back, again' + *morphe*: 'shape, form'.

Holbein's portrait of the two men – but this representation is more conventionalised in our encounters with art, so we readily take those 'distortions' in our stride: we do not even think about them. As Lacan noted, the anamorphic skull interrupts naturalised expectations and suggests a shift in perspective or doubling of vision.[138]

Sekula's attention to the fantastic and the weird does not mean that his photographs assume the type of obvious distortions of, say, André Kertész, Bill Brandt or Lee Friedlander – work often understood to be in a post-'surreal' vein, and in which photographs alighted on odd adjacencies, unusual angles, warped reflections or exaggeratedly stretched forms. Sekula takes what could be understood as an 'expanded' approach to distortion and anamorphosis, finding them as characteristics of capitalist culture, revealing them through tropes, or through the relations between text and image. 'Surrealist' or 'gothic' features help dramatise worldly matters and horrors, but they also help simply to describe them.[139] Notably, Sekula's sensitisation to social forms – recall his attention to the value form – shares WReC's consideration of form as 'forms of capitalisation'.[140]

Critical-irrealist distortions occur at the levels of *both* 'combination'–'amalgamation' *and* 'separation'–'dislocation'–'disjunction' – or, using Freudian terms, 'condensation' *and* 'displacement'. The fractured, incongruous and juxtaposed alert us to radical unevennesses. These juxtapositions can, at the same time, make us aware of comparisons, setting off concatenations and metonymic chains. Meanwhile, amalgamative tendencies can entail '"accordianising" or "telescoping"' (to use WReC's terms), expanding and compressing, zooming outwards or inwards, taking the long view or pulling close distant objects.[141] Space can be 'twisted', to wrap together multiple dimensions. Working across image sequences, and between these and the written (or spoken) prose,

138 Jacques Lacan, 'Of the Gaze as *Objet Petit a*', in *The Four Fundamental Concepts of Psycho-analysis* (1964; London: Penguin, 1994), 67–119 (79-90 for the section on anamorphosis).

139 In this regard, Alejo Carpentier's idea of *lo real maravillosa* ('the real marvellous', as opposed to the imaginary marvellous) has some interesting parallels, emphasising at once the fantastic existent in actuality and its 'rigorous documentation'. Alejo Carpentier, 'Prologue to The Kingdom of This World' (1949), *Review: Literature and Arts of the Americas* 26:47 (1993): 28–32 (31). *El reino de este mundo* concerns the Haitian Revolution. It is intriguing to compare Carpentier's and Lefebvre's criticisms of European surrealism's 'marvellous'.

140 WReC, *Combined and Uneven Development*, 69.

141 Ibid., 17, cf. ibid., 64, discussing Roberto Schwarz.

Sekula's work entails such 'telescoping', 'accordianising', 'twisting' and 'torquing'; highlighting the influence of unseen forces; bringing into adjacency radically contrasting elements or experiences; construing 'discrepant encounters, alienation effects, surreal cross-linkages, unidentified freakish objects, unlikely likenesses'.[142] Catachreses can register such dislocations, and have proven an important strategy for postcolonial criticism. By deliberately misusing the terms of the oppressors – appropriating, displacing and recoding their existing concept metaphors – the postcolonial writer captures the ethical and political ambivalence felt towards a colonial discourse (their being both *of* and *outside*).[143]

If, taken in this expanded sense, anamorphosis tends to emphasise spatial distortion (Holbein's *vanitas* notwithstanding), then anachronism highlights temporal distortions. The maritime chronotope invariably brings anachronism into play and Sekula recognises it as a source of tropes for obsolescence or nostalgia. 'Culturally, the sea becomes a vast reservoir of anachronisms',[144] he writes, later underscoring that it is 'as if the sea were indeed a bottomless reservoir of well-preserved anachronisms'.[145] In 'On *Fish Story*', he suggests that 'the maritime world is made visible only in its pastness', with 'assorted mercantilist reveries on the maritime past'; 'the problem becomes one of rescueing [sic] the maritime world from its undeserved reputation for anachronism'.[146] Echoing Thompson, Sekula alights on and rescues those 'anachronisms' that are typically dismissed by cultural adjudicators as obsolete and irrelevant. However, this defensive response to the charge of anachronism still risks preserving the negative valences of the original dismissal.

---

142 Ibid., 17.

143 Ibid., 70–3. Catachresis is formally defined as the transference of a figure from one semantic arena to another, as in 'the arm of a chair'. It is seen as the use or abuse of metaphor (intentional or unintentional). Since Quintilian, some argue that it occurs when no proper term exists (whereas metaphor, in contrast, substitutes where there is already a proper term). Catachresis's strategic displacements share some features with the discussion of chiasmus in Chapter 3. Gayatri Chakravorty Spivak has made it central to decolonial and deconstructive thought, employing catachresis to describe the deconstructive move of 'reversing, displacing, and seizing the apparatus of value-coding' ('Poststructuralism, Marginality, Postcoloniality, and Value', in *Literary Theory Today*, eds Peter Collier and Helga Geyer-Ryan (Bloomington, IN: Indiana, 1990), 219–244 (228). Catachresis is employed extensively in Spivak, *Outside in the Teaching Machine* (Abingdon and New York: Routledge, 1993).

144 'Dismal Science', 51.

145 Ibid., 106.

146 'On *Fish Story*', 55.

Anachronism proves to be much more than that for Sekula. As we saw when we looked at 'rust' in Chapter 3, Sekula's counterargument is stronger, using a chiasmatic structure to criticise the mainstream discourse and to assert the centrality of rust for contemporary working phenomena. There are other anachronisms that he enlists for their critical leverage: 'So perhaps to go forward, we must take several steps backward and recover abandoned paths.'[147] Time can be 'torqued' to achieve additional power and 'to reactivate archaic and residual forms';[148] disaggregated and re-constellated (as with the dialectical image), compressed and expanded – for example, by using a specific location to bridge different historical periods. Sekula's comparisons and collisions between images, and between image and text, entail the active construction of anachronistic relations.

Sekula's irrealism frequently works with figurations of the body – although, as emphasised in Chapter 2, this is not the body as affirmation of skill, or as the privileged site of immediacy or 'matter'. Rather, the body is always subject to, mediated by and materialised through the forces of capitalist abstraction and value, and the negative aspects of a labour theory of culture. Catachreses are frequently body-based, and the back has served Sekula as both synecdoche and catachresis. This is prominent in *Sugar Gang (Santos)*, the photographs made in the Brazilian port and added to the *Ship of Fools* cycle in 2010. This sequence focuses on the loading of sacks onto a ship, showing the continuation of forms of dock work that started well before the 'logistics revolution'. Using what was known as the *nova sistema* (introduced in the mid-twentieth century and involving trucks and winches), a team on one of the old docks transfers sacks of sugar from a flatbed vehicle; in a ship's hold, another man distributes them. Manifested quite starkly here is another exploration of the uneven but integrated character of the modern world system. Despite all the celebrated modernisation projects (containerisation and piped liquid bulk), Santos trades – and expects to continue to trade – with those ports that are unable to accommodate the deep draughts required for container vessels, and this condition requires the loading of holds by crane and hand. *Ship of Fools* is typically co-exhibited with *The Dockers' Museum*, Sekula's collection of maritime-themed objects and images – many sourced via eBay – which are displayed on tables, on

147 'On *Fish Story*', 50.

148 WReC, *Combined and Uneven Development*, 72.

plinths or in vitrines. *The Dockers' Museum* contains several images of historical Santos. A run of eight photographs from an old album, possibly anthropological, show the huts and canoes of a fishing community on a Santos beach from the years prior to the port's expansion (with captions such as 'Native Grass Huts, Santos' and 'Native Dug-Outs, Santos'). An engraving based on a late-nineteenth-century photograph by Marc Ferrez that depicts ships at anchor before the quays were built. A postcard from c.1908 of a team of men holding coffee sacks on their shoulders, standing on the same dockside as that which Sekula photographed; one of them – probably the celebrated 'Jacinto' – demonstrates his record-breaking ability to carry five sacks at once. Picking up the theme, a Toby jug is smothered by a pile of mini coffee sacks. The postcard would have been produced commercially as a souvenir for those passing through Santos, often as migrant labour. Meanwhile, the loading of bananas onto a Swedish vessel in 1914 appears in a stereoscopic photograph for the Keystone View Company for their 'Tour of the World', one from a set of 1,200. The explicit posing of the dockers for camera in the 'Jacinto' postcard is echoed by the exaggeratedly sensual gestus of 'dancing dockers' in a production still for *The Thrill of Brazil*, a 1946 film musical by Homer Van Pelt. These Brazilian-themed images – traversing varied social functions of photography (anthropological and topographical documents; touristic or memorial; fantasised entertainment) – intermingle with those from other locations, primarily Antwerp, but also Newcastle and Hong Kong. Black-and-white ethnographic photographs – from Palestine (undated), Morocco (undated), Haiti (1966) – show women carrying heavy loads on their heads. Toys, lapel badges, grotesque objects, eroticised figurines and other objects abound.

The photographs of *Ship of Fools* usually take the lead, but sometimes, as exhibited in a Lisbon suburb in 2013, the prioritisation was reversed. Here, the backbone could be said to be the axis around which the Lisbon exhibition turned, as a catachretic 'spine' holding together 'a book'.[149] Of the few photographs included, one was of the single Santos docker loading a ship's hold with sugar sacks. Sekula's camera looks

149 We have thus far pressed the physical characteristics of the 'back', but it is important to recall – as Sekula often emphasised – that this work task is also a complex mental work of planning, considering weight distribution and a foresight of how this will be impacted by the staged unloading schedules. See David Wellman, *The Union Makes Us Strong: Radical Unionism on the San Francisco Waterfront* (Cambridge: Cambridge University Press, 1995).

downwards into the cargo storage area. Seen from behind, the worker is set against the arrangement of sacks. At first glance, it appears as an exemplary image of masculine strength – at once in the traditions of social realism's affirmation of the toiling body and the eroticisation of the male form (from neoclassical sculpture to Mapplethorpe). Yet, while carrying these initial suggestions, the image develops different registers – both internal to the photograph and externally in its relation to the objects of *The Dockers' Museum*. In the photograph, the man's spine is doubled by the sacks being winched by rope, the latter 'looking like' a vertebral column. Externally, and crossing sight lines in Lisbon, the photograph links to a chiropractor's model backbone, suggesting the negative image of physical damage and vulnerability. A row of (odorous) salt cod was also included – a nod to the Portuguese culinary classic and the historical staple of its colonial fleets, but also forming a visual metaphor: as sails, as crucifixions, as rigor mortis or simply as muscular stiffness. Also nearby, in *The Dockers' Museum*, an old black-and-white postcard-sized photograph of a seal in a zoo or aquarium was placed alongside a postcard from c.1906 of Meunier's famous nineteenth-century sculpture *Débardeur du port d'Anvers* (1890; sometimes known as *The Docker*). An analogy is made between the animal's slick wet pelt and the specialist work hood worn by the docker. The port worker 'looks like' the animal – and, historically, workers who donned such apparel were dubbed 'seals' (again suggesting the mixing of human and animal). Both stevedore and animal temporarily pause from their labours and sway their vertebrae in an effort to release tension; both appear to be slippery; both echo the other backbones in the exhibit.

A projective-imaginative method sometimes emerges in Sekula's own readings of photographs and other cultural items. We already saw how – in the essay 'An Eternal Esthetics of Laborious Gestures' (1997/2014) – Sekula debunks the mystifying discourse surrounding an early daguerreotype, by interpreting a blurred smudge – the registration of a shoeshine boy – as an elision of the labour–capital relation. Technically, this is the realm of allegoresis – an allegorical interpretation of a historical object or text where no allegory was intended. Sekula's approach is more playful and ironic, his social critique ('against the grain' of the ideology presented) generating a moment in which mere description (or attentiveness to a contingent detail in a photograph) can become revelatory. In the same essay, Sekula discerns an obsession with showing the hand or artisanal work in the photographic tradition, by way of a compensation for its unauthored, machine-produced, mindless, servile status. Reworking

Marx's metaphors, he suggests that this obsession with the hand is evidence of photography's 'zombie realism'.[150] The compensatory attention to hands or gloves can take bizarre turns – some imagery of handling plutonium or nuclear bombs manifests 'the crypto-surrealist attitude of an apocalyptic and gothic view of science', where 'the instruments of science themselves take on gothic characteristics'.[151] At a less excessive level, he discusses images of working hands – photographs by Gjon Mili and Russell Lee in *The Family of Man* – observing the 'mythic dehistoricization and naturalization of work' that establishes a sort of inverted temporality in which homesteading appears more current or eternal than factory work.[152] The point, which is drawn from Barthes, is that rather than a conception of 'an eternal esthetics of laborious gestures', those gestures must be historicised as 'the personification of abstract labor'.[153]

This projective-imaginative reading again plays a role in 'Between the Net and the Deep Blue Sea'. Once more addressing Steichen's *The Family of Man*, Sekula alights on a photograph by Pat English of – so he says – a London crowd attending the coronation of Queen Elizabeth II in 1953.[154] Sekula enlarges a tiny detail of the throng, which highlights a homemade periscope – a device enabling one invisible spectator to gain a better view of the distant parade.

The photograph shows an array of white faces, prompting Sekula to argue that diasporic experience is evaded, both in this image and by the larger ensemble of *The Family of Man*. He underscores the colonial underpinnings of the United Kingdom and the postwar migrations from the British Commonwealth to answer the labour shortages in the

150 'An Eternal Esthetics of Laborious Gestures', 18 (*Art Isn't Fair*, 154).

151 Ibid., 19 (155).

152 Ibid., 20 (156). (Sekula's essay title is taken from Barthes's 'The Great Family of Man'.) In his own photographic projects, Sekula has often focused on the human hand to indicate a negative version of the 'labour theory of culture' – rather than simply affirming skill and craft, he emphasises strains and injuries. In *Shipwreck and Workers*, Sekula includes a panel board with an image of Constantin Meunier's sculpture *Puddler* (1893), annotated with arrows pointing to body parts and indicating the range of financial compensations for industrial injuries. This montage had originally appeared in the work of labour activist Crystal Eastman in 1910. Crystal Eastman, *Work-Accidents and the Law* (New York: Charities Publication Committee, 1910). Eastman's work was part of the six-volume *The Pittsburgh Survey*, edited by Paul Underwood Kellogg (and to which Lewis Hine also contributed). Sekula juxtaposed a photograph of Alberto Giacometti's bronze *Hand* (1947) surrounded by a cloud of similar arrows, but without any financial quantification.

153 'An Eternal Esthetics of Laborious Gestures', 20 (156).

154 Sekula says the photograph was used for the endpapers for the catalogue's luxury edition.

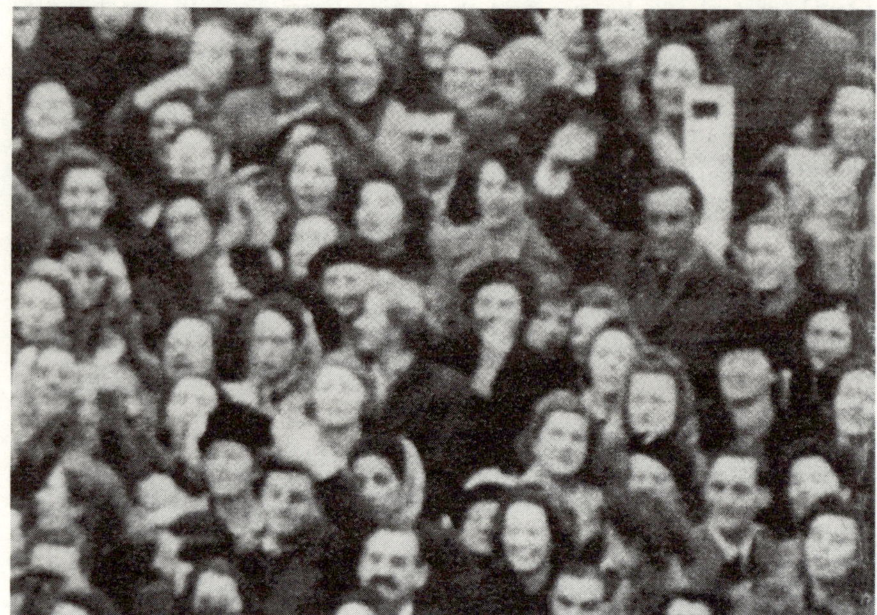

Figure 9: Detail enlarged by Sekula from photograph by Pat English

empire's metropole. He imagines an alternative to the ethnically homogeneous visages: beneath the surface of this '*sea of humanity*', straining to catch a 'submarine view' of the just-crowned Elizabeth, he visualises a child gazing through the amateur optical apparatus.[155] What if, Sekula wonders, this child had recently disembarked from the *Empire Windrush*?

It turns out that Sekula made an error, believing English's photograph to depict the street crowds attending the coronation of Queen Elizabeth in the summer of 1953. It dates from 1947: not her coronation, but her wedding to Philip Mountbatten, which took place seven months before the arrival of HMT *Empire Windrush* at Tilbury Docks in June 1948.[156] Sekula's liking for the slippery potentials of allusive connections and metalepsis got the better of him. This temporal materiality is interesting not only in itself, but also because of the context of Sekula's discussion: Steichen's exhibition had 'timeless' ambitions. Yet Sekula's mistake – his slip on his slips – remains more than just a research error: it nonetheless

155 'Between the Net and the Deep Blue Sea', 23 (Sekula's emphasis).

156 Sekula's error was drawn to our attention by Sally Stein. Sekula also mistakenly calls the ship 'HMS' *Empire Windrush* rather than 'HMT' *Empire Windrush*; the ship was attributed varying titles in historical sources even after its renaming by the British. There could also have been a confusion with the naval vessel HMS *Windrush*.

gives insights into his processes of critical thought and imaginative creativity. It shows how he uses detail, defamiliarisation and reversal to recast this terrestrial scene from the streets of London in terms of marine imagery. He counters the royal celebration with an anti-colonial vision and, in doing so, re-establishes the interconnectedness of the colonised and imperial centre. It is almost impossible not to drift on the imaginative flow and connect Sekula's 'submarine child' to the postcolonial interpretations and adaptations of *The Tempest* from Aimé Césaire onwards: shipwreck, colonisation, magic, enslavement, the desire for freedom; Caliban's misshapen and grotesque form that mixes human with fish (or animal).[157]

Sekula's use of photographic details for imaginative allegoresis might also be a riposte to Barthes's *punctum* in *Camera Lucida*, rescuing it from its acritical and narrowly subjectivised employments. What if we reject the privatised ruminations that routinely characterise the appeals to the *punctum*, along with their concomitant denigration of the *studium*? What if, he seems to suggest, we unleash a differently politicised subjectivity, one countering the worldview of capitalist extraction and desirous of traversing those many 'metaphoric registers'? The political is not merely a topic to be written about but is integrated into the figural patterning of Sekula's 'fantastic' reading. Even as they drift from their moorings, with the skein of associations sometimes breaking from the literal facts before us, his figurations always intersect with political interpretation. Sekula was keenly aware of semiotic motility – which is not to say that the unstable ('unmoored' or 'wilder') aspects of his allusions were always deliberately conjured or staged.

Fish Story's *'True Cross': Take 2*

Recall the old fort in Veracruz from *Fish Story*. Its fabric of coral stone was being damaged by the passage of time and, especially, by the dredging for the neighbouring container terminal. Conservators were trying to regenerate coral stone artificially, by passing electricity through seawater to precipitate calcified material. The first section of the accompanying essay ends by addressing their efforts – and on an irrealistic dental note: 'the science-fiction experiment of a team of

157 Caliban is described by Prospero as 'not honour'd with a human shape' (Act 1, Scene 2) and 'misshapen knave' (Act 5, Scene 1); and by Trinculo as 'a strange fish' (Act 2, Scene 2).

Frankenstein periodontists. The gum disease of the future eats away at the teeth of the past.' The figure conjured here 'en-weirds' the rest of the picture sequence. The drilling for coral samples takes on an entirely fresh aspect in light of this metaphor (#75, #76). The port surveyor's careful visual inspection through his theodolite mutates into an inspection of a mouth (#73, #74). Shipping containers even start to resemble dentures, some regular and aligned, others crooked (#72). The sand heaving against the barrier of metal boxes is 'gum-like' (#78). In the final image, the coral sample sits on a tray like an extracted tooth (#82).

Having prompted the dental references, the second part of the essay opens with the metaphor of blood. Sekula specifically highlights this as a rhetorical manoeuvre. (His writing for 'True Cross' is both a meditation on and an exercise in rhetoric.) The Zapatista Army's Subcomandante Marcos uses the loss of blood from the body to describe the economic exploitation of the state of Chiapas: the region is 'bleeding' resources and commodities; 'a thousand-some teeth' of capital have bitten its throat. The earlier dental motif now slides into the 'vampiric' incisors associated with capitalist violence. Blood is not only the 'lifeblood' of Chiapas (its wealth and resources); 'blood' also serves, Sekula suggests, as the Zapatistas' common measure, their currency or universal equivalent. Moreover, the Zapatista statement is, Sekula says, itself a twist on the modality of travel brochures, as he himself foregrounds, emulating that same voice: 'Borrowing the mock-touristic rhetorical style of the Zapatistas, suppose we stop at Salina Cruz . . .'. The words transport us from the Gulf of Mexico to the Pacific (and from there to yet other places), but key is the commencement of a play on the word 'Salina'. It is the east-coast port, Salina Cruz – 'salty cross' or 'saltmarsh cross' – the major 'bleeding' point for the resources of Chiapas. In addition, it is the name of Mexico's president from 1988 to 1994. The very first thing Sekula says about President Salinas is that he was 'the cardiologist responsible since 1988 for improving Mexico's circulatory health'. This further loads the corporeal metaphor and does so ironically: Salinas was never a medic; he was an economist. Again, the economic is figured through the corporeal: capital circulation is treated as blood circulation; the president is metaphorised as a specialist in the workings of its pump. Salinas's policies were central to neoliberal 'modernisation'. He coauthored the North American Free Trade Agreement (NAFTA) and ushered in a new age of port development. The tropes in play – bleeding, veins, circulation, heart – return us to literal facts of neoliberal capital circuits. In Sekula's prose, the 'cardiologist' comment masquerades as a passing aside. (And how many readers have taken it to be literal rather than figural, assuming Salinas to have been a former doctor?) But it does vital associative work: high consumption of sodium (*sal*) raises blood pressure and the risk of heart disease. The evocation of salinity also refers us back to the eroding coral walls of Veracruz's fort and its 'salty colonial dungeons'. Salt here is also a temporal agent: as the seawater gradually leaches through the old structure, the moment of Hernán Cortés belongs in the present.

The relationship between Sekula's image and text work is not one-way; the text does not necessarily restrain any semiotic ambivalence in the photographs. Indeed, as we have just seen (and saw earlier), the writing can have the very opposite effect, unleashing figural resonances from the images. Recall also Sekula's photograph of the monument to the heroes of 21 April 1914, when US forces occupied the city and the seven-month Battle of Veracruz began (#72). (Coincidentally, Cortés had landed on the Culúa/Ulúa reef that very day, 395 years earlier.) The memorial Sekula photographed no longer exists. (Following exhumation of the heroes' remains, a century after the invasion, the bronze statues and their plinths were incorporated into the Centinala de la Patria, on the corner of the Malecón, a stone's throw away from the demolished monument.) The monument, inaugurated in 1979, was located outside the 1950s-built Pemex tower (Petróleos Mexicanos, originally the Banco de México). Its structure comprised an open-sided square into which was set a semi-circular marble wall embracing a raised plaza, approached by a flight of shallow steps. Around the curved wall were arranged the plinthed statues of the city's defenders: Manuel Azueta (with machine gun), José Azueta (standing halfway along the curve) and Virgilio Uribe. Earlier we noted there is a gap between what Sekula photographed and what he described in his accompanying short essay, the latter effectively deprioritising this monument. Here, we point to a different text–image disjunction. The caption tells us what the monument commemorated and where it was. The photograph, though, shows more. Sekula faces the monument side-on, looking towards the city with his back to the harbour. (The previous photograph looks in the opposite direction, from a nearby standpoint: beyond a tugboat, we look across the water to the cranes of the modern industrial port and to the colonial fort.) Sekula's image of the monument incorporates three significant buildings: the Pemex; the neoclassical tower of the Faro Venustiano Carranza; and the Hotel

Emporio (which, like the Pemex, belonged to the developments of the 1950s). The Faro's tower rises behind (and visually between) the Azueta father and son – a landmark building from the comprehensive modernisation of the port undertaken from 1902 to 1910, during the presidency of Porfirio Díaz. Yet, the building is now named for Venustiano Carranza, who opposed first Díaz's regime and then Huerta's right-wing coup of 1913, before becoming the first president after the Mexican Revolution (1910–17). He then came into conflict with other forces of the Revolution, such as Pancho Villa and Emiliano Zapata (who he had assassinated). There are several historical layers, economic and political, as well as revolutionary ambivalences, built into this scene.

As we noted earlier, when Sekula visited Veracruz, landscaping work was in progress on the Pemex gardens: the photograph shows that some of the trees were wrapped for protection and temporary fences steered pedestrians away from the lawns. The 'panels' of these rickety fences are made of sugar sacks (and identifiable are the enterprises of Santa Rosalía de la Chontalpa in Tabasco, to the south of Veracruz, and Ingenio 'El Molino' in Tepic, in the west-coast state of Nayarit). Much could be said of Mexico's sugar industry, but suffice to observe that its labourers were central in the militancy and armed struggle of the Revolution; that many of the sugar haciendas were expropriated, some to be managed co-operatively, some run as alliances between state-owned mills and peasant growers. The post-Revolution social arrangements were ended with Salinas's neoliberalisation from 1988 and entrenched by NAFTA. The *ingenios* and the *ejido* lands that were at the heart of the Zapatistas' uprising were privatised. A few notes, appropriate to Sekula's radar for political and historical ironies, seem pertinent: the 'privatisation' was based on loans to, not investment from private capital; NAFTA advantaged US corn syrup over Mexican sugar and many Mexican mills had to be bailed out by the state in 2001. Mexico's dietary reliance on sugar-fuelled soft drinks and junk food grew rapidly under NAFTA, paralleled by an accelerating public health crisis in obesity, diabetes and tooth decay. The metaphorical 'cardiologist' and 'orthodontists' of Sekula's 'True Cross' return. The interventions of the 'cardiologist' led to a demand for actual medical intervention on a national scale. The container-dwelling 'nomads' – to whom are devoted three images and a passage in the short essay – make a living by selling colas to port workers. One of the containers has the Pepsi logo and among the array of belongings on the ground outside the vendor's temporary home are stacked crates of sugary soda. The informal barrier constructed near the monument can appear (like the shipping containers earlier) to be another set of dentures.

Dead Letter Office *(1997–8)*

Sekula imagined *Dead Letter Office* as an extension to his chapter on Veracruz for *Fish Story*.[158] The title derived from Melville's *Bartleby*, suggesting failed circuits of communication – more broken metonyms (and an experience that is the source of Bartleby's truculence). This relatively modest project of nineteen photographs, made between August 1996 and June 1997, was commissioned for the InSITE97 triennial as one of several artistic reflections on the Mexican–US border, and Sekula insisted on exhibiting in Tijuana.[159] The geopolitical boundary or frontier is another major chronotope, and, as Franco Moretti has noted, figural density concentrates as borders are approached.[160] A diptych structure shapes the project – or, more specifically, what Sekula calls 'broken diptychs' – with juxtapositions that enable spatial and economic comparisons, as well as temporal shifts in gesture.[161] These diptychs are often based on marginal changes to the viewpoint, as Sekula first points his camera in one direction and then adjusts his orientation to photograph another.[162]

In the first photograph, we have a distant view of a container factory, owned by Hyundai (which established its base there after Mexico lifted restrictions on foreign capital). Most containers are made in China, but this Hyundai factory is specifically geared to producing them for the US. The second photograph presents more or less the same view but with a slight shift of position and a radical change in focal depth to include in the foreground a concrete column bearing a drawing of a truck. Sekula's caption identifies this as a trucker's graffito and tells us that the word 'Chespiro', on the container's roof, alludes to a character on Mexican television, the 'little Shakespeare' 'Chespirito'; and that, with the marijuana icon on the side, the graffiti-artist trucker boasts of holding a gangster-smuggler role. The graffito provides a frontal view of

158 'Dead Letter Office (Work in Progress)', *Camera Austria* 59/60 (1997): 68–9 (68). The essay was published alongside 'On *Fish Story*'.

159 'Globalism's Discontents and the Return of the Sea'.

160 Franco Moretti, *Atlas of the European Novel 1800–1900* (London: Verso, 1998), 43.

161 'Working at the Light Table'.

162 'Globalism's Discontents and the Return of the Sea'.

the driver's cab, drawn in the anthropomorphic mode of a scowling 'Aztec' warrior or 'demon' face. As such, it is reminiscent of Diego Rivera's blending of machinic forms and pre-Columbian deities, which figure in his Ford murals for Detroit and the 'Pan-American Unity' panels in San Francisco. Less immediately obvious, and turning around the column's corner, the graffito also gives a side-on view of the attached container, depicted as if seen from a higher vantage point. This can be read, Sekula said, as a *trompe l'oeil* or post-Cubist doubling of view-points.[163] If read more 'naturalistically' – an interpretation suggested by the inclusion of lines delineating the edges of a road – it is a vehicle performing a sharp left turn. The emphatic linearity of the graffito in the second photograph is important, playing off similar forms shared with the first: rows of containers, the factory roofline and, above all, the electricity wires and open metal structures of a pylon.[164] The anthropomorphism evident and the marijuana logo in the graffito carries over to the pylon in the distance. These all carry through to the next pairing.

The second diptych shows the cranes and towers on the Fox film set for *Titanic* (it was planned to be used for twenty films) and the mast on the replica of the sinking ship.[165] A large earth bank, a sweeping track and, behind a concrete wall, cranes, and the huge model of an early twentieth-century liner, tipping nose downwards. The companion picture looks down another earth bank to an assembly of makeshift dwellings next to the sea. Looking up at us, a barefoot man and a smiling woman are grilling mussels from their day's catch. One of the most expensive films of all time – in which the poor boy expires in frigid waters while the rich girl floats to safety – confronts the everyday reality of those eking out a living from the sea. A representative of the community describes what happened: Popotla's fishing community supported itself by working off small boats, taking what they needed for their families and small restaurants. They were legally entitled to fish the Federal Zone Strip along the ocean front, but they found the law arrayed against them. Protected by armed guards behind a high wall, the American studio built a colossal tank to house its 'ghost ship'. With the complicity of local officials and police, earth-moving machines simply buried the fishing boats. The only concession to the community offered

163 Ibid.

164 We have extended the 'linear' links here, but Sekula specifically mentions the graffito and pylon in 'Working at the Light Table'.

165 'Globalism's Discontents and the Return of the Sea'.

by Fox's lawyers was to sell back a section of their own land. No local people were employed. The development proved an economic and ecological disaster. Chlorine, solvents and human waste were discharged in high concentrations, which, together with underwater explosives and noise, devastated sea life: the sea-urchin population collapsed; fish emigrated; and the submarine jungle of sea sequoia was almost eradicated.[166] Both photographs carry over the linearities of the opening diptych. On the Fox site, the cranes' lattice structures echo those of the pylon; scaffolding and the rear of a signboard, repeat rectilinearity. The fishing homes' elongated cube forms loosely mirror those of Hyundai's containers and that of the graffito truck. The sheets of corrugation, plywood and other reclaimed materials used to build them create gridded surface patterns, further emphasised by window blinds and barbeque grills.

It is as if, in response to breaks in contiguity, Sekula seeks to re-establish the linking chains with visual echoes; rhythms of lines establish associations. These opening diptychs are followed by: vignettes associated with the peripheries of a Republican convention in San Diego; a cruise ship loading at Ensenada; a woman at work in a Mexican tuna cannery; naval exercises between Los Angeles and San Diego; and the interior of a Tijuanan coffin factory. In San Diego, Sekula pairs a photograph of a scavenger with one featuring the son of a lobbyist at the convention. The gridded and grill forms recur: on the rummager's shopping trolley; on the mirrored façade of the building behind him. The emblematic character of the graffito is echoed by the tattoo of an African elephant on the right pectoral of the wealthy bather. Lines of various sorts create dancing rhythms tracking through the sequence: the rope is thrown from the cruise ship to the workers on the Ensenada dock and the cable assisting the loading of luggage; gridded camo nets, helmets adorned with grasses, radiophones and antennae at the amphibious landing; a temporary set-up for an ABC News crew is a tangle of wires.

Sekula's strategies point to a destructive and fugitive capitalism. As the five-paragraph essay to *Dead Letter Office* suggests, the project presents fragments of majority and minority worlds in a tensile relation:

---

166 The information in this paragraph is from a statement by Fernando Larios Zepeda, spokesman for the Popotla Fisherman's Association, written in 1998: archive.rhizome.org/artbase/1693/popotlaaustria.html. Several international artists decorated the film companies' barrier wall with scenes of the sea.

> The industrialized northern border of Mexico is the prototype of a grim Taylorist future. The re-floated *Titanic* is the belated harbinger of the runaway assembly-line. A reservoir of cheap labor is contained and channeled by the hydraulic action of an apartheid machine. The machine is increasingly indifferent to democracy on either side of the line, but not indifferent to culture, to the pouring of oil upon troubled waters.[167]

The passage – speaking in terms of 'prototype of a . . . future', Taylorism and 'the runaway assembly line', and of the film as 'belated harbinger' – might feed a sense of linear time. Yet, on closer inspection, matters become more temporally ambivalent. The photographs have brief captions in the published catalogue, but we glean more from the extended titles Sekula initially toyed with. The cruise ship (itself an obvious allusion to the doomed transatlantic liner) is picking up passengers transferred from San Diego to Ensenada because the travel company can circumvent labour laws requiring US crews to be hired.[168] Elsewhere, Sekula referred to cruise liners as 'the floating apartheid machines of postmodern leisure'.[169] The *Titanic* set, the Ensenada cruise terminal and the *maquiladoras* are equivalents, all moving production south of the border to sidestep legal protections and environmental regulations. Hollywood's famed factory of (American) dreams migrates to Popotla, where it constructs its phantasmagorical set and remanufactures its story of modernity in the form of the lost ocean liner: 'the dream-work performed by the "white system"'.[170] North and south are mixed unevenly through the pumping action of the passage's hydraulic metaphor.

As Sekula was preparing *Dead Letter Office*, he admitted to envisioning the accompanying essay as 'science fiction writing or speculative military fiction'.[171] For US West Coast culture, he writes, Mexican California represents 'the place of escape, drunkenness and dreams'.[172] Preserved as a *terra nova*, this fantasy is completely at odds with the industrialised border areas. (At the time of our writing, *Lonely Planet* still refers to Baja California as 'untamed', describing its roads as

167 *Dead Letter Office* (Rotterdam: Nederlands Foto Instituut, 1997), 32.
168 'Dead Letter Office (Work in Progress)', 68.
169 'Dismal Science', 51.
170 *Dead Letter Office*, 32.
171 'Dead Letter Office (Work in Progress)', 68.
172 *Dead Letter Office*, 32 (the same pagination applies throughout this paragraph).

winding 'drunkenly'.) Sekula specifically links these fantasised perspectives to the 'freedoms' of white-adventurer spirit entering a lawless space: from earlier colonists to the nineteenth-century gold rush; from fugitives depicted in old films to Hollywood itself migrating south to make *Titanic*. Sekula's choice of words and figures makes this dreamscape stranger still: many northerners 'regard the long peninsula of Baja California as a kind of vestigial organ, a primeval, reptilian tail', an evolutionary remain. The same temporal trope recurs, and shortly after, Sekula writes that the liner *Titanic* encountered 'the primordial abyss'.

The fourth and penultimate paragraph of the essay assembles several vignettes, each a single sentence in length. This is it in full:

> Extras float and shiver among the dummy corpses, flailing about and gagging on command. A veritable reserve army of the drowned. Eighty miles north, hapless immigrants stumble upon another narrative, a dress rehearsal for an amphibious landing. A California congressman, the architect of the triple fence, worries about Chinese nuclear weapons smuggled across the border in cargo containers. A former secretary of defense writes an illiterate scenario for an invasion of Mexico. The United States Marines investigate having their tank transporters built in Tijuana by a Korean conglomerate. A North American actor, reading the voice-over to a promotional film for the same Korean conglomerate, slips and speaks of the 'artesian' traditions of Mexican labor.[173]

These snippets are summary descriptions of discrete events, encountered paratactically as if we were flicking through news channels. The overall tone is relatively flat, although there is still a judgemental loading to some of the terms used ('flailing about and gagging on command', 'illiterate scenario') that hold it back from entirely neutral description. Sekula's words sketch a sequence of images that present the contradictions of the border. From movie narrative to a military practice; from naval exercises in US national security, to a politician feeling threatened, yet safely behind the border's barriers. In a quasi-filmic vision, another politician entertains the reverse fantasy: direct aggression by the US against Mexico (the reference, here, is to Caspar Weinberger).[174] Securitisation and economic interests collide: containers are projected as devices for concealing weapons; contrariwise, the US navy

173 Ibid.

174 'Working at the Light Table'.

recognises that Mexican-constructed Hyundai equipment is financially advantageous. The last sentence of Sekula's paragraph alights on a slip of the tongue where an intended reference to Mexican labour skills slides to the motif of bountiful fountains spurting from subterranean aquifers – those that, before being squandered, had once irrigated orange groves. The actor's slip is a malapropism (use of incorrect vocabulary) but also an elision based on homophonic similarity; and it can be a Freudian eruption of desire and fecundity.

Back and forth across the border go goods, people and capital, and with them go various projections and representations: the making of film narrative; a military rehearsal; political scenarios; a performer voicing a commercial.[175] There is a thematic relay – narrative, rehearsal, scenario, performance – although the passage links less by way of conventional prose development than by its adjacencies. The second sentence, at least, opens by connecting two scenes by their relative geography ('Eighty miles north'); a later statement uses retrospective comparison ('same Korean conglomerate'). Other interlinking work is handled more subtly, such as with the figure of an uncoordinated body: the 'flailing' of the opening sentence segues to the 'stumble' of the second; and is reprised by the actor's 'slips' of mouth-tongue-brain-vocal cords. The montage and word choices reveal and exaggerate the contradictions and violence of the border. This sequence of bizarre-yet-factual sketches form an irreal nightmare, retold with absurdist dark humour. The figural intensification of the border chronotope is pushed to the extreme.

This absurdism is taken further still with the culminating diptych of the Tijuanan coffin workshop, a seemingly idiosyncratic but deliberate gesture.[176] Two photographs of the factory interior depict caskets on stands. The first shows one under construction; turned side-on, it displays its internal space – as though to invite us into its void. The next presents the finished item: closed, in its correct horizonal position and displaying its decorative covering, a silvered foil with floral wreath

175 Contemporaneous with Sekula's project is Mike Davis's study of the mutual imbrication of the Mexican–US economies, with flows of labour, commodities, money and even sewage across the border. Mike Davis, *Magical Urbanism: Latinos Reinvent the U.S. City* (London: Verso, 2000).

176 Accompanying the essay are two supplementary photographs: another of the *Titanic* set, and one of metalworkers for a Hyundai subcontractor signing up to join an independent union. The coffin factory's structural 'finality' for the main run of images no doubt matters.

motifs (a naturalistic and open-form damask or 'baroque' pattern). From Sekula's earlier working captions, we learn that half the produce of the factory was destined for the home market, and half for the US. The latter is referred to as *el otro lado* ('the other side') – literally referring to the crossing of the geopolitical and economic barrier, but, as everyone knows, a popular idiom for death. Put less prosaically, it is the supernatural world of the afterlife, and sometimes also the promise of Heaven. Behind the second coffin is a large pile of shiny shavings, residues from the lamination process. The metallic application is meant to signify 'wealth', of course, and to 'elevate' the coffin from, and to fetch a higher price than one made with, mundane construction materials. Here, in Sekula's diptych, it surely also points to money in general, and more specifically to New Spain's/Mexico's role as the world economy's leading producer of silver until the late nineteenth century (supporting colonial revenue, the monetary systems of the US and Europe in the era of bimetallism, and the integration of Asia into the world economy).[177]

In both photographs, the workshop walls are pasted with magazine pin-ups – hyper-sexualised images of scantily clad, breast- and buttock-thrusting women. The proximity of Thanatos and Eros is inescapable, and in a lecture Sekula alluded to this labour as a 'daily encounter with Thanatos'.[178] The pin-ups suggest a different sort of escape to that celebrated by tourist guides and American movies. This is another 'Heaven', one of sex and not-work – a paradise, at least, for an assumed heterosexual male coffin-maker; unlikely so for the models who laboured to construct the images – and we think back, here, to Harun Farocki's *An Image* (1983), the making of a 'centrefold', as porn pictures were sometimes known. Indeed, the presence of these pin-ups inevitably prompts yet another idiom, the 'little death' (*la petite mort*) of male orgasm. Sekula himself imagines the pin-ups being shredded, like the heap of lamination foil in the photograph, to form a bed for the corpse.[179]

Discussing Cameron's film *Titanic* in 'Between the Net and the Deep Blue Sea', Sekula comments on what he sees as the director's overweening ponderousness, his meditation on historical destruction and fascination with death. He writes:

---

177 Sandra Kuntz Ficker, 'The Universal Mint: Mexico's Silver and the World Economy (1821–1870)', *Capitalism: A Journal of History and Economics* 3:2 (Summer 2022): 257–300.

178 'Globalism's Discontents and the Return of the Sea'.

179 Ibid.

> We peer morbidly into the vortex of industrialism's early nosedive into the abyss . . . Quick as a wink, cartoon-like, the angel of history is flattened between a wall of steel and a wall of ice. It's an easy, premature way to mourn a bloody century.[180]

Sekula recasts these themes in his own critical-irrealist idiom, blending Benjamin's ruminations on history, destruction and ruin with animation comedic violence in the mode of Tom and Jerry (Hanna-Barbara/MGM) or the rival Wile E. Coyote and Road Runner (Warner Brothers' Looney Tunes).

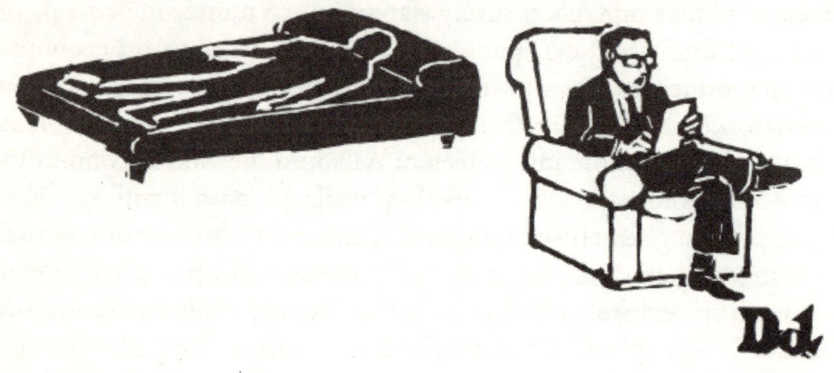

"How long have you worked on the docks?"

Figure 10: Item from The Dockers' Museum *(2010–13):*
Psychiatrist with flat docker *(Sekula's title)*
Cartoon (with different title): Drew Dernavich, The New Yorker Magazine, *9 January 2012*

Sekula's works orbit key points at which capital besieges idyll – meant in the strong sense of the genre: the cyclical time of nature and everyday life. *Fish Story* shows a fishing village in South Korea threatened by a swelling industrial plant. In *Dead Letter Office*, the contrast of the *Titanic* – a metaphor of maritime disaster – with the struggles of fishing families in Mexico is a further example. Such contrasts occur throughout his work, sometimes as diptychs, sometimes within single images; another example would be 'One Thousand Trucks' in *Freeway to China*. It is significant that the transformation of everyday life is

180 'Between the Net and the Deep Blue Sea', 17.

never presented as complete but held in suspension at critical turning points. The future remains uncertain. In a sense, Sekula's chronotope captures the classic modernist concern with 'edge of the city' or Haussmanisation – but with its spaces now globalised and displaced from the metropoles.[181] Sekula's juxtapositions, split panoramas, broken diptychs, and the interrelations of his writing and image work all take on symptomatic importance. The scenes depicted may entail adjacent views or transpositions of non-homogeneous times and places establishing new matrices. The shack often appears – perhaps as a figure for a most basic foothold on the earth. Capitalism emerges in these works as a permanent emergency, where localised personal catastrophes, such as impending unemployment or loss of economic independence, confront the Capitalocene.[182]

In this sense, Sekula's subject is not only the sea, or even commodity circulation, but also capitalist life as planetary cataclysm. For Marx, crises in the accumulation process are cyclical events; they are interspersed with periods of 'normal' economic activity, punctuated by smaller local crises. There are technical debates about this process, but the focus on a periodic economic crisis of this type can overshadow how routine accumulation assaults the lifeworld. As Henri Lefebvre noted, 'modernity is in permanent crisis'.[183] This is a perpetual crisis of overlapping but homologous levels, which often seem to float free of class relations: the commodity form's invasion of social life and the atrophy of the public sphere; colonialism, enslavement and their legacies of inequality; harrowing wars and the mass displacements of those escaping them; environmental catastrophes, from local patterns of toxification and the invasive spread of microplastics to the systemic breakdowns of the warming world; famines and pandemics; acidification of the oceans; the violence of abstract bureaucratic processes; and the crises of representation, involving a torrent of images, the hollowing-out of news media and ruptures in signification (another form of a dead letter office). It has often been argued that there will be a final crisis of capitalism, but that may yet prove optimistic.

181 T. J. Clark, *The Painting of Modern Life: Paris in the Art of Manet and his Followers* (London: Thames & Hudson, 1985).

182 The term is credited to Andreas Malm by Jason Moore in the Acknowledgements of *Anthropocene or Capitalocene? Nature, History, and the Crisis of Capitalism*, ed. Jason W. Moore (Oakland, CA: PM Press, 2016). See also Andrea Malm, *Fossil Capitalism: The Rise of Steam Power and the Roots of Global Warming* (London: Verso, 2016).

183 Henri Lefebvre, *Introduction to Modernity* (1962; London: Verso, 1995), 236.

Sekula's work is sometimes seen as a straightforward practice of social realism. We hope to have shown that it is anything but. His dialectical matrix brings into play a series of displacements and condensations. The relation of aesthetics and politics shares with critical irrealism an inner tension – its torquing and twisting qualities, and even its monstrous distortions. Sekula's project brings together contradictory forces, never quite synthesising them. They strain in different directions, pointing beyond the tethers that materially bind their (ir)reconcilability. It is not that his terms, or motifs, are simply ambiguous floating signifiers. However unruly, they are ferried aboard specific vessels, swept along by particular currents, sometimes anchored to moorings. To shift the metaphor: in Sekula's work, all the links in the chain are forged in the inferno of capitalism. In Sekula's critical ensemble, each coordinate, or vector, can be worked to illuminate other objects of attention. It is this amphibious (ir)reality that makes his practice overdetermined, cognitively rich and aesthetically powerful.

Index

Abse Gogarty, Larne, 132
abstraction, 6, 62, 64, 66–9, 73–5, 94–6, 113, 126, 129, 132, 189, 211, 241, 260, 266
accumulation, 11, 62, 66, 69, 74, 77, 95, 106, 126, 217, 283
  so-called primitive, 260
  uneven and combined, see unevenness
Adorno, Theodor W., 15, 23, 31, 62, 95, 118, 171, 209–11, 214–15, 218
aesthetics, 7–9, 16, 22–3, 26, 31, 75, 103, 140–1, 184, 215, 244, 257, 263, 284
Africa, 80, 97, 123
d'Alembert, Jean le Rond, 2–3, 100
allegoresis, 139, 268, 271
allegory, 110, 136–44, 147, 168, 179, 181, 204, 206, 247, 268
Althusser, Louis, 14, 26, 50, 52, 168, 181, 185, 190, 259
anachronisms, 7, 135–6, 263, 265–6
anal, 235–7, 243–7, 249
anamorphosis, 246, 263–5
Anthropocene, 94, 283
anthropology, 13, 188
architecture, 11, 106, 152, 214, 236, 241, 256
Aronowitz, Stanley, 51, 53
Art & Language, 31
Asher, Michael, 238
Athens, 190–1, 194–6, 200, 202–3, 217
autonomy, 15, 23, 52, 54, 63–4, 75, 140, 168, 177, 214
avant-garde, 5, 13, 32, 75, 85, 133–4, 137, 168, 171, 222, 256
Azoulay, Ariella Aïsha, 8, 13, 144

Baja California, 234, 250, 278–9
Bakhtin, Mikhail, 13, 25, 86, 118, 137, 168, 184
Bakhtin Circle, 86, 168, 183–5, 222
Baldessari, John, 29, 31
Balibar, Etienne, 67, 123, 259
Banaji, Jairus, 259
Barthes, Roland, 9, 25–6, 57–8, 143–7, 164, 167, 171–2, 180, 183, 216, 241, 269, 271
Bataille, Georges, 245
Benjamin, Walter, 5, 8, 11, 15–16, 24–5, 34, 108–12, 118, 128, 137, 140, 143–4, 146–7, 183, 204, 207–8, 214–15, 219, 231, 236, 258–9, 282
Berger, John, 39
Bensaïd, Daniel, 110, 112, 147, 259
Bertillon, Alphonse, 71–3

Bhaskar, Roy, 20, 252
Bilbao, 212–13, 228, 234, 249–50, 261
biopolitics, 6, 40–1, 70, 72–3, 147
bodies, 6, 48, 59, 70–1, 73–4, 125–6, 128, 130–1, 238, 266, 272
Boggs, James, 51
Bologna, Sergio, 87
Bolshevism, 115, 251
borders, 6, 76, 78, 86, 91, 161, 262, 275, 278–80
Borneman, Ernest, 25, 243
Braverman, Harry, 51, 53, 56, 58–9, 74
Brecht, Bertolt, 5, 11–12, 14, 20, 23, 34–5, 39, 41, 45, 67, 83, 110, 118, 134, 252
Brenner, Robert, 83
Buchloh, Benjamin, 5, 8, 30, 32, 40, 84, 140–2
Buck-Morss, Susan, 231
Bunyan, John, 120, 137
Burch, Noël, 6–7, 19, 171, 189, 190, 208, 213–14, 262
Burgin, Victor, 14, 16, 64
Butler, Judith, 73, 125

Cahiers pour l'Analyse, 179, 181
CalArts, 4, 80
Canada, 76, 241–2, 248
  the asshole of, 241
Canetti, Elias, 127, 231
cartoons, 1, 8, 116, 145, 235, 255, 282
chiasmus, 208–17, 242, 265–6
China (see also *This Ain't China* and *Freeway to China*), 40, 77, 84, 89, 91, 105, 108, 275
circulation, 26, 63, 88, 94–6, 208, 263, 272, 283
class, 4, 7, 11–13, 25, 31, 34, 37–8, 40–2, 44, 50–5, 59, 63, 66, 71, 77, 82–3, 107, 112–13, 117, 120–4, 126–7, 129, 131, 133, 136, 157, 179, 180, 183, 239, 252
  PMC (Professional Managerial Class), 51–7
  property-owning, 123
  self-abolishing, 36, 38
  technical-professional, 50
  working class, 12, 38, 40, 52, 78, 83, 89, 103, 122, 187, 204
  end of the, 78
cognitive mapping, 6, 15, 190
colonialism, 79, 81, 97–9, 121, 193, 197, 240, 248, 260, 263, 265, 268–71, 273, 281, 283
  settler, 91
colour, colour as a comrade, 98, 107, 150–64, 232
combined and uneven development, 90, 257, 260–1, 263–4, 266
conceptual art, 29, 31–2, 130, 170
containerisation, 6–7, 87–8, 91–2, 98, 266
container ports, 12, 89, 94, 189, 271
containers, 17, 30, 64, 66, 81, 84–5, 87, 89, 91–5, 97–8, 105–6, 150–3, 180, 186, 189, 191–2, 202–3, 206, 213, 229, 250, 255, 272, 274–7, 279
contradictions, 19, 26, 42, 52, 55, 60–1, 134, 216, 222, 224, 279–80
Crimp, Douglas, 141
crises, 37, 43, 45, 50–1, 78, 88–9, 274, 283
critical realism, 13, 20, 37, 130, 167, 223, 251–2, 257, 262
crowd (see also multitude, Hydra and proletariat, motley), 124–32, 155–6, 164, 269–70
culture, including image culture, 4, 10, 12, 15, 16, 38, 40, 52, 55–6, 60, 61–2, 70, 74, 81, 84, 89, 107, 113, 118, 145–6, 175, 184, 189, 207, 215–16, 221, 229, 238, 245, 248–9, 253, 256, 258, 264, 266, 269, 278
  cultural logics, 9, 106, 175
  cultural studies, 1–2, 118, 258

Daguerre, Louis-Jacques-Mandé, 115–17, 268
Davis, Mike, 29, 31, 80, 105, 108, 180, 187, 191, 239, 280
City of Quartz, 105, 108, 187
Dean, Jodi, 111–12, 127
deindustrialisation, 7, 78, 91, 108, 187, 213
Deleuze, Gilles, 73, 162, 245
democracy, 4, 13, 122, 194–7, 201, 278
Denning, Michael, 36–7, 125
dialectical image, 18, 146, 214–16, 218, 266
dialectical juxtaposition, 142
dialectics, 7, 9, 22, 24, 26–7, 90, 128, 143, 209–11, 215, 238
Díaz, Porfirio, 93, 274
Diderot, Denis, 2–3, 16, 100
diptychs, 17, 85–6, 148, 212–14, 275–7, 280, 282–3
dockers (including port and longshore workers), 23, 37, 92, 98, 114–15, 128, 137, 148–53, 188, 193, 208, 266–8, 274, 282
documentary film and photography, 5, 10–16, 18, 20–1, 31, 33–5, 42–3, 69, 74–5, 80, 83, 99, 114, 133–4, 143, 149, 168, 170, 172–3, 175–6, 186, 204–5, 218, 220–3, 247, 252, 262
Duchamp, Marcel, 230, 239

Eagleton, Terry, 118, 141, 185
Ehrenreich, Barbara, 51–5, 59, 221
Ehrenreich, John, 51–3, 59
Eisenstein, Sergei, 9, 19, 115, 145, 154, 174, 216, 247
Elbaum, Max, 40
Eley, Geoff, 121, 133
empiricism, 56
Engels, Friedrich, 43, 84, 67, 91, 104, 115, 211
engineers, 42–59, 64, 69, 83, 255
aerospace, 53
epistemological scepticism, 5, 74–5, 141, 222
Erlich, Viktor, 173, 184, 223
Evans, Walker, 47–8, 138, 141, 262

factory, 11–12, 30, 35–6, 46, 53–4, 67, 69, 89, 208, 209–11, 269, 275–8, 280–1
Fanon, Frantz, 33, 37, 257
fantasies, 4, 80, 82, 163, 198, 204–5, 229, 234, 248, 256, 261, 267, 278–9
Farm Security Administration (FSA), 31–2, 221
farmworkers, 30, 155–6
Farocki, Harun, 7, 31, 237, 244, 281
Federal Works Agency, 187
Ferenczi, Sándor, 25, 232–6, 243–4, 247
fertiliser, 192, 242, 248
fetish, 98, 106, 142, 188, 199, 245, 256–7
fetishism, 15, 20, 63–4, 117, 188–9, 211, 215–16, 241, 244, 250, 256, 260
Fineman, Joel, 140, 181, 223
fishing communities, 6, 137, 267, 276, 282
FOCs (flags of convenience), 6, 80, 88, 148, 186, 189–91, 200–1, 205, 263
form determination, 62
Fontana, 80, 105, 108, 148
Foster, Hal, 141
Foucault, Michel, 25–6, 57, 70, 72–4, 81, 120, 137, 217, 222
Frankfurt School, 258
Freud, Sigmund, 25, 111–12, 127, 145, 174, 188, 190, 229–36, 241, 243–7, 264, 280
Fried, Michael, 168, 203

Galton, Francis, 71, 73
Gdańsk, 83, 104, 255
Gehry, Frank, 106, 155–6, 212, 214, 234, 236, 249

gender, 45, 48, 89, 121–3, 187, 195, 200, 204, 245–6
Gilbreth, Frank and Lillian, 58, 62, 97
Gilroy, Paul, 121, 124
global capitalism, 6, 20, 77–9, 125, 132, 188, 216
globalisation, 4, 6–7, 77, 87, 94, 124–7, 172, 193, 211, 224, 260–1
Godard, Jean-Luc, 6, 16, 32–4, 39–41, 244, 246
gold, 98, 107, 114, 157, 198, 207, 242–5, 256, 279
Gorky, Maxim, 118
gothic, 249–51, 260–1, 264, 269
Goux, Jean-Joseph, 245
Graham, Dan, 31, 203
Gramsci, Antonio, 81, 149
Greenberg, Clement, 168–9, 249
Greimas, Algirdas Julian, 22, 24, 167
Greimas's square, 22, 24
Grimm brothers, 48–9, 243
Grundrisse, 37, 61, 66–8, 94, 96, 256
Guggenheim Museum, 212–13, 228, 234, 249, 261

Hall, Stuart, 77, 118, 181
harbour, 23, 31, 81–2, 85, 93–4, 97, 101, 105, 148, 187, 198, 202, 273
Harootunian, Harry, 259
Harris, Nigel, 78
Harvey, David, 74, 77, 80, 104
Harvey, Sylvia, 14
Hegel, G. W. F., 22–4, 118, 193, 210–11
Heinrich, Michael, 68
heteroglossia, 17, 184, 220
Hill, Christopher, 119, 122–4, 136–7
Hine, Lewis, 31, 60, 83, 100, 175–6, 269
historical time, 147, 161–2, 165
Holmes, Oliver Wendell, 63, 72, 97
Homer, Winslow, 31, 228, 250
Hollywood, 158, 205, 229, 249, 278–9
Hocquenghem, Guy, 245
Hydra, 121–3

idealism, 1, 82, 182, 185
ideology, 13–14, 24–5, 30, 52–8, 61, 63, 66, 68, 71, 74, 76, 80–1, 99, 136, 141, 151, 169, 171, 173, 175–84, 189–90, 193–4, 206, 210–12, 216, 223, 230, 236, 240–1, 262, 268
ILWU (International Longshore and Warehouse Union), 92, 151
imaginary, 6, 14, 16, 25, 34, 80–1, 84, 98, 126, 145, 190, 195–6, 204, 233, 242, 260, 264
imagination, 24, 115, 123, 129, 137, 145, 207, 230, 234, 238, 252, 261
industries, 7, 41, 51–2, 56, 59, 61, 77, 79, 80, 82–5, 92, 103, 104, 108, 171, 186, 188, 193, 200, 203, 212, 214, 231, 247, 249, 250, 274
  chemical, 248
  electronics, 35
  marine-extractive, 228
inequalities, 78, 126, 257, 283
irrealism, 27, 134, 249–84
isotype, 63–5, 97

Jakobson, Roman, 20, 25–6, 167–8, 171–80, 185, 188–9, 222–4, 228, 257
James, C. L. R., 41, 100, 115, 119, 136
Jameson, Fredric, 11, 16, 20, 22–4, 26–7, 29, 106, 128, 135, 140, 168, 181, 185, 222, 239, 257–8
Jesi, Furio, 161–2, 165

Kracauer, Siegfried, 12, 18, 46, 143–4, 258
Krauss, Rosalind, 172, 178, 203, 232

labour power, 30, 36, 38, 42, 57–9, 62, 72, 103, 250

labour process, 47, 53, 56, 59–60, 74, 92
Lacan, Jacques, 14, 17, 167, 172, 179, 181, 190, 196, 232, 245–6, 264
landscapes, 76, 80, 85, 91, 104, 108, 155, 178, 203, 241–2
language, 15, 25, 26, 56–8, 64, 74, 93, 121, 133, 144, 167–8, 172–84, 189–90, 203, 218–24, 245, 246
Lefebvre, Henri, 252, 264, 283
liberal humanism, 169, 176, 228
libidinal drives, 233, 238
libidinal substitutions, 246
Linebaugh, Peter, 121–4, 126, 136–7
linguistics, 144, 167, 173–4, 176–81, 185, 189, 214, 222, 247
  cognitive, 167, 179–80
linguistics and poetics, 172, 176–7, 185, 222–4
linguistic turn, 133, 167
Lisbon, 4, 124, 190, 267–8
Liverpool, 148–9, 151–3, 249, 261
Lockheed aerospace, 42–3, 46, 51
logistics, 6–7, 87–9, 94–6, 98, 186, 208
  multi-modal, 95
Lonidier, Fred, 29, 31
Loraux, Nicole, 195–6, 200
Los Angeles, 4, 32, 80–1, 84, 98, 104–7, 114, 129, 148–9, 153, 187, 190, 207, 214, 239, 249, 261, 277
Löwy, Michael, 90, 110–11, 147, 251–2, 256–7, 258, 259
Lukács, Gyorgi, 15, 16, 20, 23, 26, 43, 61–2, 127, 171, 251–2, 257–8

magic, 22, 174, 215, 218, 243, 248, 250–3, 253, 256, 261, 271
Mapplethorpe, Robert, 238–9, 243, 268
Marcuse, Herbert, 25, 29, 50, 200, 230, 236, 238, 258
Marker, Chris, 7, 31, 112, 134, 147
markets, 4, 6, 11, 30, 42, 77–8, 94, 96, 119, 136, 142, 163, 192, 194, 199–201, 214, 228, 231, 249–50, 263, 281
Marx, Karl, 11, 25–6, 38, 53, 56, 58, 61–4, 66–9, 94–6, 103–4, 113, 115, 121, 180, 188, 209, 211, 230, 240, 242, 244, 250–1, 256, 258–60, 263, 269, 283
Marxism, 5, 22, 26, 29, 36, 62, 67, 111, 121, 133, 188
material geographies, 74, 80, 94, 98
materialism, 1, 23, 25, 66–7, 74, 81–2, 94, 95, 120, 179, 212
Medvedev, Pavel, 168, 184–5
Melnick, Mimi, and Robert A., 239–40
Melville, Herman, 31, 48, 80, 100, 275
metaphor, 70, 73, 80, 93–4, 97, 101, 103, 106, 114, 118, 122, 129, 133, 138, 153, 167–83, 186, 189–90, 207–9, 214, 220, 223–4, 228–9, 239, 241, 254, 261, 265, 268, 269, 271, 272, 278, 282
  cult of, 168–70, 175–6, 223–4
metonymy, 167, 170, 172–6, 178–82, 186, 188–90, 201, 205, 223–4, 261
Mexico, 79, 84, 90, 92, 98, 262, 272, 274–5, 278–9, 281–2
Middle Passage, 84–6, 91–2, 96–7, 105, 232, 250, 253
modernism, 14–16, 19–20, 23, 34, 64, 67, 85, 107, 140, 167, 169–70, 176, 190, 221, 251, 257–8
money, 62–3, 72, 96, 238, 240–5, 248–9, 256, 280–1
Morris, William, 120, 255
multitude (see also crowd, Hydra and proletariat, motley), 36, 122–4, 126, 131–2
Mulvey, Laura, 7, 133, 137
Museum of Modern Art (MoMA), 31, 33, 169

myths, 4, 49, 74–5, 78, 82, 171, 176–7, 195–8, 220, 239, 242–3, 269

Nadar, Gaspard-Félix Tournachon, 178–9, 212, 215
NAFTA (North American Free Trade Agreement), 98–100, 272, 274
NAM (New American Movement), 40, 51–2, 55
negation, 19, 75, 112, 119, 130, 138, 141, 157, 190, 210, 216
  negation of the, 22
negative labour, 37–8, 42, 84, 99, 103, 113, 266, 269
Negri, Antonio, 122, 126, 147, 259
neoliberalism, 6, 12, 77–8, 90, 108
Neurath, Otto, 64
neurosis, 48, 179, 230, 243
New Topographics, 32
Noble, David F., 43, 51, 53, 57, 59
North American Free Trade Agreement. *See* NAFTA

Ochs, Phil, 191–2, 98
OECD, 188
oedipalised gender relations, 245
oil, 6, 78–9, 104, 106, 191, 205–7, 278
oil tankers, 79
Orton, Fred, 141
Osborne, Peter, 15, 146, 259
Owens, Craig, 140–1
O'Sullivan, Timothy, 178

Pacific, 105, 108, 148, 160, 272
Panama, 80, 190, 193, 200–2, 207, 224, 237
Panama Canal, 224
parataxis, 209–10, 220
Pêcheux, Michel, 168, 179–82, 189–90, 329
perspective, 17, 80, 85, 97, 131, 194, 228, 264
performative assembly, 125, 131
Piraeus, 191, 194, 199–202, 204
poetics, 10, 25, 66, 132, 167–225, 253
police, 70–1, 114, 125, 128–32, 155, 157, 161–3, 202, 205, 237, 276
political economy, 11, 25–6, 36–7, 66, 68, 80, 188, 191, 193, 238, 248, 256, 260
Pop Art, 151, 240
Popotla (discussion of *Dead Letter Office* mussel-beds and set), 276–8
ports, 4, 23, 37, 79–81, 83–4, 88–9, 92, 94, 100, 104, 115, 138, 148–9, 151–2, 186, 188–9, 191, 193–4, 196, 202, 204–5, 249, 266–8, 272–4
  deep-water, 92
  modern industrial, 273
postcolonial, 91, 121, 141, 257–8, 260, 265
postmodernism, 5, 8, 17, 34–5, 125, 133, 140–1, 186, 205, 218, 221, 239, 258, 278
Potts, Alex, 10
Poulantzas, Nikos, 51, 181
precarity, 38, 151, 223, 262
proletarians, including proletarianisation (see also working class), 36–8, 40, 53–4, 59, 63, **110,** 115, 126–7
  motley, 122–3, 126–7, 131–2
Propp, Vladimir, 44, 167
prose poetry, 218–19
prosopopoeia, 149, 191
protective clothing, 104, 164, 199, 206
protests, 6, 84, 113, 124–32, 153–65, 207, 231, 239
Proust, Marcel, 109
psychoanalysis, 9, 25–7, 145, 179, 182, 188–9, 196, 228, 230–3, 238–9, 242–9

Rabelais, 118, 237, 254
race, 36, 37, 40, 71–4, 77–9, 89,

121–2, 129, 181, 187, 191, 196–8, 200, 239, 252, 269–71
Rancière, Jacques, 118, 122, 127, 222–3
rationalisation, 53, 58–60, 72, 94, 178
realism, 5, 7, 10, 13–16, 20–1, 23, 31, 34, 41–3, 71, 75, 130, 138, 143, 167, 169–72, 174, 177–9, 190, 204–5, 218, 220, 223, 251–3, 257, 261–2, 268–9, 284
instrumental, 56–8, 60, 70
sentimental, 56, 60
technical, 56–8, 69
Rediker, Marcus, 121–4, 126, 136–7, 227
reification, 11–12, 61, 185, 211, 246
representation, 7, 10, 12–14, 19, 21, 34, 39, 41, 55, 60–1, 63, 69–70, 80, 104, 120, 125, 127–8, 132–40, 159–60, 169, 178, 184, 186, 206, 216, 218, 223, 245–6, 251, 253, 256, 264, 280, 283
repressive desublimation, 230, 236, 245
reproduction, 46, 52, 95, 122
sexual, 234–5
social, 6, 26, 36, 41–2, 46–7, 53, 77–8, 187, 262
visual and technical, 2, 107, 117, 141, 228
Richon, Olivier, 247–8
Roberts, John, 13, 15, 32, 75
romantic anti-capitalism, 55, 120, 251
Rosaldo, Renato, 135–6
Rose, Gillian, 209–11, 215
Rosenstone, Robert A., 134
Rosler, Martha, 7, 14, 29–30, 32, 34, 39, 41, 43, 141, 238
The Bowery in two inadequate descriptive systems, 14, 34, 41
Rotterdam, 83–4, 87, 92, 96–8, 104, 114
Ruscha, Ed, 31–2, 39, 138, 239–40
Rubin, Isaak, 62, 260–1
ruins, 103, 106–9, 142–3, 282
Russian Formalism (see also individual thinkers), 118, 168, 173, 184–5, 222–3

Said, Edward W., 81
sailors, 37, 80, 83–4, 115, 123, 172, 191–3, 233
Salazarist Monument, 124
Salgado, Sebastião, 17
Sarlin, Page, 158
San Diego, 4, 15, 24, 29, 35, 42, 84, 104, 107, 169, 230, 255, 277–8
San Diego Group, 31–3
San Pedro, 4, 31, 75, 104–5, 152, 186–8
Sartre, Jean-Paul, 9, 124, 145, 196
Schwartz, Stephanie, 153–4
Schwarz, Roberto, 21, 257, 260, 264
science, 2–3, 48, 56–7, 71, 80, 104, 177, 179, 212, 215, 222, 269
fiction, 144, 195, 204, 220, 229, 251, 255, 271, 278
natural, 66–8
philosophy of, 20, 68
sea, 6–7, 79–87, 91–103, 105, 115, 137–8, 153, 191–3, 196, 200, 202, 205–7, 209, 227, 229, 231–6, 240, 249, 263, 265, 270, 271, 273, 276–7, 283
seafarer, 92, 103, 137, 149, 192, 194, 202, 254, 263
Seattle, 124–8, 154, 159, 231
Sekula, Allan
Aerospace Folktales, 6, 18, 33, 42–51, 53–4, 107, 195, 219
Black Tide/Marea Negra, 5, 6, 113, 205–6
California Stories, 31–3, 75
California Stories: Attempts to correlate class with the elevation of the main harbor channel (San Pedro, July 1975), 33
Dead Letter Office, 90, 220, 227, 234, 275–84
Dear Bill Gates, 227–8, 232

Sekula, Allan (*cont.*)
The Dockers' Museum, 6, 21, 116, 171, 224, 235, 256, 266–8, 282
Fish Story, 2–3, 6–8, 11, 54, 64, 75–101, 103–9, 112–15, 124, 137–8, 142, 148, 158, 170–1, 186–7, 208–9, 217–19, 236, 238, 250, 253–5, 262, 271–5, 282
Forgotten Space, 5–7, 64, 89, 171, 188–90, 206, 208, 212–13, 249, 262–3
Freeway to China, 79, 82, 113, 138, 148–55, 209, 249, 261–2
Gala, 214, 224, 249
The Lottery of the Sea, 5–7, 11, 64, 167, 171–2, 189, 190–208, 216–17, 219, 224, 238, 249, 254
Meat Mass, 30, 40, 199
TITANIC's wake, 6, 109, 124, 138, 209, 212, 227, 249
Geography Lesson: Canadian Notes, 5, 75–6, 240–3, 248, 262
School Is a Factory, 32, 53, 63–5, 75
Ship of Fools, 6, 113, 137–8, 224, 255, 266–7
Shipwreck and Workers, 109, 262, 269
Short Autobiography, 33, 37, 42, 44, 47
Sketch for a Geography Lesson, 75–6
This Ain't China: A Photonovel, 15, 33, 35–41, 170
Tsukiji, 224
Two, Three, many . . . (Terrorism), 33
Untitled Slide Sequence, 33, 158
Waiting for Tear Gas, 6–7, 10, 113, 124–32, 152, 153–65, 227, 232
ships (including vessels), 79, 80–1, 84–5, 87, 88, 91, 92, 94–8, 100, 105–6, 115, 137–8, 150–3, 188–9, 191–2, 196–8, 200–3, 206, 208–11, 213, 217, 227, 239, 250, 254, 255, 256, 263, 266–7, 270, 284
container, 17, 64, 79, 81, 84, 87–8, 91–2, 150–1, 202–3, 229, 263, 272, 275
cruise, 12, 277–8
Empire Windrush, 270
Exxon Mediterranean (*Exxon Valdez*), 104, 106
Global Mariner, 88, 137, 159, 228, 231, 235, 255
Neptune Jade, 149, 151, 153
Sea-Land Quality, 85, 87, 91–2, 96–7, 105, 114, 253
Teal, 148, 151–3
Titanic (see also the film *Titanic*), 231, 279, 282
shipyards, 107–8, 150, 187, 214
shipwreck, 109, 112, 248, 271, 276
shit, 152, 237–8, 241–8
Shklovsky, Victor, 41, 167
Silverman, Kaja, 25, 152–5, 157, 244–6
slides, 18, 83, 84, 115, 124, 131, 142, 154–5, 157–61, 164, 170, 224
Smith, Adam, 11, 68, 172, 192–4
Smithson, Robert, 31–2, 163, 203–4, 232
social forms, 25, 63, 69, 74, 124, 264
socialism, 38, 103, 112, 147
contemporary, 126
creeping, 187
sociological poetics, 25, 168, 172, 182–5, 223
Sohn-Rethel, Alfred, 25, 56, 62, 64, 75, 241
solidarity, 103, 113, 120, 124–5, 129, 138, 149, 153, 156, 237
Solidarity (organisation), 40
South Korea, 84–5, 92, 98, 105, 282
Southern California, 43, 51, 80, 84, 89, 148, 151
Spartakus Uprising 161–2
Spinoza, Baruch, 122, 258–9
Spivak, Gayatri, 62, 265
Staten Island Ferry, 100–1, 255

Steichen, Ed, 60, 146, 228, 232–3, 236
Stein, Sally, 5, 31, 64, 117, 124, 130, 270
Steiner, Ina, 5, 31, 80, 117
Steinmetz, Phil/Phel, 29, 39
Sternberg, Fritz, 11
Stieglitz, Alfred, 100–1, 175, 223, 269–70
structuralism, 22, 24–6, 139, 145, 167–8, 172, 179, 182–3, 185, 222–3
supertankers, 81, 104
surrealism, 110, 174, 240, 251–2, 264–5, 269
synecdoche, 61, 115, 170–1, 174–5, 180, 186, 188, 202, 253, 266
Szarkowski, John, 33, 35, 169
Szewczyk, Monika, 39–40

Tamás, Gaspar, 37–8, 113, 119
Taylorism, 58–9, 72, 261, 278
Teamsters, 127, 155–6
temporalities, 10, 113, 143, 147, 151, 164, 206, 208, 210, 225, 259, 269
  allegorical, 137
Titanic (film), 230, 236, 249, 276–82
Thompson, E. P., 25–6, 37, 119–20, 124, 131, 135–7, 147, 265
Todorov, Tzvetan, 167, 222
Toscano, Alberto, 62, 67–8, 74, 87–9, 96
totality, 8, 20, 94, 103, 171, 188, 210, 228, 258, 263
Traverso, Enzo, 108–12, 147
Trotsky, Leon, 90, 115
Trotskyism, 40, 92, 115, 119, 128
trucks, 79, 84, 88, 92–3, 96, 104, 106, 150, 186, 262, 266, 275, 277, 282
  robot, 92, 263
Tsing, Anna, 89
Tynjanov, Yuri, 167, 185

underwater cables, 80, 82
unemployment, 36–7, 42, 46–7, 50–1, 82, 85, 104–5, 107, 112–13, 262, 283
unevenness, including Uneven and Combined Development, 20, 46, 89, 90–1, 104, 182, 190, 212–13, 224, 257–8, 260–4, 266, 278
utopian forms, 46, 108, 119, 128, 164, 232, 233, 245, 251–2

value form, 6, 25, 27, 38, 62–9, 260–1, 264
Verbeeck, Jeroen, 80, 113–14
Vertov, Dziga, 19, 255
Vigo, Jean, 31, 219
Vishmidt, Marina, 15, 69, 73–4, 126
Vološinov, Valentin, 13, 26, 168, 180, 182–5, 190

waged work, 36–7, 74, 77, 122, 198
Walker, Pat, 54
Wall, Jeff, 17, 74, 142, 235, 237
war, 6, 29–30, 51, 60, 76, 87–9, 100, 105, 109, 169, 187–8, 191, 195–8, 201, 202, 207, 229, 236, 238, 253, 276, 283
Warwick Research Collective (WReC), 250, 257, 260–1, 263–4
Watts uprising, 129, 239
White, Hayden, 134–5, 147, 222, 251
Williams, Raymond, 37, 81, 118, 129, 168, 183, 185
Wilson Gilmore, Ruth, 77, 79, 129
Wollen, Peter, 34, 133, 144, 147, 237
world system, 6, 20, 90, 257, 262, 266
World Trade Organization (WTO), 124, 126, 128, 155, 157, 231

Young, Benjamin J., 18, 29, 32, 40, 43, 45

Zapatistas, 98, 100, 272, 274
Žizek, Slavoj, 22, 246